Pass the 7

A Training Guide for the FINRA Series 7 Exam

by

Robert Walker

FIRST BOOKS ®
PORTLAND • OREGON
FIRSTBOOKS.COM

Contents at a Glance

The following section headings indicate how our chapters relate to the "7 Critical Functions Performed by a Registered Representative" structure of the FINRA exam outline.

Provides customers and prospective customers with information on investments and makes suitable recommendations.

Explains the organization, participants, and functions of various securities markets and the principal factors that affect them.

Evaluates customers in terms of available investment capital, current holdings, and financial needs, and helps them identify their investment objectives. Monitors the customer's portfolio and makes recommendations consistent with changes in economic and financial conditions as well as the customer's needs and objectives.

Opens, transfers, and closes customer accounts and maintains appropriate account records. Obtains and verifies the customer's purchase and sale instructions, enters orders, and follows up on completion of transactions.

Seeks business for the broker-dealer through customers and potential customers.

But Wait There's More

Detailed Table of Contents

From the Author

Everybody wants test-taking tips for passing the Series 7. My advice is to answer at least 70% of the questions right, although many people prefer to answer no more than 30% of the questions wrong. Either way, they give you the license, and—remember—you do not have to show your work for the Series 7. If you manage to choose the right answer, you get the question right, even when you really have no idea what you're doing. And that's okay—you're not trying to learn how to become a stockbroker by passing your Series 7. You're just trying to pass the test that currently stands in your way of getting a license to sell securities. It's a multiple choice test, remember, and good test takers know that you're not really looking for the right answer to the question; you're usually trying to determine the three *wrong* answers instead. If you can do that on 175 or more of the questions they throw at you at the testing center, you win.

While this book attempts to cover the important concepts for the Series 7, I do not pretend that I have listed every word and every phrase you will encounter on your exam. If I tried to do that, the book would come in a 15-volume set, each one about 1,000 pages long. And, even that wouldn't completely cover it. See, there is really no end to the scope of the Series 7. To see what I mean, visit www.FINRA.org and check out the reading list they give for the Series 7 in the exam outline. One of those books is the classic *Security Analysis* by Benjamin Graham, Warren Buffett's former professor. Great book, but it also happens to be 725 pages long, and if you read it cover to cover you'd maybe end up getting one more question right on the exam. In fact, even if you read every word of every book on that list, you still wouldn't have covered every factoid that might be thrown at you on your exam. So, what are you supposed to do?

My approach is to cover all the fundamental concepts likely to be tested on your Series 7 exam, and cover them in a way you'll both understand and remember. Rather than churning out endless bullet point lists of terms that "could show up on the Series 7," I'm going to explain the concepts that are known to not just "show up on the test" but also provide the foundation for a large number of likely questions. I'm not going to pretend you won't see a *few* questions on your Series 7 that are unfamiliar. That's the nature of the beast, and anybody who tells you they "know what's on the Series 7" is yanking your chain—the securities regulators would sue any company that somehow hacked into their database of Series 7 questions and foolishly distributed them among their customers. All anybody can do is try to cover the fundamentals of the Series 7 in a way that will help you get at least 175 of 250 questions correct. I hope you'll agree that the book you're about to read is as interesting as anything related to the Series 7 could possibly be. I tried to write it in a way you can relate to, connecting the material to your own life whenever possible. I tried to use language as simply and concisely as possible, with examples that you will be able to remember, perhaps longer than you care to. But, no matter what I did with the material, the only person who can get you to pass the Series 7 is you. Put in the time, don't take any short-cuts, and do your due diligence. This is a hard process, but it's not impossible. If you do the work.

For more information on the test itself, visit www.FINRA.org. Under "industry professionals" you'll find a list of most viewed links, one or two of which will take you to the exams & qualifications page. You can get the exam outline, find out the cost to register, etc., but I'll let the regulators tell you why you have to take *their* exam and what you can do with the license. My job is simply to help you pass the test.

Ready?

Let's get started anyway.

The Big Picture

Just down the street a company has been making and selling fruit pies for over 50 years. Frank & Emma's Fruit Pies the company is called. It's been a good business, but now that Frank & Emma have passed on, their three children have decided that the market for their fruit pies is much bigger than either Frank or Emma ever imagined. After talking to several advisers, Jeremy, Jason, and Jennifer decide it's time to raise some serious cash and invest it back into the business.

The local banks, however, aren't interested in lending the company the $100 million it needs to build a new factory, hire 100 more employees and set up distribution centers throughout the Midwest. Luckily, there are investors who might be willing to provide the capital in exchange for owning a little slice of Frank & Emma's Fruit Pies. Actually, the investors will provide the company with money, but we prefer to use words like "**capital**" because it makes us sound much smarter than we really are. In the "capital market" investors provide capital (money) to corporations in exchange for ownership positions, called "**equity** securities." Just as homeowners have equity/ownership in their homes, stockholders have equity/ownership in the corporations whose stock they hold.

Frank & Emma's Fruit Pies would use the stockholders' money to grow the business. The money (capital) that investors provide to Frank & Emma's Fruit Pies would allow the business to pay for equipment, wages, computers, and all the basic ingredients businesses need in order to grow from small companies to bigger, more fruitful corporations. What do the shareholders get in return?

Basically, slices of the big profit pie. If the company has earnings (profits), the shareholders are entitled to their share of the pie. If the profits/earnings keep growing, eventually not only will the shares get bigger, but also Frank & Emma's might start cutting checks to the shareholders every quarter and call them "dividends."

Or not. Maybe the business will hit a series of setbacks and end up owing creditors more than they can possibly repay. Bankruptcy. Game over. There is always a risk when you buy a company's equity securities. On the other hand, if things work out the way we think, your slice of the pie could end up feeding you and your grandchildren's grandchildren, the way Microsoft, IBM, and Coca-Cola enriched their early investors beyond anyone's wildest dreams.

So Jeremy, Jason, and Jennifer decide to offer 30% of the company for sale to public investors. They don't plan to do the offering themselves, though. The process of issuing stock to public investors is very complex, with little room for error. So, they hire a firm called an underwriting or **investment banking** firm. Like a bank, the firm could raise money for Frank & Emma's Fruit Pies, but this wasn't a loan. The underwriting firm would promise to buy all the stock the company was issuing and immediately re-sell it to investors, keeping a piece of the proceeds for their efforts. It was a **firm commitment** of capital on the part of the underwriters, but if everything went according to plan, they would walk away with a nice profit, and Frank & Emma's Fruit Pies would have the $100 million it needed to expand the business. Since the brothers and sister owned the majority of the company, their own wealth would most likely grow, too, right along with the company's increased profits. And if everything went as planned, the investors who bought the slices of the big pie would also see their equity/ownership stakes in the company grow, too.

The underwriters registered the stock with the **Securities and Exchange Commission**, which under the Securities Act of 1933 requires companies issuing securities to provide disclosure to investors in the form of a **prospectus**. The **registration statement** with the SEC and the prospectus delivered to investors must reveal not just the promises of success but all the chances for failure, as well. Only if an investor has been provided with essential or "material" facts, can he/she make an informed decision about buying or not buying a particular security.

So the company and the underwriters provided information on the company's story to investors: its history, plans for the future, purpose for raising the money, as well as information on the **officers** and members of the **board of directors**. Public companies like Frank & Emma's are run by corporate officers including the chief executive officer (CEO), chief financial officer (CFO), and chief operating officer (COO), and also by the members of the board. The board of directors is supposed to look out for shareholders, and if the CEO, for example, isn't delivering results, the board can replace him with someone who appears to know what the heck he's doing. Some investors would base their decision to buy or not buy a particular common stock based on who the officers and board members are and what their track record looks like. That's why this "material information" must be provided in the prospectus.

Also, a section on the risks involved in buying stock in this particular company was prepared and placed toward the front of the document. The material risks included :

- The fluctuating price of oil can unpredictably raise delivery costs and compromise profit margins.
- Unionized laborers can unpredictably raise labor costs and force slowdowns in production and delivery.
- We compete against larger, better-capitalized companies.
- We rely on a few large customers for a large share of our revenue.
- Product liability risks (contamination) would have a material negative effect on the price of the stock.

It took a long time to get the SEC to finally give the green light, but, eventually, the underwriters were permitted to sell the shares to pension funds, mutual funds, and individual investors, who all liked Frank & Emma's Fruit Pies' chances for future success, weighed carefully against their possibility for failure. The underwriting was over in a few days, and after keeping a percentage known as the "**spread**" from the proceeds, the underwriters gave the company $100 million, which was quickly invested in new equipment, employee salaries, computer systems, and an aggressive TV and radio marketing campaign. Frank & Emma's Fruit Pies was looking a whole lot sweeter with the fresh infusion of capital.

Now a public company, Frank & Emma's has to file quarterly and **annual reports** with the SEC, which is actually kind of a pain. So, they hired an in-house attorney and accountant primarily to work on the 10-Q (quarterly) and 10-K (annual) reports. In the reports, the company discloses financial information to investors, as required by the **Securities Exchange Act of 1934**. This Act, sometimes called the "People Act," requires issuers of securities to file reports so public investors have enough information to decide whether to invest or stay invested in the company.

Public investors apparently like what they read in the reports because the shares keep trading among investors at higher and higher prices. Sold at a public offering price of $10, the stock is now trading over NASDAQ as high as $25. NASDAQ, the main stocks traded "over-the-counter," and the NYSE are part of the **secondary market**. When the stock was first issued, it was issued in the **primary market**, where the issuer received the proceeds. When those shares trade back and forth among investors, we call that process the secondary market, where the issuer does not get the proceeds. Underwriters work in the primary market. Broker-dealers work in the secondary market, facilitating trades between investors and making **commissions** or markups for their services. Some broker-dealers maintain an inventory of over-the-counter stock, acting as market makers. A **market maker** allows investors to sell their securities when the time comes to sell and, hopefully, receive a decent price from an interested buyer. The market maker buys stock from one party at the lower "bid" price and sells the stock to another at the higher "ask" price. Maybe the bid for 10,000 shares of Frank & Emma's common stock is $25.00 and the ask is $25.25. If the market maker can buy 10,000 shares at the bid and immediately re-sell them at the ask, they will keep the 25-cent "spread" per share, which is a quick $2,500 profit. What if they buy the 10,000 shares and then no buyers show up to take them off their hands?

That's the risk they take by making a market in the stock. Market makers act as principals, which means they have money at risk. When a firm sells a customer a stock from its inventory, it is said to be acting as a **dealer** or **principal**. When it simply arranges the trade for a customer, it is said to be acting as a **broker**. That's why the firm is called a **broker-dealer**, since it can act either as a broker, earning a commission, or as a dealer, earning a profit or markup on a particular trade. They can't do both on the same trade; they act as either a broker or a dealer on any particular trade.

And, they also get involved in the primary market taking companies public. When they do that, they call themselves underwriters/investment bankers. When they help investors unload and purchase securities in the secondary market, they call themselves broker-dealers.

You will be working for one of these broker-dealer firms, helping investors choose investments in stocks, bonds, options, mutual funds, and other products. Some investors will need the income provided by bonds. Others will need the **growth** offered by stocks. Still others will choose to risk their money on options. So, when a new customer decides to establish an investment account with you, you will fill out a customer account form that provides basic information on the customer's financial situation and investment goals. The younger the investor, the more likely you will recommend stocks, such as the stock in Frank & Emma's Fruit Pies. Or, maybe some day Frank & Emma will decide to offer bonds to investors, whereby the company simply borrows money from the public investors and pays a rate of interest on the loan/bonds until the loan is paid off in full. Instead of offering equity, then, the company would be offering debt securities. And that would make the bondholders creditors, who have to be paid on time. If not, the company goes into bankruptcy, and all the pie makers and other equipment could be sold at auction, the proceeds returned to the bondholders.

But bankruptcy seems like a remote possibility since Frank & Emma's is now a better-established company, with manufacturing facilities in Chicago, Cleveland, Milwaukee, and Indianapolis. Their fleet of delivery vans now stocks the shelves of regional grocers like Jewel and Dominick's, as well as serving up pies to school, hospital, and large corporate cafeterias. Their cash flow is strong,

their sales are growing 20% a year, and the stock's market price keeps reflecting the good news coming out of Frank & Emma's Fruit Pies. So, while the market price for FREM common stock is important to Jeremy, Jason, and Jennifer, the three corporate officers have more important day-to-day concerns. So, let's let Frank & Emma's run their business a while, while we talk about serving *your* customers, the investors kind enough to supply growing companies like FREM with capital.

Let's say that tomorrow morning you get a phone call from a prospect named Michelle Madsen. Michelle has been referred to you through a friend, who spoke highly of your recommendations and attention to detail. First thing you do is pull out a **new account form** for Ms. Madsen, filling it in with her contact information, employment situation, financial information, and investment goals. Once this is completed, you will sign it and get the signature of your principal. Michelle does not have to sign the new account form—she'll sign other documents, but this is just a profile you can use to make recommendations.

If Michelle is showing a high net worth and high tax bracket, you might interest her in tax-free municipal bonds issued by cities and states to fund roads, schools, and other necessary infrastructure improvements. Since the IRS generally does not tax the interest, these bonds offer lower nominal interest rates (**coupon rate**s,) but high tax-bracket people still come out ahead. If you're in the 30% bracket and receive a 10% **nominal yield** on a corporate bond, you only keep 70% of that, since the other 30% goes to the IRS. Therefore a 10% corporate bond would be equivalent to a 7% municipal bond, since either way the investor keeps $70 a year. They might receive $100 on the corporate, but $30 is "shared" with Uncle Sam. The municipal bond pays $70 and the investor keeps all of it.

Equivalent.

Michelle likes the idea of some tax-free income, so you and she agree to put 25% of her money into general obligation municipal securities issued by Chicago, Cleveland, and New York City. To get a slightly higher yield, you also use some of that 25% to purchase **revenue bonds**, backed only by the revenues on sports stadiums and toll roads, issued by the same municipalities. See, the **general obligation bonds** are a legal obligation of the issuer to pay bondholders with tax money. Revenue bonds are backed by the revenues generated from the facility built with the proceeds of the bonds. If the revenue bond builds a toll road, the bonds are backed by the tolls, for example. The state or city doesn't have to step in to pay back the bondholders, so revenue bonds are riskier than general obligation (GO) bonds. Therefore, they have a higher yield.

So 25% of Michelle's money is now invested in tax-free municipals.

Michelle is 41 years old and plans to work at least another 20 years. With such a long time horizon, you suggest she invest 50% of her capital in common stock like FREM. Michelle has never considered investing in FREM, but she has seen the pies at the supermarket and was quite taken by a recent French Silk with Pecan creation that she picked up on a whim at Walmart.

You and Michelle decide to invest in common stock for the growth she'll need between here and retirement. Some of the companies have relatively few shares outstanding, making them "small cap" stocks, like FREM. These "small cap stocks" have less established histories but also potentially brighter futures than **large cap** stocks, in general. Their P/E ratios are high, since much of the perceived value is built on speculation of future profits. But, if the future is as bright as investors hope, millionaires are created, just as they were when investors took a chance on companies such as Microsoft®, IBM®, Oracle®, and Starbucks®, to name just a few former growth stocks that eventually matured into large cash-generating machines. These days, Microsoft®, IBM®, and Oracle® would be considered "large cap" stocks, since the value of their stock is relatively large. Huge, in fact.

So, you and Michelle put together a diversified portfolio of common stock, investing in FREM, as well as Walmart®, General Electric®, Starbucks®, and Oracle®.

Michelle now has 25% in tax-free municipals and 50% in common stocks of companies as small as Frank & Emma's and as large as General Electric. That's **diversification**, or the "don't put all your eggs in one basket" principle of equity investment. What about the other 25%?

Michelle puts 20% in-the-money market, which is a very boring holding place for cash. Money market securities are short-term debt obligations that will be paid back within 1 year (usually 270 days maximum) by high-quality issuers. Commercial paper, banker's acceptances, and jumbo CDs are the most common of these safe, short-term debt securities that will end up paying Michelle some interest without subjecting her principal to any significant risk.

And the final 5% Michelle decides to use speculating in equity options. **Calls** and **puts**, in other words. Although not your strong suit, you decide that 5% is not a lot to risk on these high-risk securities that derive their value from an underlying stock. Which is why options are called "derivatives."

Ever heard that you shouldn't try to time the market? Well, **options** are all about trying to time the market. If you think a stock is going up in a hurry, buy a call. If the stock goes up in a hurry, the value of the call skyrockets. What if the stock drops in a hurry, instead?

The call expires worthless and you lose.

Magically, you can make just as much money when stocks do belly flops by buying puts. If you have an ABC August 70 put when ABC drops to $10 a share, your put would be worth at least that $60 difference. And you might have bought the thing for just $5. Or not. It's all speculation, this world of options, but since Michelle has plenty of financial means and is only risking 5% of her capital on options, you decide not to talk her out of it. Instead, you send her the OCC disclosure document that lays out all the risks and characteristics of options trading and get her to sign an options agreement. As soon as your firm's options principal approves the account, Michelle can start trading.

Now that you have met your **suitability** requirements with Michelle by carefully recommending securities that make sense given her time horizon, risk tolerance, and financial means, you must continue to deal fairly and equitably with her. FINRA's Member Conduct Rules try to ensure that customers get a fair deal from their agents and broker-dealers, and if you violate these rules FINRA has a whole system in place to handle infractions, called Code of Procedure (COP). Under Code of Procedure, you could be fined, sanctioned, suspended, expelled, or even barred from doing business with any other firm.

Which is bad. You can appeal these decisions, but who wants to end up there?

No one. So, to avoid going through this Code of Procedure, make sure you take the time to evaluate your customer's needs and make suitable recommendations. Don't "borrow" money from customer accounts, even when you intend to replace it after hitting it big at the racetrack. Don't use **material inside information** to make recommendations, and always forward written complaints to your supervisor/principal at the firm. Above all, never deceive a client for financial gain. That's called **fraud**, and it cannot only get you suspended, but also get you thrown in jail.

So, here's the big picture: in order for a company to expand, it needs capital. It accesses this capital in the "primary market," where investment bankers raise money for corporations by selling the company's securities to investors, keeping a "spread" for their trouble. The issuing corporation takes the capital and buys equipment, technology, or whatever it needs for expansion. Investors can now trade their stocks and bonds with other investors on the secondary market. Securities firms like yours might work both the primary market and the secondary market. Whether offering new stock to a customer in the primary market or helping her trade securities in the secondary market, your firm's actions are regulated by their **self-regulatory organization**, FINRA, as well as the government body called the SEC. The SEC insists on truthfulness and full disclosure. Because of the SEC, companies who access the public markets have to disclose all kinds of negative information about things that have happened and things that could happen in the future to impair the value of the investor's stock or bond before issuing their securities. Then, they have to disclose all kinds of negative information through quarterly and annual reports filed with the SEC and posted all over the Internet. This way investors have a fair shot at discerning a good investment opportunity from a poor one. There is always risk, but through full disclosure, truthfulness, and fair dealings, investors can manage this risk, using a highly regulated professional such as yourself to help choose suitable investments.

Now that you have a grasp of the big picture, let's start looking at all the details your exam will expect you to know. But, no matter how detailed the material may get, please remember one thing: this is not rocket science. It isn't even close. Just learn the big concepts, and boost your score at the exam center with good test-taking skills.

Ready?

CHAPTER 1

Equity Securities

Some investors want to receive a predictable stream of income on their investment. For example, maybe they like to loan a corporation $100,000 and receive $5,000 a year in interest payments. That 5% yield is nice, but at the end of the term, the investor will only get back $100,000. Other investors will give up that steady stream of income in order to reach for growth or "capital appreciation." Rather than lending money to a corporation, these **equity** investors prefer to buy **common stock** in the company. This way, if the company becomes more profitable, so do the shares of common stock that the investor purchased.

COMMON STOCK

The most basic form of "equity" is known as **common stock**. Common stock is easily transferable, which means it can be sold without breaking a sweat. If investors get tired of looking at the stock certificates, they can sell them to other investors. That's how common stock works. You get tired of it, you sell it. You start to miss it, you buy it back.

A corporation hires a firm (usually a bank) to keep track of all of those transfers of ownership, by the way, and guess what we call them? The **transfer agent**. The transfer agent keeps the ownership records of the company's stock. Equate the word "certificates" with "transfer agent." The transfer agent deals with issuing and validating certificates, recording all the name changes when investors sell their certificates, that sort of thing. Lost, stolen, mutilated...if there's a problem with the certificates, contact the transfer agent. They can validate them or re-issue them, as the case may be. And, usually for a fee. They're a business. They like fees.

Just to make sure the transfer agent does a good job, the corporation also hires another outside firm—typically a bank—and we refer to this bank as the **registrar**. The registrar audits/oversees the transfer agent, just to make sure there aren't more shares outstanding than the company is authorized to sell.

AUTHORIZED, ISSUED, TREASURY, OUTSTANDING

Which brings us to four important terms: **authorized, issued, treasury, and outstanding**. To answer most test questions successfully, all you really have to do is take the number of "issued" shares and subtract the number of "treasury" shares to get the number of shares "outstanding." But, if you want to grasp the concept of the four terms, you'll need to read the next few paragraphs.

Sorry about that.

Authorized shares represent the number of shares a company has authorized itself to issue to the public, a number disclosed in the corporate charter. Let's say a company is authorized to issue 1,000,000 shares of common stock, according to the charter. When they first sell shares to the public during their IPO, they probably won't issue all of them the first time out. The number they actually issue would be known, surprisingly enough, as issued shares. This corporation could issue 1 million, but they only issue 500,000. Therefore, there are 500,000 issued.

For various reasons, the corporation might decide to buy back some of those shares that are out in the secondary market. These shares, which were issued but repurchased, are called **treasury stock**. Since it's sort of locked up in a vault, it has no voting rights and pays no dividends. But, it can be used in many ways by the issuing corporation. For the test, you just have to take the number of shares actually issued and subtract the number repurchased and held in the treasury. If this corporation had issued 500,000 shares and then purchased 100,000 for the treasury, they would have how many shares left outstanding?

Exactly. 400,000 shares outstanding.

So, just take "issued" and subtract "treasury" to get the number of shares "outstanding."

500,000	Issued
-100,000	Treasury =
400,000	Outstanding

No big deal, really. When we talk about a company's **earnings per share,** or **EPS**, we're only talking about the **outstanding shares**, which are also the only shares that get to vote. That's why the company can boost its earnings per share (EPS) by repurchasing their outstanding stock on the secondary market. Even if the company's total profit/earnings stayed the same, the earnings *per share* would rise if the company were reducing the number of outstanding shares. For example, if the company earned $1 million, that would be an earnings per share of $2 when there were 500,000 shares outstanding. However, after the company buys back 100,000 shares for the treasury, that same $1 million profit would be $2.50 of earnings per share. Right?

RIGHTS, PRIVILEGES OF COMMON STOCK OWNERSHIP

Owners of common stock enjoy several important rights the exam wants you to know about. The first right is the right of common stockholders to vote for any major issue that could affect their status as a proportional owner of the corporation. Things like stock splits, mergers and acquisitions, board of director elections, and changes of business objectives all require shareholder approval. But, one thing shareholders never get to vote on is whether a dividend is paid and, if so, how much it should be. Letting shareholders propose and vote on dividends would be like letting your kids propose and approve their own allowance.

Not at this time, thank you.

Shareholders vote their shares. If you own 100 shares of common stock, you have 100 votes to cast. Let's say there are three seats up for election on the Board of Directors. There are two ways that your votes could be cast for the election. Under **statutory**

voting, you can only cast the number of shares you own for any one seat. So, you could cast up to 100 votes for any one seat, representing a total of 300 votes for three seats. Under cumulative, you could take those 300 votes and split them up any way you wanted among the three candidates. You could even cast all 300 votes for one candidate and give nothing to the others. That's why the exam might want you to say that **cumulative voting** gives a benefit to the small/minority shareholders. In other words, if we can manage to get a candidate on the slate who will look out for us small shareholders, we can all cast all of our votes for her. The big guys will still get their way with the other candidates, but this gives us a fighting chance every once in a while. And remember that "the big guys," including pension funds and mutual funds, may have millions of shares (votes) versus our couple of hundred votes. Oh well. That's how it works—one vote per share, not per shareholder.

Beyond voting, common stockholders also have the right to inspect the corporation's financials through quarterly (10-Q) and annual (10-K) reports, just to see how the corporation is spending the shareholders' money and running the show up there at headquarters. Shareholders may also see the list of stockholders and the minutes of shareholder meetings.

Shareholders have the right to receive a certificate that serves as their proof of ownership. The certificate states the name of the issuing corporation, the shareholder's name, and the number of shares represented by the certificate. The certificate must be signed by an officer of the corporation. If you were to purchase 1,000 shares of Frank & Emma's Fruit Pies, your certificate would look something like this:

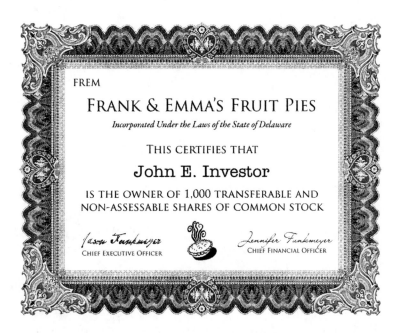

The certificate above would also include the name of the transfer agent, because shareholders have the right to freely transfer their shares to other parties, whether by selling them, donating them to a charity, giving them as a gift, or "bequeathing" them to their heirs when they pass away. The transfer agent is usually a division of a bank that keeps shareholder records for an issuer such as Frank & Emma's or Microsoft.

Common stockholders have what the test may call a "pre-emptive right" to maintain their percentage of ownership. In other words, if Frank & Emma's wants to raise more money in the future by selling more common stock, existing shareholders would get a chance to buy their percentage of the upcoming issue. If not, their ownership would be diluted.

Should a corporation go belly-up and have to be liquidated, common stockholders get in line for their piece of the proceeds. Unfortunately, they are last in line. They are behind all the creditors, including bondholders, and also behind preferred stockholders.

But, at least they are in line, and if there are any residuals left, they get to make their claim on those assets. That's known as a **residual claim** on assets, by the way, because they like to get real creative with the language in this industry. The test could also refer to common stock as the most "junior" security, since all other securities represent senior claims.

The exam might also point out that shareholders, who are owners of the corporation, have **limited liability**, which means they are shielded from the debts of the company and lawsuits filed against it. I'm not sure why they bring this up—it's not like the bondholders *are* liable, just something the exam might mention. Limited liability is a good news–bad news thing. The bad news is when you buy common stock, you can lose all your money. The good news is that when you buy common stock, you can only lose all your money.

Finally, the exam might say that common stock owners have a "claim on earnings and dividends." That's true—as owners, they have a share of the profits. Some of the profits/earnings are reinvested into the business, which tends to make the share price rise. Some of the profits might be paid out as dividends, so let's take a look at that.

DIVIDENDS

Did you know that a cash dividend is only paid if the Board of Directors decides to pay it?

That's right, if a corporation doesn't declare a dividend, the dividend doesn't get paid. End of story.

But, if they do declare a dividend, the board gets to decide three dates. FINRA/NYSE (depending on where the stock trades) decides the fourth one. Here's how it works. The day that the Board declares the dividend is known as the **declaration date**. The board decides when they'll pay the dividend, too, and we call that the **payable date**. Notice how creative the language is there—we call the day the dividend is d-e-c-l-a-r-e-d the *declaration date*, and the day the dividend is p-a-y-a-b-l-e the *payable date*. Remember, if you get yourself in a jam on the exam, break down the words and ask yourself what they probably mean, because most terms probably mean exactly what their names imply. The party in charge of transfers is the "transfer agent." The company that issues securities is called the **issuer**, and so on.

Anyway, the board of directors wonders who should receive this dividend—how about investors who actually own the stock as of a certain date? We call that the **record date** because an investor has to be the "owner of record" as of that date if she wants to receive the dividend. Now, since an investor has to be the owner of record as of the Record Date to receive the dividend, there will come a day when it's too late for investors to buy the stock and also get the dividend.

Why?

Regular Way Settlement

Because stock transactions don't "settle" until the third business day following the **trade date**, you might put in your purchase order to buy 1,000 shares of Frank & Emma's on a Monday, but you aren't the official owner until that transaction clears or settles on Thursday. Your broker-dealer has to send payment to the seller's broker-dealer, who has to deliver the 1,000 shares. Both sides have to agree that the terms of the transaction have been met, and the whole thing has cleared or settled between the buyer and seller. This process takes three business days and is known as **regular way settlement,** or "T + 3," where the "T" stands for <u>T</u>rade Date. Assuming there are no holidays, a trade taking place on Monday, would settle on Thursday, while a trade on Tuesday would settle on Friday. So, if an investor has to be the owner of record on the record date, and it takes three business days for the buyer to become the new owner, wouldn't she have to buy the stock at least three business days prior to the record date? Yes. If she buys it just two business days before the record date, her trade won't settle in time. We call that day the **ex-date** or "ex-dividend" date, because starting on that day investors who buy the stock will not receive the dividend. On the ex-date, it's too late. Why? Because the trades won't settle in time, and the purchasers won't be the owners of record (with the transfer agent) as of the record date. The answer to your exam question might be that "if the trade takes place on or after the ex-date, the seller is entitled to the dividend." Of course, if the trade takes place before the ex-date, the buyer will get the dividend.

FINRA sets the ex-date, as a function of "regular way" or "T + 3" settlement. The ex-date is two business days before the record date.

So, remember DERP. Declaration, Ex-Date, Record Date, Payable Date. The board sets all of them except the Ex-Date, which is set by FINRA/NYSE. If investors don't qualify for the dividend starting with the ex-date, guess what? The amount of the dividend is taken right out of the stock price when trading begins on the ex-date. If the dividend to be paid is 70 cents, and the stock closed at $20 the day before, it would open at 19.30 (the dividend comes out) on the ex-date.

One of the problems people have while studying for the Series 7 is that too much information seems to be "test world" and not "real world." I know from teaching live classes that candidates get tired of just memorizing chunks of information that seem completely divorced from reality. All this "XYZ" and "ABC" stuff gets a little tiring, so let's take a look at how the DERP thing would play out in the so-called "real world." Also, we *know* the date below is 2005—this is a *historical* example. The date will *always* be 2005 for this *one example,* even in the year 2018, okay?.

Equity Office declares first quarter common dividend

```
Mar 16, 2005-- Equity Office Properties Trust (EOP), a publicly held
office building owner and manager, has announced that its Board of
Trustees has declared a first quarter cash dividend in the amount
of $.50 per common share. The dividend will be paid on Friday
15 April 2005, to common shareholders of record at the close of
business on Thursday 31 March 2005.
```

So, March 16 is the Declaration Date. The Payable Date is April 15. The Record Date is Thursday, March 31st. The article doesn't mention the Ex-Date (because that's not established by the company), but we can figure that it must be…right, Tuesday, March 29th. If you bought the stock on Tuesday, your trade wouldn't settle until Friday, April 1st, which means the seller's name would be on the list of shareholders at the close of business on Thursday, March 31st.

Quick note: EOP is a REIT, and the "T" in "REIT" stands for "trust." That's why the press release refers to the board as the "Board of Trustees." EOP is a Real Estate Investment Trust, but the stock works like any other stock. It simply pays a nice dividend. As we'll see later, REITs are just shares of stock that tend to pay nice dividend yields. If you owned 1,000 shares of EOP as of the record date, what would you receive?

A check for $500. So, if the dividend stays the same or increases in Q2, Q3, and Q4, you'll collect at least $2,000 just for sitting on your shares of EOP this year. Ever heard that the rich get richer? This is partly why.

It also brings up a testable point as to how a dividend can be paid. A dividend can be paid in the following ways:

- Cash (which means they cut you a check)
- Stock (more shares of stock)
- Shares of a subsidiary
- Product (extremely rare)

Cash dividends are taxable. Stock dividends are not taxable.

PRACTICE

1. **An investor purchases common stock on a Thursday. Under regular way settlement, the transaction will settle**

    A. Friday

    B. Monday

    C. Tuesday

    D. Wednesday

2. **The Board of Directors declared a dividend on Monday, March 1st. If the record date is Tuesday, March 16th, the ex-dividend date is**

    A. Monday, March 15th

    B. Friday, March 12th

    C. Thursday, March 18th

    D. Tuesday, March 23rd

3. **Which of the following is/are true concerning Treasury stock?**

    A. has been issued and repurchased by the company

    B. reduces the number of outstanding shares

    C. tends to raise EPS

    D. all of the above

ANSWERS

1. **C,** Thursday is the trade date or the "T" in "T + 3." T + 1 is Friday, T + 2 is Monday, and T + 3 is Tuesday.

2. **B,** go back two business days.

3. **D,** they buy it back to leave fewer shares outstanding; therefore, the same total earnings/profits of the company are divided among fewer shares for a higher EPS.

STOCK SPLITS, STOCK DIVIDENDS

The big idea behind stock splits and stock dividends is that when the investor ends up with more shares, the total value of his investment is unchanged. If he had 100 shares at $10 before, that was worth $1,000. No matter how many shares he has after the split or the stock dividend, the total value is still just $1,000. So, when a corporation does a 2:1 stock split, the investor would have twice as many shares. What would the price per share be?

Half as much. The investor has $1,000 worth of stock both before and after the split. He used to have 100 shares worth $10 each. Now he has 200 shares worth $5 each. A thousand bucks, either way. The test might want you to work with an uneven split, like a 5:4 ratio. This is where the company gives investors five shares for every four that they own.

A possible exam question might read:

Joe Tidewater owns 100 shares of XYZ Corp. common stock currently trading at $50. XYZ Corp. declares a 5:4 stock split. What will Mr. Tidewater's stock position be after the 5:4 split?

I.   500 shares

II. 125 shares

III. @$50 each

IV. @ $40 each

A.   I, III

B.   I, IV

C.   II, III

D.   II, IV

Okay, if Joe Tidewater had 100 shares worth $50, what was the total value? $5,000. Well, that's what his investment will be worth after the split, too, so let's see how the numbers work out.

Just multiply Joe's 100 shares by the first number, and divide that by the second number.

$$100 \text{ X } 5 \text{ divided by } 4 = 125 \text{ shares}$$

Joe will have 125 shares.

What will each share be worth?

Well, he still has $5,000 worth of XYZ Corp. stock; he just has to divide that total amount over more shares. $5,000 divided by 125 shares, gives us a share price of $40.

The answer, then, is "D."

Why do companies do this? For one reason: to push the share price *down*. Companies have concluded that when their stock price goes up "too high," many investors, especially the Average Joe and JoAnne, get scared off. Since stock prices are determined purely through supply and demand, if we scare off the little guy, there won't be as much demand for our stock, and the stock price will drop. So, if our share price goes up to $100, let's knock it back to $50 with a 2:1 split and hope that demand for the shares will increase. At this point, it might seem shocking that a company worried about a sagging stock price will solve the problem by pushing their share price . . . down. But, trust me, you'll get used to these things the farther you go into Series Sevenland.

In any case, a stock *dividend* would work the same way in terms of more shares/lower price. If an investor receives a 20% stock dividend, that's 20% more shares of stock, but the total value of the investment is the same. It's just divided among more shares. So an investor with 200 shares of XYZ common stock @40 would have $8,000 of XYZ stock. If XYZ sent her a 20% stock dividend, she would then have 240 shares. Her $8,000 would then be divided among 240 shares, yielding a per-share price of $33.33. Companies like Frank & Emma's, which are still in a growth phase, are more likely to pay stock dividends (vs. cash dividends) than more established companies, who are more likely to pay cash dividends compared to small, growing companies.

Either way, nothing really changes after a stock dividend or a stock split. The investor simply has more shares at a lower price, which means her **cost basis** in the stock changes. 100 shares @50 might become 125 shares @40. Just keep track of your cost basis so that when you sell someday you can tell the IRS how much of a **capital gain** or loss you realized on the stock. But whether you have 100 shares @50 or 125 shares @40, you've paid $5,000 for a certain percentage of ownership. And, we'll deal with concerns such as "cost basis" and "capital gains" in more detail in the Taxation chapter later in the book.

You can think of a stock split or stock dividend like this: let's say you and a friend are on a diet. You decide to splurge and order pizza for lunch, but since you're on this diet you're not going to cut the thing in half and eat half a pizza, for crying out loud. Since you're on a diet, you can only have small pieces, so you decide to cut the pie into 20 slices, and you each eat only 10 small pieces. Or, maybe your friend is overzealous and talks you into cutting the pie into 50 slices, whereby you each consume only 25 teeny, tiny, little pieces.

Umm, you're eating half the pie either way, right?

Same thing for a stock dividend or a forward stock split. No matter how they slice the earnings pie, you own the same percentage before and after this non-event. They've made the shares smaller and "cheaper," but you have more of them. A "forward split," by the way, just means you end up with more shares. A 2:1, 3:2, or 5:4 split would be a forward split that pushes the share price down.

Well, sometimes companies have the opposite problem—their share price is so low that the big, institutional investors (pension funds, mutual funds, insurance companies) won't touch it. These entities usually won't touch a stock trading below $5, so if our company's stock is trading for $1, we might need to increase that price. One way to do it would be to become a more competitive, profitable company and let the increased profits take the share price up.

Nahhhhh, too much work. Let's do a reverse stock split instead.

If the test question says that JoAnne is long 100 shares of LMNO @$1, we might find LMNO doing a reverse split of 1:10. That means for every 10 shares she owns now, she'll end up with only one really big share. She'll have 10 shares when it's all over, in other words. If the shares were trading for $1 before the split and everybody now has shares that are 10 times bigger, the share price magically becomes…yes, $10 a share. JoAnne is now long 10 LMNO @$10.

Awesome—LMNO is a $10 stock, just like that! Doesn't the stock represent the same % ownership, though? Sure, but human beings are funny creatures—many of them will just think the stock has gone up due to, like, profits and stuff. Just remember that whether the exam is talking about a stock dividend, a forward split, or a reverse split, the investor's cost basis changes because the share price changes. But no change in *value* actually occurs. See, there's a big difference between a change in *price* and a change in *value*. It's not how many dollars you paid for the stock. It's, "How much did you pay for the *earnings*?" Remember, a share of stock represents a slice of the earnings/profits pie, so how much are you paying for these earnings/profits? A $100 stock with $10 of earnings associated with it is much *cheaper* than a $1 stock with 1 penny of earnings. The first one trades at a "multiple" or P/E of only 10, while the second one will cost you 100 times the earnings, or a P/E of 100. Looks cheaper, but the $1 stock is really 10 times more expensive than the $100 stock. P/E means "Price to Earnings." Just compare how much larger the stock price is compared to the earnings associated with each share. Guess what we call "earnings per share"?

Earnings per share. Except we prefer to be hip and abbreviate it as "EPS."

Finally, remember that shareholders vote on stock splits, whether forward (5:4, 2:1, 3:2) or reverse (1:7, 1:10, etc.). Shareholders do not vote on dividends, period.

WHAT IS A SHARE OF COMMON STOCK?

Before we move on, let's make sure we understand exactly what a share of stock is. When you buy a company's common stock, you simply own a percentage of the company. What are all owners interested in? Profits, called *earnings*. The bottom line, baby. You start your own business for one main reason—to earn a profit. You buy a <u>share</u> of somebody else's business for the same reason—to <u>share</u> in the profits. So, you only buy a share of common stock if you think the company will earn a profit, increase that profit, and, eventually, pay some of that profit out to you as a dividend. That's all there is to it—if you want to <u>share</u> in the earnings/profits of the company, buy some *shares* of common stock.

What if there aren't any earnings?

Hope for better days or sell the stock to a greater fool than the current owner.

RIGHTS, WARRANTS

As we mentioned, one of the **rights** common stockholders enjoy is the right to maintain their proportionate ownership in the corporation. We call this a "preemptive right" because the existing shareholders get to say yes or no to their proportion of the new shares before (pre-) the new shareholders get a chance to buy any. Otherwise, if you owned 5% of the company, you'd end up owning less than 5% of it after they sold the new shares to everyone *but* you, which could be called "dilution of equity" to make us sound smarter than we really are. Sort of a "first dibs for current investors" thing happening here, but the exam will probably call it "preemptive rights." For every share owned, an investor receives what's known as a right. It's an equity security with a very short life span. It works like a coupon, allowing the current shareholders the chance to purchase the stock below the market price over the course of a few weeks—called the **subscription price**. If a stock is trading at $20, maybe the existing shareholders can take two rights plus $18 to buy a new share. Those rights act as coupons that give the current shareholders two dollars off the market price. So, the investors can use the rights, sell them, or let them expire in a drawer somewhere, like most coupons. The exam might bring up a rather challenging question or two on calculating the value of a right. We will explain the two formulas required to make the calculation at the end of this chapter in order to avoid getting bogged down with numbers at this point.

Warrants have absolutely nothing to do with rights, and vice versa, but it's convenient to talk about them in the same section, so here goes. Unlike a right, a **warrant** is a long-term equity security. There are no dividends attached to a warrant. If you own a warrant, all you own is the opportunity to purchase a company's stock at a pre-determined price. If you have a warrant that lets you buy XYZ for $30 per share, then you can buy a certain number of shares at that price whenever you feel it makes sense to do so, like when XYZ is trading for a lot more than $30 per share. When issued, the price stated on the warrant is above the current market price of the stock. It usually takes a long time for a stock's price to go above the price stated on the warrant. But, they're good for a long time, typically somewhere between two and ten years.

Warrants are often attached to a bond offering. Corporations pay interest to borrow money through bonds. If they attach warrants, they can "sweeten" the deal a little and maybe offer investors a lower interest payment. Why would you take 4% when your buddy gets 6% on his bond? Doesn't he make $60 a year, while you only make $40? Yes. But if the company's common stock rises, he'll still be making $60 a year, while you could make a huge profit on the common. If you have a warrant to buy 1,000 shares @30 and those shares rise to $50, are you going to cry about that $20 a year your buddy made? Not when you just made about $20,000, right? In fact, why not give your buddy a call right after you cash in your profits and offer to buy him lunch, especially if he was ever talking trash about your decision to take 4% when he got 6%.

PREFERRED STOCK

A common stock investor might receive dividends, but the dividend is not stated by the company on the stock certificate—in fact, the company may never get around to paying a dividend on their common stock. Common stock investors are generally interested in growth or capital appreciation more than income. That means they want to buy the stock low and watch it increase in market price over time. On the other hand, income investors who want to buy a corporation's stock would likely want to buy the company's **preferred stock** instead. Preferred stock gets preferential treatment if the company has to be forcibly liquidated to pay creditors, and always receives dividends before owners of common stock can be paid. And, unlike common stock, the preferred stock dividend is printed right on the stock certificate. The par value for a preferred stock is assumed to be $100. The stated dividend is a percentage of that par value. Six-percent preferred stock would pay 6% of $100 per share, or $6 per share per year. Three percent preferred stock would pay a dividend of 3% of the par value each year.

We hope.

See, dividends still have to be declared by the Board of Directors. Preferred stockholders aren't creditors. They're just proportional owners who like to receive dividends. If the board doesn't declare a dividend, do you know how much an owner of a 6% preferred stock would receive?

Nothing.

However, if the investor owned **cumulative preferred stock**, that might be different. They wouldn't necessarily get the dividend now, but the company would have to make up the missed dividend in future years before it could pay dividends to any other preferred or common stock-holders. If the company missed the six bucks this year and wanted to pay the full six bucks next year, cumulative preferred stockholders would have to get their $12 before anybody else saw a dime.

This 6% works more like a maximum than a minimum. If an investor wants the chance to earn more than the stated 6%, he'd have to buy **participating preferred stock**, which would allow him to share in dividends above that rate, if the company has the money and feels like distributing it. Generally, if the issuer increases the dividend paid to common stockholders, they will also raise the dividend paid to participating preferred stockholders.

Another type of preferred stock has a rate of return that is tied to another rate, typically the T-bill rate. If T-bill rates are up, so is the rate on the **adjustable preferred stock**, and vice versa. Because the rate adjusts, the price remains stable.

Convertible Preferred Stock

A highly testable type of preferred stock is **convertible preferred stock**. This type lets an investor exchange one share of preferred for a certain number of common shares whenever the investor wants to make the switch. Say the convertible preferred stock is convertible into 10 shares of common stock. Therefore, the convertible preferred stock is usually worth whatever 10 shares of common stock are worth. If so, they trade at "parity," which means "equal." Just multiply the price of the common stock by the number of shares the investor could convert the preferred into. That gives you the preferred stock's parity price.

So, if the convertible preferred were convertible into 10 shares of common and the common stock went up to $15 a share, how much would the convertible preferred be worth at parity?

$$10 \text{ X } \$15, \text{ or } \$150$$

The test question will either tell you how many shares the investor can convert into, or it will make you take the par value and divide it by the conversion price given. If the question says the convertible is convertible at $10, just take $100 of par divided by that $10, and you'll see that the investor can convert to 10 shares of common. Convertible at $20 would be $100 divided by $20 = 5 shares. Either way, if it's convertible at 10, you have a 10:1 relationship. If it's convertible at $20, you have a 5:1 relationship. Use those 10:1 and 5:1 relationships as your tool. If they give you the common stock price, multiply by the first number to get the parity price of the preferred. If they give you the preferred stock's market price, divide by the first number to get the parity price of the common stock.

It's basically a gift certificate. If you have a gift certificate worth $100, how many blue jeans can you buy if they're priced at $20?

5.

What if you want T-shirts priced at $10? You can get 10.

So, when they say the preferred is "convertible at $20," or "convertible at $10," just ask how far your "gift certificate" would go. Preferred stock is a gift certificate worth $100 toward the purchase of/conversion to common stock at a set price.

Let's make sure you have it by looking at a practice question:

XYZ 4% preferred stock is convertible @25. Currently, XYZ common trades at $28 per share; therefore, the parity of XYZ preferred stock is:

A. $100

B. $112

C. $33

D. $53

The answer is "B," $112. How did we get that? How far does the gift certificate of $100 (par value) go if the stock costs $25 upon conversion?

4 shares.

What are 4 shares now worth? Four times $28 = $112.

If a security has a fixed payment, the market compares that fixed payment to current interest rates. Current interest rates represent what investors could receive if they bought low-risk debt securities. If low-risk debt securities are paying 4%, and your preferred stock pays you a fixed

6%, how do you feel about your preferred? Pretty good, right, since it's paying a higher rate than current interest rates. If somebody wanted to buy it, they'd have to pay a higher price. But, if interest rates shoot up to 10%, suddenly your 6% preferred doesn't look so good, right? In that case the market price would go down. Not the par value—par value is etched in stone. It's the market price that fluctuates.

Market prices adjust for interest rates: rates up/prices down, rates down/prices up. Well, as we mentioned, if the rate adjusts along with the T-bill rate, the price doesn't need to move. But for other types of preferred, the price moves in the opposite direction of interest rates, just like bond prices. That's because the value is really determined by a comparison of the fixed rate of return to current interest rates.

But, if we add another variable, now the security's price isn't so sensitive to interest rates. Convertible preferred has a value tied to interest rates, like other preferred stock, but its value is also tied to the value of the common stock into which it can be exchanged or converted. If rates are up, preferred prices drop. But if you're holding a convertible preferred while the common stock is skyrocketing, the price of the preferred would skyrocket right along with it. Remember, it's worth a fixed number of common shares. If the value of the common goes up, so does the value of the convertible preferred. So, the exam might want you to know that convertible preferred stock is less sensitive to interest rates than other types of preferred.

The exam might want to know all kinds of fun stuff.

Remember that unlike a bond, preferred stock generally does not have a **maturity date**, and unlike common stock, usually does not give the owner voting rights. Two specific cases where preferred stock *does* get to vote are: 1) the corporation defaults on the dividend payment a certain number of times and 2) the corporation wants to issue preferred stock of equal or senior status.

Finally, to review how common and preferred stock relate to each other, let's note the similarities and differences between the two.

SIMILARITIES	DIFFERENCES
dividends must be declared by the board of directors for each	preferred stock is a fixed-income security paying a stated rate of return
both are equity securities	preferred has a higher claim on dividends and on assets in a bankruptcy
	common stock has voting rights and pre-emptive rights

ADRs

"ADR" stands for **American Depository Receipt**, and like many of the abbreviations you'll need to know for the exam, this one means exactly what it says. It's a receipt issued to somebody in America against shares of foreign stock held on deposit in a foreign branch of an American bank. Look for an answer like "a foreign stock in a domestic market" or something that "facilitates U.S. investors in purchasing foreign stock." The investor buys shares of a Japanese corporation's stock, only the shares are held in a bank in Japan, which issues a receipt to the investor in America. The receipt is what is traded in America. It pays dividends, maybe, but they are paid in the foreign currency and then have to be converted into U.S. dollars, which is why ADR owners are subject to currency risk. Also, if the stock is worth a certain number of yen on the Japanese markets, that won't work out to as many U.S. dollars when our dollar is strong, although it would work out to more American dollars if our dollar is weak.

In the real world people often don't even realize they own ADRs. If somebody tells you he owns stock in Toyota or Nokia, he really owns their ADRs. I'm certainly not going to buy a stock quoted at 1,174.567 yen, right? Heck no. I'll buy the Toyota ADR in American dollars, thank you.

The exam might point out the holders of ADRs have receipts that represent 1 to 10 shares of the foreign stock and have the right to exchange the ADR for the actual shares of foreign stock. If the corporation sponsors the creation of the ADR, the industry cleverly calls them "sponsored ADRs," and, when feeling especially punchy, might refer to them as ADSs or "American Depository Shares" to make sure they have at least four names.

REITS

Investing in real estate has many advantages and disadvantages. The advantages are that property values usually go up and that real estate provides nice diversification to a securities portfolio. The disadvantages include the fact that real estate costs a lot of money, and it isn't liquid. It often takes months to get a house sold, or sold for a decent price, so the lack of **liquidity** keeps many investors from buying real estate, especially commercial real estate (shopping malls, skyscrapers, factories, etc.).

Which is where **REITs** come in. **A Real Estate Investment Trust** (REIT) is a company that owns a portfolio of properties and sells shares to investors. You could buy into REITs that own apartment buildings, office buildings, shopping centers, hotels, convention centers, self-storage units, timber—you name it. This way you can participate in real estate without having to be rich, and you can sell your shares as easily as you can sell shares of other publicly traded stock. REITs, then, are just equity securities that give the investor an ownership stake in a trust that owns real estate. They do not pass through losses (only real estate *partnerships* do that), they pay out nice dividend yields provided the company makes a profit, but the dividend is taxed at your ordinary income rate, not the kinder, gentler rate on **qualified dividends**.

YIELD, TOTAL RETURN

There are only two ways that I know of to make money on stocks. One, the stock price goes up, and/or, two, the stock pays me a dividend. If I'm looking only for the share price to go up, I'm a "growth investor." If I'm solely interested in the dividends, I'm an "income investor." If I want both growth and income, guess what kind of investor I am?

Would you believe "growth and income"?

But, really, that's the only way to make money on stocks. You either sell the stock for more than you bought it someday, or the stock paid you some nice dividends. Otherwise, you wasted your money.

So, measuring the return on equity securities really comes down to two concerns: **capital**

appreciation (growth) and dividends (income). If you buy a stock at $10, and a year later it's worth $20, that's a capital appreciation of 100%. If the stock pays $2 in annual dividends and costs $20 on the open market, that's a yield of 10%. **Yield** just asks how much an investor has to pay to receive how much in dividends.

Annual Dividend Divided By Market Price = Dividend Yield

Substitute the word "get" for "yield," because yield simply shows how much you get every year compared to what you put down to get it. The test may give you a "quarterly dividend" in the question. If so, multiply it by four—there are four financial quarters per year, which is sort of why they call them "quarters."

Another concept is **total return**. Here, just add the dividend received plus the capital growth/appreciation. In other words, if you buy a stock for $10 and the market price rises to $12, you have $2 of capital appreciation (sometimes called a "paper gain" or an **unrealized gain** just to make sure it has three separate names). If the stock pays $1 in dividends, you're basically "up $3" on a $10 investment.

That's a total return of "3 outa' 10" or 30%. Registered representatives must be careful when quoting "yield" or "total return" to investors. If a customer receives, say, a 5% dividend yield on a common stock investment, a registered representative might want to talk only about that and ignore the fact that the market price is down, say, 40%, and the total return is negative. The registered representative should give the customer the whole picture to avoid misleading her, right?

PRACTICE

1. **Which of the following represents the least expensive common stock?**
    A.   market price - $10, earnings per share: $.40
    B.   market price - $15, earnings per share: $.75
    C.   market price - $95, earnings per share: $5.00
    D.   market price - $100, earnings per share: 4.00

2. **An issuer's transfer agent would perform all the following tasks except**
    A.   canceling old certificates
    B.   recording transfers of ownership
    C.   transferring funds among client accounts
    D.   validating torn, mutilated certificates

3. **The registrar is responsible for which of the following?**
    A. recording changes of ownership
    B. filing the corporate charter
    C. overseeing/auditing the transfer agent
    D. selling mutual fund shares to large institutional buyers

4. **An investor is long 100 shares of XXR @50. After XXR declares a 5:4 split, the investor will be long how many shares at what price?**
    I.   100 shares
    II.   125 shares
    III. $50
    IV. $40

    A. I, III
    B. I, IV
    C. II, III
    D. II, IV

5. **Robin Danestegg owns 300 shares of QRZ @40. After QRZ pays a 20% stock dividend, Robin will be long how many shares at what price?**
    I.   300 shares
    II.   360 shares
    III. $40
    IV. $33.33

    A. I, III
    B. I, IV
    C. II, III
    D. II, IV

6. **An investor who owns which of the following securities might receive more than the stated rate of return?**
    A. common stock
    B. cumulative preferred
    C. participating preferred
    D. all of the above

7. MTG Corporation has the following dividend payment record on its 5% cumulative preferred stock. Two years ago the company paid a $3 dividend. Last year the company missed the dividend payment. If the company wants to pay dividends to other preferred and common stockholders this year, how much must owners of cumulative preferred stock be paid first?

    A. $5

    B. $10

    C. $12

    D. the difference between par value and fair market value divided by CPI

8. XXX convertible preferred stock can be converted into XXX common stock at $10. If XXX common is currently trading at $14.50, what is the parity price for XXX convertible preferred stock?

    A. $104.50

    B. $145.00

    C. $1,450

    D. not enough information provided in the question

9. All of the following statements are true of rights and warrants except

    A. Warrants are better.

    B. Warrants are sometimes attached to bond offerings.

    C. Rights are short-term instruments with an exercise price below CMV.

    D. Warrants are long-term instruments with an exercise price above CMV.

10. Which TWO of the following statements are true concerning cumulative voting?

    I.   Said to benefit the majority over the minority investor.

    II. Said to benefit the minority over the majority investor.

    III. Allows investors to cast only the number of shares owned as votes.

    IV. Allows investors to split total votes in any way they choose.

    A. I, IV

    B. I, III

    C. II, IV

    D. II, III

11. A company may pay dividends in which of the following ways?

    A. cash

    B. stock

    C. shares of a subsidiary

    D. all of the above

ANSWERS

1. **C**, the lowest P/E ratio is the cheapest stock, ignore the market price. The P/E of 19 is the cheapest stock. The other stocks trade at P/E ratios of 25 (A), 20 (B), and 25 (D).

2. **C,** the transfer agent deals with certificates and the names of those who own them.

3. **C,** the corporation files its own charter—the registrar oversees the transfer agent.

4. **D,** more shares at a lower price.

5. **D,** more shares at a lower price.

6. **D,** cumulative preferred stock might be making up for arrearages; participating preferred often raises the dividend. The stated return on common stock is zero, so any dividend paid would be more than the stated rate. A smart-aleck question, but if you like two choices, you must go with "all the above."

7. **C,** $2 in arrears plus $5 in arrears plus the current $5 = $12

8. **B,** 10 shares times the CMV of $14.50 = $145

9. **A,** nothing is "better" than anything else on this exam

10. **C,** minority shareholders could nominate a "pro-minority" candidate and cast all their votes for that one candidate

11. **D,** some things just need to be memorized.

EX-RIGHTS AND CUM RIGHTS

Just in case your exam forces you to calculate the value of a right, let's take a look at two different formulas.

CUM RIGHTS

When a stock with rights attached is trading on an exchange, it has what is called "**cum-rights**" or "with rights." As you know, a rights offering is short-term, so there is a deadline to buy the stock and receive the rights. That deadline begins 2 days before the rights record date—which is the ex-date for the rights offering. From the time of the announcement of the rights offering to the ex-rights date, the rights are attached to the stock (cum rights). During this period, we can calculate a hypothetical value for a "cum right" with the following formula:

Value of 1 Cum Right = (Stock market price − subscription price)
DIVIDED BY (# of rights needed to buy 1 new share PLUS 1)

As with most Series 7 formulae, this one is MUCH easier than it looks. Let's say that XYZ stock trades right now for $50. One right plus $45 will get you 1 new share of XYZ. So, if we plug that into our formula, we get $50 - $45 DIVIDED BY 2. That's $5 divided by 2, which means the value of 1 "cum right" is $2.50.

EX-RIGHTS

Okay, as we said, there is a record date, and you have to be an owner of XYZ stock on or before that record date. Since it takes 3 business days for a trade to settle, if you buy XYZ from somebody just two business days before the record date, your trade won't settle in time. So, on the **ex-rights** date, XYZ stock trades "ex-rights" or "without rights," and the market price drops accordingly. The formula now is exactly the same as before, *only we drop the little "+1" on the bottom.*

Value of 1 "Ex-Right = (Stock market price − subscription price)
DIVIDED BY (# of rights needed to buy 1 new share)

Again, XYZ isn't going to be trading much higher than the exercise price of the right at this point, since buyers of the stock won't get rights. What are the existing rights worth at this point? If XYZ trades at $46 now, and one right plus $45 will get you one new share of XYZ, the value of this right would be $46 - $45 DIVIDED BY 1 = $1.

WRAP-UP

Before we wrap up this discussion of equity securities, let's take a look at things from the perspective of your client, Michelle Madsen. If Michelle owns 300 shares of Frank & Emma's Fruit Pies, what does that actually mean?

Well, since FREM is still a growing company, we call it a "growth stock," which means Michelle won't be receiving any dividend checks any time soon. But that's okay. Michelle is in her early 40s—she can cash dividend checks in retirement, at which point Frank & Emma's should be paying some. What will she get in the meantime? With any luck, she'll watch the value of her shares grow right along with the growth in profits at Frank & Emma's. If the Frank & Emma's earnings pie grows, her slices of the pie—called "shares of stock"—will grow right along with it, right? What if Frank & Emma's really drops the ball and goes bankrupt?

Hate it when that happens. That "non-systematic" risk, which is the risk of one stock dropping, can be taken care of by not putting all your eggs in one basket. Michelle's FREM holdings only represent a small percentage of the equity securities she has invested in, and the equity securities only represent a percentage of the portfolio, which is also diversified into municipal securities, corporate bonds, money market securities, and a few options here and there just to keep things interesting. So, even if the worst-case scenario played out and the company went belly-up, it wouldn't take Michelle's entire portfolio with it. In fact, it's even possible that the day that unlikely event occurred, she could see a gain in another stock that outweighed the loss on FREM. Diversification—that's what it's all about.

As an owner of FREM common stock, Michelle has the right to vote for the board members and other big issues at the corporation. Well, she has the right, but she's been sort of too busy to open the proxy statements they keep sending her. However, if the company wanted to acquire a competitor or merge with a larger food service company, she'd get to vote on the merger or acquisition. If Frank & Emma's offers additional common stock to a new batch of investors, they'd have to do a "rights offering" where Michelle gets a certain number of subscription rights allowing her to maintain her percentage of ownership, if she chooses to exercise her rights. Frank & Emma's files quarterly and annual reports that Michelle can easily access online if she wants to check out their sales, their **balance sheet**, their profit margin, management's discussion of all the risks the company faces, etc.

As Michelle gets older her taste for the wild ups and downs of the stock market will probably fade, and she'll become less of a "growth" and more of an "income" investor. If so, she'll want to buy some Frank & Emma's debt securities, which are called bonds. The bonds will not give Michelle any voting rights and won't offer a huge amount of growth potential, but they will do something common stock never does—they will state the rate of return she will get every year. And, unlike with preferred stock, bond interest has to be paid.

Or else.

CHAPTER 2

Debt Securities

As we mentioned, a few years down the road Frank & Emma's Fruit Pies may decide they could use another infusion of capital (money) from investors. However, maybe they already have enough owners in the form of shareholders. After all, you can only cut the earnings pie into so many slices before everybody goes hungry. So, instead of rounding up equity investors, the investment bankers will round up lenders interested in spotting Frank & Emma's some money in exchange for interest payments. Rather than selling pieces of paper called equity securities, the underwriters would be offering pieces of paper known as "debt securities," which we usually call **bonds**. Corporate bonds represent loans *from* investors *to* the corporation. Investors buy the bonds, and the corporation then pays them interest on the loan and promises to return the principal amount of $1,000 at the end of the term.

It's like a mortgage. Your family wants to expand, so you decide to acquire a house. Trouble is, you don't seem to have enough cash on hand to buy the thing outright. So, you borrow the money by issuing a piece of paper known as a mortgage. You carry the loan for 15–30 years, returning the principal amount plus interest until the debt is paid in full. In this case, you are just like a corporation selling bonds. Only difference is you pay back the principal little by little, while a corporation returns the principal all at once, at the end when the bond matures. Or, if you're doing an "interest only" loan, you're actually doing the same thing. Only difference is, the corporation is using *other people's* money.

How much did you put down on your house—the full purchase price? Wouldn't that have been fun, to just "buy the house," literally? Since it's pretty tough to buy a house by just cutting a check, we usually use **leverage**. To use "leverage" means to use a lot of borrowed money. On the exam, when you see the word "leverage," just insert the phrase "borrowed money." A "highly leveraged" company has simply financed operations by issuing a lot of debt/borrowing a lot of money. And when we get to a truly exciting chapter on margin accounts, we'll see that investors often use leverage by borrowing half the purchase price of a stock from their friendly broker-dealer.

Anyway, a bond has a specific value known as either **par** or the **principal** amount printed right on the face of the certificate. Since it's printed on the face of the certificate, the exam could also call it the "face amount," since every concept needs at least three different names in this industry. In Series Sevenland, bonds have a par value of $1,000 and, occasionally, $5,000. This is the amount an investor will receive with the very last interest payment from the issuer. You might think of this as the investor "getting his original money back." Up to that point, the investor has only been receiving interest payments against the money he loaned to the corporation by purchasing their bond certificates. So the bond certificate has "$1,000" printed on the face, along with the interest rate the issuer will pay the investor every year. This interest rate could be referred to as the coupon rate or "nominal yield."

Don't let the word "nominal" intimidate you. It means "name." The nominal yield is named right there on the certificate. It can also be referred to as the "coupon rate" because bonds used to come with coupons that investors would present when it came time to claim their interest checks. They would present these interest coupons twice a year, because that's how often most bonds pay interest—twice a year, also called **semi-annually**. So, the interest rate a bondholder receives is a stated, known thing. That's a big difference from common stock, where you simply own a percentage of a company and hope that company becomes more valuable. If you buy a 5% bond, you get 5% of $1,000 every year, which is $50 per year. Nominal yield is a known, stated thing. But when interest rates start changing, as interest rates will do, the value of your bond will change, as we'll now look at in more detail than you probably ever wanted.

RATES, YIELDS, PRICES

Interest rates represent what new bonds have to pay in order to attract new investors. But, bonds are issued with a fixed interest rate (like a fixed mortgage). If the bond is an 8% bond, it will always be an 8% bond, and it will always pay 8% of the par value every year no matter who owns it at the time.

For some reason, that concept seems to be tough for many candidates to accept, and I'm not sure why. What do we call bonds in general? Fixed-income securities, right? Why do we call them fixed-income securities? Because the income these securities pay is *fixed*. It's fixed or named on the bond. If it's a 5% bond, it pays $50 a year. If it's a 13% bond, it pays $130 a year and I hope somebody checked the credit rating on *that* one.

So, please, remember that if a bond pays a nominal yield/coupon rate of 8%, it will ALWAYS pay 8% of par or $80 per year. So, whenever interest rates change, they will change the bond's price. When rates on new bonds go up above 8%, the existing bond's price will go down, since new bonds would be issued with coupon rates higher than 8%. When rates go down below 8%, the bond's price will go up, since new bonds would be issued with coupon rates lower than 8%.

And the yields will move right along with interest rates, like this:

DISCOUNT BONDS

Remember, even though a bond has a par value of $1,000, we don't necessarily expect the bond to trade at $1,000 in the open market. As with a stock, a bond's price fluctuates. Why?

Interest rates. If a bondholder has a bond that pays a nominal yield of 8%, what is the bond worth when interest rates in general climb to 10%? Not as much, right? If you had something that paid you 8%, when you knew you could be receiving more like 10%, how would you feel about the bond?

Not too good. But, when interest rates fall to 6%, suddenly that 8% bond looks pretty good, right?

Current Yield

When we take a bond's price into consideration, we're looking at a concept known as current yield. **Current yield** just takes the annual interest paid by the bond to an investor and divides it by what an investor would have to pay for the bond.

Current Yield = Annual Interest divided by the Market Price

It's just how much you get compared to what you put down to get it.

$80/$800 gives us a current yield of 10%.

It's the same formula used for Dividend Yield. It's just that bonds pay interest, rather than dividends. But "yield" just asks how much do I get every year compared to what I pay to get it? So, if interest rates go up to 10%, suddenly, this bond that pays only 8% isn't worth as much, right? The only motivation for buying this 8% bond sitting out on the open market would be if an investor could get it at a **discount**. And, if she can get the $80 that the bond pays in annual interest for just $800, isn't she really getting 10% on her money? That's why we say her current yield is equal to 10%, higher than the nominal yield that never, ever changes.

Rates up, price down. But the yields are going up, right along with rates.

Of course rates and yields go up together, right? Rates are what new bonds pay; yields are what existing bonds offer, after we factor in their market price.

As soon as you see a current yield higher than the coupon rate, you know you're looking at a discount bond. An 8% bond with a 10% current yield, for example, has to be a discount bond. But, there are two more yields the test wants you to be comfortable with.

Yield to Maturity

The first one is easy. It's the **yield to maturity**, the theoretical return an investor gets if she holds the bond all the way to maturity. At maturity, an investor receives the par value, which is $1,000. If the investor puts down only $800 to buy the bond and receives $1,000 when the bond matures, doesn't she receive more at maturity than she paid?

Yep. That's why her yield to maturity is higher still. She gets all the coupon payments, plus an extra $200 when the bond matures. If you see a YTM that is higher than the coupon rate, you're looking at a discount bond. For example, a 4% nominal yield trading at a 5.50 YTM is a discount bond. The YTM would also be higher than the current yield: nominal, current, yield to maturity, in that order.

Yield to Call

Like homeowners, sometimes issuers get tired of making interest payments that seem too high. That's why some bonds are issued as **callable**, meaning that after a certain time period the issuer can buy the bonds back from investors at a stated price. A bond that matures in 10 or 20 years is often callable in just 5 years. Since the investor who bought a bond for less than par is going to make money when the principal of $1,000 is returned, do you suppose he'd rather make his profit sooner or later?

Sooner, right? When you're making money, you want to make it as fast as possible. That's why **yield to call** is the highest of all for a discount bond.

PREMIUM BONDS

Of course, whatever can go up can also go down. What happens when interest rates fall? Bond prices RISE. Here's why. If you owned this 8% bond and saw that interest rates have just fallen to 6%, how would you feel about your bond?

Pretty good, right? After all, it pays 2% more than new debt is paying. Do you want to sell it? Not really. But you might sell it to me if I paid you a….. that's right, a premium.

If I paid you $1,200, you might be willing to sell it. From my perspective, I see that new debt is only going to pay 6%, which is too low for my needs. Even though I have to pay more than par for your 8% bond, it will all work out if I can get all those interest payments at a higher-than-prevailing rate.

Current Yield

So, we've just pushed the price of the bond up as interest rates went down. Dividing our $80 of annual interest by the $1,200 we put down for the bond gives us a current yield of 6.7%. That's lower than the coupon rate, which is why the CY is below our coupon rate/nominal yield. Whenever you see a coupon of 8% and current yield of 6.7% (or anything lower than that 8% printed on the bond), you know you're looking at a **premium bond**. Remember, the coupon rate/nominal yield doesn't change. Therefore, the only way to get the yield lower than the coupon is to pay more than par for the bond. Just like the only way to get the yield higher than the coupon is to pay less than par for the bond.

YTM

Now, when this investor's bond matures, how much does she get back from the issuer? Only $1,000. So, she put down $1,200 and will only get back $1,000 at maturity. Pretty easy to see why her Yield to Maturity (YTM) goes down.

YTC

Remember when we decided that a person who buys a bond at a discount wants the bond to return the principal amount sooner rather than later? Well, if you pay more than the par value for a bond, you're going to lose some money when the bond returns your principal, right? So, if you're going to lose money, do you want to do it quickly, or spread it out over time, collecting the higher-than-prevailing-rate interest payments in the meantime?

Pretty clear that we're pushing for the latter, right? That's why a person who purchases a bond at a premium will have a lower yield to call than maturity. He's going to lose money in either case, so he'd rather lose it over 10 or 20 years (maturity) rather than 5 years (call).

So, yield to call is the lowest yield for a bond purchased at a premium.

Disclosing Yield on Customer Confirmations

When a customer purchases a bond from you, the **registered representative**, your firm will send her a **trade confirmation** no later than the T + 3 settlement date. And, on this trade confirmation your firm has to disclose either the YTM or the YTC. Should you disclose the best possible yield or the worst possible yield?

Always prepare your customer for the worst or most conservative yield, so there are no bad surprises, right? Okay, for a discount bond, which yield is lower, YTM or YTC? YTM. That's what you would disclose to a customer who purchases a bond at a discount.

For a premium bond, which yield is lower?

Yield to *Call*. So, that's what you would disclose to a customer who purchases a bond at a premium.

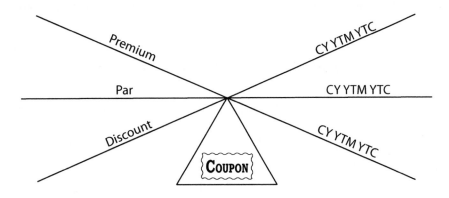

RETIRING THE DEBT

A bond has a maturity date that represents the date when the issuer will pay the last interest check and the principal. At that point, it's all over—the debt has been paid in full, just like when you pay off your car, student loan, house, etc. This can be referred to as "maturity" or **redemption**. As we saw with "yield to call," many bonds are repurchased by the issuer at a set price if interest rates drop. So, a bond might not make it to the maturity date because it might be called early.

Also, sometimes the issuer will simply make an offer to repurchase your bonds at a certain price. You can accept or reject the offer, known as a **tender offer**. You would "tender your bonds" to the issuer for payment, and that would retire the debt. Or, you could just hang onto them, unlike with a call. When a bond is called, remember, it's all over.

When we look at municipal securities in the next chapter, we'll see that many city, county, and state governments will issue a new batch of bonds before the first call date and then park the proceeds in an escrow account as they impatiently await the first call date stipulated in the indenture. That's known as "advance" or "pre-refunding," but we'll save that excitement for the next chapter.

BOND CERTIFICATES

There are four different forms that a bond can take in terms of the certificate itself. In the olden days, bonds were issued as "bearer bonds," which meant that whoever "bore" or had possession of the bond was assumed to be the owner. No owner name at all on the certificate; it just said "pay to the bearer," so whoever bore the bond received the principal at maturity. In order to receive the interest, investors holding bearer bonds used to clip coupons attached to the bond certificate every six months. There was no name on the interest coupon, either, so the IRS had no way of tracking the principal or the interest income. And you know how much that irritates the IRS. So, bonds haven't been issued in bearer form since the early '80s—that doesn't mean they don't exist. A few are still floating out there on the market, so you have to know about them for the test. Just remember: no name on certificate, no name on payment coupons.

Bonds also used to be **registered as to principal only**. That meant that we had a name on the bond certificate—the person who would receive the principal amount at maturity. But, again, with the silly little unnamed interest coupons. Therefore, only the principal was registered, thus the name "registered as to principal only." See, these vocabulary terms often mean exactly what they say…except when they don't.

Anyway, the bond market got smart in the early 1980s and started registering both pieces of the **debt service**. Now, the issuer has the name of the owner [principal] and automatically cuts a check every six months for the interest. Therefore, the IRS—which is here to help—can also help themselves to a bit of the proceeds for the interest and principal income. We call these bonds fully registered, because both pieces of the debt service (interest, principal) are registered. And you know how that pleases your friends and mine at the Internal Revenue Service.

Book entry/journal entry bonds are still fully registered. It's just that it's done on computer, rather than on paper. The investor keeps the trade confirmation as proof of ownership, but we still have an owner name on computer, and we automatically cut interest checks to the registered owner.

QUOTES

Bonds are quoted either in terms of their price, or their yield. Since the coupon rate or nominal yield doesn't change, if you give me the price, I can figure the yield. And, if you give me the yield, I can figure the price. This process is known as "interpolation," by the way, which is just a fancy word for converting bond yields into bond prices, and vice versa. If we're talking about a bond's price, we're talking about bond points. A **bond point** is worth $10. You'll need to memorize that for the test. So, if a bond is selling at "98," that means it's selling for 98 bond points. With each point worth $10, a bond selling for 98 bond points is trading for $980. A bond trading at 102 would be selling for $1,020. Although fractions have been eliminated from stock and options pricing, they are still very much alive in the world of bond pricing. If a bond point is worth $10, how much is 1/2 a bond point worth? Five dollars, right? A quarter-point would be worth $2.50, right? An eighth is $1.25, and so on. Therefore, if you see a bond priced at 102 3/8, how much does the bond cost in dollars and cents? Well, "102" puts the price at $1,020, and 3/8 of $10 is $3.75. So, a bond trading at 102 3/8 costs $1,023.75.

102 [$1,020] + 3/8 [$3.75] = $1,023.75

If we're talking about **basis points**, we're talking about a bond's yield. Yield to maturity, to be exact. If I say that a bond with an 8% coupon just traded on a 7.92 basis, I'm telling you that the price went up above par, pushing the yield to maturity down to 7.92%. In other words, the price pushed the yield to maturity to a particular percentage, or number of "basis points." A basis point is the smallest increment of change in a bond's yield. When the media talks about the Fed easing interest rates by fifty basis points, they're talking about 1/2 of 1 percent. We would write 1% as .01, right? Well, basis points use a 4-digit display system, so .01 is written as:

.0 1 0 0.

Then, we read that figure as "100 basis points." Two percent would be 200 basis points. One-half of one percent would be written as .0050 or "50 basis points." So, a bond trading at a 7.92 basis means that the YTM is 7.92% or 792 basis points. An easy way to work with basis points is to remember that all the single-digit percentages are expressed in hundreds. 400 basis points just means 4%. Anything less than 100 basis points is less than 1%. So 30 basis points is only .3 of 1%.

Fascinating, isn't it?

NOTATION

The exam might want to see the look on your face when they make you read the following:

10M XYZ 8s debentures of '13, callable @103 in '11

Huh?

Well "10M" means $10,000 par value or 10 bonds. XYZ is the issuing corporation, and they pay "8s" or 8% in interest each year. The little "s" means you get the $80 in two semi-annual payments of $40 each. Remember that—a test question might ask how much the investor receives at maturity on this bond. The answer is $1,040. Remember that interest is always paid retroactively, meaning for the previous 6 months. So, when the bond matures, you get your final interest payment (for the previous 6 months) plus the principal/par value of $1,000. This investor owns 10 bonds, so she would receive $10,400 at maturity.

Assuming we make it that far—remember, if interest rates drop in 2011, the company can buy back the bonds for $1,030, end of story. That's what "callable at 103 in '11" means.

ACCRUED INTEREST

We have been discussing the annual interest paid to the owner of a bond. Well, if we can express the interest per year, we can also express what the interest per day is, right? Heck, we could even do the interest-per-minute, but, luckily, the exam doesn't go quite that far.

And let's not give it any ideas, okay?

The tricky part is that different issuers use different days in their months and years. For a corporate or municipal issuer, we consider every month to have 30 days, and every year to have 360 days. Yes, even February has 30 days for corporate and municipal bonds. Don't ask about Leap Year. The exam has plenty it can use against you without going there.

The following table might help:

Type	Settles	Months	Years
Corporate/Municipal bond	T + 3	30 days	360 days
Treasuries	T + 1	Actual	Actual

So, if a corporate bond pays $80 in annual interest, how much is that per day?

Just divide $80 by 360 days to get about 22.2 cents per day. That's what the owner of the bond earns in interest every day.

How often does the owner receive a check for her interest?

In Series Sevenland, twice a year, or semi-annually. But, they don't always like to name the months. Like most things in the securities industry, the payment months are abbreviated. You'll only see one letter as an abbreviation, too. If you see a "J & J" bond, you'll have to think about which two "J" months would be six months apart.

January and July, right?

Here's how the chart works out for interest payment months:

J	J
F	A
M	S
A	O
M	N
J	D

Reading left to right, we pair January with July, February with August, March with September, April with October, May with November, and June with December. So if you buy an "A & O" bond, you'll receive your two interest checks on the first of April and the first of October. If it's the 8% bond we've been discussing, how much will you receive each time?

That's right, $40. $80 per year divided into two semi-annual payments.

If they don't add a number to the "A & O," that means the checks are received on the first of each month. If they add a "15" to the abbreviation, that means the checks are received on the 15th of each month, as in an "A & O 15" bond.

Now, the check might be received on the first day of April. That doesn't cover that day's interest, though. A bondholder earns interest every day she owns the bond, including weekends and holidays. Doesn't matter when the check arrives. The check covers the previous six months' worth of interest, nothing more.

Did we mention this stuff is complicated?

Anyway, the concept behind accrued interest is that a bond is usually traded somewhere between the two interest payment dates. If the bond owner got her last interest check on the first of April, then sells the bond on July 16, what happens?

Well, who is going to receive the next interest check?

The buyer of the bond, who is about to become the new owner. Should we trust the buyer to deliver the seller's portion of that check when the buyer receives it?

Not a chance. So, the buyer is going to pay the seller her portion of the interest right up front. That's what the whole accrued interest concept comes down to. The buyer has to pay the seller the price of the bond, plus the interest that belongs to the seller, who hasn't gotten a check since the last payment date.

You can answer these questions step-by-step.

Let's try one now for practice:

Dale Dawson sells Jim Jacobs an XYZ Corp. 8% A&O bond on Wednesday, June 19. How much in accrued interest must be paid, and who pays the interest?

I.   Dale pays the interest.

II.   Jim pays the interest.

III. Accrued interest is $18.44 per bond.

IV.   Accrued interest is $1.84 per bond.

A. I, III

B. I, IV

C. II, III

D. II, IV

Well, we know who pays the interest. Jim-the-buyer pays Dale-the-seller.

How much does Jim have to pay Dale in accrued interest?

Step one, find the settlement date. Corporate and municipal bonds settle "T + 3," or three business days after the trade date. That's why the test likes to make the trade date Wednesday or Thursday, so the weekends can confuse you a little.

Don't let them. Just remember that weekends don't count as business days. So "T" is Wednesday. We count Thursday as one, Friday as two, and…Monday as the third business day after the Trade date. Monday will be June 24th.

Step two, count the days.

On the settlement date, the buyer starts earning interest. So, the seller is entitled to every day up to—but not including—the settlement date. The settlement date's interest belongs to the buyer. So, if the trade settles on the 24th of June, the seller is entitled to 23 days of interest.

This A&O bond last paid interest on the 1st of April. How many days in April is the seller entitled to?

Thirty.

So, 30 days for April plus 30 days for May plus 23 days for June = 83 days of accrued interest.

Step three, find the interest-per-day that the bond pays. The bond pays $80 per year divided by 360 days, or 22.2 cents a day.

Step four, multiply the daily interest by the number of days that have accrued. Twenty-two cents a day times 83 days equals $18.44 per bond that Jim Jacobs must pay Dale Dawson, on top of the price of each bond.

The answer to that seemingly hard question, then, is "C."

Now, we already know the exam likes to challenge you as much as possible. So, once you get used to doing accrued interest questions concerning corporates and munis, you might find yourself staring at a question concerning Treasuries, also referred to as "government securities."

Don't panic. Govies work the same way, with two major differences. First, Treasuries settle the next business day or "T + 1." And, Treasuries use actual or calendar days. Now July has 31 days, and February 28.

Other than that, it's the same process. Step 1—find the settlement date. Step 2—count the days up to, but not including, the settlement date. Step 3—find the interest paid per day. Step 4—multiply the daily interest by the number of days. Step 5—move on with your life.

So, you could probably answer the following question right now:

A J & D 5% government bond trades on Wednesday, August 14th. How much accrued interest will the buyer pay the seller?

A. 13.7 cents

B. 28 cents

C. $1.65 per bond

D. $10.27 per bond

Step one—when does the trade settle? Thursday, August 15th. Govies settle on the next business day. T + 1.

Step two—count the days. This bond last made an interest payment on the first of June, so how many days have accrued?

June	30
July	31
Aug	14 (up to, not including, the settlement date of the 15th)

Looks like 75 days total, right?

Step three—find the interest per day. $50 per year divided by 365 (actual) days = 13.7 cents per day.

Step four—multiply the days by the daily interest. 75 days times 13.7 cents = $10.27 per bond. The answer is "D."

Next question, please?

Oh yeah, something that is related to yet different from accrued interest is called the "long coupon." If a bond has a payment schedule of, say, January and July, it might be issued in, say, March but not make the first payment until January. If so, that would be a coupon payment bigger than the usual six months' worth. So, they call that a "long coupon," in case you don't already have enough to memorize.

PRACTICE

1. Debbie Benture sells her XXY 6% J & J bond on Thursday, March 14. How many days of accrued interest will she pay for this transaction?

    A. 60

    B. 78

    C. 0

    D. 73

2. Debbie Benture buys an XXY 6% J & J bond on Thursday, March 14. How many days of accrued interest will she pay for this transaction?

    A. 60

    B. 78

    C. 0

    D. 73

3. What is true about a bond with an 8% coupon trading at a 10% Yield to Maturity?

    A. It is trading at a discount.

    B. The price of the bond went up.

    C. Interest rates have fallen.

    D. The bond is trading at a premium.

4. Which of the following bonds is trading at a premium?

    A. 8% coupon, 9.10 basis

    B. 8% coupon, 9.50 basis

    C. 8% coupon, 7.70 basis

    D. 8% coupon, 8.00 basis

ANSWERS

1. **C,** why would the seller pay accrued interest? It's the buyer who pays the seller.

2. **B,** step one: find settlement. If the "T" or Trade date is Thursday, March 14th, the trade will settle in three business days, or Tuesday, March 19th. Debbie has to pay the seller for every day up to (not including) the settlement date, because up to the settlement date the seller is the owner of the bond. So, Debbie pays her for 18 days in March, plus 30 days each for January (that's the first "J" in a J & J bond) and February. 18 + 30 + 30 = 78 days. How were you supposed to know it was a corporate bond? XXY looks like a corporation, right? Sure isn't the federal government.

3. **A,** if the yield is higher, it's because somebody bought it at a lower price. The coupon doesn't change, so if the yield is higher, the price is lower. If the yield had been lower than the coupon/nominal rate, the price would have been higher. So, when you see a yield higher than the coupon, you know the bond was traded at a discount, and vice versa for a premium bond.

4. **C,** if the basis (YTM) is lower than the coupon, the bond was traded at a premium.

YIELD CURVES

Municipal bonds are usually issued under a "serial maturity," which means that a little bit of the principal will be returned every year, until the whole issue is paid off. Investors who buy bonds maturing in 2015 will generally demand a higher yield than those getting their principal back in 2007. The longer your money is at risk, the more of a reward you demand, right? If a friend wanted to borrow $1,000 for one month, you'd probably do it interest-free. What if they wanted to take three years to pay you back? You could get some interest on a thousand dollars by buying a bank CD, which carries no risk, right? So, if somebody's going to put your money at risk for an extended period of time, you demand a reward in the form of an interest payment.

Same with bonds. If your bond matures in 2022 when mine matures in 2014, isn't your money at risk for 8 more years? That's why your bond would be offered at a higher yield than mine. If I buy a bond yielding 5.65%, yours would probably be offered at more like 5.89%. The extra 34 basis points is your extra reward for taking on extra risk.

This is how it works under a normal yield curve, where long-term bonds yield more than short-term bonds. Guess what, sometimes that yield curve gets inverted. Suddenly, the rule flies out the window, and folks are getting higher yields on short-term bonds than on long-term bonds.

The cause of this is generally a peak in interest rates. When bond investors feel that interest rates have gone as high as they're going to go, they all clamor to lock in the high interest rates for the longest period of time. In a rush of activity, they sell off their short-term bonds in order to hurry up and buy long-term bonds at the best interest rate they're likely to see for a long time. Well, if everybody's selling off short-term bonds, the price drops [and the yield increases]. And if they're all buying up long-term bonds, the price increases [and the yield drops]. That causes the yield curve to invert, a situation that usually corrects itself very quickly.

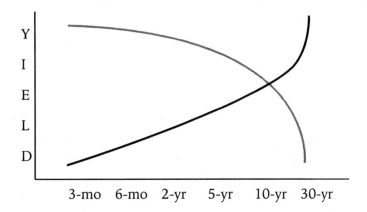

NOTE: the curve sloping upward is a "normal yield curve," where as the term to maturity increases, so does the yield. The curve sloping downward is an "inverted yield curve," a fairly rare situation where short-term debt securities yield more than long-term.

YIELD SPREAD

Another yield concept the test might throw at you considers the difference in yields between high-rated and low-rated bonds. If folks are demanding a much greater yield on low-rated bonds than on high-rated bonds, that's a negative indicator for the economy. Basically, it means folks are nervous about issuers' ability to repay. If investors don't demand a much higher yield on the low-rated bonds, that means in general they are confident about issuers' ability to repay, which is a positive indicator. So, when the "yield spread narrows," there is much reason to rejoice, although, personally, I hope I have better things to celebrate.

RISKS TO BONDHOLDERS

Credit risk is the risk of **default**, which is what Moody's and Standard & Poor's measure when they rate bonds. Treasury debt has no real **default risk**, while many corporate bonds carry major default risk. Remember that **"high-yield"** is just a polite way of saying "junk," which means "serious default risk." Event risk for a bondholder entails the chance that the corporation whose bonds they own is acquired by another company that is highly leveraged. What if S&P and Moody's decide to downgrade the bond ratings once they become the obligation of the highly leveraged acquiring company?

Hate it when that happens.

Interest rate risk is the risk that rates will suddenly shoot up, sending the market price of your bond down. The longer the term on the bond, the more volatile its price. When rates go up, all bond prices fall, but the long-term bonds suffer the most. And, when rates go down, all bond prices rise, but the long-term bonds go up the most. So, a 30-year government bond has no default risk, but carries more interest rate risk than a 10-year corporate bond.

Purchasing power risk has to do with **inflation**. If inflation erodes the value of money, an investor's return simply ain't worth what it used to be. Fixed-income investments carry purchasing power risk, which is why investors often try to beat inflation by investing in common stock. The ride might be a wild one, but the reward is that we should be able to grow faster than the rate of inflation, whereas a fixed-income payment is, well, fixed, even when inflation rises. Note that high inflation does not help stocks. It's just that in a period of high inflation, stock will probably perform better than fixed-income securities. So, during an **expansion**, where inflation tends to rise, you're better off in equities/stock. During a period of decline/contraction, bonds are the place to be, since their price will rise as interest rates fall due to the cooling demand for money/expansion.

Call risk is the risk that interest rates will drop and bondholders will have their bonds called. If this happens, they reinvest at lower rates and lose the full appreciation in price that would have resulted as interest rates kept falling. If rates were likely to fall, I'd want a non-callable bond, myself. Even though non-callable bonds offer lower yields than callable bonds, that's okay. I'd like to hang on to this one as rates go down, pushing the market price up, and the issuer has no way of forcing it out of my hands.

Reinvestment risk is somewhat related to **call risk**. When you receive the principal, you go ahead and reinvest it into new bonds—what kind of rates/yields are bonds offering now?

Low ones.

Another way to look at reinvestment risk is to remember that bonds paying regular interest checks force investors to reinvest into new bonds every few months or so. What kind of rates/yields will debt securities be offering when they go to reinvest the coupon payments?

Nobody knows, which is why it's a risk.

To avoid reinvestment risk buy a debt security that gives you nothing to reinvest along the way—zero coupons, i.e., Treasury **STRIPS**.

Notice how bondholders can get hit comin' or goin'. If it's a corporate bond—and even some municipal securities—you could end up getting stiffed (default risk). If rates go up, the price of your bond gets knocked down (interest rate risk). If rates go down, callable bonds are called (call risk), and the party's over, plus you have to reinvest the proceeds at a lower rate than you were getting (reinvestment risk). And, even if none of the above calamities strikes, inflation could inch its way up, making those coupon payments less and less valuable (purchasing power risk).

Oh well. If you want fixed income, you take on these risks to varying degrees, depending on which bond you buy and when you buy it.

So, nobody ever wins by purchasing bonds, right?

Right, except when they do.

Can you think of a situation where buying bonds could turn out extremely profitable? What if you purchased a bunch of 30-year, non-callable bonds right when interest rates were sky-high and getting ready to plummet? Wouldn't that make your purchase price extremely cheap (rates high/price low) and, then, suddenly the market price would shoot sky-high as interest rates started to fall, the faster the better?

How often is that going to happen, and how are you going to know when rates have peaked?

Beats me. But if you figure it out, please contact me at your earliest convenience.

CORPORATE BONDS

To protect bondholders, Congress passed the Trust Indenture Act of 1939. If a corporation wants to sell $5,000,000 or more worth of bonds that mature outside of one year, they have to do it under a contract or "indenture" with a trustee, who will enforce the terms of the indenture to the benefit of the bondholders. In other words, if the issuer stiffs the bondholders, the trustee/trust company can get a bankruptcy court to forcibly sell off the assets of the company so that bondholders can recover some of their hard-earned money.

Remember that a corporate bond pays a fixed rate of interest to the investor, and that bond interest has to be paid, unlike a dividend on stock that is paid only if the board of directors declares it. We'll see that a bondholder usually doesn't suffer as much price **volatility** as a stock investor. But, unlike the owner of common stock, bond holders don't get to vote on the things we looked at in the preceding chapter. The only time bondholders get to vote is if the corporation goes into bankruptcy. Creditors will be offered various little scenarios by the corporation who can't actually pay them, and the bondholders will get to vote on these terms.

Since bankruptcy is always a concern, corporations often secure the bonds by pledging specific assets like airplanes, government securities, or real estate. Would you believe we call these **secured bonds**? For a secured bond the issuer pledges title of the assets to the trustee, who just might end up selling them off if the issuer gets behind on its interest payments. Investors who buy bonds attached to specific collateral are secured creditors, the first to get paid should the company go belly up. If the collateral used is real estate, we call it a **mortgage bond**. If the collateral is securities, we call it a **collateral trust certificate**. And if the collateral is equipment, such as airplanes or railroad cars, we call it an **equipment trust certificate**. Since these bonds are the most secure, they offer the lowest coupon payment, too. Remember, if you take a small risk, you usually only get a small reward.

Most corporate bonds are backed by a promise known as the "full faith and credit" of the issuer. That's why we might want to see what S&P and Moody's have to say about a particular issuer's full faith and credit. If the credit is AAA, we probably won't be offered a huge coupon payment. But if the issuer is rated right at the cut-off point of BBB (Baa for Moody's), then we might demand a bigger pay-off in exchange for buying bonds from an issuer just one notch above junk status. Regardless of the rating, if we buy a bond backed simply by the full faith and credit of an issuer, we are buying a **debenture**. Debenture holders are general creditors and get paid after secured bondholders. Therefore, debentures pay a higher coupon than secured bonds, since they carry more risk.

"Sub" means "below," as in "submarine" for "below the water," or "subterranean" for "below the ground." **Subordinated debentures** are below debentures when it comes to liquidating a company and paying out money to the bondholders. Since these bonds are riskier, they pay a higher coupon than debentures.

If all the bondholders have been paid and there's still money left over (it could happen, right?), then we start talking about paying out some money to stockholders. Preferred gets preference, so we pay them first, and common stock is always last in line.

Liquidation Priority

So, if a company goes belly up, interested parties get paid something in the following order of priority:

1. Employees/wages
2. IRS/taxes
3. Secured creditors
4. Debentures/general creditors
5. Subordinated debentures
6. Preferred stock
7. Common stock

Yes, the IRS, an inherently benevolent society, makes sure that employees get paid first…that way they can tax the wages as they come for all the other taxes the corporation has failed to pay.

Warms your heart, doesn't it? Also note that I didn't say everybody above gets his money back, or even that he gets *any* money back. Those are *claims* on corporate assets. Common stock usually receives nothing, and even the unsecured bondholders may be lucky to get back $80 or $90 per bond. It all depends on how the bankruptcy court process works out.

Speaking of bankruptcy, remember that an **income bond** only pays income if the company has income. It's usually issued by a company coming out of bankruptcy and usually offers a high coupon, just in case it ever gets around to making a payment. The re-organized company gets some breathing room from the creditors and maybe this breathing room will help it finally get its act together long enough to start paying interest on its "income" or "adjustment" bonds.

Moody's, S&P & Fitch

There's nothing worse than lending some corporation $1,000 and then finding out they're, like, not going to pay you back. What? But, dude, you *owe* me. This is known as a "default," and it's the worst thing that can happen to a bondholder. How likely is it that a bond will go into default? Well, it isn't going to happen on a United States Treasury bill, note, bond, or STRIP. It might happen on some municipal securities. But when you get into the category of corporate bonds, you see that it happens much more than you'd like. Luckily, Moody's, S & P, and Fitch all give bond ratings designed to help you gauge the likelihood of default. Remember that this is *all* that the bond rating agencies are talking about—the risk of default. They aren't making any recommendations with these ratings. The highest quality issuers have AAA/Aaa (S&P/Moody's) ratings. The **investment grade** issues go from AAA/Aaa down to BBB/Baa. And below that, dude, watch out!

Standard & Poor's (& Fitch)	Moody's
AAA	Aaa
AA	Aa
A	A
BBB	Baa
BELOW THIS IS JUNK, NON-INVESTMENT GRADE, HIGH-YIELD, SPECULATIVE	
BB	Ba
B	B

So, credit quality is the highest on the AAA/Aaa-rated bonds. As credit quality drops, you take on more default risk, right? So, you expect to be compensated for the added risk through a higher yield. High yield and low quality go hand in hand, just as low yield and high quality do. How does a bond become "high yield" or "junk"? That just means that a brand new issue of low-rated bonds would have to offer fat coupons to get you interested in lending the money, and existing bonds would simply trade at lower and lower prices as people get more and more nervous about a possible default. As the price drops, the yield...*increases.*

Remember that—it's not just interest rates that can knock down a bond's market price. When S&P, Moody's, or Fitch downgrade an issuer's credit rating, the market price of those bonds will drop, increasing their yield. In fact, when the first headline comes out that the ratings agencies are sort of keeping a real close watch on a particular company, that doesn't usually do a lot for the market price of that company's bonds. Although it, by definition, sure does boost the yield, right? Price down, yield UP.

Not sure how detailed the exam will get, but please note that an S&P rating such as "BBB" actually has three levels: BBB+, BBB, BBB-. Just like in school, S&P can add plusses and minuses to the A's and B's. Moody's uses 1, 2, and 3. After "Aaa," Moody's then subdivides the next three ratings into: Aa1, Aa2, Aa3, then A1, A2, and A3, and, for those unafraid to teeter on the cut-off, they have Baa1, Baa2, and Baa3. So, what's the lowest investment-grade rating from S&P? BBB-. For Moody's, it would be Baa3. In the Wall Street Journal, the story would probably read, "XYZ has recently been downgraded by S&P (or Moody's) to one notch above junk status." That means their bonds are now rated BBB- (Baa3), and one more notch below that puts them in the exciting world of junk bonds. Of course, you're a good salesperson. You aren't going to call me up and try to sell me some junk bonds, are you? Heck no. But you might try to interest me in some "high-yield" bonds, instead.

Oh, high-yield? Sure, I'm into that—just don't try and sell me none of that junk.

As you can see above, it's just a different name for the same darned thing. Some investors will go for the higher yield offered on the lower quality bonds. But they better not come crying to us if the corporation goes into default. Risk versus reward—you want a big reward, you take on a big risk. You want low-risk bonds, you get lower returns. Most customers would really like you to sell them a no-risk, high-yield bond. They'd probably also like a good-tasting beer with no calories and a 30-year mortgage fixed at 2%.

Sinking Fund

Since the issuing corporation has to return the principal value of the bond at some point, they usually establish what's known as a **sinking fund**. If you actually held your interest-only mortgage 30 years, maybe your spouse would have to gently remind you, "Remember to add the $300,000 to this month's interest check, honey. Gotta pay the principal back." Since that's how corporations pay back the principal (all at once), they set some money aside in escrow, which means they park it in safe, dependable U.S. Treasury securities. With this sinking fund established, the company would be able to return the principal, make a "tender offer" where they offer to buy back the investors' bonds, or complete a "call." Having this money set aside sure can't hurt the old rating with S&P and Moody's either, right?

Callable and Convertible

The "callable" concept is easy. Just means that after a certain period of time, the issuer might be able to call up the bondholders and announce that they're buying back the bonds at a certain price already agreed upon. A bond might be callable starting in the year 2009 at 104, meaning that in the year 2009 the issuer can retire the debt by giving each bondholder a check for $1,040 plus any accrued interest.

When might they want to call a bond? Probably when interest rates have fallen, right? Isn't that when homeowners refinance their homes? Works the same way for bond issuers. When rates go down, they start to think maybe the outstanding debt could be replaced with brand-new, much cheaper debt. If interest rates fall to 6%, they reason, let's issue new debt at 6% and use the proceeds to retire the outstanding debt we're currently paying 8% on.

Pretty simple.

Replacing one bond issue with another is called "refunding." It tends to happen when interest rates fall. It allows the issuer to issue less-expensive debt and retire more-expensive debt.

It's not such a great deal for the bondholders, though. What can they do with the proceeds of the call? Reinvest them. At what rate? A lower rate. This is called reinvestment risk. Upon reinvestment, the bondholders will get a lower rate of return, since interest rates have now fallen. And, what happens to bond prices as rates decline?

Right, they go up.

Only they stop going up when the bonds are called away, meaning the bondholder doesn't get the full appreciation in price he would have otherwise gotten. So, since the bondholder takes on this risk, callable bonds yield more than non-callable. As always, if you want something good from the corporation, they take something away. Just like we saw in the equity chapter—if the preferred stock is convertible, you get a lower dividend. If the bond comes with a warrant, you get a lower yield on the bond.

Then, there are convertible bonds, which can be converted into a certain number of shares of the issuer's common stock. Bonds have a par value of $1,000, so the investor applies the $1,000 of par value toward purchasing the company's stock at a pre-set price. When a convertible bond is issued, it is given a conversion price. If the conversion price is $40, that means that the bond is convertible into common stock at $40. In other words, the investor can use the par value of her bond towards the purchase of the company's common stock at a set price of $40. Bonds have a par value of $1,000, so if she applies that $1,000 toward the purchase of stock at $40 per share, how many shares would she be able to buy? 25 shares, right? $1,000 of par value divided by $40 per share of stock tells us that each bond can be converted into 25 shares of common stock. In other words, the two securities trade at a 25:1 relationship, since the big one (bond) can be turned into 25 of the little ones (stock). The company sets the conversion price; they have no control over where their common stock trades on the open market, right? If the price goes up, the value of the convertible bonds goes up. Just like if the price goes down, that drags down the market value of the bonds.

So how much is this particular bond worth at any given moment?

Whatever 25 shares of the common stock are worth.

Just take Par and divide it by the conversion price to find out how many shares of common stock the bond could be converted into.

In this case it's 25 shares, since $1,000 would go exactly that far when purchasing stock priced at $40 a share.

Par/Conversion price = # common shares
1,000/40 = 25 shares

So how much is the bond worth?

Depends. How much are 25 shares of the common stock worth?

Since the bond could always be converted into 25 shares, it generally has to be worth whatever 25 shares of the common stock are worth. When the bond trades for exactly what the 25 shares are worth, we call this relationship "parity," which is just a fancy word for "same" or "equal." Since one's price depends on the other, the two should have a price that is at "parity."

So, if a bond is convertible into 25 shares of IXR common stock, and IXR is trading @50, what is the bond's price at parity?

25 X $50 = $1,250.

And, if the common stock went up to $60 a share, the bond would be worth 25 times that number, right?

25 X $60 = $1,500.

Sometimes the test gets tricky and gives you the bond's market price, asking for the stock's parity price.

Don't sweat it.

It's a 25:1 relationship, so instead of multiplying the stock price by 25, just divide the bond's price by 25. If the bond trades at $1,250, just divide that by 25 to get to the common stock's parity price of $50.

See, once you get that 25:1 relationship determined, you're good to go. If the relationship is 25:1, either multiply the stock's price or divide the bond's price by 25. Just depends on what the question gives you. So, when you see a question on convertibles, look for the conversion price. Divide par by that conversion price, and now you have the relationship. If the bond is convertible at $40, it trades at a 25:1 relationship to the stock. What if the bond were convertible at $50?

20:1.

Convertible at $25?

40:1.

And so on.

Sometimes the question will come right out and say that the bond is convertible into a certain number of shares.

Great, now they've already done the work for you. If it's convertible into 50 shares, it trades at a 50:1 relationship. Usually you have to divide par by the conversion price to get that number. Sometimes the test just gives you that relationship straight up. Either way, just work through the problem step by step. It isn't that difficult really. Just ask yourself how far the par value would go if divided by the conversion price of the stock. Whatever you come up with will allow you to answer the question.

So, all you have to do is find the ratio. $1,000 of par value divided by $40 per share gives us a ratio of 25:1. If the question gives you the stock price, multiply by 25 to find the bond's parity price. If it gives you the bond price, divide by 25 to find the common stock's parity price.

PRACTICE

1. **MMY Corporation has convertible debentures that can be exchanged for shares of MMY common stock at a set price of $40. If MMY common is currently trading at $57 dollars, what is the parity price of the MMY convertible debentures?**

   A. $1,017

   B. $1,425

   C. $1,000

   D. $1,765

2. **Which TWO of the following statements are true of callable bonds?**

   I. Bonds are typically called when interest rates are rising.

   II. Bonds are typically called when interest rates are falling.

   III. Bonds trading at a discount are more likely to be called.

   IV. Bonds trading at a premium are more likely to be called.

   A. I, III

   B. I, IV

   C. II, III

   D. II, IV

3. **Which TWO of the following are associated with falling interest rates?**

   I. bond prices rising

   II. bond prices falling

   III. coupon rates rising

   IV. coupon rates falling

   A. I, III

   B. I, IV

   C. II, III

   D. II, IV

4. **Which of the following bonds is most susceptible to a call?**

    A.   6% nominal, matures in 2013, callable @103

    B.   6% nominal, matures in 2015, callable @par

    C.   9% nominal, matures in 2020, callable @par

    D.   9% nominal, matures in 2020, callable @103

5. **If a company is liquidated, the following parties will be paid in which order?**

    I.   preferred stockholders

    II.   secured bondholders

    III.   subordinated debenture owners

    IV.   common stockholders

    A.   I, II, III, IV

    B.   II, I, III, IV

    C.   II, III, I, IV

    D.   I, II, IV, III

6. **Which of the following represents a true statement concerning bearer bonds?**

    A.   They no longer exist.

    B.   The government called all bearer bonds in 1983.

    C.   They no longer exist on the primary market.

    D.   They yield more than book-entry bonds.

7. **50 basis points is equal to**

    A.   50%

    B.   5%

    C.   .5%

    D.   .05%

8. **Which of the following bond ratings implies the highest yield?**

    A.   Aa

    B.   Baa

    C.   BBB

    D.   Ba

9. **If the yield curve inverts, which of the following would carry the lowest price?**

   A. T-bond

   B. T-bill

   C. T-note

   D. 10-year debenture

10. **All of the following represent secured bonds except**

   A. collateral trust certificate

   B. debenture

   C. mortgage bond

   D. equipment trust certificate

11. **All of the following would increase the market price of an outstanding bond except**

   A. interest rates fall

   B. S & P upgrades the credit rating

   C. Moody's upgrades the credit rating

   D. the company undergoes a reverse stock split

ANSWERS

1. **B,** "convertible at 40" means 1 bond can be exchanged for 25 shares. If each share is now worth $57, 25 of them are worth $1,425. Parity.

2. **D,** bonds are called when rates fall. Issuers of bonds are borrowers, so, just like people with mortgages, when rates fall, they refinance their debt at a lower rate. Why would a bond be trading at a premium? Because rates have fallen.

3. **B,** bond prices refer to bonds trading on the secondary market. As rates on new bonds fall, the market prices of existing bonds rise. Rates down, price up—commit that to memory. Coupon rates ARE interest rates, so if the exam says that rates are falling, it is also saying that coupon rates on new bonds are falling. Which, again, makes the bonds already out there on the secondary market look more attractive.

4. **C,** if you held these four mortgages, which one would you refinance first? The one with the highest

interest rate—9%. Which 9% mortgage should you refinance first, the one you can pay off at par, or the one you can pay off with a $30 per bond penalty? Right?

5.   **C,** memorize it, but it also makes sense. Pay the secured creditors, then the general creditors (debentures), then the SUB-ordinated creditors. If there's still money left—and I'm not sure why there would be—give PREFERENCE to preferred. Common is last—that's why it's called "common."

6.   **C,** they don't get issued this way on the primary market, but there are still some bearer bonds in investors' safe-deposit boxes.

7.   **C,** anything less than 100 basis points is less than 1%.

8.   **D,** the lowest credit rating scares buyers the most—as they pay less and less for the bond, what happens to the yield?

9.   **B,** an evil question. The inverted yield curve makes the T-bill yield the most—so what does that say about its price?

10. **B,** debentures are backed by the issuer's promise to pay, nothing more.

11. **D,** stock splits don't really achieve much of anything.

U.S. GOVERNMENT DEBT SECURITIES

U.S. Government debt is very safe stuff. If you buy a bill, note, or bond from the United States Treasury, you do not have to worry about default risk. You're going to get your money back. You just aren't going to get rich in the process. In fact, you usually need to be rich already to get excited about U.S. Government debt, but that's another matter. For the test, just remember that U.S. Government/Treasury debt is just about the safest debt known to humankind. Safe and boring. Also remember that the interest income is exempt from state and local taxes. I mean, usually, it's the tax rate you pay the federal government that bothers you, but it is nice to avoid paying state and local taxes on interest earned on your U.S. Treasuries. If you live in a high-tax state such as Maryland, you have to enjoy earning lots of interest on **T-bills**, **T-notes**, **T-bonds**, etc., knowing that your state can't touch any of it. T-bills, T-notes, T-bonds, STRIPS, and TIPS are all securities that can be traded on the secondary market, what we call "negotiable" securities. The final three Treasury products for investors—I-Bonds, Series EE Bonds, and Series HH bonds—are not "negotiable," meaning they can't be traded/sold to other investors.

T-BILLS

T-bills pay back the face amount, and investors try to buy them for the steepest discount possible. If the T-bill pays out $1,000, you'd rather get it for $950 than $965, right? In the first case you make $50 interest; in the second case you make only $35. That's why the BID *looks* higher than the ASK for T-bills trading on the secondary market. The bid is the discount that buyers are trying to get; the ask is the discount the sellers are willing to give up.

So, the quote might look like this:

BID	ASK
5.0%	4.75%

In other words, the buyers want a 5% discount; the sellers are only willing to give up a 4.75% discount from the par value.

These bills mature in one year or less (4 weeks, 13 weeks, 26 weeks, 52 weeks), so there are no coupon payments. These work like short-term "zero coupon" bonds, where the difference between the discounted purchase price and the face amount IS the investor's return. T-bills are offered in minimum denominations of $100 and, like all Treasuries, T-bills are issued in **book entry**/journal entry form. I mean, if the U.S. Government had to pay for all the paper, ink, and printing services on all their T-bills, T-notes, and T-bonds, they could end up running, like, a *deficit*. The maturities available change from time to time. Currently (as you can see at www.treasurydirect.gov) the available maturities are 4 weeks, 3 months, 6 months, and something I don't expect the test to mention: extremely short-term "cash management bills." That website, by the way, offers a great primer on bills, notes, bonds, etc. As you'll see, T-bills are auctioned every Monday by the **Federal Reserve Board**. The big institutions put in "competitive tenders," trying to buy the bills for the lowest possible price. A pipsqueak like me puts in a "non-competitive" tender that will be filled, since I'm not trying to lowball Uncle Sam. Yes Morgan Stanley will probably get a better price on T-bills today, but they also might not get their bid filled at all. I'm going to let that website mentioned above take us home on T-bills:

Key Facts

- Bills are sold at a discount. The **discount rate** is determined at auction.
- Bills pay interest only at maturity. The interest is equal to the face value minus the purchase price.
- The minimum purchase (face amount) is $100.
- Bills are auctioned every week.
- Bills are issued in electronic form.
- You can hold a bill until it matures or sell it before it matures.
- In a single auction, an investor can buy up to $5 million in bills by non-competitive bidding or up to 35% of the initial offering amount by competitive bidding.

T-NOTES, T-BONDS

T-notes are offered with 2- to 10-year maturities. T-bonds mature in 30 years. These both make semi-annual interest payments, and are both quoted in 32nds. A quote of 98.16 means $980 plus 16/32nds or 1/2. So a T-bond priced at 98.16 costs $985. A price of 98.24 would be $987.50. In other words "24/32nds" is the same thing as "3/4s." If they hit you with a tough question here, one that doesn't reduce nice and easy to 1/2s or 1/4s, just multiply the number of 32nds by ".3125," and move on with your life.

Also note that 30-year T-bonds are callable in the last five years. For example, the T-bonds issued in 1980 were finally called in 2005.

Key Facts

- The yield on a note or bond is determined at auction.
- Notes and bonds are sold in increments of $100. The minimum purchase is $100.
- Notes and bonds are issued in electronic form.
- You can hold a note or bond until it matures or sell it before it matures.
- In a single auction, an investor can buy up to $5 million in notes or bonds by non-competitive bidding or up to 35% of the initial offering amount by competitive bidding.

STRIPS

The Treasury Department can also take T-notes and T-bonds and "strip" them into their various interest and principal components. Once they strip the securities into components, they can sell interest-only or principal-only **zero coupon bonds** to investors. We call these STRIPS, an acronym which stands for the "separate trading of registered interest and principal of securities." Of course, if you can tell someone what a STRIP is and the fact that it stands for the "separate trading of registered interest and principal of securities," chances are you're going to impress them enough to buy whatever the heck you're pitching. Either that, or they'll think you're an egghead with no social life, but go ahead and memorize it, anyway. As long as you're already going to be memorizing more information than you ever wanted to or ever thought possible, why not also know that STRIPS stands for.... well, you know what it stands for. Enough already.

For the test, if an investor needs to send kids to college and needs to have an exact amount of money available on a future date, put him into STRIPS. This way, he'll pay a known amount and receive a known amount on a future date. He won't get rich, necessarily, but he won't lose the kid's college fund day-trading debit call spreads, either.

TREASURY RECEIPTS

Broker-dealers sell the same basic product, only they call them **treasury receipts**. For both receipts and STRIPS, just remember that they are purchased at a discount and mature at the face value. And remember that the STRIP is guaranteed by Uncle Sam, while a Treasury Receipt is not.

TIPS

As if government securities weren't safe enough, the Treasury department recently decided to protect investors from inflation. The Treasury Inflation-Protected Securities adjust for inflation, meaning that if inflation rises, you receive more money, and when it falls, you receive less. Inflation is measured through the Consumer Price Index (CPI), which tracks the basic things that consumers buy. The CPI surveys certain major metropolitan areas of the US to find out what consumers are paying for, say, blue jeans, movie tickets, a gallon of milk, or a loaf of bread. If prices in general are rising (CPI is positive), the principal amount of the TIPS is adjusted upwards. That's a little surprising, since most readers would assume the principal amount/par value would stay the same, with the coupon rate adjusting. No. That would probably make too much sense to ever fly in Washington, DC. In any case, if the (fixed) coupon rate on the security is 3%, suddenly the investor could be receiving 3% of, say, $1030 to reflect inflation/rising consumer prices. If the economy is experiencing falling prices (the CPI is negative) the principal amount of the TIPS could be lower than $1,000 when calculating the semi-annual interest payment. Even if the principal amount used to calculate an interest payment could be less than $1,000, the TIPS will pay out the $1,000 face amount at maturity, period. So, there is no default risk and no purchasing power/inflation risk on a TIPS. Basically, if you can find a safer security than a TIP, please buy it.

Just don't expect to get much of a yield for your money.

I-BONDS

Like all the other Government Securities above, TIPS are "negotiable securities," meaning you can sell them to other investors on the secondary market. I-Bonds, on the other hand, are "non-negotiable," meaning there is no secondary market for them. An investor buys the I-Bond from the US Government and can only sell it by redeeming it to the US Government for payment. In other words, they're not securities; they're merely "savings bonds." An I-bond is a savings bond issued by the U.S. Treasury, which means it's absolutely safe and also exempt from state and local income taxes. An I-bond pays a guaranteed rate that is fixed but also pays more interest income when inflation rises. The semi-annual inflation rate announced in May is the change between the CPI (inflation) figures from the preceding September and March; the inflation rate announced in November is the change between the CPI figures from the preceding March and September. So, since they adjust the interest income to levels of inflation, there's no default risk and no real purchasing power risk, either. There are also tax advantages. First, the interest isn't paid out; it's added to the value of the bond. You can, therefore, defer the taxes until you cash in the bond. And, if you use the proceeds for qualified education costs in the same calendar year that you redeem the bonds, the interest is tax-free. The investor does not even have to declare that the I-bonds will be used for educational purposes when she buys them. As long as she uses the proceeds in the same year she redeems the bonds—and meets the other requirements of the Education Savings Bond Program—the interest is tax-free.

SERIES EE BONDS

As the US Treasury states at www.treasurydirect.gov: EE Bonds are reliable, low-risk government-backed savings products that you can use toward financing education, supplemental retirement income, birthday and graduation gifts, and other special events. Series EE Bonds purchased on or after May 1, 2005, earn a fixed rate of return, letting you know what the bonds are worth at all times. EE Bonds purchased between May, 1997, and April 30, 2005, are based on 5-year Treasury security yields and earn a variable market-based rate of return. Paper EE Bonds are still available for purchase through most local financial institutions or participating employers' payroll deduction plans. Treasury is phasing out the issuance of paper savings bonds through traditional employer-sponsored payroll savings plans. As of September 30, 2010, federal employees will no longer be able to purchase paper savings bonds through payroll deduction. The end date for all other (non-federal) employees is January 1, 2011. Since their website does a fine job of explaining things, let me just keep copying-and-pasting:

Key Facts:

Buying Electronic EE Bonds
- Sold at face value; e.g., you pay $50 for a $50 bond and it's worth its full value when it's available for redemption.
- Purchase in amounts of $25 or more, to the penny.
- $5,000 maximum purchase in one calendar year.
- Issued electronically to your designated account.

Buying Paper EE Bonds
- Sold at half their face value; e.g., you pay $25 for a $50 bond but it's not worth its face value until it has matured.
- Purchase in denominations of $50, $75, $100, $200, $500, $1,000, and $5,000, and $10,000.
- $5,000 maximum purchase in one calendar year.
- Issued as paper bond certificates.

If you redeem EE Bonds in the first 5 years, you'll forfeit the 3 most-recent months' interest. If you redeem them after 5 years, you won't be penalized.

SERIES HH BONDS

I don't have a lot to say about Series HH savings bonds, since this is what the US Treasury has to say about them at www.treasurydirect.gov:

HH/H Bonds

Notice: As of September 1, 2004, the U.S. Treasury is no longer issuing HH/H Savings Bonds. Investors are no longer able to reinvest HH/H Bonds or exchange EE/E Bonds for HH Bonds.

About HH/H Bonds
- HH Bonds are current-income securities.
- HH/H Bonds are no longer issued by the U.S. Treasury.
- HH Bonds were once available in exchange for EE/E Bonds or on reinvestment of matured HH/H Bonds.

GOVERNMENT AGENCY SECURITIES

The U.S. Government also has agencies that issue debt securities. Investors are often attracted to this category because the securities are relatively safe but also offer yields that are higher than on comparable T-bills, T-notes, and T-bonds. Part of the reason for the higher yields is that Government agency securities are not direct obligations of the US Government, unless we're talking specifically about "Ginnie Mae." That's right, securities issued by "Fannie Mae" and "Freddie Mac" are not direct obligations, while securities issued by "Ginnie Mae" *are* backed by the full faith and credit of the United States Treasury. Either way, Fannie Mae (**Federal National Mortgage Association**), Freddie Mac (**Federal Home Loan Mortgage Corporation**) and Ginnie Mae (**Government National Mortgage Association**) all issue mortgage-backed pass-through securities. The concept behind these mortgage-backed securities is a little tricky, so let's take a little time to explain things. First, Fannie Mae and Freddie Mac provide liquidity for mortgages, meaning that lenders can make a mortgage to a homeowner and then sell the thing to Fannie or Freddie and, thereby, make more mortgages to more homeowners. In fact, you may have been alerted that "Fannie Mae" or "Freddie Mac" have purchased your mortgage at some point. Why? Well, a big pool of mortgages can be packaged together by a financial institution and then turned into mortgage-backed "pass-through certificates" that are sold to investors. If an investor buys a pass-through certificate, she receives a monthly check representing both interest and principal that is being paid by the homeowners whose mortgages are now in the pool. When will all the principal on these mortgages be paid off? Nobody knows for sure, which is why the securities all carry **prepayment risk**. Prepayment risk is the risk that interest rates will drop, folks will pay off their mortgages by refinancing at a lower rate, and investors will get their money back sooner than they wanted it, reinvesting it at a lower rate going forward. On the other hand, if interest rates start to rise, investors may experience **extension risk**, as homeowners take longer to pay off the principal, since, by definition, there aren't any great refinancing activities available when rates are even higher than what homeowners are currently paying. So, an investor who owns pass-through certificates or mortgage-backed securities issued by Fannie, Freddie, or Ginnie really owns an undivided or proportional interest in a big pool of mortgages. Rather than *paying* monthly interest and principal, these investors are *receiving* most of the monthly interest and principal being paid off by the homeowners in the pool—with the creator of the product taking a few basis points for its trouble, of course. Ginnie Mae (GNMA) is the only one of the three that is backed by the full faith and credit of the U.S. Government, which insures all the mortgages in the pool. Fannie (**FNMA**) and Freddie (**FHLMC**) are public companies, so you can buy stock in them. There is no stock in Ginnie because it's not a company. Fannie and Freddie are also referred to as "government sponsored enterprises," which Freddie Mac explains on its website as "a shareholder-owned company created by Congress to serve a public purpose." That's exactly right, of course, so even if you've heard that the US Government has "bailed out" Fannie and Freddie, remember that Fannie and Freddie are both still just shareholder-owned companies, with the US Treasury now the biggest and highest-ranking shareholder. Turns out, the US Treasury likes to buy senior convertible preferred shares in these instances. That way, after they pump in a few hundred billion dollars in exchange for senior convertible preferred shares, the US Treasury can determine if and when any dividends get paid on the many different issues of preferred and common stock, and if the companies finally get their acts together, the US Treasury can buy the appreciated common stock at a set price, make a profit, and "return it to the taxpayers."

That's the plan, anyway, as if things ever go as planned in Washington, DC. In any event, please remember that GNMA has always been a direct obligation of the US Government, while Fannie Mae and Freddie Mac have never been direct obligations.

Ginnie Mae requires a $25,000 minimum investment, in case the exam feels like playing Trivial Pursuit the day you take it.

I would expect the exam to stick more to the Ginnie, Fannie, and Freddie side of things, but it could also mention a few others. With that in mind, please note that other government sponsored enterprises—not direct obligations of the U.S. Government—include:

- Federal Farm Credit Banks (FFCBs)
- Federal Home Loan Banks (FHLBs)
- Student Loan Marketing Association (SLMA)

These "GSEs," or "**Government-Sponsored Enterprises**" are publicly chartered by Congress but privately owned by shareholders. The GSE raises money by letting a selling group of dealers offer its securities to investors, with the proceeds then loaned to a bank, which, in turn, makes loans to individuals including farmers, homeowners, and students. **The Federal Farm Credit Banks** provide funds for Banks for Cooperatives, Intermediate Credit Banks, and Federal Land Banks by issuing both short-term discount notes and interest-bearing bonds with both short and long-term maturities. These enterprises help farmers stay in business, a goal that the US Government obviously (and rightfully) considers an important one. The Federal Home Loan Banks (there are 12 of them) help to provide liquidity for savings and loan (S & L) institutions. Like the Federal Farm Credit Banks, the Federal Home Loan Banks issue both short-term discount notes and also interest-paying bonds of various maturities. Finally, the **Student Loan Marketing Association** (SLMA) or "Sallie Mae" provides liquidity to institutions making student loans. Sallie Mae purchases both uninsured loans and loans insured under the Guaranteed Student Loan Program (GSLP)

In all cases, remember that only Ginnie Mae (GNMA) is a direct obligation of the US Government. All other securities issued by "government-sponsored enterprises" are considered relatively safe, but still not directly backed by the United States Treasury's full faith and credit. The interest that investors earn on the securities discussed in this section are assumed to be taxable by the federal, state, and local governments.

FOREIGN BONDS

Some investors choose to purchase bonds issued outside the U.S.—why? Higher yields. Doesn't that imply that this international investing is riskier? Absolutely. Yes, your clients would love to buy a safe bond with a high yield, but they'd also like to be able to eat a dozen hot, glazed donuts or three orders of super-sized cheese fries every day without putting on weight. Doesn't work that way. If you want absolute **safety**, you sacrifice yield. If you want high yield, you sacrifice safety. Investing in foreign bonds is risky, but there is a big difference between a "developed market" and an **emerging market**. In general, the following countries enjoy securities markets and economies that are considered developed: U.S., Canada, European Union countries, Australia, New Zealand, and Japan. Emerging markets would include everyone else, though South Korea and Singapore are much more advanced than China, India, and other "emerging" nations. If you purchase bonds issued and traded in emerging markets, you're investing in regions characterized by low per capita incomes, primitive securities markets, and/or economies that are not fully industrialized. In other words, there is a promising future, but it inconveniently hasn't shown up yet, sort of like the Chicago Cubs, who haven't won a World Series in over 100 years in spite of how bright "next year" often appears.

Whether the foreign market is considered developed or emerging, investors have to deal with currency risk. If your bond pays interest and principal in yen or bot, you have to convert that to U.S. dollars; if the dollar is strong, you get fewer dollars. Luckily, not all foreign bonds pay interest and principal in foreign currencies. Your exam might bring up the difference between "U.S. Pay Bonds" and "Foreign Pay Bonds." If your bond pays you in U.S. dollars, currency risk is eliminated, but if it pays in another currency (foreign pay bond), then you, obviously, do have **currency exchange risk**. Types of so-called "U.S. Pay Bonds" include "Eurodollar bonds," which are issued and traded outside the U.S. but are denominated in U.S. dollars. Another type is called the "Yankee bond," which allows foreign issuers to borrow money in the U.S. marketplace. Eurodollar bonds are not registered with the SEC and cannot be sold to U.S. investors until a certain number of days after being issued. Yankee bonds, on the other hand, are registered with the SEC.

We already looked at **political risk**, which is associated with emerging markets. And, there are "operational risks" when investing in foreign markets, especially emerging markets. That just means that the securities markets are less liquid/efficient, and usually carry much higher transaction costs. In the U.S. we can assume that "government" bonds are *much* safer than bonds issued by U.S. *corporations,* but I'm not sure I would make that assumption in foreign markets, where governments have been known to "pull a Russia" on investors and declare, as Russia did in 1994, "Very sorry, comrades, but we cannot pay."

Oh, and just in case the exam has not met its quota of trivial information, you may need to know that "Brady bonds" are issued by the governments of emerging markets, usually in Latin America. And, just to be on the safe side, remember that if the exam calls something a "developed market," that would be the opposite of a "develop-ing market," which is another name for an "emerging market."

No, the regulators certainly do *not* want you to pass their exam, but won't it be fun to pass it anyway?

CMOs

CMOs or collateralized mortgage obligations are derivative securities and are inherently complex products. Generally, a financial institution takes either a pool of mortgages or a pool of mortgage-backed securities issued by GNMA, FNMA, or FHLMC and creates a CMO. The CMO offers various classes of bonds called **tranches**. The tranches are bonds that offer different rates of interest, repayment schedules, and levels of priority for principal repayment. Investors can choose the yield, maturity structure, and risk level that best suits them. Let's look at a very simple example of a "plain vanilla" CMO product. The investors in the CMO are divided up into three tranches, A, B, and C. Each tranche differs in the order that it receives principal payments, but it receives interest payments as long as it is not completely paid off. Class A investors are paid out the principal first with prepayments and repayments until they are paid off. Then class B investors are paid off, followed by class C investors. In a situation like this, class A investors bear most of the prepayment risk, while class C investors bear the least.

CMOs are usually rated AAA, so default risk is not a major concern. You just never know if you'll get your money back sooner [rates fall] or later [rates rise]. The risk of receiving your principal sooner than expected is called **prepayment risk**, which is associated with falling interest rates. The risk of receiving your principal later than expected is called **extension risk**, and is associated with rising interest rates. Two specific types of CMOs are called **PACs** and **TACs**. A "PAC" is a **planned amortization class**, while a "TAC" is a **targeted amortization class.** Since there is a "plan" with the PAC, the exam might say that it protects the investor more against prepayment and extension risk. A TAC does offer some protection against prepayment risk but not extension risk. In either case, there is a "support class" created to protect against prepayments—if the principal is repaid more quickly than expected, it goes into a support class. For the PAC, if interest rates rise and principal is being repaid more slowly, money will be transferred from the support class to protect that PAC owner against extension risk. This would not happen for the owner of a TAC. If the exam is in an especially bad mood the day you take it, it might even bring up the methods of estimating prepayment rates on CMOs. One method is called the "average life" method in which CMOs are compared to other types of fixed-income securities, with an average maturity calculated for each tranche. The **"PSA model"** estimates the speed of prepayments against a benchmark. If the "PSA" is 100, that means that prepayment rates will remain stable. If the PSA is greater than 100, prepayments are expected to speed up. If the PSA is less than 100, prepayments are expected to slow down.

Beyond the PAC and TAC, the exam might mention the **Z-tranche**, which is basically a zero coupon bond inside the CMO that returns principal (and, therefore, accrued interest) only after all the other tranches have been paid off/retired. And, there are "principal only" and "interest only" securities which are pretty much what they sound like. The principal and the interest is separated so that principal-only investors are concerned with how quickly they receive the principal—the *faster* the better. Interest-only investors enjoy a higher yield when prepayments slow down and a lower yield when prepayments speed up. That is because interest payments are based on the remaining principal amount on the loans—as that principal declines, so does the amount of interest paid by homeowners and received by the interest-only investors in the CMO. The faster that principal declines, the lower the yield to the investor; the longer it takes homeowners to pay off the principal, the *higher* the yield to the investor.

CMOs are not extremely liquid and are often too complex to be suitable for many investors. Registered representatives should get the customer's signature on a suitability statement when selling these products. Also, advertising and sales literature on CMOs must be filed with FINRA ten days *before* its first use, subject to any revisions that FINRA demands before the firm uses the piece. The communication must refer to the securities as "collateralized mortgage obligations" and not some other name, and CMOs can not be compared to *any* other product, since they are totally unique. The following disclosure statement has to appear in an advertisement for a CMO: the yield and average life shown above consider prepayment assumptions that may or may not be met. Changes in payments may significantly affect yield and average life. Please contact your representative for information on CMOs and how they react to different market conditions.

FINRA has even gone so far as to offer a standardized CMO print advertisement that broker-dealers can use, but even if the firm uses that format, they still have to submit the ad to FINRA prior to first use. Broker-dealers have to offer educational material about the features of CMOs to customers that must include:

- A discussion of the characteristics and risks of CMOs. This would include: how changing interest rates may affect prepayment rates and the average life of the security, tax considerations, credit risk, minimum investments, liquidity, and transactions costs.

- A discussion of the structure of a CMO. This would include the different types of structures, tranches, and risks associated with each type of security. It is also important to explain to a client that two CMOs with the same underlying collateral may have different prepayment risk and different interest-rate risk.
- A discussion that explains the relationship between mortgage loans and mortgage securities.
- A glossary of terms applicable to mortgage-backed securities.

MONEY MARKET

Debt securities maturing in greater than one year are sometimes called **funded debt**. Money market securities, on the other hand, are debt securities maturing in one year or less. They are considered to be safe, liquid investments. The exam may refer to money market securities as "cash equivalents" because, basically, they are just as good as cash. Better actually, because unlike cash sitting in a drawer somewhere, money market instruments are earning interest. It's not necessarily a high *rate* of interest, but at least you're putting your cash to work and you're not risking it in the stock market, where anything can happen, or the bond market, where interest rates could rise and knock down the value of your holdings. Of course, the problem with investing too much of your money into cash equivalents is that you will miss out on the big growth opportunities that arise when the stock or bond markets decide to go off on a run. Sounds like opportunity cost, right? Also, these things do not keep pace with inflation, leaving the investor with purchasing power risk.

T-bills

Most investors devote a certain percentage of their portfolio to the safe, boring, interest-bearing world of "cash" or "money market" securities. Buying T-bills is about as safe as it gets, as we saw with the Sharpe ratio, which uses the return on the 3-month T-bill as the "riskless rate of return." The "T" is for "Treasury," and T-bills are guaranteed by the United States Treasury.

Guaranteed? But, but…no buts. The interest and principal are guaranteed, and the US Treasury has never stiffed anyone so far. So, if you don't need to withdraw a certain amount of money for several months or longer, you can buy the 3-month or 6-month T-bill and earn higher yields than you'd earn in a savings account. There are no fees to buy T-bills if you buy them directly through www.treasurydirect.gov.

Bank CDs usually yield about the same as T-bills, but the bank's FDIC insurance stops at $250,000 per account. T-bills, on the other hand, are simply guaranteed no matter how large the denomination. Any given Monday T-bills are available by auction through the website mentioned above from as small as $100 par value to as large as $5 million. No matter how big your bill, it's fully insured/guaranteed by the US Treasury.

Bankers' Acceptance

A **bankers' acceptance** is a short-term credit investment created by a non-financial company and guaranteed by a bank as to payment. "BAs" are traded at discounts to face value in the secondary market. These instruments are commonly used in international transactions, and the exam might associate them with "importing and exporting." As with a T-bill, bankers' acceptances are so short-term that it would make no sense to send interest checks to the buyer. Instead, these short-term debt securities are purchased at a discount from their face value. The difference between what you pay and what you receive *is* your interest income. The "BA" or "bankers' acceptance" is backed both by a bank's full faith and credit and the goods being purchased by the importer. I'm not sure you need to know this to answer test questions, but this is how the BA is created. First, a computer manufacturer in California imports computer parts from a Japanese company but—like most Americans—is not in the mood to, like, pay. So, the California company issues a "time draft" to the Japanese company, which is really a post-dated check that is good on a future date and backed up by their bank's line of credit. The Japanese company can sit now sit on this time draft until the due date and receive the full amount. Or, if they get antsy, they can cash it immediately at their bank at a slight discount. If they do the latter, the Japanese bank would then have a "bankers' acceptance" guaranteed by the American company's bank and the computer parts purchased by the American importer. The Japanese bank can either wait until the due date or sell the thing on the secondary market at a discount.

Commercial Paper

Normally people have to pay much higher interest rates to borrow long-term as opposed to borrowing short-term. But, in order to build major items such as an $800 million factory, a company generally bites the bullet, issues long-term bonds (funded debt), and pays the lenders back slowly, in the same way that you are probably currently paying off the mortgage on your house. But if Microsoft needs a mere $50 million to tide them over for a few months, they would probably prefer to borrow it short-term at the lowest possible interest rate. If so, they issue a piece of **commercial paper** with a $50 million face amount, selling it to a pension or mutual fund for, say, $49.8 million. Again, the difference between the discounted price and the face amount *is* the interest earned by the investor. Commercial paper is generally issued only by corporations with high credit ratings from S&P, Moody's, or Fitch. Unfortunately, each of the three ratings agencies uses different nomenclature, so I have decided not to tell you about the P-1 down to P-3 ratings issued by Moody's, let alone the A1 down to A3 ratings issued by S & P or the F1 down to F3 ratings issued by Fitch. Do know that a rating below any of those "3's" would be considered speculative commercial paper and would, therefore, not be found in the typical money market mutual fund portfolio. Some large corporations issue their commercial paper directly to the lenders/investors, which may be mutual funds, pension funds, etc. The industry cleverly calls this "directly placed commercial paper." Would you, therefore, believe that when corporations use commercial paper dealers to sell to the investor, the industry refers to this as "dealer-placed commercial paper"? Either way, retail investors typically get their commercial paper exposure when they buy money market mutual funds as opposed to, like, fronting Microsoft $3 million dollars until a week from next Tuesday.

Repurchase Agreements

Large financial institutions borrow money at low interest rates over the short term by taking your money and paying whatever a savings account or CD currently offers. They then lend your money out to someone else long-term at a higher interest rate. As long as they're able to borrow at a lower rate than they lend, they're fine. But this business model also puts them at risk in terms of fluctuating interest rates. Think of the flat and inverted yield curves we looked at, or even a positive yield curve with only a tiny spread between short-term and long-term interest rates. These interest rate environments are no good for bankers, who live by the time-tested motto: borrow at three, lend at six, golf at three. If they suddenly have to pay high interest rates to borrow short-term while they're earning lower and lower rates when they lend the money out long-term, that's got to hurt. In order to shield themselves from interest-rate risk over the next 30, 60, 90 days, large financial institutions engage in **repurchase agreements** and **reverse repurchase agreements**. Basically, one party sells the other party something today with the agreement to repurchase it at a set price in the near future. The difference between what you pay today and what you receive in the near future would be your fixed rate of return over that time frame. If one bank calls another to propose the arrangement, that's a repurchase agreement. If they call the other bank and ask to do it the other way around, that's a reverse repurchase agreement. Although definitely part of the money market, they're more of a private arrangement than a piece of paper that gets bought and sold.

Tax-Exempt Municipal Notes

We'll look at municipal securities in a moment, but for now just know that cities, counties, school districts, etc., can borrow money long-term by issuing bonds, and they can borrow short-term by issuing notes. "Anticipation notes" are very common, and their name tells you exactly what's going on: there is money coming into the city's coffers in the near future, but there are some bills due *right now*. For example, property taxes are collected twice a year. If the city wants some of that money now, they can issue a **tax anticipation note**, or TAN. If it's backed up by revenues—from sewer and water services, for example—it's a **revenue anticipation note**, or RAN. If the note is backed up by both taxes and revenues, they call it a **tax and revenue anticipation note**, or TRAN. But my personal favorite of these short-term municipal notes has to be the **bond anticipation note**, or BAN. In this case, the issuer borrows money from somebody now and backs it up with part of the money they're going to borrow in the near future when they issue more bonds.

Seriously.

The interest paid on these municipal notes is lower than the nominal rates paid on a corporation's commercial paper, but that's okay—the interest paid is also tax-exempt at the federal level. So, if an investor or an institution is looking for safety, liquidity, and dependable, tax-exempt interest over the short-term, they purchase these anticipation notes directly or through a tax-exempt money market mutual fund.

Negotiable/Jumbo CDs

Some people like to step outside the realm of FDIC insurance and purchase **jumbo** or **negotiable CDs**. The denominations here are at least $100,000 and often several millions of dollars. Therefore, jumbo CDs are usually not fully insured by the FDIC but are, rather, backed by the issuing bank. That makes their yields higher. Also, if you've ever pulled out of a bank CD early, you know how painful that can be. With a jumbo CD you have a negotiable/marketable security that you can sell to someone else. That's what the word "negotiable" means.

Long-Term CDs

Then, there are long-term certificates of deposit with maturities from 2 to 20 years. Alert readers may be thinking, "Then what the heck are you talking about them under money market securities for?" To which I would respond, "Because I have to talk about them somewhere."

So there. These long-term CD's may have limited or even no liquidity and investors might actually lose money by selling these things on the secondary market. So-called "brokered CDs" may have call features that limit any capital appreciation on the things should rates go down, and they also subject the investor to reinvestment risk. Also, the interest payments are frequently funky, as the CDs are issued with variable rates determined in ways few normal people understand. Broker-dealers selling these long-term CDs need to be sure that investors understand how these products differ from traditional bank CDs and must disclose all potential risks.

Fed Funds

Banks typically lend out much more money than they take in through deposits. To keep the banks from going belly-up when the borrowers can't repay the loans, the Federal Reserve Board requires banks to maintain a minimum amount of their deposits in reserve. In case somebody, you know, wants her money this afternoon at the teller window. If a bank in Sandusky, Ohio, is a few million dollars short of meeting their reserve requirement, they might borrow excess funds from a bank in Biloxi, Mississippi, at the **fed funds** or federal funds rate. This is the interest rate that banks charge other banks for overnight loans. The fed funds rate fluctuates daily and is considered an indicator of interest rate trends in general. For example, if the fed funds rate rises, it's likely that the prime rate that banks charge their most creditworthy corporate borrowers will also rise in the near future. As will rates charged on mortgages, car loans, and unsecured personal loans

Last Word

Finally, while the textbook definition of a money market security is a debt security maturing in one year or less, the usual maturity is a maximum of 270 days. There is an exemption to registration under the Securities Act of 1933 based on that 270 days, and no one wants to register a short-term debt security, since by the time they got it through registration interest rates would have changed. Also, if the test writers want to mess with your head, they might ask if a T-note could be a money market security. At first glance you think, no, a T-note matures in 2 - 10 years, so there's no way it could be in a money market portfolio. Well, when it's issued the thing might have a 10-year maturity. The next year it would be nine years from maturity. Eventually, it would be one year or less from maturity, so, yes, *any* debt security one year or less from maturity is a money market instrument, regardless of the original maturity.

CASH ALTERNATIVES

Remember that another name for "money market securities" is **cash equivalents**. The term "cash equivalents" implies a level of safety and liquidity, so broker-dealers have to be careful when selling so-called "cash equivalents" or "cash alternatives" to their customers. As FINRA reminds member firms, T-bills and CDs are guaranteed by the federal government. Money market mutual funds have historically been reliable and liquid, but some things that have been marketed as "cash alternatives" have or could turn out to be a real mess for investors. Not long ago "auction rate securities" caused a huge mess that led to multimillion-dollar settlements and repurchases of the securities by the broker-dealers who ran the auctions. Retail and institutional investors had been told that their auction-rate securities were a totally liquid investment designed to pay a higher yield than safe, boring, traditional money market securities. The "auction" meant that investors could always liquidate their securities to a new group of buyers if they needed to turn them back into cash, and, as it turned out, they always could, except when they couldn't. For a while broker-dealers wanted to sweep the impending problems under the rug, so when there was a shortage of buyers for the auctions, they posed as buyers themselves and bought back part of their own offerings just to keep the market flowing. Well, eventually, even that neat trick didn't work, the auctions failed, and suddenly St. John's Lutheran Church can't pay salaries, or print bulletins, or pay the utility bill etc., because the money they put into these "cash alternatives" was, like, gone. Gone? Umm, that's not exactly the *alternative* we had envisioned for our cash.

So, FINRA now reminds firms that if they're going to sell "cash alternatives," they need to avoid overstating a product's similarities to a cash holding and:

- provide balanced disclosure of the risks and returns associated with a particular product
- conduct adequate due diligence to understand the features of a product
- conduct appropriate suitability analyses
- monitor market and economic conditions that may cause the description of an investment as a "cash alternative" to become inaccurate or misleading, and adopt procedures reasonably designed to ensure that the firm responds to those changing conditions; and
- train registered persons regarding the features, risks and suitability of these products

Firms need to be careful in their **sales literature**, **advertising** and other communications concerning "cash alternatives." As FINRA says, "In virtually all cases, a statement to retail investors that an investment is a **'cash equivalent**,' that it is as 'safe as cash' or that it carries no market or credit risk would raise serious questions under FINRA's advertising rules." Firms "must take reasonable steps to ensure that any communication that presents an investment as a cash alternative discloses, if applicable, that it is not federally guaranteed and that it is possible to lose money with the investment." So, a T-bill is a **cash equivalent** but is guaranteed by the U.S. Treasury. If another so-called "cash equivalent" is *not guaranteed*, that little difference needs to be made very clear to investors.

Not only must firms implement the above general approach to "cash alternatives," but FINRA also reminds them that they "must *reasonably* believe that a product is suitable for a particular customer seeking a cash alternative before recommending it." FINRA cautions firms that the fact that an investment may meet established accounting standards for treatment as a "cash holding in a financial statement does not conclusively establish that the investment is an appropriate cash alternative for a particular investor." Good point—a corporation might be able to take on bigger risks with its excess cash that would make no sense for a retail investor. If MSFT, for example, loses a billion dollars chasing after a high yield in some complex "cash alternative" investment, they probably have 20 times that amount sitting in safer alternatives, like T-bills. And if not, they should have.

PRACTICE

1. **All of the following pay interest subject to state taxes except**

    A. GNMA

    B. FNMA

    C. municipal securities

    D. T-bills

2. **The quote on your customer's T-bond is BID 101.12 - ASK 101.16. Therefore, she can sell her T-bond for**

    A. $1,013.75

    B. $1,015.00

    C. $1,011.20

    D. $1,011.60

3. **A quote for a T-bill is BID 5% - ASK 4.5%. What is true in this case?**

    A. the bid represents a higher price

    B. the bid represents a lower price

    C. the ask represents a lower price

    D. the ask represents the suggested price by the FRB

4. **BID 98 3/4 - ASK 99 1/2 would be a quote for a**

    A. T-bill

    B. municipal serial bond

    C. T-bond

    D. corporate bond

5. All of the following are true of corporate zero coupon bonds except

   A.   interest is received at maturity

   B.   interest is taxed annually

   C.   the return to the investor is zero

   D.   the bonds pay no interest

6. Which of the following CMOs leaves the investor with the most prepayment risk?

   A.   PAC

   B.   TAC

   C.   ZAC

   D.   MAC

ANSWERS

1.   **D**, the states can't tax Treasury securities. The Feds don't tax most municipal securities, but the states can do what they want with munis. GNMA, FNMA, and FHLMC are subject to tax at all levels.

2.   **A,** 101 means $1,010. The "and 12" means "and 12/32nds." Multiply each 32nd by .3125 and move on with your life.

3.   **B,** the steeper the discount, the lower the price. Wouldn't you rather buy something at a 5% discount than a 4.5% discount? So would the market maker.

4.   **D,** has to be a corporate bond. T-bills are quoted as a % discount from par. T-bonds have the weird "spot + 32nd" thingie. And a "serial" issue is quoted in terms of yield.

5.   **C,** be a good test taker. A good test taker would never believe choice "C," which is why choice C is the answer.

6.   **B,** a TAC has a "target," while a PAC has a "plan." The other two are fictitious.

SUITABILITY

Let's not forget Michelle Madsen, our loyal client who seems to be bringing home more and more money every paycheck, most of which she wants to invest. Her risk tolerance only allows her to buy so much stock (equity); therefore, much of the new money she puts into her investment account goes into bonds and bond mutual funds. In fact, that's a pretty typical pattern—the older somebody gets, the more money she puts in bonds as opposed to stock. No big surprise there. The older people get the more Republican they get, so why wouldn't their investments become more conservative as well?

Even most younger and middle-aged investors get spooked by the stock market's volatility, so they usually put a percentage of their investment capital into debt securities: bonds, certificates, notes, whatever we want to call them. What type of bonds should Michelle purchase? Well, she isn't such a wimp that she requires the absolute umbilical safety provided by Treasuries. She is in a high tax bracket, and as we'll see in the exciting chapter on municipal securities, municipal securities are for folks in high tax brackets. So, we originally allocated 25% of her money toward general obligation and revenue bonds issued by Cleveland, Chicago, and New York City, and we'll keep that as-is.

As she gets closer to retirement, let's stop putting new money into equities and put it, instead, into corporate bonds. Michelle enjoys receiving interest checks every six months, and who can blame her? She can either go shopping for clothes, or go shopping for more bonds that pay more interest allowing her to buy more bonds that pay more interest. After running a risk profile, we conclude that Michelle is not a junk bond investor. The thought of default would keep her up at night, and as the great JP Morgan once told a panicked investor, "Sell down to the sleeping point."

Still, we don't want to insist on AAA (Aaa) ratings for *all* of the corporate bonds. That would put too much emphasis on safety and end up giving Michelle crummy yields. So, let's diversify her corporate bond holdings by allocating 20% to AAA, 20% to AA, 20% to A, and 40% to BBB. Those are all investment grade bonds, and while she takes on more default risk on the BBB-rated bonds, she balances that by putting 60% into bonds rated in the top three credit tiers.

That's how we deal with default risk—what about interest rates? As we saw at the beginning of this chapter, interest rates jump all over the place, sending bond prices all over the place as well. Should we be wimps and buy bonds with short maturities? We could protect against interest rate risk that way, but what kind of yield do we get on short-term bonds? Really low rates, which is why corporations often borrow money short-term through commercial paper and why municipalities often borrow money short-term through anticipation notes (TANs, BANs, etc.). When you borrow short-term, you pay lower rates. So when you lend money short-term (buying short-term bonds) you *receive* low interest rates. Okay, so let's go as far out on the yield curve as possible to get the maximum yield possible. Sure, and as long as rates don't go up suddenly, we won't get crushed.

Hmm, too risky.

Here's an idea, let's buy some short-term, some intermediate-term, and some long-term bonds. Maybe you've heard a financial planner talk about building a "bond ladder" before. There are different ways to do it, but here's one way:

Let's buy an equal number of bonds that mature in one year, two years, three years, and so on up to a ten-year maturity. The bond that matures in one year will pay out the principal of $1,000 next year, and we'll simply use it to buy a 10-year bond. At that point, we'll again have bonds maturing in one year, two years, three years…up to 10 years. Every time the one-year bond matures, use the proceeds and buy a 10-year bond. This way, no matter where interest rates go, she'll have some short-term bonds that don't get hurt so much, and only so much of her money will be in the 10-year notes/bonds, whose market price will suffer the most.

So, we've now dealt with both default risk and interest rate risk by staggering the credit ratings and staggering the terms to maturity.

What happens if inflation rises? Well, that basically means that interest rates rise, and we just dealt with that by building our bond ladder, which puts only some of the bonds at high risk. The fact that her coupon payments will be less valuable…well, that's why we put money into equities, which are the most resilient in terms of fighting the ravages of inflation. What do we do about call risk, which is the risk that rates will go down? Well, we could give up some yield by purchasing non-callable bonds, or we could just live with the fact that some bonds will be called when rates fall. We'll take the proceeds and keep climbing the bond ladder all the way to retirement.

Also notice that within her municipal bond allocation we didn't buy bonds issued by just one municipality. While it's pretty rare that a city or state goes bankrupt, it can happen. And, if it did, wouldn't we look silly trying to explain to Michelle (and possibly her attorneys) why absolutely *every* last bond we bought was issued by the state that just did the unthinkable—defaulted on its bonds. Or economic conditions in the Rust Belt could deteriorate, so we don't want all of our bonds issued in Indiana, Ohio, and Pennsylvania. Or the Southwestern U.S. could go into a tailspin, which is why we wouldn't want all the bonds issued by or within New Mexico, Texas, and Arizona. Or, Hurricane Katrina could hit and wipe out entire cities in three or four different states, making it really tough for the issuers to pay bond interest and principal.

Of course, we could theoretically make higher returns by buying the riskiest securities, but Michelle Madsen is a human being who has to sleep at night. Let's help her manage her risk and maintain her sanity. Remember that a customer's psychological profile is just as important as her financial needs when it comes to recommending an investment portfolio. Yes, Warren Buffett will make much higher returns than Michelle Madsen will with his big, well-researched-but-still-risky-as-heck bets. Then again, if Warren Buffett loses $10 million buying junk bonds, something tells me the lights will still be on at his house. And, I don't know about you, but if Michelle's $500,000 portfolio suddenly plummets to $100,000, I don't want to take her next phone call and try to explain the value of p-a-t-i-e-n-c-e, especially when her attorneys get on the line and start explaining the value of a-r-b-i-t-r-a-t-i-o-n.

Whenever Michelle has a short-term need for liquidity, we'll put some of her money into the money market. She started out with 5% there, and I don't see why we'd need to allocate more than that, unless she's planning on buying a house or investment property in the near future.

So, Michelle is invested in corporate stock and corporate bonds. She has a small percentage in "cash," which is like a hip way of saying "money market." And the rest of her portfolio is devoted to municipal bonds, which just happens to be the LARGEST section on your exam. And, coincidentally, the very next chapter in the book.

CHAPTER 3

Municipal Securities

OVERVIEW

Across the street from my office sits an old brick industrial building that was supposed to be turned into a major townhouse/condo development. Unfortunately, the developers borrowed $15 million but sold only one condominium, and now the property sits in foreclosure, owned by a very unhappy bank. So the park district, whose land presses right up against the foreclosed property, would like to use the building for offices, conference rooms, exercise rooms, and also some green space after tearing down the back part of the massive and outdated structure. They need $6 million to acquire and re-hab the property and, therefore, want to raise that amount by issuing municipal bonds. So in a recent election, a majority of Forest Parkers voted to allow the park district to raise property taxes slightly in order to create the funds needed to pay off a $6 million bond issue.

At this point, the park district is still in negotiations with the bank sitting on the foreclosed property. But, assuming they can work out the price, the park district will end up buying the property and issuing $6 million worth of **general obligation** bonds in order to finance the project. The bonds will pay investors tax-exempt interest at the federal level. Illinois residents will also escape income tax on the bond interest, which is why I might just buy a few bonds, myself. The bonds will be offered by a group of broker-dealers who form a temporary **syndicate** just long enough to get the bonds sold to investors, give the park district its $6 million and keep a percentage as their profit or **spread.** And then most investors will probably hold the bonds until maturity, collecting tax-exempt interest checks every six months along the way. Meanwhile, some investors may want to turn those bonds into cash before maturity; if so, their broker-dealer will either find a buyer on the secondary market and charge a **commission** to complete the sale, or the firm will buy the bonds themselves and make a **markdown** when acting in a **principal** capacity.

For me, all it takes to see the connection between this municipal securities chapter and the so-called "real world" is to walk 15 steps to the front window and look at this ⎯⎯⎯➤

So, if anybody tells you that municipal securities or the Series 7 in general have nothing to do with the so-called "real world," they obviously didn't do their homework.

THE EXCITING DETAILS OF MUNICIPAL SECURITIES

There are two main types of municipal bonds: **general obligation** and **revenue**.

GENERAL OBLIGATION BONDS

The phrase **general obligation** means that the municipality is legally obligated to pay the **debt service** (interest and principal) on the bonds issued. GOs are backed by the **full faith and credit** of the municipality. Where does a municipality get the money they'll need to pay off the bonds? Well, if necessary, they'll dip into all the sources of general revenue generally available to a city or state, like sales taxes, income taxes, parking fees, property taxes, fishing licenses, marriage licenses, whatever. And, if they have to, they'll even raise taxes in order to pay the debt service on a general obligation bond.

Whoa! Raise taxes?

You bet they will. That's why "GOs" require **voter approval**. States get most of their revenue from sales and income taxes, while local governments rely on property taxes. Since local governments (cities, park districts, school districts) get a major chunk of their revenue from property taxes, a "GO" bond will be associated with property taxes. The test wants you to know a fancy phrase for property taxes, which is **ad valorem**. Just need to memorize it. It means property taxes. A municipality might assess property at 50% of its market value. So, a home with a market value of $500,000 would have an **assessed value** of only half that, or $250,000. As a homeowner, you take the assessed value of your home and multiply it by a rate known as the **millage rate** to find your tax bill. If the millage rate is "7 mills," that just means you multiply the assessed value of $250,000 by .007 to get a tax bill of $1,750. And then pretend that you can actually have a house worth half a million and a tax bill of only $1,750. See—*that's* where people get the idea that the test has no connection to the real world. But, that just exposes lazy thinking. Yes, the *amount* of that little pretend tax bill might be lower than what you pay, but everything we just explained is still accurate, even in the "real world." If you don't believe it, take a look at your recent property tax bill. It might use slightly different terms, but it still matches up with the test-world version pretty well.

Anyway, if you see the term **millage**, you're looking at a GO bond. If the test makes you figure somebody's tax bill, remember that "mill" means "thousand." Seven "mills" means there is a 7 in the thousandth place (.007). Multiply the assessed value by that many thousandths and move on.

Some municipalities limit the number of mills that can be levied against property. If so, they might end up issuing **limited tax bonds**, which means property tax rates can only go so high to pay the debt service on a particular GO. School districts are often limited as to how high property taxes can go to support their bonds, while other governmental units have no such limits. So if you see limited tax bonds, associate the terms with GOs.

Whenever the issuer's full faith and credit backs the bonds, we refer to the bonds as "general obligations." There is also a type of municipal bond that is backed by that full faith and credit but also by the revenues generated at the facility being built with the bond proceeds. These bonds are called **double-barreled.** For example, a hospital is something that all residents of a municipality can benefit from, which is why the issuer might put its full faith and credit behind the bond issue. However, hospitals also generate revenues, which can be used to pay debt service. In this case, the issuer has two sources of revenue to pay debt service, which is why we call it a double-barreled bond. Anything backed by the issuer's full faith and credit as well as revenues is called a double-barreled bond. Since the full faith and credit of the issuer backs the issue, we consider this to be a GO.

REVENUE BONDS

Revenue bonds are the same thing only different. Rather than putting the full faith and credit of the issuer behind it, a revenue bond identifies a specific source of revenue, and only that revenue can be used to pay the interest and principal on the bond. **User fee** is the first phrase you should associate with "revenue bond." Have you ever driven on a toll way? What did you drop in the basket? A user fee, right? Well, that money you put in the toll basket helped to pay the debt service on the revenue bond issued to build the toll way. If money problems arise, they won't raise property taxes. They'll raise the tolls, the user fees. You don't like the higher tolls? Use the freeway. But, homeowners aren't affected one way or another since their property taxes cannot be used to pay off revenue bonds—only your generous quarters or E-Z Pass account can be used for that.

Since we don't have property tax on the table, the municipal government doesn't need any type of voter approval. So you never want to associate "voter approval" with a revenue bond. That belongs under the "GO" heading.

There are other ways that a municipality could identify specific sources of revenue for a bond issue. For example, if the residents of a county wanted their roads paved, the county could add a special tax on gasoline throughout the county and let motorists pay for the new roads each time they fill up their tanks. This **special tax** will be used to pay the debt service on the revenue bonds, which are issued to raise the money required to pave the roads. That's an example of a **special tax bond**, a type of revenue bond. Any tax that is not a property or sales tax is considered a special tax, including taxes on business licenses, excise taxes, and taxes on gasoline, tobacco, hotel/motel, and alcohol. The exam might even refer to these as "sin taxes" if it's feeling especially judgmental on testing day.

There are also **special assessment bonds**. Say that a wealthy subdivision experiences problems with their sidewalks. The concrete is chipped, threatening the property values of the homes in the exclusive subdivision. The residents want the municipality to fix the sidewalks. The municipality says, okay, as long as you pay a special assessment on your property, since you're the only ones who'll benefit from this improvement. That special assessment will be the revenue used to pay the debt service on a special assessment bond, which is issued to raise the money to fix the sidewalks.

Isn't it a neat process? They identify a future source of revenue, like tolls, park entrance fees, or special taxes on gasoline. Then, since they need all that money right now, they issue some debt securities against this new source of revenue they're creating. They take the proceeds from selling the debt securities and get the project built. Then those revenues they identified come in, and they use them to pay the interest and, eventually, the principal due to investors who bought the bonds.

Cities like Chicago and New York have public housing projects, which are under HUD, a unit of the federal government. Municipalities issue **PHA (Public Housing Authority)** or **NHA (New Housing Authority) bonds** to raise money for housing projects. The debt service is backed by the rental payments, which are in turn backed by contributions from Uncle Sam. PHAs and NHAs are considered the safest revenue bond because of this guaranteed contribution from the federal government. Sometimes they are referred to as "Section 8" bonds because everything needs at least three names in this business. Note that they are not double-barreled bonds, because it's not the issuer's full faith and credit backing the things.

Industrial Development Revenue Bonds are used to build or acquire facilities that a municipal government will then lease to a corporation. These **IDRs** carry the same credit rating as the corporation occupying the facility. The issuing municipality does not back the debt service in any way. Again, the debt service will be paid only from lease payments made by a corporation, so it's the corporation that backs the debt service. As you know, corporations have been known to go belly-up occasionally. If they're the ones backing up the debt service, you can imagine what happens when they themselves no longer have any assets behind them.

Ouch. And if it happens, the issuer won't be there to bail out the bondholders.

A special type of revenue bond is known as a **moral obligation** bond. While revenue bonds are only serviced by specific sources of revenue, a moral obligation bond provides for the possibility of the issuer going to the legislature and convincing them to honor the "moral obligation" to pay off the debt service. This is a moral obligation, not a legal one, and it would take legislative action to get the money authorized. But it is comforting to know that the safety of your bond investment is guaranteed by the morality of your local and state politicians, isn't it?

SHORT-TERM MUNICIPAL SECURITIES

Anticipation Notes

Remember how corporations borrow money short-term at low interest rates by issuing commercial paper?

Sure you do, we just talked about it in the previous chapter. Anyway, municipalities can borrow money more cheaply by borrowing short-term (just like you get a lower interest rate on a 5-year than a 30-year mortgage). Municipalities issue **anticipation notes**, meaning the notes will be paid off by some money they anticipate receiving very soon. If property taxes won't be collected for another three months, why wait? Why not borrow the money now from a pension fund or a tax-exempt money market mutual fund? We call that a **TAN** for **tax anticipation note**. Maybe the revenues from the toll way system will be collected in a few weeks, but, again, why wait? Why not borrow the money from an institution by selling them a **RAN** or **revenue anticipation note**? Maybe we want to back up the note with both taxes *and* revenues—if so, let's get real creative and call it a **TRAN** for **tax & revenue anticipation note**.

But my personal favorite has to be the **BAN** or **bond anticipation note**. The city has a big bond issue coming out that will supply hordes of cash, but, again, why wait? Why not borrow the money now by issuing a bond anticipation note. In other words, the issuer goes to the money market mutual fund and says, "Hey, we'd like to borrow some money and pay you back as soon as we borrow some more money."

Whatever. As long as you pay us back and it's tax-free, why not?

Since the Series 7 knows no limits, you might also need to know what a **GAN** or **grant anticipation note** is. In this case, the municipality has applied for a grant of money from the US Government, which will be used to pay off the note. Also **CLNs**, or **construction loan notes**, are typically issued to finance construction of a housing facility. The CLN helps the issuer get the project going and is then paid back from the proceeds of the permanent financing raised through a bond issue.

How do you know if these notes are good credit risks? Moody's and S&P both rate them. If the note receives an "MIG" rating, that means it is high enough to be a "Moody's Investment Grade" obligation. S&P uses "SP1, SP2, and SP3" to indicate how solid the note is.

So, when they need to borrow money for a new school, municipalities borrow long term by issuing bonds. When they just need a few million for a few weeks or months, they'll issue notes and pay lower interest rates. No different from how the federal government borrows long-term through T-bonds and short-term through T-bills. Different needs, different rates of interest paid.

Auction Rate Securities

With all the other financial calamities going on at the time, most investors completely slept through the recent disaster of **auction rate securities**. An auction rate security is a debt security with a variable rate of interest or a preferred stock with a variable dividend rate that is re-set at regular auctions. In theory, they're great. The problem was the way they were marketed to investors, who were told that these things were good alternatives to "cash investments," due to their excellent liquidity. Well, as with many new ideas on Wall Street, this one didn't quite pan out as described. I mean, it worked great up on the whiteboard, but when investors were eventually unable to turn their auction rate securities into cash, the you-know-what hit the fan. Suddenly companies, churches, school districts, etc., were unable to pay their bills because these so-called "liquid" securities had absolutely no buyers. To make matters worse, some of the broker-dealers running the auctions started to secretly pose as "buyers" with their own money to make it appear that the auction process was working just fine and dandy, when, in fact, the process was starting to fail. See, although auction rate securities are usually sold as an alternative to short-term money market securities, they are actually long-term securities that are nowhere near as liquid as they were originally described. The way it's *supposed to work* is basically that interested buyers put in bids in an auction process expressing the yields they want to receive. After all the bids have been submitted, a **clearing rate** is established as the rate that all buyers receive—similar to the rate set for T-bills sold through a similar auction process every Monday by the Federal Reserve Board. The clearing rate is the lowest interest rate that buyers will accept to purchase all the available auction rate securities that sellers want to unload. So, the interest rate is re-set regularly based on these auctions, and the owners of the auction rate securities are *supposed to be* able to turn their investment into cash through this auction process. What happens if there aren't enough buyers to take the securities off the sellers' hands? Gee, apparently, nobody never thought a' that, although, now that bazillions of dollars worth of auctions have failed, the regulators have decided to clamp down on the process. Going forward, a registered representative pitching auction rate securities must disclose to a client that, if the auction fails, the client may not have immediate access to her funds. The registered representative has to consider the customer's need for liquidity when recommending this type of product, as well as the fact that the interest rate is re-set at specified intervals. In other words, if the investor can live with fluctuating rates of return and the potential inability to turn her investment into cash, auction rate securities may be suitable.

When we get to the chapter on Investment Companies and talk about closed-end funds, we'll bring up the fact that they issue auction-rate preferred shares to attempt to boost the returns on their portfolios. For now, just know that the issuers of auction rate securities include municipalities, corporations, closed-end funds, and even student loan organizations.

Variable Rate Demand Obligations

Another long-term security that is sold as a short-term investment is the **variable rate demand obligation** or **VRDO**. The variable rate demand obligation also pays a rate of interest that is regularly re-set, though not through an auction process. The big difference between VRDOs and the auction rate securities we just discussed is that the variable rate demand obligation can generally be sold back to or "put" to the issuer or a designated third party for the par value plus any accrued interest. The auction rate securities, as you recall, have to be sold at auction, in which sellers receive whatever the "clearing rate" happens to be, if they can actually sell the things at all.

PRACTICE

1. **Which of the following projects is most likely financed by a GO bond?**
   A. prison
   B. sports stadium
   C. toll-way
   D. airport

2. **Which of the following projects funded by municipal bonds is least likely to require voter approval?**
   A. building a public middle school
   B. constructing a turnpike
   C. building a prison
   D. building a public high school

3. **Which of the following is a double-barreled bond?**
   A. Section 8 bond
   B. NHA
   C. PHA
   D. Hospital bond backed by revenues and full faith and credit of the issuer

4. **All of the following projects would probably be funded with bonds awarded by a competitive sealed bid except**
   A. public school
   B. prison
   C. highway
   D. turnpike

5. **All of the following projects would probably be funded with bonds issued through a negotiated underwriting except**
   A. public school
   B. sports stadium
   C. golf course
   D. turnpike

ANSWERS

1. **A**, the other projects could easily generate revenue to pay off the debt service.

2. **B,** the turnpike is most likely financed by a revenue bond, which does not require voter approval.

3. **D,** the issuer's full faith and credit is not backing NHA/PHA/Section 8 bonds—the US Treasury backs those.

4. **D,** the turnpike/toll road is most likely awarded through a negotiated underwriting.

5. **A,** the public school, financed by a GO bond, would be awarded through a competitive, sealed bid.

ISSUING MUNICIPAL SECURITIES

In order to issue municipal bonds, the issuer puts together a **bond resolution** in which they legally authorize the process of issuing bonds for a specific purpose. This document, or set of documents, describes the nature of the bond issue and the issuer's duties to the bondholders, as well as the issuer's rights to do X, Y, and Z. Issuing municipal bonds involves a very detailed legal process, so the issuer hires a **bond counsel** (attorney) to guide them through the legalities.

Bond Counsel

A bond counsel is a law firm specializing in public finance and the complexities of guiding a bond issue through the city council, the voters, the state legislature, etc. The bond counsel provides a **legal opinion** in which they attest to the issuer's legal authority to issue the bonds and a statement as to whether the interest will be tax-exempt, taxable, or subject to AMT.

There are two types of opinions that the bond counsel could render: qualified and unqualified. While we always want our attorneys to be qualified, we don't necessarily want their opinions to be qualified. A **qualified opinion** means that something is in doubt; the attorneys have attached "qualifiers" to their opinion. What the issuer hopes for is an <u>un</u>**qualified opinion** from the bond counsel. That means everything looks fine to the bond counsel or that he/they can render their opinion without attaching any lengthy explanations to qualify it. Or, think of it this way: if you came into the office tomorrow for some tutoring, I might say, "You look great today!" That would be my UN-qualified opinion. A qualified opinion would sound like this: You look great today, much better than you usually look.

Oops. Adding the qualifier shook your confidence in the opinion, right?

Finding the Underwriters

Municipalities are forever borrowing money. They raise money by selling bonds, and those bonds are taken to the capital markets by underwriters, who keep part of the proceeds for their trouble. We call the part of the proceeds kept by the underwriters "the spread." Underwriters are the municipal securities firms who raise money for municipalities by lining up interested investors. The big underwriting firms of Wall Street typically have municipal underwriting departments. Also, there are several small firms that specialize in this particular industry, e.g., Loop Capital Markets here in Chicago. How do municipalities find underwriters interested in taking their bonds to the capital markets in order to fund their projects? By advertising in the daily **Bond Buyer**. Let's use our initial example of the park district that wants to raise $6 million here in Forest Park to buy and re-purpose the unused industrial building across the street. The park district will attract underwriters by publishing an **official notice of sale** in the Bond Buyer. In this official notice of sale the issuer announces to prospective underwriters that they would like to raise $6 million. They tell the underwriters what type of bond they want to issue—GO or revenue—what they need the money for, how much principal they want to pay back each year of the serial maturity, when the bids will be accepted, where to send the bid, how much of a **good faith deposit** is required, etc. Underwriters interested in winning this business will join a group of underwriters called a "syndicate" and submit a bid on the **bid form** included with the official notice of sale. First thing the syndicate does is figure out the coupon rates that the issuer will have to pay on the bonds, with each maturity year paying a slightly higher yield. Then, they figure out how much they'll have to pay the issuer for the bonds.

Municipalities want the lowest debt service they can possibly get, which is why they always award their business to the group of underwriters who can sell bonds to the public at the lowest cost to the municipality. We call that cost the **net interest cost**, or NIC. That's all the municipality cares about—the lowest net interest cost, which is their cost of borrowing money from the public. Net interest cost is basically the total cost of all the interest payments the issuer will make until the bonds are retired. If bonds are purchased from the issuer at a discount, that amount is *added* to the net interest cost, and if bonds are purchased at a premium, that amount is *subtracted*. In other words, if the issuer pays back more than they received, that has to be added to their cost of borrowing, and when they receive more now than they pay out at maturity, that's subtracted. TIC stands for **true interest cost**. TIC factors in the time value of money. Whether the issuer is using NIC or TIC, they're looking at the cost of borrowing the money, which is all they care about.

If it's a GO, the municipality will take **competitive, sealed bids** from potential underwriters. If it's a revenue bond, they'll just select a group of underwriters and hammer out the terms in a **negotiated underwriting**. What the issuer is looking for in either case is the lowest cost of borrowing available, whether measured as NIC or TIC. So, if it's a competitive underwriting, maybe the Park Board President will open the sealed bids at Park District Headquarters at noon on such-and-such a date, awarding the underwriting to the syndicate who turned in the lowest NIC or TIC. Why open sealed bids in public? Because, believe it or not, some politicians might otherwise try to rig the bidding process to help their cronies and make a little dirty money on the side. How? If the bids aren't sealed, maybe the mayor accidentally looks at all the bids submitted so far and then calls a particular underwriting firm to tell them how low they need to bid if they want to win the business, meeting somebody later that night under a bridge to collect a small, brown bag of cash. Of course, I'm from Chicago, but still.

The bidding syndicates have already made a good faith deposit, which is usually 1–2% of the par value of all the bonds. Kind of like earnest money—if an interested "buyer" can't come up with this amount, he isn't much of a buyer now is he? The ones who lost the bid get their deposit back, while the winning syndicate has simply made their deposit on the bonds that need to be purchased from the issuer and unloaded to investors in the near future. Most municipal underwritings are done on a **firm commitment** basis, which means the winning syndicate is going to buy all the bonds from the issuer, whether they end up selling them to investors or not. The exam may say that the underwriters act in a "principal capacity," and you'll note that the word "principal" can mean many different things on the Series 7. It means to have capital/money at risk in a transaction. The "principal" is also a supervisor of a broker-dealer. And, the "principal" amount of a debt security is what the buyer receives at maturity.

The Syndicate

The syndicate makes the "spread," which is just the difference between what they pay the municipality for the bonds and the price (re-offering yields) at which they sell the bonds to the public. Say the issuer gets $990 per bond, and the syndicate sells the bonds to the public for $1,000 each. That's a spread of $10 per bond. How does that $10 get split?

Into three pieces. One of the underwriters will act as the manager. They'll take some money right offa' the top, known as the **manager's fee**. Then, all syndicate members will get the next piece of the spread, known as the **additional takedown**, split according to each member's share of the bonds. Finally, whoever sells a bond gets the last and biggest piece, the **concession**. A syndicate member who sells a bond from their allotment would get the additional takedown plus the concession. Those two pieces are known together as the **total takedown**. If you want the total takedown, you have to sell the bond; if somebody else sells one of your bonds, you give up or "concede" the concession, keeping only the "additional takedown," which is the piece that syndicate members get, one way or the other.

See, in order to make sure the bonds get sold, the syndicate might let other broker-dealers help sell them. If another broker-dealer sells a bond for the syndicate, the syndicate gives the B/D the concession. They "concede" that portion of the spread, in other words. These broker-dealers outside the syndicate make up a group of sellers, so the industry creatively dubbed them the "selling group."

Okay. A bond point is worth $10. How much is a half-point worth?

$5.

Quarter-point?

$2.50

Eighth of a point?

$1.25.

And so on.

So let's say the spread is $10. That means that each bond is sold for $10 more than the issuer receives—how does that $10 get split up?

Let's say the manager gets 1/8 point or $1.25. That's the Manager's Fee.

The syndicate members get 3/8 of a point or $3.75. That's the additional takedown.

Whoever sells the bond gets the 1/2 point concession, or $5.00.

So, if the managing underwriter sells a bond, they keep the whole **underwriting spread** of $10.00. If a syndicate member sells one of their bonds, they keep the "total takedown" or $8.75. In other words, the manager gets their $1.25, and the rest of the $10 goes to the syndicate member who sold their bond. The syndicate typically lines up broker-dealers interested in helping to sell the bonds to their clients, with no capital commitment whatsoever. These firms make up the **selling group.** If a selling group member sells bonds, the dealer whose bonds they sold keeps the additional takedown and gives up the **selling concession** to the selling group member who made the sale. In that case the member of the "selling group" keeps $5.00, the syndicate member who let them sell their bond gets $3.75, and the manager—as always—gets the manager's fee of $1.25.

As Al Capone would attest, it's good to be the syndicate manager.

ISSUER RECEIVES	SPREAD		MANAGER'S FEE	$1.25 1/8
	$10		ADDITIONAL TAKEDOWN	$3.75 3/8
$990			CONCESSION	$5.00 ½

Investor Pays $1000

Since the syndicate is at risk for these bonds, the big question is, "What happens if we don't sell all of them?" Answers to these and other questions are agreed to among the underwriters in a document called, ironically, the **agreement among underwriters**. To make sure it has at least two names, the exam might also call this the **syndicate letter**, where the terms of the underwriting are laid out for all syndicate members to see. Whatever we call it, this agreement spells out each firm's responsibilities, the order period, and the priority of orders coming in for the bonds. As you might expect, the document governs the operations of the syndicate only, and the issuer of the bonds could not care less about it.

There are two types of syndicate accounts: western and eastern. Under a **western/divided account**, a syndicate member only has to worry about selling their share of the bonds. If they sell their allotment, they walk.

Western walks.

Under an **eastern/undivided account**, all syndicate members are responsible for selling their bonds, as well as their share of any unsold bonds. If a syndicate member gets 10% of the bonds and sells its entire allotment, that's great. But if the other clowns don't do so good, leaving the syndicate with 1,000 unsold bonds, the member is going to be responsible for 10% of those, too. So even though the member sold its allotment, they're going to have to sell 100 more bonds, worth about $100,000. If they can't sell them, they eat them.

Eastern eats.

Remember:

Western walks.   Eastern eats.

Sometimes the darned munis sell like hotcakes, though, and we don't worry about unsold bonds. Now we have the opposite problem as a syndicate, which is that there are more buyers than bonds. What happens if the issue is "oversold" or "oversubscribed"? Well, we could do several paragraphs on this process, or we could just remember the following mnemonic:

Please
Sell
Da'
Munis

Which is designed to help you remember the order for allocating oversold municipal securities:

Pre-Sale
Syndicate (or "Group Net Order")
Designated
Member

The syndicate may publish a tombstone advertisement, which lays out just the basic facts, and is not considered an offer to sell the securities, just an announcement, including amount of the bond issue and purpose of the proceeds, interest payment dates, maturity years and yields to maturity, and the bond counsel. The date on which interest begins to accrue is known as the **dated date** and would be included in the tombstone. The "dated date" means that buyers of the bonds may have to pay accrued interest calculated from the dated date up to—not including—settlement. Bonds are not considered to be issued until they are delivered to the buyers, so if there is lag time between the dated date on the issue and the delivery of the bonds to purchasers, purchasers will end up paying accrued interest, since their first interest payment will be larger than it should be. I would not recommend spending a lot of time trying to wrap your head around the "dated date." It's only used in a new issue. It's used to calculate accrued interest. Can't imagine how much further this exam would take the concept.

Settlement

The most detailed information about an issuer's financial condition is found in the **official statement**. This is what is delivered with final confirmation of the purchase to the investor. If the official statement isn't quite ready, the issuer can prepare a **preliminary official statement**. Either way, municipal underwriters have to make sure that if an official statement is prepared it is delivered to all buyers of the bonds. As the MSRB explains, "official statements typically include information regarding the purposes of the issue, how the securities will be repaid, and the financial and economic characteristics of the issuer with respect to the offered securities. Investors may use this information to evaluate the credit quality of the securities. Although functionally equivalent to the prospectus used in connection with registered securities, an official statement for municipal securities is exempt from the prospectus requirements of the Securities Act of 1933."

There you have it.

So, the syndicate will hopefully have all the buyers they need to unload the bonds they're responsible for. After the orders are taken and filled, buyers often receive **when-issued confirmations** because the bonds have not actually been issued yet. The confirmations prove that the buyers will receive a certain number of bonds, *when* they are *issued*. At this point, interest may be accruing from the dated date up to the settlement date, which has not occurred yet. So, the exam might have a question in which you tell it that "total dollar amount of the transaction can not be calculated" for a when-issued confirmation. Why not? If we don't know the settlement date, we can't calculate the accrued interest owed by the buyer. But, of course, the bonds are eventually ready to be delivered. On the delivery date, the purchasers make full payment for the bonds, plus any accrued interest, and the syndicate delivers the bonds, a final confirmation, and the official statement.

REVIEW

So, what just happened? Essentially this: the issuer (Forest Park Park District) needed to raise $6 million by issuing general obligation bonds. They found potential underwriters by publishing an official notice of sale in the Bond Buyer. Interested syndicates submitted competitive bids, and the lowest bid won. The winning syndicate sold the bonds to investors, keeping a spread when they sold the bonds at a higher price to the investors than what they paid the issuer for the bonds. When the bonds were ready for delivery, the sales were finalized, the issuer received their money, the underwriters kept their pieces of the spread, and the investors received their confirmations plus the official statement. Now that the bonds are out there, investors can either sit back and cash the tax-exempt interest checks every six months, or they can sell their bonds to other investors on the secondary market.

And, as we saw in the previous chapter, the issuer might decide to buy the bonds back before maturity in order to refinance at a lower interest rate going forward. So, let's look at that process.

REFUNDING/ADVANCE REFUNDING

When do homeowners refinance their mortgage loans? When interest rates are falling, right? Homeowners paying 8% might get tired of servicing their debt at that rate when prevailing interest rates are falling well below 8%, right? Well, municipalities feel the same way. If a municipality is paying 8% on a bond issue when interest rates are falling to 6%, they might want to pay off the outstanding debt and issue new, cheaper debt. If the bond issue has passed its legal call protection period, the municipality could issue new bonds at 6% and use the proceeds to call/pay off the bonds issued at 8%. That's known as **refunding**. Just means replacing expensive debt with cheaper debt.

If the bond issue had not reached the first call date, the municipality could still issue cheaper debt at 6% and put the proceeds in escrow. The proceeds earn interest on Treasury securities, and as soon as the first call date is reached, the municipality uses the proceeds to call/buy back the outstanding bonds. Here, they've refunded the outstanding debt in advance of the first call date, which is why we call this **advance refunding** or **pre-refunding**. The bonds that are outstanding and will be called at the first or next legal call date are called "pre-refunded bonds." If the issuer creates an escrow account that is large enough to pay off all the interest and principal through the last maturity date, the industry cleverly calls those outstanding bonds **escrowed to maturity.**

The exam might expect you to know that once a bond has been advance refunded or escrowed to maturity, its credit rating becomes triple-A, since the money needed to pay off the debt is already parked in an escrow account. Or, to mess with you, they might say that "its liquidity increases," which is another way of saying the same thing. Finally, know that municipalities often invest the proceeds of an advance refunding issue of bonds in **SLGS**, which stands for "State and Local Government Series" securities. These are special securities created by the US Treasury to help municipalities do an advance refunding and comply with IRS rules and restrictions on such transactions.

PRACTICE

1. **All of the following deal with the primary market except**

   A. Markups

   B. Notice of Sale

   C. Syndicate

   D. Bond Counsel

2. **None of the following statements is true concerning municipal securities except**

    A.   they have no exemption under the Act of 1933

    B.   they usually yield less nominally than corporate bonds

    C.   they must be sold with a prospectus

    D.   they must be issued with a trust indenture

3. **Which of the following has liability for unsold bonds?**

    A.   underwriter in a best efforts underwriting

    B.   syndicate manager in a best efforts underwriting

    C.   member of the selling group in a firm commitment

    D.   member of the syndicate in a firm commitment

4. **Which of the following is usually the largest piece of the underwriting spread?**

    A.   manager's fee

    B.   additional takedown

    C.   concession

    D.   total takedown

5. **When an issue of municipal securities is oversold, orders generally are given the following (from highest to lowest) priority**

    I.   designated

    II.   syndicate or group net

    III.   pre-sale

    IV.   member

    A.   I, II, III, IV

    B.   IV, III, II, I

    C.   III, II, I, IV

    D.   III, II, IV, I

ANSWERS

1. **A**, markups and markdowns are made on the secondary market when the dealer sells to or buys from the customer.

2. **B,** they yield less nominally because the interest income is tax-exempt.

3. **D,** selling group members never have liability. Syndicate members have liability in a firm commitment underwriting.

4. **D,** a trick question, since the total takedown includes two pieces of the spread.

5. **C,** Please (pre-sale) Sell (syndicate) Da' (designated) Muni's (member).

BOND BUYER

If they still offer it, get a free two-week subscription to the Bond Buyer. Seriously. The Bond Buyer is the information source for the primary market, meaning the new-issue market where municipalities raise money through their underwriting syndicate. If your firm is a municipal securities underwriter, you're receiving this newspaper and reading it every day. The exam might want you to say that the Bond Buyer provides information on the primary market, even though there is actually some secondary (trading) market info in there as well. Underwriters could see the total par value of municipal securities that are about to be offered in the near future. This is called the **visible supply**. If we're about to do a primary offering of municipal securities, we might want to know how many other bonds are trying to be absorbed by the market, right? We also might want to see how well the market absorbed the bonds offered last week, called the **placement ratio**. The placement ratio tells us the dollar amount sold out of the dollar amount offered the previous week. If the market tried to absorb $100 million par value of municipal securities last week but only ended up absorbing $90 million, that's a placement ratio of 90%, meaning some of the underwriters are sitting on some bonds they would have rather sold. Since everything needs at least two names in this industry, remember that the "placement ratio" can also be referred to as the "acceptance ratio" by a test question writer with nothing better to do.

The Bond Buyer is where underwriters find official notices of sale announcing the issuer's need to raise X amount of money by a certain date in order to build a school, road, hospital, etc. Actually, what we see in the Bond Buyer is a summary official notice of sale, which gives us info on how to get the full official notice of sale, complete with a bid form that we can use to try to come up with the lowest NIC/TIC required to win the underwriting business through a competitive bid. Or, maybe we prefer to contact the issuer willing to do a negotiated underwriting in order to, you know, negotiate.

There are also various indices published in the Bond Buyer, which I'll simply list as bullet points:

- REVDEX 25: yield-based index tracking the revenue bond market. A weekly index of 25 revenue bonds with 30 years to maturity rated A or higher. Remember, rising yields equals falling prices.
- 40 Bond Index: a daily price-based index comprised of 40 GO and revenue bonds. This one's based on price, remember, which is inversely related to yield, as we may have mentioned about 1,000 times at this point.
- 20 Bond Index: weekly index comprised of 20 GO bonds with 20 years to maturity rated A or higher.
- 11 Bond Index: weekly index comprised of 11 of the 20 bonds from the 20-bond index, rated AA or higher. These yields will be lower than yields on the 20 Bond Index because the average quality of these 11 bonds is higher.

SECONDARY MARKET

Municipal bonds do trade in the secondary market, but not as actively as corporate stocks and bonds or Treasury bonds. If a school district raises $2,000,000 by issuing bonds, how many bonds are there to trade?

2,000 if the denominations are $1,000, and just 400 if the denominations are $5,000. In other words, there's very little liquidity in some of these issues. That's why a municipal bond dealer will usually only provide *either* a bid or an offer price. If you want to buy a municipal bond, the dealer will quote you an offer price; if you want to unload a municipal bond, the dealer will give you a bid. If you like the dealer's price, you have a deal. If not, storm out of the showroom and wait for the inevitable phone call explaining the amazing discount that was just approved four seconds ago by the sales manager.

Sometimes a broker-dealer will have a customer come in trying to liquidate some municipal bond no one at the office has ever heard of. The broker-dealer will submit a "bids wanted" to see what various municipal bond dealers will pay for the customer's funky municipal bond. If the customer wanted to buy a funky municipal bond no one's ever heard of, the firm could send out an "offers wanted" to see how much the various dealers would charge for the bonds.

Since most municipal securities are issued under a serial maturity with different yields for different maturity years, quotes are usually given in terms of yield to maturity. If the municipal bond dealer says "it's offered at 5.60," that means he'll sell the bond at a price that makes the yield to maturity 5.6%. That was a firm quote, by the way, meaning the dealer will do the deal at that price. Had he said, "looks like the offer is around 5.60," that would have been a nominal quote. He's just sharing information there, but if he gives a firm quote, he has to honor it. Municipal securities dealers who publish quotes can only publish firm quotes. The nominal quotes are between the dealer and an interested party. Sometimes we'll call these "workable indications." The nice little old lady sitting in the broker-dealer's office wants to liquidate 1,000 bonds issued 20 years ago by a small school district in rural South Dakota. The broker-dealer calls a municipal bond dealer asking for a workable indication or a "likely bid" the dealer would pay for the bonds.

The language used by the municipal securities dealer would be vague, with phrases such as the following attached to his nominal quote:

- It looks like
- Subject
- Last I saw
- It's around

When we get down to doing the deal, the dealer will then give a firm quote, but right now they're just feeling the situation out.

Since most municipal securities usually don't trade actively, time isn't as critical as it is when trading stocks. Therefore, dealers sometimes give "out firm" quotes. Maybe the dealer will give you a firm quote that's good for the next hour. However, if somebody else calls, he'll call you back and give you five minutes to make up your mind.

The test will probably bring up the term **broker's broker**. A broker's broker executes securities transactions exclusively with other broker-dealers and not with public investors. Broker's brokers generally do not take inventory positions in securities . . . since that would make them principals/ dealers and not brokers. The broker's broker keeps the identity of the client confidential, allowing municipal dealers to get maximum exposure to the marketplace without telegraphing that they need to sell a bunch of bonds in a hurry. In the real world a big broker's broker is Cantor Fitzgerald. They provide a wire service through which dealers who want to put a block of bonds out for bids can see what buyers will pay, without divulging the identity of the seller. Buyers who subscribe to the service can put in their bids, and at the end of the day the broker's broker will notify the sellers of the high bid. If the seller accepts, the broker's broker informs the high bidder that the bid was accepted, congratulations. The broker's broker charges the seller a fee, pretty much as they do on eBay.

Municipal securities transactions are reported by dealers through an electronic reporting system known as **"RTRS"** for **"Real-Time Transaction Reporting System."** As the **MSRB (Municipal Securities Rulemaking Board)** states, RTRS is a trade reporting facility "operated by the MSRB. RTRS receives municipal securities transaction reports submitted by dealers pursuant to Rule G-14, disseminates price and volume information in real time for transparency purposes, and otherwise processes information pursuant to Rule G-14." Since we'll be mentioning MSRB Rule G-14 in a later segment, we won't ruin the suspense by adding further details here.

PRACTICE

1. **Which of the following is associated with the secondary market?**

   A.   notice of sale

   B.   broker's broker

   C.   bond counsel

   D.   Bond Buyer

2. **All of the following deal with the primary market except**

   A.   Quotes

   B.   Notice of Sale

   C.   Legal Opinion

   D.   Bond Counsel

ANSWERS

1.   **B**, broker's brokers help municipal dealers buy and sell on the secondary market.

2.   **A,** on the primary market, bonds are sold at the public offering price—bonds are only quoted when trading among investors in the secondary market.

CREDIT RISK ANALYSIS

United States Treasury bills, notes, bonds, etc., do not carry default risk. On the other hand, while municipal bonds are generally safer than corporate bonds, municipal bonds do carry default risk. How would an investor know a strong municipal securities issuer from a weak one? Same way he'd do it for a corporate bond—he would check the Moody's, S&P, and Fitch credit ratings. Perhaps you have seen recently that your county, city, or state has suffered a "credit downgrade" recently from Moody's, S&P, and/or Fitch. Maybe the issuer used to be a double-A borrower, but now has to pay the higher yields offered by single-A or triple-B borrowers. In other words it affects the borrower the same way a lower credit score would affect you when applying for your next mortgage.

GO Analysis

A general obligation bond (GO) is backed by the full faith and credit of a municipality. Where does a municipality get the money needed to back up this sweeping promise to pay debt service? Mostly from taxpayers. So, how do these taxpayers generally feel about taxes and debt? A municipality whose voters typically approve bond issues will receive a higher rating than one populated by conservative voters who typically shoot down all bond referendums. Are residents moving in and bringing their tax dollars with them, or are they moving away and taking their tax dollars with them? Are jobs coming in or fleeing the municipality? What's the economic health? High unemployment? Scary. Is the economic base diverse, or is it too dependent on just one industry or one or two big employers who might decide to go bankrupt or outsource to China? Are the residents affluent? Let's hope so. What are the property values looking like? Trending upward? Excellent. Dropping? Not good. What is the issuer's **collection ratio**? The collection ratio is found by dividing the taxes collected by the taxes assessed, because no matter how many property tax bills get sent out, it only helps the issuer when people actually pay them. A high collection ratio is a positive sign to a GO bond analyst and vice versa.

The issuer has a **debt statement** that analysts review. On the debt statement we find the amount of general obligation debt that the issuer is fully responsible for and the debt it is partly responsible for. The **direct debt** is the GO debt that only the issuer is responsible for paying off. Sometimes a school district lies in more than one village; if so, the villages and the school district are **coterminous**. That means that when the analyst looks at the debt of the villages, they also factor in the debt of the school district. This debt is called **overlapping debt** for obvious reasons. So the issuer's **net overall debt** is the total of GO bonds for which it is solely responsible and the total of overlapping debt for which it is partly responsible. To protect residents from excessive taxes municipalities typically impose a maximum on how much general obligation debt they can have outstanding at one time, so how close is the municipality to this **debt limit**? If it's already close to the limit, an analyst might not like to see another bond issue going out at this point, just as a mortgage lender is not going to be thrilled to see that you came up with your down payment by maxing out all your credit cards. What is the issuer's **debt per capita**, which is the debt divided by the population ? If that's already a high number, this new GO issue is probably going to have a lower credit rating than the issuer would like.

What about the city's, county's or state's budget—are there any big **unfunded pension liabilities** that they are *also* legally obligated to pay? If an analyst is judging the issuer's ability to repay the bondholders and sees that the issuer has also promised to pay out about $2 billion more than they apparently have to teachers, police officers, or fire fighters, that fact is not going to help the credit rating.

In short, the issuer is the borrower. Do they have enough money from tax revenues versus their obligations to assure that bond holders will not get stiffed? If so, they get a good credit rating. If they're in way over their heads, their bonds get a lower rating, which means they have to offer higher yields to investors, just as someone with a low credit score has to pay a higher rate on his mortgage.

Revenue Bond Analysis

Revenue bonds aren't backed by the issuer's taxing ability, so an analyst rating a revenue bond would not look at anything we just looked at for general obligation bonds. Revenue bond analysts need to know if the facility will be able to generate enough revenue to maintain operations and pay back the bondholders their interest and principal (debt service). A good place to start is the **feasibility study** that the issuer paid a consulting firm to put together. The feasibility study includes an **engineering report** that focuses on the design and construction of the facility. The feasibility study also predicts how many people will use the facility and how much they'll pay to use it, versus all the expenses and costs associated with the convention center, sports stadium, airport, etc. The most important factor for assigning a credit rating to a revenue bond is the project's **debt service coverage ratio.** In the indenture, we see whether the project uses a **net revenue pledge** or a **gross revenue pledge.** The most common by far is the "net pledge," in which the issuer states that the first priority of payment will be operations and maintenance of the facility. After operations and maintenance are covered, then debt service is taken care of. Under the rarer "gross pledge," the first priority is the debt service. Since most projects use a "net pledge," let's look at how the numbers might work out here. Let's say that a football stadium will pull in $20 million in revenue each year, with operations and maintenance at $10 million and debt service payments of $5 million. The first priority is operations and maintenance, so we take the $20 million of revenue and subtract the $10 million of operations and maintenance. The *net* revenue is now $10 million. That $10 million covers the $5 million of debt service at a 2:1 ratio. A 2:1 debt service coverage ratio is considered adequate and would boost the revenue bond's credit rating as opposed to a lower coverage ratio. This might sound like rocket science at first, but that's only because the terminology is new. You, like the issuer of a revenue bond, like to borrow money at the lowest possible rate. Whoever issues your credit score looks at your income versus your expenses to calculate how likely you are to pay off your debts. You get your credit score from Experian, TransUnion, and Equifax. The revenue bond issuer would get their credit score from S & P, Moody's, and/or Fitch.

Revenue bonds are issued under what's known as an **indenture.** As we saw in the previous chapter, most corporate bonds have to be issued with an indenture, a contract in which the issuer makes promises to protect the bondholders, which are enforced by the trustee. Municipal bonds aren't actually covered by the Trust Indenture Act of 1939, but since revenue bonds are only as solid as the revenue generated by the facility being built, usually revenue bonds are sold with an indenture in order to calm the lenders enough to buy the bonds. The indenture includes **protective covenants.** Some of the covenants include raising user fees to meet the debt service (**rate covenant**), keeping the facility properly maintained and insured (**maintenance covenant, insurance covenant**) and making sure the finances are subject to outside audit (**financial reports and audit covenant**). The **nondiscrimination covenant** is a promise that even local politicians and their girlfriends have to pay to park at the sports stadium or to drive through the toll booths along the turnpike. We would also see a **catastrophe call** described in the indenture, which means that if, for example, the convention center is destroyed by a hurricane, the entire bond issue will be called—assuming the place was properly insured, as the insurance covenant specified.

The **flow of funds** statement is also found in the bond's indenture. Most revenue bonds use a series of funds/accounts that provide for the security of the bonds as funds generated by the facility are used to pay operations and maintenance expenses, debt service, and also a reserve fund for a rainy day. The flow of funds statement details the priority for allocating the revenues of the facility among the various accounts/funds. Basically, the revenues generated by the facility fill each account to a certain level and then flow to the next account. A fairly typical "flow of funds" would go in this order:

- Revenue Fund: all receipts (gross revenue) are recorded and deposited here first
- Operations and Maintenance Fund: a prescribed amount of gross revenue is deposited here to pay operations and maintenance expenses
- Debt Service Fund: the required amount to meet interest on existing bonds and return principal on bonds that are about to mature
- Debt Service Reserve Fund: extra money that might come in handy if revenues are a little light but bondholders expect to be paid anyway
- Reserve Maintenance Fund: extra money to cover unexpected maintenance expenses
- Replacement and Renewal Fund: extra money to cover new equipment and repairs to existing equipment, based on the engineering report
- Sinking Fund: extra money that can be used to retire the bonds early through a refunding or advance refunding
- Surplus Fund: extra money to be used in emergencies

A revenue bond indenture would also include the bond counsel's legal opinion and the maturity features of the bonds.

PRACTICE

1. **What would an analyst look at when determining the creditworthiness of a General Obligation bond?**

    A.   debt service coverage ratio

    B.   feasibility studies

    C.   flow of funds statement

    D.   public's attitude toward debt, taxes

2. **Bend, Oregon has included a net revenue pledge in the indenture for a recent revenue bond issue. During the first year total revenues are $20,000,000. Expenses are $15,000,000. Interest expense equals $4,000,000 with $1,000,000 for principal repayment. What is the debt service coverage ratio?**

    A. 20:1
    B. 4:1
    C. 1:1
    D. 5:1

3. **All of the following might lower the credit rating on a GO bond except**

    A. Unemployment rates are rising
    B. Population has decreased
    C. Unemployment rates are falling
    D. Lack of economic diversity

4. **All of the following might raise the credit rating on a GO bond except**

    A. Unemployment rates are falling
    B. Unemployment rates are rising
    C. Population has increased
    D. Economic diversity

5. **One would expect to see a flow of funds statement in the indenture for which of the following?**

    A. General Obligation bonds
    B. TAN
    C. PHA
    D. Revenue bonds

ANSWERS

1. **D**, the other choices are relevant for revenue bonds.

2. **C,** net revenue is $5 million, to cover $5 million at a 1:1 ratio.

3. **C,** falling UN-employment is a good thing.

4. **B,** rising unemployment is a bad thing.

5. **D,** revenue bonds have flow of funds statements.

TAXATION

If the bond is issued for "public purpose" and is providing an essential service, the federal government will not tax the interest on the bond. That's the interest.

Capital Gains

Capital gains are a different story. If you buy a municipal bond from somebody at $900 and sell it later for $980, you have a capital gain to deal with. Figuring your gain or loss involves many steps, unfortunately. In fact, you might feel as if you've mistakenly signed up for the CPA exam, but this is actually much easier than it seems.

No, really.

Premium Bonds

First of all, if a municipal bond is purchased at a premium, that premium has to be **amortized** or "stepped down" over the **holding period**. If you buy a bond for $1,100, you've paid $100 above the par value. If you hold that bond until maturity, you'll lose $100 when the thing pays out only $1,000. Well, the IRS doesn't want you to wait until maturity to take a big loss all in one year. The IRS wants you to take a little bit of that loss every year that you hold the bond. If the bond matures in 10 years, the IRS wants you to take 1/10 of your loss every year, or $10. So, if you buy a bond that matures in ten years for $1,100, you will take a $10 loss each year on your tax returns.

The template that you'll use for the test question looks like this:

> Price
> – Par =
>   Premium
> Divided by Term =
> Amortize/Year
>   X
> Holding Period =
> Adjustment

Say the test question looked like this:

An investor buys a municipal bond at 120. The bond will mature in 10 years. What is the capital gain or loss at maturity?

No problem.

The price paid was $1,200, so we put that on top and see that we have a $200 premium. Like this:

Price	$1,200
- Par =	$1,000
Premium	$200

The bond will mature in 10 years, so we divide the $200 over 10 years, like this:

Price	$1,200
- Par =	$1,000
Premium	$200
Divided by Term	10 years
Amortize/Year	$20/year

How long did the investor hold the bond?

The full term. So, we multiply the $20/year by the full 10 years to get a total adjustment of $200. Like this:

Price	$1,200
- Par =	$1,000
Premium	$200
Divided by Term	10 years
Amortize/Year	$20/year
X	X
Holding Period	10 years
Adjustment	$200

Now, we go to the master template for capital gains/losses, which just takes Proceeds minus Adjusted Cost. The proceeds when the bond matures would be $1,000. The investor originally paid $1,200, but we adjust that cost DOWN by the $200 adjustment to get an adjusted cost of $1,000, too. So, the investor has no gain/loss at maturity:

Proceeds	$1,000
- Adjusted Cost	$1,000 ($1,200 paid less $200 adjustment)
Gain/Loss	ZERO

For a premium bond, remember to subtract the amount of the adjustment from the original price paid by the investor. Amortize = subtract.

Whenever an investor holds the bond for the full term there is no gain or loss at maturity… simply because it was dealt with year by year. Let's say in that question we just examined the investor had held the bond only six years before selling it @110. We would use the same template, but some of the numbers would change:

Price	$1,200
- Par =	$1,000
Premium	$200
Divided by Term	10 years
Amortize/Year	$20/year
X	X
Holding Period	6 years
Adjustment	$120

So now the investor's proceeds are $1,100 (sold @110) and the adjusted cost is the original $1,200 minus the $120 adjustment, or $1,080.

Proceeds	$1,100
- Adj Cost	$1,080 (original $1,200 minus the $120 adjustment)
Gain	$20

In this case the investor has a gain, then, of $20. And he'll pay capital gains taxes on that money to your friends and mine at the IRS.

So, if the investor holds the bond the full term, there will be no gain or loss at maturity. If the investor sells the bond after a few years, he could have a gain or a loss, depending on the numbers you plug into the template.

Discount Bonds

All premium bonds are amortized on the test, so it doesn't matter whether the investor bought it from the issuer at a premium or from some investor for a premium. Discount bonds are a different story. If Max Gaines buys a bond from Joe Kuhl @98, you don't do anything special. If Max holds the bond until maturity, he'll make $20 on it (buy at $980, matures at $1,000). That twenty bucks will be taxed as interest income by the IRS, which likes to keep everything nice and simple.

Only if the bond is originally issued at a discount (**OID**) do we have to do something special. That something is called **accretion**, which is a fancy word for "adding to." Amortization means subtract from; accretion means add to. Accountants would probably call it stepping down (amortize) or stepping up (accrete) the investor's cost basis, but everybody's really saying the same thing. Whatever we call it, the concept is that only original issue discount (OID) bonds are accreted. This is where the concept of zero coupon bonds intersects with the concept of tax-free interest on a municipal bond. Remember how zero coupon bonds work—the investor's interest income received is the difference between the price paid and the amount received at the end. So, that's not a buy and a sell; it's just a funky way of receiving interest all at the end. A municipal bond could be sold as a zero coupon bond at $500 (originally issued at a discount), maturing in 10 years at par, or $1,000. That means the investor would make the $500 difference as interest income. Interest income is tax-free on municipal securities, so we aren't going to tax the poor guy on the difference between $500 (paid) and $1,000 (received). He's not realizing a capital gain—this is just how a zero coupon bond pays interest. So, we let him step up/accrete/add to his cost basis a little bit for every year he holds the bond. The template we use here looks a lot like the one we used for premium bonds, actually:

Price
Vs. Par =
    Discount
Divided by Term =
Accrete/Year
    X
Holding Period =
Adjustment

Notice how only two words were changed: discount, accrete. Instead of paying more for the bond, this investor pays less (a discount). Instead of subtracting from his cost basis (amortize), we'll be adding to it (accrete).

Let's say an investor buys a zero coupon/OID bond @500, and the bond matures at par in 10 years. If so, our numbers would look like this:

Price	$500
Vs. Par =	$1,000
Discount	$500
Divided by term	10 years
Accrete/year	$50/year
X	X
Holding Period	10 years
Adjustment	$500

So, if the investor holds the bond the full 10 years, he'll receive the $1,000 proceeds (par). His original cost base was $500, but he gets to add another $500 (accrete) to his cost base, stepping it up to $1,000. The difference between his proceeds and adjusted cost, then, is zero, which is why he has no gain or loss at maturity. Remember, that $500 is interest income, so this is how we prevent him from being taxed on a tax-free municipal bond. We just step-up or add to his cost basis so everything "zeroes out" in the end.

Now, if he held the bond only 6 years and sold it @88, things would be different. Now he would only adjust his cost by $300, right? $50 per year times a six-year holding period = $300 adjustment. So, his adjusted cost would be $800. His proceeds are $880 (@88), so he would realize a **capital gain** of $80 here. If he had sold it for anything less than $800, he would have realized a **capital loss**. As before, when the investor holds the bond the full term, there is no gain/loss at maturity. If the investor holds the bond a few years and then sells it, you never know what will happen until you run the numbers.

Aren't you glad you signed up for your Series 7?

We've explained the OID as if it's always issued at a deep discount; it might not be on the test. If the test question says the bond is originally issued at 93, then you're working with a discount of $70 divided over the term to maturity. Why would an issuer sell a bond @93? Well, it really doesn't matter, does it? If it's in the test question, you just take it and run with it. But if you're an inquiring mind that has to know, think of it this way. Perhaps this is one of the bonds that mature at the very end of a serial maturity, and this is how we offer a higher yield to the buyers of these longer-term bonds, by issuing them at a discount. In this case, the coupon rate on the bond issue will be the same for all bonds, but the early maturing bonds will be sold at a premium, while the later maturing bonds will be sold at a discount. That way the yields are higher for the later maturing bonds.

Whatever.

Again, all premium bonds are amortized. For **discount bonds**, only OIDs are accreted. Secondary market discounts are NOT accreted—the difference is taxed as ordinary income.

Interest Income

So that's the capital gains part. The interest part is nowhere near as simple as we've led you to believe up to now. So, I guess it's time to tell you the truth—can you handle the truth?

Here goes. The interest on general obligation bonds is going to be tax-exempt at the federal level, but your state could tax the interest if you buy a bond from an out-of-state issuer. If you live in Georgia and buy a bond issued by the State of Alabama, Georgia can tax that interest. Plus if you live in Atlanta, Georgia, and Atlanta has a tax on bond interest, your city could tax you as well.

How could you avoid being taxed by Georgia and the city of Atlanta?

Buy a bond issued by Atlanta, Georgia. The State will give you a break, and so will Atlanta.

Finally, if you live in Atlanta and buy a bond issued by Valdosta, Georgia, the federal government will give you the tax break, and so will the State of Georgia, since both Valdosta and Atlanta are in that state. But, what about Atlanta—did you help them out? Not at all—so they can tax you. How do you get Atlanta off your back? Buy one of *their* municipal securities—hey, now you're catchin' on, boy. You help us finance our schools, we'll help you deal with your little tax problem.

Nice and simple, the way the tax code always works.

SITUATION	FEDERAL	STATE	LOCAL
Resident of Topeka, KS, buys a Toledo, Ohio, municipal bond	EXEMPT	TAXABLE	TAXABLE
Resident of Topeka, KS, buys a Wichita, KS, municipal bond	EXEMPT	EXEMPT	TAXABLE
Resident of Topeka, KS, buys a Topeka, KS, municipal bond	EXEMPT	EXEMPT	EXEMPT

And if you thought that was confusing, check this out—not *all* municipal securities pay tax-free interest. The ones used for public purpose/essential services do, but if the IRS code says that the bond is a "private activity" bond, the interest is subject to **alternative minimum tax (AMT)**. Most municipal bond investors are subject to AMT, which would force them to add some of the interest received on a private activity bond back into their taxable income. For that reason private activity bonds usually offer higher yields (before tax). An example of a private activity bond would be a bond issued to finance a parking garage that will be operated by a private company, or bonds issued to build a sports stadium used by an NFL or NBA team. If the exam says your customer wants a municipal bond but is concerned about AMT, put her into a general obligation bond, such as a school bond. Or look for the concept of "essential, public purpose." And, if the exam really wants to hit hard, it might bring up the fact that some municipal bonds are simply taxable. For example, if a public university has already issued a certain amount of GO debt that is outstanding, additional bond issues could be taxable, requiring the issuer to offer much higher yields to investors. Speaking of taxable municipal bonds, let's say a few words about **Build America Bonds** here. Build America Bonds (BAB)s are issued by states and cities, but, unlike typical municipal bonds, these are taxable to the investor. The issuer has to, therefore, pay a higher nominal yield to investors, but the issuer receives a big chunk of the interest they pay right back from the US Government. The Build America Bonds are designed to stimulate the rebuilding of infrastructure (roads, bridges, sewers, etc.) and are authorized under the American Recovery and Reinvestment Act of 2009. Basically, the federal government is helping municipalities to rebuild infrastructure by allowing them to sell bonds to a bigger group of investors compared to those who typically buy the tax-exempt municipal bonds. See, since the interest payment the investor receives is taxable, any bond investor might be interested, not just high-bracket investors who typically buy tax-exempt municipal bonds. As the US Treasury explains, low-income investors, corporate bond investors, and pension funds—who would normally not buy municipal bonds—will in many cases be interested in buying the taxable municipal bonds called "BABs." How does the issuer benefit by paying a higher interest rate? The federal government reimburses the issuer for 35% of the interest paid to investors. As the US Treasury explains, if an issuer sells a 10% bond to an investor, the issuer receives 35% of that back from Uncle Sam, making their net borrowing cost just 6.5%, while being able to sell bonds to a wider spectrum of investors. The way I just described BABs actually applies to just one type of them, which we could call the "BABs - Direct Payment." There is another type in which the tax credit is given to the investor, and we could call these "BABs - Tax Credit." The investor's tax credit is also equal to 35% of the interest payable on the bonds. The effective savings that the bond issuer realizes is not as high on the "tax credit" BABs, but these bonds also don't carry as many restrictions. Basically, as long as the "tax credit" bonds would normally pay tax-exempt interest and are issued before January 1, 2011, they can be used for virtually any purpose. On the other hand, with "direct payment" BABs, issuers have to use virtually all the money raised to build something (capital expenditures), while the money raised through "tax credit" BABs can be used for both capital expenditures (building stuff) or working capital (paying bills). They can also be used to perform refundings and no more than one advance refunding.

If the test brings these Build America Bonds up at all, I would anticipate that it would focus on the main points:

- they pay taxable interest to the investor
- the issuer receives a direct payment (refundable credit) from the US Treasury of 35% of the interest paid on the bonds for "direct payment" BABs
- the investor receives a tax credit of 35% of the interest received from the issuer for "tax credit" BABs
- BABs are not guaranteed by the federal government/not direct obligations

By the way, *why* wouldn't pension funds normally purchase tax-exempt municipal bonds? Because pension funds already pay no tax on the income they generate. Oh, and in case the Series 7 hasn't already overwhelmed you with factoids, please know that a **bank qualified municipal bond** is simply a municipal bond that gives banks incentive to hold it. Since banks would invest the deposits of their customers into such municipal bonds, they would, of course, have to pay interest to those depositors. The IRS will allow the bank to deduct 80% of those interest costs associated with investing in these bank qualified municipal bonds.

TAX-FREE AND TAX-EQUIVALENT YIELD

The exam might ask you to determine whether a particular GO bond pays a higher or lower "equivalent yield" compared to a particular corporate bond.

For example, the exam could ask you something like this:

Jeremiah Jones is in the 30% tax bracket. Jeremiah is trying to determine whether he should purchase a 7% New Haven general obligation bond or a 9.5% XYZ Corp. debenture. As his registered rep, you should recommend that Jeremiah:

A. Buy the XYZ debenture

B. Buy the New Haven GO

C. Stop pestering you about municipal securities

Well, we can probably weed out choice "C." But, we still have to figure out whether the GO or the corporate gives Jeremiah Jones a better yield. Sure, 9.5% is a bigger number than 7%, but the GO provides interest that is not taxed. What happens to the interest Jeremiah earns on a corporate bond?

30% goes to Uncle Sam. So, which bond would put more money in Jeremiah's pocket?

A couple of easy math formulas will provide you with the right answer every time. If you know the yield for the GO or "tax-free" bond, you take that percent and divide it by 100% minus the customer's tax bracket. In other words, divide .07 by .70, because Jeremiah is in the .30 tax bracket. 100 - .30 = .70.

So, .07 divided by .70 = 10%

That would be the **tax-equivalent yield**. Means the corporate debenture would have to be offering Jeremiah that much for him to get an equivalent yield.

And it isn't. It's only offering 9.5%, right? So, we'd have to recommend that Jeremiah buy the New Haven GO.

If we knew the taxable yield on the corporate, we could find the tax-free equivalent yield by multiplying the 9.5% by .70. That would tell us that Jeremiah's "tax-free equivalent yield" is 6.65% on this bond that says 9.5% on the bond certificate. If the GO (municipal bond) offers anything higher than 6.65%, let's buy that muni.

The GO, in fact, offers 7%, which is higher than the 6.65% that the corporate bond yields after taxes are taken out.

Again confirming that the GO offers a higher yield. So, if you have the tax-free yield, divide it by (100 - tax bracket). If you have the taxable yield, multiply it by (100 - tax bracket).

And, if the question gives you both the coupon rate and the YTM, use the YTM.

Did we mention this stuff is hard?

Good.

PRACTICE

1. Your customer is concerned about AMT. You would most likely recommend a municipal bond issued to complete which of the following projects?

    A. Parking garage

    B. Convention center

    C. Dome sports stadium

    D. Public school

2. A general obligation bond pays a 7% coupon. A comparable corporate bond pays a 9.5% coupon. Therefore

    A. A customer in the 15% tax bracket should buy the municipal security

    B. A customer in the 30% tax bracket should buy the municipal security

    C. A customer in the 30% tax bracket should buy the corporate bond

    D. Both customers should purchase the municipal security

3. A customer purchases an 8% municipal security @105, maturing in 20 years. After 8 years, she sells the bond @101, realizing a

    A. capital gain of $20

    B. capital loss of $20

    C. capital gain of $200

    D. capital loss of $50

4. Your customer is in the 30% marginal tax bracket and sees that a corporate bond offers a 10% yield. This would be equal to a municipal bond paying

    A. 4.5%

    B. 13%

    C. 7%

    D. .7%

5. **Your customer buys a zero coupon municipal bond on the primary market @500, maturing in 10 years. After holding the bond for six years, she sells the bond @85, realizing**

    A. gain of $50

    B. no gain or loss

    C. loss of $50

    D. capital gains tax plus penalties and interest

ANSWERS

1. **D**, schools are not "private purpose" bonds. Assume they are all GO's.

2. **B,** the customer in the 30% bracket would have a tax-equivalent yield of 10%, vs. the corporate bond's 9.5% yield.

3. **B,** she reduces her cost basis by $2.50 per year ($50 premium over 20 years). After 8 years, her adjusted basis is $20 lower, or $1,030. She sells the bond for $1,010, realizing a capital loss of $20.

4. **C,** multiply the 10% by 70%.

5. **A,** the cost basis rises (tax-free) by $50 per year, or $300 after six years. The adjusted basis is now $800. The bond is sold for $850.

THE MSRB

The SEC is the ultimate securities regulator and is part of the federal government. National securities **exchanges** and associations such as FINRA, CBOE, etc., are "self-regulatory organizations" or "SROs." The SRO that regulates municipal securities firms is the MSRB, which stands for the "Municipal Securities Rulemaking Board." This organization has lots to say about how municipal securities dealers do business. They have nothing to say about the issuers. They have no power over an issuer like California or New York City. They have all kinds of power over the folks who do municipal securities business with them.

But they don't actually enforce anything.

Ever heard the phrase, "We don't make the rules; we just enforce them?"

Well, at the MSRB the motto is, "We don't enforce the rules, we just make them."

If you can remember that just about everybody can enforce an MSRB rule except the MSRB, you'll probably get another test question right there. Specifically, you need to know that the following bodies can enforce MSRB rules: for bank dealers we have the FDIC, FRB, and the Comptroller of the Currency; for broker-dealers we have FINRA and the SEC. But not the MSRB itself.

All right, so that's who the MSRB is. Unfortunately for you, they have 41 "General" rules, and they are all highly testable. Since they are the "General" rules, they all start with the letter "G." We'll list them in order, but we're not telling you to memorize each rule by rule number, unless you happen to be a savant. You'll need to know what the rules mean and how they're applied.

MSRB Rules

Rule G-1. A separately identifiable department or division of a bank…is that unit of the bank which conducts all of the activities of the bank relating to the conduct of business as a municipal securities dealer.

Comment: some banks have departments/divisions that conduct municipal securities business. The exam might refer to them as "bank dealers."

Rule G-2. No municipal securities dealer shall effect any transaction in, or induce or attempt to induce the purchase or sale of, any municipal security unless such municipal securities dealer and every natural person associated with such municipal securities dealer is qualified in accordance with the rules of the Board.

Comment: the firm, the principals, and the representatives have to meet the qualifications and registration requirements of the MSRB. They then clarify that with the next rule.

Rule G-3. No municipal securities dealer or person who is a municipal securities representative, municipal securities principal, municipal securities sales principal or financial and operations principal (as hereafter defined) shall be qualified for purposes of rule G-2 unless such municipal securities dealer or person meets the requirements of this rule. The term "municipal securities representative" means a natural person associated with a municipal securities dealer, other than a person whose functions are solely clerical or ministerial, whose activities include one or more of the following:

(A) underwriting, trading or sales of municipal securities;

(B) financial advisory or consultant services for issuers in connection with the issuance of municipal securities;

(C) research or investment advice with respect to municipal securities; or

(D) any other activities which involve communication, directly or indirectly, with public investors in municipal securities; provided.

Comment: the words "clerical or ministerial" are often used in regulations to distinguish between those who are actively involved in the investment business of the firm and those who are maybe just working as the receptionist or performing filing, word processing, or other general office work. As we can see, if the individual (natural person) is involved with underwriting, trading, or selling municipal securities, he is a "municipal securities representative" and must register. Also, if he is involved with financial advisory/consulting activities for issuers, providing research/advice on municipal securities, or communicating with public investors, he is a "municipal securities representative" and subject to registration requirements. This rule goes on to state that municipal securities representatives brand new to the securities business must go through a 90-day apprenticeship period. During this period, they can be paid a salary (no commissions) and can only deal with other dealers or institutional investors, not with public investors. A public investor is the "retail investor," the average Joe and JoAnne, and we protect them much more than we protect other dealers or big institutions. In fact, the basic idea is that an **institutional investor** will know if the apprentice screws up and will generally be quite happy to point out the mistake in a very pleasant, encouraging, professional tone of voice. The apprentice also must pass the appropriate exam within 180 days or stop all sales activities immediately. Of course, if you had already worked in the business with a Series 6 or Series 7 for at least 90 days, you would have already completed your apprenticeship period.

The term "municipal securities principal" refers to the individuals who are "directly engaged in the management, direction or supervision of" all the activities mentioned for representatives, plus:

- maintenance of records with respect to the activities enumerated
- training of municipal securities principals or municipal securities representatives

The rule then goes into extreme details concerning the fact that the qualification exams (52, 53, etc.) are confidential and that people who fail must wait 30 days to retest the first time, 30 days to retest the second time, and then 6 months every time after that. Of course, that's the way all of these exams work, so there's nothing surprising there. Continuing Education requirements are also discussed, but we'll leave the rest of the details alone for now to avoid overexciting you.

Rule G-4. No municipal securities dealer or natural person shall be qualified for purposes of rule G-2 if, by action of a national securities exchange or registered securities association, such

municipal securities dealer has been and is expelled or suspended
from membership or participation in such exchange or association,
or such natural person has been and is barred or suspended from
being associated with a member of such exchange or association
for violation of any rules of such exchange or association which
prohibit any act or transaction constituting conduct inconsistent
with just and equitable principles of trade, or which requires any
act the omission of which constitutes conduct inconsistent with
such just and equitable principles of trade.

Comment: in English, the above might be translated to, "Look, if you've already been in trouble with other regulators, your chances of getting registered ain't lookin' too good." Notice the phrase "conduct inconsistent with just and equitable principles of trade." That phrase is used by FINRA, the NYSE, and the MSRB. If the conduct of a firm, a principal, or a representative is not consistent with being fair to customers, and being fair *among* all customers, then we've got ourselves a problem. For example, there are plenty of reps out there who have told customers to cut checks for investments in *their* name. The rep then either puts the money in his own bank account or maybe establishes a little joint account at an online broker. You know, two grand of his own money and fifty grand of the customer's money, split right down the middle. In order to conceal the fact that he's investing or simply spending the client's money, he sends monthly account statements to the client that are totally bogus making it appear that the investment is doing just fine. This would be conduct that is sort of "inconsistent with just and equitable principles of trade." And, this happens much more frequently than you might believe.

The SEC, called "the Commission," under the Securities Exchange Act of 1934 has the power to allow or disallow somebody from registration with the MSRB. But, if you accidentally spent all of your client's money while lying to her with bogus account statements, I would not anticipate the SEC going out of its way for you.

Rule G-5. This rule makes it clear that is a violation of MSRB rules to violate any SEC rules or rules of the other SROs that the firm belongs to. As usual, the regulators are pretty much on the same page when it comes to what constitutes "conduct inconsistent with just and equitable principles of trade."

Rule G-6. This rule states that since firms are members of FINRA, they have to meet the fidelity bond requirements of FINRA. Let's see how FINRA defines the "fidelity bond" issue:

Each member required to join the Securities Investor Protection
Corporation who has employees and who is not a member in good
standing of the American Stock Exchange, Inc.; the Boston Stock
Exchange; the Midwest Stock Exchange, Inc.; the New York Stock
Exchange, Inc.; the Pacific Stock Exchange, Inc.; the Philadelphia
Stock Exchange, Inc.; or the Chicago Board Options Exchange shall:

(1) Maintain a blanket fidelity bond, in a form substantially similar
to the standard form of Brokers Blanket Bond promulgated by the
Surety Association of America, covering officers and employees

which provides against loss and has agreements covering at least the following:

-Fidelity

-On Premises

-In Transit

-Misplacement

-Forgery and Alteration (including check forgery)

-Securities Loss (including securities forgery)

-Fraudulent Trading

Comment: so, certain firms that have employees need to meet fidelity bonding requirements just in case anyone accidentally loses securities or tries to steal them.

Rule G-7. This rule stipulates that municipal securities firms have to get all kinds of information about their principals and representatives. The firm needs to check the individual's employment history over at least the past 10 years, a record of all residences over the past five years, a record of any disciplinary history involving the SEC, state regulators, banking regulators, SROs, etc., and—of course—any felonies or misdemeanors related to forgery, fraud, burglary, perjury, bribery, etc. In other words, submit a U4, which is the standard form used whenever an agent or principal associates with a firm.

Rule G-8. This rule illustrates what a pain in the neck it is to keep all the required records. Member firms have to keep "account records for each customer account and account of such municipal securities dealer. Such records shall reflect all purchases and sales of municipal securities, all receipts and deliveries of municipal securities, all receipts and disbursements of cash, and all other debits and credits relating to such account." Firms also need to keep a daily itemized record of everything mentioned above in something called a "blotter" or "other records of original entry." There needs to be a record of each security carried by the member for its own account or the accounts of its customers. The firm needs to obtain customer account information, just as FINRA firms are required to do. In fact, if you're a broker-dealer involved in municipal securities, you're a member of FINRA. You follow both sets of rules, which are usually on the same page, more or less. The firm needs:

- customer's name and address
- whether customer is of legal age
- tax identification or social security number
- occupation
- name and address of employer
- information about the customer used for suitability/recommendations
- signature of municipal securities representative and signature of a municipal securities principal indicating acceptance of the account
- with respect to discretionary accounts, customer's written authorization to exercise discretionary power or authority with respect to the account, written approval of municipal

securities principal who supervises the account, and written approval of municipal securities principal with respect to each transaction in the account, indicating the time and date of approval
- whether customer is employed by another broker, dealer or municipal securities dealer

As we'll see when we look at FINRA rules in oppressive detail, firms like to get their customers to sign a pre-dispute **arbitration** agreement. Once that's signed, the customer cannot sue the firm in civil court. Instead, all claims are taken to arbitration, as they are in Major League Baseball. In arbitration, there is one decision and no appeals. The arbitrators don't have to explain their decision, and some of them come from the securities industry. Therefore, the rules state that firms need to make it very clear what arbitration is and what the heck the customer is being asked to sign. We'll save the details for the even more fascinating discussion of FINRA rules covering the same darned thing.

The firm needs to keep records of all customer written complaints, including the action taken to resolve the complaints. Records of political contributions made to issuers must be kept; in fact, there are so many rules to be kept that we're going to move on from here. But, we are definitely encouraging you to go to www.msrb.org and scan each of the 41 "General Rules" yourself. Regulations are just things to be memorized. You may or may not get comfortable with the concepts surrounding options, stop and limit orders, bond yields, etc., but you can memorize any regulation with pure effort and determination.

Rule G-9. This rule simply explains that some records must be maintained for three years, and some for six years. Customer complaints, for example, are kept for six years, possibly because after six years it's too late to file an arbitration claim. Written and electronic communications, written agreements, customer account information, powers of attorney, transaction records, etc., are kept for three years.

Rule G-10. When the firm receives a written customer complaint, the firm must send an "investor brochure" that explains the customer's remedies, such as the arbitration we mentioned above.

Rule G-11. This rule provides mind-numbing detail for syndicate procedures. It's actually a good one to review, as it brings up concepts we've mentioned in this chapter. But to prevent this book from weighing in at 30 pounds, let's keep moving.

Rule G-12. This is the "uniform practice" rule, so it's extremely detailed. It defines the terms "settlement date" and the specific types of settlement: cash, regular way, when/as/and if issued. Cash settlements occur on the day of the trade. Regular way settlement is "T + 3 business days." A "when, as, and if issued" settlement is what the buyer of a new issue receives. In other words, the bonds have been sold but not actually created and delivered yet. Dealers must confirm transactions with one another, and this rule provides an amazing level of detail on that process.

When firms deliver securities to the buyer's broker-dealer, there are all kinds of rules about the denominations they have to come in and all the special ways they might have to be marked. The test could ask about a "mutilated certificate," which is not good **delivery** unless it is validated by the "trustee, registrar, transfer agent, paying agent or issuer of the securities or by an authorized agent or official of the issuer." If there's no legal opinion, the bond must be marked "ex-legal," or else delivery can be rejected by the other dealer. If the bonds have those funky, old-fashioned coupons, those coupons must be attached. If you get some weird question about a coupon bond that is in default, tell the test that all coupons would need to be attached for purposes of good delivery: past due coupons, currently due coupons, coupons due in the future. You see, there is really no end to the exam's ability to delve in trivialities.

Don't worry, though. This nightmare will be over soon.

Although, technically, you are only on page 105 so let's keep moving.

Rule G-13. This rule covers quotations. The phrase "bona fide" means that a quotation that is published has to be legitimate. So, don't be publishing BID prices unless you're prepared to actually buy some of those municipal securities at that price, for example. Also, make sure that your Bid and Offer prices represent your best judgment of the fair market value for those securities, rather than, say, gouging the heck out of your loyal customers. And, if a member is participating in a joint account, meaning that several firms control the same securities, the members cannot put out different quotes on these bonds to different parties. The exam might say that they cannot "indicate more than one market for the same securities" since the exam doesn't get out much.

Rule G-14. Municipal securities firms have to report transactions to "RTRS," which is the MSRB's "Real-Time Transaction Reporting System." As this rule explains, reporting transactions is important for the purpose of regulatory enforcement and also provides transparency to the public, meaning it allows investors to quickly know the market price and volume for a particular security. Trades must generally be reported within 15 minutes to RTRS. Also, municipal securities firms need to be sure they are not reporting transactions that did not actually occur, or reporting prices that are fictitious. See, there are always a few bad apples out there who will try to manipulate the securities markets. Maybe they purchase a block of bonds and then artificially drive up the price by having sloppy or dishonest firms publish trades that did not even occur at higher and higher prices until a buyer can be lured in to pay much more than the bonds are actually worth. The MSRB would appreciate a lot less of that sort of thing. Or, two traders will form what are really two joint accounts at different firms but conceal each other's names from the account documents. Now, they spend all day buying and selling the securities back and forth, when there is really no change in ownership taking place. Municipal securities firms not only must avoid such conduct themselves, but also make sure they're not being used as pawns by criminals much smarter than themselves.

Rule G-15. When a firm executes a trade with or for a customer, they must provide a written trade confirmation no later than settlement/completion of the transaction. Confirmations must include information such as:

- Name, address, telephone # of the dealer
- Customer name
- Purchase from or sale to the customer
- Capacity in which firm acted (agent for customer, principal for own account)
- Trade date and time of execution
- Par value
- CUSIP #
- Yield and dollar price
- Accrued interest
- Extended principal (total amount paid for the bonds, before commissions or accrued interest)
- Total dollar amount of the transaction

The trade confirmation must always disclose the most conservative or lowest yield to customers. For discount bonds, they must disclose the YTM. For premium bonds, they must disclose YTC. Only exception is if a bond has been advance refunded. In this case, we know for sure when the bond will be called, so yield-to-call is the only yield we have to disclose. No longer matters what yield to original maturity would have been at this point, since we'll never get there now that the bond has been called.

If the bond is insured against default, as many revenue bonds are, the customer must receive evidence of that insurance, either on the face of the certificate or in a document attached to the certificate.

> Rule G-16. At least once each two calendar years, each municipal securities dealer shall be examined to determine, at a minimum, whether such municipal securities dealer and its associated persons are in compliance with all applicable rules of the Board (MSRB) and all applicable provisions of the Act (Securities Exchange Act of 1934) and rules and regulations of the Commission (SEC) thereunder.

Comment: that one's very clear as is—I just added the parenthetical clarifications. This next one is a real shocker, though.

> Rule G-17. In the conduct of its municipal securities activities, each broker, dealer, and municipal securities dealer shall deal fairly with all persons and shall not engage in any deceptive, dishonest, or unfair practice.

Comment: there isn't time or space here to imagine all the ways that a municipal securities dealer could take advantage of customers. But, let's look at one example to make the above dead language come alive. Let's say that Mrs. Jenkins, an 85-year-old customer, comes in with some bonds that nobody at the firm has ever heard of. Nobody ever trades these securities, but the firm, being so nice and all, tells Mrs. J that they will buy those bonds from her "at the market price" of $700. *Is* there a market price of $700? No. There is no market for the securities at all, so the firm is taking advantage of the client with the low price and deceiving her by pretending she's getting an objectively fair price for the bonds. The firm should be clear that these are illiquid securities with no active secondary market; if she still wants to sell them for $700, maybe the transaction will pass the smell test. Though not if the firm quickly resells the bonds for $900, right? Or, maybe a particular high-yield (junk) municipal bond fund pays the highest 12b-1 fees to firms and their agents. Therefore, even when conservative investors ask for recommendations, they are routinely routed to the higher-risk, high-yield mutual fund, not because it's suitable for the investors but because it's lucrative to the firm and the agents. Again with the whole "deceptive, dishonest, or unfair practice" thing.

> Rule G-18. Each broker, dealer and municipal securities dealer, when executing a transaction in municipal securities for or on behalf of a customer as agent, shall make a reasonable effort to

> obtain a price for the customer that is fair and reasonable in relation to prevailing market conditions.

Comment: notice how it doesn't say "the best possible price." Just says that if you're acting for a customer who wants to buy or sell a municipal security, try to make a reasonable effort to get them a good price. Is that too much to ask? It might be tempting for two firms to trade favors by getting their customers to pay way too much whenever buying municipal bonds on the secondary market. Unfortunately, the regulators are saying that the firm needs to do some due diligence in obtaining a fair and reasonable price. It's not that hard for the regulators to review the prices reported throughout the day. If it's clear that a particular member firm is gouging their clients, there will be hell to pay in the form of sanctions, fines, and possibly even suspensions.

Rule G-19. This rule is sort of a re-statement of G-8. It tells the dealer which account information it must obtain before executing transactions with or for customers in municipal securities. For a non-institutional investor (regular Joe and JoAnne), the firm must obtain the following:

- the customer's financial status;
- the customer's tax status;
- the customer's investment objectives; and
- such other information used or considered to be reasonable and necessary by such broker, dealer or municipal securities dealer in making recommendations to the customer.

The rule states that all recommendations to customers must be suitable and if granted **discretion**, the firm needs to be sure that what they're purchasing for their clients (without even talking to them first) is suitable. And, as always, churning is considered impolite. **Churning** is defined as "executing transactions that are excessive in size or frequency in view of information known to such municipal securities dealer concerning the customer's financial background, tax status, and investment objectives."

Rule G-20. It's okay for a principal or a member firm to give gifts to their employees. But, in general, this rule forbids members from giving to anyone other than an employee or partner of the firm anything worth more than $100 per year. You can probably imagine how many exceptions I'm going to have to lay on you now. First, the rule states that an occasional ticket to a sporting, theatrical, or other entertainment event that is sponsored by the firm is okay, as long as it doesn't happen so often and so extensively that it raises questions of propriety. Second, the firm can sponsor legitimate business functions recognized as deductible expenses by the IRS. Third, gifts of reminder advertising (pens, coffee mugs, golf balls, etc.) are usually okay. A municipal firm could contract somebody for services, as long as there is a written agreement that spells out exactly what the heck this person is going to be doing for the firm and how much they'll be compensated, and the agreement is approved by the employer of the person whose services are being contracted. This rule also states that in connection with primary offerings, it is not okay to make or accept payment of non-cash compensation. Non-cash compensation would be, for example, merchandise, gifts and prizes, travel expenses, meals and lodging. But, of course, there are exceptions. Gifts that aren't preconditioned on somebody meeting a sales target can be given if they don't exceed $100. The occasional ticket to an entertainment venue is okay, as long as it's not excessive or preconditioned on meeting a sales target. And, if it's legitimate and by-the-book, an education seminar can be paid for by the "offeror" to a representative or principal, as long as the attendance is not preconditioned on the meeting of a sales target, only the associated person's expenses (not the guests') are reimbursed, the firm approves the attendance ahead of time, and the location is appropriate to the purpose of the meeting. In other words, if the offeror's headquarters are in LaCrosse, Wisconsin and the associated person works in Appleton, why again does the "seminar" always have to be held in Maui?

Hmm. Again, try not to raise any question of propriety.

Finally, the member can provide non-cash compensation to its reps for doing a great job. But the rule states that the compensation has to be "based on the total production of associated persons with respect to all municipal securities within respective product types distributed by the firm. And, the credits are equally weighted for each product type."

> Rule G-21. (a) Definition of "Advertisement." For purposes of this rule, the term "advertisement" means any material (other than listings of offerings) published or designed for use in the public, including electronic, media, or any promotional literature designed for dissemination to the public, including any notice, circular, report, market letter, form letter, telemarketing script or reprint or excerpt of the foregoing. The term does not apply to preliminary official statements or official statements, but does apply to abstracts or summaries of official statements, offering circulars and other such similar documents prepared by brokers, dealers or municipal securities dealers.

Comment: okay, I see several potential test questions here. The exam will ask you which of the following must be approved by a principal. Advertising must be approved, but as we see above, listings of offerings are not included in this definition, and neither are preliminary or official statements. Official and preliminary official statements are prepared by the issuer. The MSRB has nothing to say about issuers. Then again, if a firm creates a summary or abstract of either document, the MSRB considers that advertising, which must be approved by a principal. A listing of offerings would just be a statement of fact—the firm has these bonds for sale at this price. Advertising is something that presents a message that could, perhaps, be misconstrued. Rather than a straight-up statement of fact, maybe the piece exclaims, "Our firm can make you rich!" Unfortunately, that's not going to make it past compliance. How about, "Wealth management and tax-relief strategies for the discerning investor." Perfect. See, the regulators get quite upset when important facts are left out of a presentation, or when an advertisement implies more safety than an investment actually provides, or higher returns than anyone is likely to see.

Rule G-22. What if somebody just happens to be a principal at an underwriting firm while also serving as mayor of the city issuing the bonds? He would be in a position to control both parties; therefore, a control relationship exists. In this case, the firm would have to disclose the control relationship to customers before executing transactions in that issuer's securities. If the disclosure is made verbally, a written disclosure has to be sent no later than settlement. If it's a discretionary account, this is one time when the customer would have to be notified before the trade is executed. As we'll see in a later section, a discretionary account allows the firm to execute trades without first contacting the customer. If it's a transaction in a security where a control relationship exists between the issuer and the firm, however, the customer would have to be notified in order to authorize the transaction. You know, just in case you didn't have enough details to keep straight.

Rule G-23. This rule regulates financial advisory activities. Issuers usually pay a financial firm to advise them "with respect to the structure, timing, terms and other similar matters concerning such issue or issues." These advisors charge handsome fees for their expertise. Rule G-23 states that if the firm acts as a financial advisor to an issuer, there must be a written agreement that "sets forth the basis of compensation for the financial advisory services to be rendered." Now, believe it or not, some of these municipal securities firms are pretty darned interested in making as much money as possible. So, they sure appreciate the advisory fees, but now maybe they would like to help underwrite this new issue of bonds they just advised the issuer on. For a competitive, sealed bid (GO), the underwriter would need the written permission of their client, the issuer, in order to participate in the syndicate. For a negotiated bid (revenue bond) the financial advisory relationship has to be terminated in writing, the issuer has to consent to the advisor getting involved with the underwriting process, and the firm must disclose the underwriting compensation and the potential conflict of interest to the issuer and get a written acknowledgment from the issuer that the disclosure was received. See, if the firm changes from a disinterested adviser charging a fee to a very interested buyer of the issuer's bonds who might just like to buy the bonds a bit cheaper than they're worth, that's a different relationship where the firm isn't necessarily on the same side anymore. For a sealed, competitive bid, there is no reason to terminate the financial advisory relationship, since the issuer has to award the business to the lowest bid, end of story. For a negotiated underwriting, the firm that was just giving disinterested advice for a fee is now negotiating the price they'll pay for the issuer's bonds. Note, this rule is currently "in play," with the MSRB submitting a draft of the changes and asking interested parties to comment. Check www.passthe7.com/updates to see if anything has been finalized. Not that this change is going to be a make-or-break topic on your exam, but it's always good to be a little over-prepared.

Rule G-24. Municipal securities firms sometimes perform services for an issuer and may, thereby, find out information that could be used to their advantage. For example, maybe they act as the paying agent, which means they cut the interest and principal checks to the bondholders. How much creativity would it take for this "paying agent" to send a slick, colorful marketing piece that says, "Has your bond matured? Why not buy a new one from us?" with the final principal and interest checks? Not much, of course. So, this rule states that no firm "shall use information discovered through performing [such] services for the purpose of soliciting purchases, sales, or exchanges of municipal securities or otherwise make use of such information for financial gain except with the consent of such issuer or such broker, dealer, or municipal securities dealer or the person on whose behalf the information was given."

Rule G-25. This rule is called "Improper Use of Assets." It tells firms not to offer guarantees against loss to customers. Investing in securities involves risk, and that's just the nature of the beast. Your firm cannot shield the investor from risk, acting as an insurance company. Now, the exception here is that the dealer can sell the investor a put option giving him the right to sell the bond back prior to redemption, usually for par. Or, the dealer can enter into one of those **repurchase agreements** that we glossed over in the Debt Securities chapter. In those two cases, there would be a written agreement with all of the terms spelled out, not some empty promise that the investor "can't possibly lose when investing at this firm." A representative or principal might want to "share" in the profits and losses of a customer account, which makes the regulators rightfully nervous. If an associated person wants to share in the account of a client, he'll need to establish a joint account with the customer, and the exam might say he needs "the client's written consent, the consent of the employing firm, and must share in proportion to his investment in the account." In other words, even if you could get a joint account going with one of your customers, you can't put in $50 to his $50,000 and split everything "right down the middle."

Rule G-26 has to do with the process of transferring a customer account to another firm. We will save that excitement for a later chapter called "Customers and Brokerage Procedures." In other words, FINRA and MSRB rules, as usual, are on the same page.

> Rule G-27. Supervision. (a) Obligation to supervise. Each municipal securities dealer shall supervise the conduct of the municipal securities activities of the dealer and its associated persons to ensure compliance with Board rules and the applicable provisions of the Act and rules thereunder. Each dealer shall specifically designate one or more associated persons qualified as municipal securities principals, municipal securities sales principals, financial and operations principals in accordance with Board rules, or as general securities principals to be responsible for the supervision of the municipal securities activities of the dealer and its associated persons as required by this rule. A written record of each supervisory designation and of the designated principal's responsibilities under this rule shall be maintained and updated as required under rule G-9.

Comment: stuffy legalese aside, the above ramble is actually self-explanatory. This rule also stipulates that the firm must have written supervisory procedures that "codify the dealer's supervisory system for ensuring compliance." What are the principals responsible for?

- Handling of customer complaints
- Supervision of municipal securities representatives
- Monitoring of correspondence between representatives and customers
- Approval of new accounts
- Approval of all transactions on a daily basis
- Required maintenance and retention of required books and records
- Reviewing at least annually the written supervisory procedures of the firm
- Updating the written supervisory procedures in response to rule changes by the MSRB and other regulators

> Rule G-28. Transactions with Employees and Partners of Other Municipal Securities Professionals. No municipal securities dealer shall open or maintain an account in which transactions in municipal securities may be effected for a customer who such municipal

securities dealer knows is employed by, or the partner of, another
municipal securities dealer, or for or on behalf of the spouse
or minor child of such person unless such municipal securities
dealer first gives written notice with respect to the opening and
maintenance of such account to the municipal securities dealer by
whom such person is employed or of whom such person is a partner.

Comment: in English that just means that before opening an account for somebody who works for a municipal securities firm, or for the spouse or minor child of somebody who works for a municipal securities firm, the municipal securities dealer has to notify the employer in writing. And, after every transaction for this person, the municipal securities dealer has to send a duplicate trade confirmation to the employing dealer and has to act in accordance with any instructions that the employing broker-dealer has provided for the handling of this account. Also, this rule doesn't cover transactions in municipal fund securities, just municipal securities purchased "a la carte."

Rule G-29. Each broker, dealer and municipal securities dealer
shall keep in each office a copy of all rules of the Board (MSRB)
and shall make such rules available for examination by customers
promptly upon request.

Comment: yes, the MSRB Rules contain a Rule about MSRB Rules. Keep a few copies on hand and make sure you provide them to customers upon request. Why is a customer requesting a copy of the MSRB Rulebook? A, she's ticked off at something your firm did, and, B, she doesn't realize the rules are available online at www.msrb.org.

Rule G-30. (a) Principal Transactions. No municipal securities
dealer shall purchase municipal securities for its own account from
a customer or sell municipal securities for its own account to a
customer except at an aggregate price (including any mark-down or
mark-up) that is fair and reasonable, taking into consideration
all relevant factors, including the best judgment of the municipal
securities dealer as to the fair market value of the securities
at the time of the transaction, the expense involved in effecting
the transaction, the fact that the municipal securities dealer is
entitled to a profit, and the total dollar amount of the transaction.

(b) Agency Transactions. No municipal securities dealer shall
purchase or sell municipal securities as agent for a customer for
a commission or service charge in excess of a fair and reasonable
amount, taking into consideration all relevant factors, including
the availability of the securities involved in the transaction, the
expense of executing or filling the customer's order, the value of
the services rendered by the municipal securities dealer, and the
amount of any other compensation received or to be received by the
municipal securities dealer in connection with the transaction.

Comment: small transactions usually carry higher mark-ups, as is the case whenever we buy in small quantities, but then the flip side is that large transactions should get a better deal. While the firm is "entitled to a profit," they aren't entitled to rob their clients blind by purchasing bonds from them @98 and immediately reselling them @108, pocketing $100 per bond. Not that the regulators would give a maximum or minimum mark-up; instead, they use phrases that imply that there is some leeway here but that firms need to use their best judgment when determining what is "fair and reasonable." Basically, either the firm can do a good job of making those judgment calls, or FINRA can schedule a hearing to help them at their earliest convenience.

> Rule G-31. No municipal securities dealer shall solicit transactions
> in municipal securities with or for the account of an investment
> company as defined in the Investment Company Act of 1940, as compen-
> sation or in return for sales by such municipal securities dealer
> of participations, shares, or units in such investment company.

Comment: FINRA prohibits the same "shelf space programs" in its "anti-reciprocity rules" codified in FINRA Rules. What they're saying is that the firm cannot approach a municipal bond mutual fund with a pitch like this, "So, if you were willing to execute all of your trades through our firm, we would be willing to sell your fund to our investors ahead of all other funds." I know, many of you just can't see what the heck is wrong with this one-hand-washes-the-other approach, especially if you ever worked in city government. But, the point is that the mutual fund uses their investors' money to pay for everything, including trading commissions. It would be sort of nice if the fund would, then, obtain "best execution" on all of their trades, since they are using the customers' money to buy and sell portfolio securities. If they're cutting sleazy little deals with broker-dealers in which they pay fat commissions in exchange for the broker-dealer pushing the fund to new investors, the mutual fund investors are getting screwed. See, when the fund gathers new investors, that doesn't help the existing investors at all. It does give the fund more assets against which to charge management and 12b-1 fees, and it also gives them more assets to park in money market securities in order to generate enough interest to pay ever higher board of directors salaries. But, that's not helping the investors. Plus, the broker-dealer making this pitch should probably take the radical approach of recommending mutual funds to their customers based on suitability, rather than pushing whatever piece-of-crap fund pays them the most in commissions.

Rule G-32 stipulates the information that must be disclosed to investors who purchase new issues of municipal securities. In a new offering, the dealer has to deliver the official statement no later than the due date for confirmation. If the issuer is not putting an official statement together, that has to be disclosed to investors in writing. If the dealer is involved in a negotiated underwriting, they must disclose the following to investors:

- The underwriting spread
- The amount of any fee received by the municipal securities dealer as agent for the issuer in the distribution of the securities
- The initial offering price for each maturity in the issue that is offered or to be offered in whole or in part by the underwriters

Underwriters now file Official Statements and Advance Refunding Documents to the "EMMA" electronic system that the public can access through a website. And, in those cases in which no official statement or advance refunding document will be prepared, underwriters must notify the EMMA system of that fact.

Rule G-33. This rule standardizes how accrued interest must be calculated. If you take a quick look at this one, you'll see something rather scary: even though the Series 7 information seems difficult, it is really just an entry-level view of the industry. Imagine if one of *those* formulae were actually on the exam.

Rule G-34. This rule is about CUSIP numbers and is probably too detailed to make a good test question.

Rule G-35. This rule simply makes bank dealers subject to FINRA Code of Arbitration procedure. We'll look at FINRA Arbitration in more detail in the final chapter of this book.

Rule G-36. This rule was replaced with changes to Rule G-32 and the EMMA system referenced there. The status is "reserved," as you'll see at www.msrb.org.

Rule G-37. Political Contributions and Prohibitions on Municipal Securities Business. As a resident of Chicago, I find this rule especially interesting. See, a municipal underwriting firm in Chicago wouldn't take too long to figure out that the best way to get invited to the table for a bunch of lucrative, no-bid "negotiated" underwritings of municipal bonds would be to contribute, say, half of whatever they make to the mayor's political campaign. Not to mention that the governor and certain members of the state legislature might turn out to be really helpful allies in their quest to underwrite lucrative municipal bonds issued by the State of Illinois. Hint: the state recently did a $10 *billion* pension bond underwriting, so what's a few percentage points of $10 billion work out to be?

So, the MSRB takes the radical view that municipal securities dealers should not buy their way into the underwriting process. Let's see how the MSRB explains the rule:

> (a) Purpose. The purpose and intent of this rule are to ensure that the high standards and integrity of the municipal securities industry are maintained, to prevent fraudulent and manipulative acts and practices, to promote just and equitable principles of trade, to perfect a free and open market and to protect investors and the public interest by: (i) prohibiting brokers, dealers and municipal securities dealers from engaging in municipal securities business with issuers if certain political contributions have been made to officials of such issuers; and (ii) requiring brokers, dealers and municipal securities dealers to disclose certain political contributions, as well as other information, to allow public scrutiny of political contributions and the municipal securities business of a broker, dealer or municipal securities dealer.

Okay, so if the dealer has made political contributions to an official of the issuer in the past two years, they may not underwrite any of that issuer's municipal bonds. If the contribution was made by the firm, a municipal finance professional associated with the firm, or any political action committee (PAC) controlled by the firm or any municipal finance professional with the firm, the above prohibition would apply.

Except when it wouldn't. As the MSRB explains in its page-turning prose, "this section shall not prohibit the municipal securities dealer from engaging in municipal securities business with an issuer if the only contributions made by the persons and entities noted above to officials of such issuer within the previous two years were made by municipal finance professionals to officials of such issuer for whom the municipal finance professionals were entitled to vote and which contributions, in total, were not in excess of $250 by any municipal finance professional to each official of such issuer, per election.

So, notice there are two requirements there—first, the municipal finance professional has to be eligible to vote for the official they're contributing to, and the contribution cannot exceed $250.

To make sure everything's on the up and up, member firms have to submit quarterly statements to the MSRB concerning political contributions on Form G-37. For anything other than the little $250 contribution by a municipal finance professional eligible to vote for the official, the MSRB wants the name and title of each official and/or PAC receiving contributions, listed by state, amount of the contribution, and whether it was made by the firm, a municipal finance professional, a non-municipal finance executive, or a PAC controlled by any of those folks. The form also lists which issuers the firm has done underwriting business with in the preceding quarter, listed by state.

Rule G-38. Speaking of Chicago, I remember reading an interesting story in the *Sun-Times* a while back that pointed out how the mayor's brother was paid something like $180,000 a year as a "consultant" for a large Wall Street firm that happened to be the largest underwriter of Chicago municipal bonds. When the press asked the firm exactly what sort of "consulting" the mayor's brother might do for them, they got no answers. Well, that was then—this is now. In fact, if you diligently peruse these MSRB rules, you'll see how they often mention "former rule G-38." In the old days, a firm could use a so-called "consultant" as long as they followed some rather lax rules requiring a written agreement and a little bit of disclosure. Now, check out what the current Rule G-38 thinks about the use of so-called "consultants" . . .

> Prohibited Payments. No municipal securities dealer may provide or agree to provide, directly or indirectly, payment to any person who is not an affiliated person of the municipal securities dealer for a solicitation of municipal securities business on behalf of such municipal securities dealer.

Okay, so what is an "**affiliated person** of the municipal securities dealer"? Here we go:

> The term "affiliated person of the municipal securities dealer" means any person who is a partner, director, officer, employee or registered person of the municipal securities dealer (or, in the case of a bank dealer, any person occupying a similar status or performing similar functions for the bank dealer) or of an affiliated company of the municipal securities dealer.

Hmm. So, I didn't notice an exemption for the mayor's brother in there. Why would the MSRB have a rule such as this? Think how easy it would be for an underwriting firm to "hire" the immediate family of mayors, governors, and other key politicians to act as so-called "consultants" when, in fact, it's just a glorified bribe. If we give the governor's sister-in-law $125,000, she can get us the negotiated underwriting deal on about $25 million of upcoming revenue bonds. To make it look legitimate, we'll hire her as a consultant and let her work from home. As long as she sends in a few emails, maybe even a spreadsheet or two, we got ourselves a "consulting engagement" at about $40,000 an hour to a person who's never had a finance class and can't even balance her own checkbook.

And, it's not just the underwriting firms who might abuse the system. This rule actually protects firms from being basically shaken down by seedy family members of key political figures. "Hey, I hear you'd like to get in on that next big bond issue. Turns out, as the Governor's baby brother, I'm looking for a little, uh, you know, *consulting* work, myself, so maybe we should, you know, talk." At least now they can say that they are precluded from pursuing such a consulting arrangement due to MSRB Rule G-38. Which they would be happy to explain in a darkened parking garage, say, around two am down by the canal?

Rule G-39. Everybody hates **telemarketing** these days it seems. We'll see the FINRA Rule in the final chapter, which is going to mirror this one very closely. Basically, the SROs are stipulating that firms need to be very careful about their telemarketing practices. Callers have to identify the firm they represent and the fact that they are calling about securities investment opportunities. If someone says she isn't interested and asks to be put on the do-not-call list, put her on the do-not-call list and do-not-call her. There is a firm-specific list and a national list, so you have to make sure that your next victim—I mean, prospect—is not on either list. Prospects are not to be called before 8 am or after 9 pm in their time zone.

Rule G-40. This rule just stipulates that firms need to establish an Internet electronic mail account to allow for electronic communications with the MSRB. A Primary Electronic Mail Contact has to be established to serve as the official contact person for purposes of electronic mail communication between the municipal securities dealer and the MSRB. The firm may also establish an Optional Electronic Mail Contact. The firm needs to file a Form G-40 electronically informing the MSRB who these electronic mail contacts are. And the testing committee really needs to find better things to talk about on the Series 7.

> Rule G-41. Every municipal securities dealer shall establish and implement an anti-money laundering compliance program reasonably designed to achieve and monitor ongoing compliance with the requirements of the Bank Secrecy Act ("BSA"), and the regulations thereunder.

Comment: this rule then states that if the firm complies with the anti-money laundering compliance program of FINRA, then they comply with MSRB Rule G-41. We will discuss the FINRA rule in the final chapter, which means we're finally done talking about MSRB rules at this point.

You, however, are just getting started. Please become an expert on MSRB rules for this exam. Visit www.msrb.org and go through their glossary as well as skim all the "General" Rules (G-1 through G-41). That will provide a major edge at the exam center. You may also find it useful to sign up for a two-week subscription to the daily Bond Buyer at www.bondbuyer.com.

PRACTICE

1. **Which of the following are regulated by the MSRB?**

   A. Municipal bond issuers

   B. FINRA

   C. FDIC

   D. Municipal bond dealers

2. **The principal at a municipal securities firm must approve which of the following?**

   A. official statement

   B. preliminary official statement

   C. listings of offerings

   D. abstract of the official statement

3. **To whom must a customer direct a request for a copy of the MSRB rulebook?**

   A. SEC

   B. MSRB

   C. Broker-dealer

   D. FINRA

4. **The principal at a municipal security firm would do all of the following except**

   A. approve each new account

   B. approve the preliminary official statement

   C. approve customer transactions

   D. review the copy of a newspaper advertisement

5. **When a registered representative of a municipal securities firm receives a written complaint from a customer, she should**

   A. ask where the shredder is located

   B. file the complaint promptly with FINRA

   C. take the complaint to her supervisor/branch manager

   D. file the complaint promptly with the MSRB

6. **A municipal securities firm is about to open an account for a registered representative of another municipal securities firm. All of the following actions should be taken by the executing member firm except**

    A. obtain written permission from the employing member

    B. notify the employing member in writing

    C. send duplicate trade confirmations to the employing member

    D. fill out a new account form

7. **When a member firm sells a customer municipal bonds from inventory, it must**

    A. indicate the bond's rating from at least two recognized ratings agencies

    B. take into consideration the total dollar amount of the transaction in order to determine the markup

    C. follow the 5% FINRA guideline

    D. disclose the commission on the trade confirmation

8. **Which of the following indicates a control relationship?**

    A. lead underwriter is a registered voter in the issuing municipality

    B. lead underwriter voted for the mayor of the municipality

    C. mayor of the issuer is on the underwriting firm's board of directors

    D. mayor's wife bought securities from a member of the selling group

9. **All of the following could disqualify a representative from associating with an MSRB member firm except**

    A. the representative was suspended two years earlier from FINRA

    B. the representative was suspended two years earlier from the NYSE

    C. the representative was convicted of felony embezzlement eight years ago

    D. the representative failed his Series 6 twice

10. **Your firm would like to be invited to participate in future syndicate accounts. In order to gain influence with an underwriter, you are permitted to give**

    A. gifts in excess of $100 per month

    B. gifts not to exceed $1000 per donor per year

    C. gifts not to exceed $100 per person per year

    D. reasonable gifts as determined by the compliance officers of the firms involved

ANSWERS

1. **D,** the MSRB only regulates municipal bond dealers. They have no authority over the cities, states, etc., who *issue* municipal bonds.

2. **D,** if the firm alters the official statement (summary, abstract) that document must be approved by a principal.

3. **C,** broker-dealers must provide copies of the MSRB rulebook to customers upon request.

4. **B,** the preliminary official statement is put together by the issuer.

5. **C,** always take written complaints to a principal/supervisor.

6. **A,** *permission* is going too far—notification is all that is required.

7. **B,** municipal bonds are not subject to the 5% guideline. If the firm is selling form inventory, it does not add a commission. It sells at a markup to the customer.

8. **C,** the mayor apparently represents both the issuer and the underwriter.

9. **D,** there is no maximum number of attempts allowed on these exams.

10. **C,** it's not just up to the compliance officers. The gift limit is set by the MSRB.

SUITABILITY

The printout you receive at the testing center will tell you exactly how many options (derivatives) questions you got, but we have to make assumptions on how many questions you got on municipal securities, since they're lumped in with a lot of other topics (rules and regulations, taxation, issuing securities, trading securities, etc.). Still, we expect you to get at least as many questions on municipal securities as you get on options, probably more. Is all this stuff related only to the test world? Not at all. The big broker-dealers do a lot of municipal securities underwriting, so you might actually work the primary market for municipal financing, helping school districts, park boards, and other taxing districts build facilities by raising money through bond sales. Many underwritings are done on a negotiated basis, remember, so schmoozing with convention center boards, park district officials, and city finance department heads is definitely part of the game. Which is why there are MSRB rules that try to prevent a pay-to-play atmosphere in which underwriting business ultimately paid for by taxpayers is granted in exchange for political contributions or payments to political cronies posing as so-called "consultants." But you would never cross that line yourself, of course.

Even if you never participate in a municipal securities underwriting, it's almost certain that some of your customers will invest in municipal securities, either a la carte or through mutual funds. Customers like Michelle Madsen. As we said in The Big Picture: Michelle likes the idea of some tax-free income, so you and she agree to put 25% of her money into general obligation municipal securities issued by Chicago, Cleveland, and New York City. To get a slightly higher yield, you also use some of that 25% to purchase **revenue bonds**, backed only by the revenues on sports stadiums and toll roads, issued by the same municipalities. . . so 25% of Michelle's money is now invested in tax-free municipals.

This implies that Michelle is in a high tax bracket and that when you run those crazy tax-equivalent yield calculations, you keep determining that the tax-free municipal bond gives her more of an after-tax yield compared to corporate or Treasury bonds of similar credit quality and term to maturity. For example, a 5% tax-exempt municipal bond would be equivalent to a taxable corporate or Treasury bond yielding 7.7% if Michelle is in the 35% marginal tax bracket. Therefore, if taxable bonds are offering only 7% when similar tax-exempt municipal securities are yielding 5%, Michelle comes out better with the municipal bond.

But she doesn't hold tax-exempt municipal securities in a Traditional IRA, 401k, or any other tax-deferred account in which withdrawals will be taxed at ordinary income rates someday. Oddly, the only way to get the tax-exempt interest on a municipal bond is to hold the thing in a taxable account.

Well, even though municipal securities is probably the biggest section on the test, the fact is that most people spend more time learning the next chapter, Options. That doesn't mean that Options questions are the hardest ones you'll deal with at the testing center. They just require a lot of effort on the front end. Once they begin to make sense, Options questions actually become some of the easiest questions you'll encounter on your Series 7. So, let me ask you this: have you got, say, 40 hours to kill?

Excellent.

CHAPTER 4

Options

A guy steps into a tavern. After a hard day at the office, he's full of attitude. He plops down at the last open stool and slaps a stack of twenties on the bar, just loud enough to get the bartender's attention. The bartender, an attractive redhead in a pressed, white shirt and green bow tie, looks up from the pitcher of ale she's pouring.

"Just a sec'," she says, afraid to take her eyes off the thick head of foam gathering at the top.

"No hurry," the guy says, although it's clear he's not in the mood to wait.

Bartender finally comes up and takes his order. Bourbon and Pepsi. Not Coke—Coke's for losers. He wants *Pepsi* with his bourbon, okay?

The waitress shrugs and mutters something as she mixes him his drink.

Three guys sitting to his right take the bait.

"You don't like Coke, huh, buddy?" says the dark-haired guy in the denim shirt.

"Nope," the guy says. "Don't like the drink, don't like the stock."

"What, you're a trader?" the blond dude with the big shoulders says, wiping foam from his mustache.

"Just a guy who says Coke is headed where it belongs—down the toilet."

The three friends all raise their chins to the same level.

"That's a bold statement," the dark-haired guy says. "My dad drove a route for Coke twenty years by the way."

"Good for him," the guy says. "Used to be a decent company—that's history, though. I say Coke is a dog, and I'll bet anybody at this bar it won't go above twenty-five bucks a share the rest of the year."

He says the last part loud enough to get everyone's attention. Even the jukebox seems to quiet down at this point.

"Oh yeah?" somebody shouts from a corner booth. "I'll take that bet."

"Me, too!" somebody cries from over by the pool tables.

Pretty soon the guy has over a dozen loud-talking, well-lubed happy hour customers standing in line to bet the cocky newcomer that Coca-Cola common stock will, without a doubt, rise above $25 a share at some point between today (March 1) and the rest of the year.

How do they make this bet?

The guy breaks out a stack of cocktail napkins and on each one he writes the following:

BUY 100 SHARES
COCA-COLA
@25
THRU 3rd Friday December

Anybody who thinks Coca-Cola stock will rise above $25 a share has to pay the guy $300. Guy ends up collecting $300 from 15 different customers, walking out with $4,500 in premiums.

What's his risk as he steps onto the rainy sidewalk outside?

Unlimited.

See, no matter how high Coca-Cola common stock goes between today and the 3rd Friday of December, this guy would have to sell it to any holder of the cocktail napkin for $25 a share. Theoretically, his risk is unlimited, since there's no limit to how much he'd have to pay to get the stock.

What if the stock never makes it above $25 in the next 9 months?

That's what he's hoping! If it never makes it above $25, nobody will ever call him up and ask to buy the stock for $25. In short, he'll walk away with the $4,500 in premiums, laughing at all the suckers at the bar who bet the wrong way.

What the guy sold everybody at the bar was a Coca-Cola Dec 25 call @3. As the writer of that option, he granted any buyer willing to pay $300 the right to buy Coca-Cola stock for $25 per share any time between today and the end of the contract. When would the person holding that option want to use or exercise it?

Only if Coca-Cola were actually worth more than $25 a share. In fact, since they each paid $3 a share for this right, Coca-Cola will have to rise above $28—their breakeven point—before it ever becomes worth the trouble of exercising the call.

Either way, the guy who sold/wrote the calls gets the $4,500 in premiums. If Coke never makes it above $25, he'll never have to lift a finger. Just smile as the calls expire on the third Friday of December.

Think of a call option as a bet between a buyer and a seller. The buyer says the price of a particular stock is going up. The seller disagrees. Rather than argue about it all day, they put their money where their mouths are by buying and selling call options.

The buyer pays the seller a **premium**. Because he pays some money, he gets the right to buy 100 shares of a particular stock for a particular price within a particular time frame. If the buyer has the right to buy the stock, the seller has the obligation to sell the stock to the buyer, if the buyer chooses to exercise his right.

Buyers have rights. Sellers have obligations.

The buyer pays a premium, and he receives the right to buy a particular stock at a particular price. That particular price is known as the **strike price** or **exercise price**.

CALLS

A "MSFT Aug70" **call** gives the call buyer the <u>right</u> <u>to buy MSFT common stock for $70</u> at any time up to the **expiration date** in August. If the stock goes up to $90 before expiration, the call owner could still buy the stock for $70. If MSFT went up to $190, the call owner could still buy it at the strike price of $70. So you can probably see why call buyers make money when the underlying stock goes up in value.

That's right. Call buyers are betting that the stock's market price will go up above the strike price. That's why they're called "bulls." Bull = up. If you hold an Aug 70 call, that means you're "bullish" on the stock and would like to see the underlying stock go UP above 70. How far above?

As far as possible. The higher it goes, the more valuable your call becomes. Wouldn't you love to buy a stock priced at $190 for only $70?

That's what call buyers are hoping to do.

So for a call, just compare the strike price to the stock's market price. Whenever the underlying stock trades above the strike price of the call, the call is said to be **in-the-money**. A MSFT Aug 70 call would be in-the-money as soon as MSFT began to trade above $70 a share. If MSFT were trading at $80 a share, the Aug 70 call would be in-the-money by exactly $10.

PRACTICE

1. **A MSFT Jun 50 call is in-the-money when MSFT trades at which of the following prices?**
   A. $49.00
   B. $50.00
   C. $51.00
   D. $49.05

2. **How far is a MSFT Jan 90 call in-the-money with MSFT trading at $85?**
   A. $5
   B. $90
   C. $87.50
   D. none of the above

3. **How far are the IBM Aug 70 calls in-the-money if IBM trades at $77?**

    A. $77

    B. $7

    C. $0

    D. none of the above

ANSWERS

1. **C,** there is really no way to miss that question. Only one price is above $50.

2. **D,** would you pay $90 for an $85 stock? If so, please give me a call ASAP so we can set up some trading opportunities for you.

3. **B,** take the market price minus the strike price.

THE PREMIUM

The money you pay for your life or auto insurance policy is called a "premium." That's also what we call the money paid for an option; in fact, as you'll see with hedging, options can be used as insurance policies to protect against the risk of owning securities.

How much does an investor have to pay in premiums for an option?

Depends.

Option **premiums** really just represent the probability that a buyer could win a particular bet. If the premium is cheap, it's a long-shot bet. If the premium is expensive, the bet is probably already working in favor of the buyer with time left for things to get even better. As with everything else, you get what you pay for when trading options.

Time and Intrinsic Value

There are only two types of value that an option can possess: **intrinsic value** and **time value**. For calls, intrinsic value is another way of stating how much higher the stock price is compared to the strike price of the call. If the underlying stock is trading at $75, the MSFT Aug 70 call is how far in-the-money? Five dollars. The stock price is above the call's strike price by $5; therefore, the call has intrinsic value of five dollars. That just means that an investor could save $5 by owning that call and using it to buy the underlying stock.

But, if the stock is trading below the strike price, the option is out of the money. With MSFT trading at $65, the Aug 70 call would have absolutely no intrinsic value. So, if there is a premium to be paid for this "out-of-the-money" call, it's only because there's plenty of time for things to improve. In other words, if the option doesn't expire for another three months, speculators might decide that the stock could easily climb more than 5 points in that time period. If so, the market will attach time value to the call. Time value simply means that the option could become more valuable given the amount of time still left before expiration.

Whenever a call is at or out of the money, the premium represents time value. Whenever a call is in-the-money, you can find the time value attached to it by subtracting intrinsic value from the premium. Let's say MSFT is trading at $72, and the Aug 70 calls are selling for a premium of $5. That means the call is in-the-money by $2 ($72 market vs. 70 strike price), yet an investor has to pay a premium of $5. So, where is that extra three dollars coming from?

Time value. If there is still plenty of time on the option, speculators might gladly pay an extra $3, even if the stock is only above the strike price by $2 at this point.

Premium of $5 minus intrinsic value of $2 = time value of $3.

PREMIUM	5
- INTRINSIC VALUE	-2
TIME VALUE	3

So for calls, intrinsic value is a way of stating how much higher the stock price is than the strike price. Time value equals whatever is left in the premium above that number.

What if MSFT were trading at $69 with the MSFT Aug 70 calls @5—how much time value would that represent?

PREMIUM	5
- INTRINSIC VALUE	-0
TIME VALUE	5

All time value. In other words, with the stock trading at only $69, the right to buy it at $70 has NO intrinsic value. (If you disagree, please call us at your earliest convenience; we have some options we'd like to sell you here in friendly Chicago, IL.) In fact, if the stock were trading right at the strike price of 70, there would still be no intrinsic value to the MSFT Aug 70 call, right? If you want to buy a $70 stock for $70, do you need to buy an option?

No.

You only buy the call because you want to end up buying the stock for LESS than it's currently trading, which will happen if the stock moves above the strike price.

So, if you pay $5 for a MSFT Aug 70 call with the stock trading at $70 (at the money) or below (out of the money), you're paying purely for the time value on the option.

BREAKEVEN, MAX GAIN, MAX LOSS

So far we've been talking about the option itself. If we're looking at the options *investor*, we have to remember that he won't begin to profit until the stock starts trading above the strike price by an amount greater than what he paid for the call. If an investor paid $5 for an Aug 70 call, he will only start making money when the stock goes above $75. So, he breaks even (BE) at $75 and begins to profit above $75.

$$\text{Strike Price} + \text{Premium} = \text{Breakeven}$$
$$70 + 5 = 75$$

Another way to remember the **breakeven** on a call is to "Call UP from the Strike Price." If you see a test question about the breakeven for an investor who buys a MSFT Aug 70 call @5, just add the $5 premium to the strike price of 70 to get a BE of $75. Or "call up" from 70 by the premium of five.

What about the guy who sells the MSFT Aug 70 call @5. Where does that investor break even?

Same place:

Strike price plus premium.

That might be tough to accept at first. To be honest, it would be much easier if you did just accept it, but perhaps you're an inquiring mind who just has to know.

So here goes. See, if the stock goes up five bucks to $75, the buyer's 70 call is worth $5 (intrinsic value). He could then sell it for exactly what he paid and be "even." The seller, however, sold the option for $5 and could now (to avoid being exercised) buy it back for its intrinsic value of $5, leaving him even. In other words, the breakeven point is where the buyer and seller "tie." Nobody's made anything, but nobody's lost anything.

And, if you don't quite understand that, just remember that the breakeven on a call is the same for the buyer and the seller: strike price + premium.

The Series 7 will ask you to figure the breakeven point, the maximum gain, and the maximum loss for either the buyer or the seller of the call. Those are all hypothetical situations. See, sometimes you calculate what actually happened for an options investor; sometimes you figure out what *could* happen. If the test is talking about breakeven, maximum gain, or maximum loss, it is asking you to look at what could happen. This is how it works for calls:

Buyers

The maximum loss is the premium they pay. Why? Because buyers can only lose whatever they pay for the option, end of story. There are no "loser fees," in other words.

To find the breakeven point add the premium to the strike price. A MSFT Aug 70 call @5 would have a breakeven point of $75. Strike price of 70 + premium of 5 = 75.

There is no limit to the call buyer's maximum gain. How high can the price of the underlying stock go before expiration?

Nobody knows. That's why the buyer's maximum gain is unlimited. His purchase price is fixed as the "strike price." The sell price is unlimited; it's wherever the market takes the stock, with no limit on the upside.

Sellers

What's the most that the seller can win on this call option?

Sellers can only make the premium. Always. So, the seller's maximum gain is the premium.

The breakeven point is the same for buyers and sellers: strike price + premium, end of story.

The call seller's maximum loss is unlimited. If the buyer has an unlimited maximum gain, what do you suppose the seller's maximum loss is?

That's right, unlimited. His sale price is fixed at the "strike price." His purchase price is wherever the market takes the stock, which could be as high as infinity.

More, even.

We're not saying it will happen; we're saying it could happen.

Remember that whatever the buyer can win, that's what the seller can lose. Whatever the buyer can lose, that's all the seller can win. Buyers and sellers break even at the same place.

• Call BUYER	• Call SELLER
• Max Loss = Premium	• Max Gain = Premium
• Max Gain = Unlimited	• Max Loss = Unlimited
• Breakeven = Strike Price + Premium	• Breakeven = Strike Price + Premium

GAINS AND LOSSES

Before we move forward, let's remember that options go in-the-money or out-of-the-money. People don't do that. People have gains and losses, based on how much they paid for an option versus how much they received for the option. So, terms such as time value, intrinsic value, in-the-money, out-of-the-money, and at-the-money refer only to options. Terms such as gains, losses, and breakeven refer to the options investor. Like this:

THE OPTION	THE INVESTOR
Time value	Gains
Intrinsic value	Losses
In-the-money, out-, at-the-money	Breakeven

The T-Chart

When the exam wants you to tell it whether an investor ends up with a gain or a loss, and exactly how much he or she gained or lost, approach the problem step-by-step. These are essentially bookkeeping questions, where you track everything the investor paid and everything he/she received. This might seem complicated, but luckily you have a friend who is here to help.

Your friend's name is Mr. T-chart. Mr. T-chart wants to help you pass your exam. Say, "Hello, Mr. T-chart."

$ Out	$ In

Mr. T-chart's job is to help you track debits and credits. Whenever you buy or go long, you have a debit (Dr). Whenever you sell or go short, you have a credit (Cr). So debits are for the money going out of the account; credits are for money that comes into the account. If you end up with more money coming in than going out, you have a gain. If you end up with more money out than in, you have a loss. The rest simply involves running the numbers.

So let's start running.

Here's a possible Series 7 question:

An investor with no other positions buys an XYZ Jun 50 call @4 when the underlying instrument upon which the derivative is based is trading at 52. If the stock is trading at $52 at expiration and the investor closes his position for the intrinsic value, what is the investor's gain or loss?

A. $1,000 loss

B. $100 loss

C. $200 gain

D. $200 loss

Whoa! They actually expect people to know that kind of stuff for the Series 7? You betcha. And this is one of the easiest questions they could ask you about options, so let's get on top of this one right now. First of all, draw your T-chart and use whichever labels you prefer: - and +, "$ out" and "$ in", "Dr" and "Cr," whatever works for you:

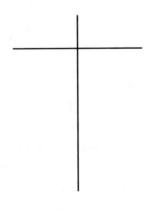

Okay. When the investor buys the call for $4, that's money out, so let's place "4" in the debit column.

The next part looks tricky but really isn't. The phrase "at expiration" means the last day of trading. At this point, all time value has evaporated. Since the option will soon expire, it is only worth the in-the-money amount. The intrinsic value. At expiration, an option either has intrinsic value, or it is worthless. So, what is the intrinsic value of the Jun 50 call when the stock is trading at $52? Two dollars. So, at expiration, the Jun 50 call would be worth exactly $2. In this question the investor is closing his position for the intrinsic value. If he bought to open the contract, he sells it to close. When he sells the call for its intrinsic value of $2, that represents a credit, right? When you buy something, money comes out of your wallet. When you sell something, money comes into your wallet. Same for an options investor.

All right. So, if $4 went OUT of his account, and only $2 came back INTO his account, he ends up with a loss of how much? Two dollars. An option covers 100 shares, so just multiply $2 by 100 to get a total loss of $200.

The answer to the question is "D," a $200 loss.

See? It's really not that hard. You just have to do it step by step. Many students get into trouble by trying to arrive at the answer all at once. Doesn't work that way for options. You have to weed through all the information thrown at you and break the problem down into steps. These options questions might look like math questions, but really they're just testing your ability to organize information. If you need two numbers, they'll be sure and give you five or six. They're testing your ability to separate relevant information from irrelevant, and then sort all the information into neat, usable steps. Just remember the basics, watch out for traps, and let Mr. T-chart sort everything out for you.

Would you like another question?

Let's do one, anyway.

On June 12 June Jorgenson bought an XYZ Jun 50 call @ 3 when XYZ Corporation's common stock was trading at $47. On June 15, June exercises her Jun 50 call when the underlying stock is trading at $55 and immediately sells the stock on the open market. What is June's gain or loss on the Jun 50 call that she purchased on June 12?

A. $300 gain

B. $300 loss

C. $200 gain

D. none of the above

This is a good way for the exam to challenge your ability to separate relevant from irrelevant information. In the above question most of the information is unnecessary and, at best, distracting. It's mostly weeds, so let's grab the only information we need and forget all the rest. The question is just asking you whether June Jorgenson made any money on her Jun 50 call and if so, how much?

So, break out the best weapon in your arsenal, the all-powerful Mr. T-chart. On a separate piece of paper, draw your chart and fill it in with the following numbers.

June Jorgenson paid how much for the call? Three dollars. Place "3" in your debit column.

When she exercises the call, what happens? That's right, she buys the stock at the strike price of $50. So, let's write "50" in the debit column. If she immediately sells the stock on the open market, where the stock is trading at $55, she'll have "55" coming in, right? So, we'll place "55" in the credit column.

What are we left with? $53 went out, $55 came in. Looks like a gain of $2 per share times 100. The answer must be "C" then, a gain of $200.

EXERCISE, TRADE, EXPIRE

Notice how in the first question, the investor bought an option and sold it. That's called trading options, where you'll see terms such as "opening" and "closing." No stock is involved in that case. In the question we just did with June Jorgenson an option was **exercised**. Now stock <u>was</u> involved, which is why the strike price and market price ended up in our T-chart. Sometimes options are exercised; sometimes they are opened and closed; and sometimes they **expire** worthless. So, when figuring gains and losses for questions like the ones above, remember that only three things can happen once an option contract has been opened:

- Exercise
- Close Position
- Expire

If the call goes in-the-money, the investor could choose to exercise it. That means he buys stock at the strike price and sells it immediately at the current market price. If so, you'll be entering both the strike price (Dr) and the market price (Cr) into your T-chart—just make sure you place the numbers in the correct columns. The investor could also close his position for the intrinsic value. To calculate intrinsic value just compare the higher market price to the strike price and place the difference in your T-chart. To close the position, remember that if he bought to open, he sells the option to close. If he sold to open, he buys the option back to close. And, finally, the option could expire worthless—put a zero in the T-chart to signify expiration. The exam questions will give clues as to which of the three events has occurred. Just make sure you read the question carefully so you'll know what the exam expects. In terms of expiration, know that ordinary options expire in 9 months or sooner. There are also long-term options called **LEAPS**, and these have much longer shelf lives—12 to 39 months. So, if you think it's hard to predict where Google common stock will close a week from next Friday, how about buying a LEAPS contract that allows you to predict where it will close 38 months from next Friday

Sounds like a bit of a leap, doesn't it? Because of the extra time on the contracts, LEAPS premiums are much higher than they are on similar ordinary options.

PRACTICE

1. **Joe Schmoe is long an XYZ Dec 50 call @2.50. On the third Friday of December, XYZ is trading @56 and Joe closes the contract for its intrinsic value. What is the result?**

   A. gain of $250

   B. loss of $250

   C. gain of $350

   D. loss of $350

2. **Joe Schmoe buys an ABC Apr 85 call @3.25. With ABC trading @89.50, Joe exercises the call and immediately sells the stock for a**

   A. loss of $125

   B. gain of $125

   C. loss of $50

   D. gain of $450

3. **Joe Schmoe shorts an XYZ Jun 50 call @3.75. With XYZ @51, Joe closes the contract for its intrinsic value, realizing a**

   A. loss of $375

   B. gain of $375

   C. gain of $275

   D. loss of $1,000

ANSWERS

1. **C**, use the T-chart. He pays the premium of $250, so put that in the debit column. When he closes the contract, he sells it, so he takes in the intrinsic value of $6 per share or $600 total. $250 out - $600 in. That's a gain of $350.

2. **B,** use the T-chart again. Step one, he pays $3.25, so put that in the debit column. When he exercises the call he has the "right to buy stock at the Strike Price," so put the strike price in the buy/debit column, too. Now you have $3.25 per share and $85 per share in the debit column. He sells the stock for $89.50, so put that in the credit column. With $88.25 in the debit column and $89.50 in the credit column, he gains the difference of $1.25 or $125 total.

3. **C,** anything "short" goes in the credit column, so put $3.75 per share in the credit column. He buys it back to close, and it's worth exactly $1 per share when he does. He makes the difference between $3.75 and $1 per share, or $275 total.

THE LANGUAGE MAKES IT FUN

It would be a lot easier if we could just refer to the two parties in the options contract as the buyer and the seller. Unfortunately, we have other ways of referring to each. The exam might talk about the buyer of an option, or it might refer to him as being "long the option." Or, maybe he is referred to as the owner or the "holder" of the option.

It's all the same thing.

To sell an option is to write an option. If you sell an option, you are said to be "short" the option.

All means the same thing. Why would they use the word "hold" instead of "buy" or "own"? Think back to our guy in the tavern. When he sold the little cocktail napkins, the buyers were now holding the option in their hands. And, we call the seller the "writer," because, as you remember, our guy in the tavern literally wrote the terms of the contract on each cocktail napkin.

Buyer-holder-owner.

Seller-writer.

Why would we call the buyer "long" and the seller "short"?

Because it blows people's minds and, therefore, makes them confused and us the experts.

Long = buy. Short = sell.

Just because.

BUYER	SELLER
Long	Short
Holder	Writer
Owner	

So far, we've been talking about calls, which give investors the right to buy stock. Let's take a look at **puts** now, which give investors the right to sell stock at the strike price before expiration.

PUTS

If we clipped the following coupon from the newspaper, what would it allow us to do?

```
SELL
100 SHARES
IXR @40
THRU 3rd Friday October
```

That coupon represents an IXR Oct 40 put. As the holder/owner/buyer of this put we have the right to sell IXR stock for $40.

What if IXR is only worth $2?

Awesome! We get to sell the stock for $40 at any time before the end of trading on Friday, October 20, even if it's worth only two bucks on the open market. In fact, even if it's worth zero, we can still sell it for the $40 strike price.

That's how a **put** works. A put buyer gets the right to sell IXR at the strike price before the contract expires. No matter how low IXR goes, the holder of an Oct 40 put has the right to sell 100 shares of IXR for $40 each before the end of trading on the third Friday of October.

Who buys puts? Investors who think a stock is about to drop in price. Bears. Bear = down. (Bulls point UP, like the horns on a Bull. Bears point DOWN, like the claws on a Bear, or just remember "bear down.")

Strange as it seems, as the stock price drops below the strike price, the value of the put goes up.

Think of it like this—if a stock is now at $20, wouldn't you like to sell it to somebody for $40? If you were ready to exercise the put, you could just buy the stock for $20, then immediately sell it to the put writer for $40. That would involve exercising the put. As we saw with calls, though, options investors don't always exercise their options, but, rather, close the positions for their intrinsic value. If they take in more than they spend, they end up with a profit. And if they spend more than they take in, they don't.

For puts, intrinsic value is the amount of money that a put's strike price is above the market price, which is another way of saying that the market price has fallen below the strike price. An October 40 put has how much intrinsic value when the underlying stock trades at $20?

$20. Wouldn't you love to sell something worth only $20 for $40?

Talk about putting it to somebody, huh? The owner of a put profits when he can sell higher than the market price. He needs the stock price to go down, below the strike price. That's when he profits, when the stock is losing value. Sounds illegal, perhaps, but it's not. In fact, it's a beautiful opportunity to make money as a stock loses money.

So puts go in-the-money when the market price of the stock drops below the strike price. And, if you've already noticed that buying puts is very similar to selling stock short, I really like your chances of passing this exam the first time. Not that I'm particularly worried about those who didn't see that. In any case, let's take a second to look at how the two strategies are the same, and how they're different:

Buying a Put	Selling Stock Short
Bearish (profits when stock goes down)	Bearish (profits when stock goes down)
Limited loss (just the premium paid)	UN-limited loss
Less of a capital commitment	More capital, plus margin interest
Loses time value quickly	Stock can drop slowly, still profitable

TIME AND INTRINSIC VALUE

IXR Oct 40 put @5 with IXR trading at $38

PREMIUM	5
- INTRINSIC VALUE	-2
TIME VALUE	3

IXR Oct 40 put @5 with IXR trading at $40

Premium of $5 minus intrinsic value of $0 = time value of $5.

PREMIUM	5
- INTRINSIC VALUE	-0
TIME VALUE	5

So, in the first case, the put has $2 of intrinsic value, since it would allow the buyer to sell the stock for $2 more than it's worth. The premium costs $5, so the additional $3 is time value. In the second case, the put has zero intrinsic value, since nobody needs the right to sell at $40 when the stock is at $40. So, the $5 premium is ALL time value.

PRACTICE

1. **A MSFT Jun 65 put @3 has how much intrinsic value with MSFT @65?**

    A. $3

    B. $2

    C. $65

    D. 0

2.   An IBM Mar 75 put @3 has how much time value with IBM @74?

A. $1

B. $3

C. $2

D.   none of the above

ANSWERS

1.   **D**, the right to sell a $65 stock at $65 has no intrinsic value. The premium represents pure speculation or "time value."

2.   **C**, there is $1 of intrinsic value, since the $74 stock can be sold for $75. The rest of the premium ($2) equals its "time value."

Easier Than They Look

There are exactly two things you can do with stock: buy it, or sell it. How do you make money? By buying low and selling high. When you buy an option, you're hoping to buy the stock low and sell it high, which you can do with either a call or a put. If you buy a call, you're picking your buy price—hopefully, the market price will go above that, so you can buy the stock low (strike price) and sell it high (market price). If you buy a put, you're picking your sell price—hopefully, the market price will go below that, so you can buy the stock low (market price) and sell it high (strike price).

Okay. So you can see why a bearish investor might buy puts.

Why would anyone sell them?

Max Gain, Max Loss, Breakeven

Back to our tavern. It's Monday after that third Friday in December, and our hero is back at the bar buying all the call buyers cheap beer just so they'll stick around long enough for him to rub it in.

Yes, unfortunately, for everyone but the seller/writer of the calls, Coca-Cola only made it to $22, and the calls all expired worthless. So, with the $4,500 still in his pocket, the guy is in a pretty good mood. He's in such a good mood that he can't keep himself from not only trashing Coca-Cola but talking up his favored Pepsi. Pepsi is such an awesome stock, he swears, stirring his bourbon and Pepsi, that it couldn't possibly fall below $70 a share in the next nine months. He's so confident his favorite stock won't fall below $70 that he'll take a bet with anyone who says the stock is a loser. You have to pay him three hundred dollars to make the bet, but it gives you the right to sell him 100 shares of Pepsi for $70, no matter how low it goes in the next nine months. Even if the stock drops to ZERO dollars, you can make him pay you $70 a share.

The 15 losers look at each other and decide the temptation is just too great. They imagine how much fun it will be to see the dude's face when they all make him give them $70 a share for a worthless stock. What if they're wrong? Then, just like before, they lose part or all of their premium. But that's all they can lose, too.

How much can our Pepsi-loving dude make? Same as before—just the premium. That's all the seller of an option can ever make. In fact, if you can remember that any time somebody starts with a credit in their T-chart, that's ALL they can ever make (maximum gain), you will save yourself lots of frustration and probably snag a few more test questions.

How much can he lose on this Pepsi put?

The good news for him as the writer/seller/short dude of a put (as opposed to a call) is that his maximum loss is NOT unlimited. In fact, you won't see the word "unlimited" associated with puts. A stock can only go down to zero, which caps the maximum loss for the seller and the maximum gain for the buyer. If this guy collects $3 a share ($300 total) granting the right to sell him stock at $70 per share, the worst that could happen is that he'd pay $70 for a stock worth zero and would have only collected $3 per share. A maximum loss of $67 per share, and it could only happen if PepsiCo, like, went out of business in the next nine months. Which could never happen, unless it did.

So, like before, the guy lines up the same 15 buyers and takes $300 from each one. He takes out a cocktail napkin for each buyer and writes:

So, after finishing his drink and buying the house another round, the guy walks out with $4,500 and the obligation to buy Pepsi for $70 a share, no matter what it's actually worth at the time. Oh well. He's confident that the stock will remain at $70 or above. If so, those Pepsi puts will end up just as worthless as the Coke calls did.

So, the buyer and seller of a put have the following maximum gain, maximum loss, and and breakeven:

• BUYER	• SELLER
• Max Loss = Premium	• Max Gain = Premium
• BE = SP - Premium	• BE = SP - Premium
• Max Gain = BE down to zero	• Max Loss = BE down to zero

PRACTICE

1. **IBM is trading at $93. Which of the following options would, therefore, command the highest premium?**
   A. IBM Aug 90 call
   B. IBM Oct 90 call
   C. IBM Aug 95 put
   D. IBM Nov 100 put

2. **Which position exposes the investor to the greatest risk?**
   A. Long XYZ Mar 80 call @3
   B. Long XYZ Mar 85 put @4
   C. Short XYZ Mar 80 put @2
   D. Short XYZ Mar 20 put @2

3. **Paula Padilla purchases a put for $300. Three hundred dollars represents**
   A. the price per share
   B. Paula's maximum gain
   C. Paula's maximum loss
   D. Paul's breakeven

4. **An investor buys an ABC Apr 45 put @2.50. With ABC trading @41, he exercises his put for a**
   A. loss of $250
   B. gain of $250

C.   gain of $150

D.   loss of $4,500

5.   **An investor shorts an ABC Apr 45 put @2.50. Which of the following stock prices would prove the most profitable for the put writer?**
   A. $44
   B. $43
   C. $42
   D. $45

ANSWERS

1.   **D,** the option with the most intrinsic value ($7) AND the most time would have to be the most expensive, right?

2.   **C,** the most risk is always on the short/sell/write side of the contract. Which put has a bigger maximum loss? The first one has a max loss of $78, which is much more than the max loss of $18 in choice D.

3.   **C,** Paula, like any put buyer, or ANY buyer of anything, can only lose what she pays.

4.   **C,** he pays $2.50 per share for the put and pays $41 for the stock. $43.50 in the debit column. He has the "right to sell stock at Strike Price," so put the $45 in the credit column. The difference of $1.50 per share or $150 total is his gain.

5.   **D,** when you sell/write/short an option, you want it to expire worthless. Only the price of $45 would cause the option to expire worthless. The other three prices would leave intrinsic value on the contract, which the seller never wants to see at expiration. If you sell something, you want to walk away and never pay another dime. That happens if the thing expires at-the-money or out-of-the money. At which point it's worthless.

So far we've discussed the lion's share of what the exam will focus on, so please make sure you're comfortable with everything we've looked at before worrying about everything that comes next. What comes next can be a bit mind boggling, but, still, I'm confident that most of your exam questions will focus on the concepts we've discussed. We've discussed single options so far, and now we're going to have even more fun discussing multiple options. Multiple options include **straddles** and **spreads**, where the investor is dealing with two options at the same time. If the investor is dealing with two options that don't quite make a straddle or spread, we simply call it a **combination**. For combinations, break out Mr. T and pity the fool who wrote the question.

THE STRADDLE

A **long straddle** means that an investor has bought a call and a put with the same strike price and the same expiration month. Like this: buy 1 XYZ Jun 50 call, sell 1 XYZ Jun 50 put.

Why would somebody want to do a thing like that?

Say an investor sees that the XYZ Corporation is trading at about $50 a share. He hears that a major news release is due out the next day that could cause the stock to shoot way up or way down. In other words, the investor expects volatility; he's just not sure in which direction the stock will move. Not that he's really "sure" it's going to move at all, but the point is, he *thinks* he is and you want to earn commissions filling his orders.

So, he buys or "goes long" a straddle, buying a Jun 50 call and a Jun 50 put. In other words he is "straddling the market" at $50, with one foot on the call side, and one foot on the put side. Right? He's standing on both sides of the 50-yard line to use a football analogy. As long as the stock advances in a big way, in either direction, he's happy. His risk is that the stock won't move. Remember that calls go in-the-money when the stock price goes above the strike price, and puts go in-the-money when the stock price goes below the strike price. One way or the other, this investor is convinced he'll make some money. One option will expire; the other one will go in-the-money.

He hopes.

Of course, he has to buy two options, which is why he has a "total premium." If he buys a Jun 50 call @3 and a Jun 50 put @2, he has a total premium of $5. Like any other options buyer, if he starts with a debit (money out), he has to recover that amount just to break even. In other words, if the call goes in-the-money by $5, he breaks even; if the put goes in-the-money by $5, he breaks even there. If you ever see two breakeven points in a test question, they must be talking about a straddle. In this case the breakeven points for the buyer are $45 and $55.

SP + Both Premiums *and* SP - Both Premiums

Let's find the maximum gain and loss for the buyer of this straddle. The buyer can lose the total premium of five. We've already established the two breakeven points—45 and 55. And, since the buyer holds a call, his maximum gain is unlimited.

Easy stuff. Let's try a tougher question then:

An investor anticipating volatility goes long an XRQ Oct 60 call @4 and an XRQ Oct 60 put @3. If XRQ is trading @54 at expiration and the investor closes both positions for their intrinsic value, what will be his gain or loss?

A. $700 loss

B. $700 gain

C. $100 loss

D.   not enough information provided in the question

Okay, let's break out the T-chart and attack this question.

Ready? The investor bought two options, so he has two premiums in the debit column. On a separate piece of paper let's place "4" and "3" in debit, then. Now we need to find the intrinsic value for each position. If XRQ is trading at $54, what's the right to buy it at $60 worth?

Zero. So the call he bought at $4 could be sold back for zero. Write "0" under credit.

If XRQ is trading at $54, what's the right to sell it at $60 worth?

Right, six dollars. So we put "6" under credit.

Run the numbers, and we see that $700 went out, and $600 came back in. The answer is "C, a $100 loss."

$ Out	$ In
$4	0
$3	$6

If you use a T-chart, note that you can either use the per-share amounts (4, 3, 6), or you can use the per-contract amounts of $400, $300, and $600 above. Just pick the method that works and stay consistent.

Now let's try a question for the seller of a straddle:

An investor who anticipates stability shorts a Jun 90 call @4 and a Jun 90 put @3.5. He closes both positions for their intrinsic value at expiration, when the underlying stock is trading at $111. What is the investor's gain or loss?

A. $5 loss

B. $13.5 loss

C. $13.5 gain

D. $1 loss on the put, not too sure about the call

No need to panic. The above question is no harder than the question before it, especially when we use the awesome power of our T-chart.

The investor places the "4" and the "3.5" under credit, right, since he sold both options?

Okay. Now we have to find the intrinsic values because that's what he pays when he buys back both positions to close out the straddle. So, if the stock is at $111, what's the right to sell it at $90 worth at expiration?

Nothing. Place "0" under debit, then, since that's what he'd pay to buy back the put.

If the stock is at $111, what's the right to purchase it at $90 worth?

Right, $21. That's a debit, because he'd have to buy back the call to close the position.

Add it all up, and we see that $7.5 came in, with $21 going out. Looks like a loss of about $13.5, doesn't it? The answer, then, is "B, $13.5 loss."

Why would somebody sell/write a straddle? Well, like all sellers of options, they simply think the buyer is wrong and can't wait to watch him lose. They're like White Sox fans here in Chicago. It makes no difference what the Sox do on any given day; as long as the Cubs lose, they're happy. I've never experienced the joy of rooting *against* someone, but if you're drawn to that sort of thing, you could become a White Sox fan and laugh at the Cub fans when the north-siders lose. Or, you could write options and laugh at the buyers when they expire. The test will say that the writer of a straddle expects stability or a lack of volatility. True. But take it a little farther—they aren't necessarily expecting both options to expire worthless—that kind of hope-against-all-odds stuff is for rookies or fools sitting at their computer screens in their boxer shorts. The writer of a straddle simply feels that the two premiums collected are much greater than the stock is likely to move. Take in $5 a share and maybe pay out just $2 or $3 when the stock moves up or down by less than the buyer imagined. Sell enough contracts, and you could get rich writing straddles.

Or lose all your money really fast. What is the maximum loss to the writer of a straddle?

Take your time. That's okay, I'll put on a pot of coffee.

Got it? That's right, the maximum potential loss to the writer of a straddle is *unlimited*. Why? He's writing a naked call, and the stock could hypothetically go up forever. If the stock drops, the loss won't be as bad, but that, by definition, is not the *maximum* loss. Remember that the maximum loss is always the absolute worst-case scenario. What's the best-case scenario for the writer of a straddle? As always, sellers can only make the premiums collected. So the guy in the practice question above can make $750 per contract, since that's what he's collecting. And, I hope he's not expecting to make all that, since it could only happen if the stock ended up trading at exactly the strike price of $90. Any higher or lower, and he'll have to pay some money to close out either the call or the put. As long as he pays out less than $7.50 per share ($750 per contract) he wins.

His breakeven, as always, is the same as the buyer's. Strike price plus both premiums *and* strike price minus both premiums. I suppose we could call "both premiums" "total premiums." Lord knows the exam will probably find still more names to use, no matter how creative we get. Since I know my readers pretty darned well, I'm going to assume that now would be a real good time to present a chart. Here you are:

POSITION	EXAMPLE	STRATEGY	MAX GAIN	MAX LOSS	BREAKEVEN
LONG STRADDLE	Long ABC Oct 50 call Long ABC Oct 50 put	Expects volatility in either direction	unlimited	total premiums	SP +and– total premiums
SHORT STRADDLE	Short ABC Dec 50 call Short ABC Dec 50 put	Expects stability	total premiums	unlimited	SP +and– total premiums

PRACTICE

1. **If an investor expects the price of a stock to remain unchanged over the next three months, which of the following would be most suitable?**

    A.   long straddle

    B.   short call

    C.   short put

    D.   short straddle

2. **What are the breakeven points for the following position? :**
    Long XYZ Oct 50 call @1.50
    Long XYZ Oct 50 put @1.50

    I. $53

    II. $51.50

    III. $47

    IV. $48.50

    A.   I, IV

    B.   I, III

    C.   II, III

    D.   II, IV

3. **An investor is long an Oct 40 call and short an Oct 35 put. This position is best described as a(an)**

    A. long straddle

    B. debit spread

    C. combination

    D. iron butterfly

4. **An investor buys an ABC Apr 45 call @1 and writes an ABC Apr 45 put @2. At expiration, ABC trades at $46. Therefore the investor realizes a**

    A. loss of $300

    B. gain of $300

    C. gain of $200

    D. loss of $500

5. **If an investor anticipates volatility but does not have an opinion on market direction, he would most likely**

    A. sell a straddle

    B. buy a call

    C. buy a straddle

    D. buy a put

ANSWERS

1. **D**, never buy an option if you think the market will remain unchanged. If you buy an option, you need the market to change in a hurry. Otherwise, the time value comes off your option and you sell it for less than you paid, if it doesn't expire on you. If you think the market will be flat, sell an option. Why sell just one, though, when you can sell both a call and a put with the same strike price? Short straddle. 75

2. **B,** for a straddle, enter the premiums in the T-chart. Add and subtract their total from the strike price. $50 plus $3 and $50 minus $3. It's really nothing new from single calls and single puts. Just that we're doing both at the same time.

3. **C,** if it's not quite a straddle and not quite a spread, just call it a combination.

4.   **C,** he breaks even on the call, and the put expires, letting him pocket the premium.

5.   **C,** volatility assumed, direction unknown. Buy/long a straddle.

SPREADS

A **spread** is another type of multiple options position the exam will expect you to work with. With a straddle, we saw that the investor bought two options or sold two options. The two options were different types. One was a call, the other a put. For spreads, the **type** of option is the same. We're either talking about two calls for a **call spread**, or two puts for a put spread. To open a call spread, an investor buys a call and sells a call. To open a put spread, an investor buys a put and sells a put. Usually the expiration months are the same. For example, the investor buys a Jan 50 call and sells a Jan 60 call.

That would be a call spread. A debit call spread to be exact.

DEBIT SPREAD

Why is it a **debit spread**?

Well, which call is worth more, the Jan 50 or the Jan 60? In other words, would somebody rather buy a stock at $50 or at $60?

Fifty dollars. Calls with lower strike prices are always worth more money. So even before we attach premiums, do you suppose this investor has more money coming in or going out of his T-chart?

Well, the Jan 50 call is worth more—did he buy or sell it?

He bought it. So he paid more for the Jan 50 call than he received for selling the Jan 60 call. We call this a debit call spread because the investor starts out with a debit. And, like any options investor who starts with a debit, the debit represents the investor's maximum loss.

Okay, let's say the investor went long the Jan 50 call @5 and shorted the Jan 60 call @3. Go ahead and enter that in a T-chart. We place "5" in the debit column, since that's what he paid for the Jan 50 call. We place "3" in the credit column, since that's what he received for selling the Jan 60 call. He starts with a net debit of $2, so his maximum loss is $2.

What's his maximum gain?

This part is easy. What's the difference between the two strike prices?

Jan	60 call
Jan	50 call

Ten.

So just take ten and subtract the loss of two.

10 minus 2 = 8.

So, his maximum gain is $8. That's one of the great things about spreads: the max gain and max loss will always add up to the difference between the two strike prices.

Max gain + Max loss = Strike price difference

So, if the max loss is 2, the max gain is 8 when the difference between strike prices is 10. If the max gain is 7, the max loss is 3, and so on. You'll never see the word "unlimited" associated with spreads, because the max gain and max loss are always going to be known numbers that add up to the difference between the two strike prices.

Breakevens for spreads are even easier. For call spreads, just add the net premium of $2 to the lower strike price. The lower strike price is $50. Add 2 to get $52. That's where the investor would break even.

So, how does the investor who establishes a debit call spread make money?

When both options go in-the-money, becoming much more valuable.

If the stock goes up to $70 a share, how much is the right to buy it at $60 worth? $10.

Long Jun 50 call

Short Jun 60 call @3 (now worth) $10

What's the right to buy it at $50 worth?
$20.

Long Jun 50 call @5 (now worth) $20

Short Jun 60 call @3 (now worth) $10

So the option he bought for $5 he could sell back for $20. And the option he sold for $3, he could buy back for $10. If he did that, he'd have a total of $15 going out, and $23 coming in. Looks like he just made his maximum gain of $8, right? 23 in vs. 15 out = a gain of $8. Great. And where did he make his maximum gain? When both options went in-the-money, meaning they were "exercisable." When we started, the difference between the two premiums was $2. When the options went in-the-money, the difference widened to $10. For a **debit spread**, the investor wants the difference in premiums to WIDEN and/or wants both options to be EXERCISED. Just like so many Americans have allowed themselves to widen and are in dire need of exercise.

Debit = widen and exercise.

You have to know that for the test.

It might help to remember that "d-e-b-i-t" has five letters, as does the word "w-i-d-e-n."

Also, if you look at the investor's position, you can see why he'd love to see both options exercised:

Long Jun 50 call

Short Jun 60 call

Looking at the position, we see that he's obligated to sell stock at $60, but if so, that means he has the right to buy it for $50. Buy for $50, sell for $60. Not a bad thing. So, he can make a maximum of that $10 difference, minus what his initial debit is.

CREDIT SPREAD

To make the debit spread a **credit spread**, all we'd have to do is switch the words "buy" and "sell" so that our investor sells the Jan 50 call @5 and buys the Jan 60 call @3. If he did that, he'd start out with a net credit of $2. As always, if the investor starts with a credit, that credit represents his maximum gain. So, his maximum gain is 2. Gee, the difference in strike prices is still 10, right? 10 - 2 = 8, right?

So the investor's maximum loss is $8.

Buyers and sellers break even at the same place, so the credit spread also breaks even at the lower strike price plus the net premium. Call UP from the lower strike price by the net premium to get $52 as the breakeven point.

Now, if the underlying stock were at $40 at expiration, how would the investor fare?

Well, if the stock is trading at $40, what's the right to buy it at $50 worth?

Zero.

What's the right to buy it at $60 worth?

Zero.

As Billy Preston sang years ago, "nothing from nothing leaves nothing." A premium of zero means the options have expired worthless, and the difference between zero and zero is zero. When we started, the premiums were $3 and $5, exactly two dollars apart. Now how far apart are they?

Not at all.

Their difference has narrowed, and they have expired. Credit spread investors want the difference between premiums to narrow, and the options to expire worthless. Narrow and expire. Might help to remember that "n-a-r-r-o-w" has six letters, just like the word "c-r-e-d-i-t."

And, if you look at his position, you see that he is obligated to sell at $50 and has the right to buy at $60. Buying at $60 to sell at $50 is the worst that can happen, which is why he can lose that $10 difference, minus what he starts with as a credit.

BULL AND BEAR SPREADS

What if the exam asked you to identify the two spreads as either "Bull" or "Bear?"

Easy. Just use the following acronym:

B
U
L
L
S

Which stands for "Because U are Long the Lower Strike." If you are long the lower strike, then you are a bull. If not, you're a bear.

So, the following spreads are all BULL spreads, because "u" are long the lower strike:

Long MSFT Oct 50 call @4

Short MSFT Oct 60 call @1

Long IBM Mar 45 put @4

Short IBM Mar 50 put @7

Notice this "BULL" thing works for both call and put spreads. If you're long the lower strike price number (50 vs. 60, 45 vs. 50), you're a BULL. Which is why the following would be BEAR spreads:

Short MSFT Oct 50 call @4

Long MSFT Oct 60 call @1

Short IBM Mar 45 put @4

Long IBM Mar 50 put @7

PUT SPREADS

Put spreads work exactly like call spreads. An investor buys a put and sells a put. If he spends more than he takes in, he has a debit put spread. If he takes in more than he spends, he has a credit put spread. For example:

An investor buys an Apr 50 put and sells an Apr 40 put. The investor will profit if which of the following events occur:

I. difference in premiums narrows

II. difference in premiums widens

III. the puts expire worthless

IV. the puts go in-the-money

A. I, III

B. I, IV

C. II, III

D. II, IV

Okay, this almost looks like a difficult problem. You might even think the test forgot to include some necessary information.

It didn't. Although we don't see any premiums attached to the puts, we still know which one is worth more money. Would you rather sell your computer for $300 or $100? Three hundred, right? So the right to sell something at a higher price is always worth more than the right to sell it at a lower price. Puts with higher strike prices are worth more money.

So the Apr 50 put is worth more than the Apr 40 put. Which one did the investor buy? The more expensive put. So, he starts with a debit.

We can now answer the question. Debit = widen and exercise. You don't see the word "exercise" in choice "IV"?

That's okay. Only options that are in-the-money can be exercised. So the correct choices are "II" and "IV." The answer is "D."

His position gives him the obligation to buy at $40, but if that occurs, he can sell the stock for $50. Which is why his maximum gain would be that $10 difference minus the debit he starts with.

One way the exam likes to make test-takers sweat is by asking options questions that do not even provide the premiums. That's okay. We don't always need the premiums in order to answer the questions. Let's say the exam asked you the following:

An investor with no other positions is long a Jun 50 call and short a Jun 60 call. This investor will profit if:

I.   difference in premiums narrows

II. difference in premiums widens

III. both options expire worthless

IV. both options are exercised

A.   I, III

B.   I, IV

C.   II, IV

D.   II, III

Step one, which option has more value?

Long 1 Jun 50 Call

Short 1 Jun 60 Call

Look at the right side to complete step one. A "call" is the "right to buy," so would you rather buy a stock at $50 or at $60?

$50, right? So let's put a plus-sign by the more valuable option, like this:

Long 1 Jun 50 Call+

Short 1 Jun 60 Call

Step two, did the investor buy or sell the more valuable option? The investor went "long," which means he bought the more expensive option. So, he starts with a DEBIT.

Step three, what do debit spreads want? Debit spreads want two things: widen, exercise. So the answer to this seemingly tough question is "C," widen-exercise.

PRACTICE

1. **All of the following positions represent spreads except**

    A.   Long 10 XYZ Oct 50 calls, short 10 XYZ Oct 60 calls

    B.   Long XYZ Oct 50 call, short XYZ Oct 40 put

    C.   Long XYZ Nov 30 call, short XYZ Nov 40 call

    D.   Long XYZ Nov 70 put, short XYZ Nov 60 put

2. **Which of the following positions is BULLish?**

    A. Short XYZ Dec 20 put, long XYZ Dec 30 put

    B. Short XYZ Jan 40 call, long XYZ Jan 30 call

    C. Buy DFZ Sep 90 put, write DFZ Sep 80 put

    D. Hold XYZ Oct 30 call, write XYZ Oct 20 call

3. **What does an investor with the following position need in order to profit?**
   Long XYZ Oct 40 call
   Short XYZ Oct 50 call

    I.   difference in strike prices narrows

    II.   difference in premiums widens

    III. both options expire

    IV.   both options go in-the-money/are exercised

    A. I, III

    B. I, IV

    C. II, III

    D. II, IV

4. **What does an investor with the following position need in order to profit?**
   Long XYZ Oct 40 put
   Short XYZ Oct 50 put

    I.   difference in premiums narrows

    II.   difference in premiums widens

    III. both options expire

    IV.   both options go in-the-money/are exercised

    A. I, III

    B. I, IV

    C. II, III

    D. II, IV

5. **What does an investor with the following position need in order to profit?**
Short XYZ Oct 40 call
Long XYZ Oct 50 call

I. difference in premiums narrows

II. difference in premiums widens

III. both options expire

IV. both options go in-the-money/are exercised

A. I, III

B. I, IV

C. II, III

D. II, IV

6. **What does an investor with the following position need in order to profit?**
Long XYZ Oct 60 put
Short XYZ Oct 50 put

I. difference in premiums narrows

II. difference in premiums widens

III. both options expire

IV. both options go in-the-money/are exercised

A. I, III

B. I, IV

C. II, III

D. II, IV

ANSWERS

1. **B**, a spread is two calls or two puts. One is long, the other short.

2. **B,** go to the lower strike price. If they're long, they're a bull. If not, they're a bear.

3. **D,** it's a debit spread, since he bought the more valuable call.

4. **A,** it's a credit spread, since she sold the more valuable put.

5.   **A,** it's a credit spread, since she sold the more valuable call.

6.   **D,** it's a debit spread, since he bought the more valuable put.

MORE JARGON

There are still other ways to refer to spreads. Rather than explain them in detail, I'm going to opt for the handy-dandy table format:

EXAMPLE	DESCRIPTION	NAME(S)
Long Jun 50 call Short Jun 60 call	Same expiration, different strike PRICE	Price spread, vertical spread
Long Jun 50 call Short Aug 50 call	Same strike price, different expiration	Time spread, calendar spread, horizontal spread
Long Jun 50 call Short Aug 40 call	Different strike price, different expiration	Diagonal spread

If the exam really wanted to make you sweat, it could use several different terms at once. For example, the following position can be referred to as a bear call spread, a credit call spread, a price spread, and/or a vertical spread:

Long XYZ Jun 50 call

Short XYZ Jun 40 call

COMBINATIONS

This is a straddle:

Long 1 XYZ Jun 50 call

Long 1 XYZ Jun 50 put

Notice how EVERYthing is the same except for the "type" of option. One is a call, the other a put. The same is true of a short straddle:

Short 1 XYZ Jun 50 call

Short 1 XYZ Jun 50 put

The investor buys a call and a put with the same strike price and expiration, or he sells a call and a put with the same strike price and expiration.

This, on the other hand, is a s-p-r-e-a-d:

Long 1 XYZ Jun 50 call

Short 1 XYZ Jun 40 call

Now, the only thing that is the *same* is the type—they BOTH have to be calls, or they both have to be puts. The investor always buys one option and sells the other. Something is always different about the two calls, or the two puts—different strike price, different expiration month, or both.

A spread could also look like this:

Long 1 XYZ Jun 50 call

Short 1 XYZ Aug 50 call

That's a horizontal/time/calendar spread in which the Aug 50 call is worth more than the June 50 call.

So, what if the test gives you a position that is not quite a straddle, and not quite a spread? Identify it as a **combination**. For example, take a look at the following and tell me whether it's a straddle or a spread:

Long 1 XYZ Jun 50 call

Short 1 XYZ Jun 45 put

It can't be a straddle, because he's buying one option and selling the other—not to mention that the strike prices are not the same. It can't be a spread, because they're not both calls or puts. Remember, they call them *call* spreads and *put* spreads for a reason. So, this position is neither a straddle nor a spread. Instead, we call it a "combination." In the "real world" there are many crazy names for multiple options positions, but to avoid confusing you I refuse to even mention gut strikes, strangles, iron butterflies, condors, or any of that nonsense. Luckily, the test apparently lumps many of the multiple options positions that aren't straddles or basic spreads under the heading of "combination." Chances are, you will only have to identify the position as a combination. If you have to calculate a gain or loss, use the T-chart and figure out the intrinsic value of the two options based on the stock price. For example, in the position above, what happens if XYZ trades for $52 at expiration? The Jun 50 call would be worth $2, while the Jun 45 put would expire worthless. Or, if XYZ trades for $42, the Jun 50 call expires worthless, and the Jun 45 put is worth $3.

Another example of a combination would look like this:

Long 1 XYZ Jun 50 call

Long 1 XYZ Jun 45 put

Can't be a spread because he's buying two options, and they're not even the same type of option. It's almost a straddle, though almost never counts in this sport. Some folks might call it a "poor man's straddle" because one of these options is out-of-the-money and, therefore, cheaper than buying two options with the same strike price. Right? If the stock is at $50 right now, the

Jun 50 calls and the Jun 50 puts are at-the-money and trade with lots of time value. The Jun 45 put would be pretty far out-of-the-money and, therefore, cheaper. Is this more thought than you cared to put into options? Me too. Oh well, as I was saying, this position is not a long straddle. The test might call it a "long combination," which is almost a straddle except that the strike prices are different. If the test says that the Jun 50 call trades @3 and the Jun 45 put @1, you could figure the breakeven by adding the total premium ($4) to 50 and subtracting the total premium from 45. The two breakeven points, then, would be $54 or $41. Notice how going the poor man's route requires the poor man to hope for some extreme volatility on the stock. It either has to go up to 54 or way down to 41, just to break even.

HEDGING

If you buy stock, you're betting that it's going up. If it doesn't go up, or—worse—if it goes down, you lose. If you sell a stock short, you're betting that it's going down. If it goes up, you lose. Maybe the problem with both strategies, then, is that the investor is betting all one way. What he could do, instead, is hedge his bet. To **hedge** a stock position means to "bet the other way, too." If you bet your buddy that the Atlanta Falcons will win the Super Bowl this year, you can also bet another buddy that they won't. To "hedge your bets" you could bet $100 that the Falcons would win and $45 that they won't. This way, you can't have a total loss, since the Falcons will either win or lose the game. Unfortunately, you also can't win as much, right? If the Falcons win, you coulda'/shoulda' made $100, but you'll have to give the other buddy $45 of it now. But, this way if the Falcons do not win the Super Bowl, at least you get $45 from the second buddy, losing only $55 total, while you could have lost $100 with just one bet in one direction.

The word "hedge" is based on the way people grow hedges to establish the boundaries on their property. Your property is your stock—with a hedge, you can establish the boundaries in terms of what you're willing to lose. Notice how hedging questions *always* involve a stock position. Without a stock position, there is nothing to hedge.

HEDGING LONG POSITIONS

Let's say one of your favorite stocks looks like it's about to do a belly flop. What should you do about it? Sell the stock? Yes. You could sell the stock, but that's a drastic measure, especially when it's also possible that the stock will rally, and you'd sure hate to miss out if it did. If you've ever taken a 50% profit on a stock, only to watch it go up 300% from there, you know exactly what I'm talking about.

So, instead of taking a drastic measure, maybe you could buy an option that names a selling price for your stock. Let's see, which option gives an investor the right to sell stock at a particular price?

A put. So, if you thought one of your stocks might drop sharply, you could buy a put, giving you the right to sell your stock at the put's strike price, regardless of how low it actually goes.

Protection

It's like a homeowner's insurance policy. If you own a home, you buy insurance against fire. Doesn't mean you're hoping your house burns down, but, if it does, aren't you glad you paid your premium? Buying puts against stock you own is a form of insurance. Insuring your downside, you might say. In Series Sevenland we call it "protection."

A question might look like this:

Vito Spadafora purchases 100 shares of QSTX for $50 a share. Mr. Spadafora is bullish on QSTX for the long-term but is nervous about a possible downturn. To hedge his risk and get the best protection, which of the following strategies would you recommend?

A. sell a call

B. buy a call

C. sell a put

D. buy a put

Okay, first of all, when we say "hedge," all we mean is "bet the other way." If an investor buys stock, he is bullish, or betting the price will go up. To hedge, he'd have to take a bearish position, betting that the stock might go down. There are two "bearish" positions he can take in order to bet the other way or "hedge." He could sell a call, but if the test wanted you to recommend that strategy, the question would have said something about "increasing income" or "increasing yield."

And this one doesn't. This one gives you the key phrase:

and get the best protection

Whenever you see the word "protection," remember that the investor has to BUY an option. If an investor is long stock, he would buy (or go "long") a put for protection.

Max Gain, Loss, Breakeven

Let's see how the protection might work for Mr. Spadafora. Let's say he bought that stock for $50 and paid $3 for an Oct 45 put. That Oct 45 put gives him the right to sell the stock for $45, regardless of how low the stock actually drops. Downside insurance for a premium of $3. With a "deductible" of how much? $5 per share (buy stock at $50; right to sell for a loss of only $5 per share). It really is a $500 deductible insurance policy good through the third Friday of October. Just like a car owner, who can handle the first $500, after that, damaged or destroyed property is passed off to the other side of the contract, who probably isn't too happy about having to cut a check but hey that's life.

When the test asks you about the investor's breakeven point, be careful. It is NOT "strike price minus premium." That only works for a single put option—if there is a stock position, the investor does not want the stock to drop. Just like the homeowner who pays a premium to insure his house, this investor would rather not have to use the insurance. Right? If you have to use your insurance, something bad just happened. It's a lot better because of the insurance, but your car or house is now totaled, just as your stock could be wiped out in the stock market equivalent of a tropical storm or hurricane. The insurance just gives somebody the ability to sleep at night, knowing that he can replace his property for a fair price should calamity strike.

So, what he wants is for his stock to go UP. And, since he paid $3 to protect his $50 stock, how much ground does the stock have to gain before he breaks even?

Exactly. It has to go up to $53. Remember, he doesn't want to use this put; he's just hedging his risk, buying temporary portfolio insurance. Insuring his downside. He paid three for the put; the stock has to make three bucks a share before he breaks even.

So, the investor breaks even at the stock cost plus the price of the premium.

Long 100 shares QSTX @50

Long 1 QSTX Oct 45 put @3

Might be easier to just use a T-chart. Put the price of the stock and the price of the put in the T-chart, and you'll see why the breakeven becomes 53. Wouldn't the stock have to rise to $53, so we could put that number in the credit column and make the T-chart "even"? You can always find the breakeven on a hedged position just by entering the stock price and the premium on the correct side of the T-chart. If it's a buy or a "long" position, place that number on the debit side. If it's a sell or a "short" position, place that number on the credit side. Then just ask yourself what number would make both sides equal.

What's the maximum gain for this investor, who owns stock and a put to protect his downside?

Well, how high could his stock rise? It's unlimited, right? So his maximum gain is still unlimited.

What about his maximum loss?

Easy. When he bought the stock at $50, what was the most he could have lost?

All of it—fifty bucks. If the stock went to zero, he would have had no protection. But, in the question he has purchased a sale price of $45 by purchasing the Oct 45 put. If that stock collapses to zero now, he can sell it for $45. Looking at his T-chart, we would place "45" in the credit column, since that's the amount of money he would get for selling his stock at the strike price.

So, what's his maximum loss? Well, under the worst scenario $53 went out, $45 came back in. The most this investor could lose is $8 per share, or a total of $800.

He's not happy about losing $800, but he's probably giddy over not losing $5000.

That's what we mean by "protection." If my basement floods next summer, ruining the furnace, washer, dryer and water heater, I have to absorb the first $1,000 (my deductible) and then State Farm would cover the rest of the damage up to a maximum of $5,000. Only costs me a premium of $85 a year to be able to sleep even when I hear the thunder a few miles away. Will I be happy as I wade through the mess in my bathrobe and soggy slippers? No. But I'll be a lot happier than any of my neighbors who chose to take on all the risk themselves, even if they did save a few hundred bucks on premiums. I could have reduced the deductible to $500, just like a stock investor could purchase a put with a strike price closer to his purchase price, but in both cases the premium would be . . . higher.

And you were afraid options might turn out to be dull. Hah!

Increasing Overall Return

So, Mr. Spadafora paid for protection. However, the question might have looked like this:

Barbara Bullbear purchases 100 shares of QSTX for $50 a share. Ms. Bullbear is bullish on QSTX for the long-term but is nervous about a possible downturn. To hedge her risk and increase income, which of the following strategies would you recommend?

A. sell a call

B. buy a call

C. sell a put

D. buy a put

Well, as we saw, you don't increase your income by buying a put. When you buy something, money comes out of your wallet. In this case, Barbara Bullbear has to sell an option. What's the only bearish option she could sell?

A call. Call sellers are bearish. Since Barbara already owns the stock, this would be a **covered call**. Let's say she bought the stock at $50, then writes a Sep 60 call at $3. If the stock shoots up to the moon, what would happen? Ms. Bullbear would be forced to honor her obligation to sell the stock at the strike price of $60. Well, she only paid $50 for the stock, so she just made ten bucks there. And, she took in $3 for writing the call. So, she made $13, which represents her maximum gain.

Max gain = (stock cost vs. strike price) + premium

Her maximum loss is much larger than the investor who bought the put in the preceding question. In this case Ms. Bullbear has not purchased a sale price for her stock. All she did was take in a premium of $3. That is the extent of her downside insurance. She paid $50 for the stock and took in $3 for the call. So, when the stock falls to $47 she has "broken even." And, if you prefer to use the T-chart, place the 50 that she paid for the stock in the debit column and the 3 that she received for selling the call in the credit column. What number would balance both sides? 47.

Now that Ms. Bullbear has broken even at $47, what's to prevent her from losing everything from that point down to zero?

Right, nothing at all. So $47 is her maximum loss. Breakeven down to zero.

Notice the difference between Long Stock–Long Put and Long Stock–Short Call. When an investor goes long stock–long a put, she leaves her upside totally unimpeded. Her maximum gain remains "unlimited." And, her maximum loss is usually much smaller than the writer of the **covered call**. Only problem is she has to pay some money. Long Stock–Short a Call investors get limited downside protection and also cap their upside. But, they also get to take in some money.

Just depends on what they want to do, which is why the exam will give you the clue.

Okay, so that's half of it. In both cases so far the investor started out long the stock. The exam could also ask you what an investor who is short stock should do in order to hedge his risk.

HEDGING SHORT POSITIONS

The trouble with short sellers is that they turn everything upside down. Since they sell something they'll eventually have to buy back, they're hoping the stock's price goes . . . down. Short sellers have heard all about "buy low–sell high." They just prefer to do it the other way around: Sell High. Buy back Low. So if an investor sells a stock short for $50, what's his risk?

That the stock could go above $50. Remember, he still has to buy this stock back, and he definitely doesn't want to buy it back for more than he first sold it for. Which option gives an investor the right to buy stock at the strike price?

Calls.

Protection

If this investor wants protection, he'll have to buy a call.

The test question could look like this:

An investor shorts 100 shares of ABC at $50. In order to get the best protection against a possible increase in price, which of the following strategies would you recommend?

A. buy a put

B. sell a put

C. sell a call

D. buy a call

The answer is "D," buy a call. Again the word "protection" means the investor has to buy an option. If he is concerned about his purchase price, he buys a call, which gives him the right to purchase stock at a strike price. Maybe he's willing to risk having to repurchase the stock at $55 but not a penny higher. Therefore, he buys a Sep 55 call for $2. Using our T-chart, where would we plug in the numbers?

Max Gain, Loss, Breakeven

Well, if he shorts (sells) the stock at $50, that's a credit, right? So, let's place $50 in the credit column. He paid $2 for the call, so that's "2" in the debit column.

Okay, where does this investor break even, then? $48, right? 50 in the credit column, 2 in the debit column, so 48 would make things even.

And if you prefer to analyze the position, start with step one—look at the stock position. He shorted the stock at $50, which means he wants it to go down. If he paid $2 for the option, doesn't the stock have to work his way by exactly $2 before he breaks even?

You bet it does. So when the stock goes down to $48, this investor breaks even. Is there anything to prevent him from making everything from that point down to zero? No. So $48 is his maximum gain, too. Breakeven down to zero.

What about his maximum loss? Well, let's say disaster strikes. The stock skyrockets to $120 a share. Does he have to buy it back at that price in order to "cover his short"? No. At what price could he buy back the stock?

The strike price of $55. That was the protection he bought. And, if he exercised his call, his T-chart would show that $50 came in when he sold short, while $57 came out (when he bought the stock at $55 after buying the call at $2). That's a loss, but it's only a loss of $7, which ain't too bad considering how risky it is to sell a security short.

So if a short seller needs protection, he buys a call. It's the same thing as long stock–long a put, only upside down.

Increasing Overall Return

Now, let's look at the mirror image of the covered call. Say this same short seller wanted to hedge his bet while also increasing income. If he starts out bearish, he hedges with a bullish position. To increase income, he'll have to sell a position. Only bullish position he can sell is a put. So, he goes short stock–short a put.

If he shorts the stock at $50 and sells a Jun 40 put @ 3, where would he break even? Well, short sellers want to see the stock go down. However, since he took in $3, he can let his stock position work against him by $3. This investor breaks even at $53.

Right? That's what selling an option does for a hedger; it offsets the potential loss by the amount of premium collected. And, your T-chart tells you that $50 came in when he sold the stock short, plus $3 that came in for selling the put. So 53 is the breakeven point.

What's the most he can lose? Well, how high could the stock jump? Unlimited. Does he have the right to buy the stock back at a particular price? No. So, his maximum loss is unlimited.

Like the covered call writer, he has also capped his "upside" or his maximum gain. His upside is down, remember. When the stock goes down to zero, does he get to buy it back at zero?

Not after writing that put option. The investor who bought the Jun 40 put is going to make him buy the stock for $40. Now the investor realizes his maximum gain. Shorted at $50, bought it back at $40. That's a gain of $10. He also took in $3 for writing the put. So, his maximum gain is $13. Stock price vs. Strike price + Premium.

PRACTICE

1. **An investor long stock would receive best protection if she**

    A. bought calls

    B. sold puts

    C. sold calls

    D. bought puts

2. **An investor long stock wants to hedge and increase income. What should he do?**

    A. buy puts

    B. sell puts

    C. sell calls

    D. buy calls

3. **An investor short stock would get best protection by**

    A. buying puts

    B. selling calls

    C. selling puts

    D. buying calls

4. **An investor short stock wants to hedge and increase yield. She should**
    A. buy calls

    B. buy puts

    C. sell puts

    D. sell calls

5. **What is the maximum loss for the following position?**
    Long 100 shares XYZ @60
    Long 1 XYZ Apr 60 put at 3.35

    Answer: _____

6. **What is the maximum loss for the following position?**
    Long 100 shares XYZ @60
    Short 1 XYZ Apr 75 call at 3.85

    Answer: _____

7. **What is the maximum loss for the following position?**
    Short 100 shares XYZ @60
    Long 1 XYZ Apr 60 call at 3.75

    Answer: _____

8. **What is the maximum loss for the following position?**
    Short 100 shares XYZ @60
    Short 1 XYZ Apr 40 put at 3.20

    Answer: _____

ANSWERS

1. **D,** to "protect," you buy an option. If you're long stock, you hedge by betting the other way—buy a put.

2. **C,** to increase income/yield, you have to sell an option. Its "arrow" has to be pointed the other way. Long stock—sell a call.

3. **D,** to "protect," you buy an option. If you're short stock, you hedge by betting the other way—buy a call.

4. **C,** to increase income/yield you have to sell an option. Its "arrow" has to be pointed the other way. Short stock—short a put.

5. **$335,** if you buy at 60 and can sell at 60, you can't lose on the stock. You can only lose the premium in this case. It's like a "zero deductible" insurance policy.

6. **$5,615,** if that stock goes to zero, the only thing working in the investor's favor is the premium. If you lose $6,000 on a stock but took in $385, you lost your maximum of $5,615.

7. **$375,** if you sell and buy stock at the same price, you lose zero. You can only lose the premium in this case.

8. **Infinity,** you're short stock. If it goes up, you have no "right to buy." You would only be forced to buy if the stock went your way—down. If it goes up, it just keeps a-goin' up to infinity. More even.

NON-EQUITY OPTIONS

The bad news is there's still more that the exam wants you to know about options.

The good news is it's all based on the stuff we've discussed so far. It's just that these options cover things other than stock. These options cover stock indexes, Treasury prices, Treasury yields, and foreign currencies. The numbers will look a little different, but they still come down to calls and puts, which can be bought or sold.

Simple. Just like the other options we've discussed.

Sort of.

The options we just covered are called **equity options**, by the way, because the underlying instrument is an equity security, common stock. The options we'll cover now are not based on common stock. That's why they're called **non-equity options**.

First, let's introduce two more terms in case your head isn't quite full at this point: **American style** and **European style**. An American style option can be traded throughout each trading day and even exercised before the contract expires. That means that if you hold a MSFT May 30 call, you can exercise it in April, March, February, etc., if the common stock rises above $30 per share. All equity options are American style. They can be exercised early if the buyer wants to do that. Non-equity options, however, can be either American style or European style. A European style option can be *traded* throughout each trading day, but it can only be exercised *at expiration*. Many students remember it this way: "A is for <u>anytime</u>" and "E is for expiration only. WW, people. Whatever works.</u>

INDEX OPTIONS

The first type of non-equity option, the **index option**, derives its value from various stock indexes. You're probably familiar with the S&P 500 index. Did you know you could buy puts or calls on the value of that index? Sure. The symbol for that option, by the way, is SPX. Here's how it works. The S&P 500 index is a big basket of stocks hand-picked by the experts at Standard & Poor's. These 500 stocks represent the most important in the overall market. By tracking these 500 stocks, we can track the overall movement of the market. So, when investors buy or write calls on the SPX, they're betting on the point value of the S&P 500, which gets figured every trading day.

The buyer of an SPX call says the point value of the S&P 500 is going up in the short-term, while the writer says the point value of the index is not. Exercise involves the delivery of cash rather than stock. That's right, if the buyer exercises the call, the seller would pay the buyer cash. How much cash? The intrinsic value or "in-the-money" amount.

Let's say the call has a strike price of 500. If the holder exercises the call when the index is at 520, the call would be in-the-money 20 points, so the seller would have to send the buyer 20 points' worth of cash. How much is a point worth?

$100. Twenty points times $100 each equals a total of $2,000 that the seller would deliver to the buyer. And he would deliver it by the next business day. No need for a T + 3 thing, since no stock is changing hands, only money.

All you have to do with index options is multiply everything by 100. The real point value of a "500" call is "50,000." 520 is really 52,000, which is why the seller pays the buyer $2,000 in cash upon exercise.

The premium is also multiplied by $100.

Here's an example:

Long 1 SPX Jun 500 call @ 8

In this case, the investor has a strike price of 500 (or 50,000), for which he pays 8 X $100, or $800. In order to break even, the SPX option would have to go in-the-money by 8 points. That would be 508.

Here's your practice question:

An investor buys 1 SPX Mar 600 call when the index is @590 for a premium of 9. What is the investor's gain or loss if he exercises the option when the SPX closes at 612?

    A. $100 loss

    B. $300 loss

    C. $300 gain

    D. $100 gain

As always, let's get serious and break out Mr. T-chart.

The investor buys the call for $9, so let's place "9" in the debit column. How much money comes in upon exercise? Well, how much is the call in-the-money? That's right, by 12 points, so let's place "12" under credit. That's what the writer would pay the buyer upon exercise. Total it up, and we see that $9 went out, while $12 came in, for a net gain of $3. Multiply $3 by 100 to get our answer, which is "C, $300 gain."

Remember that the index is valued as of the end of the trading day, so it would be real dangerous to exercise your index option in the morning. If your call went deep in-the-money at 11 o'clock in the morning, you would still need to wait and see where the index closes. The S&P and other indexes often go up for part of the day before finishing in negative territory. I highly doubt the test would go there, but the OCC Disclosure Document does indicate that if you exercise an option before the index has been officially totaled up for the day, and that option ends up going *out of the money*, you would have to pay the *seller* the amount that your option is out of the money.

And then drop and give everybody at the exchange 200 push-ups.

So, here are some key things to remember about index options:

- exercise involves delivery of cash, not stock
- index is valued at the end of the trading day
- multiplier is $100

The S & P 500 and the Dow Jones Industrial Average are **broad-based indexes**. That means they don't focus on a particular industry. Even if the Dow is only 30 stocks, the companies are so diverse as to include Microsoft, Home Depot, Johnson & Johnson, Walmart, American Express, and Disney. Then again, these stocks are all issued by huge companies with a huge number of shares outstanding—the way those shares trade is pretty close to what the whole market is doing that day.

A **narrow-based index** is pretty easy to spot, since it names the industry it focuses on. A "transportation index" would be narrow based, as would a "utilities index." Therefore, the exam could get nasty. It knows you know the "Dow" is a broad-based index. But that's true only of the Dow Jones Industrial Average. There is also the Dow Jones Utilities Index and the Dow Jones Transportation index, both of which are obviously following just one sector at a time and are, therefore, narrow-based indexes.

So, if an investor is heavily weighted in a particular industry sector, he needs to hedge his risk with the associated narrow-based index options. If the guy is overweighted in pharmaceutical stocks, he needs to find a pharmaceutical index that mirrors his own portfolio—the broad-based indexes won't help him. On the other hand, an investor exposed to the broad market would hedge with broad-based index options. Index options are frequently used to hedge stock portfolios. They can also, of course, be used to speculate that the market, or a market sector, is about to go up, down, or stay the same.

Capped Index Options

Hypothetically, there is no limit to how high an index can rise, and that's what makes selling calls on an index mighty dangerous. Therefore, **capped index options** may be available. If we set the cap interval at 30 points, as soon as the buyer's option goes up that high, it's automatically exercised. That way the seller knows what his maximum loss is and, therefore, the buyer knows his maximum gain. If it's an SPX Aug 400 call, it would be automatically exercised as soon as the S&P 500 hit 430 or higher, assuming the cap interval is 30. If it's an OEX (S&P 100) Aug 400 put, it would be automatically exercised if the S&P 100 hit 370 or lower.

Very similar to the way commodities will stop trading once they "hit the limit" for the day. To prevent the price of cocoa or corn from spiraling out of control, once the price moves a certain amount, the contract stops trading. The movement is "capped."

Now, if you're a former CBOE trader, you may be wondering what the heck I'm smoking with these "capped index options" that don't even exist. If they don't "exist," why are they still explained in the OCC Disclosure Document called "Characteristics and Risks of Standardized Options" that all new options customers must receive?

Hmm. Like it matters.

INTEREST RATE OPTIONS

My opinion is that the Series 7 is likely to ask several questions on **interest rate options**, because it gives the exam yet another excuse to talk about the relationship of bond prices and interest rates/yields. Since they can throw in that sometimes confusing concept along with some funky options few people have ever worked with, they can make you sweat.

And, like any elite fraternity, FINRA is looking forward to making all of you pledges sweat.

Don't let them.

Price-Based Bond Options

Okay, remember the "bond see-saw" from Debt Securities? It might have seemed a bit overwhelming, but all it does is provide a model of what happens when interest rates go up or down. Remember that on a bond the borrower/issuer prints a stated interest rate. Since that rate is fixed, whenever prevailing interest rates change, they change in relation to that fixed rate on the bond. So, the price or value of the bond changes accordingly, as does its yield. You don't have to do a lot of calculations for the exam, and the exam doesn't ask that you become an expert on debt securities. You just have to master the relationships of interest rates, bond prices, and bond yields.

If interest rates go up, bond prices go down. If interest rates go down, bond prices go up.

And yields move with interest rates.

So, who might be looking at a **price-based option**? Well, the manager of a bond portfolio would be concerned about the price of bonds. What would cause the price to go down? Right, rising interest rates. So, her risk is that interest rates will go up and push down the value of the bonds in her portfolio.

How could she hedge her risk?

Well, with options, there are always two ways to hedge. If you want protection, you buy an option. If you want to increase income, you sell an option. If the portfolio manager is bullish on bond prices, she'd have to take an appropriate bearish position to hedge. Bears buy puts and sell calls; therefore, the portfolio manager could hedge against rising interest rates by selling calls to increase income or buying puts for protection.

That's the concept behind it.

Let's look at an example.

First of all, the bond prices we're talking about are U.S. Government T-bonds. The amount of T-bonds covered in one option contract is $100,000. In other words, a lot of money. The strike price of a T-bond call is the percent of par at which a call buyer could purchase $100,000 worth of T-bonds. So, you might see something like this on your exam:

Aug '21 T-bond Sep 101 call @1.16

The "Aug '21" means that this series of T-bonds matures in August of 2021. Upon exercise, the buyer of this call could purchase $100,000 of T-bonds for 101% (the 101 strike price) of par, or $101,000, before it expires in September. Obviously, this investor would be bullish on the price of T-bonds. Must believe that interest rates are going which way?

That's right, down.

How much does he pay for this option?

Well, the "1" stands for 1% of par. 1% of $100,000 is $1,000, so the investor would pay $1,000 and some change. Remember, these are Treasury bonds, so the point-16 isn't a decimal. It's the number of 32nds. 16/32 times $1,000 gives us $500, so the premium is $1,500. If the price of T-bonds shoots up, this call goes in-the-money, just like any other call.

Back to our portfolio manager. Would she buy the above call?

No. She's only worried about the price of bonds falling. She might sell this call, to profit from her risk side. Or, she could buy a T-bond put if she wanted "protection" from her risk side. Her only hedge would be a bearish position on the price of T-bonds. If she wants to "increase income," she sells a call. If she wants "protection," she buys a put.

Guess what?

Yield-Based Options

She could also use **yield-based options**. The portfolio manager is only concerned that interest rates might go up and push down the price of her bonds, right? Well, if interest rates go up, what else goes up?

That's right, yields. Yields go the same way interest rates go.

It's prices that move the other way.

The portfolio's enemy is higher yields. So, if she can't beat them, why not join them?

That's the concept behind hedging. If the other side is about to win, you bet on the other side a while. You profit from a temporary situation that otherwise would have left you with a loss.

So if the portfolio manager is bearish on prices, she's bullish on yields. Therefore, if she wants protection, she can either buy a price-based put, or buy a yield-based call. Right? If bond prices are going down, bond yields are going up. To increase income, she could sell price-based calls, or sell yield-based puts. Both options would work for her if she's right about interest rates rising.

Remember, it's all based on simple math. You just have to break things down and organize them properly. Never forget the premise:

If rates are up, prices are down, and yields are up.

If rates are down, prices are up, and yields are down.

Let's say our portfolio manager wanted protection. Her hedge is a bearish position on bond prices, which is the same thing as a bullish position on bond yields. So, she might protect against a drop in price by betting on the corresponding increase in yields. Maybe she goes long the following position:

Long 1 Mar 75 call @1

That "75" is notation for a yield of "7.5%." In basis points, it would be expressed as 750 basis points. The premium of $1 needs to be multiplied by $100, which is what the investor would pay to buy this yield-based call. Remember, no Treasury securities are delivered upon exercise—just cash.

So if she pays $100 for the call, she has to make $100 to break even. She needs to make 10 basis points. Each basis point is worth $10, so she needs to make ten of them to break even. That would happen if yields go to 7.6%, or 760 basis points. Upon exercise, she would receive 10 basis points times $10 each, or $100 and break even because 760 basis points is 10 points above her strike price of 750 basis points.

Simple, right?

Finally, yield-based options are "European style," meaning they can be traded at any time but only exercised on the expiration date. Of course, if you get that question, your odds of making it through the rest of the day alive are statistically zero.

FOREIGN CURRENCY OPTIONS

When you're talking about currency exchange rates, this is what it all comes down to:
If one goes up, the other goes down.

That's what you have to remember about foreign currencies. If the U.S. dollar's value goes up, the other currency you're measuring it against goes down, and vice versa. The easy way to attack these questions is to remember the following mnemonic:

E
P
I
C

American Exporters buy Puts. American Importers buy Calls. And, of course they sell the opposite positions.

Let's say we make computers in Keokuk, Iowa. We import hard-drives from a company in Canada that insists on being paid in Canadian dollars within 60 days of issuing the purchasing order. Okay, so we have to pay a certain number of Canadian dollars for those hard-drives 60 days from now, eh?

What's our risk, eh?

That the value of the Canadian dollar could skyrocket, forcing us to use more of our hard-earned American dollars to buy enough Canadian dollars to satisfy the contract terms. Let's say the contract price is $1 million Canadian dollars. How much is that in U.S. dollars?

Depends on the exchange rate, which is why importers and exporters constantly have to hedge their foreign currency risks with **foreign currency options**. If the exchange rate between the U.S. dollar and the Canadian dollar is as follows:

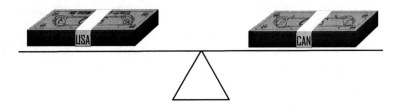

Then, we will be paying $1 million American for those hard drives. That's because we'll take one of our dollars and turn it into one of their C$, one million times.

But if the exchange rate should tip, and suddenly their C$ has shot up in value against our weak dollar, it's going to take more of our dollars to buy their C$.

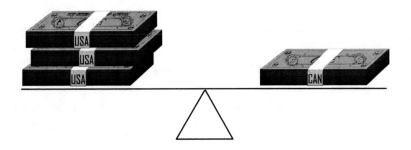

If our dollar weakens against a strengthened Canadian dollar, it might take three of our dollars to convert to just one C$. We have to pay 1 million C$, regardless of the exchange rate. If it takes three of ours to get one of theirs, how much are we really going to pay for those hard drives? That's right, *three* million dollars. Hope you bought a call on the Canadian dollar, eh? A call gives you the right to buy C$ at a strike price, even if the underlying C$ goes up in value.

That's why American "Importers buy Calls."

Now, let's say that we're going to export our assembled personal computers to a retailer in Japan, who is going to pay us in yen in 60 days. We agree that they'll pay us 100 million yen for a certain number of our computers. What's that amount going to be worth to us in 60 days? That's our risk, right?

If the exchange rate right now is 100 yen = 1 U.S. dollar, then we actually receive U.S.

$1,000,000, when we take their 100 million yen and divide them into 1 million piles of a hundred. Not too bad. But what if our dollar strengthens against their suddenly weakened yen? Suddenly, their currency is so weak that it takes not 100, but 1 million of theirs to equal one of ours? Yikes! Sixty days later they send us that box of 100 million yen, and we put 1 million yen in each pile, ending up with 100 piles, each one worth exactly a dollar.

In other words, we get $100 when we were expecting $1,000,000!

Oops. Hope somebody bought a put on the yen. Or at least sold a call to offset the major loss we just took on the exchange rate. You can now answer some of the exam questions, just by understanding the risks, and remembering that American Exporters buy Puts, American Importers buy Calls.

E
P
I
C

What if the test question is talking about a *foreign* company? Then the wise guy who wrote the question is clearly hazing you—big deal? He wants to turn it all around on you—turn the EPIC thing around on him and keep moving. Or, think through the story problem. If the Japanese country is going to receive American dollars in 90 days, they worry that its value could drop. Since there are no puts on the U.S. dollar, they simply buy calls on the yen. Remember, if one currency is dropping, by definition, the other one is rising. Seriously. No, just take it on faith—you have enough to think about.

The size of each foreign currency option varies by currency, so the exam should give you the amount in the question.

If you see something like:

Canadian dollar (50,000) Oct 75 call at .60

This is what it breaks down to. The "50,000" refers to the number of Canadian dollars covered by this one contract. The "75" is the strike price. Remember that these options are quoted in terms of American cents. So, the "75" means that each Canadian dollar can be purchased at the strike price of 75 American cents, regardless of how high the Canadian dollar goes relative to the American dollar. The ".60" means "six-tenths of one penny," so it just has to be multiplied by the penny (.01) to get .006. This contract covers 50,000 Canadian dollars, so multiply that by .006 to get $300.

$300 is what an investor would pay for this call.

If this investor were concerned that the Canadian dollar might skyrocket, chances are he's an importer who has to pay for a product in Canadian dollars. This call would tell him the maximum cost of the contract, and could also be used to profit, should his risk materialize.

One more pain-in-the-neck: Japanese yen are quoted in hundredths of American cents. So, if you're given a premium of ".52," you'll have to put two zeroes in front of it (.0052) before multiplying by the penny (.01).

Physically settled foreign currency options are no longer traded—instead retail investors settle all foreign currency options in U.S. dollars. This eliminates the risks associated with physical delivery of currency (which has to be stored, could be lost or destroyed). The exam might expect you to know that **"New World Currency Option"** contracts (WCOs) have been created to better fit the needs of retail investors by making the contracts smaller and having them settled in U.S. dollars. The exam might expect you to know all kinds of neat stuff.

OPTIONS ACCOUNTS

Now that we've sufficiently analyzed how options work, let's talk about further testable points. If you're a little worn out from all the hedging, straddling, and spreading that's been going on in the previous pages, you may find this stuff refreshingly simple.

First, there is nothing stopping you from obtaining the "OCC Disclosure Document" yourself. In fact, you can get one by visiting www.cboe.com or www.optionsclearing.com and poking around a bit. It's called "Characteristics and Risks of Standardized Options," and it's basically the prospectus used by the OCC (which *issues* the options) to comply with the Securities Act of 1933. When a customer opens an options account, he/she must receive this disclosure brochure, which explains how options work and discloses all the many risks involved. At what point must the customer receive this document? No later than when the account is approved for trading by the registered options principal.

OPENING THE ACCOUNT

Here are the steps for opening an options account:

1. Registered rep discusses suitability issues with the customer: net worth, experience with options, types of options trades anticipated.
2. Registered rep sends OCC Disclosure Brochure either now or *at the time the* Options Principal approves the account. Registered rep also indicates when the **OCC Disclosure Brochure** called "Characteristics and Risks of Standardized Options" was sent/delivered to customer.
3. As soon as the Options Principal approves account, first options trade may occur.
4. Customer has 15 days to return a signed options *agreement*. If not, only closing transactions would be allowed—no new positions.

POSITION LIMITS

The customer's signature on the options agreement means that he/she understands the devastating risks associated with options but chooses to trade anyway, and that he/she will abide by the rules of the options exchange. For example, they won't take the electronic quotes they get and re-sell them on a website. They won't write calls and then flee the country whenever they go deep in-the-money. And, they'll abide by any position limits that may be in place. A **position limit** means that a customer, or a group of customers "acting in concert," will not try to corner the market, so to speak. If a standardized option has a position limit of 25,000, that means that an investor can have no more than 25,000 bull or bear positions in that option. If he buys 20,000 calls, there are 5,000 bull positions left. He could, therefore, buy 20,000 calls and write 5,000 puts. I'm talking about "per class" here, meaning all MSFT calls or puts, not all MSFT Oct 30 calls, which would be a series. He could also establish 25,000 bear positions (buy puts, sell calls) on a particular underlying security. The OCC provides a list of options and their position limits, and I hope to sell enough Pass the 7™ books someday to have to check myself before establishing 25,000 contracts, but that's another issue. I don't think the exam would ask for some hard-and-fast number for the maximum number of contracts. That number is subject to constant revision; a better test question would have you remember which two positions are bullish, and which two are bearish. Also know that the same numbers used for position limits are used for exercise limits. That means that if the option is subject to a limit of 25,000, that number represents the maximum number of open bull or bear positions you can have at one time and also the maximum number of contracts you can exercise over five consecutive business days. As I write these fascinating words, the maximum number for position/exercise limits is 250,000, so if you ever find yourself hampered by that constraint, chances are it's time for a new hobby.

As I read through the exciting rules of the CBOE this afternoon, I see that if a customer has 200 or more positions on the same side of the market, the firm has to notify the exchange of that fact. That seems a bit too arcane even for a Series 7 question, but you never know considering how infrequently the test writers have been getting out lately.

REGISTRATION OF REPRESENTATIVES, PRINCIPALS

As CBOE Rule 9.2 declares:

> No member organization shall be approved to transact options business with the public until those persons associated with it who are designated as Options Principals have been approved by and registered with the Exchange. Persons engaged in the management of the member organization's business pertaining to option contracts shall be designated as Registered Options and Security Futures Principals (ROSFPs).

The Options Principal approves the new accounts and approves all the orders executed at the firm to ensure suitability. We just mentioned the principal when we said that the customer must receive the OCC disclosure document either at or before the time that the "principal" approves the account. The CBOE says that the Options Principal "shall be responsible to review and to propose appropriate action to secure the member organization's compliance with securities laws and regulations and Exchange rules in respect of its options business."

CBOE Rule 9.21 states:

> All advertisements and sales literature issued by a member pertaining to options shall be approved in advance by the Options Principal or designee. Copies thereof, together with the names of the persons who prepared the material, the names of the persons who approved the material and, in the case of sales literature, the source of any recommendations contained therein, shall be retained by the member or member organization and be kept at an easily accessible place for examination by the Exchange for a period of three years.

So, as with NYSE, FINRA, and MSRB firms, options firms who belong to the CBOE keep their communications on file three years, two years readily accessible, and they approve communications before they go out. Of course, it isn't feasible to pre-approve all correspondence between the firm and customers, so correspondence has to be regularly monitored. But, when the communications are called advertising or sales literature, the stuff needs to be both pre-approved and filed internally.

This next rule says it quite clearly, so let's just copy and paste:

> Exchange Approval Required for Options Advertisements. In addition to the approval required by paragraph (b) of this Rule, every advertisement of a member pertaining to options shall be submitted to the Department of Compliance of the Exchange at least ten days prior to use (or such shorter period as the Department may allow in particular instances) for approval and, if changed or expressly disapproved by the Exchange, shall be withheld from circulation until any changes specified by the Exchange have been made or, in the event of disapproval, until the advertisement or has been resubmitted for, and has received, Exchange approval.

So, advertising on options is subject to some pretty uptight scrutiny. I mean, FINRA firms usually just file communications internally. Even when they have to file sales literature/advertising pertaining to investment companies with FINRA, it's within 10 days *after* first use in most cases. Oh well. If you thought people could lose money in mutual funds, you wouldn't believe how fast they can piss it away on puts and calls. So, the regulators figure let's go ahead and see what you intend to tell your customers *before* they start shorting spreads and straddling things they have no business straddling, shall we?

Options communications now use the same definition of "correspondence" used by FINRA. That definition states that if the written communication goes to one or more existing customers (regardless of #), it is considered correspondence, which is not subject to pre-approval by an options principal. Also, if the written communication is sent to fewer than 25 prospects in a 30-day period, it meets the definition of correspondence rather than sales literature, which requires pre-approval. So, the exam could easily throw a question at you about written communications being sent electronically to 30 prospects in a 25-day period; if so, that would be sales literature, since it goes to 25 or more prospects. The exam plans to take what you've learned/memorized and put some very weird spin on it, like a really good ping-pong player. Remember that "written communications" are now much broader than the printed page; they include email, fax, and text/instant messaging.

FINRA rules require all firms to ensure that their options communications to retail investors include a statement that supporting documentation for any claims (including the benefits or performance of certain programs or the options expertise of sales persons) will be supplied upon request. As FINRA states:

> Communications regarding standardized options that are used prior to delivery of the Options Disclosure Document must be limited to general descriptions of the options being discussed. This text, however, may contain a brief description of options, including a statement that identifies the registered clearing agency for options (OCC, for example) and a brief description of the general attributes and method of operation of the exchanges on which such options are traded, including a discussion of how an option is priced. Additionally, such options communications must contain contact

information for obtaining a copy of the ODD and must not contain recommendations or past or projected performance figures, including annualized rates of return, or names of specific securities.

So, before the disclosure document is delivered, the material presented to customers cannot look anything like a recommendation for a particular options strategy or position. General information on options, the OCC, the options exchanges, etc., is fine at this point.

The Options Disclosure Document can be delivered electronically—what the exam might call "by hyperlink" just to haze you—if the customer has already consented to receiving communications electronically from the firm. For example, many customers receive trade confirmations, proxy statements, and Account Statement account statements electronically from their broker dealer. These customers, if they started an options account, could also receive the Options Disclosure Document (Characteristics and Risks of Standardized Options) electronically.

Since we're having such a good time with this, let me make just one more point about all this stuff straight from the mouth of the CBOE:

Any statement referring to the potential opportunities or advantages presented by options shall be balanced by a statement of the corresponding risks. The risk statement shall reflect the same degree of specificity as the statement of opportunities, and broad generalities should be avoided. Thus, a statement such as "with options, an investor has an opportunity to earn profits while limiting his risk of loss," should be balanced by a statement such as "of course, an options investor may lose the entire amount committed to options in a relatively short period of time."

Just so we're clear—that's copied and pasted text from the CBOE. Didn't want you to think I had inserted a little humor into that with the "of course, an options investor may lose the entire amount committed to options in a relatively short period of time." Of course, I would have rewritten it to say something like, "With options, an investor always earns fantastic profits while limiting his risk except in those situations where he loses all his money really fast."

Good to see the CBOE has a sense of humor, though. Must be a Chicago thing.

Anyway, I lied when I said "one more point." I really wanted to make *three* more points but was afraid you'd stop reading if I gave it to you straight. The CBOE also offers the following comments about communications for options firms:

- It shall not be suggested that options are suitable for all investors.
- Statements suggesting the certain availability of a secondary market for options shall not be made.

That last bullet point means that sometimes you go to close out 10,000 contracts and, guess what, nobody wants to buy your stupid little 10,000 contracts. Unless you'd be interested in reducing your asking price by, say, 75%?

Now, here's another case where we have to keep the terms "sales literature" and "advertising" separate in our minds. Advertising may not "use recommendations or past or projected **performance**

figures, including annualized rates of return." What's the big deal? Well, I, myself once got lucky and bought some PCLN calls for $35 which I quickly sold for $285. What kind of profit percentage is that? There were three contracts since I'm such a big-time player, which means my little T-chart had $855 in-the-money-in column versus $105 in-the-money-out column. That's a profit of over 700%. Since it took just one week to do it, let's annualize that by multiplying by 52—your firm can now put out a TV ad that says, "One of our customers recently made an annualized return of 36,400% without even knowing what the heck he was doing!"

No, the truth is, I only made about $100 when all the transactions were totaled out for the year, which is just a little bit contradictory of the "36,400% annualized return" the advertisement is using to sucker people into trading options.

Then there's sales literature, and this stuff can use projected performance figures, as long as a whole bunch of disclosure is provided including the fact that the quoted rate of return is not a certainty, all related costs of commissions, margin, etc., are disclosed, and all risks are disclosed. Also, the sales literature must state that supporting documentation for the impressive claims and scenarios being laid out will be provided upon request. And, as with the advertisements of an investment adviser, if the firm is touting the performance of their awesome recommendations/trades, the period quoted should cover at least the most recent 12-month period.

A test question may expect you to know that a Registered Options and Security Futures Principal (ROSFP) must review the following:

- Advertising, sales literature
- General prospecting letters
- Seminar transcripts
- Allocation of exercise notices

Not long ago, there were distinct types of Options Principals (CROPs and SROPs), but now the regulators refer to an options principal as a "Registered Options and Security Futures Principal (ROSFP)." In case there isn't already enough stuff for you to memorize for the exam.

TAXATION

As we said earlier, three things can happen once an option contract is opened:

- Expire
- Close
- Exercise

Let's see about the tax implications for each event.

EXPIRE

Ordinary options expire within 9 months, so all gains and losses will be short-term. A short-term gain, as discussed in the Taxation chapter, is taxed at the investor's ordinary income rate. If you buy an option this November, and it expires next April, you lose all the money you paid. It will be a short-term loss that you claim for April's tax year, which is when you "realize" the loss.

Back in November you were just putting down some money. Only in April of next year will you actually realize your loss. If you sell an option in November that expires the following April, you'll realize a **short-term capital gain** in April.

CLOSE

Options can be closed for either a gain or a loss. The investor/trader doesn't realize the gain or loss until both sides of the T-chart have been completed, so to speak. If she buys an option in November for $300 and sells it to close next April for $400, she realizes a $100 **short-term capital gain** in April. Obviously, if she only sells it for $200, she would realize a $100 **short-term capital loss** in April.

Same thing for the seller of the option. When they close with a "closing purchase," they realize either a short-term capital gain or loss when they do so.

EXERCISE

It gets trickier when an option is exercised. The options premium will affect either the cost basis or the proceeds on the stock transaction. For example, when a call owner exercises her call, maybe she gets to buy the stock for $50 a share. If she paid $2 for the right to buy at $50, her cost basis on the stock acquired through exercise is really $52. Her proceeds will only come into play if and when she sells the stock.

The seller of that call took in her $2 a share. Upon assignment of the contract, the seller also sells the stock for $50, meaning he's taken in a total of $52 for selling that stock. Proceeds are what you take in when you sell.

So, the premium was added to the call buyer's cost basis on the stock. The premium was added to the call seller's proceeds on the stock.

Nice and simple, as always.

If you buy a put, you get the right to sell stock, so the premium will affect your proceeds. If you buy a Jun 50 put @2, you pay $2 for the right to sell stock at $50. If you exercise the put and actually sell the stock at $50, did you take in $50 per share? No, you only took in $48 per share, so $48 is your proceeds. Your cost basis is whatever you bought the stock for before putting it in somebody's reluctant face.

The reluctant face who sold you that put has the obligation to buy the stock at $50. So, the cost basis on the stock will be $50 per share, right?

No, since he took in your $2 first, the IRS—which is here to help—says he really only has a cost basis of $48.

Position	Upon Exercise	Premium	Affects
Long Call	Buys stock	Add to strike price	Raises cost base
Short Call	Sells stock	Add to strike price	Raises proceeds
Long Put	Sells stock	Subtract from strike price	Lowers proceeds
Short Put	Buys stock	Subtract from strike price	Lowers cost base

LEAPS

Ordinary options expire in 9 months or sooner. Then, there are long-term options called **LEAPS.** Since the time value is, by definition, greater on these contracts that can go out over three years, LEAPS contracts trade at much higher premiums. The strategies are the same. You buy a call if you think the stock is going up—you simply pay more for a MSFT Oct 50 call expiring in 2 or 3 years versus the one expiring in 2 or 3 months.

The taxation is a little tricky. For the buyer of the contract, capital gains and losses are considered long-term. But a short seller never establishes a holding period, so any capital gains and losses are considered short-term.

FUNDAMENTALS OF OPTIONS

The Series 7 will have plenty of questions concerning which options are in-the-money or out of the money; plenty of questions on max gain, max loss, and breakeven for both buyers and sellers of calls and puts; and plenty of questions where you calculate a pretend options trader's gain or loss on a position. I would much rather discuss this material, but, luckily for you, many options questions are based simply on a set of facts that can be memorized. Whenever we get to an area that is mostly memorization, I try to shift to bullet point mode, saving the witty, side-splitting prose for other sections of this fascinating book.

So, let's load up the bullets:

- Each equity options contract covers 100 shares.
- Contracts are adjusted for stock splits, stock dividends.
- Equity options expire at 11:59 pm Eastern on the Saturday immediately following the 3rd Friday of the expiration month.
- Last opportunity to close/trade an option is 4:02 pm Eastern on the 3rd Friday.
- Last opportunity to exercise an option is 5:30 pm Eastern on the 3rd Friday.
- Options contracts are issued by the OCC (Options Clearing Corporation).
- OCC guarantees performance of the contract, even if the seller disappears.
- Buyers open with an "opening purchase" and can close with a "closing sale."
- Sellers open with an "opening sale" and can close with a "closing purchase."
- Ordinary options are offered 9 months into the future.
- LEAPS are long-term options that can last from 12 to 39 months.
- Options are called "derivatives."
- American style exercise means the contract can be exercised anytime up to expiration.
- European exercise means the contract can be exercised on the expiration day only.
- Options allow for leverage—less money down, but a higher % gain potentially.
- Buying puts is safer than selling short—less money can be lost.
- Bulls buy calls or sell puts.
- Bears buy puts or sell calls.
- Buyers have more upside potential.
- Sellers have more risk.
- Buyers have rights.
- Sellers have obligations (to the buyer of the contract).

- Options transactions settle T + 1.
- When exercised, the stock purchased or sold through the contract settles T + 3.
- Options are paid in full—not bought on margin.
- Options are bought inside margin accounts, but they're paid in full.
- Advertisements must be submitted to the exchange 10 days prior to initial use.
- All advertisements must be maintained on file by the member firm for three years.
- Foreign currency options expire on the Friday before the third Wednesday of the month (seriously).

ADJUSTING CONTRACTS FOR STOCK SPLITS, DIVIDENDS

If you own a MSFT Oct 50 call, you own the right to buy 100 shares of MSFT for $50, meaning you get to buy $5,000 of Microsoft common stock if you want to between now and late October. Well, what if you had attended the annual meeting in Redmond, Washington, last year after a few shots of Jack Daniel's and started giving Steve Ballmer a hard time, calling him an "incompetent, bald-headed bureaucrat" and calling the board of directors a "den of do-nothing dunces." They might then find out you're holding calls on the stock and decide to make them go suddenly out of the money. They get wind that you own 100 Oct 50 calls that have just gone in-the-money. So, they effect a 2:1 stock split. Suddenly, the stock drops from $52 a share to $26 a share, sending your calls from in-the-money to worthless.

Well, they could try that, except it wouldn't work. If they do a 2:1 stock split, each MSFT Oct 50 call you own would become 2 MSFT Oct 25 calls. Remember, with each contract you have the right to buy $5,000 worth of MSFT stock, no matter how they decide to slice $5,000 worth of stock.

If it's a 5:4 or 3:2 split, just treat the test question like a question on 100 shares of stock. If you have 100 shares of stock @50, it becomes 125 shares of stock @40 after a 5:4 split. Actually, it becomes the same thing after a 25% stock dividend, too. Either way, an Oct 50 call would become an Oct (125 shares) 40 call. So, rather than creating some handy-dandy table, just know the concept. If it's a 2:1 split, you get twice as many contracts at half the strike price. If it's an uneven split or a stock dividend, just treat the question as if it were asking what happens when somebody is long 100 shares at that particular strike price.

Oh heck, maybe I should just give you the table:

Position	Event	Becomes
Jul 50 call	2:1 split	2 Jul 25 calls
Jul 50 call	5:4 split, 25% stock dividend	Jul (125 shares) 40 call
Jul 50 call	3:2 split	Jul (150 shares) 33.33 call

EXERCISING A CONTRACT

Let's say Mr. Long is holding a MSFT Oct 50 call with MSFT trading at $57. Since Mr. Long only paid $2 a share for the contract, he's in a pretty good mood today. He could just sell the contracts and walk away with a profit of about $5 a share, or he could exercise his *right to buy* 100 shares of Microsoft for $50 a share.

Today, Mr. Long decides to exercise the contract, just to be difficult. So, your firm sends notice to the OCC. The OCC (in the middle of all trades) passes the contract off to any firm that has at least one customer short that series of option. See, the folks who end up getting hurt with Mr. Long's call didn't necessarily sell one to Mr. Long. But, if it's a MSFT Oct 50 call, it can be assigned to anybody who wrote a MSFT Oct 50 call to anybody. Options, like dollar bills, are **fungible**. That means that if 50 people put dollar bills in a box, shook up the box, and let everybody pull out a dollar bill, nobody would end up getting cheated, right? A dollar bill is a dollar bill. A MSFT Oct 50 call is a MSFT Oct 50 call.

So, the OCC assigns the contract to a broker-dealer at random.

Now, the broker-dealer who receives the assignment notice didn't write the call. One of their customers did. Which one should they pass it off to? How about the guy who makes all the pesky phone calls and writes all those nasty letters? Why not?

Because the firm can use only the following methods to decide who gets hit with this hot potato known as an assignment notice:

- Random
- FIFO
- Any other fair method

Of course, if it isn't "random" or "**FIFO,**" what, exactly, *would* be "another fair method"? Rock-paper-scissors?

Also random.

Oh well—they can't use LIFO, which might be a false answer choice. It's "first-in-first-out," not "**last-in-first-out,**" in other words.

Nobody wants the assignment notice, so the firm has to be fair in how they assign it. Unless that letter-writing guy takes it too far. Then, they can start sticking it to 'em. For real.

Anyway, when Mr. Long bought that call way back when, the transaction settled T + 1. In other words, Mr. Long bought the call, and the OCC issued it next business day. Now that he's exercising the call, he's buying stock, though. This transaction is a stock transaction that will settle regular way T + 3. If Mr. Long were exercising a put, his stock would end up being sent to the seller's broker-dealer, and the sell side would deliver cash T + 3, just like any other stock transaction.

OPTIONS – BIG IDEAS

1. Whenever somebody starts with a Debit, that's all he/she can lose. If an investor is long an option, the premium is the maximum loss. If someone buys a straddle, the two premiums he paid represent the maximum loss. And the debit that a debit spread investor starts out with represents the maximum loss. In other words, if you start with a debit, that's all you can ever lose.

2. Whenever somebody starts with a Credit, that's all he/she can gain. If somebody is short an option, short a straddle, or doing a credit spread, the credit they begin with is their maximum gain.

3. People do not go in-the-money or out-of-the-money, only options do that. If XYZ stock trades at $83, the XYZ 80 calls are in-the-money by $3. An investor can easily have an option go in-the-money and still lose money himself. If you buy an XYZ Mar 80 call for $5 back in January and the stock only rises to $83 by expiration in March, your option will only be worth $3 at expiration, meaning that you paid $2 too much for it. So, in that case your option went in-the-money, while you had a $2 loss.

4. Breakeven, max gain, and max loss. Investors have breakeven points. For a call, just add the premium to the strike price. For a put, just subtract the premium from the strike price. Doesn't matter if the investor bought or sold. If they bought, the option needs to make back the amount they spent. If they sold, the option can move in favor of the buyer by the same amount that they received. Max gain and max loss tell an investor the most he/she can make and lose on the deal. If you buy a call, you have an unlimited max gain, since a stock could theoretically run forever. You can only lose your premium paid. If you sell a naked call, you could lose everything that the buyer could win, which is unlimited. You can only make the premium received. A put buyer can only lose the premium paid. Their max gain is just strike price minus premium. A 50 put at 2 means the buyer could make 48. The seller can only make the $2 premium and could lose 48.

5. Buyers pay money and won't break even until the stock moves by the amount of the premium paid. If you buy a 50 call at 2, the stock needs to move up $2 so that even if it never goes beyond there by expiration, it will still have an intrinsic value of $2, meaning you could sell it for the exact amount you paid for it. Even-steven.

6. Sellers receive money and won't break even until they lose the bet by the amount of the premium. If you sell a 50 call at 2, the stock can move up $2 and you're okay. If it never goes beyond there by expiration, it will have an intrinsic value of $2, meaning you could buy it back for the exact amount you sold it. Even-steven.

7. Buyers are gamblers; sellers are bookies. Buyers make bets. They can only lose the amount they put down and can usually win a whole lot more, just like gamblers at a casino. Sellers are the bookies, the house. They can only make the money that gamblers put down and could (theoretically) lose a whole lot more. Call buyers and put sellers are both bullish, but call buyers can make a whole lot more, theoretically. If you're bullish on MSFT, you could buy a MSFT Oct 70 call at 5. Or you could sell a MSFT Oct 70 put at 5. If the stock goes to 85, who makes more money? The put seller makes the $5 as the put expires worthless. But the call buyer makes $10, since he paid $5 and can now sell the call for $15 (difference between Strike Price of 70 and the market price of 85, right?). Plus, the stock could have gone even higher, at which point the buyer keeps making money, but the put seller maxed out long ago at the premium of $5. Buyers have bigger upsides. Sellers can make the premium and nothing more; they can also lose much more than the premium.

8. Buy low. Sell high. Calls with lower strike prices are worth more. Always. A Mar 50 call is always worth more than a Mar 60 call. One gives you the right to buy at 50, one at 60. Which one is more valuable? The right to BUY at 50. Puts with higher strike prices are worth more. Always. A Mar 60 put is always worth more than a Mar 50 put. One gives you

the right to sell at 60, one at 50. Which is more valuable? The right to sell at 60. So, when determining whether an investor wants a spread to widen or narrow with no premiums given, determine which option is worth more. If he bought the more valuable one, it's a debit spread. If he sold the more valuable one, it's a credit spread. Debit = widen, Credit = narrow. Long the 50 call/Short the 60 call—widen or narrow? He bought the more expensive option, the option to buy a stock cheaper, so it's a debit spread. Long the 50 put/Short the 60 put—widen or narrow? He bought the cheaper option and sold the more expensive option, the right to sell higher, so it's a credit spread. Debit = widen, Credit = narrow.

9. If a debit spread widens, the investor makes the amount that it widened. If an investor buys one option at $4 and sells one at $1, that's a spread of $3. If the options premiums are $10 apart at expiration, the investor makes the difference between where the spread started (3) and finished (10). He makes $7, in other words.

10. If a credit spread narrows, the seller makes the amount that it narrowed. If an investor sells one option at $4 and buys one at $1, that's a spread of $3. If the options premiums are $0 apart at expiration (both expire worthless), the investor makes the difference between where the spread started (3) and finished (0). He makes $3, exactly what he started with.

11. For hedging, identify the risk and bet that way. If you are long stock, you want the stock to rise. What's your risk, though? That the stock could fall. So, your risk is pointing down. Who bets that something might go down? Long puts, short calls. If you are short stock, you want the stock to fall. Your risk is that it could rise. Who bets that stock might rise? Long calls, short puts.

12. Buy protection, sell to increase income/yield. For the "best" hedge or protection, buy an option. Best-buy. To increase income or yield, sell an option. If you're long stock, you buy a put for protection or sell a call to increase income. If you're short stock, you buy a call for protection or sell a put to increase income.

13. If the stock goes beyond the breakeven point, the buyer makes the difference. If it's an XYZ Oct 50 call at 3, both the buyer and the seller have a breakeven point of $53. If the stock finishes at $57, the buyer makes the difference of $4.

14. If the stock fails to hit the breakeven point, the seller makes the difference. If it's an XYZ Oct 50 call at 3, and the stock finishes at $48, the option expires worthless, so the seller makes the difference between $3 (what he received) and $0 (what he paid).

It's also a good idea to obtain the OCC Disclosure Document and spend ½ hour reading it. Approximately ½ hour, like you'll actually do it.

CHAPTER 5

Investment Companies

(Open- and Closed-end Funds, UITs, Face-amount certificate companies.)

Imagine what it's like to allow a perfect stranger into your home and let him ask a bunch of awkward personal questions about finances, health problems, death, disability, you name it, and then ask you to trust him with your life savings. As if trusting this person weren't hard enough, this "financial services representative" is also asking you to understand all the different investment options available and all of their implications. How do you decide how much risk to take? How do you do an accurate comparison of all the **sales charges** and **operating expenses**, knowing that the sales representative helping you with your decision will only get paid if you invest through him?

That's pretty much what it's like to be your client, so let's take a look at mutual funds from your clients' perspective. They meet with you, maybe at the kitchen table, and you all share a cup of coffee or maybe a cold drink depending on the time of year and their willingness to be nice to a salesperson. You ask them to bear their soul concerning how much money they make, how much credit card debt they've been silly enough to amass at this point, how far they've stretched the equity in their home trying to cover that credit card debt, and how miserably they've failed to save any money over the years. Then, you pull out a slick, colorful catalog of various mutual funds they can choose from.

MUTUAL FUND CATEGORIES

First, they don't know a mutual fund from a hole in the ground. Second, they're even less curious about mutual funds than the average Series 7 candidate, which is scary. And, third, they don't understand half of what you're saying about 12b-1 fees, expense ratios, Morningstar ratings, and contingent deferred sales charges. Even before they settle on a particular fund from a particular family, they have to decide on the following *categories* of mutual funds:

Domestic Equity Funds
- Small Cap Growth
- Small Cap Value
- Small Cap Blend
- Mid-Cap Growth
- Mid-Cap Value
- Mid-Cap Blend

- Large Cap Growth
- Large Cap Value
- Large Cap Blend
- Specialty—natural resources
- Specialty—real estate
- Specialty—communications
- Specialty—technology
- Specialty—financial services
- Specialty—utilities
- Specialty—healthcare

Balanced Funds
- Target-Date 2030+
- World Allocation
- Target-Date 2015–2029
- Convertibles
- Moderate Allocation
- Conservative Allocation

International Stock Funds
- Specialty—precious metals
- Latin America Stock
- Diversified Emerging Markets
- Foreign Small/Mid Growth
- Foreign Small/Mid Value
- Foreign Small/Mid Blend
- Foreign Large Cap Growth
- Foreign Large Cap Value
- Foreign Large Cap Blend

Fixed-income Funds
- High-Yield Bond
- Emerging Markets Bond
- Short-Term Bond
- Short-Term Government
- Intermediate-Term Bond
- Intermediate-Term Government
- Long-Term Bond
- Long-Term Government
- Inflation-Protected Bond

Municipal Bond Funds
- High-Yield Muni
- Short-Term Muni
- Intermediate-Term Muni
- Long-Term Muni

Money Market
- Taxable
- Tax-Exempt

We haven't even begun to show the investor all the different names of particular funds from different fund families—the above represents just *categories* under which most funds could be placed. Do they want the Fidelity Intermediate-Term Municipal Bond Fund or the Intermediate Tax-Exempt Bond Fund from T. Rowe Price? Which of the 29 domestic stock funds that you sell would they like to choose this evening? The one that returned 10% over five years but was negative last year, or the one that returned 8.5% over five years but was up 2.7% last year?

Since mutual fund investing can be extremely baffling and overwhelming to an investor, FINRA insists that you can help your clients sort it all out without stepping all over yourself.

WHAT IS A MUTUAL FUND?

First of all, what the heck *is* a mutual fund?

Think of a mutual fund as a big portfolio pie that can serve up as many slices as investors care to buy. Investors send in money to buy slices of the big pie; the fund uses the money to buy ingredients, like IBM, MSFT, and GE. When an investor sends in, say, $10,000, the pie gets bigger, but it also gets cut up into more slices—however many she is buying with her $10,000. That way each slice stays the same size. The only way for the slices to get bigger is for the pie to get sweeter, which happens when securities in the fund go up in value.

Su-weet!

Now, couldn't an investor bypass the mutual fund and just buy stocks and bonds in whatever companies or governments he chooses? Sure, but most people refuse to change the oil in their car—why would they suddenly become do-it-yourselfers with six and seven-figure retirement nest eggs? Takes a lot of work to decide which stocks or bonds to purchase. If you only have $400 to invest, you can't take a meaningful position in any company's stock, and even if you tried, you'd end up owning just *one* company's stock. **Diversification** would protect against that risk, and mutual funds own stocks and bonds from many different issuers, usually in different market sectors. Plus, the portfolio is run by professionals who know when it's time to rebalance the portfolio as sure as the crew at Jiffy Lube knows when it's time to rotate your tires.

ADVANTAGES OF MUTUAL FUND INVESTING

The exam may bring up the many advantages of mutual fund investing over picking stocks and bonds individually, so let's take a look:

- Investment decisions made by a professional portfolio manager
- Ease of diversification
- Ability to liquidate a portion of the investment without losing diversification

- Simplified tax information (1099's make tax prep easier)
- Simplified record keeping (rather than getting 50 annual reports from 50 companies, you get two reports per year from one mutual fund)
- Ease of purchase and redemption of securities
- Automatic reinvestments of capital gains and income distributions at **net asset value** (**NAV**)
- Safekeeping of portfolio securities
- Ease of account inquiry

Most of the above bullet points are self-explanatory, but let's add some clarification since you were nice enough to buy the materials from us. The first point is probably the main reason people buy mutual funds—no way are they willing to try this stuff at home. They have no knowledge of stocks, bonds, taxation, etc., and they have even less interest in learning. Let a professional portfolio manager—often an entire *team* of portfolio managers—decide what to buy and when to buy or sell it. As we mentioned, it's tough to have your own diversified portfolio in individual stocks and bonds because a few hundred or thousand dollars will only buy a few shares of stock or a few bonds issued by just a few companies. Any one company could turn out as profitable as Enron, WorldComm, and eToys, and with their luck, many investors would end up purchasing two out of the three. On the other hand, a mutual fund would usually hold stock in, say, 50 or more companies, and their bond portfolios are also diversified. Therefore, even with the smallest amount of money accepted by the fund, the investor is immediately diversified. The exam calls this the "undivided interest concept." That just means that your $50 owns a piece of all the ingredients in the portfolio, just as the rich guy's $1 million does. Yes, you own a much smaller piece, but you're also just as diversified as the rich guy is—you both own your percentage of everything inside the portfolio. Notice that another bullet point said, "Ability to liquidate a portion of the investment without losing diversification." See, if you own 100 shares of IBM, MSFT, and GM, what are you going to do when you need $5,000 to cover an emergency? If you sell a few shares of each, you'll pay three separate commissions. If you sell 100 shares of any one stock, your diversification is seriously reduced. With a mutual fund, you redeem a certain number of shares and remain just as diversified as you were before the sale. And, you can usually redeem/sell your shares without getting hit up for any fees.

What exactly do we mean by "diversification"? As the FINRA exam outline indicates, mutual funds can diversify their holdings by:

- Industries
- Types of investment instruments
- Variety of securities issuers
- Geographic areas

If it's a stock fund, it is basically a growth fund, a value fund, an income fund, or some combination thereof. No matter what the objective, the fund will usually purchase stocks from issuers across many different industries. In a mutual fund prospectus you'll often find a pie chart that shows what percentage of assets is tied up in a particular industry. Maybe it's 3% in telecommunications, 10% retail, 1.7% healthcare, etc. That way if it's a lousy year for telecommunications or retail, the fund won't get crushed like a small investor who owns only one telecomm company's and one retailer's stock or bonds. A bond fund can be diversified among investment interests.

That means they buy some debentures, some secured bonds, some convertible bonds, some zero coupons, some mortgage-backed securities, and even a few money market instruments to be on the safe side. Even if the fund did not spread their investments across many different industries (telecomm, pharmaceutical, retail, etc.) and chose, instead, to focus on just a few industries, they would still purchase securities from a variety of issuers. So, if they like retail, they can still buy stock in a variety of companies—Walmart, Target, Sears, Nordstrom, Home Depot, etc. And, since any geographic area could be hit by an economic slump, a tsunami, or both, most funds will spread their holdings among different geographic areas. I mean, the Pacific Rim countries sure look promising, but I don't want all my holdings in companies from Japan, Taiwan, and Singapore.

If the exam is in an especially trivial and mean-spirited mood, it might require you to regurgitate some rather useless information about the definition of a **diversified fund**. Let's go to the most important document on mutual funds, the Investment Company Act of 1940, which defines a diversified fund like so:

> "Diversified company" means a management company which meets the following requirements: At least 75 per centum of the value of its total assets is represented by cash and cash items (including receivables), Government securities, securities of other investment companies, and other securities for the purposes of this calculation limited in respect of any one issuer to an amount not greater in value than 5 per centum of the value of the total assets of such management company and to not more than 10 per centum of the outstanding voting securities of such issuer.

So, how does the "Act of 1940" then define a **non-diversified company**?

> "Non-diversified company" means any management company other than a diversified company.

Oh. Thanks.

That just means that if the fund wants to promote itself as being "diversified," it has to meet the definition—no more than 5% of its assets are in any one company, and they don't own more than 10% of any company's outstanding shares. If it doesn't feel like meeting the definition, it will have to refer to itself as a "non-diversified fund."

Many students seem miffed that I don't buy a lot of mutual funds, myself. That's because I like to own pieces of particular companies of my own choosing and am willing to do a little research myself. Unfortunately, I also end up getting proxy (voting) materials and annual reports from, like, 20 different companies, and keeping track of all the dividends I've received from the various sources is slightly annoying. With a mutual fund, I'd get one **1099-DIV** that would keep track of all the dividends and capital gains distributions, and I'd also get just one semi-annual report and one annual report from the fund.

TYPES OF MUTUAL FUNDS

We already took a look at the overwhelming array of mutual funds available. Now, let's get into the nitty-gritty.

EQUITY FUNDS

The primary focus of **equity funds** is to invest in equity securities. Might have been easier to just call them "stock funds," but we like to use fancier language whenever possible to make ourselves sound smarter than we really are.

Within equity funds, we find different objectives. **Growth funds** invest in companies that appear likely to grow their profits faster than competitors and/or the overall stock market. These stocks usually cost a lot compared to the profits that they might or might not have at this point. For example, Amazon and Starbucks are "growth stocks," but you have to pay dearly for this perceived growth. As I write this sentence, Amazon trades at 45 times the earnings/profits of the company, while Starbucks trades at 57 times the earnings. In other words the market price compared to the earnings is very high. What should we call the comparison of price to earnings?

How about the "price to earnings" ratio? The **p/e ratio** just compares how high the stock price is to the earnings per share. A share of stock is just a slice of the company's profit pie—how much of the profits belong to each slice of the pie? That's the earnings per share. The question is, how many times the earnings per share are you willing to pay for the stock? If you're willing to pay high "p/e ratios," you're a growth investor. Also note that dividend income, if any, would be incidental (not important) to the fund's goal of finding growth opportunities. In other words, if your investor is seeking income, by definition, they don't want growth funds.

What if you prefer to buy stocks trading at low price-to-earnings ratios? You're looking for *value*, so the industry decided to call you a "value investor." **Value funds** simply seek out companies trading for much less than the geniuses on the portfolio management team decide they're actually worth. GM is in a world of hurtin' as I write this witty monologue. But, if a value fund thinks the stock is worth a lot more than folks realize, they'll snap it up now at a low price-to-earnings multiple and wait for the turnaround that inconveniently hasn't happened yet. The exam might say that value funds buy stocks in established companies that are currently out of favor. Or, to show how unbelievably smart he is, a test writer might want you to declare that value funds "seek to purchase stocks trading below their estimated intrinsic value." Right—they like stocks trading cheaper than they should be. Since the share price is depressed while the dividend keeps getting paid, value stocks tend to have high dividend yields. Therefore, they are considered more conservative than growth funds.

What if you just can't make up your mind between a growth fund and a value fund? Luckily, there are funds that blend both styles of investing, and the industry cleverly calls these **blend funds**.

If your investor's objective is to receive income from equities, the industry would be happy to sell her an **equity income fund**. Believe it or not, what these funds do is buy equities that provide fairly dependable income. Receiving dividends tends to reduce the volatility of an investment, so equity income funds are lower risk than equity growth funds.

What if you can't decide between a mutual fund family's growth funds and its income funds? Chances are, they'll get real creative and sell you a "growth and income fund."

Hmm, maybe this *is* rocket science. Right, and Miley Cyrus will still be a big star 5 years from now. A growth and income fund buys stocks in companies expected to grow their profits and also in companies that pay dependable, respectable dividends. Since we've added the income component, growth & income funds would have lower volatility than growth funds. So, from highest to lowest volatility, we would find growth, then growth & income, and then equity income funds. I have a catalog from one of the largest mutual fund families in the world which puts them in exactly that order, and even uses the color red for the highest volatility—growth—as in, "Warning! This stuff can jump up and down in a hurry."

That same catalog places **balanced funds** in a lower volatility category than growth, growth & income, and equity income funds. Why? Because a balanced fund keeps a large percentage of its assets in both the stock and the bond markets. The bond market is not as volatile as the stock market, so if the fund devotes, say, 40% or more to the bond market, that will reduce the price fluctuation/volatility of the fund. What percentage is devoted to the stock and to the bond markets? Read the prospectus, and don't expect the fund to maintain an exact mix, either. One of the prospectuses on my desk says, basically, that the balanced fund will always maintain a mix of 80% stocks–20% bonds, except when it maintains a mix of 80% bonds–20% stocks.

And you wonder why I talk from both sides of my mouth.

BOND FUNDS

In any case, stock is not for everybody. Even if an investor wants to own some stock/equity, chances are you'll still put a percentage of her hard-earned money into bond funds. A rule-of-thumb is that whatever your age is, that's the percentage that you should put into fixed-income. So, which type of fixed-income (bond) funds should the investor purchase? If the investor is not in a high tax bracket or is investing in an IRA, 401(k), etc., we'll be recommending taxable bond funds—corporate and U.S. Government bonds, in other words. The investor's time horizon will determine if we should purchase short-term, intermediate-term, or long-term bond funds. Her risk tolerance will tell us if she needs the absolute umbilical safety of U.S. Treasury funds or is willing to party with high-yield corporate bond funds. If the investor is in a taxable account and wants to earn interest exempt from federal income tax, we put her into—get this—a tax-exempt bond fund, which purchases municipal bonds. If the investor is in a tax-addicted state such as Maryland, Virginia, or California, we can sell her the "Tax-Exempt Fund of Maryland," Virginia, or California. Now, the dividends she receives will generally be exempt from both federal and state income taxes. Whether she ends up getting ahead or not, at least she'll know that Uncle Sam and her state governments will get squat from her dividend distributions (notice how we said nothing about capital gains except in this cheap little parenthetical). But, we're not done just because we put her into a tax-exempt bond fund—how much of a yield does she want and how much risk can she withstand? If she's willing to roll the dice, we can put her into the "High-Yield Tax-Exempt Fund" and pray that not too many of the states or water and sewer districts actually stiff us on the interest and principal they're supposed to pay. If her risk tolerance is lower, we'll buy funds that stick primarily to investment-grade municipal bonds.

MONEY MARKET FUNDS

We've also seen that an investor's need for liquidity tells us how much to park in the safe, boring money market. There are both taxable and tax-exempt money market mutual funds. The tax-exempt money market funds buy short-term obligations of states, counties, cities, school districts, etc. They pay *really* low rates of interest, but since it's tax-free, rich folks still come out ahead. We're talking about TANs, RANs, BANs, etc.

In case they're not overwhelmed enough with choices, the industry has also developed a bunch of other funds, which the exam outline calls **specialized funds**. As we saw at the beginning of the chapter, there are categories such as "specialty—healthcare." You may be shocked to learn that this mutual fund actually specializes in purchasing stocks in healthcare companies. That means that during a slump in that industry, we can't expect the fund to do particularly well. What about when the industry is on a tear? Everything's great. So, the trick is to buy when the industry is in a slump and sell on the day that the industry hits a peak. And, if you can do that, stop studying for this silly exam and start doing exactly that at your earliest convenience. Some funds specialize in a particular industry, some in geographic regions. As we said, you can buy the Latin America, the Europe, or the Pacific Rim fund. You would then hope that those regions don't go into a major economic slump or suffer a natural disaster. See, when the fund concentrates heavily in a particular industry or geographic region it, generally, takes on more volatility. There are **asset allocation** funds, and—believe it or not—what they do is allocate their assets. The percentage for equity, fixed-income, and money market is fairly rigid, so if you're too lazy to buy your own equity, fixed-income, and money market mutual fund, you can buy an asset allocation fund and let them subdivide things for you. I've seen definitions that say that asset allocation funds are another name for balanced funds, and I'm not sure how I could argue with that. I mean, if a balanced fund invests a percentage in equity and a percentage in debt, how is that different from an asset allocation fund, which invests a percentage in equity and a percentage in debt securities?

Both international and **global funds** appeal to investors who want to participate in markets not confined to the U.S. The difference between the two is that an **international fund** invests in companies located anywhere but the U.S. A global fund would invest in companies located and doing business anywhere in the world, including the U.S. Remember that when you move away from the U.S., you take on more political/social risk as well as currency exchange risk.

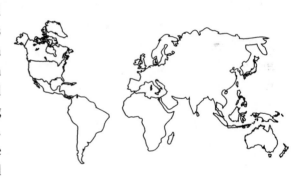

Could you take a guess as to what a precious metals fund would invest in? I thought so.

What if you don't believe that portfolio managers are likely to beat an index such as the S&P 500 over the long-term? First of all, you're in good company with plenty of evidence to support your notion. Secondly, if you can't beat the S&P 500 index, join it. Just buy an index fund that contains the same 500 stocks and only trades a stock if Standard & Poor's kicks it out of the index, forcing you to sell that one and buy the one that S&P is welcoming into the club. Passive management, in other words, as opposed to active management. An index is just an artificially grouped basket of stocks. Why are there 30 stocks in the **Dow Jones Industrial Average**, and why are the 30 particular stocks that are in there in there?

Because the Dow Jones publishing company says so. Same for the S&P 500. S&P decided that these 500 stocks make up an index, so there you have it. Investors buy index funds because there are no sales charges and very low expenses. Since there's virtually no trading going on, the **management fees** should be—and typically are—very low. So, for a no-brainer, low-cost option, you can put your money into an index and expect to do about as well as that index, no better, no worse.

Since FINRA decided to add a few new items to this exciting list of fund types, we will now devote a disproportionate amount of verbiage to "funds of funds" and "principal protected funds."

FUNDS OF HEDGE FUNDS

Mutual funds are open to the average investor, not just to the big, sophisticated individuals and institutional investors that include pension funds, insurance companies, university endowments, etc. Since the mutual fund is open to the average Joe and JoAnne, they can't focus on extremely risky investment strategies. It would be sort of rude to take the average Joe and JoAnne's retirement nest egg and lose it all on a couple of ill-placed foreign currency bets or ill-timed short sales. But, when the investors are all rich folks and institutions, the regulators can relax a little bit.

This is where **hedge funds** come in. In general, hedge funds are only open to institutions and to individuals called "accredited investors." We'll look at these **accredited investors** when we discuss another fascinating topic called "Reg D private placements under the Securities Act of 1933." There, too, the well-moneyed accredited investor can do things the average Joe and JoAnne cannot, but we'll save that excitement for another section. An accredited investor has over $1 million in net worth and makes > $200,000 per year. If it's a married couple, the assets held jointly count toward that $1 million figure, and the annual income needs to be > $300,000, just to make sure you have even more numbers to learn for your exam.

Why does the investor need to be rich? Because these hedge funds use some very high-risk strategies including short selling, currency bets, risky options plays, etc. If you're an average Joe and JoAnne, it wouldn't be cool to let you risk all of your investment capital on such high-risk investing. On the other hand, if you're a rich individual or a big institution, chances are your hedge fund investment is just a percentage of the capital you invest. So, if you lose $1 million, chances are you have several more million where that came from.

A typical arrangement for a hedge fund is to have a limited number of investors form a private investment partnership. The fund typically charges 2% of assets as a management fee and extracts the first 20% of all capital gains. Then, they start thinking about their investors (we hope). Once you buy, there's a good chance you will not be able to sell your investment for at least one year, even if it sucks. Rather than trying to beat an index such as the DJIA, hedge funds generally go for "absolute positive investment performance"—usually 8% or so—regardless of what the overall market is doing.

Now, just to keep everything nice and simple, although a **non-accredited investor** cannot invest directly in a hedge fund, there are mutual funds called "funds of hedge funds," which she can invest in. As the name implies, these mutual funds would have investments in several different hedge funds. In most cases, the investor would not be able to redeem her investment, since hedge funds are illiquid (they don't trade among investors). Also, these investments would involve high expenses, since there would be the usual expenses of the mutual fund, on top of the high expenses of the hedge funds the mutual fund invests in.

So, other than the fact that they're really expensive, very risky, and make it really tough for the investor to liquidate her position, they're a great investment. The main testable points on hedge funds would seem to be:

- Open to sophisticated, accredited investors with high net worth
- Illiquid—usually can't be sold for at least one year
- Employ riskier, more diverse strategies
- Charge high management fees and usually 20% of all gains
- Non-accredited investors can buy mutual funds that invest in hedge funds

PRINCIPAL-PROTECTED FUNDS

Would you believe that **principal-protected funds** focus on protecting investors' principal? Why these people can't just buy Treasuries, I do not know. Perhaps they prefer paying expenses to getting the principal guarantee for free. These funds take a lot of steps to keep the principal invested stable, but those steps usually cost something—buying puts on indexes or individual stocks, for example, carries a cost. So, these funds can be rather expensive. In exchange for the guaranteed principal, the fund also might limit the upside that the investor can make. Reminds me of an "indexed annuity," but let's not get into that right now. Principal-protected funds would be suitable for a very conservative investor who needs a **lump sum** at a fixed point in the future. These are not for income investors, as there will be no income for a long while. Generally, the investor has to deal with a lock-up period of 5 to 10 years, during which no redemptions can be taken and all dividends/capital gains must be reinvested. The guaranteed principal begins after this lock-up period.

Now, this should be way ahead of the curve, but the mutual fund industry has recently added a new spin to this notion of promising a certain value to investors. There are actually funds now that will guarantee that when you sell, you will receive the *highest NAV* that the fund ever achieved during your holding period. No, that is not a typo. The fund does a bunch of sophisticated hedging strategies (just like a hedge fund does) in order to make money comin' or goin', and that adds to the already high expense ratio. But some people like knowing that they'll be able to sell at the highest price the fund reached over a certain holding period and are willing to pay higher expenses for that feature, God love 'em.

COMPARISONS OF MUTUAL FUNDS

Once we decide that the investor wants to invest in a growth fund or a value fund, how do we go about comparing one growth or value fund to another? The mutual fund prospectus would be a darned good place to go. In this handy piece of sales literature we will find the fund's investment objectives and style. Do they focus on companies valued at $5 billion and above? $1 billion and below? Do they use fundamental analysis, poring over income statements and balance sheets, possibly meeting with senior management of the companies whose stock they hold? Or, do they rely more on technical analysis—charts, patterns, trends, etc.? Is a company's dividend payout important when selecting investments for the portfolio, or is the fund really only looking at the growth potential? Is this a small cap, mid-cap, or large cap fund, and how is the fund defining "small, mid-, and large cap," anyway? There are also investment policies disclosed in the prospectus and the statement of additional information. Maybe the fund is telling you that it may invest up to 10% of its assets in securities of issuers outside the United States and Canada and not included in the S&P 500. Or, that they allow themselves to invest 10% of their assets in lower-quality debt securities rated below BB/Ba by S&P and Moody's, or even in debt securities no one has *ever* actually rated. If that stuff all sounds too risky for the investor, well, that's why we're disclosing it here in the prospectus before we ever think about taking his or her money.

The prospectus provides information on the party managing the portfolio. We call that party the **investment adviser** or the portfolio manager. Often, it's a team approach, so we can see the names of the individual portfolio counselors and how much experience they have doing this sort of thing. The prospectus I happen to be looking at now has a team of eight advisers, and their experience in the industry ranges from 18 to 40 years.

One of the most misunderstood aspects of mutual fund investing has to do with the fees and expenses. You'll often hear people say, "No, there's no expenses on any of my mutual funds— they're all no-*load*." As we'll see in more detail later, whether the fund is "no load" or not, all funds charge operating expenses. You might not get a bill for your share of the expenses, but the fund takes out enough money from the portfolio to cover their expenses, whether this happens to be a "no load" fund or one that charges either front- or back-end sales charges. Sales charges are one thing; expenses are another. Not all funds have sales charges, but all funds have expenses.

In the prospectus the investor can see how much of her check is going toward the sales charge, and how much of the dollars she then invests will be eaten up by ongoing operating expenses. The section that details the fees and expenses of the fund has been entitled "Fees and expenses of the fund" in the prospectus sitting on my desk at the moment. If two growth funds have similar 10-year track records but one has expenses of 1.5% while the other charges just .90%, that could certainly be the tiebreaker the investor is looking for. Expense ratios, in other words, are important factors when determining your investment into a particular fund. A large fund family that starts with "V" has been playing up the significance of expense ratios on long-term returns quite success-fully lately. Perhaps you've seen the print ads or heard the radio commercials.

How well does the fund perform? The prospectus will show you "total return," usually as a bar chart and a table of numbers. Since I'm looking at a growth fund prospectus, the red bars are often very long and pointing in both upward and downward directions. Over the past 10 years, the fund has gone up as high as 45% and down as much as 22%. As we said, investing in growth stocks requires a higher risk tolerance and a longer time horizon. There was a 3-year period here where the fund averaged returns of *negative* 9%. Gee, sure hope you didn't need any of this money for a while or anything.

What is **total return**? As usual, it's much simpler than you might assume. The point of buying a mutual fund share is that it might go, you know, up. We call that "**capital appreciation**" since "going up" doesn't sound nearly as sophisticated. The mutual fund will usually also pay out divi-dends from all those stocks and bonds they're sitting on. And, at the end of the year, if they took more profits than losses while trading their stocks and bonds, they will distribute a capital gains check to shareholders. Total return takes all three of those things and compares it to where the fund started. If the fund started out with a "net asset value" or "NAV" of $10 and finished the year at $11 per share, that's $1 of "capital appreciation." If the fund also paid a dividend of 50 cents per share and a $1 capital gains distribution, we would add that $1.50 to the capital appreciation of $1 for a total of $2.50 of good stuff. Comparing that $2.50 to where we started—$10—gives us a total return of 25%. How likely is it that a fund could have a total return of 25%? The prospectus I happen to be looking at did 26%, 31%, and 45% during 1997, 1998, and 1999. So, naturally, it had a similar return the next three years, right? No, after that, it was anybody's guess: 7% in

2000, negative 12% in 2001, negative 22% in 2002. Which means the following year was probably even worse, right? No. In 2003 the fund had a total return of nearly 33% in a positive direction. Now we see why the prospectus says that "past results are not predictive of future results." Yeah. I guess not.

See, mutual funds are not short-term investments, especially not equity funds. You need a long time horizon, as this prospectus tells you on the very first page. Nobody knows what will happen this year or next. We can show you the returns over 1, 5, and 10 years and let you be the judge. If we've only been in existence four years, we'll show you the figures for one year and also "life of fund" or "since inception." But no one can tell you which funds will go up this year, let alone which funds will go up the most. If they could do that, why the heck wouldn't they just buy the funds that will go up the most each year and quit their day job?

As we've seen, taxation always plays a part on an investor's returns, so the prospectus will also show results after taxes have been figured in. Of course, this is a little tricky, as we see from the caveat in the prospectus on my desk:

> Your actual after-tax returns depend on your individual tax situation and likely will differ from the results shown below. In addition, after-tax returns may not be relevant if you hold your fund shares through a tax-deferred arrangement, such as a 401(k) plan, IRA, or 529 Savings Plan.

Remember that funky stuff about the "duration" of a bond or the "beta" of a stock? Those are what the exam may refer to as "quantitative risk measurements." A mutual fund could be compared to another based on how much interest rate risk they take on (duration) or how aggressive they are in their stock selections (beta).

SALES CHARGES AND EXPENSES

If you and your friends wanted to launch a new mutual fund, how would you go about doing that? Forget the nightmare of SEC registration, I mean just from a business standpoint—how would you go about launching this mutual fund? You would need investors, right? Okay, how do you find investors? You have to advertise the fund and give people a number to call or a website to visit for more information. You'd have to print up a bunch of colorful prospectuses and mail them out whenever somebody requests one. And, most of these customers are going through a sales representative, and—believe it or not—sales representatives like you do not generally work for free. So those distribution costs are going to have to be covered somehow. You can cover them with a sales charge. If the **net asset value (NAV)** of our aggressive growth fund is $9.50, we might actually charge people $10.00 for a stock worth $9.50 and call the difference of 50 cents a sales charge. What's more, we will get away with it. Yes, mutual fund investing is somewhat unique in this way. It's a little bit like going into Nordstrom and hearing the sales clerk say, "That will be $274.50 for the ridiculously overpriced sandals, plus $12.50 to cover the cost of the ad we had to put out to bring you into the store."

What? They're charging the customer an additional fee to cover advertising/distribution expenses?

Absolutely.

If the mutual fund is sponsored/underwritten/distributed by a member firm, there will be a sales charge on purchases or redemptions of the fund. This sales charge covers the distribution expenses of printing, selling, mailing, and advertising the fund, and also leaves a really nice profit for the underwriter/sponsor/**distributor** of the fund. How much of a sales charge will the investor pay?

Depends on the fund. 5.5% is not uncommon for small investments. The maximum allowed sales charge is 8.5%, but anything over 5.75% is generally considered impolite. So, if a mutual fund charges a maximum sales charge of 5.5%, that means that when the investor cuts her check, 5.5% of it goes to the distributors. Only the other 94.5% goes into the mutual fund for investment purposes.

So, if the NAV is $9.45 but the **public offering price** or "**POP**" is $10.00, the difference of 55 cents is the sales charge. How big is that sales charge? It is exactly 5.5% of the investor's $10 check. There are few calculations on the Series 7 exam, but you could be expected to know that the sales charge as a percentage equals:

POP minus NAV divided by the POP

If we plug our numbers into that quasi-formula, we see that $10 minus $9.45 is 55 cents. 55 cents divided by the POP of $10 equals 5.5%.

A-, B-, AND C-SHARES

A mutual fund that levies sales charges can get the sales charge from investors either when they buy or when they sell. "A"-shares charge a **front-end load** when the investor acquires them. A = "acquire." "B"-shares charge a **back-end load** when the investor sells them. B = "back end." For a "B"-share, the investor pays the NAV, but she will leave a percentage behind when she sells. The percentage usually starts to decline in the second year, and after several years (6 to 8), the back-end load goes away completely—effectively, the "B"-shares are converted to "A"-shares. "B"-shares are associated with **contingent deferred sales charges**. Break down those words. The sales charge is deferred until the investor sells, and the amount of the load is contingent upon when the investor sells. For a test question on the proceeds of a B-share redemption, just take the NAV and deduct the appropriate percentage from the investor's proceeds. If the NAV is $10, the investor receives the $10, minus the percentage the fund keeps on the back end. So, if she sells 100 shares and there is a 2% back-end sales charge, she gets $1,000 minus $20, or $980 out the door.

So, since the back-end or deferred sales charge eventually goes away, as long as the investor isn't going to sell her shares for, say, seven years, she should purchase B-shares, right?

Wouldn't it be great if things were *ever* that simple in the world of investing? See, we've been acting as if distribution expenses are covered only by sales charges, either on the front-end (**A-shares**) or back-end (B-shares). Turns out, distribution expenses are covered only by the sales charge, unless the fund has a **12b-1 fee**.

What?

Yes, a "12b-1" fee *also* covers distribution costs, and if you're annoyed at these things right now, you'll eventually learn to love them, as they will put money in your pocket once you begin to sell. 12b-1 fees, like sales charges, go to salespersons like yourself. No doubt you've heard about so-called **no-load funds**. Well, you may not have gotten the whole story. A no-load fund can still charge a 12b-1 fee, as long as it doesn't exceed .25% of the fund's assets. Every quarter, when they take money out to cover expenses, these so-called "no load funds" can also take an amount not to exceed 25 basis points. Money market mutual funds have to be "no load," but that also means they can charge 12b-1 fees up to .25%.

Hmm. So, again, should the investor buy the A-share or the B-share? The choice has to do with this 12b-1 fee I'm currently babbling about. See, the A-shares for our aggressive growth fund might be as high as 5.5%, but the 12b-1 fee we tack on will often be .25%, while the B-shares will pay a 12b-1 fee of, say, 1.00%. That complicates things, doesn't it? While the person who bought the B-shares is waiting for that contingent deferred sales charge schedule to hit zero, he's paying an extra .75% every year in expenses. .75% times seven years is an extra 5.25%. Yeah, but still, the A-shares start out with a maximum of 5.5% upfront sales charge, so the B-shares are still better.

Oh, if things were only that simple. See, this 12b-1 fee is a percentage. As your assets are growing over time, that .75% is also taking more *money* from you, even if it's a flat percentage—almost like the reverse of compounded interest. We're probably going beyond the depth of the exam, but I just can't stop myself. See, if you invest $10,000 into a fund, the first year's 12b-1 fee would be $75.00. If your investment grew to be $11,000 (as it should, since it's sort of the whole "growth" part of the so-called "growth fund"), the 12b-1 fee is going to be $82.50. If the assets are eventually $13,000, the extra .75% in 12b-1 fees equals $97.50.

And, as we'll soon see, 5.5% would probably be the *maximum* sales charge on the A-shares. If the investor puts in more money, she can maybe knock down the sales charge to 3 or even 2%, which is why long-term investors with a decent amount of money should almost always buy the A-shares.

Just to make the decision harder, there are also C-shares, which usually don't charge an upfront load but do carry a 1% 12b-1 fee. The level 1% 12b-1 fee (which is so much higher than the .25% allowed for a "no load" fund) is where we got the clever **level load** nickname, by the way. Some C-shares also charge a contingent deferred sales charge if the investor sells in less than 1 year or 1½ years, just to keep things nice and simple.

So, which type of share should an investor buy? Although I think this concept is a little too subjective (like what makes something "small cap" versus "mid cap"), I'd recommend the following answers.

- Long-term investor with $50,000+ to invest – A-shares
- Long-term investor with small amount to invest – B-shares
- Short-term investor – C-shares

The only difference in expenses between A-shares on one hand, and B- and C-shares on the other has to do with the 12b-1 fee. The fund also charges a management fee to cover the cost of hiring a portfolio manager. That would be the same for everybody and would have to be a separate line item—remember that. A mutual fund can't bury their management fees under the 12b-1 fees or sales charges. Sales charges and 12b-1 fees cover distribution costs. The management fee covers portfolio management—the fund has to keep the two separate. The next item in the expenses table of the prospectus would be "other expenses." When you add the management fee, the 12b-1 fee, and the "other expenses" fee, you have the **expense ratio** for the fund. For the A-shares, maybe the expense ratio is .70%. But, the expense ratio for the B- and C-shares could be 1.45%, due to that extra .75% 12b-1 fee. Please don't assume that the difference would always be .75%, though.

I'm just using that as a typical, credible number. The fact that I'm too lazy to get up and look at a different prospectus has nothing to do with it.

If the investor purchases a B-share, she pays the NAV or "net asset value." Only if/when she sells would the fund take a sales charge from her. If the investor purchases the A-shares, she pays more than the NAV. That extra that she pays is the sales charge, as we said. When you add the sales charge to the NAV, you get the public offering price (POP). So, another little formula the exam could throw at you is:

NAV *plus the* Sales Charge *equals the* POP

It looks so much more intimidating as a formula. All we're saying is that if the NAV is $9.45 and the Sales Charge is 55 cents, the POP is $10.00. Or, they could really mess with you and ask you to *determine* the amount of the sales charge. That formula would be:

POP *minus the* NAV *equals the* Sales Charge

Which, again, looks much more intimidating as a formula. All we're saying is that if the POP is $10 and the NAV is $9.45, the Sales Charge must be 55 cents. As we saw earlier, that sales charge would be 5.5%, since the public offering price of $10 has a sales charge built into it representing exactly 5.5%. That's the percentage that goes to the distributors of the fund, leaving the other 94.5% for the investor to, you know, invest.

So, how and when is this net asset value (NAV) figured? The exam wants you to know that mutual funds use **forward pricing**. That means that if you take my check for $10,000 at 11 am, you won't know how many shares I'll end up buying. The fund will refigure the NAV when trading closes that day, and then put my $10,000 into the fund at the NAV they come up with then. Same thing for a seller. A seller "redeems" her shares to the fund. When she turns in a redemption order at 1 pm she won't know the exact dollar amount of her check because the NAV won't be determined until after the markets close at 4 pm Eastern. The NAV is nothing more than the value of one slice of the portfolio pie. The assets of the portfolio would be the value of the securities plus any cash they've generated minus any liabilities. Where did the liabilities come from? The fund might borrow money from time to time to handle redemptions—they don't always want to sell off stocks and bonds to pay investors ready to sell their shares, so they borrow some money. If the fund has $10,000,000 in assets and $550,000 in liabilities, the net assets of the fund would be $9,450,000. If there are 1 million shares, the NAV per share is $9.45. Sellers will receive $9.45 per share when they redeem their A-shares today, but they'll pay a POP higher than that if they're buying. Buyers of the B-shares will pay $9.45, but those redeeming/selling their shares will receive $9.45 per share minus whatever percentage they leave behind to the contingent deferred sales charge.

Just to keep everything nice and simple.

As we just said, the value of a mutual fund share is just the net assets of the fund divided by the shares. If a fund takes some of that cash and pays it out as a dividend or capital gains distribution, they reduce the net assets of the fund *without* reducing the number of shares. Hmm—so they're depleting the size of the pie but still cutting it into the same number of shares.

You bet. And that's why whenever a mutual fund distributes a dividend or capital gain to the shareholder, the NAV per share is reduced by the amount of the dividend. So, tell the exam that on the "ex-dividend date" for a mutual fund, the NAV drops by the amount of the dividend or capital gain distributed to the shareholders.

Also remember that the NAV is sometimes referred to as the "bid" price, because that is the price the investor receives when selling. So, the answer to an exam question could be, "redemptions are executed at the next calculated bid price," or they could substitute "NAV" for "bid price," just to keep everything nice and simple.

REDUCING THE SALES CHARGE

Although A-shares do charge the front-end sales charge, you can also reduce that sales charge by employing various methods laid out in the prospectus.

Breakpoints

Perhaps you've noticed that in general the more you want to buy of something, the better the deal. Doesn't a small box of Lucky Charms™ at the convenience store cost a lot more per ounce than a shrink-wrapped pack of 10 boxes from Sam's Club? Same with mutual funds. If you want to invest $1,000, you're going to pay a higher sales charge than if you want to invest, say, $100,000. For mutual funds, investors are rewarded with breakpoints. Let's say that the L & H Fund had the following sales charge schedule:

INVESTMENT	SALES CHARGE
<$25,000	5.5%
$25,000 – $49,999	5.0%
$50,000 – $99,999	4.0%
$100,000 – $199,999	3.0%

That means that an investor who buys $100,000 worth of the fund will pay a much lower sales charge than an investor who invests $20,000. In other words, less of her money will be deducted from her check when she invests. A breakpoint means that at this point the fund will give you this break. A lower sales charge means that an investor's money ends up buying more shares. For mutual funds, we don't pick the number of shares we want; we send in a certain amount of money and see how many shares our money buys us. With a lower sales charge, our money will buy us more shares. Keep in mind that fractional shares are common. For example, $1,000 would buy 12.5 shares if the POP were $80.

Letter of Intent

So, what if we didn't have the $100,000 needed to qualify for that breakpoint? We could write a **letter of intent** explaining to the mutual fund our intention to invest $100,000 in the fund over the next 13 months. Now, as we send in our money, say, $5,000 at a time, the fund applies the lower 3% sales charge, as if we'd already invested the full amount. The lower sales charge means we end up buying more shares, right? So, guess what the fund does? It holds those extra shares in a safe place, just in case we fail to invest that $100,000 we intended to. If we don't live up to our letter of intent, no big deal. We just don't get those extra shares. In other words, the higher sales charge applies to the money actually invested.

Also, that letter of intent could be backdated up to 90 calendar days in order to cover a previous purchase. If an investor bought $3,000 of the L & H fund on March 10, he might decide in early June that he should write a letter of intent to invest $50,000 over 13 months. He could backdate the letter to March 10 to include the previous investment and would then have 13 months from that date to invest the remaining $47,000.

Breakpoints are available to individuals, husbands & wives, parents & minor child in a **custodial account**, corporations, partnerships, etc. So, if the mom puts in $30,000 and also puts in $20,000 for her minor child's UGMA account, that's a $50,000 investment in terms of achieving a breakpoint. The child cannot be an adult; he must be a minor. Corporations and other businesses qualify for breakpoints. About the only folks who don't qualify for breakpoints are investment clubs.

Another important consideration for breakpoints is that a sales rep can never encourage an investor to invest a lower amount of money in order to keep him from obtaining a lower sales charge offered at the next breakpoint. That's called **breakpoint selling** and is a violation punishable by death or dismemberment. Likewise, if a rep fails to point out to an investor that a few more dollars invested would qualify for a breakpoint, that's just as bad as actively encouraging him to stay below the next breakpoint. Remember, sales reps (broker-dealers) get part of the sales charge. It would definitely be to their advantage to get the higher sales charge. Unfortunately, they have to keep their clients' interests in mind, too.

Yes, unfortunately, they take all the fun out of this business.

Rights of Accumulation

If an investor's fund shares appreciate up to a breakpoint, the investor will receive a lower sales charge on additional purchases. In other words, when an investor is trying to reach a breakpoint, new money and account accumulation are counted the same way. So, if an investor's shares have appreciated to, say, $42,000 and the investor wanted to invest another $9,000, the entire purchase would qualify for the breakpoint that starts at $50,000. In other words, the $42,000 of value plus an additional $9,000 would take the investor past the $50,000 needed to qualify for the 4% sales charge.

This is known as **rights of accumulation**.

Please note that this has *nothing* to do with a letter of intent. If you write a letter of intent to invest $100,000, you'll need to invest $100,000 of new dollars into the fund to get the break-point you're intending to get. Rights of accumulation means that you could save money on future purchases, based on the value of your account.

Combination Privilege

Most "funds" are part of a "family" of funds. Many of these fund families will let you combine your purchase in their Income Fund with, say, their Index or Growth Fund in order to figure a break-point. They call this, very cleverly, a **combination privilege**. So, if the individual invests $20,000 in the Income Fund and $30,000 in the Growth Fund, that's considered a $50,000 investment in the family of funds, and that's the number they'd use to figure the breakpoint.

Just trying to keep everybody in our happy family.

Conversion/Exchange Privilege

The fund might also offer a **conversion/exchange privilege**. This privilege allows investors to sell shares of, say, the L & H Growth Fund, in order to buy shares of the L & H Income Fund at the NAV, rather than the higher POP. If we didn't do that, the investor might get mad enough to leave our happy family, since there would be no immediate benefit to his staying with us. I mean, if he's going to be charged the POP, why not look for a new family with a growth fund that might actually, you know, grow?

But remember that buying the new shares at the NAV is nice for the investor, but the IRS still considers the sale a taxable event. So if you get a test question on the tax treatment, tell the exam that all gains or losses are recognized on the date of the sale.

And then move on with your life.

BUYING AND SELLING YOUR MUTUAL FUND SHARES

We already looked at the detailed and slightly perplexing options for purchasing mutual fund shares. A "no load" fund is purchased at the NAV, but every quarter 12b-1 fees are deducted from the fund's assets to cover the cost of distribution. If the fund has a "load," you can pay it upfront by buying an A-share and then save money on expenses going forward. You can also knock down your front-end sales charge by purchasing in quantity either all at once or through a Letter of Intent (LOI). If you buy the B-shares, you avoid the front-end sales charge, but you have two other concerns to keep in mind: 1) you'll leave a percentage on the table if you sell for the first several years and 2) the fund will take a much higher 12b-1 fee on your behalf every quarter, driving up your expenses. If you were only going to hold a fund for, say, two or three years, the C-shares would probably make sense. You would pay no front-end or back-end sales charge, and even though the 12b-1 fee of 1% is a bit annoying, it's only being charged for two or three years.

PURCHASING SHARES

Who do you buy your mutual fund shares from? Or, for you English majors, from whom do you buy your mutual fund shares? Usually, through a well-dressed, overly caffeinated financial sales representative such as yourself. However, an investor could also just set up an account with the fund company and buy shares directly from them. Usually, the fund company will strongly encourage you to go through a financial adviser/registered representative, though, who is licensed to discuss investments with clients and maybe even get paid for it. If you go directly through the fund, the folks on the phone are just taking whatever order you'd like to place—don't ask 'em nothin' about suitability. Would you save money by bypassing the registered representative? No. The distributor of the fund would just keep all of the sales charge, rather than sharing it with the registered rep's broker-dealer and the registered rep. Believe it or not, most people do not wake up thinking, "Gee, I think I need to buy some shares of a well-diversified growth & income mutual fund today," so a registered representative such as yourself will be the one getting the ball rolling 99% of the time. Even if somebody calls the fund company, the person on the other end will probably recommend that he/she consult with a financial representative such as yourself (once you pass your exams and get licensed). Once you've set up an account through the registered representative, you can purchase additional shares in any of the following ways:

- Contacting your registered representative

- Mailing in your payment to the fund's customer service department (transfer agent)
- Telephoning the fund company
- Purchasing online
- Wiring the money from your bank account

Many people choose to set up an automatic investment program whereby, say, $300 per month is drawn from their bank account and sent to the fund company. This puts them on a disciplined schedule of investing and also makes sure they don't purchase all their shares at just one price. With their luck, some investors will put in $50,000 at the absolute highest price of all time. The automatic plan uses **dollar cost averaging**, which will be explored later in exciting detail.

When the investor opens her account, the fund needs to know if she wants to receive dividends and capital gains in the form of a check, or in the form of more shares. If she decides to automatically reinvest, there will be no tax advantages, but there is a big advantage to her in that she gets to reinvest at the net asset value, avoiding sales charges. Her money will grow faster this way, since every dollar she reinvests goes back into the fund and not a dime to the distributors. If she's in a retirement plan, she will automatically reinvest, since there are penalties for early withdrawals from retirement plans.

Mutual funds have minimum initial investments that are usually lower for IRA accounts than taxable accounts. Some funds will let you in the door for as little as $25 or $50. Others are upscale clubs that won't talk to you for less than $3,000. The minimum initial investment would be found in the prospectus, along with all the other vital information.

SELLING SHARES

Open-end mutual fund shares are not traded with other investors. When you want to sell your L&H Aggressive Growth Fund, you don't sell it to me; you sell it back to the L&H Aggressive Growth Fund. This is called a **redemption** or "redeeming your shares." When you redeem your shares, you receive the NAV per share if it's an A-share and the NAV minus the back-end sales charge if it's a B-share.

How do you go about putting in your redemption order?

- By contacting your registered representative
- By writing to the fund company
- By telephoning or faxing the fund company
- By going through the fund company's website

The fund company reserves the right to require what's known as a "signature guarantee" on any redemptions. A signature guarantee is an official stamp that officers of a bank can put on the required paperwork. When I inherited shares from a family member a few years back, I had to go to my bank for a signature guarantee in order to transfer ownership from the individual to the individual's **estate**, of which I am the executor. A "signature guarantee" is just a very common requirement when stock is being transferred or sold. They are usually obtained from a bank officer, or a member of a stock exchange.

The prospectus I've been using to write most of this fascinating chapter tells me that the fund reserves the right to require the pain-in-the-neck signature guarantee on any redemptions. The fund *will* require a signature guarantee if the redemption is:

- Over $75,000
- Made payable to someone other than the registered shareholder(s); or
- Sent to an address other than the address of record, or an address of record that has been changed within the last 10 days

Of course, if the Series 7 expects you to memorize even that bullet point list, God help us all. Also note that some mutual fund shares are (or were) actually issued as paper certificates. If that's the case, the investor will have to send in the certificates after signing them and also getting the signature guarantee.

Mutual funds are not exactly in love with redemptions. In fact, many will charge a redemption fee during the first year or so just to encourage you to sit tight. If you sell too soon, you might leave 1% of your investment behind. Note that this is not a back-end sales charge going to the distributors. This is just a little penalty that compensates the fund for the hassle of having to pay out redemptions.

But, whether mutual funds enjoy redeeming shares or not, the fact is that they have to redeem your shares promptly. The answer to the test question is "within 7 days." That requirement could only be suspended if an emergency shut down the exchanges and there was no way to value the fund's portfolio. So, be very skeptical of any answer that's trying to convince you that the fund can "halt redemptions." They'd *like* to do that, the same way you'd like to start selling mutual funds without having to sit for your Series 7.

SYSTEMATIC WITHDRAWAL PLANS

Many investors choose to invest into the fund systematically through an automatic deduction from their bank account. This way they actually invest rather than procrastinating, and they also use "dollar cost averaging," which avoids buying all the shares at an inconveniently high price. Well, when you go to sell/redeem your shares, it sure would suck to sell them all at the *lowest* price of all-time, right?

Therefore, some investors set up systematic **withdrawal plans**. You might think of this as "dollar-cost-average on the way in, dollar-cost-average on the way out," in case you don't have enough to think about at this point. In order to set up a systematic withdrawal plan the investor must have a minimum account value, often $5,000 or so. Payments are made first from dividends and then capital gains. If the dividends and capital gains don't cover the amount the investor wants to withdraw, the fund then starts redeeming shares. It's also a good idea to stop putting money into the fund once you begin the withdrawal plan. If you recall our wash sale rule, buying shares of a fund that were just sold a few days ago is going to make tax season even more annoying than it already is.

There are several payout or withdrawal options that might pop up on the exam.

Fixed-dollar Periodic Payments

As the name implies, if the investor wants to receive a fixed dollar payment periodically, we can offer her the cleverly named "fixed-dollar periodic payment." If she wants $300 per month, the fund will send her $300 a month. How long will her investment last? Until it's all gone. She's not fixing the time period—she's fixing the monthly payment, which will keep coming until all the funds have been withdrawn.

Fixed-percentage Periodic Payments

The investor might prefer to receive 2% of her account value each month, or maybe 5% each quarter. How much will the investor receive with each withdrawal? Who knows? Whatever 2% or 5% of the current account value happens to be.

Fixed-shares Periodic Payments

The investor can also have the fund redeem/liquidate, say, 10 shares per month and send a check. How large will that check be? Whatever 10 shares are worth that month. As we'll soon see, that's pretty much how a variable annuity works during the annuitization phase.

Fixed Time

Finally, if the investor wants her account liquidated/withdrawn over, say, three years, she'll give the fund an exact date, and they'll figure out how much to redeem each month (or other period) in order to exhaust the account by that date.

STRUCTURE AND OPERATION OF THE MUTUAL FUND COMPANY

So far we've been looking at a mutual fund in terms of what they are, who buys which ones, and how investors go about buying and selling them. Now, let's take a look at a mutual fund as a company—who performs which functions at, say, Fidelity, American Funds, AIG, etc.?

BOARD OF DIRECTORS

A mutual fund has a **board of directors** that oversees operations of the fund or family of funds. The board's responsibilities include:

- establish investment policy
- select and oversee the investment adviser, transfer agent, custodian
- establish dividends and capital gains policy
- approve 12b-1 plans

Remember, the board of directors does not manage the portfolio; it manages the company. The shareholders of the fund elect and re-elect the board members. Shareholders also vote their shares to approve the investment adviser's contract and 12b-1 fees. Those with enough moxie to open the proxy do, anyway.

INVESTMENT ADVISER

Each fund has an **investment adviser**, whose job is to manage the fund's investments according to its stated objectives. Shareholders and the board vote to hire/retain investment advisers, who are paid a percentage of the fund's net assets. That's why they try so hard. The more valuable the fund, the more they get paid. Their fee is typically the largest expense to a mutual fund. Investment advisers have to advise the fund (select the investments) in keeping with federal securities and tax law. They must also base their investment decisions on careful research of economic/financial trends rather than on hot stock tips from their bartender. Since everything needs at least two names, the investment adviser is also called the "portfolio manager."

CUSTODIAN

The fund also keeps its assets in a safe place at the **custodian** bank. Under very strict rules, some funds do this themselves, but most still let a bank take custody, since banks have vaults and security guards and stuff. Keeping track of all the dividends received from common and preferred stock held in the portfolio, interest payments from the bonds and money market instruments owned by the fund, purchases and sales, etc., is a big job, and the custodian performs it. The exam might say that the custodian is responsible for the payable/receivable functions involved when the portfolio buys and sells securities. That means they release the money and receive the securities purchased, and they accept the money and deliver the securities sold by the portfolio manager.

TRANSFER AGENT

The **transfer agent** is incredibly busy. This is the party that issues new shares to buyers and cancels the shares that sellers redeem. Most of these "shares" are simply electronic files (book entry), but it still takes a lot of work to "issue" and "redeem" them. While the custodian receives dividends and interest payments from the portfolio securities, it is the transfer agent that distributes income to the investors. The transfer agent acts as a customer service rep for the fund and often sends out those semi-annual and annual reports that investors have to receive. As we just saw, investors can purchase and redeem shares directly with the transfer agent, should their registered representative develop an attitude or an unhealthy love of golf.

UNDERWRITERS/DISTRIBUTORS/WHOLESALERS

Some funds are sponsored by underwriters, who bear the costs of distributing the fund up front and then get compensated by the sales charge that they either earn themselves or split with the broker-dealers who make the sales. Underwriters (AKA "wholesalers," "distributors," or "sponsors") also prepare sales literature for the fund, since they're the ones who will be selling the shares, either directly to the public or through a network of broker-dealers. If a fund distributes itself, it usually covers the distribution costs through a 12b-1 fee, as we mentioned. The fund can call itself "no load" as long as the 12b-1 fee does not exceed .25% of net assets. There is also a very famous mutual fund family that sells "100% no load funds." That means there is no sales charge and no 12b-1 fee. How are they able to stay in business?

Through the management fees—the "100% no load" label helps them pull in more assets.

The management fee is simply a % of those assets, so .50% of $1 million is nice, but .50% of $1 *billion* is even nicer.

Don't worry—mutual funds have figured out how to make a profit.

These are the methods of distribution for mutual fund shares:

- Fund/to underwriter/to dealer/to investor (assume sales charge here, a nice big one, probably)
- Fund/to underwriter/to investor (underwriter cuts out the other middleman but still gets a sales charge)
- Fund/to investor (no-load funds, which can charge 12b-1 fees no larger than .25% of assets, deducted quarterly)

SHAREHOLDER VOTING

In class, I usually see some very confused faces when I tell students that mutual fund shareholders get to vote. Perhaps my students have been too busy to notice. Or perhaps they file all their proxy materials with the junk mail. In any case, mutual fund shareholders are, obviously, shareholders, so they get to vote their shares in matters of major importance. If you get a test question about voting rights, tell the test that mutual fund shareholders vote on:

- Changes in investment policies and objectives
- Approval of investment adviser contract
- Approval of changes in fees
- Election of board members
- Ratification of independent auditors (PricewaterhouseCoopers, Deloitte-Touche, any accounting firm not named Arthur Andersen)

CLOSED-END FUNDS

The third type of investment company defined by the Investment Company Act of 1940 is the **management company**. Within this category, we find both open-end funds and closed-end funds. So far, we've been talking about the open-end funds. Let's say a few fascinating words on the closed-end variety at this point. The main difference between the two is that **open-end fund** companies continually issue and redeem shares. When you find an investor for the L&H Aggressive Growth Fund, the fund will issue brand new shares to the investor, which is why you had to sell them with a prospectus. Open-end funds don't do an IPO and then force shareholders to trade the fixed number of shares back and forth. Rather, they issue new shares every time somebody wants to buy them, and they let the shareholders sell back/redeem the shares when they get tired of looking at them.

On the other hand, closed-end funds do an IPO, at which point there is a fixed number of shares. What if you want to sell your closed-end fund? You trade it the same way you trade any other share of stock. How much will you receive? Whatever a buyer is willing to pay. These things can trade at a discount to their NAV, or at a premium. It just depends on the supply and demand for these shares. So, if the test question says that the NAV is $9.45 with the POP at $9.00, something's up, right? You can't buy an open-end fund at a discount. As we saw, the cheapest you can buy them is at the NAV. B-shares are sold at the NAV and so are "no load" funds. But, no way can a public investor buy open-end shares at a discount—only dealers, who are members of FINRA, get to do that. So, if the fund shares are selling below NAV, they have to be closed-end fund shares. Doesn't mean they *always* trade at a discount. If people really want your shares, they might pay a premium. In fact, some folks simply try to buy closed-end funds when they're trading at a discount and then sell them later if/when they begin trading at a premium. To be honest, the test question isn't entirely fair. I mean, if they say "NAV" and "POP," they're really talking about an open-end fund. A closed-end fund, like any other share of stock, would have a BID and an ASK price. But, the exam wants you to equate NAV with BID and POP with ASK. NAV or BID represents what the investor receives when selling. POP or ASK represents what the investor pays when purchasing. So, we're not saying that closed-end funds always trade at a discount to their NAV; we're saying that *only* the closed-end fund could do that. Since closed-end shares trade the same way that GE or MSFT shares trade, investors can both purchase them on margin and sell them short. To "sell short" involves borrowing shares from a broker-dealer and selling them, with the obligation to buy them back and replace them later. If the price falls, you buy low after you already sold high. If the price pulls a Google on you, you're screwed.

Another difference between open and closed-end funds is that you would purchase, say, 100 shares of the closed-end fund and pay whatever that costs. For an open-end fund, you would just cut a check for, say, $1,000, and see how many shares you end up with. In almost all cases, you'll get "full and fractional shares," which is just a lame way of saying that $100 would turn into 12.5 shares if the POP were $8.00. That little "point-5" of a share is the **fractional share**. For a closed-end fund, you would either buy 12 shares or 13 shares, not 12.5. In fact, if the investor is not a total nancy-boy, he would buy at least a "round lot" of 100 shares.

The exam might also bring up the fact that open-end funds only issue common stock to investors. That's right—even if it's a bond fund, the investor isn't buying bonds in the mutual fund company. The investor is buying a percentage of the bond portfolio. How do you evidence ownership? Common stock. A closed-end fund can use leverage by issuing bonds to investors—I mean, borrowing their money and paying them back a rate of interest. They can also issue preferred stock and even common stock with greater/lesser voting rights, should the exam care to be that difficult the day you sit down to take it.

The investment objectives between an open-end and a closed-end fund could be exactly the same—there are closed-end corporate bond funds, tax-exempt bond funds, aggressive growth funds, etc. Here in Chicago, in fact, Nuveen Investments (www.nuveen.com), the largest issuer of closed-end municipal bond funds, offers a darned nice primer on open-end and closed-end funds, by the way. Why would you want those versus the open-end variety? Well, what happens to your yield when the price of the bond drops—it goes up, right? So, if you can buy somebody's closed-end bond fund at a discount, you just goosed your yield a little bit. What about when you want to sell your shares? Well, let's hope they're trading at a premium by then. If not, welcome to the NFL.

ETFs

Perhaps you have heard of "ETFs" or seen advertisements for the well-known varieties called "Spiders," "Diamonds" and "QQQ." An **ETF** is an **exchange-traded fund**. Why did they name it that? Because it is a fund that trades on an exchange and this is not an industry brimming with creative types.

Trade Like Shares of Stock

An ETF is typically an index fund that trades throughout the day among investors. That means that if an investor wants to do as well as a particular index, she can track that index with an exchange-traded fund (ETF). To track the S&P 500, she can buy the "Spider," which is so named because it is an "SPDR" or "Standard & Poor's Depository Receipt." Of course, she could already have been doing that with Vanguard's S&P 500 open-end index fund. But, that is a boring old open-end fund, and how does an investor buy or sell those shares? Directly from the open-end fund. No matter what time of day, if we put in a redemption order, we all receive the same NAV at the next calculated price—forward pricing. So, if the S&P 500 drops 80 points in the morning and rises 150 points by mid-afternoon, there is no way for us to buy low and then sell high.

But with the ETF version investors can buy and sell their shares as often as they want to. They can try to buy when the index drops and sell when it rises. Unlike the open-end versions, these ETFs can be bought on margin and can be sold short for those who enjoy high-risk investment strategies. The test might say that ETFs facilitate "intra-day trading," which just means that you can buy and sell these things as many times as you want throughout the day. An ETF is organized as a UIT (unit investment trust), but the shares trade back and forth among investors.

Cost Comparisons

So, are the ETFs cheaper than the open-end index fund versions?

Depends how you do it. If you were only going to invest $500, the open-end fund by Vanguard would be cheaper. By the way, I don't work for Vanguard. I'm just using them because they have a low expense ratio, and their S&P 500 index fund is the biggest fund in America. Anyway, you wouldn't pay a sales charge and the expenses are only .18% (18 basis points) at the time of this writing. The ETF has an expense ratio of only .11% (11 basis points). But, since the ETF version (Spider) is a stock, you would pay a commission to buy it, just as you would pay to buy shares of GE, Walmart, etc. So, if you invested $500 into the ETF and paid a $10 commission, that commission would work out to be 2% (200 basis points), which is much higher, and that's before we factor in the expenses. On the other hand, if you're investing a larger amount, such as $100,000, the same $10 commission is now 1 basis point (.0001) versus the 18 basis points (.0018) for the open-end index fund's operating expenses. So, I think it's safe to say that for a small amount of money—as usual—the open-end mutual fund is a great option. For larger amounts of money, though, the ETF might be cheaper, assuming the investor is paying low commissions.

Diversification

As with the open-end index funds, ETFs offer diversification. For a rather small amount of money, an investor can own a little piece of, say, 500 different stocks with the SPDR, or 100 stocks with the QQQ. It is also easy to implement asset allocation strategies with ETFs. An investor can find ETFs that track all kinds of different indexes (small cap, value, growth, blue chip, long-term bonds, etc.). If an investor wanted to be 80% long-term bonds and 20% small-cap stock, that goal could be achieved with just two low-cost ETFs. This point is not necessarily a comparison to the open-end index funds, which would offer the same advantage. Rather, it is a comparison to purchasing individual bonds or small cap stocks. In order to spread the risk among many bonds and small cap stocks, an investor would have to spend large sums of money. With an ETF (as with the open-end index funds) diversification can be achieved immediately with a much smaller investment.

Taxation

The exam may point out that there are some tax advantages with ETFs. That is because an investor can turn her ETF into what's known as "creation units," rather than actually selling anything. See, even though ETFs aren't redeemable for cash, the investor can basically exchange them for the underlying security, which is called a "creation unit." Another tax advantage would be the same as the open-end index fund variety—there is virtually no selling of shares within the portfolio, so there are few capital gains distributions.

Suitability

An ETF such as the SPDR (SPY) or Mid-Cap SPDR (MDY) would be appropriate for most investors with a time horizon and risk tolerance suitable for stock (equity) investing in general. But not every ETF is the same. Due to their popularity, ETFs have spawned new versions that make the regulators nervous. FINRA has put out a notice to member firms that "inverse" or "leveraged" ETFs may not be suitable for many investors. Therefore, firms need to be very diligent when recommending these particular versions of exchange-traded funds. FINRA is perfectly clear when they write: "Leveraged ETFs seek to deliver multiples of the performance of the index or benchmark they track. Some leveraged ETFs are 'inverse' or 'short' funds, meaning that they seek to deliver the opposite of the performance of the index or benchmark they track." Right there, I'm getting nervous for retail investors—will they understand that when a leveraged ETF loses the bet, it loses *big time*. Will they understand that when the rest of their friends are cheering about the "market being up lately," that they should not be cheering along with them? If not, educate them carefully and understand the higher risks yourself if you're going to recommend them to investors. Again, FINRA says it perfectly clearly when they write, "While the customer-specific suitability analysis depends on the investor's particular circumstances, inverse and leveraged ETFs typically are not suitable for retail investors who plan to hold them for more than one trading session, particularly in volatile markets."

Summary

The main testable points concerning ETFs would seem to be:

- Organized as Unit Investment Trusts (UITs)
- Trade like shares of stock, intra-day
- Investors pay a commission rather than a sales charge
- Shares can be bought on margin, sold short
- ETFs have low expense ratios
- ETFs are convenient for investors seeking diversification/asset allocation
- ETFs are very low cost when purchased in larger quantities
- Indexes include small cap, mid-cap, large cap, growth, value, S&P 500, Dow Jones, NASDAQ, even fixed-income
- Offer certain tax advantages

To help you prepare for the exam, it would be a good idea for you to obtain several mutual fund prospectuses, especially those with A-, B-, and C-shares. Read through the document carefully.

CHAPTER 6

Retirement Planning

(Including Annuities)

NOTE: In the following chapter we generally avoid providing maximum annual **contribution** limits for retirement plans. Although these maximum contributions could surface on your exam, we do not think that books are the best place to publish information that is ever-changing. Please visit our website www.passthe7.com/updates or use another trusted source for maximum contribution limits. And please do not be surprised to see zero questions on the Series 7 asking for the maximum contribution limit to a retirement plan.

OVERVIEW

Chances are you already know something about IRAs, 401(k)s, Keoghs, and pension plans. Let's take a look at what the exam wants you to know about this stuff.

The two big categories for retirement accounts are "qualified" and "non-qualified." If a retirement plan is "qualified," that means it qualifies for special tax treatment by your friends and mine at the IRS and, therefore, has to comply with certain rules. It's covered by **ERISA**, which means it has to include all eligible employees and various other stuff we'll look at later if we haven't fallen asleep. It also involves pre-tax contributions, for the most part.

NON-QUALIFIED BUSINESS PLANS

If a plan is "non-qualified," it is an informal plan that does not have to comply with ERISA and does not need formal IRS approval. All employees do not have to be covered by a non-qualified plan. In fact, that's what makes a plan "non-qualified." If any type of employee can be excluded from the plan, the plan is "non-qualified." Common examples include **deferred compensation** and the workplace savings plan or **payroll deduction**. In either case, the employer runs the plan and basically just puts some of the employee's money into an account, where it will be held until retirement. Payroll deductions on behalf of employees can then go towards a life insurance policy or an investment account such as an IRA. Deferred compensation means, "We'll hold back some of your salary now, let you invest it, and give it to you when you retire, at which point you'll be in a lower tax bracket." These are usually for executives only. Unfortunately, these assets are not segregated, so if the company goes into bankruptcy, creditors could attach those assets, which would be bad news for those executives.

Small Businesses

A small business can establish a **SEP-IRA**, which stands for "Simplified Employee Pension" IRA. This allows the business owner to make *pre-tax* contributions for herself and any eligible employees. Twenty-five percent of compensation can be contributed to a SEP, up to the current maximum. SEP contributions are not mandatory on the part of the business owner. It's just that if the business makes *any* contributions, they have to be made to all eligible employees as stipulated in the plan agreement. To establish a SEP, the employer uses a model agreement put out by the IRS (download it at www.irs.gov) that they and the employee sign. It does not have to be filed with the IRS, who does not issue an opinion or approval. That's another sign of a non-qualified plan— more informal, no IRS sign-off required. All contributions to the SEP-IRA come through payroll, so remember that individuals do not contribute to their SEP if they work for a small business—the business makes the contributions.

Another type of plan for small businesses is called the **SIMPLE IRA** plan. This is for businesses with no more than 100 employees. The SIMPLE IRA may allow participants to save more money than the SEP. Of course, that depends on how much they earn. If they earn a lot, a SEP might be better. But, if the participant made only, say, $15,000 and wanted to sock a bunch of cash away for retirement, the SIMPLE would allow her to put in more than what her employer could have contributed in a SEP-IRA. So, SEPs allow high earners to save more than they could save in a SIMPLE IRA, while SIMPLE IRAs allow lower earning employees to save more than they would be able to put away in a SEP, should the exam really feel like harassing you. Both provide for *pre-tax contributions*, meaning all the money will be taxable when it's distributed during the golden years.

In a SIMPLE plan business owners must match the employee's contributions up to 3% of compensation or contribute 2% of the employee's compensation, whether he contributes or not. There is also a funky thing about SIMPLE IRAs in the first two years. During that time, the participant could only roll the money into another SIMPLE IRA to avoid tax. During this phase, if she tried to roll it into a Traditional IRA, she'd get dinged with a 25% penalty (not 10%), plus ordinary income tax on all of it, plus it could be treated as an excess IRA contribution (6% penalty), so, all in all, not a real good idea. Once the two years have passed, everything's fine. Go ahead and transfer it to a **401(k)**, traditional IRA, **403(b)**, etc. A big difference between the SEP and the SIMPLE IRA is that both the employer and employee may contribute to a SIMPLE IRA, while only the employer contributes to a SEP-IRA, on behalf of employees.

In a **money purchase** plan the employer has to make a contribution as a percentage of an employee's salary, regardless of profitability. The exam might indicate that money purchase plans do not offer much flexibility.

QUALIFIED BUSINESS PLANS

Defined Contribution

401(k) plans are considered **defined contribution plans**, because an employer defines how much they will contribute on behalf of the employee. Employers generally match all or part of an employee's contributions up to a certain level, as stipulated in their plan literature. Since this plan is qualified, it has to follow all the guidelines of ERISA, covering all eligible employees, whether the company wants to or not. Even though most 401(k) plans offer a matching contribution up to a certain percentage of the worker's salary, not all of them do. Some folks would participate, anyway, because the 401(k) has much higher contribution limits than a Traditional IRA or Roth IRA, for example. Although 401(k) plans offer pre-tax contributions, as of January 1, 2006, employees can designate some or even all of their contributions as being after-tax "Roth" contributions. That means they'll get no tax break now, but when the money comes out later, it will be tax-free if they do it right. The maximum contribution limit is the same whether you do pre-tax contributions, after-tax (Roth) contributions, or a combination of both. As with a Roth IRA, all the individual needs to do is wait five years and reach at least age 59½, and the money comes out tax-free. If they don't meet the qualifications, though, the money could be taxed. These designated "Roth" contributions are not matched by the employer. Unlike the Roth IRA, it doesn't matter how much income the individual earns. Finally, designated Roth 401(k) contributions cannot be rolled into a Roth IRA, just to make sure you have more details to remember.

Profit-sharing is also a "defined contribution" plan, but the contributions can be very flexible. It's based on corporate profits, so in a year of no profits, guess what?

No sharing. Profits have to be shared according to some sort of formula, but there is no rule that says a contribution has to be made this year or next year, whether the company makes a profit or not.

Sole Proprietors

Keogh Plans, sometimes referred to as HR-10s, are for the self-employed. Not for S-corps, C-corps or other entities, only sole proprietors. If the individual in the test question has side income or is self-employed, he or she can have a Keogh. They can contribute a certain percentage of their self-employment income into the Keogh.

How much?

A lot. A self-employed individual can put in 20% of compensation up to nearly $50,000 currently, a number that will continue to change every year except when it doesn't. The employer can contribute up to 25% of the employee's compensation. If you have a book talking about "100% of compensation," first that's because they don't like to bother themselves with facts and, secondly, that means that the workers could actually put in more money than what the sole proprietor contributes, taking it up to an amount equal to 100% of compensation. A sole proprietor doesn't actually pay him or herself a "salary," so the 100% thing is not available.

Non-profits

TSAs are **tax sheltered annuities**. They are for school and other non-profit organization employees. Non-profit organizations are tax-exempt and called either "403b" or "501c3" organizations, so the exam can refer to these plans by those labels, too. In one class a student said, "Aren't these kind of like 401(k)s for non-profits?"

Basically. Only the investments are more limited and are usually annuities, thus the name **tax-sheltered annuity**. On the exam, assume that these plans are funded with a pre-tax contribution, and the employees will pay ordinary income tax on all the money when they pull it out at retirement. But, as with the 401(k), individuals can now designate some or all of their contributions as after-tax "Roth" contributions. Whatever we said about the exciting "Roth" 401(k), we'd say again here if we were certain that we wouldn't die of boredom.

Students don't qualify; janitors at the school do. Gotta be an employee. The 403b/TSA is also a

qualified plan because the school may not exclude, say, janitors while covering teachers, or cover administrators while leaving teachers out in the cold.

Section 457 plans are for state and municipal government workers. The current maximum contribution is the same as it is for 401(k) plans offered by businesses in the private sector. The contributions are made pre-tax, so all money coming out is taxed as ordinary income.

Defined Benefit

Defined benefit pension plans are the opposite of defined contribution plans. For a defined contribution plan, the employer says something like, "We'll match your contributions up to 10% of your salary." For a defined benefit plan, the employer has to get sufficient returns on their investments to pay a defined benefit, such as 70% of your average salary over the last three years of service. These plans are great for folks who have put in many years at the company—usually the plan bases the payout on the final years of service, where the salary is the highest for the employee. The employer gets to take a deduction for tax purposes on the amount contributed to the plan. The employee doesn't recognize the contributions or earnings until he/she finally receives payments in retirement. Some employers prefer to contribute shares of the company's stock to employees as opposed to cash-money. This helps the employer with its cash-flow challenges, but it also subjects the employees to big risk, especially if they can't sell those shares for a certain period of time. If you already depend on your employer for your paycheck, do you also want to put all your retirement money at risk, knowing that if the company goes belly-up, you lose both? Probably not.

ERISA

Qualified plans offered by businesses are covered by ERISA, which stands for Employee Retirement Income Security Act. It governs retirement plans in the private sector. It spells out things like **vesting, funding,** disclosure, etc. Vesting means that at some point even the employer's contributions belong to the employee. Or, at least some percent of those contributions. If you're in a 401(k) and your employer has put in $10,000 in matching contributions, you'd walk away with only $3,000 if you were only 30% vested. If you were 70% vested, you'd probably forego the temptation to accidentally key your supervisor's car in the parking garage as you walk out with $7,000. And, if you were 100% vested, you might even go back to meet a former colleague for lunch once in a while. The vesting schedule has to be laid out, and there is a maximum time frame that a company can use before an employee becomes fully or "100% vested." There has to be money in the plan and the contributions are governed by the section on **funding**. The section on **reporting** makes sure that employees are provided regular updates on the account. The employee also gets to choose a beneficiary.

Who is eligible for these qualified plans? Gotta be 21 years old and work at least 1,000 hours a year. That's ERISA in a nutshell, a really small nutshell.

INDIVIDUAL PLANS

Traditional IRA

The first thing you need to remember is: The I stands for INDIVIDUAL. An IRA is an Individual Retirement Account, so don't let the exam trick you into saying a husband and wife should open a "joint IRA." There is no such thing. If a spouse is non-working, an individual can contribute the current maximum on his or her behalf in the spouse's INDIVIDUAL Retirement Account. They can do this if they file jointly for income taxes. But under no circumstances can two people jointly own an IRA.

Who can have a **Traditional IRA**? Anyone with **earned income**. How much can they contribute? 100% of earned income up to the current maximum, and there are also "catch-up provisions" that allow people 50 and older to put in an extra amount. Remember on the exam—they might not get to *deduct* their contributions, but if they have earned income, they can have and contribute to an IRA. So, don't let the exam trick you into saying a wealthy executive with a 401(k) is somehow prohibited from having an IRA. He can contribute to his IRA; if he's covered by an employer plan or makes too darned much money, he might not get to deduct the contribution, but the contribution can still be made. What is "earned income"? Basically, it's the money earned through salary, bonuses, tips, writer's royalties and—get this—alimony. Earned income does not include income from investments or passive income, like the stuff we looked at with direct participation programs (limited partnerships).

There are two types of IRAs, Traditional and Roth. Traditional IRAs can be funded with pre-tax dollars. That means if you make $25,000 a year and contribute $5,000 to your traditional IRA, you're only taxed on the remaining or "post-contribution" amount of $20,000. Of course, when you pull the money out at retirement, you'll pay ordinary income tax on all of it. See, with retirement plans, you either pay tax before it goes in, or when it comes out. Luckily, you don't have to pay tax on both ends. You shouldn't take any money out until you're 59½ years old unless you want to pay a 10% penalty on the money taken out. Luckily, there are a few ways to avoid the penalty (but not the ordinary income tax):

- Become disabled
- Die
- Buy a first home for residential purposes (up to $10K)
- Use $ for certain medical and educational expenses
- **72(t)** series of substantially equal payments

An individual should wait until he's 59½ to take distributions; he also has to start taking it out by the time he's 70½. If not, the IRS will slap a 50% insufficient distribution penalty on him, which seems a little harsh but is unfortunately how it is. To keep things nice and simple, it's not the year in which the individual turns 70½ (like anybody actually celebrates or notices their 70½th birthday). It's April 1st (not the 15th, which would have made too darned much sense) of the year following the year in which the individual turns 70½.

Gives you a whole new respect for CPAs and retirement specialists, doesn't it? And this is called the **required minimum distribution** the IRS is sort of requiring him to take.

Roth IRA

The **Roth IRA** is funded with after-tax dollars. Therefore, the money comes out tax-free as long as the individual is 59½ years old and has had the account for at least 5 years. For the Roth there is no requirement to start taking the money out at 70½. Since the IRS isn't going to tax that money, they couldn't care less when it starts coming out.

The contribution limits for both the traditional and the Roth are 100% of earned income up to the current maximum. For people 50 and older, an additional amount is allowed as a "catch up" provision, as in, "Social Security ain't lookin' so secure, so let's everybody try and catch up." If an individual has both a Traditional and a Roth IRA, the contribution limit would be the total allocated among the two accounts. If the maximum is $5,000 maybe $3,700 for the Traditional and $1,300 for the Roth.

Income Limits

In the "real world" there are income limits for Roth IRAs, but I would not expect the exam to hit you with those. Do remember, though, that there are no income limits for the Traditional IRA. Don't worry about how much money somebody makes in the test question, or if she's covered by an employer plan. All that would change is the amount she can deduct from her contribution. See, nothing is simple. We'd like to say that all contributions to a Traditional IRA are pre-tax, but, if the individual is covered by an employer plan or makes what the IRS deems a high salary, she might only get to deduct some of her contribution, or even none of it.

So what?

Either way, she can make her maximum contribution. She'd just have to keep track of how much went in after-tax or her "cost basis," so she doesn't get taxed twice on that money when it comes out with everything else. So, it's a hassle, but if she has earned income, she can contribute to her Traditional IRA. She might not deduct 100% or even any percent of it, but it can still go in there.

Whether you deduct or not, the real beauty of these plans is that the earnings grow tax-deferred. Since you don't have to remove cash or sell stocks to pay the current tax bill, your principal is larger, which means that more money can make more money, which can make more money all the time...compounded returns is what we call that. In other words, if you can get a 5% return on your investments, it's better to make 5% of a bigger and bigger number, as opposed to shrinking the size of your principal each year by paying the tax collectors.

So tax-deferred earnings provide a major benefit to the individual.

Investment Restrictions

IRAs are not really for high-risk speculation. Toward that end, there are to be no short sales, margin trading, or naked options in these accounts. Also no tangibles or life insurance. And municipal bonds make no sense for a Traditional IRA. Municipal bonds pay tax-exempt interest, which is why their coupon payments are so low. All money coming out of the IRA is taxed, so the municipal bond's tax advantage is destroyed and all the individual is left with is a lower coupon payment. That and a good arbitration case.

Rollovers and Transfers

If you want to move your IRA from one custodian to another, your best bet is to do a transfer. Just have the custodian cut a check to the new custodian, nice and simple. You can do as many of these direct transfers as you want. If, however, you do a *rollover*, things get tricky. First, you can only do one per year, and, second, it must be completed within 60 days. Plus, the custodian with-holds 20% of the money, and that will become a huge hassle, so, if at all possible, do the transfer.

In a rollover, the custodian cuts a check in your name. You cash it and then send the money to the new custodian, but you have to make up the 20% that was withheld. Otherwise, what they withheld is treated as an early distribution, and now the 10% penalty thing plus ordinary income, plus much heartburn and lost sleep, etc. Imagine rolling over a $100,000 IRA, where you receive a check for only $80,000 and then have to come up with an additional $20,000 within 60 days or get penalized and taxed.

No thanks. Also note that what the "real world" calls a "direct rollover" is considered a "transfer" on the exam. A "rollover" on the test means the individual has the check cut in *her* name.

EDUCATION SAVINGS PLANS

529 PLANS, COVERDELL EDUCATION SAVINGS ACCOUNTS

These are not retirement plans, but we usually talk about them when discussing retirement plans because of the tax deferral.

529 Savings Plan

The 529 Savings plan allows investors to save/invest for education. Usually, it would be a family member socking away money for a nephew's or grandchild's education, but, actually, the **donor** and the beneficiary do not need to be related. The beneficiary also does not have to be a child. The person who opens the account is the owner; the beneficiary is the person who will use the money for education. Lots of flexibility in these plans. The donor can contribute up to the **gift tax** exclusion ($13,000 currently) without incurring gift taxes and can even do a lump sum contribution for the first five years ($65,000) without incurring gift tax hassles. A married couple—grandpa and grandma, for example—could double that amount and contribute $130,000 currently. Note that if somebody uses the five-year-up-front method, they can't make any more gifts to the beneficiary for the next five years without dealing with gift taxes. We're talking about avoiding gift taxes—the states would actually set the maximum that may be contributed on behalf of a beneficiary.

Contributions are made after-tax, and the withdrawals used for qualified education expenses are tax-free at the federal level. A qualified withdrawal would be taken to cover tuition, room & board, books and no more than seven pitchers of beer per week. Kidding with the last item—the expenses do need to be directly related to education; otherwise, you'll get hit just like you do for an early IRA distribution (10% penalty plus ordinary income tax). Once per year, the account can be transferred to a different 529 Savings plan without tax hassles. Also, if the beneficiary decides he doesn't need the money, the account can name a second beneficiary without tax problems, as long as the second beneficiary is related to the first.

The plans are state-specific, so some states may actually allow the donors who are residents to deduct their contributions for purposes of state income taxes. Or, maybe they'll tax the withdrawals if little junior decides he's too good for any of the little colleges in his little old home state. Also note that the MSRB and FINRA are actively increasing the regulatory protections for these plans. Believe it or not 529 plans are classified as "municipal securities" and the MSRB and FINRA are going to raise the requirements for selling these plans to what they are for selling mutual funds. In other words, lots of disclosure about tax implications, fees, and the fact that folks like you aren't selling them just to be nice. We'll discuss the "Coverdell" plan below, and see that the 529 Savings Plans differ from them in the following ways:

- Higher annual contributions allowed
- Maximum contribution is per-donor, not per beneficiary
- Used only for post-high school education (not Kindergarten through private high school)
- Always remain the property of the account owner, not the beneficiary

Coverdell Education Savings Account

The Coverdell plan is also funded with after-tax dollars, but the maximum contribution is per-child, not per-donor. At the time of this writing, the maximum contribution per-child is only $2,000, a figure that could rise by the time you read this, though not by very much. Investments in the account grow tax-deferred and withdrawals are tax free when used for qualified education expenses.

In summary, the 529 Savings Plan and the CESA differ in the following ways:

529 SAVINGS PLAN	CESA
Always remain the property of the account owner, not the beneficiary	Assets become the property of the beneficiary at the age of adulthood (age of majority)
Maximum contribution is per-donor, not per beneficiary	Maximum contributions are per-beneficiary
Used only for post-high school education (not Kindergarten through private high school)	Withdrawals can be used for education expenses for Kindergarten through post-high school
Higher annual contributions allowed	

VARIABLE ANNUITIES

With a mutual fund the investor gets taxed on dividends and capital gains whenever she receives/takes them. As much as modern Americans love to procrastinate, imagine how much we love to procrastinate when it comes to paying taxes. Not only is it psychologically appealing to just keep putting off the big tax bill, but also there is a major financial advantage to this strategy. See, whether we reinvest our mutual fund dividends or go shopping, we pay tax on that dividend for the tax year it was received. That tax bill reduces the amount we have invested. So, if the account gains 4% next year, it's 4% of a reduced number. This tax burden keeps knocking down our principal, slowing down our ability to earn compounded returns. See, even though a bond might pay 5% fixed, if you're reinvesting those interest payments into more bonds, you will have more money earning interest next year, and even more the year after that. That's called compounded interest. Of course, we can't predict that we'll be able to keep reinvesting at 5%, but there's probably about a 50-50 chance that it will be reinvested at 5% or higher. Reinvestment risk doesn't always work against us, right? Yes, it stinks to reinvest a 5% coupon at 3%, but it is kind of fun to reinvest a 5% coupon payment at 9%. The market price of your bond is down—so what? You aren't thinking about selling, anyway. Just the fact that you're taking your returns and reinvesting them so that you have a bigger principal amount earning some rate of return is a beautiful thing. In fact, since we've stumbled onto one of the few interesting topics related to the Series 7, let's give you a sneak peak at what most of you will see up ahead, whether they've informed you of it or not—the Series 65/66. In the Series 65/66 you'll learn that an investment that grows at 5% for five years in a row is worth a lot more than just 5% more at the end. In fact, if you get 5% for 5 years, your dollar is worth $1.27 at the end of five years. To check my math, just take $1 and multiply it by 1.05. That's one year. Times 1.05 again. That's two years. Keep multiplying by 1.05 until you've done it five times, just as a dollar invested for five years at five percent would do. You end up with $1.27. And, if you're really curious, keep doing it and notice how much faster the principal grows every year. The money would *double* every 14.4 years, as those of you hip to the "rule of 72" already know. If the Series 7 has the audacity to bring up the "rule of 72" concept, what it's saying is that you can take a rate of return and divide it into the number 72. Your answer tells you how many years it takes for the money to double. So, if you get returns of 10%, it takes 7.2 years for your money to double.

That assumes you're not taking any withdrawals and are, instead, reinvesting all the dividends, interest, and capital gains into more securities throwing off more dividends, interest, and capital gains, and so on. So, if you can avoid having to sell a bunch of stock to pay this year's tax bill on your investments, your money will grow faster. That's what tax deferral is all about.

Tax deferral is the main thing that separates a mutual fund from a variable annuity. A mutual fund held in a regular ole' taxable account will subject investors to taxation every year. The dividend and capital gains distributions are taxable, and if the investor redeems some shares for a gain, that's also taxable for the year it occurs. A **variable annuity**, however, is really a retirement plan where you get to keep all the dividends and capital gains in the account, adding to your principal, and compounding your returns forever and ever and ever.

Whoa, sorry. Not forever. You get to defer taxation until you take the money out, which is usually at retirement. Your money grows much faster when it's not being taxed for 10, 20, maybe 30 years, but every dance reaches the point where you have to pay the fiddler. It's been a fun dance, for sure, but the reality is that you will pay ordinary income tax rates on the earnings you've been shielding from the hungry hands of the IRS all these years.

Ordinary income rates, remember. If you're in the 35% tax bracket, the gains coming out of your variable annuity are taxed at that rate. Which complicates things, since long-term capital gains taken in a regular ol' taxable account are now taxed at no more than 15%.

Oh well. The tax deferral is still a big advantage, and there are other advantages of the variable annuity. I'm looking at a very handy brochure that compares mutual funds and variable annuities. The company, which sells both, is pointing out that no matter how diligently you save for retirement, you could end up outliving your nest egg. Unless you buy an annuity, that is. An annuity comes with a **mortality guarantee**, which means that as long as you are alive, you can receive a monthly check. Many readers already know this because they have sold their share of fixed annuities. A **fixed annuity** is an insurance contract where somebody puts money into the contract, and the insurance company promises to pay a certain rate of return and keep making monthly payments for as long as the annuitant is alive. A variable annuity doesn't promise a particular rate of return, which is where they got the "variable" part, but since investors are investing in little mutual funds of their choosing, maybe they'll end up doing much better than the modest rate that the fixed annuity guarantees. In other words, in a variable annuity, the annuitant bears the investment risk rather than having the insurance company promise a certain rate of return. In exchange for bearing the risks we've looked at in the bond and stock markets, the variable annuitant gets the opportunity to do much better than he would have in a fixed annuity.

Could he do worse?

Sure, but what does he want? If he wants a guarantee, he buys a fixed annuity where the insurance company guarantees a certain rate of return. Now he lives with "purchasing power risk," because if the annuity promises 4%, that's not going to be sufficient with inflation rising at 6%. If he wants to protect his purchasing power by investing in the stock market, he buys a variable annuity, but now he takes on all the investment risks we've discussed.

Life is full of tough choices like that. Just like when I chose "English" as a major when I should have chosen "Finance" or "Anything that could potentially lead to employment." Bottom line is, a variable annuity is really just a mutual fund investment that grows tax deferred. The insurance company has basically crossed a mutual fund with a retirement plan here. Insurance companies then cross-pollinated that concept with an insurance policy, offering a **death benefit** to folks buying variable annuities. In a regular ol' mutual fund investment, you could put in $80,000 and when you die the investment could be worth $30,000, which is all your family would inherit. In a variable annuity, the death benefit would pay out the $80,000. In fact, if the value of your investments was worth more than the $80,000 you had put in, your family would receive the $90,000 or whatever the account was worth.

Insurance companies sell peace of mind, and that death benefit helps a lot of investors sleep better. Pretty tough to put a price tag on that.

Although, actually, I'm going to be pointing out that price tag in great detail throughout our fascinating discussion of variable annuities, but I don't want to hit you with too much excitement all at once. For now, just know that a variable annuity offers the investment choices that you'd get from a family of mutual funds (growth, value, high-yield bonds, etc.), the tax deferral you'd get from an IRA or 401(k) plan, plus a death benefit similar to what you'd get from a life insurance policy.

PURCHASING ANNUITIES

The two major types of variable annuities are "immediate" and "deferred." Those terms simply define how soon the contract holder wants to begin receiving payments. These are retirement plans, so you do need to be 59½ to avoid penalties, unless you qualify for an exemption. So, some customers might want or need to wait 15 or 20 years before receiving payments. We call that a **deferred annuity**, because "deferred" means "I'll do it later," the way some readers may have "deferred" their study process for a while before opening the book and realizing there's, like, a lot to know for this exam.

If the individual is already in her 60s, she may want to start receiving payments immediately. As you can probably guess, we call that an **immediate annuity**.

Customers can buy annuities either with one big payment or several smaller payments. The first method is called "single premium" or "single payment." The second method is called "periodic payment." If an investor has a large chunk of money, she can put it in a variable annuity, where it can grow tax-deferred. If she's putting in a big single premium, she can choose either to wait or to begin receiving annuity payments immediately. She has to be 59½ years old to start annuitizing, but if she's old enough, she can begin the pay-out or "annuity phase" immediately. That's called a **single-payment immediate annuity**. Maybe she's only 42, though, and wants to let the money grow another 20 years before taking it out.

That's called a **single-payment deferred annuity** (SPDA). This way she buys **accumulation units** with her money and holds them as they—we certainly hope—increase in value, just like mutual fund shares. In fact, the accumulation units will increase in number, too, because all dividend and capital gains distributions from the little mutual funds will be reinvested into more accumulation units—that's the compounding we were discussing a few moments ago.

Many investors put money into the annuity during the accumulation phase (pay-in) gradually, over time. That's called "periodic payment," and if they aren't done paying in yet, you can bet the insurance company isn't going to start paying out. So, if you're talking about a "periodic payment" plan, the only way to do it is periodic deferred. No such thing as a "Periodic Immediate Annuity."

To review, then, there are three methods of purchasing annuities:

- Single-Payment Deferred Annuity
- Periodic-Payment Deferred Annuity
- Single-Payment Immediate Annuity

There is no such thing as a "periodic-payment immediate annuity," which just looks like a test question waiting to be written.

THE SEPARATE ACCOUNT

An insurance company is one of the finest business models ever constructed. See, no one person can take the risk of dying at age 32 and leaving the family with an unpaid mortgage, a bunch of other bills, and a sudden loss of income, not to mention the maybe $15,000 it takes just for a funeral these days. But, an insurance company can take the risk that a certain number of individuals will die prematurely by insuring a huge number of individuals and then using the very precise laws of probability over large numbers that tell them how many individuals will die each year with only a small margin of error. Once they've taken the insurance premiums that individuals pay, they then invest what's left after covering expenses and invest it very wisely in the real estate, fixed-income, and stock markets. They have just as much data on these markets, so they can use the laws of probability again to figure out that if they take this much risk here, they can count on earning this much return over here within only a small margin of error.

And, of course, insurance companies are very conservative investors. That's what allows them to crunch a bunch of numbers and know with reasonable certainty that they will never have to pay so many death benefits in one year that their investments are totally wiped out. This conservative investment account that guarantees the payout on whole life, term life, and fixed annuities is called the **general account**. In other words, the general account is for the insurance company's investments.

They then created an account that is separate from the general account and, believe it or not, decided to name it the "separate account." It's really a mutual fund family that offers tax deferral, but we don't call it a mutual fund, even though it's also covered by the same Investment Company Act of 1940. The Investment Company Act of 1940 defines a separate account like so:

> "Separate account" means an account established and maintained by an insurance company pursuant to the laws of any State or territory of the United States, or of Canada or any province thereof, under which income, gains and losses, whether or not realized, from assets allocated to such account, are, in accordance with the applicable contract, credited to or charged against such account without regard to other income, gains, or losses of the insurance company.

Well, that certainly clears things up, doesn't it?

Anyway, you will get a few questions talking about the "general account" versus the "separate account," so please keep the two separate. When your premium dollars are invested into the general account, you are guaranteed a certain rate of return—whole life, fixed annuity. When your premium dollars are invested into the separate account, welcome to the stock and bond markets, where anything can happen and usually does.

From the perspective of the nice couple sitting across from you at the table, it all looks pretty much the same. You were talking about the Platinum Equity Income Fund a few minutes ago—now that you've switched to your variable annuity pitch, we're still seeing the same darned Platinum Equity Income Fund. What's up with that?

It's the same darned fund, but if you buy it through an annuity purchase, we call it a **subaccount**, just to keep everything nice and simple.

FEATURES OF THE VARIABLE ANNUITY CONTRACT

The insurance company makes some promises when you buy the annuity. They promise that if you die during the **accumulation period**, your beneficiary will receive the greater of the contract's value or what you put in. That death benefit, of course, comes at a price, but it gives you peace of mind knowing that your wife, for example, won't receive less than you put in should you pass away prematurely. And—if the investments have done well, she'll receive the higher value, too. Most people end up taking the money out as monthly payments for the rest of their life. The insurance company promises to make these monthly annuity payments for as long as the annuitant shall live, even if she ends up living an inconveniently long time. Notice how an annuity gives the insurance company a different kind of "mortality risk." In a life insurance policy, their risk is that somebody will put in $10,000 and die the next month, forcing the company to pay out hundreds of thousands, maybe a million. In an annuity, their mortality risk is that the annuitant will end up living to the ripe old age of 101. The insurance company makes a mortality guarantee, which promises to pay the annuitant each month for the rest of her life. But—as always—they cover their risk with a fee, called a mortality risk fee. An insurance company has the risk that their expenses will rise. They promise to keep expenses level, but they charge you an "expense risk fee" to cover their risk. In fact, usually, the two are combined and referred to as a "mortality and expense risk fee," or "M & E" for those in the real world who love to abbreviate. If the whole thing just doesn't work out, you can **surrender** the contract for its "surrender value," but watch out here. The first seven or eight years is typically your "surrender period." During that time if you decide to cash in the annuity, you will get hit with a surrender charge, which is often called a "contingent deferred sales charge" just as we saw on the B-shares. These surrender charges start out pretty high—maybe 7 or 8%—which is one reason that deferred annuities are long-term investments.

Don't be pitching a deferred annuity to a senior citizen, who might need to access her money for an emergency. You need to be pretty sure the individual can leave the money alone for at least as long as the surrender period. And, be honest and upfront with the investor—don't tell her money is "safe" if it's going into subaccounts with names like the International Opportunities Fund or Small Cap Growth Fund. The investor chooses among stock and bond investments primarily in the annuity, so make sure they don't think it's "like a fixed annuity." A fixed annuity is *guaranteed* as to value. A variable annuity is not. Kind of an important difference, right?

When the individual purchases the annuity, the following are deducted from the check:

- Sales charge (if they have a front-end load)
- Administrative fee
- State premium tax

Most annuities use the contingent deferred sales charge called the "surrender period," but some are still sold with front-end sales charges. Either way, there is a premium tax and administrative fees taken out of the check. The individual then allocates what's left to the various subaccounts, the little mutual funds. Maybe 20% goes into the income subaccount, 20% into the growth subaccount and 60% to the high-yield long-term bond subaccount. From the money invested there are plenty of fees that will be deducted. We have all the operating expenses we saw for mutual funds: management fee, 12b-1 fee, other expenses. And, we also have the "mortality & expense risk fee."

What is the maximum that an insurance company can charge for sales charges and expenses? The current regulations just say that the charges and expenses have to be "reasonable."

Seriously.

Bonus Annuities

As if annuities weren't complicated enough already, the exam may expect you to know something about **bonus annuities**. With a bonus annuity the annuity company may offer to enhance the buyer's premium by contributing an additional 1 to 5% of what he/she puts in. Of course, this comes with a price. First, there are fees attached and, second, the surrender period is longer. Third, if the investor surrenders the contract early, the bonus disappears. Remember that an investor will get penalized by the annuity company with a "surrender charge" if they pull all their money out early. For "bonus annuities" that period where the investor could get penalized is longer.

Bonus annuities are not suitable for everyone. Variable annuities in general are not good for short-term investment goals, since the surrender charge will be applied during the first 7 years or so. Should you switch a customer into a bonus annuity? Maybe. But, remember, even though the annuitant can avoid taxes through a 1035 exchange, when she exchanges the annuity, her surrender period starts all over again. And, yes, FINRA will bust you if it looks like you did the switch just to make a nice commission, forcing the investor to start the surrender period all over again. In general, investors should maximize their 401(k) and other retirement plans before considering annuities. Annuities are ideal for those who have maxed out those plans, since the annuity allows investors to contribute as much as they would like.

Voting Rights

Just like owners of mutual fund shares, owners of variable annuities get to vote their units on important decisions such as:

- Electing the Board of Managers
- Changing the Investment Objectives, Policies
- Ratifying the Independent Auditor/Accounting Firm

PAYING IN, PAYING OUT

Most annuities are **non-qualified**, which means that they are purchased with after-tax dollars. When you cut the check for, say, $50,000 for the annuity, you get no tax deduction from the IRS. So they won't tax that money again when you take it out. That $50,000 will be your cost basis. You will only pay taxes on the amount of earnings above that and only when you finally take out the money. But, if the exam specifically mentions a "tax-qualified variable annuity," you'll have to adjust your thinking. A "tax-qualified variable annuity" is funded with pre-tax or tax-deductible contributions with the same maximums used for Traditional IRA accounts. Also, like the Traditional IRA—and unlike the non-qualified variable annuity—withdrawals from the account must begin at age 70 ½. The IRS refers to these plans as "individual retirement annuities," and they are basically just IRAs funded with an investment into a variable annuity. Why do that? Probably for the death benefit during the accumulation phase that guarantees your beneficiaries will receive at least the amount you contributed. Or, some people like the idea of an annuity payout that lasts as long as they live, perhaps longer, as we'll see. So, most questions—maybe all of them—will focus on non-qualified variable annuities funded with after-tax dollars. But, don't be shocked if you get a question or two about variable annuities funded with pre-tax dollars.

When you are allocating your investment among the little subaccounts, you are in the "accumulation phase." Since this is a tax-deferred account, the dividend and capital gains distributions from the equity income or bond subaccount will be automatically reinvested into more **accumulation units**. Therefore, part of the answer to a likely question is that "both the number and value of accumulation units varies." That's right. You're investing in the unpredictable stock and bond markets, so the value of the "accumulation units" varies right along with the markets. The number varies too, because you don't take the dividends and capital gains now—they automatically reinvest them into more units.

When you reach the magic age of 59½ you can annuitize the contract. And, you can certainly wait longer than that, too. It's just that, without a qualifying reason, you'd have to pay a 10% penalty tax on the earnings portion of the contract, plus ordinary income rates, *plus* maybe surrender charges to the annuity company. So, when you reach retirement age, you shift from putting money in to taking money out. When you decide to **annuitize**, the insurance company converts your accumulation units into a *fixed number of* **annuity units**. Did you catch the italics? This concept would make a nice, little Roman-numeral-type question. Remember—the *number* of annuity units is fixed. It's their *value* that varies. How does the insurance company calculate your first payment? They take the following into consideration:

- Life expectancy
- Age and gender

- **AIR**
- Settlement option

Insurance companies are experts when it comes to knowing when you are going to die. No, they don't know when *you* are going to die. I mean, they are really good at knowing what percentage of people are going to die in any given year. They don't know the exact percentage, but they can pick a tight range of outcomes that is so darned dependable that they will win as often as the house wins in Vegas. Yes, a few individuals will always beat the house, but the other 99% will keep the house rolling in dough for years to come. You *might* have a life expectancy of 82 years and still manage to see 100. But only a tiny percentage of folks will end up that far from what's expected. As long as we make enough off the other 99%, we can easily cover the few who end up beating the house.

So, the older you are, the bigger your monthly payment will be. Why? You'll be gone sooner if you're 92 compared to someone who's only 62.

Why would gender matter? Women still manage to live longer, so they'll receive a slightly lower monthly payment. It will all work out the same, though—they're just using the separate mortality tables for men and women. Men, high-strung and risk-taking that we are, still consistently drop several years before women.

We'll explain the funky "AIR," which stands for "assumed interest rate" below, right after we take an exciting look at "settlement options."

SETTLEMENT OPTIONS

When the individual gets ready to annuitize the contract, he tells the insurance company which payout option he's choosing. For the biggest monthly check, he'll choose the "life only" or "straight life" option. That means the company only has to make payments for as long as he lives. As soon as he ceases, so do his payments. If that seems too risky, he can buy a "unit refund life annuity." This way he is guaranteed a certain number of payments. If he dies before receiving them, his beneficiary receives the balance of payments. If he chooses **life with period certain**, the company will make payments for the greater of his life or a certain period of time, such as 10 years. If he dies after 2 years, the company makes payments to his beneficiary for the rest of the term. And if he lives longer than 10 years, they just keep on making payments until he finally expires. The **joint and last survivor** option would provide the smallest monthly check because the company is obligated to make payments as long as either one of the parties is still alive. The contract pays the joint beneficiaries when it is annuitized, and keeps paying until the last beneficiary expires. Covering two persons' mortality risks (the risk that they'll live an inconveniently long time) is an expensive proposition to the insurance company, so those monthly checks are going to be the smallest.

AIR AND ANNUITY UNITS

As we said, once the number of annuity units has been determined, we say that the number of annuity units is fixed. So, for example, maybe every month he'll be paid the value of 100 annuity units.

Trouble is, he has no idea how big that monthly check is going to be, since nobody knows what 100 annuity units will be worth month-to-month, just like nobody knows what mutual fund shares will be worth month-to-month. Remember the "fixed-shares systematic withdrawal plan" from a mutual fund? We said that the fund will redeem a fixed number of shares and pay you whatever they happened to be worth. Again, the units really are mutual fund shares; we just can't call them that. During the pay-in phase, we call the shares **accumulation units**. During the pay-out phase, we call them **annuity units**, just to keep things nice and simple.

So, how much is an annuity unit worth every month? All depends on the investment performance of the separate account compared to the company's expectations of its performance.

Seriously.

AIR

If the separate account returns are better than anybody expected, the units increase in value. If the account returns are exactly as expected, the unit value stays the same. And if the account returns are lower than expected, the unit value drops from the month before. It's all based on the actuary's best guess, known technically as the **Assumed Interest Rate**. If the **AIR** is 5%, that just means the actuary expects the account to return 5% every year. If the account actually gets a 6% annualized rate of return one month, the individual's check gets bigger. (Remember, during the payout phase, the investor is paid the value of his fixed number of annuity units, so to say that the annuity units have increased in value is the same as saying the individual's check gets bigger.) If the account gets the anticipated 5% return next month, that's the same as AIR and the check will stay the same. And if the account gets only a 4% return the following month, the check will go down.

Don't let the exam trick you on this concept. If the AIR is 5%, here is how it would work:

Actual Return:	5%	7%	6%	5%	4%
Check:	$1,020	$1,035	$1,045	$1,045	$1,030

When the account gets a 7% return, the account gets much bigger. So when it gets only a 6% return the following month, that's 6% of a bigger account, and is 1% more than we expected to get. So, just compare the actual return with the AIR. If the actual return is bigger, so is the monthly check. If it's smaller, so is the monthly check. If the actual return is the same as the AIR, the check stays the same.

FIXED VS. VARIABLE ANNUITIES

Notice how the payout varies and, thus, the clever name "variable annuity." If an individual doesn't like the variable part of the annuity she can buy an insurance product called a fixed annuity. In a fixed annuity, the insurance company invests her payments into its general account and guarantees a certain monthly payment. Maybe the payment is $750. That's a guaranteed $750, but that $750 is also just about guaranteed to lose value to inflation. If you keep getting the same flat payment even as prices rise, your payment won't go very far at Walmart, right?

If you want the guaranteed payout, you subject yourself to this "purchasing power" or "constant dollar" risk. If you want to fight inflation, you buy a variable annuity so you can invest at least part of your money in stocks, which are the best protection against inflation. To combat inflation/purchasing power risk, though, you take on investment risk.

Always trade-offs in this business.

But, since Americans simply have to have it all, the industry has also created "combination annuities," which are a hybrid of fixed and variable. Some of the payments the individual makes are put in the general account to guarantee a certain rate of return; some of the payments are allocated to the separate account to try to beat the rate of inflation. So, remember that when the individual is allocating money to the various subaccounts, one of the options is a fixed-return investment into the general account.

Just to keep things nice and simple.

EQUITY-INDEXED ANNUITIES

What is a so-called **equity-indexed annuity**? Basically, it is an annuity that guarantees a minimum rate of return backed by the insurance company's claims-paying ability. The "equity-indexed" part means that the individual can make excess upside when the S&P 500 or other index rises. Some quick bullets on the indexed annuity include:

- Equity-Indexed Annuities are considered to be insurance products, not securities.
- EIAs are sold by insurance agents who do not need a securities license.
- EIAs pay a guaranteed rate of return (minimum) but also offer higher returns if a particular stock index rises.
- Investors do not typically get all of the increase on the index, usually capped at some percentage.
- EIAs typically have surrender charges during the early years of the contract, so if the agent says "you can't lose money," he must point out the surrender charges.
- EIAs and deferred annuities are appropriate as long-term investments only due to the surrender charges.

For more information on indexed annuities contact:

Sheryl J. Moore
President and CEO
LifeSpecs.com • AnnuitySpecs.com
Advantage Group Associates, Inc.
Office number (515) 262-2623

TAXATION OF ANNUITIES

The tax implications of variable annuities are a little tricky.

Accumulation Period

During the accumulation phase, the investment is growing tax-deferred. So, all the dividends and capital gains distributions from the subaccounts are being reinvested into more units, just like most people reinvest their distributions back into a mutual fund. If the individual dies, the death benefit is paid to the beneficiary. The death benefit is included in the annuitant's **estate** for estate tax purposes, and the beneficiary would have to pay ordinary income tax on anything above the cost basis. If the husband bought the annuity for $50,000, and it's now worth $60,000, she'll receive $60,000 and pay ordinary income rates on the $10,000 of earnings.

Sometimes people just can't stop themselves from cashing in their chips. Not that they haven't been given incentives not to. If they're under 59½ and don't have a qualifying exemption, they will not only pay ordinary income tax on the earnings, but also a 10% penalty tax, too. So, if it's a $60,000 annuity, and a 49-year-old surrenders the contract that he bought for $50,000, he'd pay his ordinary income rate on the $10,000 of earnings and also a 10% penalty of $1,000. You didn't think the IRS would, like, penalize him 10% and then take his ordinary income rate on what's left, did you? It's his ordinary income rate *and* 10% of the excess over his cost basis.

Notice how only the excess over cost basis is taxed and/or penalized on a non-qualified annuity. The after-tax cost basis is just the cost basis, which means the IRS taxed that money a long time ago and quickly lost interest in it. The earnings part—that part really intrigues them.

So, if you're not 59½ yet, the IRS is giving you all kinds of reasons not to surrender your contract. And, we already mentioned that the insurance company will keep a percentage on the back end if you surrender during the early years of the contract. So, you can have your money if you want to, but if you take it out too soon, you'll be penalized by the IRS and possibly the annuity/insurance company, too.

Also, this isn't the same thing as a life insurance contract. With a life insurance policy, people often cash in part of their **cash value**. If they're only taking out what they put in—or less—the IRS treats it as part of their cost basis. In an annuity, however, if somebody does a **random withdrawal** for, say, $10,000, the IRS considers that to be part of the taxable earnings. So, if you get a test question where some dude put in $10,000 and with the annuity at $30,000 this dude takes out $10,000, remember that that is *not* treated as his cost basis. The way the IRS sees things, the dude has $20,000 of earnings. So, whatever comes out is treated as part of that $20,000. So, the entire $10,000 random withdrawal is taxed as ordinary income. And, if he's not 59½ yet, the IRS will also penalize him $1,000.

Loans

Some insurance companies allow contract owners to take a loan against the value of the annuity during the accumulation period. Usually, the interest charge is handled by reducing the number of accumulation units owned. If the owner pays back the loan in full, the number of units goes up again. Unlike a loan against a life insurance policy, however, a loan from an annuity is treated as a distribution. In other words, it is not tax-free.

1035 Exchanges

We've mentioned that both annuities and insurance policies allow people to exchange their contract for another without paying taxes. That's fine, just don't forget the surrender period. If somebody still has a 6% surrender fee (contingent deferred sales charge) in effect, and you push them to do a 1035 exchange, the IRS won't have a problem with it, but FINRA almost certainly will. Especially if you get caught.

Annuity Period

When the annuitant begins receiving monthly checks, part of each check is considered taxable ordinary income, and part of it is considered to be part of the cost basis. Once the annuitant has received all of the cost basis back, each additional annuity payment will be fully taxable.

Also, if the beneficiary is receiving annuity payments through a "life with period certain" or a "joint and last survivor" settlement option, she will pay ordinary income tax on part of each monthly check, too—as always, on the "excess over cost basis."

72(t) and Substantially Equal Periodic Payments

We've mentioned that the magic age for taking distributions is 59½ because, otherwise, the individual is hit with early withdrawal penalties. Remember that annuities are by nature retirement plans and are subject to the 10% penalty for early withdrawals made without a good excuse. One good excuse is to utilize IRS rule "**72(t).**" As with an IRA, an individual can avoid the 10% penalty if the withdrawal qualifies for an exemption. For example, if the individual has become disabled and can't work, or has certain medical expenses, money can be taken out penalty-free. Notice how I didn't say tax-free.

Basically, a reference to "72t" has to do with an individual taking a series of substantially equal periodic payments. Of course, the industry quickly turned that phrase into the acronym "SEPP." The IRS won't penalize the early withdrawal if the individual sets up a rigid schedule whereby they withdraw the money by any of several IRS-approved methods. Once you start your little SEPP program, stay on it. See, the IRS requires you to continue the SEPP program for five years or until you are the age of 59½, whichever comes last. So, if the individual is 45, she'll have to keep taking periodic payments until she's 59½. If the individual is 56 when she starts, she'll still have to continue for 5 years. Either that, or cut the IRS a check for the very penalties she was trying to avoid.

VARIABLE LIFE INSURANCE

AN INSURANCE PRIMER

I've always felt that it would be awfully rude of me to die unexpectedly and leave family and friends footing the bill for my funeral. That's why I basically "rent" insurance coverage through something called **term life insurance**. It's very cheap ($5.50 a month in my case), but it's only good for a certain term—maybe it's a 5-, 10-, or 20-year term. The individual pays premiums in exchange for a guaranteed death benefit payable to a beneficiary if the insured dies during that period. If the insured does not die during that period, the policy expires. If the policyholder wants to renew, he can, but he's older now and more costly to insure. In other words, his premiums will go up, even though the death benefit will stay the same. Plus, he's older and more likely to have some medical condition that raises his rates. So, as with all products, there are pluses and minuses.

Also note the language used in insurance:

- Policyholder: the owner of the policy, responsible for paying premiums
- Insured: the person whose life is insured by the policy, usually the policyholder
- Beneficiary: the party that receives the death benefit upon death of the insured

- Death benefit: the amount payable to the beneficiary upon death of the insured, minus any unpaid premiums or loan balances
- Cash value: a value that can be partially withdrawn or borrowed against

So, let's say that Joe Schmoe buys an insurance policy with a $100,000 death benefit payable to his wife. He's the policyholder and the insured. If he dies, the death benefit of $100,000 is paid to the beneficiary, his wife. As we'll see, most insurance also builds up cash value, which can be withdrawn or borrowed while Joe is still alive. (Note that term does not build up this cash value, which is also why it's relatively cheap insurance.)

Permanent vs. Temporary Insurance

Just as with housing, some prefer to rent for a term, some prefer to buy. Some feel that if you're going to be putting money aside, you might as well end up with something should you have the misfortune of living. Death benefits are only worth something when you die, and, as they say, you can't take it with you. You can leave it behind for your beneficiaries, but many people end up at age 55 realizing that their home is paid off, they've got a $2 million 401(k) that already names their spouse as beneficiary, so why do they need a $1 million death benefit? They're covered for the death part.

With term, they would really have nothing of value at this point to show for all those premiums. With **permanent insurance** however, there would be something called **cash value** that they could tap. They could borrow against it, or maybe withdraw some of it just for fun. The most common type of permanent insurance is called **whole life insurance**. You pay premiums for your whole life (thus the clever name "whole life"). Some policies have the policyholder stop paying premiums at a certain age, but it's still pretty darned close to his or her "whole life." The premiums are much higher than on the term insurance you sort of "rent," but insurance companies will guarantee a minimum cash value, and you can also pretty well plan for an even better cash value than that. This way it works to protect your beneficiaries if you die unexpectedly and also acts as a savings vehicle where the cash value grows tax-deferred. Maybe at age 55 you decide to borrow $50,000 of the cash value and put in a new kitchen with granite countertops, cherry cabinets, and other shockingly expensive amenities. Plus, remember that to renew a term policy means you pay a higher premium. Premiums are "level" in a whole life policy, meaning they don't go up.

So, term is "cheap," but after a few years you end up with nothing. And to keep it going, you'd have to pay more for the same benefit. Reminds me of how I spent five years paying "cheap" rent to a landlord. It was definitely lower than any mortgage payment would have been, so every month I "saved" at least $300. Only, at the end of this 5-year term, I had forked over 40 g's to the landlord and was left with nothing but the opportunity to renew my lease at a higher rate. I covered myself with a roof over my head for 5 years, and at the end of the 5 years I owned absolutely no part of that roof, not even one cracked, loose shingle.

Whole life is more like buying the house, which is exactly what I did after five foolish years of renting. I had to come up with a down payment, and my monthly mortgage is now $200 more per month than my rent was. But, at the end of 5 years, I'll have some equity in the house that I can tap into for a loan maybe (kind of like cash value). Just like with a whole life policy, I'll be getting at least something back for all those payments I've made over the years.

So, whole life involves premiums that are higher than those for term life insurance, but you end up with something even if you stop paying into the policy. There is a guaranteed cash value, whereas term leaves you with nothing. As with term, the death benefit is guaranteed, too, so this is a very popular product for people who want to protect their families and also use the policy as a savings vehicle, where all that increase in cash value grows tax-deferred. Both term and whole life insurance are purely insurance products, and many readers are not only selling them already, but also could probably tell you infinitely more about insurance products right now. Don't let them—remind them that they, too, are studying for a very difficult securities exam and have no extra time for holding court at this point.

Well nothing is simple in either the securities or insurance industry. Since some clients crave flexibility, the industry bent over backwards to come up with a flexible form of permanent insurance called **universal life insurance**. Think "flexibility" when you see those words "universal life insurance." The death benefit and, therefore, the premiums can be adjusted by the client. They can be increased to buy more coverage or decreased to back off on the coverage and save some money. If the cash value is sufficient, premiums can actually stop being paid by the client and start being covered by the cash value. The cash value grows at a minimum, guaranteed rate, just like on traditional whole life policies, and if the general account does particularly well, the cash value goes up from there. As mentioned, at some point the policyholder may decide to withdraw part of the cash value, or may usually borrow up to 90% of it.

So, whether it's term, traditional whole life, or universal life insurance, we're talking strictly about insurance products. Death benefits and cash values (term has no cash value) are guaranteed by the insurance company, which invests the net premiums (what's left after deducting expenses, taxes, etc.) into its general account. Once you start attaching cash value and death benefits to the ups and downs of the separate account, however, you have created a new product that is both an insurance policy and a security. Opens a whole new market for the company, but it also means that those who sell them need both an insurance and a securities license.

Hey, doesn't that sound familiar? For many readers, this explains why they're reading a book they otherwise wouldn't touch with an 11-foot pole.

Variable vs. Whole Life

Whole life and term life insurance policies tell clients exactly how much they will pay out upon death. And unlike most securities, when an insurance company says a policy is worth $100,000, it's really worth $100,000. If it's a whole life policy with a death benefit of $100,000, $100,000 is the death benefit paid upon death of the policyholder, as long as the premiums are paid and no loans have been taken out.

So, in term and whole life policies, the investment risk is borne totally by the insurance company through its "general account."

Well, with **variable insurance** products, the death benefit—as well as the cash value—fluctuates just like it does in a variable annuity. That's what they mean by "variable." It all varies, based on the investment performance of the separate account. The separate account, as we discussed under variable annuities, is made up of subaccounts. The investor chooses from these little quasi-mutual funds trying to meet different investment objectives: growth, long-term bonds, short-term Treasuries, etc.

He can even choose to invest some of the premiums into a fixed account, just to play it safe, and he can switch between the subaccounts as his investment needs change without a tax problem. This stuff all grows tax-deferred, remember.

The cash value is tied to account performance, period. So if the test question says that the separate account grew, it doesn't matter by how much. The cash value increases when the separate account increases. But death benefit is tied to actual performance versus AIR, just like an annuity unit in a variable annuity. So, if the AIR is 6% and the account gets a 4% return, the cash value will increase due to the positive return, but the death benefit will decrease because the account returned less than AIR.

Variable Life Insurance (VLI) policies will pay out the cash value/surrender value whenever the policyholder decides to cash in the policy. But, there's no way to know what the value might be at the time of surrender. If the little subaccounts have performed well, the cash value might be better than expected. But if the market has been brutal, the cash value could go all the way down to zero. Probably not gonna' happen, but it could.

A minimum or fixed death benefit is guaranteed, however. Some refer to it as the "floor." No matter what the market does, the insurance company guarantees a minimum death benefit that could be depleted only by failure to pay premiums or by taking out loans against the policy. Remember that any guaranteed payments are covered by the insurance company's general account. So, the minimum is guaranteed, and the policyholder also has the chance of enjoying an increased death benefit, depending on how well the little subaccounts (inside the separate account) do. As we said, that's tied to AIR, so if the market is kind, the death benefit increases, but if the market is unkind, it could, theoretically, drag the death benefit all the way down to the floor.

Sound familiar? Sounds a lot like investing in...yep, securities.

Again, that's why many insurance agents have to sit for this wonderful exam, called the Series 7. They have strayed far from the safe, guaranteed territory of term and whole life into the less predictable world of variable insurance.

When the customer pays the premium, the insurance company deducts S-A-S. That stands for State premium tax, Administrative fee, and Sales load. The "net premium" is then placed in the separate account, allocated among the little subaccounts that work like little mutual funds.

After the money's been allocated to the little subaccounts of the separate account, the insurance company charges regular fees, just like it does in variable annuities:

- mortality risk fee
- expense risk fee
- investment management fees

The value of the subaccounts and, therefore, the cash value is calculated daily. The death benefit is calculated annually. If the separate account has several below-AIR months, it will take several above-AIR months until the customer's death benefit starts to increase.

Variable Universal Life

Remember that flexibility we discussed that separates traditional whole life from universal life? Well, it probably isn't too surprising that somebody eventually crossed that with variable life to get **Variable Universal Life** (VUL). Now, we have the death benefit and cash value tied to the separate account (variable), plus we have the **flexible premium** thing (universal) going on. Regular old variable life is called **scheduled premium**.

That means the insurance company puts your premium payments on a schedule, and you better stick to it. Variable Universal or Universal Variable Life policies are funded as "flexible premium." That means the client may or may not have to send in a check. With a VUL policy, the customer has to maintain enough cash value and death benefit to keep the policy in force. If the separate account rocks, no money has to roll in from the customer. If the separate account rolls over and dies, look out. Since that's a little scary, some VULs come with minimum guaranteed death benefits.

Advantages of Variable Insurance

The advantages of variable life insurance include the ability to invest some of the premiums into the stock market, which has historically enjoyed relatively high average returns and done very well at beating inflation. A robust investment market can increase the cash value and death benefit, often faster than the rate of inflation. A traditional whole life policy, on the other hand, that promised to pay $50,000 when it was purchased in 1964 represented a lot of money. But if it pays that $50,000 out in 2004, the $50,000 doesn't go very far, due to inflation. In other words, choosing between whole life and variable life is pretty much the same as choosing between a fixed annuity and a variable annuity. If you worry about purchasing power and trust both your luck and the securities markets, you buy the variable stuff. If you'd rather deal with purchasing power risk in exchange for the comfort of the guarantee, you buy fixed annuities and whole life.

Policy Loans

Variable policies make at least 75% of the cash value available to the customer as a loan after 3 years, and maybe as much as 90%. Never 100%, though. 100% means "game over." Guess what, though—they charge interest on that loan. If the loan is not repaid, that reduces both the cash value and the death benefit of the policy. And if the customer takes out a big loan and then the separate account tanks, he'll have to put some money back in to bring the cash value back to a sufficient level or risk having the policy lapse. Don't worry, though. Some people take out a loan with absolutely no intention of repaying it. They simply don't need as much death benefit, so why not have some fun with the money right now?

Settlement Options

The policyholder can choose from many options concerning the method of payment to the beneficiary. These are called "settlement options." The "lump-sum" method is self-explanatory. "Fixed-period" means that the insurance company will invest the proceeds of the policy into an interest-bearing account and then make equal payments at regular intervals for a fixed period. The payments include principal and interest.

How much are the payments? That depends on the size of the principal, the interest rate earned by the insurance company, and the length of time involved in this fixed period.

The "fixed-amount" settlement option has the insurance company invest the proceeds from the policy and pay the beneficiary a fixed amount of money at regular intervals until both the principal and interest are gone. The amount received is fixed, but the period over which the beneficiary receives payments varies.

So, for "fixed-period" versus "fixed-amount," the decision comes down to this: do you want to receive some money for a fixed period of time, or do you want to receive a fixed amount of money for an uncertain period of time? In other words, do you want to be paid something like $25,000 for exactly three years (fixed-period)? Or, would you prefer being paid exactly $25,000 for about three years (fixed-amount)?

In a "life-income" settlement option, the proceeds are annuitized. That means the insurance company provides the beneficiary with a guaranteed income for the rest of his or her life. Just as with annuities, the beneficiary's age and life expectancy are taken into account to determine the monthly payout, along with the size of the death benefit and the type of payout selected.

There is also an "interest only" settlement option, whereby the insurance company keeps the proceeds from the policy and invests it, promising the beneficiary a guaranteed minimum rate of interest. The beneficiary might get more than the minimum, or not, and may receive the payments annually, semi-annually, quarterly, or monthly. She also has the right to withdraw all the principal, if she gets antsy, or change settlement options.

General Features

Since these variable policies are a little confusing to some, the company has to give the policyholder at least 2 years (24 months) to switch back to traditional whole life without having to provide proof of insurability. The new whole life policy will have the same issue date as the original variable policy.

As with contractual plans, variable policies have a free-look period, which is 45 days from execution of policy application or 10 days after policy delivery. During the first year the customer gets all sales charges in excess of 30%. During the second year the customer gets all sales charges in excess of 10% of the second year's premium.

1035 Contract Exchange

If you buy a variable life policy, you have the opportunity to exchange it for a different policy even if issued by a different company. You don't have to pay taxes since you aren't taking the cash value and, like, going on a fly fishing trip to Alaska. You just cash in one policy and exchange it, tax-free, for another insurance policy. Or, believe it or not, you can even exchange a life policy for an annuity.

You can't turn an annuity into a life policy, though.

Sorry about that.

Regulations

Four federal acts are involved with variable life insurance and variable annuities.

The Securities Act of 1933 covers variable life insurance (and annuities). These products must be registered with the SEC and sold with a prospectus. Even though the company that issues these contracts is an insurance company, the subdivision that sells the securities products has to be a broker-dealer registered under the Securities Exchange Act of 1934. The separate account is defined as an investment company under the Investment Company Act of 1940 and is either registered as a UIT or an Open-End Investment Company as defined under that act. The investment adviser has to register under the Investment Advisers Act of 1940.

And at the state level both securities and insurance regulators are watching these products and those who sell them, too.

The Prospectus

The prospectus is intended to fully inform the client and fully disclose all sales charges and expenses. It must be delivered either before or during the sales presentation to the client (which just sounds like the answer to a test question to me). The sales rep must believe that the product is suitable, and that the client understands and can afford any risks associated with it. The sales charges and expenses must be reasonable, as determined by regulations, as well. Such expenses in a variable life policy are deducted from the net premium after it's been invested by the client in the various subaccounts:

- Investment Management Fee
- Cost of Insurance: based on the policyholder's current age and the amount that the insurance company has at risk (the difference between the death benefit and the policy's cash value)
- Administrative Charges: compensate insurance company for expenses involved in issuing and servicing policies after they are sold, e.g., record keeping, processing death claims, loans and surrenders, sending required reports to policyholders
- Mortality and Expense Risk Charges: the risk that the insured will die earlier than expected (opposite of mortality risk in an annuity)

Most policies have an "expense guarantee provision," which limits the amount the company may raise the administrative charges, no matter what.

Variable life insurance policyholders get to vote their units pretty much like variable annuitants and mutual fund investors. They get to vote for the folks running the show, and would get to approve any major changes to investment objectives.

Taxation of Life Insurance

When you pay your life insurance premiums, you don't get to take a deduction against income, so they are made after-tax. They usually grow tax-deferred, however, which is nice. When the insured dies, the beneficiary receives the death benefit free and clear of federal income taxes.

Cool!

But the death benefit will be added to the insured's estate to determine estate taxes.

Uncool.

It's that simple when the beneficiary has the lump-sum settlement option, anyway. If we're talking about those periodic settlement options that generate interest, some of those payments could be taxed as interest income.

Rather than take a loan, the policyholder can also do a **partial surrender**, whereby the policyholder takes out some of the cash value, not enough to make the policy lapse, of course. Depending on how much has been paid in premiums, taxes may be due on the amount withdrawn. Unlike for variable annuities, the IRS uses FIFO here, assuming that the first thing coming out is the cost basis, not the earnings. Only the part taken out above the premiums paid would be taxed.

If a loan is taken out, there are no immediate tax consequences.

PRACTICE

1. The AIR for a variable annuity is 3.5%. Last month, your client received a check for $1,000 based on actual performance of 6%. If the actual performance is 5% next month,

    A. your client will receive slightly less than $1,000
    B. your client will receive $1,000
    C. your client will receive more than $1,000
    D. AIR will be increased

2. Annuities may be purchased in all the following ways except

    A. single premium immediate
    B. single premium deferred
    C. periodic deferred
    D. periodic immediate

3. The major difference between variable annuities and mutual funds involves

    A. tax deferral
    B. investment objectives
    C. bonds vs. stock
    D. EPS

4. An annuitant requiring the largest possible monthly check should choose

    A. life only (straight life)
    B. periodic immediate
    C. period certain
    D. joint and last survivor

5. **Your 60-year-old client contributed $10,000 to a non-qualified variable annuity many years ago. Now that the account is worth $40,000, the client takes a lump sum withdrawal of $35,000. If his ordinary income rate is 28%, he will pay**

    A.   no taxes until age 65

    B.   no taxes

    C. $8,400 in taxes

    D. $9,800 in taxes

ANSWERS

1.   **C**, it's hard to see how the check will go up if the return next month is lower than the return this month. Don't do that—don't compare next month's return to this month's return. Only compare the returns to AIR. AIR is 3.5%, so anything higher than that makes the check go up. Seriously.

2.   **D,** "periodic" means the individual has not finished paying in and will continue to pay in periodically. The word "immediate" means the annuity company starts paying out immediately—not if the annuitant hasn't finished paying in, right? If the individual makes a single payment and is old enough, she can immediately go into the annuitization/pay-out phase, but not if she's still making periodic payments into the contract.

3.   **A,** mutual funds give no tax deferral; annuities do. The other three choices don't distinguish the two: either could invest in bonds or stock, and they both have investment objectives. No idea what "EPS" could even mean in this context.

4.   **A,** if the company only has to bear one mortality risk, they'll be more generous with the monthly pay-out. As soon as the annuitant ceases, so do the payments, unlike a "period certain" that locks in payments for a minimum number of years.

5.   **C,** why would there be a penalty? He's over 59½. Also, remember only the earnings are taxed. He only had 30K of earnings, the difference between his 10K contribution and 40K value.

CHAPTER 7

Direct Participation Programs

FORMS OF BUSINESS OWNERSHIP

Before we dive into the details of direct participation programs, let's start with a quick look at various types of ownership structures that business use.

SOLE PROPRIETOR

If you're a handyman or a hair stylist, you typically have to pay for state and municipal licenses, so you might not want to also pay an attorney to set up a corporation or other business structure for you. Therefore, it might be tempting to just run your business as a sole proprietor. Perhaps you've noticed that a lot of folks who can fix your plumbing or coif your hair are just doing business as, you know, themselves. Unlike for a corporation or other business structure, setting up a sole proprietorship doesn't require much in terms of time and expense. So, the advantages of opening your business as a sole proprietorship include:

- Faster, easier, cheaper set-up (corporations require set-up fees, often attorneys)
- Easy tax preparation (1040)

The trouble with being in business as a sole proprietor is that you remain personally liable for the debts and lawsuits against the business. In other words, you have not created a separate legal entity—you and the business are one and the same. If the sole proprietorship called Harry's Hotties accidentally sells 1,000 tainted hot dogs that send swarms of sick people to the emergency room, Harry is in a whole lot of trouble. All the lawsuits will be filed against Harry personally, and the creditors who used to spot him buns, hot dogs, and condiments are going to come after Harry personally for all the unpaid bills. Even if he has insurance, once the insurance is exhausted, the angry parties move directly to Harry, not to some corporate structure that would have added a layer of defense. The disadvantages of owning a business as a sole proprietor include:

- Personal liability (no separate legal entity)
- Harder to obtain loans or attract investment capital due to lower financial controls (financial statements and minutes not required)

PARTNERSHIPS

As Robert Kiyosaki explains in his *Cash Flow Quadrant*, there is a big difference between being a self-employed professional and owning a business. Many business owners are really just cantankerous codgers who can't take criticism, let alone orders, from other people. So, they "go into business for themselves" and run everything as a sole proprietorship in which they control every aspect and answer to no one. We just looked at the pros and cons of that business structure.

Another approach is to take on a partner, maybe several partners. What we're talking about here, of course, is a partnership. In a partnership, the income and expenses of the business flow through directly to the owners. The business entity, in other words, is not taxed. The percentage of profits and losses flowing through to the owners is stated in the partnership agreement. Does the partnership create a separate entity that shields the owners from liabilities of the business? Yes and no.

General Partnership

The main difference between general and limited partnerships has to do with liability. In a general partnership, two or more persons own the business jointly and are still subject to creditors and lawsuits personally. Unless otherwise stated in the agreement, the general partners control the business jointly, equally, with one vote each. So, if Moe, Larry, and Curly want to open a restaurant and maintain 33.3% ownership each, a general partnership may be the way to go. Of course, all three are personally liable should Curly spill hot soup on the wrong customer pursuant to a poke in the eye from Moe or Larry.

Basically, a general partnership is like a sole proprietorship with more than one owner. The owners agree to be in business together. They do not shield themselves personally from debts of the business. But, the income and expenses do flow through directly to the partners rather than being taxable to the business.

Limited Partnership

To form a **limited partnership**, there still has to be at least one *general partner*, who, as we just saw, has personal liability for debts of and lawsuits against the business. But a limited partnership then has limited partners who maintain limited liability status, meaning they can only lose what they invest into the business. By "invest into the business" I mean the money they put in as well as any debts that they personally guarantee. A debt that a limited partner signs his name to may be called a **recourse note** on the exam, meaning that creditors have recourse to come after him for the amount he guaranteed personally. A non-recourse note, then, would mean that the creditors have no recourse to collect this debt out of the investor's personal assets. The exam might say that a limited partner's cost basis "equals the capital he contributes initially plus the capital he agrees to contribute later." The exam might say a lot of things. For example, it might expect you to know that there is no maximum number for GPs and LPs, but there must be at least one GP and at least one LP to form a limited partnership.

A limited partner is very interested in maintaining its/their limited liability status. To maintain the shield of protection, limited partners must stay out of day-to-day management decisions. So, if the exam asks if limited partners should be making regular management decisions, the answer is no. But, the LPs do get to vote on the big issues through something the exam might call "partnership democracy." Partnership democracy would be used to allow the LPs to have a voice on a limited number of items, such as:

- Dissolving the partnership
- Suing the GP for negligence, breach of fiduciary duty
- Inspecting certain records

The General Partner has a "fiduciary relationship" to the LPs, which means he/they must put the LPs' needs first. In legal terms, the GP's fiduciary duty is "two-pronged," meaning he has a duty of loyalty and a duty of good faith. His duty of loyalty means he can't compete with the partnership. His duty of good faith means he has to do whatever he possibly can to run the business successfully and in accordance with the LPs' best interests. The GP can end up getting sued by the LPs if it becomes clear that he/they are not meeting their duty to the limited partners through negligence or even outright fraud. If the GP is a lousy businessman who is really just using the partnership as a front for a bunch of personal expenses or gambling activities, that is not going to sit well with the LPs or the courts.

Since the GP has unlimited liability, the general partner is often a corporation rather than a natural person (human being). The corporate structure, as we'll see, provides a layer of protection. Finally, when the partnership is liquidated, the senior creditors are paid first, then the unsecured creditors. The next priority is the limited partners, with the general partner last in line.

The advantages of the partnership structure include:

- Flow-through of income and expenses directly to the partners
- Limited partners have limited liability

The disadvantages of the partnership structure include:

- General partner has unlimited liability
- Distribution of profits not as flexible as LLC

Keep in mind that for now, we're merely putting limited partnerships in the context of other business ownership structures. There will be more details on limited partnerships up ahead.

LLC (Limited Liability Company)

A limited liability company (LLC) is a type of business ownership combining several features of the corporate and the partnership structures. Although it combines features of the corporation and the partnership, the limited liability company is *neither* a corporation *nor* a partnership. Because the LLC is neither a corporation nor a partnership, the owners are neither shareholders nor partners. They are, instead, called "members." We will see that the S-corp is limited to 100 shareholders, but the LLC has no limit on the number of members, who can be individuals, corporations, or *other LLCs*. The owners and any officers and directors are protected from the liabilities of the company, including for their own negligence in operating the business. Advantages of setting up an LLC include:

- Limited liability
- More flexible profit distributions (compared to most partnerships)

- No minutes (meetings not required, as opposed to corporations)
- Avoids double taxation of income

The exam may bring up the fact that to be structured as an LLC rather than a corporation, the LLC needs to avoid two of four corporate attributes. That means that it needs to avoid two of the following characteristics associated with corporations:

- Perpetual life
- Centralized management
- Limited liability
- Freely transferable assets

It's almost impossible to avoid the centralized management, since the GP runs the business while the LPs put up and shut up. It's also tough to avoid limited liability as a, you know, limited liability company. So, how do they avoid the perpetual life and freely transferable assets associated with corporations? Unlike a corporation, an LLC has a limited life. For example, when the business is set up, perhaps it has a stated term of 30 years. The members also agree that they won't sell their interests except according to a certain strict set of rules. For example, if you want to sell your interest to a stranger, the other members might have the right to buy the interest first to prevent that from happening, because who wants to suddenly be in business with a stranger? If one of the members got himself into debt, the members might discover they're in business suddenly with the guy's bookie, who wants to collect the debt through the seized profit interest in his hand. Much to the bookie's frustration, the other members could vote to *not* distribute profits. In any case, the disadvantages of setting up an LLC include:

- Limited life
- Harder to attract financing (creditors don't like the idea explained above)
- More complexity than sole proprietorship (paperwork)

To set up a limited liability company, the business would file its articles of organization with the Secretary of State and pay the filing fees. The owners would also typically draft and sign an operating agreement. Similar to corporate bylaws or partnership agreements, these operating agreements spell out important points about ownership, responsibilities, and the distribution of profits.

S-corps

A very popular form of business ownership is the S-corp. The S-corp is a separate legal entity, so it offers some protection against debts and lawsuits compared to running the business as a sole proprietor. The income and expenses pass directly to the owners, so it's like a partnership or limited liability company in that sense. In other words, it avoids being taxed as a business entity, even as it provides that separate legal structure known as a corporation. The advantages of using the S-corp structure include:

- No corporate tax (the entity is not taxed itself)
- Liability protection (compared to sole proprietor)
- Write-offs (early losses can offset personal income of the owners)

Of course, there are also disadvantages to the S-corp, including:

- One class of stock
- 100 shareholders maximum
- Corporate meetings required

If your business is hoping to attract venture capital, the VC firms will not like the S-corp structure with its direct flow-through of income and expenses and the limit of 100 shareholders. Also, all stock has equal voting rights and claims on profits, tying the hands of the financiers. And, even if it is a good idea, many business owners hate having to hold an annual meeting where they have to talk like Thomas Jefferson and write down the minutes to the most boring two and a half hours this side of C-SPAN.

Oh well. If you want to create a business structure that offers some protection against debts and lawsuits and still avoid the double taxation of income, the S-corp is an attractive option. More details on S-corps include:

- The corporation can have no more than 100 shareholders with a husband and wife counting as one shareholder.
- Shareholders can be individuals, estates, and certain trusts.
- Shareholders must be American residents.
- The S-corp must be a domestic company in any state

C-corps

The C-corp is the traditional corporate structure. When we were talking about common stock in General Electric, Microsoft, Oracle, etc., we were talking about C-corps. In other words, since Microsoft has over 10 billion shares outstanding, it would be difficult to also be an S-corp, with its limit of 100 shareholders. This means that Microsoft is a separate legal entity that is taxed as a corporation—the profits do not flow directly through to large shareholders like Mr. Gates or even small shareholders like me. The corporation gets taxed on all those billions of dollars it makes year after year. Then, when the shareholders receive dividends on the stock, they are also taxed on that income.

The by-laws of the corporation and the corporate charter govern the operation of the corporation. A broker-dealer or adviser would look at the corporate resolution to see who has the authority to place trades and/or withdraw cash and securities. When opening an account for a corporation, the broker-dealer or adviser would get the officers who are authorized to transact business on behalf of the corporation to sign a "certificate of incumbency," which the firm keeps on file.

TYPE	ADVANTAGE	DISADVANTAGES	TAXATION	LIABILITY
Sole proprietor	Fast, cheap set-up No meetings	Personal liability	Personal income	Yes
General partnership	Flow-through of income, expenses	Personal liability	Flow-through to owners	Yes
Limited partnership	Flow-through of income, expenses	Must have 1 general partner, with unlimited liability	Flow-through to owners	Not for limited partners
LLC	Flow-through of income, expenses	Not good for attracting VC	Flow-through to owners	No, not even for negligence while running business
S-corp	Flow-through of income, expenses	Annual meetings Not good for attracting VC One class of stock	Flow-through to owners	No
C-corp	Attracting capital	Double taxation of income Annual meetings	Taxed as business entity	No, not even for negligence while running business

DETAILS OF DIRECT PARTICIPATION PROGRAMS (DPPs)

So, we looked at limited partnerships, a form of "direct participation program," but since the exam will ask probably 10 or more questions on this topic, we need to drill down a little harder. The basic characteristic of a **Direct Participation Program (DPP)** is that rather than paying taxes at the business level, the partners all take a share of the income and expenses on their own personal income taxes. The partners who provide most of the money to the business are the **limited partners**, meaning their liability is limited to their investment. If they put up $100,000, then $100,000 is all they could ever lose as passive investors in the partnership. To maintain their limited liability status (which means they can't be sued for personal assets) they have to stay out of day-to-day management of the business. Day-to-day management is up to the **general partner**. The general partner either runs the show himself or appoints someone to do it. Either way, it's his responsibility to get the thing managed. If he's the manager, he can also be compensated for his efforts through a salary. While the LPs provide most of the capital, the GP (general partner) must have at least a 1% financial interest in the partnership. The GP can enter into legally binding contracts on behalf of the partnership and has the authority to buy and sell property. As we said, the general partner has unlimited liability. His fiduciary responsibility to the limited partners means he can not:

- compete with the partnership
- borrow money from the partnership
- sell property to the partnership
- commingle personal assets with partnership assets

The GP can't compete with the partnership through some other business venture and also can't charge some bogus "no compete" payment, since they can't compete anyway. Also, while the

GP can't borrow money from the partnership, he/they could provide a loan to the partnership at prevailing interest rates.

Limited partners definitely stay out of day-to-day management decisions, but because of "partnership democracy" they do get to vote on the big issues like suing the GP, dissolving the partnership, switching GPs. Why would they sue the GP? Maybe the oil & gas program turns out to be a big scam in which the guy is using partners' money to fund a gambling habit or a high-rolling lifestyle. Maybe the GP misleads the LPs about the problems and risks of the partnership, causing them to lose money—if they're American limited partners, trust me, they'll find a reason to sue. This is why the GP usually forms a corporation or an LLC. As we saw, those structures separate the individual human being from the corporate or LLC structure. Through partnership democracy, the LPs also get regular financial reports, what the exam could refer to as "the right to copy certain partnership records." So, if you're talking about deciding which assets should be sold, the LPs don't get to decide that. If you're talking about changing the partnership from a baseball team to a soccer team...now the LPs get to vote. Just like common stockholders don't get to decide on every day-to-day issue that pops up at corporate headquarters, but if the corporation wants to change business objectives or buy another company, the stockholders get to vote. If the exam asks if LPs can make loans to the partnership, the answer is yes.

SUITABILITY

These partnerships or DPPs must have economic viability. They can't just be money-losing schemes devised by wealthy folks over several snifters of brandy. If the IRS suspects the thing never had a chance to make money, they can deem it an abusive tax shelter and go after folks with the full force of the IRS: audits, penalties, interest, seizure of assets...all falling safely under the "don't go there" category.

So, economic viability is the first consideration for a potential investor. The second would be tax benefits. If folks have a lot of **passive income**, they can receive passive losses from DPPs and use them to offset the gains for tax purposes. Public-assisted housing and historic rehab partnerships also offer tax credits to investors.

The third consideration is liquidity because, basically, there isn't any. You buy an interest in a limited partnership—it's yours, baby. Don't think you're going to be calling your broker a few weeks later to sell your position. These things are for the long-term. You buy in as a limited partner and you become a direct participant in the business. A passive participant, but you are directly participating in the gains and losses. That's why they call them Direct Participation Programs in Series Sevenland.

So what do these partnerships do? For test purposes, they seem to be either in the oil and gas business or real estate. The exam wants you to know which programs are the riskiest and which are the safest. Well, if you're talking about oil, which is riskier: drilling for oil, or selling oil that's already coming out of the ground? Obviously, drilling for oil is riskier, since most folks who drill never actually find any oil. **Exploratory programs** for oil and gas are the riskiest programs and, therefore, carry the highest return potential.

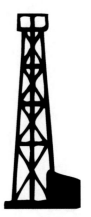

Sometimes folks drill for oil in an area where oil has already been found. It's still risky, but a lot less risky than exploratory programs. They call these **developmental programs**. They're a little less risky than exploratory with a lower return potential.

The safest program just buys existing production. They call these **income**

programs. They have immediate cash flow and are, therefore, the safest programs with the lowest potential reward.

In real estate, which is riskier, buying raw land or buying into an apartment complex already filled with renters? **Raw land** is purely speculative and is, therefore, the riskiest type of real estate DPP. You buy a chunk of land betting that an airport will be built nearby in the next five years. If you're right, the land skyrockets in value. If you're not, it doesn't.

New construction programs buy land and put up apartment buildings or office complexes. They're speculative, but once the projects are completed folks can move in and start paying rent. So they're a little safer than raw land and provide a lower reward potential.

Existing properties is sort of like the income program for oil. The business is already flowing; let's buy in. Immediate cash flow. Lower risk, lower reward.

Tax credits are the benefit for **government-assisted housing** programs. That means that if the partnership builds, acquires, or rehabs a government-assisted housing project, it will benefit from tax credits, and possibly from subsidy payments form the federal government. Remember that a tax credit is always better than a tax deduction. Just to make sure, let's compare a $100,000 tax deduction to a $100,000 tax credit:

$1,000,000 Income	$1,000,000 Income
- $100,000 Deduction	x .30 30% tax rate
$900,000 Net Income	$300,000 Tax
x .30 30% tax rate	-$100,000 CREDIT
$270,000 Tax Owed	$200,000 Tax Owed

Notice how a deduction is subtracted from the top line—revenue. For a credit, you figure the amount of tax you were going to have to pay, and then apply the credit dollar-for-dollar against that amount.

Another common type of limited partnership is the **equipment leasing program.** These partnerships typically lease equipment that other companies do not want to actually own. For example, computers, transportation equipment, construction equipment, etc., might not be cost-effective for the users to own; therefore, it makes more sense to simply lease such equipment from an equipment leasing program.

There are, of course, risks involved when investing in limited partnerships. First, the venture might not make any money, a risk that is higher on, say, an exploratory program vs. an income program. Second, the IRS might determine that the partnership is really just an abusive tax shelter, set up to generate deductions without ever intending to be economically viable. If that happens, the IRS can suddenly disallow deductions that the partners previously claimed, causing investors to pay back taxes *plus* interest and penalties on the back taxes. A DPP may be considered abusive if it's based on a false assumption or if the partnership overstated property values in order to take large depreciation deductions.

INVESTING IN DPPs

The general partner is also known as the **sponsor** of the program. In some cases, the sponsor will do a private placement (explained in Issuing Securities) in which he sells only to investors directly. In other cases, the sponsor will hire an underwriting firm to line up investors. Either way, if your investor wants to buy into a DPP, he fills out the **subscription agreement** and attaches his check. By signing the agreement, your investor (LP) attests to his net worth and indicates that he understands all the risks involved. Only when the General Partner (GP) signs the agreement does he become a limited partner (LP). When selling the partnership interests, the syndicator/sponsor can take a "syndication fee" of 10%. So, for a $100,000 partnership interest, a syndication fee of $10,000 could be taken. Most of these interests are sold through private placements. As we'll see in the chapter on issuing securities, private placements are generally sold only to accredited investors, so the LPs will disclose their income and net worth on the subscription agreement. Some interests are sold through public offerings, and then, of course, we would need a prospectus. Either way, investors get disclosure of the risks involved, as they do for any new investment that is not specifically excused from the registration requirements of the Securities Act of 1933. If the partnership assets are disclosed, we call it a **specified program**. If the assets are not disclosed, we call it a **blind pool offering**. Maybe the partnership is going to wildcat/speculate on some oil patches—they don't necessarily want anyone else to know where they think the oil is located. Or, if it's raw land, maybe they don't want others to know which area they think is the next hot market. If so—blind pool offering. Can you imagine a riskier investment than turning your money over to a sponsor who isn't even telling you where the assets of the partnership are located or what they are? Me neither.

FINRA now requires firms offering DPPs (and unlisted REITs) to provide some specific disclosure about liquidity. If the GP running the program that's being offered has done, say, 10 previous partnership deals, in how many of them were people *actually* able to sell their interests if they wanted to by the target date laid out in the offering document? Two times? Three times? FINRA isn't saying that meeting the target date for investors to liquidate/sell is always imperative, but they're saying investors should have an idea of how liquid their investment might *actually* be. A member firm may be receiving these liquidity stats from the sponsor of the program, and FINRA says they can just rely on his numbers unless they have reason to believe he's fudging.

No, they don't actually use the word *fudging*.

Sharing arrangements will also be laid out in the offering document, so the LP knows how he and the GP will share expenses and income. Let's do a quick bullet list here:

- overriding royalty interest: this would give the sponsor no responsibility for costs, only a share of the royalty stream when oil/gas is sold
- functional allocation: General Partner bears the capitalized costs (oil rig, other equipment) while LPs bear the deductible expenses (intangible drilling costs like labor and geological surveys)
- reversionary working interest: LPs bear all the costs and the GP doesn't get a share of income until all of those costs have been recovered
- disproportionate working interest: the GP receives a disproportionate share of income and bears very little of the costs

The GP has already filed the **certificate of limited partnership** with the state. This is a public document that provides the following information:

- Name and address of partnership
- Description of the partnership's business

- Life span of the partnership
- Conditions for assignment/transfer of limited partnership interests to others
- Conditions for dissolving the partnership
- Conditions for admitting new partners
- Projected date for return of capital (if one is determined)

The **partnership agreement** is signed by all partners and is the foundation for the partnership. In this agreement we would find the following information:

- business purpose of the partnership
- terms and conditions
- powers and limitations of the GP's authority

This document binds the partnership and authorizes the GP to run the business. It's a private document, for partners' eyes only. If the partnership is liquidated, either because it went belly-up or because it's time to pull the plug, interested parties would be paid off in the following order:

1. Secured creditors
2. Other creditors
3. Limited partners
4. General partners

Notice that the General Partner has unlimited liability, a fiduciary responsibility to the limited partners, and is also the last one to get paid should the whole thing go belly up?

Oh well. That's the nature of being the GP. Lotta risk, lotta reward.

CASH FLOW AND INCOME

Since we're running numbers, make sure you know the difference between the Cash Flow statement and the **Income Statement**.

Let's say a limited partner in a real estate partnership takes the following share of income and expenses from operations:

Rental income: $50,000
Operating expenses: $20,000
Interest expense: $25,000
Depreciation: $10,000

So, the Income Statement (P & L) looks like this:

$50,000 Income
-20,000 Expenses
-25,000 Interest
-20,000 Depreciation
-$15,000 Income

The limited partner, assuming he had sufficient passive income to offset, could deduct $15,000 for purposes of tax relief.

But, if we're talking about "cash flow" we add back that non-cash subtraction called "depreciation." Why? Well, depreciation is not an actual outlay of cash. If you buy a printing press for $1 million and it has a useful life of 10 years, you would subtract 1/10 of its value or $100,000 each year on your income statement. Since you're not actually paying out $100,000 in cash each year, you would add that back when figuring "cash flow," just to keep things nice and simple.

So, if we add back the "depreciation" of $20,000, we'd see a positive cash flow of $5,000. In case the exam gets really nasty the day you take it, tell it that we figure cash flow by adding back depreciation.

With that loss of (-$15,000) from his share of the income and expenses, the investor can offset other passive income that he might have from other partnerships or from owning rental properties. Only *passive* income, though—not portfolio or earned income. The test might point out that real estate investment trusts (REITs) do *not* pass through losses. But, remember, real estate limited <u>partnerships</u> do pass through losses to the partners, which is what the partners are often hoping for, especially in the early years. At some point, though, income from the partnership will start to exceed the fancy little deductions we've been discussing. This is known as the **crossover point**, should the exam decide to go there.

Let's make sure you understand depreciation/depletion…these are just accounting entries that allow partnerships to write down the cost of equipment and other assets over time. If a chair costs the business $100 and has a useful life of 10 years, they'll write down $10 of its cost each year for 10 years. If the partnership leases equipment, they'll depreciate the cost of that equipment a little bit every year. If they have to buy an oil rig, same thing. Depletion is for natural resources only. As you take oil out of the ground and sell it, you get to take a "depletion allowance" for every barrel of oil sold. It's just a method of cost recovery. You don't really have to understand it. If you can remember that depreciation is for equipment and depletion is only for natural resources, you'll probably be good to go. Also, raw land is not depreciated. Raw land should do the opposite—appreciate, right?

The exam might bring up "depreciation recapture." Let's say that the partnership has been using accelerated depreciation. That means they aren't subtracting the value of a fixed asset the nice and neat way I explained. I explained "straight line depreciation," where something with a useful life of 10 years is simply depreciated over 10 equal subtractions. But, many businesses use "accelerated depreciation" whereby they take much larger deductions in the early years. If an LP sells his interest/unit to somebody else, he may have taken larger deductions based on accelerated depreciation. So, the IRS, which as always is here to help, will help themselves to some of that benefit through "depreciation recapture." Basically, they will tax the difference between the cost basis arrived at through accelerated versus straight line depreciation, and I actually can't believe I just wrote a sentence that boring. Sorry—there was no way around it.

RECOURSE DEBT

If a limited partner signs a "recourse note," that means that the creditors/lenders have recourse to go after his personal assets if the partnership defaults. If the LP buys a limited partnership interest for $100,000 and signs a recourse note for which he is responsible for $50,000, his cost basis in the investment is now $150,000, since that is the amount he can lose.

Of course, if it's a non-recourse note, then the creditors have no recourse. So, the recourse debt adds to cost basis, while, of course, the non-recourse debt does not. Except when it does—real estate programs do allow the LP to add non-recourse debt to his basis, mostly to make sure your Series 7 is that much harder to pass.

CHAPTER 8

Issuing Securities

In The Big Picture we told the story of Frank & Emma's Fruit Pies, which raised money from investors by completing an initial public offering of common stock. As we said, Frank & Emma's had done quite well as a private company, getting financing from the local bank through lines of credit, and financing next year's projects with this year's profits. But, in order to take things to the next level, the corporate officers (Jeremy, Jason, and Jennifer) decided to sell a percentage of ownership to investors. They went through a group of underwriters, who kept a spread for their trouble, and raised $100 million for the company to use for expansion. The investors, who now hold shares of common stock, can either hang onto their investment or sell it to other investors on the secondary market. That liquidity, or ability to turn an asset into cash-money, is a big reason investors are willing to buy the stock in the first place. Few investors, in other words, want to be like the limited partners we just looked at, who might not be able to sell their investments for a while, if at all. Frank & Emma's common stock trades on **NASDAQ**, so liquidity has not been a problem.

Or, maybe you don't like little pretend companies like Frank & Emma's Fruit Pies; so, let's use another example. Several years ago Google made headlines with its famous **initial public offering** or **IPO** in which they sold stock to investors at $85 and those investors then watched the stock climb to the high 600s. The difference between the initial $85 price and the eventual price of, say, $650, is the difference between the primary and secondary markets. Securities are issued to investors in the **primary market** to raise capital for the issuer. Securities are traded among investors in the **secondary market**.

To do an initial public offering on the primary market, a company simply sells an ownership stake to investors in exchange for a big infusion of cash that can be used to expand the business. The company takes the money and invests the capital in manufacturing equipment, computers, more employees, a fleet of delivery vans, etc., and the investors end up owning a percentage of the company. Now, nothing makes the securities regulators more nervous than to hear that a company wants to raise money from investors. Let's face it, many business owners would say anything investors wanted to hear in order to get their hands on a few billion dollars. That's why the state and federal securities regulators like to slow down the issuers in much the same way they're slowing you down right now. Just tying you up with a little paperwork, giving you a chance to rethink your whole decision, making sure it's something you really, really want to do.

The SEC wants to see exactly what the issuers will be telling their potential investors in the **prospectus**. They want the issuers to provide the whole story on the company: history, competitors, products and services, risks of investing in the company, financials, board of directors, officers, etc. And, like a fussy English instructor, they want it written in clear, readable language. Only if investors clearly understand the risks and rewards of an investment do they really have a fair chance of determining a good investment opportunity from something better left alone. If investors consistently get burned on the primary market, pretty soon investors will stop showing up to provide companies with capital, which means companies would have one heck of a time expanding, hiring more workers, and pushing along the local and national economies. So, the government is very much interested in what goes on in the securities markets, which is why Congress passed the **Securities Act of 1933**. Sometimes referred to as the "Paper Act," the Securities Act of 1933 simply requires issuers of securities to register the securities and provide full disclosure to investors before taking their hard-earned money. The SEC will make the issuer write and rewrite the registration statement, just like a hard-nosed composition instructor might make you do four rewrites of a research paper before finally agreeing to let you graduate. If this section is awkward and this paragraph is unclear, rewrite it. The SEC calls their equivalent of red pen marks, **letters of deficiency,** and sometimes, when they're feeling especially punchy, **deficiency letters**.

Now, an issuer such as Oracle would know all kinds of interesting things about relational database applications in a non-Unix environment. But, they probably know jack about issuing securities. So, they hire **underwriters**, also called "investment bankers." An underwriter or **investment banker** is simply a broker-dealer who helps issuers raise money by issuing securities to investors. All the big-name Wall Street firms have major underwriting or investment banking departments. In fact, I may just go ahead and name names such as Morgan Stanley, Goldman Sachs, and Merrill Lynch. The Series 7 is required to work in the investment banking/underwriting side of the business or the secondary market/trading side of the business, by the way. In any case, once these underwriters help the issuer file a **registration statement** under the Securities Act of 1933, the **cooling off period**, which will last a minimum of 20 days, begins. This process can drag on and on if the SEC is copping an attitude against the registration statement, but no matter how long it takes, the issuer and underwriters can only do certain things during this "cooling off" period. Number one, they can't sell anything. They can't even advertise. About all they can do is take **indications of interest** from investors, but those aren't sales, just names on a list. And those who indicate their interest have to receive a **preliminary prospectus** or "**red herring**." This disclosure document contains almost everything that the **final prospectus** will contain except for the **effective date** and the final **public offering price** or "**POP**." Remember that the registered representative may NOT send a research report along with the red herring and cannot highlight it or alter it in any way.

It is what it is. Part of the registration statement is the prospectus that investors will receive. Please understand that the SEC is reviewing the documents for clarity and to make sure that at least the boiler plate disclosures have been made. If a section looks incomplete or unclear, they'll make the issuer/underwriters rewrite it. But at no time is the SEC determining that the information is accurate or complete. They couldn't possibly do that—they don't know the issuer's history, and the financial statements the issuer provides—who knows if they're accurate? Since the SEC can't and does not verify information, the issuer and the underwriters hold a **due diligence meeting** during the cooling-off period, which just means they make sure they provided the SEC and the public with accurate and full disclosure. The issuer does not have to, but they are allowed to publish one very specific type of "advertising" during the cooling off period—a **tombstone advertisement**. A tombstone, as we saw in the Municipal Securities chapter, just lays out the basic facts: the issuer, the type of security, number of shares, amount to be raised, and then the names of the under-writers. I'm not convinced it's a hugely testable document, but it may help to make this process more tangible if we glance at an actual tombstone ad:

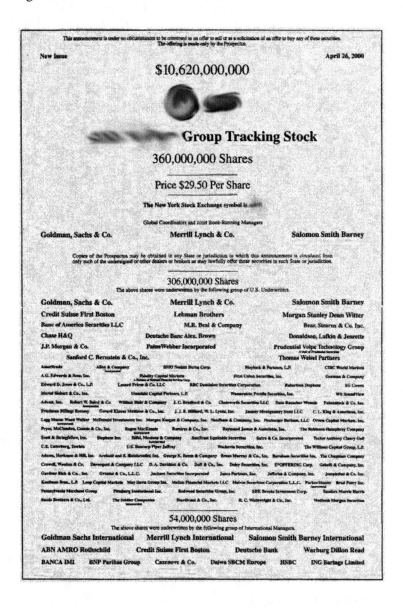

The lead underwriters often have a commemorative tombstone made in Lucite that the various players receive as souvenirs of the journey once the offering is completed. The regulators actually write this item into the gift rules as an exception, no matter how much it costs to make the "gifts." In other words—they're kinda cool, but their re-sale value would be pretty low. And how much influence could really be purchased at other firms by sending a paper weight?

Anyway, even though the SEC makes issuers jump through all kinds of hoops, once it's all done, the SEC pretty much washes its hands of the whole affair. They don't approve or disapprove of the security. They don't guarantee accuracy or adequacy of the information provided by the issuer and its underwriters. In other words, if this whole thing goes belly-up because of inaccurate disclosure, the liability still rests squarely on the shoulders of the issuers and underwriters, not on the SEC.

And there has to be a disclaimer saying basically that on the prospectus. In fact, take a look at the cover of any mutual fund prospectus. The one I'm looking at now says it this way:

```
The Securities and Exchange Commission has not approved or disap-
proved of these securities. Further, it has not determined that
this prospectus is accurate or complete. Any representation to the
contrary is a criminal offense.
```

If the issue of stock is authorized for listing on **NYSE**, **AMEX**, or **NASDAQ**, the issuer and underwriters will only register with the SEC. But, if the issue will not trade on those exchanges, the stock will have to be registered with all the states where it will be offered and sold. This state-level registration could be referred to as **blue sky-ing** the issue. Both the securities and all the firms and their agents must be registered in all the states where these securities will be offered and sold.

So, to review the timeline, remember that nothing really happens until the registration statement is filed with the SEC. At that point, the cooling off period begins. During this period, investors are asked by underwriters (their registered representatives, really) to give indications of interest, and those who do must receive a preliminary prospectus (red herring). No advertising is taking place and no sales literature is used during this cooling off period. No binding agreements to buy or deliver securities are entered into. The due diligence meeting is held to make sure all the information in the prospectus is as accurate and complete as possible. When the issuer is finally given the effective date (release date) by the SEC, sales from the underwriters to the investors are finalized, all buyers receive a final prospectus, and the issuer receives the capital it needs, with the syndicate keeping the spread for its trouble.

EXEMPTIONS FROM REGISTRATION REQUIREMENTS

So, everybody has to register their securities with the SEC, except for everybody who doesn't. The Act of 1933 is a piece of federal legislation, so it's not surprising that the federal government, who came up with the Act, doesn't have to abide by it. That's right, government securities are exempt from this act. They don't have to be registered in this way. Neither do municipal securities.

Why is that? Well, when a corporation tries to take an investor's money, there is always a good chance the investor will lose his money. Companies go out of business all the time, so if their earnings start to evaporate, the bonds go into default, and the shares of common stock are no longer worth the paper they're printed on. That's not the case when the U.S. Treasury sells you a T-note or T-bond. That's just a loan backed by the full faith and credit (the vast taxing powers) of the United States Government.

In other words, you'll get your money back. The U.S. isn't going to pull a Russia on you and suddenly declare, as Russia did back in 1998, "Very sorry—we cannot pay you."

Same for municipal securities. You'll get paid back on a general obligation bond, because it's backed by the full faith and credit of a fiscally responsible state (you hope). Either way, there is such a small chance of default on municipal securities that the issuers (cities, counties, states, school districts, etc.) got an exemption from the arduous registration process laid out under the Securities Act of 1933.

But we're not done handing out excuses; in fact, we're just getting started. Charitable organization securities, such as church bonds, are exempt from the act. So are bank securities, which are already plenty regulated by bank regulators (FDIC, FRB, Comptroller of the Currency). Finally, securities issued by small business investment companies (VC firms) also get a hall pass.

Debt securities that mature in 270 days or less—commercial paper, banker's acceptances, other promissory notes—are also exempt from this arduous registration process. Why would you need a prospectus when loaning GE some money for a few months? Just look at their credit rating and charge them an interest rate commensurate with that rating (commercial paper). What would a prospectus tell you that you couldn't get from Moody's or S&P or your own credit analyst department, right?

And, securities issued by Small Business Investment Companies (SBICs) are also exempt, since they are only offered and sold to institutions and other sophisticated investors who don't require so much protection.

So, the state of Oregon is an exempt issuer. Commercial paper is an **exempt security**. There are also transactions that qualify for exemptions. Believe it or not, we call these **exempt transactions**. That just means that if you sell the securities in a certain way you can either avoid registration altogether, avoid registration with the SEC, or perhaps just do a "fast-track" method using a scaled-down disclosure document like an "offering memorandum" or an "offering circular" as opposed to the telephone-book-size standard registration statement or "S1."

Still with us?

Boy, you must really want your Series 7. Good for you!

Under **Reg A**, an issuer can sell up to $5,000,000 worth of securities in a year without having to jump through all the usual hoops. Rather than filing a standard registration statement, the issuer files an offering circular, a much more scaled-down document. This is a small offering, so think of a small, Caribbean island where they play lots of Reg-A. But, please save the rest of that fantasy until after passing the test.

The SEC is in charge of interstate commerce, meaning commerce among many states. Therefore, if the issuer wants to sell only to residents of one state, the SEC doesn't have to get involved—there is already a state securities regulator who can deal with this one. So, if the issuer agrees to sell the stock to residents of only one state, they will qualify for a **Rule 147** exemption. The issuer's main business is located in this state, and 80% of its assets are located here. Also, the buyers can't sell the security to a non-resident for nine months. The issuer registers with the state, rather than the SEC, since it's all taking place in that one state. This is also called an **intrastate offering**, which means it all takes place within (intra) one state.

The SEC is out to protect the average Joe and JoAnne from fast-talking stock operators pushing worthless paper. But, the SEC doesn't have to provide as much protection to big, sophisticated investors such as mutual funds, pension funds, or high-net-worth individuals. If anybody tries to scam these multimillion-dollar investors, they'll be in just as much trouble as if they scammed an average investor, but the SEC doesn't have to put up as much protection for the big, institutional investors, who can usually watch out for themselves to a large extent. Therefore, if the issuer wants to avoid the registration process under the Act of 1933, they can limit the sale to these big institutional, sophisticated investors. These investors are often referred to as **accredited investors**. They include institutions and the officers and board of directors of the company. Also if an individual or married couple meets the net worth or the income requirements, he/she is accredited. So, an issuer can place their securities under a **Reg D** transaction with as many of these folks as they want. This "private placement" is, by definition, not being offered to the general public, so the SEC eases up a bit. As much as the SEC ever eases up, anyway. So, a **Reg D/private placement** transaction is exempt from the Act of 1933's registration requirements because it is offered to an exclusive group of investors. There is no general advertising or soliciting going on—the underwriters must have an established relationship with the individual investors. Why? Because, if they're advertising the offering, they're actually doing a *public* offering, which requires registration of the securities. To keep thinks as clear as mud, the regulators also allow the issuer and underwriters to sell to no more than 35 non-accredited investors. Either way, if the investor is an individual, he has to hold the stock for a certain time frame before selling it. Or, he has to hold it for "investment purposes" as opposed to buying it and immediately flipping it. After the holding period, a **non-affiliated investor** (not on the board, not an officer, doesn't own 10% or more of the company) would have to comply with volume limits on any sales of the stock for only a specified time period, while an **affiliated investor** (10% owner, officer, or director of the issuer) would have to comply with volume limits all the time because they're, you know, affiliated.

See, if you're an affiliate of the company, you always have to file Form 144 with the SEC, announcing that you intend to sell a certain amount of your stock over the next 90 days. We don't want the huge shareholders to dump too much stock at once, which usually drives the price down for everyone else who might want to sell. The volume to be sold over the 90-day period is limited to 1% of the shares outstanding or the average weekly trading volume over the four most recent weeks, whichever is larger. That's surprising, too, because you might think the SEC would stick you with the smaller number.

Go figure.

So you can bet that if it shows up at all the test will give you at least five weeks—only average the four most recent. And then compare that number to 1% of the outstanding shares. Whichever is larger, that's what an insider/affiliate could sell over the next 90 days. Or, that's what a non-affiliated investor could sell while subject to volume limits on his or her sales.

Rule 144 also covers both "restricted stock" and "control stock." Nothing different about control stock *per se*—it's the people who hold the stock that are different. If you're the CEO of a corporation, or the CFO, or the owner of a major chunk (10%) of the stock, you could control the success of the company and even the share price by buying and selling huge chunks of your stock at strategic times. Therefore, you tell the SEC what you're planning to do with your stock every time you think about selling some of it. You do this by filing a Form 144, which also covers **restricted stock**.

What is restricted stock, you may be wondering. Well, stock sold through a private placement (Reg D) is unregistered and therefore restricted. Restricted means its transfer or sale is restricted—investors have to hold it for a specified time period before selling it. Currently, investors not affiliated with the issuing company have to hold the stock for 6 months before selling, and then conform to volume limits until the first year is up, after which they can sell as many shares as they want. Affiliates of the company (officers, directors, 10% shareholders, immediate family of insiders) also have to hold restricted stock for 6 months and—as always—must report their sales, which are subject to the volume limits under Rule 144, always. This is one of those rules that is changed frequently, so see the updates at www.passthe7.com/updates before taking the exam, assuming the test will go this far into trivial pursuits. When selling restricted shares under Rule 144, investors must file a Form 144 with the SEC no later than concurrently with (at the time of) the sale. The filing is good for 90 days. Also, in case the Series 7 doesn't have enough trivia for you to memorize, you may be expected to know that if the transaction is not larger than 5,000 shares and $50,000, the sale can be made without reporting. Basically, a transaction that small does not make the regulators nervous as it won't impact the price of the stock due to the low volume of shares traded.

And, those people can never sell the company's stock short. They can't profit from their company's poor stock performance, in other words. And, if they make a profit on their company's stock held less than 6 months, they'll wish they hadn't. This is called a short-swing profit, and it has to be turned back over to the company with the gain still being taxed by the IRS, which, as always, is here to help.

FINRA is very concerned that agents and their firms sometimes help clients sell unregistered restricted securities, which violates federal securities law. In other words, if the customer does not conform to all the stipulations we just went over, but wants to just take his unregistered restricted shares and sell them, firms need to be sure they don't help him skirt securities law in this manner. FINRA alerts its member broker-dealer firms that some customers are really companies trying to sell their shares illegally. If the customer deposits certificates representing a large block of thinly traded or low-priced securities, that's a red flag. If the share certificates refer to a company or customer name that has been changed or that does not match the name on the account, that's another red flag. If a customer with limited or no other assets under management at the firm receives an electronic transfer or journal transactions of large amounts of low-priced, unlisted securities, that's another red flag. Broker-dealer firms need to do a reasonable inquiry to make sure that they are not helping people get around securities law. The SEC has said that "a dealer who offers to sell, or is asked to sell a substantial amount of securities must take whatever steps are necessary to be sure that this is a transaction not involving an issuer, person in a control relationship with an issuer, or an underwriter." For this purpose, it is not enough for him to accept "self-serving statements of his sellers and their counsel (attorneys) without reasonably exploring the possibility of contrary facts."

Rule 144a allows the restricted securities that we just discussed to be re-sold to institutional investors including banks, insurance companies, broker-dealers, investment advisers, pension plans, and investment companies without meeting the usual registration requirements under the Securities Act of 1933. So, if an investor acquires restricted securities through a private placement, he/they can actually re-sell them to **qualified institutional buyers** such as those mentioned without messing up the exemption the issuer is claiming from the registration requirements. As usual, the regulators want to prevent the shares from being distributed in a general public offering without registration requirements being met. When the buyers are all sophisticated (allegedly) institutions, the regulators can ease up and let the professionals play hardball.

This SEC rule also states that the seller needs to be reasonably certain that the buyers are qualified institutional buyers, which generally means that the institution invests on a discretionary basis at least $100 million, or is a registered broker-dealer, an investment company, a bank, or a federal covered investment adviser. To check that the buyers are qualified institutional buyers, the SEC says that the seller can rely on the buyer's most recent publicly available financial statements, or a certification from the CFO or other officer of the institution.

Rule 145 has to do with disclosure requirements to investors involved with a merger or a reclassification of securities. When Procter & Gamble acquired Gillette for example, they gave the Gillette shareholders a certain number of PG shares for each share of Gillette currently held. Those PG shares have to be registered on a special form (S-4), and the Gillette shareholders have to receive all types of disclosure of material information. Or, if an issuer has decided to give all current warrant holders shares of convertible preferred stock instead, this is a reclassification subject to Rule 145. Remember that stock splits, stock dividends, and changes to the par value of a security are not subject to Rule 145.

To review, the Act of 1933 says that non-exempt issuers (corporations) have to register their securities with the SEC. Exempt issuers, exempt securities, and exempt transactions all find a way around the arduous process set forth by the Act of 1933.

UNDERWRITING SECURITIES

We already looked at the underwriting process for municipal securities. Many of those same firms also underwrite securities for corporations. When they do, issuers receive different levels of commitment from the underwriters. Under a **best efforts** commitment, the underwriters act as agents. In other words, no money at risk. They try to sell, and whatever they can't sell goes back to the issuer. Two similar types of underwritings are **All or None** and **Mini-Max**. In either case, the underwriters have no money at risk. They just have to sell a minimum amount, or cancel the whole underwriting and return all the money to investors. Only difference between the two is that mini-max has both a minimum and a maximum number. So, if the underwriters reach the minimum level, they can continue to sell more shares, up to the maximum.

Underwriters only have money/capital at risk when they give **firm commitments**. Now, they're agreeing to buy the securities outright, then turn around and sell them to the public. The difference between where they buy from the issuer and sell to the public is known as the **spread**. The managing underwriter takes a management fee, the underwriters split up the underwriting fee, and whoever makes the sale gets the selling concession. If the total spread is 80 cents, only the managing underwriter can make that amount, and they'd have to make the sale; otherwise, they'd have to concede the selling concession to the party who made the sale. A typical spread might be made up of 10 cents for the management fee, 20 cents for the underwriting fee, and 50 cents for the selling concession. For a total spread of 80 cents per share.

If you see a reference to a **green shoe clause**, just remember that this would allow the syndicate to increase the number of shares sold by 15% over the original number of shares in the offering. People must really want the security in that case, right? They're all "green with envy," so this "green shoe" clause would take care of them.

Sorry to resort to such cheesy memory joggers, but many people swear by them.

How does the issuer decide how to price the security being offered to the public? The underwriters are the experts, so they advise the issuer as to how to structure the offering, and they determine the final public offering price (POP) based on the following:

- Current market conditions for securities offerings
- Current market value of competitors' securities
- Current climate for the industry in which the issuer competes
- Level of interest from indications of interest

We mentioned that the preliminary prospectus/red herring does not contain the final public offering price. It may, however contain a range of likely offering prices. The level of enthusiasm for the shares during the cooling off period will help determine whether the final POP ends up at the high or low end of that range. Of course, if there isn't enough interest for the shares, the offering can end up being delayed until the market is more favorable or, in some cases, the issuer might decide to stay private. Remember, there's no law that says companies have to "go public." Many big, ultra-successful companies are privately owned. There are simply advantages and disadvantages to accessing the public capital markets. If the issuer decides it makes sense to use money from public investors, they pay for that decision by having to file all kinds of paperwork and disclosing all kinds of bad news that private companies can keep between themselves, their owners, and their lenders.

Whatever the final public offering price (POP) is determined to be, remember that all investors pay this price, and that the compensation to the underwriters is already built in. There are no commissions or markups added to the final public offering price that investors pay. The spread is already in that POP, remember, and it represents the underwriters' compensation. But, no matter what the POP is, once the stock begins to trade on the secondary market (NYSE, AMEX, NASDAQ) among investors, the price could fall below the final public offering price (POP). If so, the syndicate is allowed to attempt to prop up the price by placing bids to buy the stock, as long as they don't try to bid it up above the POP. This process is called **stabilization** and is, surprisingly, legal. The prospectus would announce the syndicate's plans to do this, if necessary. This is intended to protect the IPO buyers from paying, say, $10 for a stock that immediately freefalls to $1. So, if the POP is $10 and the stock starts dropping to $8 in the secondary market, the syndicate could put in bids to buy the stock at higher prices, as long as they don't try to buy it above $10.

Finally, know that a **shelf registration** allows an issuer to register its securities all at once, but then sell them gradually over a two- or three-year period, depending on how large and well-known the issuer is.

FINRA RULES

If the underwriters have set the public offering price (POP) of a stock at $10, what happens if the stock shoots up to $20 on the secondary market, while they're still selling shares at $10? Wouldn't it be tempting to hold all the shares for their own account and let the price rise even further?

FREERIDING & WITHHOLDING

Might be tempting, but it's not allowed by FINRA, who calls the violation "freeriding and withholding." These public offerings have to be bona fide (good and true) distributions. That means that if your firm is an underwriter or a selling group member, it has to sell all the shares it is allotted to investors, no matter how tempting it might be to keep most of them for its own account and take a "free ride" by "withholding" the securities from hungry buyers. In other words, investment bankers can not pretend to be offering stock to the public and then sort of change their minds and keep the good ones for themselves.

THE NEW ISSUE RULE

Your firm has to watch whom they sell the new issue to. A person who may not purchase a new issue of common stock is called a **restricted person**. Restricted persons include:

- Member firms and their owners
- Broker-Dealer personnel
- Finders and fiduciaries (finders, accountants, consultants, attorneys, etc.)
- Portfolio managers for institutions (banks, S&Ls, insurance companies, etc.) buying for their own account

Of course, it would be fun to help your immediate family members profit from a wildly successful IPO such as the one pulled off by Google not so long ago. Unfortunately, FINRA prohibits the offering of new issues to immediate family members, defined as:

- parents
- mother-in-law or father-in-law
- spouse, brother or sister
- brother-in-law or sister-in-law
- son-in-law or daughter-in-law
- children
- any other individual to whom the person provides material support

Notice that the above list did not mention *all* family members. Specifically, aunts, uncles, grandparents, and cousins are not considered to be restricted. And, the immediate family members above are only restricted if they give or receive "material support," which FINRA defines as:

> "Material support" means directly or indirectly providing more than 25% of a person's income in the prior calendar year. Members of the immediate family living in the same household are deemed to be providing each other with material support.

Or, they would be restricted only if the family member working for a broker-dealer works for a firm that is actually selling the new issue (not a ban for employees of *all* broker-dealers), or if the employee has the ability to control the allocation of the new issue to investors. The new issue rule also requires that before selling a new issue to any account, a member firm must obtain a representation that the account is eligible to purchase new issues in compliance with this rule. The firm can obtain these "affirmative statements" either in paper form or electronic, but must not rely on oral statements from customers. And, these affirmative statements have to be re-verified every 12 months, with copies maintained at least three years. Note that an investment club could buy a new issue, but not if a registered rep is part of the club.

Finally, remember that the new issue rule only covers initial public offerings (IPOs) of common stock. The following are not subject to this rule:

- Secondary offerings
- Debt security offerings
- Preferred stock
- Investment company offerings
- Exempt securities
- REITs
- DPPs

SPECIFIC TYPES OF SECURITIES OFFERINGS

Your exam might throw some vocabulary terms at you that I need to mention. The first is the **registered secondary**. The key word is *secondary*—remember that while shares are being offered to the public, the proceeds are not going to the issuer; rather, they are going to, for example, a former CEO or board member who is now offering his or her restricted shares to the public. The restricted shares were not registered; now they are being registered and offered to investors on the secondary market—registered secondary offering. Remember that if the issuing corporation does an additional offer of stock, it is *not* a **"secondary offering."** Rather, it is a "subsequent primary distribution." Remember that when the issuer gets the proceeds, the word is "primary," not "secondary."

Often when a company is offering securities, so are certain large shareholders such as the venture capital firms that financed the company along the way. If so, we call this a **combined offering**, since it's both primary and secondary, with proceeds going to both the issuer and to persons who are not the issuer.

PRACTICE

1. **What is the maximum number of institutional buyers in a Reg D offering?**
   A. 35
   B. 1% of outstanding shareholders
   C. 100
   D. none of the above

2. **Which of the following may a registered rep do during the cooling off period?**
   A. highlight the most important points of a red herring for a favored customer
   B. attach a research report to the preliminary prospectus
   C. use the red herring to gain the SEC's approval of the issue
   D. send a red herring to customers who have given indications of interest

3. **None of the following has liability for unsold shares except**
   A. member of a selling group in a firm commitment
   B. member of a syndicate in a firm commitment
   C. member of a selling group in a best efforts underwriting
   D. member of a syndicate in a best efforts underwriting

4. **All of the following are exempt issuers except**
   A. U.S. government
   B. XYZ Bank Holding Corporation
   C. Chicago, Illinois
   D. Fernwood State Bank

5. **All of the following may issue common stock except**
   A. GNMA
   B. XXR corporation
   C. FNMA
   D. FHLMC

6. **Which of the following parties takes on liability for unsold shares?**
   A. member of a syndicate in a best efforts underwriting
   B. member of the selling group
   C. member of a syndicate in an all or none underwriting
   D. none of the above

7. **Which of the following securities would have to be registered with the SEC prior to an initial public offering?**
   A. ADRs
   B. XXR Corporation's preferred stock
   C. XXR Corporation's common stock
   D. all of the above

8. **Which of the following securities would have to be registered with the SEC prior to an initial public offering?**
   A. church bonds
   B. ADR
   C. Chicago 7% General Obligation bond
   D. T-notes

9. **The Securities Act of 1934 addressed all the following except**
   A. anti-fraud regulations
   B. registration of new issues
   C. registration of agents
   D. registration of broker-dealers

10. **Which of the following parties has capital at risk in a transaction?**
    A. agent
    B. underwriter
    C. registered representative
    D. broker

11. **Which of the following securities would require that a customer receive a prospectus?**
    A. variable annuity
    B. open-end share
    C. closed-end share during the offering period
    D. all of the above

12. **The Securities Act of 1933 applies to which market?**
    A. first
    B. secondary
    C. primary
    D. third

13. **ARC, Inc., is planning to make an initial public offering of $10,000,000 in only three states, all west of the Mississippi River. Therefore, ARC will**
    A. file an S1
    B. qualify for a Reg A exemption
    C. qualify for a Rule 147 exemption
    D. qualify for a Reg D exemption

14. **If a corporate insider sells stock of her company held five months for a profit**
    A. she will be prosecuted for fraud by the SEC
    B. she will be prosecuted for fraud by FINRA or other DEA
    C. the profit must be disgorged to the corporation
    D. she must distribute 1% to the members of the board

15. When must the final prospectus be delivered?
  A. before accepting payment from the client
  B. at or before the time payment is accepted
  C. no later than receipt of confirmation
  D. no later than settlement

ANSWERS

1. **D,** a trick question—there is only a maximum number for non-accredited investors. And, remember, the firm has to have an existing relationship with these investors—they cannot do a general solicitation to round up investors.

2. **D,** no sales literature is allowed during the cooling off period, and if the rep were to highlight a prospectus, that would imply the reader only needs to pay attention to that section. The SEC does not *approve* securities.

3. **B,** selling group members have no capital at risk, ever. Only in a firm commitment do the syndicate members have capital at risk.

4. **B,** bank holding companies have to register their stock—e.g., FMBI or BXS. Banks themselves are regulated by the FRB, Comptroller of the Currency, and the FDIC.

5. **A,** there is no stock in GNMA "Ginnie Mae."

6. **D,** again, selling group members have no capital at risk, ever. Only in a firm commitment do the syndicate members have capital at risk.

7. **D,** none of these securities is exempt. Unless there is an exemption available, the securities must be registered.

8. **B,** the US Government and municipal governments do not have to register their bonds. Non-profits generally don't have to register their securities, either. Anti-fraud rules still apply, meaning if a church puts out bogus numbers in the offering circular, they could still be sued or prosecuted.

9. **B,** the "Act of 1933" has a narrow focus—the registration of securities. The "Act of 1934" covers many, many aspects, including the other three choices.

10. **B,** an agent never has his own money/capital at risk. The words "broker," "registered representative," and also "account executive" are synonyms for "agent."

11. **D,** during the offering period, securities are sold with a prospectus. Open-end funds and variable annuities are in a state of continuous offering of new shares, so their shares are sold with a prospectus.

12. **C,** the primary market is where issuers receive the proceeds of the securities offering. The terms "first, second, third (and fourth)" apply only to the secondary market, where securities are traded.

13. **A,** there is no exemption available to this issuer.

14. **C,** this is called a "short swing profit." She should have held the stock longer than 6 months to avoid giving back or "disgorging" the profit.

15. **C,** this is a memorization point.

CHAPTER 9

Trading Securities

In the primary market underwriters help corporations and governments raise money by selling securities to investors. The investors would never buy those securities if they didn't have a **secondary market** where they could later trade the securities and turn them into cash. The primary and secondary markets are inseparable, so let's make sure you understand the concept of the "secondary market" before we start filling your head with details.

When I was a kid, my friends and I liked to buy and trade baseball cards. Of course, we couldn't buy a baseball card until it was *issued* by the bubble gum company. After we'd acquired our newly issued cards on the primary market, we were free to <u>trade</u> the cards on the secondary market among ourselves. We weren't sophisticated enough at age 10 to think of listing standards, hand signals, or regulations, but we managed to do a pretty nice volume without anybody feeling cheated, which is probably more than can be said for most adult-run exchanges. And it was, in fact, a secondary market, where prices were determined purely by supply and demand. After all, what *was* a Nolan Ryan rookie card worth? As much as you could get for it. Maybe as much as a Pete Rose and a Joe Morgan special edition combined.

For the exam, remember the difference between the primary and secondary markets. Securities are issued in the primary market, where the issuer takes money from the investor. Securities are traded on the secondary market among investors—with no money going to the issuer.

This chapter is about trading securities on the secondary market.

DIVISIONS OF SECONDARY MARKET

A big focus of trading securities has to do with four different markets. First of all, you have to remember that "primary" and "secondary" are different terms altogether. The primary market refers to a situation whereby an issuer receives the proceeds of a transaction. In the secondary market, other folks buy and sell securities, at no direct financial benefit to the issuer. The Topps bubble gum company and their underwriters (the retail stores) got our money only one time for each pack of baseball cards. That was the primary market. When we traded our cards among ourselves, we didn't send any money to Topps. That was our secondary market. Similarly, Google's IPO took place on the primary market. The price rose to the stratosphere on the secondary market, where demand outstripped supply.

FIRST MARKET – NYSE AND REGIONAL EXCHANGES

Within the secondary market, there are four separate components. Let's start with the **first market**. Imagine a clanging bell and the roar of frantic buyers and sellers in funny-looking jackets all day long until the bell rings again at four o'clock Eastern Time. That's the New York Stock Exchange, the first market. The exam will likely ask you to associate this with the phrase "**auction market**" or "**double auction market**." It really is a lot like an auction: confusing hand signals, really fast pace, and people shouting out prices all day long. There are also regional exchanges in Chicago, Philadelphia, Boston, and San Francisco that are based on the NYSE. They tend to focus on regional stocks, but they still fill orders for NYSE-listed securities, such as GE, IBM, or GM. There is also a Cincinnati Stock Exchange and, just to keep things nice and simple, they decided to locate it in Chicago. Seriously. Actually, that one was renamed the "National Stock Exchange," but they still use the "C" on the ticker tape for the "Cincinnati" exchange, located—of course—in Chicago.

Anyway, the exam will refer to the first market as a physical location where buyers and sellers gather at trading posts to bid for and offer securities. Lots of shouting and shoving going on down on the floor, sort of like an NBA playoff game.

The exam wants you to know about four different players who can play down on the floor. The first one is a quick-moving point guard called the **commission house broker**. He works for a brokerage house and fills their orders for a commission. Go figure. The more orders he can fill, the more money he can make, which explains why he's always in such a hurry. If he's too busy to fill an order, he can call in somebody off the bench known as a **two-dollar broker**, who gets a commission to help out when the commission house broker is too busy scoring his own points. Then there are the big power forwards who compete for themselves only. These **competitive floor traders** make a fortune if they can buy low and sell high, in either order, more often than not. The exam is probably most inclined to talk about the fourth player, the big man known as the **specialist**. Like a 7-footer on the basketball court, the specialist plays the game with certain inherent advantages. For example, if I want to buy 10,000 shares for $36, I put in a buy-limit order, and the specialist sees that I'm willing to take a pretty good number of shares off his or her hands for $36. Therefore, if they would like to go for an easy slam dunk, they can pay $36.01 per share and see where it goes. If it goes up, it's a slam dunk profit when they sell it to a higher bidder. If it goes down, they already know they can pass it off to me for just one penny less than they paid for it.

Nice work if you can get it.

The specialist trades for their own account, carrying an inventory. Specialists are exchange members whose responsibility is to maintain a "**fair and orderly market**" in a particular listed security. If you want to trade some IBM today, you end up dealing with the specialist in IBM. They aren't exchange employees—they are business people doing business on the floor of the exchange, trying to buy low and sell high, pretty much like everybody else. If no one is trading, the specialist has to step in and start buying to get the stock moving again. They trade in between the highest buy-limit and the lowest sell-limit price among all the fancy limit orders we'll get to in a minute. That's what enabled me to take the cheap shot at them when I talked about their being able to buy stock for one penny above the highest buy-limit order. Sometimes, that's not such a great thing, I guess. But, every job has its price, like having to pass some nightmare of an exam called the Series 7.

Anyway, let's dive into a few testable concepts and then move onto the second or "over-the-counter" market.

Reporting Prices

As we mentioned, if I place an electronic order to buy 1,000 shares of, say, GE, my order could be filled in New York, Philadelphia, Boston, San Francisco, or Chicago. In fact, that just happened the other day. As I was purchasing shares in several listed securities through my online broker, I noticed that some stocks were filled in Boston, most in New York, and one in Chicago. That's because they're all part of the "first market."

The Series 7, you see, is not as divorced from the "real world" as some would have you believe.

Consolidated Tape

When a listed security is sold, it doesn't matter whether it's sold in the Big Apple, Chi-Town, Beantown, Philly, or San Francisco...the prices are all *consolidated* on the consolidated tape. That means that the seller has to report the price he just sold a certain number of shares at within 90 seconds, whether it was sold in Philly, Boston, etc. Which is why you yourself can now waste perfectly good work time staring at prices streaming endlessly at the bottom of a television monitor. Yep, all that "10s GE 35.55" stuff actually means something. It means that somebody sold (and bought) 1,000 shares of GE for $35.55 per share. The number of round lots comes first, then the stock symbol, and then the price at which the transaction took place. Let's take a look at some more pretend stock trades on a consolidated tape:

GE36.55...10s.IBM95.04... 99s.C.75.15...13,000s. GE.36.70

The first thing we see is the stock symbol GE. If there is no number before the symbol, we know that one round lot (100 shares) of GE just traded for $36.55 per share. In the next case "10s" means 10 round lots, or 1,000 shares. So, 1,000 shares of IBM just traded at $95.04 per share. Next, we see that 99 round lots, or 9,900 shares of "C" (for Citigroup) just traded at $75.15 per share. But, when the number of shares gets up to 10,000 or more, they stop talking in round lots and just list the actual number of shares. In other words a trade for 10,000 shares would not be indicated as "100s." Rather, it would be "10,000s" just to keep things nice and simple. Therefore, we read the tape to indicate that 13,000 shares of GE just traded for $36.70 per share.

Also note that for stocks trading at $175 a share or higher, a round lot is now just one share. For these stocks, a transaction for less than 100 shares will no longer be reported as odd-lot transactions.

As usual, things get more complicated. What if you saw the following on your exam and were asked to interpret the report? :

MCD12s35 .35

That means 1200 shares of McDonald's traded at $35, followed by a trade for 100 shares at $35. Remember, if there's no number before the price, that means one round lot or 100 shares traded at that price. You also might be fortunate enough to be asked what the following means:

MCD35 .15

That means 100 shares of MickyDee's traded at $35, followed by another round lot that traded at $35.15. Just to keep things nice and simple. In other words, there is a world of difference between

"35.15" and "35 .15." In the first case, 100 shares sold at $35.15. In the second case, 100 shares sold at $35, followed by 100 shares at $35.15."

No wonder these traders are so uptight, huh?

For preferred stock, a round lot is just 10 shares, and they indicate that the only way possible, with an "s/s." Therefore, what does the following report mean? :

ABC pr 7s/s.85.05

It means that 70 shares of ABC preferred traded for $85.05 per share.

And, just in case the exam is in an especially foul mood when you sit for it, also memorize the following abbreviations used on the consolidated tape:

- SLD: means that this price is being reported late, long after the actual trade. Oops.
- Halt: sometimes trading in a stock is halted, usually when big news is about to come out on it
- OPD: the first trade that happens after a delayed opening or a trading halt
- Pr: preferred stock (also look for the s/s thingie)
- R/T: somebody's trading rights
- W/S: somebody's trading warrants

Finally, since NYSE stocks can be traded all over the place, the exchange where the transaction in, say, IBM, took place is also indicated with an abbreviation. Rather then delve, I'll just give it to you in a nice little table:

NYSE N	Boston B	INSTINET O
AMEX A	Pacific P	Philadelphia X
FINRA T	Chicago M	National C

Quote Screens

In the old days, customers had to call their registered rep to get an idea on the price of a particular stock. Now, of course, stock quotes are all over the Internet. I'm currently logged into my online brokerage account, looking at a quote on Abbott Labs. This is what I see:

ABT Abbott Labs
Bid – 44.90 Ask – 45.00 B/A size – 300x300
Last – 44.95 Open – 44.85 Close – 44.63
Change - +.32 Change % - .71%
High – 44.99 Low – 44.85
Volume – 925,000

What the heck does all that mean? It means that the last reported trade in Abbott Labs was at $44.95. You could sell ABT at the bid price of $44.90, or you could buy some ABT at the ask price of $45.00. In other words, buyers are trying to take your stock for a little less and sellers are trying to sell you the stock for a little more than the last traded price. The stock previously closed (yesterday) at $44.63, so if the last trade took place at $44.95, that represents a change of + .32, which is less than 1% higher than the previous close. The newscaster would say, "Abbott Labs is up 32 cents," and many people would consider that to be news. The high and low for the day (so far) are self-explanatory, and the number of shares that have changed hands is nearly 1 million, even though trading has only taken place for about an hour at this point. The "size" of the B/A just means that the bid and ask prices are associated with orders to buy or sell 300 shares at those prices. If you saw that the B/A size were 900x200, that means there are a lot more buyers than sellers. You could easily sell 900 shares at the bid price to willing buyers, or buy 200 shares at the ask price from willing sellers.

In case the test wants to pretend that all that information is still abbreviated, memorize the following abbreviations and what they stand for:

- B – Bid
- A – Ask
- O – opening price
- C – closing price
- H – highest price today
- L – lowest price today
- LT – last traded
- NC – net change (how much the last trade is up or down from the previous close)
- V – volume or number of shares traded

Trading Curbs, Halts

Sometimes trading gets a little chaotic, so the NYSE steps in to straighten things out. Many people trade through computer programs. If the stock goes to this price, sell 10,000 shares; if the stock goes to this price, buy 5,000 shares, etc. That's a lot of activity set on "auto-pilot," so if the market gets a little too volatile, the NYSE dictates that trading curbs be turned on. According to NYSE Rule 80A, when the Dow Jones Industrial Average (DJIA) changes by 2% from its previous day's close, trading **curbs** (restrictions) would be put into effect on program trading and index **arbitrage**, but not on all trading. The NYSE would also decide when program trading could begin again.

If the market gets extraordinarily volatile, the NYSE will **halt** trading in all stocks for a certain amount of time, as follows:

- When the DJIA declines by 10% from the previous close, trading halts for one hour.
- When the DJIA declines by 20% from the previous close, trading halts for two hours.
- When the DJIA declines by 30% from the previous close, everybody goes home.

Of course, the Dow is currently in the range of 10,000, so a drop of 10% would be a drop of about 1,000 points, which would make for one screaming headline, not to mention the mileage CNBC could get out of the Dow dropping 3,000 points in a single session. This is known as NYSE Rule 80B, in case the exam absolutely loses its mind the day you take it.

THE SPECIALIST

Priority, Precedence, Parity

The specialist uses **priority**, **precedence**, and **parity** to determine which orders get filled in which order. This means that if more than one order is the same, orders will be filled as follows:

- Priority: the order received first gets filled first
- Precedence: if the time and price are the same, the larger order gets filled
- Parity: if all conditions are the same, orders are matched in the crowd and the shares are split among the orders

Specialist's Book

It takes a large amount of capital (money) to play the role of the specialist, which is why the "specialist" is generally an employee of a specialist firm. If you're the specialist for IBM, all trades in IBM take place in front of you. Your job is to maintain a "fair and orderly market," which means that if there are no public buy orders, you have to step in and start buying to get the stock moving. If there are no public sell orders, you have to start selling some of your inventory.

Let's say the market for XYZ is:

	Bid	Ask
5 x 5	$20.05	$20.15

That means that 500 shares can be sold at $20.05, and 500 shares can be purchased right now for $20.15. If a public order to buy came in, the specialist could not charge $20.15 or higher for their own account. They would have to improve the price by charging less than $20.15. Similarly, if a public order to sell came in, the specialist cannot buy for his own account at $20.05 or lower. They'd have to pay more than $20.05 to improve the price.

Where did we get that inside market of Bid-20.05, Ask-20.15? From the buy and sell limit orders placed by exchange members. As we'll discuss a little later, traders can name the price they want to pay when they buy or the price they want to receive when they sell. We call these "buy-limit" and "sell-limit" orders. The orders aren't ready to be filled yet, so the specialist puts them on his/her book. The specialist's book for XYZ might look like this:

BUY	XYZ	SELL
2 Bear	20	
3 Morgan 2 Goldman	20.05	
3 Merrill Stp	20.10	
	20.15	2 Prudential 3 Smith Barney
	20.20	2 JP Morgan

What's going on here is that we are looking for the highest price somebody's willing to pay and the lowest price somebody's willing to sell XYZ for, and that becomes the specialist's quote.

The "Stp" for "stop" order is ignored here. As we'll see, stop orders are triggered when an actual trade takes place at that price. Limit orders are executed as soon as somebody is willing to meet your limit price. So, ignoring the "Stp" order, we see that the highest price anyone's willing to pay is $20.05, and there are 5 round lots ready to be bought at that price. The lowest price people are willing to sell XYZ for is $20.15, and there are 5 round lots ready to be sold at that price.

So, the specialist's quote becomes Bid-$20.05, Ask-$20.15 with the size at 5x5. Everybody wants to buy low and sell high, so the quote simply represents the lowest price you can buy a stock for (ask) and the highest price you can sell it for (bid).

The specialist accepts stop and limit orders that are not ready to be executed. They do not accept the following orders for their book:

- Market orders
- Not held orders

A market order is simply executed at the best available price in the crowd. Now, the specialist can execute a market order, but there is no reason to put it on his book. The book is for orders that will be executed (or not) later, if the market price moves a certain way. A **not held** order lets the floor broker decide when to enter the order and at what price, so that's all up to the floor broker, not the specialist.

Finally, if the exam uses the phrase **stopping stock**, that just means that the specialist has guaranteed an execution price for a public order and will also allow the broker to seek a better price among the crowd. If the specialist says "you're stopped at $30" that means the buy order will be filled for no more than $30, or the sell order will be filled for no less than $30. And a better price may actually be obtained.

Listing Standards for NYSE

In order to have your company's stock listed on the NYSE, you'd have to meet the exchange's listing requirements, which include:

- At least 2,000 shareholders owning at least 100 shares each
- At least 1.1 million publicly owned shares
- Certain earnings/valuation requirements

It's actually more complicated than that, but I'm not even sure those numbers will show up on your exam, let alone that the company could meet the requirement with 2,000 shareholders who own 100 shares each *or* 2,200 shareholders as long as the average monthly trading volume is 100,000 shares for the most recent six months. Now it seems we're getting too trivial even for the Series 7, which is a pretty scary thing, actually. The exchange also charges listing fees to these companies since they feel that making money is sort of a good thing.

Nine Bond Rule

Some bonds are listed for trading on the NYSE, and the NYSE is a little bit protective. So, if an order for less than 10 NYSE-listed bonds comes into your broker-dealer, you have to route that order to the NYSE. If you can't get the trade executed at a decent price, *then* you can route it to the OTC (over-the-counter) market.

OVER-THE-COUNTER

The over-the-counter market is sometimes called the second market. It's not a physical market-place, but it's definitely a market. Also known as the **interdealer** or **negotiated market**. So, the first market is an "auction market," while the second or OTC market is "negotiated," which is a very likely testable point.

Since we don't all gather together on the floor of an exchange, we need big dealers to maintain inventories of over-the-counter stocks. We call these behemoth buyers and sellers **market makers**, because they, literally, make a market. What is a "market maker?" Just a broker-dealer who carries an inventory of a particular security and stands ready to either buy or sell it throughout the day. Investors are able to trade shares of MSFT, ORCL, and CSCO only because there are broker-dealers who make a "market" in those securities. What IS a market? It's a two-sided quote, allowing buyers to buy at the ask price and sellers to sell at the bid price. Without these two-sided quotes, what would we do, call up our Aunt Ginnie and see if she'd like to go long 1,000 XYZ at $47.72? Again, liquidity is a big deal when it comes to securities—if you can't sell the thing, are you really prepared to hold it, no matter what?

Luckily, there are market makers who put out a **bid** and **ask** (or offer) price and stand ready to take either side of the trade, for at least one round lot. For stocks a round lot is 100 shares. So if a market maker says their quote is 20.00–20.11, they stand ready to buy 100 shares at $20.00 or sell 100 shares at $20.11. The difference between where they buy and where they sell is called the **spread**, just like the difference between what a car dealer will pay for your trade-in, and what you'll pay for the new car he wants to sell you. Broker-dealers can act as **brokers**, whereby they charge commissions, or they can act as **principals** in the transaction by selling stock from their own inventory to customers, or buying stock for their inventory from customers. The exam might point out that the OTC market usually has several different market makers willing to buy and sell the same stock, while the first market has only one "market maker," the specialist. All of these terms (agent, broker, dealer, market maker, bid, ask, etc.) are highly testable, by the way, which is why I'm making this chapter much denser than you or I would probably prefer.

NASDAQ

Over-the-counter stocks have more than three letters in their symbols, by the way. So if you see a symbol like "IBM," you know that one is on the first or "exchange" market, whereas if you see "MSFT" or "CSCO," you know that one is considered "OTC." People trade these stocks by computer rather than gathering at a big building on Wall Street. The "big guys" of the OTC market are quoted all day long through an electronic quotation system known as **NASDAQ**, which stands for National Association of Securities Dealers Automated Quotation system.

NASDAQ used to be divided into the "NASDAQ National Market System" and the "NASDAQ SmallCap Market." Now, NASDAQ National Market is called the "NASDAQ Global Market Companies." This group consists of over 1,450 companies that have applied for listing after meeting and continuing to meet stringent financial and liquidity requirements and agreeing to meet specific corporate governance standards. The former "NASDAQ SmallCap Market" has been renamed the "NASDAQ Capital Market Companies." This group of stocks consists of over 550 companies that have met and continue to meet financial and liquidity listing requirements and agree to meet specific corporate governance standards.

Non-NASDAQ

Stocks that do not meet NASDAQ's financial and liquidity and corporate governance standards may be referred to on your exam as **Non-NASDAQ OTC Securities**. These securities trade on the OTC Bulletin Board and the Pink Sheets, where spreads are wider and stock prices generally more volatile. When a company no longer meets NASDAQ's listing requirements, the stock symbol changes, and the security begins to trade in the nether regions of the OTC market, where professional investors generally won't touch it with an 11-foot pole. At www.otcmarkets.com we see that the Pink Sheets are called "the speculative trading marketplace," which is the perfect description. If you want to acquire a huge position in a cheap stock, in a company you're convinced is going to go a lot farther than people yet realize, buy yourself some speculative stocks trading here. You'll notice at that website that some companies provide current information to investors and some don't. There is even a tier called "caveat emptor," which is Latin for "buyer beware." But, we can only have so much fun at one time so let's keep moving.

NASDAQ Level 1, 2, 3

Back to NASDAQ. There are three levels of NASDAQ quoting that the test wants you to know about. The first is called **Level 1**, which represents the best bid and the best ask. Buyers want to pay the lowest ask price and receive the highest bid price when they sell, which is what Level 1 displays. Among all market makers, Level 1 displays the highest bid and the lowest ask. That makes up a very important concept known as the "inside market" or "inside quote." Everything is based on that. When a dealer sells a security, they have to be close to that inside market, which might look like this:

Bid	Ask
19.75	20.00

Those two prices represent the highest bid and the lowest ask among all market makers currently quoting the stock. If any particular dealer sells to a customer at a price higher than 20 or buys lower than 19.75, they have to remain somewhere within 5% in order to conform to the 5% markup rule, which we'll explain in more detail.

Level 2 looks more like the following. Let's say there are three market makers quoting this stock and their quotes look like this:

	Bid	Ask
Dealer 1	19.11	20.00
Dealer 2	19.75	20.50
Dealer 3	19.23	20.25

Among the three market makers, we find the highest bid at 19.75 and the lowest ask at 20.00.

That's what makes up the inside quote, shown on Level 1. So, Level 2 identifies each market maker's quote, from which Level 1 pulls the highest bid and lowest ask to provide the "inside market."

Level 3 has input fields that market makers use to enter their quotes. If you're not a market maker, you don't have Level 3. Levels 1 and 2 report quotes. Level 3 lets market makers provide quotes; it's interactive, rather than just a display.

5% Markup Guideline

As it says in the FINRA Manual, the 5% "rule" is a guideline that dealers must use to ensure that customers are charged reasonable commissions or markups/markdowns. A firm can act as either a broker or a dealer. When the firm brokers a trade, they add a commission that must be reasonable. When the firm deals stock to the customer, they must charge a markup that is reasonable.

Back to the inside market. The inside market in our example above was Bid-19.75, Ask-20.00. That's the "interdealer market," which means that among all the dealers in the security, the two best prices are $19.75 to a seller and $20.00 to a buyer. So, what happens if that one market maker does sell the stock for $20.50? That's a markup of 50 cents, and the markup generally needs to be around 5% above the "inside ask" of $20.00. If they charged "$20.50," we could judge the fairness of that markup by simply taking the excess of 50 cents compared to/divided by $20.00. That represents a markup of 2.5%, well within the 5% guideline. If they charged $21.00, that would be exactly 5%. But, 5% is not an absolute—even if they're charging 5% or less, they could still be violating the rules. If the stock is extremely liquid—like MSFT or CSCO—maybe they shouldn't be charging anything close to 5%. Or, for some securities, a markup above 5% might be okay. The dealers can (and must) take the following into consideration when determining the fairness of a markup or commission:

- The Type of Security Involved – stocks are riskier than bonds and carry higher charges.
- Availability of the Security – inactive securities might take more time and expense to buy or sell.
- Price of the Security – low-priced securities usually end up carrying markups that are higher as a percentage of the price. A markup of 10 cents is a big percentage when the stock costs $1.00, while a markup of 50 cents is pretty low on a $100 stock.
- Amount of Money Involved – sorry, kid, if you want to buy 50 dollars' worth of stock, you aren't going to get such a great deal.
- Disclosing the higher markup or commissions before completing the transaction usually takes care of the situation…though not always. If you're truly gouging your clients, prior disclosure isn't going to make it okay.
- Nature of the Services Provided – full-service broker-dealers can charge more in commissions and markups because they provide more services. The old "you get what you pay for" thing.

Broker-dealers can act as an agent/broker on a transaction, in which case they add a commission. Or, they can act as a principal/dealer, in which case they add a **markup** when they sell, or a **markdown** when they buy from the customer. The 5% guideline covers the fairness of both commissions and markups. Remember that this is an either-or situation. *Either* the firm gets a commission *or* they get a markup—not both. In other words, they acted *either* as a broker (agent) *or* a dealer (principal). Also note that when a firm acts as a principal, they are selling a security held in their inventory to a customer—as opposed to simply matching the customer with a seller. When they act as a principal/dealer in a transaction with a retail customer, the firm has to get the customer's written consent and acknowledgment that he/she understands the significance of the terminology, as if your customers are ever going to read one word of any document you ask them to sign.

Proceeds Transaction

If a customer sells one stock and uses the proceeds to buy another on the same day, we call this a **proceeds transaction**, for obvious reasons. When applying the 5% guideline, the firm has to treat both the sale and the purchase as one transaction. In other words, they can't ding the customer 5% on the sale and on the purchase. The combined commission or markup/markdown must be in the neighborhood of 5%. The FINRA Manual says it well when it writes, "the mark-up shall be computed in the same way as if the customer had purchased for cash."

Riskless Principal Transaction

The difference between "broker" and "dealer" is important. When the firm acts as a broker, they are simply finding a buyer or seller for their customer. When the firm acts as a dealer, they are taking the other side of the trade by either buying from the customer or selling to the customer. The firm acts either as a broker or a dealer on a particular transaction, which is why the industry got all clever and named these firms broker-dealers.

So, if you need some stock, maybe the broker-dealer will simply find a seller and get you a decent price. They're acting as a broker/agent, and they would charge you a commission. A-B-C... agents are brokers and they charge commissions. If the firm already had the stock in inventory, they might deal it to you at a markup. They would indicate on your trade confirmation that they acted in a "principal" capacity. To act as a "principal" means that they're taking the other side of the trade, rather than just arranging the trade for a commission (agent/broker).

Well, sometimes a customer will call up and express an interest in buying, say, 1,000 shares of XYZ. The firm puts the customer on hold and then purchases the 1,000 shares for their own inventory. They get the customer back on the line, and they deal the stock to him. There was no risk on this principal transaction, since their holding period is about 3 seconds. Therefore, the industry cleverly named this situation where a principal takes no risk a **riskless principal transaction**. As long as the markup conforms to the 5% guideline, everything is hunky dory.

Remember that the 5% markup guideline does provide guidance for markups and commissions on corporate (but not municipal) bonds. As FINRA points out in its notice to members, a broker-dealer would generally use its "contemporaneous cost" when determining the fairness of a markup to a customer. That means that they would use the prevailing market price that they themselves would or did have to pay at that time. There are, of course, exceptions to that: if interest rates, credit ratings, or news announcements change the whole reality for that debt security immediately after the dealer buys it, then the firm can factor that in. And, if there *is* no current market for the security, the firm would not be able—let alone required—to use their contemporaneous cost, but if the exam expects you to know that, too, well...

Anyway, the 5% markup guideline would not apply to anything sold with a prospectus, since that's a primary market transaction. A variable annuity or mutual fund, therefore, is simply sold at a public offering price, just like an IPO. The public offering price (POP) already includes all the compensation to the underwriters and selling group members. Also, municipal securities aren't covered by this 5% guideline. The firm just follows the MSRB rule, which says customer transactions must be executed at a fair and reasonable price.

How Firm Is Thy Quote?

When a dealer contacts a market maker, they need to be really clear as to what the market maker actually means with his cryptic little phrases. For example, if the market maker simply responds with a straight answer, that's a **firm quote** that has to be honored for at least one round lot of 100 shares. If the market maker says, "Bid-20.00, Ask-20.15," that's a firm quote. He doesn't have to say "firm" to make it firm. It's what he *doesn't* say that makes it firm. See, sometimes the market maker is just talking, just giving the dealer a ballpark figure. These are called **subject quotes,** which means they are subject to being reconfirmed before the deal goes down. A quote of "25 to 25.30 subject," would be, not surprisingly, a subject quote. Also know that the market maker's firm quote is only firm for 1 round lot unless some specific number of shares is mentioned. If the buy side says, "What's the quote on XYZ?" and the market maker says, "Bid-20, Ask-20.25," the market maker only has to sell 100 shares at $20.25. If the buy side says, "Great, we'll take 1 million shares at the offer," the market maker would first laugh hard enough to spit water through his nose and then remind the buyer that there was, in fact, this exam called the Series 7 which did, in fact, make it clear that a firm quote is good for 100 shares. Beyond that, we may need to talk. So, in a test question, if somebody asks for a quote on 500 shares, a firm quote given in response would be firm for 500 shares. But, a firm quote is only firm for 1 round lot. There may only be so many round lots available at a particular price, so larger orders may have to be negotiated.

Automated Confirmation Transaction (ACT) Service

For the first market, sellers report to the "consolidated tape" within 90 seconds. The OTC market uses ACT, and, again, sellers report the price to ACT within 90 seconds.

THIRD MARKET

The **third market** is just a term used when an **exchange-listed security** gets sold over-the-counter. Maybe an institutional buyer can get a better, negotiated price for an order of 10,000 IBM, a listed security, so they decide to buy it over-the-counter. When a listed security trades OTC, we refer to that situation as the "third market." The **Consolidated Quotation Service** (CQS) displays quotations on all common stock, preferred stock, warrants, and rights that are registered on the American Stock Exchange or the New York Stock Exchange and trading in the OTC market (third market). Although executed in the over-the-counter market, these transactions must still be reported to the consolidated tape.

FOURTH MARKET

The **fourth market** involves direct trading between institutional investors, completely bypassing brokers by using **Electronic Communications Networks (ECNs)**. Institutional investors include insurance companies, mutual funds, pension funds, big trust departments, broker-dealers, etc. They're professionals with millions/billions of dollars flowing in and out of the market. Basically,

ECNs work like an eBay for securities transactions by matching up buyers and sellers. Some broker-dealers use a market maker to execute client transactions during normal business hours and then use an ECN to execute orders after normal business hours (after 4 p.m.). Here are some essential facts on ECNs:

- If the ECN system cannot match a buyer and seller, a client's order can have a limited ability to be executed
- Some ECNs will only accept certain types of orders, such as limit orders
- Electronic communications networks allow market participants themselves to display quotes and execute transactions
- Participants are referred to as *subscribers* and pay a fee to the ECN in order to trade electronically through the system
- ECNs allow subscribers to trade after-hours, quote and trade anonymously
- ECNs act in an agency capacity and do not buy or sell for their own account (not a market maker)

SELLING SHORT

You've probably heard that every investor should try to buy low and sell high, right? Well, some investors take that same principle and simply try to do it in reverse: they prefer selling high, then buying back low. We call these people "short sellers," because calling them high-risk lunatics wouldn't be polite or good for business.

It works like this. You go to your friend's house and see that she has a new mountain bike that she paid way too much money for. Mind if I borrow your mountain bike, you ask, to which your friend agrees. On the way home you run into another friend, who admires the bike very much. She likes it so much, in fact, that she offers you two thousand bucks for it.

Two thousand bucks? Sold! You take the two thousand bucks and put it in your pocket.

Wait a minute, that wasn't even your mountain bike! No problem. All you have to do is replace it with an identical machine. A few weeks later you go to the bike store to replace the borrowed bike, and—as predicted—the price has fallen to just $1,000. Perfect! You sold the bike for $2,000 and you can get out of your position by paying just $1,000, keeping the $1,000 difference as your profit. Just buy the bike for $1,000, wheel it over to your friend, and everybody's happy. Notice that you made money when the price went down. The exam would say that you were "bearish" on the price of mountain bikes, because the exam doesn't get out much.

Short sellers don't sell bikes or search engines short, but they can certainly sell the stock of the companies who make bikes or search engines short. If you think that Google is wildly overpriced and headed for a big drop, borrow the shares from your friendly broker-dealer and sell them at what you think is the top. Sell Google for $100 and, you hope, buy it back later for $30, keeping $70 per share as your profit.

However, many people tried that soon after Google went public (primary market) at $85. When it got to $100 many folks were convinced the stock would only go down from there, so they sold it short at $100. Expecting to buy it back or "cover their short positions" for less than $100, these poor souls must have been really embarrassed to see the stock soon climb up to $400 per share.

Hate it when that happens. Selling something for $100 and buying it back for $400 is not a particularly good business model. That's no different from buying something for $400 and then selling it for $100. It's just more dangerous. When you buy something, you've already lost all you could ever lose. But when you sell stock short, there is no limit to how much you'll have to spend to get out of your position. I mean, reality would tell us that Google was never going to hit $1,000 a share, but, hypothetically, it could have. Higher even.

So, short sellers are bearish. They profit when the stock goes DOWN. But, they have limited upside and unlimited risk. If you short a stock for $5,000, $5,000 is the maximum you could make, and only if the stock went to zero. Your potential loss is unlimited, since no one can tell you for sure how high the stock could go up against you. When you buy stock, we refer to that as "being long the stock," because we also don't get out much. Long means "buy." Short means "sell." In case your brain hasn't been overloaded, please know that stock is not the only thing that can be "sold short." Treasury securities are frequently sold short, as are corporate bonds, ETFs (exchange-traded funds), and their kissing cousin, the closed-end fund. You probably also recall that writers of options are "short the option" and that they complete the trade when they buy it back or allow it to expire.

REGULATION SHO

The SEC does not like it when short sellers abuse their chosen pastime by selling shares that don't actually exist. Allowing them to do so would distort the downward (bearish) pressure on a stock by distorting the laws of supply & demand that determine the stock's market price. Therefore, broker-dealers have to "locate" the shares their customers are selling short and document it before effecting the short sale—that means they reasonably believe the securities can be delivered by the settlement date (T + 3) as required. In olden days a short sale could only be executed at a price that was higher than the previous price for the security, or at the same price if the price before had been an "uptick." Reg SHO now requires that before executing a short sale, broker-dealers have to locate the securities so that the laws of supply and demand are not distorted by "naked short selling," in which people sell stock that doesn't even exist short, artificially depressing its price. If the broker-dealer executes a short sale without reasonably believing the shares can be delivered by the lender, they have violated the rule.

In May 2010 Reg SHO was updated to impose a temporary version of the old uptick rule that applies when a "circuit breaker" is tripped for a particular security. Starting in May, if a security drops during the day by 10% or more below its most recent closing price, short sellers will not be able to sell short at or below the current best bid price for the security. In other words, people "selling long," which means selling the shares they own, will have priority and will be able to liquidate their holdings before short sellers can jump onto the pile. As the SEC states in their unique brand of English:

> a targeted short sale price test restriction will apply the alter-
> native uptick rule for the remainder of the day and the following
> day if the price of an individual security declines intra-day by

10% or more from the prior day's closing price for that security. By not allowing short sellers to sell at or below the current national best bid while the circuit breaker is in effect, the short sale price test restriction in Rule 201 will allow long sellers, who will be able to sell at the bid, to sell first in a declining market for a particular security. As the Commission has noted previously in connection with short sale price test restrictions, a goal of such restrictions is to allow long sellers to sell first in a declining market. In addition, by making such bids accessible only by long sellers when a security's price is undergoing significant downward price pressure, Rule 201 will help to facilitate and maintain stability in the markets and help ensure that they function efficiently. It will also help restore investor confidence during times of substantial uncertainty because, once the circuit breaker has been triggered for a particular security, long sellers will have preferred access to bids for the security, and the security's continued price decline will more likely be due to long selling and the underlying fundamentals of the issuer, rather than to other factors.

BOND TRADING

CORPORATE BONDS

Corporate bonds traded over-the-counter are reported to FINRA's **TRACE** system, which stands for **Trade Reporting and Compliance Engine**. Brokerage firms are now required to report price and volume data on all corporate bond transactions to TRACE, within 15 minutes. FINRA publicly disseminates that transaction data immediately on virtually 100 percent of over-the-counter corporate bond activity (approximately 22,000 transactions and $18 billion in volume every day!). Recently, FINRA fined a firm $1.4 *million* for failing to report a huge percentage of their bond trades to TRACE. The whole purpose of the TRACE system is to provide transparency (what's going on) in the bond market, so by failing to report the trades, the firm deprived the market of the transparency it needs to remain effective. Several smaller fines have recently been levied for failing to report trades in "TRACE-eligible securities." FINRA insists that dealers provide the market with accurate and transparent data on securities transactions, and they are quite happy to remind them with disciplinary actions and fines.

The NYSE also provides a bond trading platform, and I'm simply going to let them tell you about it:

> The NYSE Bonds trading platform provides a more efficient and transparent way to trade bonds. The platform incorporates the design of the current NYSE Arca all-electronic trading system. This system provides investors with the ability to readily obtain transparent pricing and trading information, enabling them to make better

investment decisions. The system has also been expanded to include the bonds of all NYSE-listed companies and their subsidiaries without the companies having to list each bond issued. NYSE Bonds operates the largest centralized bond market of any U.S. exchange or other self-regulatory organization. It offers investors a broad selection of bonds: corporate (including convertibles), agency and government bonds.

The majority of NYSE bond volume is in corporate debt, with some 94% in straight, or non-convertible bonds, and 6% in convertible debt issues. As of Monday, December 1, 2008 all NYSE Amex (formerly American Stock Exchange) listed bonds transferred to an electronic trading platform based on NYSE Bonds called NYSE Amex Bonds. Like NYSE Bonds, this electronic trading platform is based on the design of NYSE Arca's comprehensive matching technology allowing NYSE Members to enter orders to buy or sell bonds electronically.

No, there is, apparently, no limit to the amount of detail and trivia that FINRA expects you to know when you sit down to take the Series 7 exam. Luckily, they can only ask 250 questions—if we only knew *exactly* which 250 they planned to ask you, we could seriously cut down on the page count. But we don't, so let's keep moving.

MUNICIPAL BONDS

MSRB Rule G-14 requires that transactions in municipal bonds be reported within 15 minutes of trade execution to the MSRB's Real-time Transaction Reporting System (RTRS). The MSRB disseminates trade data about all reported municipal securities transactions almost immediately at www.investinginbonds.com. You may have noticed that for both TRACE and RTRS, bond transactions are reported within 15 minutes, but when we're talking about stock transactions, the report is due within 90 *seconds*. Yet another indication of the increased volatility and faster pace of the stock—as opposed to the bond—market.

TYPES OF ORDERS

MARKET ORDER

The exam will ask you to work with **market orders**, **limit orders**, **stop orders**, and even the dreaded **stop-limit** order. Market orders are easy. You want to buy 1,000 shares quickly, you place a market order. It will get filled as quickly as possible. We don't know exactly the price it will be filled at, but if we fill it fast enough it will probably be the same price we're looking at right now. *Now* is always the best time to fill a market order, which is also why those players down on the floor are running around like crazy people most of the day. The specialists at the NYSE have the following specialized, nit-picky orders on their "books," which are really computer screens. When somebody wants to name a specific price where a purchase or sale would happen, those orders go on the specialist's book, your exam might say. That's not to imply you can't do the same orders for

OTC/NASDAQ stocks. You can. But the test may mention the specialist's "book," so remember that the book has the stop and limit orders on it that we're about to take apart.

LIMIT ORDER

Sometimes customers like to name their price. If a stock is at 43, maybe they're starting to get interested in selling it. They'd be a lot more interested if they could sell it for $45, so they enter a **sell limit** order above the current market price. Sell limit @45 means the investor will take 45 or better (*more* is better for a seller). If he can get 45 or 45.15, or even higher, he'll sell his stock.

Another investor is interested in buying a stock currently trading at 30. He'd be a lot more interested in buying it at $25, so he places a **buy limit** order below the current price. That means he'll buy the stock if he can get it for $25 or better (*less* is better for a buyer). If the ticker comes in like this, he'll get filled at $25, his limit price:

30.00, 29.25, 28.75, 27.00, 26.25, 25.25, 25.00

And, if the last two prices had been 25.25, 24.50, he could have been filled at 24.50, which is "or better" than 25.00 when you're a buyer.

Sometimes the stock's price fails to perform like an investor wants it to. If it's entered as a day order, the limit order either gets executed that day or it goes away. If the investor is going on vacation for three weeks and doesn't want to look at his stocks while he's gone, he can leave the order open by entering it **GTC**, which stands for good 'til canceled. If the order doesn't get filled and the investor doesn't cancel it, the order remains open. Twice a year (April, October) the firm calls the customers with open orders on the books to see if they still want them, a process called "confirming" for obvious reasons.

STOP ORDER

Stop orders are even more fun. Let's say a technical analyst sees that a particular stock is trading in a narrow range, between 38 and 40. The technical analyst sees no reason to tie up his money in a stock that is stuck in a narrow trading range, known as consolidation. He decides if the stock can break through resistance (40), it will probably continue to rise, which is why he'd like to buy it on the way up. So he places a **buy stop** above the current market price. Buy stop @41 means that the price first has to reach 41 or higher, at which point the order is triggered. It will be <u>executed</u> at the <u>next available price</u>, whatever that is. Stop orders have a trigger price, at which point they become market orders. So if the ticker came in like this:

40.00, 40.50, 40.75, 41.00...his order would now be triggered or "activated" at 41.00. It would then be filled at the next available price, regardless of what that is. And, if the last two prices had been 40.75, 41.50, the order would have been triggered at 41.50, at which point the price has passed through the stop price of 41. Notice that stop orders don't guarantee a price for execution. The price named as the stop is just the price that triggers or elects the order. The order—now a market order—is filled at the next available price. Again, the stop price is not the exact price, either. A "buy stop at 41" is triggered at 41 or any price higher than that. It's then filled as soon as possible.

A day trader decides to take a large position in a high-risk security, because, well, that's what day traders do. But this particular day trader decides to play it safe and limit his loss. He buys 1,000 shares at $50 a share and immediately enters a **sell stop** order at 49. This means that as long as the stock stays above $49 he's in. As soon as it slips to 49 or lower, though, he's out. A sell stop at 49 would be triggered as soon as the stock's price hit 49 or lower, at which point it would be sold at the next available price. The exam might tell you that a customer is bullish on a stock but fears a possible downturn in the short-term. What should she do?

Well, if she originally bought in at $20 and the stock is now at $50, you should tell her that selling for more than $50 would be great. At this point, however, she should make sure she doesn't lose too much of the $30 profit she has within her grasp. Many investors end up snatching defeat from the jaws of victory at this point, probably because they don't know how to use sell stops or **"stop loss"** orders. Not going to happen to us. We'll give up one dollar from here, you tell her, but if it falls to $49 or lower, she's selling and taking her profit. So, if it goes up, great, and if it goes down, she takes a profit, and you immediately put her into another stock...assuming it's suitable, of course.

If somebody wants to get really tricky, they can enter a stop-limit order. Now their stop order also names the most they'll pay or the least they'll accept for a particular stock. A buy stop @50, limit 52 would start out as a stop order. The stock has to hit 50 or higher before it's triggered, but the investor also won't pay more than $52 for it. A sell stop @30, limit 29 would be triggered if the stock hit 30 or lower, but the investor will not take less than $29 a share. If the order gets triggered and then the price falls lower than 29, this sell order simply won't get executed, and the investor will end up holding a loser that would have otherwise been sold with a sell-stop (not a stop-limit) order.

FURTHER SPECIFICATIONS

These orders can also be entered as "specialized orders." A **fill or kill** (FOK) order has to be executed immediately or the whole thing is killed. Fill it or kill it. An **immediate or cancel** order also has to be filled immediately. If the whole thing can't be filled immediately, fill what you can and cancel the rest. So this is the only one that will take a partial execution. An **all or none** (AON) order will *not* take a partial execution. Fill all of it or none of it. You don't necessarily have to fill it right away, though. Just don't come back here with half of it filled, okay?

At-the-open and at-the-close (market-on-close) orders are filled, surprisingly enough, at the opening price of the trading session and at the closing price, respectively. If the customer's order can't be filled at the opening price (at-the-open) or the closing price (market-on-close) the order is cancelled.

And, just in case the exam feels it has not sufficiently harassed you, remember that the FOK and the AON orders are no longer accepted by the NYSE. NASDAQ trading and bond trading still use the funky orders, though.

Also, buy-limit orders and sell-stop orders are placed below the current market price of the stock. As we saw in the chapter Equity Securities, stock prices drop by the amount of the dividend on the ex-dividend date. So, both the buy-limit and the sell-stop order would be reduced by the amount of the dividend. Except when they wouldn't. If the customer wants the order marked **DNR (do not reduce)** then the price of the order would not be reduced because of a dividend. Would sell-limit and buy-stop orders be reduced? No, they're placed above the current market price, so they would not be triggered and/or filled due to the reduction of the stock's market price in response to a dividend.

STOPS AND LIMITS REVIEWED

Let's drill down on the stop and limit orders a little harder, since I suspect you'll be hit with at least three questions on this stuff, and I know from experience just how much most people enjoy working with these concepts. Here goes. Right now, XYZ's last reported price is $25. The BID is $24.90, the ASK is $25.10. Notice how the bidders (buyers willing to let you sell to them) want to buy your stock for 10 cents less, and the offerors/askers would like an extra 10 cents if you want to buy from them. You could certainly enter a market order to buy and pay $25.10, or you could enter a market order to sell and receive $24.90.

Or, you could get fancy. If you want to buy this stock for less, enter a buy-limit order below the inside ASK/offer price. The ASK is $25.10, but you aren't willing to pay one penny more than $24. Fine, enter a buy-limit @24. Nothing will happen unless and until the ASK/offer price drops to $24 or lower.

Three hours later, the ASK price does, in fact, drop to $24, and your order is filled. Congratulations, you just bought a stock whose price is dropping faster than a big league curve ball. But, this time you get lucky, and the stock turns around and starts going up in your favor. Well, heck, you're not greedy or anything, so as soon as this stock could be sold for $30, you'd be okay with a 25% profit, and you enter a sell-limit @30. So, if/when the BID price moves up to $30, you'll sell it to the bidder. You've concluded that this stock isn't likely to move above $30, anyway, so you might as well take your profit at $30. This isn't going to happen in the space of an afternoon, so you mark the order GTC, or "good 'til canceled."

Three weeks later, XYZ begins to move conveniently in your favor. The BID finally rises to $30, and you sell your stock for a $6 profit, minus commissions. Great, that was all the upside there was in the stock, anyway, right?

Wrong. As soon as you sell the stock, it starts to *really* take off, leaving you behind like the sad child nobody ever waits up for. Ouch! This stock is going up without you. But, maybe it's a temporary blip. Maybe there are only a few more points of upside on this stock—let's find out. How? Let's assume that it could easily go to $35 and then drop. But, if it goes above $35, it will keep going. How do we know that?

We don't. Remember, nobody really knows anything when it comes to trading stocks. But, we figure if XYZ breaks through resistance @35 it will continue to go up, which means if the stock goes UP to a certain level, we'll buy it. What kind of weird order is that?

A buy-stop. Let's place a buy-stop @36. That way, if the stock breaks through resistance of $35, we'll buy it just as it's about to make a real break. What if it never makes it to $36?

Then, we never really wanted it. Now, stop orders aren't based on the BID/ASK the way limit orders are. They're based on actual trades or the "last trade" price. Just means there will have to be an actual transaction at $36 or above before our order gets thrown into the game.

It takes a while, but after a few days, XYZ does break through resistance, and we end up buying shares at $36.15. Remember, stop orders aren't filled at the stop price necessarily. If you're that much of a control freak, you need to add the word "limit" to your buy-stop. But we didn't do that, because we just wanted to make sure we got the stock. You get fussy with a limit price and you might not get the stock at all.

But we did. Turns out, we were exactly right—this stock is a rocket ship headed nowhere but up. But then, in a moment of clarity, we remember that they said the same thing about CSCO, JDSU, and QCOM. Yes, stocks do occasionally reverse directions and go the wrong way on us, so just in case that happens here, let's have a sell-stop. The stock has gone from our $36.15 purchase price to $45, which is known, technically, as "a real good thing." Let's not let this real good thing slip away, though. If it continues to go up, we want to hold it. But, if it starts to drop, we want to walk away with a profit. So, we enter a sell-stop @44. Remember, we bought at $36.15, and we're sitting on a profit of $8.85 at this point because the stock is trading at $45. With our sell-stop @44, we will only sell if the stock drops. If it goes up, we continue to hold it and enjoy the upside. If it starts to drop, we walk away with a profit.

Turns out, three days later, the stock opens at $43, which triggers our sell-stop (triggered at or below the trigger price of 44). The stock is sold a few ticks later at $42.95, and we walk away with a decent paper profit, while everybody else is in denial, talking about "doubling down," "lowering their average cost," and various other clichés often uttered before disaster finally strikes.

And, disaster does finally strike. Two weeks later, the CEO is indicted for fraud, the company re-states earnings for the past five years, and the whole thing makes the WorldComm debacle look mild by comparison.

Only, it doesn't really affect us. We protected our paper profit and got out with a sell-stop.

PRACTICE

1. **An investor originally purchased 100 shares of INTC at $20 a share. Now the stock is at $60. The investor is still bullish on the stock for the long-term but fears a possible downturn in the short-term. As her registered rep, you would tell her to place a**

   A. market order to sell

   B. sell limit order at $59

   C. buy stop order at $61

   D. sell stop order at $59

2. **A sell stop order would be activated when**

   A. the stock price passes through the trigger price

   B. the stock price hits or passes through the trigger price

   C. the stock price hits the trigger price and conforms with the NYSE uptick rule

   D. none of the above

3. A sell stop at 45 would be triggered at all the following prices except

    A. 44.00

    B. 44.37

    C. 44.87

    D. 46.00

ANSWERS

1. **D,** you had to eliminate any "buy" order, since the investor already owns the stock. If the investor only wants to sell if the stock drops, place a sell-stop.

2. **B,** it doesn't have to pass through the trigger price—if it hits the trigger price OR passes through, the order is elected.

3. **D,** at the trigger price or below. Not above the trigger price. That's for buy stops.

WRAP-UP

Well, that sure was fun, wasn't it? Trading Securities is, in many ways, one of the toughest sections on the exam. You'll need to be able to define all the terms (bid, ask, markup, markdown, commission, broker, dealer, agent, principal, limit, stop, etc.). And, you'll need to understand all the concepts.

Perhaps that will become easier if we look at the preceding information from another angle. Let's say that your favorite customer, Michelle Madsen, is interested in buying some stock with some money she recently inherited when her Aunt Marta passed away. You and she, of course, discuss suitability, and you've narrowed it down to three different stocks. The first one is the old dependable General Electric, or GE. Michelle is willing to commit $30,000 to buying GE. How many shares can I get, she asks you. You pull up your quote screen and see that the market for GE is:

Bid	Ask
$29.75	$29.95

Looks like she can get a round lot. She's not interested in naming an exact price or placing a fancy buy-stop order above the inside ask, so you decide to take the simplest route and enter a market order. You quickly fill out the order ticket, indicating that she wants to buy 1000 GE "at the market." You hand the ticket to the wire room, who wires the order to your commission house broker jumping around like a lunatic on the floor of the NYSE. The commission house broker runs to the trading post and buys the 1,000 shares at the best price he can pay right now—$29.95. He sends back an execution report, and you tell Michelle that her order for 1,000 shares was filled at $29.95 per share. Later that day a trade confirmation is printed and delivered to Michelle, showing that she paid $29,950 for 100 shares of GE, plus a $50 commission.

Another stock Michelle would like to purchase is an Internet security company trading on NASDAQ. This one is fairly speculative, trading at just $3.67 a share. While not technically a "penny stock," since it is on NASDAQ, it is still trading below $5 a share, which usually gives prudent investors the willies. "Let's see if it goes above $5 a share first, Michelle," you tell her, to which she replies, "but I don't have time to watch the price all day long."

You don't have to, you inform her. And then you explain that if you place a buy-stop order at, say, $5.10, nothing will happen unless and until the stock trades at $5.10 or above. What if it never makes it that high? Then we never wanted it. You mark the order ticket "GTC" and three weeks later the company releases impressive earnings and the stock starts trading above $5.10. Michelle's order is triggered and filled, and, once again, a trade confirmation is created and sent to the customer.

The third stock happens to be one in which your firm makes a market. When Michelle decides she would like 200 shares of QRZ, your firm simply sells some of the stock in their inventory directly to Michelle. Her order confirmation this time would indicate "principal," and the price indicated per share is "$19.75 net." That means that the inside ask was actually a little lower than $19.75 at the time of the trade, but your firm is entitled to a markup/profit, as long as it's reasonable. With the inside ask at $19.50, this represents a 25-cent markup. What is 25 cents divided by (compared to) the inside ask? A markup of 1.28%, well within the fairness guideline.

Now that she has invested a few thousand dollars in common stock, what can she do to protect her investment? She could buy put options, allowing her to sell the stocks for a set price if need be. Or, she could enter sell-stop orders below the purchase price for each stock. You and she decide on the sell-stops. You decide that if these stocks drop 20% or more, it's time to bail. Rather than staring at the computer all day, you simply place sell-stops about 20% below the price she paid for the stock. This way, if the stock stays where it is or goes up, excellent. You might cancel the sell-stops and place new ones a little higher up. If the stock goes down in a hurry, it will be sold in a hurry, cutting Michelle's losses to a level she can live with.

CHAPTER 10

Taxation

As you probably know, people like interstate highways, national parks, social security, and a strong national defense. Unfortunately, the federal government has no money to pay for any of that stuff unless taxpayers are willing to pitch in. Similarly, your state government provides roads, public schools, parks, state troopers, state fairs, etc., and they use the taxes you pay to fund that good stuff.

There are different types of income that taxpayers may owe taxes on. **Earned income** is what you make through salaries, commissions, wages, bonuses, and—get this—alimony. In the chapter Retirement Planning we noted that contributions to an IRA, for example, can only be made from earned income. Other types of income, discussed below, can't be used to fund an IRA account. Earned income is taxed at what the exam might call the investor's **ordinary income rate** or **marginal tax rate**. The income tax system is graduated, called a **progressive tax** system. That means that at higher amounts, the rate increases, so that some earners might be paying only 15% on their earned income, while high earners might be paying 35% or more on most of their earned income. Whether this is fair or desirable is, of course, beyond the scope of the Series 7. It does beg the question, though: what is a re-gressive tax? A **regressive tax** is a flat tax including sales, gasoline, and excise taxes. If you think about it, lower earners generally pay a bigger percentage of their income to these sorts of taxes. Even if it's a small amount, people who don't earn a lot spend every last dollar they do earn, and most of those dollars are subject to sales and gasoline taxes. In any case, we looked at **passive income** in the exciting chapter on DPPs (direct participation programs). The tax shelter provided by certain partnerships only works if the investor has some passive income to offset with his share of partnership losses. Passive income is received from some type of business venture in which the investor plays no active role. So, if an investor is receiving income from a partnership that owns and manages apartment units, he could then offset some of that passive income by buying into another limited partnership that is building new units and will, therefore, be showing losses for a year or so. But passive losses generated from that new construction program would not offset anybody's earned income or income received on stocks and bonds. So, if you don't have any passive income, you really shouldn't be looking for passive losses, since you can't, you know, use them. Passive income is taxed the same way that earned income and—the next type—portfolio income is taxed. The important point is that passive losses can only be used to offset/reduce passive income. They can not be used to offset earned or portfolio income. I think we can leave that idea alone now. We discussed **deferred income** in the chapter Retirement Planning. This is exactly what it sounds like—income that will taxed someday, but not now. In your 401K account, any dividends you receive from mutual fund investments, and any increase in the share price of those mutual funds, avoid taxation currently, allowing the account to compound or grow more quickly. Someday, of course, you'll have to pay tax on the distributions that you take. And, you will pay your ordinary income rate on that money. But, for now, it's all deferred income, not subject to taxation. Yet.

Okay, I told you all that so I could tell you this: the Series 7 is interested almost exclusively in the next type of income, called either **portfolio** or **investment income.**

INVESTMENT (PORTFOLIO) INCOME

Portfolio income is what an investor receives through bond interest payments, cash dividends, capital gains on securities sales, and capital gains distributions from mutual funds. It would be lots of fun to take, say, five years off work and live completely on your investment/portfolio income. I guess the downside would be that none of that income could be used to fund retirement contributions. But, still, it's a tempting idea. And, if you could earn, say, $80,000 a year just managing your investment portfolio, you could probably get by, even after paying taxes to the IRS and your state tax collectors. Let's start with the tax implications of bond investing.

INVESTING IN BONDS

Interest

We've actually already covered the taxation of bonds in the Debt Securities chapter, but let's do a quick review, anyway, since taxation is of major importance on the Series 7 exam. U.S. Treasury securities (which include T-bills, T-notes, T-bonds, I-bonds, TIPS, and STRIPS) pay interest that is taxed at ordinary income rates, but only at the federal level. Much to their disappointment, state and local governments can't tax that interest. Not even Maryland. Municipal securities pay interest that is tax-exempt at the federal level. At the state level, it depends on where the bond was issued. If you live in Kentucky and buy a general obligation of Little Rock, Arkansas, Kentucky can tax the interest, and so can your local government. Of course, if you buy the general obligations of Louisville or the State of Kentucky, you'll get a break. Corporate bonds—and also Ginnie, Fannie, and Freddie—pay interest that is taxable at all three levels: federal, state, and local.

And, don't forget the funky zero coupon bonds. These are issued originally at a discount, which is why the creative types named them original issue discount bonds, which immediately became OIDs to make sure the industry had enough acronyms. If you buy a zero coupon issued for $500 with a par value that will become $1,000 in 10 years, you basically report the $50 increase each year on a 1099 OID. Yes, the interest income you haven't collected yet is still taxable at this point. If it were a municipal OID, the tax would be avoided, but corporate and US Treasury zero coupon bonds force investors to pay tax on interest income they haven't even received yet. Some folks call this "phantom tax exposure," which is a pretty good name for it.

Capital Gains on Bonds

Bond interest is the income you receive for holding a bond. A capital gain only occurs if you sell your bond for more than you bought it, or the bond matures for more than your purchase price. Even though states can't tax the interest income you receive on US Treasury securities, they can tax the capital gains that you take for selling your US Treasury securities for more than you bought them. Also, even though municipal bond investors receive tax-exempt interest at the federal level, any capital gains they take on municipal bonds are taxed at capital gains rates. Capital gains taken on corporate bonds would be subject to taxation at all three levels: federal, state, and local.

Capital gains are either **short-term capital gains** or **long-term capital gains**. A short-term capital gain occurs when the investor sells a bond for a profit within 12 months or less. If the bond is sold for a profit after being held for at least 12 months plus 1 day (more than a year), that is a long-term capital gain. What's the difference? Generally, a long-term capital gain is taxed at a much lower rate than a short-term capital gain. Short-term capital gains are taxed at the investor's ordinary income rate, while a long-term capital gain might be taxed at just 20%. And investor with capital gains can also sell other bonds at a loss, and use that loss to offset the other gains. But, when the investor sells a bond at a loss, he needs to invest the proceeds into a substantially different bond. If not, the IRS won't let him take the loss he was trying to take. To do a **bond swap** or **tax swap** correctly, the investor needs to alter the issuer, the coupon rate, or the maturity on the new bond. So, if he sells a GE 6s debenture of '15 at a loss, he could utilize the loss if he bought any of the following bond issues:

- MSFT 6s debenture of '15
- GE 4.5s debenture of '15
- GE 6s debenture of '22

INVESTING IN STOCK

Cash Dividends

Bonds are not the only securities that provide income to investors. Preferred stock is an income security paying a stated rate of return. And even some common stocks are associated with high dividend yields. Cash dividends from preferred and common stock are taxable.

Also note that if an American investor owns shares of a foreign company, say through an ADR, and that foreign government withholds dividend income as a tax, the American investor can claim a tax credit on his US taxes for that same amount.

Capital Gains on Stock

So, the income paid to shareholders is taxable. And, when the shareholders decide to sell their stock to other investors, they could end up selling for more than they paid, and nothing seems to get the IRS's attention faster. See, if you buy $10,000 of GE stock in, say, 1993 and have the audacity to sell that stock for $15,000 in 2011, you have "realized a capital gain" of $5,000. First of all, congratulations on making a profit and, secondly, don't forget your friends and mine at the IRS. At the end of the year when you figure your taxes, you'll have to report the $5,000 capital gain and maybe end up paying taxes on it.

Why just "maybe"? Because, if you're like most investors, you usually have even more stocks that moved in the opposite direction. See, if you bought JDSU, there's about a 99.9% chance that you're sitting on a big, fat "capital loss" at this point. So, if you had purchased, say $15,000 of JDSU in 1999 and sold it for a whopping $1,000 in 2011, you would have realized a $14,000 capital loss, which would more than offset the gain you took on GE. Investors subtract their capital losses from their capital gains taken during the tax year. If they end up with more gains than losses, they have a "net capital gain" for the year. If the stock is held for at least 12 months plus one day, it is treated as a long-term capital gain, which is generally a lower tax rate compared to the investor's ordinary income rate. If the capital gain had been taken on stock held one year or less, that's a short-term capital gain, taxed at the investor's ordinary income bracket just to keep things nice and simple the way the IRS and the United States Congress like it.

As with capital gains taken on bond investments, the "long-term" and "short-term" labels have to do with what the exam will call the investor's **holding period**. The holding period begins the day after the trade date and stops on the day the stock is sold. So, if you buy stock on September 5th, 2011, you can sell it on September 6th, 2012 for a long-term capital gain. But if you sell it sooner than that, it will be treated as a short-term capital gain.

To determine if the sale triggered a gain or loss, the investor compares the proceeds of the sale with the cost basis on the stock. The fancy phrase "cost basis" means all the money the investor has put into the thing up to this point. If you buy $5,000 of Microsoft common stock and pay a $25 commission, your cost basis is $5,025. The IRS has already taxed that money and won't tax it again. If you sell that stock later for $6,000 and pay another $25 commission, your "proceeds" will be $5,975. So, you would take the proceeds of $5,975 minus the cost basis of $5,025 for a capital gain of $950. If you held it for at least one year plus one day, it's a long-term capital gain taxed at the kinder, gentler rate. If your holding period was less than that, it's a short-term capital gain, which is probably taxed at a higher rate.

The exam might try to mess with you by mentioning **unrealized capital gains**, so let's take a look at that. If you buy 1000 shares of Starbucks for $10 a share, and the stock is now trading at $55 a share, how much of a capital gains tax do you have to pay at this point?

Not a penny.

This is just a gain on paper, called an "unrealized capital gain." It gives you major bragging rights around the water cooler, but you haven't sold anything yet. It's only when you "realize" your capital gain that the IRS gets concerned. To realize a capital gain means that you've sold the stock. Until you sell it, there are no capital gains taxes to pay. But don't you have to sell the stock eventually?

Not really. Some people hate the IRS so much that they will *never* sell it. Instead, the stock will pass to their children or grandchildren when they die. Or they'll just give the stock to somebody. Or, maybe they'll donate it to a charity.

The test may also ask how a customer determines which shares he sold when he tells the IRS he sold 100 shares of GE out of, say, 500 shares. He may have purchased those 500 shares at different prices and on different dates, so which of the following three methods is he using to determine is cost basis:

- FIFO: first-in, first-out, the securities sold are always the first ones that he bought. Whenever the IRS has to determine which shares were sold, they use this method
- Share identification: the customer determines which particular shares he sold
- Average cost: the customer keeps a running average cost that is applied to any/all of the shares sold

INHERITED SHARES

Let's say that Grandma purchased 1,000 shares of Harley-Davidson back in 1967 for $10 a share. On the day she dies in 2011 the fair market value is $50 a share. If you inherit the shares, what is your cost basis?

$50 a share. So, if you sell it a few days later for $55, that's only a capital gain of $5 per share, not $45. It's also treated as a long-term capital gain, even if you sell it right away. The IRS actually explains this quite clearly at www.irs.gov:

> If you inherit investment property, your capital gain or loss on any later disposition of that property is treated as a long-term capital gain or loss. This is true regardless of how long you actually held the property.

See, they do have a heart at the IRS. Imagine if you had to take Grandma's original cost basis. First, that would have made the capital gains tax much, much higher. Secondly, where the heck did Grandma keep her trade confirmations from 1967? Doesn't matter. You just take the "fair market value" as of the date of death. And, again, you can sell it as soon as you want—it's still a long-term capital gain.

Gifts of Stock

On the other hand, if Grandma is still tooling around on her Harley and just, like, *gives* you this stock that has risen about $40 a share, you would have to take her original cost basis of $10. That would lead to a higher capital gains tax if you sold it right away, although you would take over her holding period, which means you could get a long-term capital gain without waiting 12 months plus 1 day. Still, taking the original basis is a bit of a drag, so if Grandma offers to just make a gift of the stock, you might want to say something like, "Actually, Grandma, it would work out better for me if you died first."

Charitable Donations of Stock

Maybe Grandma has a more worthy cause than, say, you, and decides to donate the stock to her favorite charity, the National Association of Septuagenarian Hog Enthusiasts. If so, she can deduct the fair market value of the stock on the day of the donation from her ordinary income and reduce her tax bill that year.

You, however, would get squat on that deal, so you may want to talk to her before she goes and gets all philanthropic suddenly.

Capital Losses

As mentioned, investors often end up selling stock for less than they paid, which sort of stinks. Then again, it's not the end of the world. When you sell stock for less than you paid, you get to use that capital loss to reduce the capital gains you may have taken on other sales. And that reduces your capital gains taxes for the year. Some people go overboard. If they take a $10,000 capital gain, they then take a $15,000 capital loss just to make sure they pay no capital gains taxes that year. That extra $5,000 "net capital loss" could be used in future years to offset capital gains. $3,000 of it can also be used to reduce the investor's ordinary income for the current tax year. So, if his **adjusted gross income** was going to be $50,000, now it's only $47,000. He would only save a percentage of that $3,000, remember. It's not a tax credit; it's a tax deduction. You have to lose a dollar in order to save 25 or 35 cents, in other words. I mean, it's nice, but I wouldn't make it a cornerstone of your long-term investment strategy.

<u>Wash Sales</u>

When the investor realizes the capital loss on his stock, the IRS is cool with that. But, he has to wait a full 30 days and not repurchase that company's stock until the 31st day. Otherwise, he can't use the loss if it's declared a **wash sale**. Also, he could not have purchased that company's stock 30 days before selling it at a loss. So, there is a 60-day window pointing 30 days before and after the sale. Stay out of the stock if you want to use the loss to offset gains for the year.

What if you promise not to buy the stock back for 30 days but simply can't stop yourself? First of all, I can recommend a good therapist, and, secondly, you simply can't use that loss. However, if you took a loss of, say, $5 a share that is now going to be disallowed due to the wash sale, you can add that $5 to your cost basis on the new purchase, meaning you will eventually get the benefit of that loss you tried to take this year.

Just to keep things nice and simple. The IRS, again, actually explains this all very clearly at www.irs.gov, which is becoming, like, one of my favorite websites lately:

> If your loss was disallowed because of the wash sale rules, add the disallowed loss to the cost of the new stock or securities. The result is your basis in the new stock or securities. This adjustment postpones the loss deduction until the disposition of the new stock or securities.

The Series 7 might also have an investor sell, say, 500 shares at a loss and then promptly repurchase 300 shares. If so, it's only a wash sale on 300 shares. Always something, huh?

<u>Short Sales</u>

The Series 7 might ask whether a short seller's capital gain is short-term or long-term. If so, it's a trick question. All gains realized by a short seller are short-term because he never establishes a holding period. How does a short seller realize a capital gain? By buying back the shares he borrowed for less than he sold them a while ago. He wouldn't realize a gain or loss until he "covered" or "closed" his short position. But whenever he does close out/buy back the position, he then realizes a gain or a loss. Either way, it's considered short-term.

TAX IMPLICATIONS FOR MUTUAL FUND INVESTORS

When you own shares of a mutual fund, tax treatment will depend on the source of the income you receive.

Stock Funds

If it's a stock fund, the taxation will be a little different from a bond or money market fund. We haven't gotten into the details of mutual funds yet, but they're really just gigantic portfolios of stocks, bonds, etc. You can buy little slices of the gigantic portfolio, which is much easier than picking your own stocks and bonds. Let the mutual fund do that—you'll just own a percentage of whatever they decide to invest in. The mutual fund portfolio will receive dividends from some of the stocks they own, and since they trade their stocks all the time, they'll usually end up with a capital gain for the year. Investors in the mutual fund receive dividends and capital gains distributions from the fund, and these are taxable. The 1099-DIV that the fund sends to investors will show how much they received in qualified versus ordinary dividends, and how much they received in capital gains distributions. Is it a short-term or long-term capital gain? The 1099 will tell you that, too. Remember, the holding period is based on how long the fund held the securities before trading them. It has nothing to do with how long the investor has been in the fund—the investor didn't sell anything. She's just receiving her fair share of the income generated by the mutual fund portfolio. Usually, the fund makes sure the gains distributed are long-term gains, since the maximum tax rate is a lot easier to swallow than the rate some folks pay on short-term gains. Can the fund distribute short-term capital gains? Absolutely. And when they do, they're taxable to the investors as short-term capital gains. The higher a fund's "turnover rate" the more likely it will generate short-term capital gains. But, really, all of the capital gains distributions from mutual funds to investors are long-term, except for the ones that are short-term.

Notice how I separated the dividends from the capital gains. Dividends are what you get for holding the stock; capital gains are what you make for getting rid of the stock. In a mutual fund, as we'll see, investors get charged for many expenses. The portfolio manager charges a management fee, and investors pay for that. The board of directors likes their six-figure salaries, and shareholders pay for that. There are legal and accounting fees, transfer agent fees, custodial fees, and 12b-1 fees that cover all the sales and marketing costs. How does the fund cover these expenses? They use the dividends they receive from the portfolio stocks and the interest payments from the bonds and money market securities that they hold. When the fund takes the dividends and the interest, then deducts all the expenses, they are left with net income. The IRS, which is here to help, generally likes to share profits with companies showing net income, but they will allow the fund to use something funky called the "conduit" or "pipeline theory." If the fund has $1 million in net income, they can distribute 90% or more ($900,000+) to the shareholders and, thereby, avoid being taxed on that $900,000. The shareholders will get taxed on that money, instead. The fund only has to pay taxes on what they did *not* distribute—in this case, $100,000. The fund may also end the year taking more profits than losses trading the portfolio. If so, they realize a net capital gain and also distribute that to the shareholders. They usually only do that once a year, and usually in December.

What can you do with these dividend and capital gains distributions? A, you can tell them where to send the check and go shopping. B, you can automatically reinvest the money into more shares of the fund. So, the IRS would only tax you if you cashed the check, right? No. As it turns out, the IRS could sort of care less what you *do* with the distribution. Whether you cash the check or reinvest into more shares, you get taxed on the distributions. People reinvest these things to avoid paying sales charges to the fund, but it doesn't help them in the least with their pals at the IRS. Remember that whether the dividend or capital gains distribution is paid in cash or reinvested into more shares, the investor is taxed. And that means that when you reinvest a dividend or capital gain, your cost basis rises by that amount. So, if the test question says that Melody has invested $10,000 into the Argood Aggressive Growth Fund and reinvested dividends of $2,000, her cost basis equals $12,000. Cost basis is basically the money you've put into an investment that the IRS has already taxed. The capital gain that may someday materialize is just the amount you manage to sell it for above that amount.

Should you be so fortunate.

Bond Funds

For bond funds, there is really nothing to add to our discussion of bonds held individually. The "dividends" paid are really coming from bond interest received by the portfolio. So, U.S. Treasury funds would pay dividends that are taxable as ordinary income on federal returns but exempt from state or local taxation. Tax-exempt Municipal Bond funds would pay dividends that are tax-exempt for federal returns but may be subject to state and local taxation. This is why some fund companies have rolled out, say, the Maryland Tax-Exempt Fund or the Tax-Exempt Fund of California. That way residents of those high-tax states can buy mutual funds that pay income exempt from both federal and state taxes. If you're in a state that wants, say, 14% of your income, it might be a good idea to avoid that whenever possible, right? Corporate bond funds, unfortunately, would pay dividends subject to taxation at all three levels.

Capital gains would also be taxable to investors, including capital gains distributions to investors in municipal bond funds. Municipal bonds pay *interest* that is exempt from federal taxation, but nobody said nothin' about no capital gains. Those are still taxable as capital gains.

Money Market Funds

As the IRS also states at their highly entertaining website, "Report amounts you receive from money market funds as dividend income." Money market funds are a type of mutual fund and should not be confused with bank money market accounts that pay interest.

TAX TREATMENT OF VARIABLE ANNUITIES

A non-qualified variable annuity is basically a cross between a mutual fund, a retirement plan, and an insurance policy. In a non-qualified variable annuity, the investor contributes money that has already been taxed. Therefore, the money she puts into her annuity is her cost basis. The IRS won't tax the money she puts in; they'll only tax the money she takes out above that someday. The money grows tax-deferred, which means all the dividends and bond interest being paid to the investor will not be taxed until money is finally taken out. She put in a total of $10,000. Let's say at retirement, the annuity is worth $50,000. That means that $40,000 of earnings have accumulated. No matter how she takes the money out, she will pay ordinary income tax on that $40,000. The exam will probably call the $40,000 the "earnings" or "the excess over cost basis," just to make you sweat a little. The annuitant can take a lump sum distribution, just like somebody who retires from General Motors. Gimme' all my money right now, please. Fine. But, she'll have to pay ordinary income rates on that $40,000, and that money might push her into a higher tax bracket. Since that might push her into a higher bracket, maybe she does a "random withdrawal" of $10,000. Here's where the exam is looking to snare a few insurance agents. Insurance agents might think that since she put in $10,000 and is only taking out $10,000, there will be no tax hassles. Unfortunately, the IRS, which is here to help, considers all of the money coming out to be the earnings portion first. The exam might call that LIFO for "last-in-first-out." The earnings were the last thing into the account, so we consider them to be the first thing coming out. Why?

Because we can.

So, not only will this $10,000 random withdrawal be fully taxable as ordinary income, but also so will the next withdrawals that take us through the $40,000 of earnings.

Many people just **annuitize** the contract, which means they want to receive a monthly check for the rest of their lives. Depending on how long their life expectancy is, each monthly payment will represent part cost basis and part earnings. So, the exam wants you to know that part of each annuity payment is taxable, and part is considered a return of the cost basis.

When people annuitize the contract, they can choose to receive payments for as long as they live, or they can choose to cover a beneficiary. We'll talk about "period certain" and "joint with last survivor" later on. For now, just know that if the wife or the daughter is receiving annuity payments from the annuity purchased by a husband or parent, she is going to pay ordinary income tax on the "excess over cost basis," too. Somebody, in other words, always pays ordinary income tax on the amount above what the annuitant put into the contract. That's the deal you make in exchange for the tax deferral.

What if the annuitant dies while he's still putting money into the contract? This is known as the "accumulation phase," by the way, and if the annuitant has put in $10,000 when he dies, the death benefit will pay his beneficiary the greater of that $10,000 or whatever the contract is currently worth. So, if the annuity is worth $13,000 now, the beneficiary receives $13,000. If the value had dipped to $8,000 due to a tough stock or bond market, the beneficiary would still receive $10,000. And, as always, if the beneficiary receives more than the annuitant has contributed, that excess is taxable to her as ordinary income.

Someday you may meet up with a client who was sold a really lousy annuity from some sketchy company. You might be able to talk her into selling that one and exchanging it for an annuity that you sell. If so, she can do a 1035 tax-free contract exchange. In other words, this is different from selling one mutual fund to buy the proceeds of another fund in the same family—that would still be a taxable event. But annuities are retirement plans, really, so there is a special provision here for tax-free exchanges, just as there is for life insurance.

Since they're retirement vehicles, the individual needs to wait until she's 59½ before taking money out. Otherwise, she'll pay not just her ordinary income rate on the excess over cost basis but also a 10% penalty to the IRS.

72(T) and Substantially Equal Periodic Payments

Speaking of early withdrawal penalties, remember that annuities are by nature retirement plans and are subject to the 10% penalty for withdrawals made before age 59½ or made without a good excuse. One good excuse is to utilize IRS rule "72(t)." As with an IRA, an individual can avoid the 10% penalty if the withdrawal qualifies for an exemption. For example, if the individual has become disabled and can't work, or has certain medical expenses, money can be taken out penalty-free. Notice how I didn't say tax-free.

Basically, a reference to "72t" has to do with an individual taking a series of substantially equal periodic payments. Of course, the industry quickly turned that phrase into the acronym "SEPP." The IRS won't penalize the early withdrawal if the individual sets up a rigid schedule whereby they withdraw the money by any of several IRS-approved methods. Once you start your little SEPP program, stay on it. See, the IRS requires you to continue the SEPP program for five years or until you are the age of 59½, whichever comes last. So, if the individual is 45, she'll have to keep taking periodic payments until she's 59½. If the individual is 56 when she starts, she'll still have to continue for 5 years. Either that, or cut the IRS a check for the very penalties she was trying to avoid.

TAXATION OF LIFE INSURANCE

When you pay your life insurance premiums, you don't get to take a deduction against income, so they are made after-tax. They usually grow tax-deferred, however, which is nice. When the insured dies, the beneficiary receives the death benefit free and clear of federal income taxes.

But the death benefit will be added to the insured's estate to determine estate taxes. It's that simple when the beneficiary has the lump-sum settlement option, anyway. If we're talking about those periodic settlement options that generate interest, some of those payments could be taxed as interest income. Rather than take a loan, the policyholder can also do a "partial surrender," whereby the policyholder takes out some of the cash value, not enough to make the policy lapse, of course. Depending on how much has been paid in premiums, taxes may be due on the amount withdrawn. Unlike for variable annuities, the IRS uses FIFO here, assuming that the first thing coming out is the cost basis, not the earnings. Only the part taken out above the premiums paid would be taxed.

If a loan is taken out, there are no immediate tax consequences.

TAXATION OF OPTIONS

As we said earlier, three things can happen once an option contract is opened:

- Expire
- Close
- Exercise

Expire

Ordinary options expire within 9 months, so all gains and losses will be short-term. A short-term gain, as discussed in the Taxation chapter, is taxed at the investor's ordinary income rate. If you buy an option this November, and it expires next April, you lose all the money you paid. It will be a short-term loss that you claim for April's tax year, which is when you "realize" the loss. Back in November you were just putting down some money. Only in April of next year will you actually realize your loss. If you sell an option in November that expires the following April, you'll realize a **short-term capital gain** in April.

Close

Options can be closed for either a gain or a loss. The investor/trader doesn't realize the gain or loss until both sides of the T-chart have been completed, so to speak. If she buys an option in November for $300 and sells it to close next April for $400, she realizes a $100 **short-term capital gain** in April. Obviously, if she only sells it for $200, she would realize a $100 **short-term capital**

loss in April. Same thing for the seller of the option. When they close with a "closing purchase," they realize either a short-term capital gain or loss when they do so.

Exercise

It gets trickier when an option is exercised. If you'd like to review the step-by-step explanation, it's in the Options chapter. For now, let's review with the following handy-dandy chart:

Position	Upon Exercise	Premium	Affects
Long Call	Buys stock	Add to strike price	Raises cost base
Short Call	Sells stock	Add to strike price	Raises proceeds
Long Put	Sells stock	Subtract from strike price	Lowers proceeds
Short Put	Buys stock	Subtract from strike price	Lowers cost base

LEAPS

Ordinary options expire in 9 months or sooner. Then, there are long-term options called **LEAPS**. Since the time value is, by definition, greater on these contracts that can go out over three years, LEAPS contracts trade at much higher premiums. The strategies are the same. You buy a call if you think the stock is going up—you simply pay more for a MSFT Oct 50 call expiring in 2 or 3 years versus the one expiring in 2 or 3 months.

The taxation is a little tricky. For the buyer of the contract, capital gains and losses are considered long-term. But a short seller never establishes a holding period, so any capital gains and losses are considered short-term.

PRACTICE

1. **An investor has contributed $20,000 to a periodic deferred non-qualified variable annuity. The contract is worth $50,000 at retirement. If the investor takes a random withdrawal of $35,000, what are the tax consequences?**

    A. $50,000 taxed as ordinary income

    B. $20,000 taxed as ordinary income

    C. $35,000 taxed at long-term capital gains rate

    D. $30,000 taxed as ordinary income

2. **An investor in a municipal bond fund receives both income and capital gains distributions. What is true of the tax treatment of these distributions?**

   A. Both are taxed at ordinary income rates.

   B. Both are taxed as long-term capital gains.

   C. The income distribution is most likely tax-exempt at the federal level, while the capital gains distribution is fully taxable.

   D. Both distributions are tax-exempt at the federal level.

3. **If an individual makes qualified contributions to her IRA, her cost basis is**

   A. equal to her contributions

   B. equal to her contributions times a cost of living index multiplier

   C. zero

   D. equal to her average income over the preceding five years

4. **All of the following plans are funded pre-tax except**

   A. IRA

   B. SEP-IRA

   C. 529 Plan

   D. Tax-sheltered annuity

5. **All of the following are funded with after-tax contributions except**

   A. Coverdell plan

   B. 529 Plan

   C. Roth IRA

   D. 403b/TSA

6. **Interest earned on all of the following is taxable at the state level except**

   A. GNMA

   B. FNMA

   C. T-bill

   D. Municipal bonds

7. **All of the following are subject to taxation at the federal level except**

   A. common stock

   B. preferred stock

   C. municipal bond

   D. Treasury note

8. **Which of the following allows an individual to make the largest contribution?**

   A. Roth

   B. Traditional IRA

   C. Keogh

   D. variable annuity

9. **Which of the following represents a violation for a securities agent?**

   A. recommending that an income investor purchase shares of the ABC Equity Income fund simply because it pays regular dividends

   B. providing a mutual fund prospect with a prospectus before beginning the solicitation

   C. recommending that an income investor purchase shares of the ABC Equity Income Fund primarily to receive an upcoming dividend distribution

   D. following up oral recommendations with accompanying statements of risk

10. **All of the following offer tax deferral except**

   A. insurance policy

   B. non-qualified annuity

   C. qualified annuity

   D. mutual fund

11. **An investor originally invested $10,000 in the XYZ Growth & Income Fund. After reinvesting a $2,000 income distribution and a $1,000 capital gains distribution, her cost basis is**

   A. $10,000

   B. $7,000

   C. $13,000

   D. not determinable without marginal tax bracket provided

ANSWERS

1. **D**, there is only $30,000 of earnings or "excess over cost basis." The extra $5,000 is part of her cost basis—she already paid tax on $20,000, remember.

2. **C**, the only thing tax-exempt about a municipal bond is the interest/income. Capital gains are fully taxable on all bonds.

3. **C**, if the contributions haven't been taxed yet, she has no cost basis. It will all be taxed when it's distributed at retirement.

4. **C**, the plans for education (Coverdell, ESA, 529) are all funded with after-tax dollars. The distributions are tax-free as long as everybody plays by the rules.

5. **D**, TSA/403b-501c3...all means the same thing. Pre-tax contributions, zero cost basis, all distributions taxed at ordinary income rate.

6. **C**, states can't tax the interest on Treasury securities, period.

7. **C**, municipal securities offer tax-exempt interest at the federal level. Treasury securities definitely get taxed at the federal level, but only at the federal level.

8. **D**, assume there are NO limits to the amount you can put into an annuity. Which is what makes them so much fun to sell.

9. **C**, choice C represents "selling dividends." Choice A is fine—the agent is selling the fund. In choice C he's trying to sell the dividend—the NAV will drop, and the investor will be taxed. So you don't buy a fund for the upcoming dividend. You buy funds because they make regular dividend payments. See the important difference?

10. **D**, mutual funds offer no tax advantages per se.

11. **C**, she gets taxed on reinvested distributions, just as if she'd taken the check and cashed it. If you get taxed, it adds to your cost basis.

CHAPTER 11

Economics

<u>G</u>ross <u>D</u>omestic <u>P</u>roduct (**GDP**) measures the total output of the American economy. It's the total value of all goods and services being produced, provided and sold. If GDP is increasing, the economy is growing. If GDP is declining, so is the economy. The American economy rides a continuous roller coaster known as the **business cycle**. All this means is that the economy goes up (expands), hits a peak, contracts, hits bottom (**trough**), and then comes back up again...just like a roller coaster. Although we refer to the period following the "trough" as a "recovery," it's really just the next expansion, so I would say there are four phases to the business cycle if I got that question on the exam: **expansion, peak, contraction, trough.**

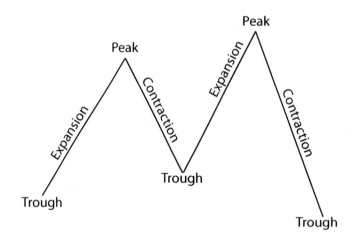

Also remember that rising prices (known as inflation) are factored into this GDP calculation to arrive at "real GDP." In other words, we don't want to kid ourselves that rising prices is the same thing as rising economic output. We use the CPI (**consumer price index**) to factor in the effects of inflation, which we'll discuss shortly. Note that the word "real" generally means to subtract the rate of inflation from something. If you got a test question that said Orville Olmeyer has an investment that grows 6% while the CPI rises 3%, Orville's "real rate of return" is 3%—the amount above inflation.

When GDP is rising at a healthy pace, the economy is in a period of expansion. In a period of expansion we would expect to see the following: low unemployment, high industrial production, rising prices (inflation), rising interest rates. When the GDP is stuck in low gear or reverse, we're in a period of contraction or maybe in the trough. Whatever we call it, this period of economic decline can be referred to as either a **recession** or a **depression**. A recession is strictly defined as 6 months (2 consecutive quarters) of GDP decline and can last as long as 18 months. After that, we call it a depression. Technically, a recession is when your neighbor loses his job. A depression is when you lose *your* job. Associate the following with recessions and depressions: falling prices, falling interest rates, high unemployment, low industrial production.

INFLATION, DEFLATION

Ever noticed how the "Fed" often seems obsessed with the price of stuff? If the economy grows/expands too fast, prices can go higher and higher until they're out of control. That's called inflation. Inflation is indicated/measured by the CPI, or "consumer price index." The CPI surveys the prices consumers are paying for the basic things consumers buy (movie tickets, milk, blue jeans, gasoline) and tracks the increases in those prices. They actually give more weighting to the stuff people buy more of (milk over lame Adam Sandler movies) and sometimes they exclude certain items which are volatile (food and energy) because how many people actually buy food or gasoline in any given month? When we exclude food and energy, we're measuring "core inflation," which will not be on the exam, unless it is. The exam might say that inflation occurs when the demand for goods and services is growing faster than the supply of these items. Or, it could say something like, "too many dollars chasing too few goods." I like to think of inflation in terms of what would happen if they ran out of beer during the third inning at Wrigley Field and then somebody stood up and said he'd be happy to sell a cold six-pack he somehow managed to smuggle past security. How high would the price of cold beer rise on a hot August afternoon with 40,000 thirsty fans vying for six cold, sweaty cans of beer?

Believe it or not, the exam might mention two different types/causes of inflation. Cost-push inflation is when raw material prices rise and producers pass on the cost to consumers. The exam might want you to know that the "PPI" stands for the "producer price index," which measures cost-push inflation. Demand-pull inflation, on the other hand, is when the demand for stuff outstrips the supply of that stuff. Back to Wrigley Field on a hot day. What I described was demand-pull inflation, since the demand for cold beer far outstripped the limited supply and you know some well-moneyed commodities trader wouldn't rest unless he could say he paid "10 g's" for the last cold six-pack in the ball park. Cost-push inflation would result if the cost of hops, barley, and malt used to manufacture the beer, or even the gasoline used to transport the beer, went up. Just like at Frank & Emma's—if the cost of wheat, sugar, flour, cherries, apples, corn syrup, etc., goes up, the company will have to both spend more on ingredients and charge more for their products.

Anyway, that's IN-flation. DE-flation is also a problem. While inflation can make things too expensive for consumers to buy, **deflation** can make things ever cheaper. Cheaper goods sounds okay until you consider that profit margins at businesses will be ever shrinking, as they pay last month's prices for raw materials and then struggle to sell them at next month's cheaper prices. Assuming they can sell anything to anyone—would you rush out to buy something today if you knew it would be cheaper tomorrow? Wouldn't you be tempted to put off your purchases indefinitely, waiting for the price of DVD players, clothing, and automobiles to drop in your favor?

That's an economic slowdown, right? Everybody sitting around waiting to see who'll be the first one to open up his or her wallet. Which is why deflation—while rare—is just as detrimental to the economy as inflation. And that's why the Fed is forever manipulating interest rates in an attempt to find the right economic temperature—not too hot, not too cold. Like Goldilocks, they hope to find the economic porridge just right. Which is another way of saying that demand for stuff and the supply of that stuff are in the right balance. If we have strong demand and tight supply, prices will rise, just as the demand for a Dave Matthews Band concert in a 1,000-seat venue will send the ticket price into the stratosphere. If demand for stuff is weak and the supply of that stuff is high, prices will fall, like the price of a ticket to see the Spin Doctors at a college football stadium.

To review, if the economy grows too fast, we can end up with inflation. And, as we'll soon see, the Federal Reserve Board (or **FOMC**) will raise interest rates to let some air out of the over-expanding economy. If the economy starts to sputter and stall, we can end up with deflation. And, as we'll soon see, the Fed will have to pump some air back into the economy by lowering interest rates.

ECONOMIC INDICATORS

The Fed monitors many economic indicators to get an *indication* as to whether inflation is trying to rear its ugly head. The exam tends to focus on employment indicators. As you might guess, employment indicators are based on employment. The following indicators tell us how many people are working and how much compensation they're receiving. If people aren't working, that signals an economic slowdown. If employment compensation is rising too fast, that signals inflation, and the Fed might have to step in by raising interest rates.

- Average Weekly New Claims for Unemployment Insurance: if people are showing up for unemployment insurance at a higher rate, that's a bad sign, right? It means their employers don't have enough work for them. If the number of new claims drops, that means economic activity is picking up.
- Unemployment Rate: since everything needs two or three names, this is also called "payroll employment" or "non-farm payroll." It's a figure released by the Bureau of Labor Statistics and includes full-time and part-time workers, whether they're permanent or temporary employees. In other words, if they're on the payroll, we count them as workers, just like they do at City Hall here in Chicago. As the "nonfarm" thing may have tipped you off, we don't count farm workers, since that stuff is very seasonal, and we also don't count employment at tiny businesses or at government agencies. So, this figure tracks how many people are working in the private sector, basically. It is released monthly.
- Employment Cost Index (ECI): this measures the growth of wages and benefits (compensation) because if wages are rising really fast, inflation can't be far behind. It's a quarterly figure, so it's not the most timely of statistics. Still, it tracks trends in compensation. While the monthly employment rate is useful, the ECI gives us more detail, since it tracks the change in benefits paid to workers, rather than just the number of workers.

> ## Economic Indicators
>
> Leading – show up before reflected in the economy
>
> - the average weekly hours worked by manufacturing workers
> - initial claims for unemployment insurance
> - manufacturers' new orders for consumer goods and materials
> - the speed of delivery of new merchandise to vendors from suppliers
> - the amount of new orders for capital goods unrelated to defense
> - the amount of new building permits for residential buildings
> - the S&P 500 stock index
> - monetary supply (M2)
> - consumer sentiment/confidence
>
> Coincident – show up at about the same time as reflected in the economy
>
> - the employment/unemployment rate (non-farm payrolls)
> - the Index of Industrial Production
> - the level of manufacturing and trade sales
> - personal income levels
> - Gross Domestic Product (GDP)
> - Consumer Price Index (CPI)
>
> Lagging – show up after the fact
>
> - the value of outstanding commercial and industrial loans
> - the change in the consumer price index for services from the previous month
> - the change in labor cost per unit of labor output
> - inventory
> - average length of employment
> - corporate profits

FISCAL AND MONETARY POLICY

Once we have these indicators, what can we do with them? Depends on whom you talk to. As George Bernard Shaw said, if you laid every economist in the world end to end, they still wouldn't reach a conclusion. But, of course, economics is a tough science. Kind of hard to put an economy under a microscope, and you sure can't recreate one in the laboratory. So, we will probably always have economists with sharply different viewpoints. The Keynesians feel that **fiscal policy** is the best way to control the economy. Fiscal policy is what the president and congress do: tax and spend. Keynesians recommend that fiscal policy be used to increase aggregate (overall) demand. To stimulate the economy, just cut taxes and increase government spending. Lower taxes leaves more money for Americans to spend and invest, fueling the economy. If the government is spending more on interstate highway construction, that means a lot more folks are going to be hired for construction crews. Or maybe the federal government orders 10 million pies from Frank & Emma's for cafeterias at various Department of Defense, Treasury, Commerce, etc., buildings. Frank & Emma's would suddenly buy more equipment and raw materials and hire more workers, which is how to push the economy forward.

On the other hand, if we need to cool things down, the Keynesians suggest that the federal government increase taxes and cut spending. Higher taxes leave less money for Americans to spend and invest, and decreased spending puts less government money into projects that would otherwise be hiring subcontractors, laborers, etc.

Monetarists feel that controlling the money supply is the key to managing the economy. What is the money supply?

It's the supply of money. Money, like any commodity, has a cost. The cost of money equals its "interest rate." If there's too much demand and too little supply, the cost of money (interest rate) goes up. That slows down the economy and fights inflation. If there's too little demand and too much supply, the cost of money (interest rate) goes down. That helps to stimulate the economy and pump some air back into a deflated economy.

Wait, money has a cost? I thought I paid the cost of things *with* money. Sure, but if I want to start a business, I need money. How much do I have to pay to borrow this money?

That's the interest rate—the cost of borrowing money.

So, how can the money supply be influenced? Through monetary policy, enacted by the Federal Reserve Board. Because of that embarrassing little fiasco known as the 1930s, the Fed likes to make sure that banks don't lend out and invest every last dollar they have on deposit. So, the Fed requires that banks keep a certain percentage of their customer deposits in <u>reserve</u>. This is called, surprisingly enough, the **reserve requirement**. If the Fed raises the reserve requirement, banks have less money to lend out to folks trying to buy homes and start businesses. So if the economy is overheating, the Fed could raise the reserve requirement in order to cool things down, and if the economy is sluggish, they could lower the requirement in order to make more money available to fuel the economy. However, this is a drastic measure because of the multiplier effect, which means that $1 more or less in reserve has more than just $1's effect on the economy. So it's the least used Fed tool.

The most used tool is open market operations. The Fed can either buy or sell T-bills to banks. If they want to cool things down/raise interest rates, they can take money out of banks by selling them T-bills. If they want to fuel a sluggish economy/lower interest rates, they can buy T-bills from banks, thereby pumping money into the system.

Again, interest rates can be thought of as the price of a commodity known as money. Whenever a commodity—corn, sugar, concert tickets—is scarce, its price rises. Whenever something is widely available, its price drops. When money is tight, its cost (interest rate) rises. When money is widely available, its cost (interest rate) falls. So, if the Fed wants to drop rates, they make money more available by buying T-bills from banks. If they want to raise rates, they make money scarce by selling T-bills to banks (who pay for them with…money). Just follow the flow of money.

Then there's the tool that gets talked about the most in the news, the discount rate and the target for the **fed funds rate**. When people talk about the Fed raising interest rates by 25 basis points, they're talking either about the discount or the fed funds rate. The discount rate is the rate the Fed charges banks that borrow directly from the Fed; the fed funds rate is what banks charge each other for loans. If banks have to pay more to borrow, you can imagine that they will in turn charge their customers more to borrow from them. So, if the Fed wants to raise interest rates, they just raise the discount rate or the target for the fed funds rate and let the banking system take it from there. The Fed doesn't directly set the **prime rate** or the fed funds rate, but they do have influence over the rates. And, of course, they never, ever have anything to do with taxes.

So, think of the Fed as the driver of the economy. If the economy starts going too fast, they tap the brakes (raise interest rates) by raising the reserve requirement, raising the discount rate, and selling T-bills. If the economy starts to stall out, the Fed gives it gas by lowering the reserve requirement, lowering the discount rate, and buying T-bills.

Money Supply

The exam may get more specific about the money supply that the FRB/FOMC can tighten and loosen in order to either fight inflation (tighten) or stimulate the economy (loosen). The money supply can be divided into three separate categories for those with clearly too much time on their hands. To save time and to avoid overexciting you, let's just dispense with the cheap bullet points here. Remember that M2 includes M1 plus some more stuff, and M3 includes M2 plus some more stuff:

- M1: cash, coins, checking, NOW accounts. Considered to be the most "narrow" idea of money, the money that's in circulation.
- M2: M1 + savings deposits, and non-institutional money-market funds
- M3: M2 + large time deposits, institutional money-market funds, short-term repurchase agreements, along with other larger liquid assets

INTEREST RATES

As we saw, a tight money supply leads to higher interest rates, which will slow the economy to fight inflation. Loose money leads to lower interest rates, which will pump a little inflation back into a sputtering economy. So, let's take a look at this concept of "interest rates." Interest rates represent the cost of money. If you want $50,000 to start a beauty salon, chances are you have to borrow it. How much you pay for that "capital" is what we call interest rates. When there's a ton of money to be lent out, lenders will drop their rates in order to get you to borrow. When money is tight, however, borrowers have to compete with each other to get a share of the limited capital and pay higher and higher rates. Again, if the concert is a sell-out, fans bid the price of the tickets ever upward; and when the performer is a has-been, the price of the tickets plummets.

Okay, so one way to borrow money is by selling bonds to investors. How much should you pay the buyers of your bonds?

How about zero? Zero percent financing sure sounds tempting to a borrower; unfortunately, the buyers of debt securities demand compensation. They're the lenders of the money, and they demand current interest rates in return for lending their hard-earned cash. So, debt securities pay investors exactly what they have to pay them in order to entice them to lend money through the purchase of these debt securities (bonds, notes, bills, certificates, etc.). If a corporation could get by with paying zero percent in order to borrow money through a bond issuance, you know they would. Since they can't do that, they offer investors only as much as they have to in order to obtain the loan. Sort of like you would do when applying for a mortgage. Would you give anyone even one extra basis point for a mortgage? Probably not. When you borrow money through a mortgage you have to pay the current rate of interest, just as the issuer of a bond must pay.

The exam may ask you to work with the following interest rates. They don't really warrant an in-depth discussion, so here's a quick list that should suffice:

- Discount rate: the rate banks have to pay when borrowing from the FRB
- Fed funds rate: the rate banks charge each other for overnight loans in excess of $1 million. Considered the most volatile rate, subject to daily change
- Call money rate or "broker call loan rate": the rate broker-dealers pay when borrowing on behalf of their margin customers
- Prime rate: the rate that the most creditworthy corporate customers pay when borrowing

LIBOR: stands for "London Interbank Offering Rate," which is the average rate that banks charge each other on loans for London deposits of Eurodollars

Whether we use fiscal or monetary policy, our efforts will influence interest rates. And interest rates can either make it easier or harder for companies to do business and for consumers to consume. The exam might bring up the term **disintermediation**. This is a situation in which money is being withdrawn from banks and savings & loans by depositors in order to reinvest the funds into higher yielding money market instruments (Treasury bills, certificates of deposit, money market funds). Disintermediation would occur when interest rates at savings banks are lower than money market instruments. The cause could be that the FRB is pursuing a "tight money policy," which is causing a rise in interest rates, creating a demand for the higher yielding money market securities.

YIELD CURVES

City, county, and state governments borrow money by issuing municipal bonds. Municipal bonds are usually issued under a "serial maturity," which means that a little bit of the principal will be returned every year, until the whole issue is paid off. Investors who buy bonds maturing in 2030 will generally demand a higher yield than those getting their principal back in 2012. The longer your money is at risk, the more of a reward you demand, right? If a friend wanted to borrow $1,000 for one month, you'd probably do it interest-free. What if they wanted to take three years to pay you back? You could get some interest on a thousand dollars by buying a bank CD, which carries no risk, right? So, if somebody's going to put your money at risk for an extended period of time, you demand a reward in the form of an interest payment.

Same with bonds. If your bond matures in 2030 when mine matures in 2012, isn't your money at risk for 18 more years? That's why your bond would be offered at a higher yield (interest rate) than mine. If I buy a bond yielding 5.35%, yours might be offered at more like 5.89%. The extra 54 basis points is your extra reward for taking on extra risk.

This is how it works under a normal yield curve, where long-term bonds yield more than short-term bonds.

Guess what, sometimes that yield curve gets inverted. Suddenly, the rule flies out the window, and folks are getting higher yields on short-term bonds than on long-term bonds. The cause of this is generally a peak in interest rates. When bond investors feel that interest rates have gone as high as they're going to go, they all clamor to lock in the high interest rates for the longest period of time. In a rush of activity, they sell off their short-term bonds in order to hurry up and buy long-term bonds at the best interest rate they're likely to see for a long time. Well, if everybody's selling off short-term bonds, the price drops [and the yield *increases*]. And if they're all buying up long-term bonds, the price increases [and the yield *drops*]. That causes the yield curve to invert, a situation that usually corrects itself very quickly. There are also "humped yield curves," where the intermediate maturities have the highest yield, and a "flat yield curve," which has to be the best example of an oxymoron you're likely to see. A flat curve?

Whatever, dude.

A "flat yield curve" would imply that short-, intermediate-, and long-term bonds are all yielding about the same, meaning that demand and supply for all maturities is similar. Believe it or not, as I write these words, the yield curve is close to flattening out, as if I didn't already have enough excitement in my life. Basically, the Fed keeps raising short-term rates, but the bond traders are driving down the yield on the long-term bonds so that the difference between short-term, inter-mediate-term, and long-term yields is not very great…it's all flattening out.

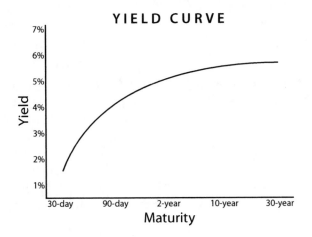

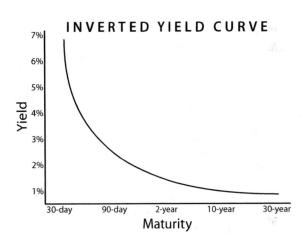

To figure your way out of any yield curve jam, just remember that yields and prices are inverse. So, if the short-term debt has a higher yield (inverted or "negatively sloped" yield curve), its price has gone down due to low demand/high supply. In a normal yield curve, short-term debt would have a lower yield/higher price due to a high demand for the short-term debt relative to supply… why are the long-term bonds yielding more on the right side of this yield curve? Long-term commit-ments scare investors, so their demand for these long-term commitments is lower than the supply, pushing price *down* and *yield* up.

Another yield concept the test might throw at you considers the difference in yields between high-rated and low-rated bonds, known as a yield spread. Remember that coupon rates don't change—they're simply printed on the bond. So, how could the yield of a bond that's already been issued go up? Only if its price starts to fall. If you get 5% a year, that's $50. If you get that $50 by paying $400, your yield is higher than for someone who bought that same bond paying $50 a year for $800. In fact, it's twice as high, right? Then again, why the heck is your $1,000 face value bond worth only $400 in the open market? Because it's a poor credit risk, a **junk bond**, a high-yield bond—whatever the heck we decide to call it. So, if folks are only willing to pay cheap prices for these higher-risk bonds, that makes the yield spread widen, and that's a negative indicator for the economy. Basically, it means folks are nervous about issuers' ability to repay. If investors don't demand a significantly higher yield on the low-rated bonds (they're willing to pay higher market prices for junk bonds), that means in general they are confident about issuers' ability to repay, which is a positive indicator.

Aren't you glad they signed you up for this test?

BALANCE OF TRADE, BALANCE OF PAYMENTS

Balance of trade tracks money in and money out of the economy specifically for goods. If we export more than we import, we have a trade surplus. If we import more than we export, we have a trade deficit. Imports and exports are directly affected by the value of the American dollar relative to foreign currencies.

As our dollar strengthens, our exports become less attractive to consumers in other countries, whose weak currency can't buy our expensive stuff. When our dollar weakens, our exports are more attractive because suddenly their strong currencies can buy lots of our relatively cheap stuff. Likewise, a strong dollar makes foreign travel less expensive for Americans, whereas a weak dollar makes foreign travel *more* expensive. It's just a way of asking how much of their stuff does our dollar buy?

Balance of payments tracks all money coming in versus going out of the economy. So, it counts both imports vs. exports and also investments. If more money is coming in than going out, we have a surplus. That could happen if the Japanese are suddenly buying lots of American securities. If more money is going out than coming in, we have a deficit, which could happen if Americans start buying Japanese securities.

So if we had a trade deficit with France, would a strong dollar or a weak dollar help to bring us back to a surplus?

Well, if we were already importing more from France than we're exporting, we would want to make our exports more attractive to the French and our imports from France less attractive to Americans, which would happen as the dollar...weakens.

The value of the dollar compared to another currency also comes into play when an investor buys an ADR, especially when it comes time to pay dividends. If the U.S. dollar increases in value, when the underlying stock pays a dividend in the foreign currency, the foreign currency received by the bank will need to be converted to U.S. dollars for distribution to the holder of the ADR. As a result of the rise in the value of the dollar relative to the foreign currency received by the bank, the foreign currency will purchase fewer U.S. dollars for distribution to the holder of the ADR. As a result of the rise in the value of the U.S. dollar, the dividend payment received by the holder of the ADR is lower.

Similarly, if the dollar is strong (yen is weak), the ADR won't be worth as many dollars, since 1,000 yen would suddenly be worth fewer of the strong American dollars.

TYPES OF INDUSTRIES

That ends the big view of the overall economy. Now let's look at industries within the economy: defensive, cyclical, and growth. Remember the business cycle and GDP? Well, **defensive industries** do okay regardless of where we are in the business cycle. These industries produce products that consumers buy no matter what, like food, cigarettes, and alcohol. You know, the important stuff. Prescription drugs and bandages also represent defensive industries. Certainly utilities also qualify. When you come home at night do you check the current economic figures before turning on the heat or air conditioning? Heck no.

But if we're in a recession, you might put off the purchase of a new car, which is why automobiles represent a **cyclical industry**. In good times, people load up, but in bad times they hold off. If you think of steel and products made from steel, like cars, heavy equipment, and big industrial machinery, you're thinking of cyclical industries. During expansions, these industries do well. During contractions, they don't. All depends on the business *cycle*. Warren Buffett often likes to buy stocks of companies that make things people buy day after day without much deliberation: soda pop, razor blades, underwear, paint, bricks, etc. If it has a strong brand name (Coca-Cola®, Gillette®, Dairy Queen®), so much the better. So, he favors the defensive, or "non-cyclical" industries, and you sort of have to like his results so far. In case the exam is in a sophisticated mood, it might ask a question about *counter*-cyclical stocks. These don't just weather the storm of a recession/contraction better than cyclical stocks, but actually do *better* in a recession. For example, a discount travel agent such as Priceline™ or a precious metals fund focusing on gold might actually *improve* in a tough economy. When times are tight, people are willing to spend time bidding for airfare and hotels, and in a recession people start buying into end-of-the-world scenarios and no longer trust the currency printed by the U.S. and other governments. Exactly what one would do with gold in an end-of-the-world scenario, I'm not sure. Me, I'd prefer a storage room full of water and canned goods to one full of gold bullion, but what the heck do I know?

Then there are growth industries, like technology, which Mr. Buffett typically avoids like the plague. Growth stocks tend not to pay dividends because they're reinvesting their earnings into *growth*. So, if the test tells you that one company pays a lot of dividends (high dividend pay-out) and another pays low dividends, the former is probably a utility or a REIT, while the latter is a growth company. While Frank & Emma's is in an old, mature boring business—manufacturing—they are a growth *company*. A company whose earnings are growing fast and which appears to have a lot more room to grow…guess what we call stock in that growth company?

Growth stock.

Again with the lack of creativity.

PRACTICE

1. **If the American dollar weakens relative to the Japanese yen, which of the following statements is true?**

    A.   American exports to Japan become more competitive with Japanese goods.

    B.   American exports to Japan become less competitive with Japanese goods.

    C.   Americans vacation dollars go farther in Japan.

    D.   none of the above

2. **Which of the following is a leading indicator?**

    A.   housing starts

    B.   GDP

    C.   savings

    D.   personal income

3. **In order to stimulate a sluggish American economy the Federal Reserve Board might take which of the following actions?**

    A.   cut taxes

    B.   raise taxes

    C.   cut the discount rate

    D.   raise the reserve requirement

4. **In order to stimulate a sluggish economy, the administrators of fiscal policy have which of the following tools available?**

    A.   reserve requirement

    B.   discount rate

    C.   tax rates

    D.   LIBOR

5. **Which of the following is the least defensive industry?**

 A. aerospace

 B. tobacco

 C. alcohol

 D. prescription drugs

ANSWERS

1. **A**, if our currency weakens, the stuff we make is cheap to the Japanese, making it easier to export our cheap American goods to Japan.

2. **A,** housing starts/building permits tell us if there is a big wave of construction up ahead or a big slowdown in construction of new homes.

3. **C,** lower interest rates make it easier to buy houses and other big-ticket items, stimulating the economy. The FRB has nothing to do with setting tax policy.

4. **C,** tax and spend—that's all there is to fiscal policy.

5. **A,** when the economy sputters, people travel less and airlines order fewer planes. Surely no one is expected to forego alcohol and tobacco just because the economy is in a slump.

CHAPTER 12

Portfolio Analysis

INCOME STATEMENT

Whether you buy bonds or stocks, the security is only as solid as the company who issued it. The company can only pay the interest on your bond if they have enough revenue to cover it. Your stock will only rise over the long term if the profits at the company rise. The place to check the company's revenues, expenses, and profit is the company's **income statement**.

We'll be looking at another financial statement called the **balance sheet**, and it may help to remember the inherent difference between the two statements, which are each put out by the same company. The balance sheet is a snapshot of the company's financial strength at a particular point in time. The income statement shows the results of the company's operations over a particular *period* of time. A public company probably had to register its stock and/or bonds with the SEC under the Securities Act of 1933. That same company almost certainly is required to file quarterly and annual financial reports with the SEC under the Securities Exchange Act of 1934. This allows the shareholders and bondholders who were bold enough to invest in these public companies to see what kind of financial condition (balance sheet) their company is in and whether the sales and profits are increasing, decreasing, or flattening out (income statement). If you go to your favorite financial website or do a Google search on a particular company's "10-K" or "annual shareholder report," you can see both the balance sheet and the income statement for companies such as Microsoft, Oracle, or Exxon-Mobil. For now, though, let's start small.

The Lemonade Stand

Let's say you're an 11-year-old kid again, and you have launched your own lemonade stand this summer. Each glass of lemonade sells for $1. The dollars you take in this summer we'll call your **revenue**. As it turns out, you sell 10,000 glasses of lemonade. Your revenue is exactly $10,000, and that's the top line of the income statement. Okay, $10,000 in revenue is fairly impressive for an 11-year-old, but let's not confuse making sales with making a profit. That lemonade you sold didn't just fall from the sky. Rather, it was produced by a combination of the following ingredients: purified water, fresh lemons, lemon juice, sugar, and ice. Those are the goods you bought to make the product you sold, which is why the money you spent on them is called the "cost of goods sold." You also have to serve your product in biodegradable, compostable cold cups, which cost $1,000, on top of the $2,000 paid for the ingredients. So, now your $10,000 in revenue is down to $7,000 after subtracting the "cost of goods sold" and packaging. Seven grand is your **gross profit**, and if you're left with $7,000 out of $10,000, your **gross margin** is exactly 70%.

Way to go, kid!

But we're not done subtracting yet. While you staffed the lemonade stand yourself most of the time, you are still an 11-year-old kid with a life. In order to attend guitar lessons, you had to hire your older sister a few hours each week. Guess what—she expects to be paid. Luckily, you only have to pay her five bucks an hour, but she did put in 100 hours. Her $500 paycheck represents an operating expense to you—what many income statements will list as "SG&A," for **"Selling, General, and Administrative"** expenses. There are other **operating expenses**, including the advertising you do by putting up signs at both ends of the block and running a classified ad in the local paper. Your advertising expense was $500 over the summer.

And you didn't just throw up a folding table and slap a piece of cardboard on a stick with the words "Cold Lemonade - $1." No, sirree. You got the boy next door to build you a stand for $200, and that is a different type of expense. See, you're going to be in business for the next five years, and you'll be using that stand each summer. So, you only have to subtract 1/5 of that $200 on your income statement each year. Instead of subtracting $200, we only have to subtract $40 to **"depreciate"** this vital piece of equipment. Even though you spent the money all up front, next year you will also subtract $40 as a depreciation expense on your income statement. You will do that five times until you have depreciated the cost of the stand to zero. Last, you have to factor in a few other things used to make lemonade and sell it. You had to buy several large thermoses, a couple of blenders, a little money drawer, a calculator, and a copy of QuickBooks™. That all works out to $300, which you depreciate over three years, subtracting another $100 this year.

So, after subtracting the cost of the ingredients, the cups, the labor, the advertising, and the depreciation of assets, you're left with $5,860. Compare that to the $10,000 in revenue, and you see that your "operating profit" of $5,860 represents an "operating margin" of 58.6%. Another name for "operating profit," by the way, is "EBIT," or "earnings before interest and taxes." Companies that issue bonds need to cover the interest payments, so bond analysts often compare the EBIT to the annual interest expense to arrive at the "times interest earned."

Speaking of interest coverage, your mom had to spot you some cash to buy your first batch of ingredients and other essentials and, unfortunately, she actually charges you interest on the loan. On the plus side, you do get to deduct that interest before figuring your taxable income, just as homeowners deduct the interest paid on their mortgages. So, you subtract the $20 of interest, and your taxable income is $5,840. You have a "pre-tax margin" of 58.4%. Your taxes work out to $40, and after paying those, you have a net profit, or net income, of $5,800. That represents an astounding 58% "net margin," a number that Bill Gates could only dream about.

Lucky for you, you have no shareholders who might be grumbling for dividends. Remember, you capitalized your operations through leverage, which sounds a lot more impressive than saying you borrowed money from your mom. But, the fact is, you have no equity partners—all you have to do is pay your mom back and pay her on time. The profits are all yours. Of course, at public companies, there are shareholders, so when we look at a company's "bottom line" or "net income," we then start figuring out how much of that net income belongs to each share of stock.

MEASUREMENTS SUCH AS EPS, P/E, ETC.

So, let's pretend that you *do* have shareholders in your lemonade stand. You just reported **net income** of $5,800. If you had raised your money by issuing stock, you would have been issuing "shares," right?

Well, it's time to start sharing. Who gets dividends first? Preferred stockholders. If you pay a preferred dividend of $800, that leaves exactly $5,000 of "earnings available to common." This is like an earnings pie that your company bakes each year for the shareholders. The question your shareholders ask is, "How big is the pie, and how many slices does it have to be cut into?" If your company has $5,000 in earnings available to common with 1,000 shares of common stock outstanding, that represents $5 of earnings per share. EPS = $5. Each slice of the earnings pie is worth $5, in other words.

We could apply a more stringent test that assumes all convertibles (bonds, preferred, warrants) are actually turned into common stock. In other words, the holder of a convertible security can decide to turn his bond or preferred stock into a certain number of common shares. He brings no earnings to the table—he only wants his fair share of the earnings pie, like an uninvited guest who brings nothing with him to the party. When these investors convert to common stock, your $5,000 in earnings could end up being divided among more shares, sort of like sharing a pizza pie big enough for eight friends among 50 friends. We'd all get a piece, but it probably wouldn't be worth eating. If your company ended up with 1,250 shares outstanding after conversion, your diluted EPS would be only $4. Same old earnings pie cut up into more slices.

Now that we have our earnings per share, we can also find out how much gets paid out in dividends. Not surprisingly, we call this the dividend payout ratio. This just takes the annual dividends paid and divides it by the EPS. Your company has earnings-per-share (EPS) of $5. If you paid out $1 in common dividends, you paid out 20% of your earnings, which is called your "dividend payout ratio." When we examine mutual funds, we'll see that an equity income fund buys stock in companies with high dividend payout ratios, while a growth fund would not consider dividends an important factor. And while we're playing with numbers and earnings and ratios, note that stocks trade at various "multiples" such as the **price-to-earnings ratio**. This simply compares the market price of the stock to the earnings per share. If you were a growth lemonade stock, you might trade for 30–50 times your earnings, which in your case would take the stock up to $150–$250 per share. If you were a value lemonade stock, you might trade at just 10–15 times your earnings, or around $50–$75 per share.

In any case, let's examine your lemonade stand's income statement once again:

Revenue	$10,000
Cost of Goods Sold	- $3,000
SG&A Expenses	- $1,000
Depreciation, Amortization	- $140
OPERATING INCOME	= $5,860
Interest Expense	- $20
PRE-TAX INCOME	= $5,840
Taxes	- $40
NET INCOME after tax	= $5,800

The numbers above show us that for every $1 your lemonade stand brings in, you keep 58 cents. And, if you're wondering how depreciation differs from amortization, basically, they're the same thing only different. Depreciation is used for tangible assets such as a lemonade stand; amortization is for intangible assets that you can't quite see or touch. If your company enters into a legal agreement to produce medicine or software under another company's patent, that agreement would have a limited life, so the accountants would gradually write down the cost of that patent, just as we wrote down the cost of the lemonade stand. We can't touch a patent, but it's still an asset that helps deliver sales and profits.

Cash Flow

We looked at a couple of subtractions on the income statement that do not really involve an outlay of cold, hard cash. Depreciation and amortization spread an asset's historical cost over an estimated useful life, but no cash is actually being spent when we record the expense on the income statement. Therefore, analysts often ignore such things when focusing on **cash flow**, which is simply how much cash is being generated by a company. One way to calculate cash flow is to take the net income and then add back two non-cash charges: depreciation and amortization. It's not a huge deal for your lemonade earnings. It'd be a bigger deal for Boeing.

Anyway, maybe next summer the local Starbucks will begin to feel the pressure of your competitive beverage kiosk and offer you seven times cash flow for your business. Whether we calculate your cash flow as EBIT, EBITDA, or some variation, Starbucks would be offering around $40,000 for your lemonade stand. Or, if you were a public company, analysts would compare your stock price to your cash flow, calling it, surprisingly, "price-to-cash flow," or "price-to-cash" for those in a hurry. As we'll see, a stock's market price can be compared to the earnings (price-to-earnings), the book value (price-to-book), the sales (price-to-sales), or the cash flow (price-to-cash). The market price of the stock is being quoted all throughout the day. The earnings, sales, and cash flow can all be pulled from the income statement. And the book value can be determined from the next financial statement on our menu, the balance sheet.

BALANCE SHEET

The income statement shows the company's sales, expenses, and profits over a particular period of operations. To see how solid the company's overall financial condition is at a particular moment, we look at the balance sheet. The basic formula for the balance sheet is expressed as:

Assets = Liabilities + Stockholders' Equity

Or:

Assets – Liabilities = Stockholders' Equity

Assets represent what a company owns. Liabilities represent what a company owes. You take what a company owns, subtract what it owes, and that's the net worth of the company. Another name for **net worth** is **"stockholders' equity."** That just implies that the stockholders are the owners of the company, so what we want to know is what that ownership is actually worth.

Assets

Assets are divided into three types. The first type is current assets. **Current assets** represent cash and anything that could easily be converted to cash quickly: cash & equivalents, accounts receivable, inventory. Cash is cash, and it's a good thing. "Equivalents" are money market instruments earning some interest, which is also a good thing. If they mature in three months or less, commercial paper, banker's acceptances, repurchase agreements, and T-bills are considered "cash equivalents" here on the balance sheet.

Back at the lemonade stand, you very wisely deposited $560 into a savings account at the end of the summer, as you know how important it is to have some dough on hand for expenses and investments into the business. File that under "cash." **Accounts receivable** is what customers owe the company. You were nice enough to sell two of your best friends lemonade on credit throughout the summer, and they ran up a tab of $40 between them. You fully intend to be paid for those sales in the near-term, so you list that payment as an asset (money coming IN).

Inventory is the stuff the company makes and plans to sell (convert to cash) just as soon as possible. When temperatures dropped suddenly and the cold rain started up in late August, you were left holding a rather large quantity of lemons, sugar, etc. You very creatively made up as much lemonade as possible and turned it into popsicles. Next season, you intend to sell that inventory for $40 cash money, making the inventory a current asset. Ah, but what if the inventory develops a hideous flavor sitting in a deep freezer all winter and spring? That's always something to keep in mind when assigning a value to—or trusting the value of—a company's inventory. As we'll see, the "quick ratio" excludes inventory from current assets for that very reason—the company might not be able to sell the stuff sitting in storage. But, for now, let's assume you will sell it and list its value as a current asset called "inventory."

Fixed assets include factories, equipment, furniture, etc. This stuff could all be converted into cash, but it would take a while, and we wouldn't get anywhere near what we paid for the stuff if we liquidated it. Not to mention that this stuff was not purchased in order to be sold; it was purchased in order to generate revenue—for example: printing presses, industrial control systems, fleet of delivery vans, etc. A large corporation would list the value of the real estate, as well as the value of the assembly line equipment, as well as the furniture and even the artwork hanging on the walls of the visitor lobby. Those are all fixed assets. They get depreciated over time, so the company's balance sheet usually reflects the original cost of the equipment and then shows how much value has been depreciated (written down) at this point. For your lemonade stand, we said that the stand itself, plus some very basic capital equipment including blenders, ice trays, software, etc., totaled $500. We depreciated $140 of that on your income statement, so we're showing the original cost of $500 and then subtracting the "accumulated depreciation" at this point to show that the net book value is now $360.

Then there are **intangible assets**. What is the value of the brand name JIF™?

Who knows, but it must be worth millions. When a company such as J.M. Smucker's purchases the JIF™ peanut butter brand, that brand name has huge value and leads to sales and profits just as a jam vat or delivery fleet or other tangible pieces of equipment would. So, it's intangible because you can't hold a brand name in your hand, but it's also an asset—an intangible asset. Intangible assets would include patents, trademarks, and goodwill. What is goodwill? When a company buys/acquires another company, they usually pay more than just the value of the equipment, land, inventory, etc. They're paying for the brand-identity, the customer base, etc. So, that excess paid above the hard, tangible value of assets you can touch and see is called "goodwill." Let's face it, your lemonade stand has no intangible assets at this point, but if you ever purchase the goodwill of a rival lemonade stand up the street, we would list that intangible here. Then, we would add all three types of assets and call it your Total Assets.

Liabilities

On the other side of the equation we find **liabilities**, which represent what a company owes. Anything that has to be paid out in the short term is a **current liability**. **Accounts payable**, **accrued wages**, and **accrued taxes** all represent bills the company has to pay currently, which is why they're called current liabilities. Your mom picked up a few batches of ingredients over the summer and put them on her credit card. Just as soon as she remembers doing so, you fully intend to pay her back the $60, listed under accounts payable. And, you still owe your sister $100, which is listed under "accrued wages."

The principal amount of a loan or a bond that has to be paid more than a year out is simply a **long-term liability**. You still owe your mother $240 in principal, which is why it's listed under "long-term liabilities." Add the current and the long-term liabilities together and you have total liabilities of $400.

Stockholders' Equity

Stockholders' Equity is sometimes called Shareholders' Equity or "net worth." Whatever we call it, remember that equity equals ownership, and the stockholders own a percentage of the company. What is that ownership worth at the time the balance sheet is printed? That's stockholders' equity. Companies place the total par value of their preferred stock under this heading. Common stock is assigned a par value of, say, $1, so if a company has 1,000,000 shares of common, they would list the par value of their common stock as $1,000,000 and place it under stockholders' equity. If investors bought the stock in the IPO at $11, that represents a surplus of $10 above the par value, so the company would list **paid-in surplus** of $10,000,000, as well. And then any earnings that have been retained are listed as retained earnings. Why did you only retain $600 this year? Because you're smart enough to know that a business that involves very little capital equipment, very little financing, and very little recurring costs can afford to pay out big distributions to the owners. As the sole owner, you cut yourself a $5,200 dividend check on September 1st and smiled all the way to and from the bank.

Measurements Such as Working Capital, Current Ratio, etc.

Current assets represent what a company owns. Current liabilities represent what a company owes. Hopefully, the company owns more than it owes, right? Fundamental analysts take current assets and subtract current liabilities in order to measure **working capital** (sometimes called "net working capital"). This is a measure of how able a company is to finance current operations. We're talking about short-term liquidity. When a company's liabilities exceed its assets, that company is in great danger of going belly up and being picked apart by hungry creditors in a bankruptcy proceeding. Likewise, if a company's assets exceed its liabilities, that company is in a strong position to fund current operations, just as your lemonade operation would be if you had $1,000 in total bills and $4,000 in the bank.

Working Capital = Current Assets – Current Liabilities

Your lemonade stand shows current assets of $640 and current liabilities of $160. Your working capital is, therefore, the difference of $480. Analysts also express current assets and current liabilities as a ratio, known as the **current ratio**. Instead of subtracting $160 from $640, we would say that $640, divided by (over) $160, gives you a current ratio of 4 to 1. Basically, for every $1 of short-term debt, you have $4 of short-term assets to cover it. Not bad.

Analysts could also apply a more stringent test, known as the **quick ratio**. The "I" in the word "quick" reminds us that "inventory" is subtracted from current assets before we compare them to current liabilities. Why do that? Again, those frozen lemonade pops might go bad in storage, or simply might not strike your customers' fancy next summer. So, in case you didn't sell your inventory, what would your short-term financial condition look like then? We would deduct the $40 of inventory from your $640 of current assets first, and then compare that $600 to the $160 of current liabilities. At which point we would still see a very impressive ratio of 3.75 to 1 for your quick ratio. For every $1 of short-term debt, you have $3.75 to cover it, even if the inventory completely spoils.

Current ratio and working capital measure short-term liquidity. For a picture of the company's long-term solvency or ability to remain afloat, analysts calculate the **debt ratio**. The debt ratio shows us how much debt a company has compared to its assets. We compare the total debt to the total assets; the smaller the number, the smaller the amount of leverage the company has used. For your lemonade stand we would take the total liabilities of $400 and divide that by (compare it to) your total assets of $1,000—your debt ratio is .40 or 40%. That means that less than half of your "total capitalization" came from borrowed money. You are not "highly leveraged" and should therefore be able to meet your obligations over the long haul.

Let's take a minute and find the important measurements that we just discussed, including working capital, current ratio, quick ratio, etc.

ASSETS			
Current Assets			
Cash & Equivalents	$560		
Accounts Receivable	$40		
Inventory	$40		
Total Current Assets		$640	
Fixed Assets	$500 – $140 deprec.	$360	
Intangible Assets		$0	
TOTAL ASSETS			$1,000
LIABILITIES			
Current Liabilities			
Acct's Payable	$60		
Accrued Wages, Taxes	$100		
Total Current Liabilities		$160	
Long-Term Liabilities		$240	
TOTAL LIABILITIES			$400
STOCKHOLDERS' EQUITY			
Common stock @par		$0	
Retained Earnings		$600	
TOTAL STOCKHOLDERS' EQUITY			$600
TOTAL LIABILITIES & STOCKHOLDERS' EQUITY			$1,000

FOOTNOTES

In a company's quarterly and annual reports, the financial statements are accompanied by **footnotes** that help clarify the numbers. For example, is the inventory valued as LIFO or FIFO? What does the company mean by "equivalents" in its "cash and equivalents" line item—debt securities with six months to maturity? Three months? How/when does a company recognize "revenue"? Is it when the company ships pies to a distributor, or only when somebody has actually paid for the product? Whenever the numbers in the annual report or other filing require further clarification, the footnotes section is used to provide it.

TECHNICAL ANALYSIS

Okay, so that's what a fundamental analyst looks at. **Technical analysts** don't care about that stuff. They don't care about EPS, P/E ratio, current ratio, debt ratio, etc. Technical analysts primarily look at charts of stock prices. They study past trends and price patterns in order to predict future trends and price patterns. If you tried to give a technical analyst a hot stock tip concerning Frank & Emma's, he'd cut you off as soon as he had the stock symbol FREM. See, he couldn't care less if they make pies, computers, cars, or loans. All he wants to see is what the stock has been doing and, based on that, try to figure out what it's going to do next.

CHARTS AND PATTERNS

If a technical analyst sees that a stock has been trading between 20 and 25 for the past three months, he'll call the low number—20—**support** and the high number—25—**resistance**, like this:

This just means that whenever the stock goes up, it meets resistance at $25, and whenever it falls, it finds support at $20. Resistance is often referred to as the market being "overbought" and support is called an "oversold" market, since everything needs at least two names in this business. So, maybe the technical trader consistently tries to buy close to $20 and sell as soon as it nears $25. Or, maybe he waits until the stock breaks through resistance before buying it, reasoning that if it hits a breakout it will keep running up. He could enter a buy-stop order slightly above the resistance point, based on the idea that if the stock price breaks through resistance it will keep going up a while. Or, maybe he hangs onto a stock until it loses support before selling, known as a breakdown/breakout. The technical trader could place a sell-stop order to sell the stock short below the support line, figuring if the stock lost support it would go into a free fall from there. That way, even if 5,000 factory workers lose their jobs and the company's bondholders get stiffed, at least this guy will make a quick profit on a well-timed short sale.

No, short-sellers are not the most popular folks on Wall Street.

There are **head and shoulders** patterns for those with clearly too much time on their hands. A head and shoulders pattern signals the reversal of a trend. So, a head and shoulders "top" indicates the bull trend is about to end—a bearish signal. A head and shoulders bottom indicates the bear trend is about to end—a bullish signal.

A head and shoulders top would look something like this:

So, when you see that right shoulder beginning to form, you're supposed to conclude that the stock price is headed for a big drop. And, if this pattern were flipped upside down, just flip what I said upside down.

But, please, don't try this at home. Especially when you should be studying for a difficult test called the Series 7.

If a stock is trading in a narrow range between support and resistance, it is consolidating. A chart of a stock in **consolidation** appears to be moving sideways, like this:

The exam might talk about consolidation as the place where sophisticated investors (mutual funds, pension funds, big Wall Street traders, etc.) are getting into or out of the stock. Since these geniuses are so sharp, when we see them buying, it must mean the stock is going up, and when we see them selling, it must mean the stock is heading down. At this accumulation or distribution point, the price moves "sideways," which is also known as "consolidation."

Technical analysts look to see how many stocks advance versus how many stocks decline. Guess what we call this? **The advance/decline line**. If advancers outpace decliners by 2:1, that means that twice as many stocks went up that day. And if decliners outpace advancers 2:1, that means that twice as many stocks went down that day. This tells the technical analyst something about buying/selling opportunities, based on pure supply and demand of shares in the marketplace.

Volume is also of interest to the technical analyst. Volume just indicates the total number of shares traded on, say, the NYSE, AMEX, NASDAQ, or the regional exchanges in Chicago, Philadelphia, Boston, etc. Analysts expect stock prices to rise on increasing volume. They would tend to place more significance on the fact that stock prices increased minutely on decreasing volume. Often, that situation is considered a reversal of a bullish trend, which is, of course, a bearish signal.

The exam may bring up the **200-day moving average**, which is a very important technical indicator. A moving average smoothes out temporary blips and makes it easier to spot trends. To track a moving average, we continuously kick out the oldest data and replace it with the newest. For example, a batting average tells us the percentage with which a baseball player successfully hits the ball over the entire season. A 30-day moving average would track his batting average just over the previous 30 days. The difference between the two approaches is the difference between, "How is he hitting this year?" and "How has he been hitting lately?" Technical analysts want to know how many and which stocks closed at a price above or below their 200-day moving average. If a stock has been trading below its 200-day moving average, it may be in a clear downtrend, or vice versa for a stock trading above its 200-day moving average. So, a technical analyst may want to buy stocks trading above their moving average and sell short those stocks trading below their moving average. Rather than focusing on what a particular stock did, technical analysts might prefer to predict the direction of the overall market or index based on the number of stocks trading above or below their 200-day moving averages.

The exam might also talk about a market being "oversold" or "overbought." First, let's look at the "oversold" thing. If the broad indices such as the S&P 500 are declining, but the <u>number</u> of stocks declining versus those advancing is actually shrinking, the market is considered to be "oversold." Huh? What that means is, yes, the market is still dropping, but it seems to be losing energy in that direction, since the *number* of stocks dropping is, uh, dropping. So, the **bear market** is losing steam, and that means we're due for a rally. How do you know when it's done being "oversold" as opposed to having maybe seven more days of shock and awe in store for naïve early comers? I have no idea. I'm just telling you about a point that has a chance of showing up on the exam. An "oversold" market is basically a bear market that is losing steam and about to reverse in an upward, bullish direction. Maybe the market rises a while, until it is "overbought." An "overbought" market is a situation where the overall indices such as the S&P 500 and the Dow have been advancing, but the <u>number</u> of advancers compared to decliners is shrinking. In other words, the **bull market** is losing steam. It's about to stall out completely and tumble back downhill at a violent, breakneck pace. Time to sell short, buy puts, sell calls, what have you.

THEORIES

The technical analyst knows how incredibly smart he is. So much smarter than the small-time investor, in fact, that all he has to do is track what odd lot investors are doing and bet the other way. If odd-lotters are buying, he sells. If odd-lotters are selling, he buys. Why? Because folks who can only afford an **odd lot** (a small transaction) of stock at a time always buy too high and sell too low. This is known as the odd-lot theory, and please do not try this at home.

The **short interest theory** has to do with how many open short sales are out there. Now, we know that short sellers profit when a stock's price drops, but this theory also recognizes that short sellers eventually have to cover or buy back their shorts. So, if there are a lot of uncovered or "open" shorts out there, they might all suddenly be forced to buy the stock in a hurry. That would create buying pressure that would drive up the stock's price, which is why a large number of open short positions is a *bullish* indicator.

Technical analysts also use indexes such as the Dow (30 huge "industrial" stocks), the S&P 500 (the overall market), NASDAQ Composite (mostly technology), the Russell 2000 (small cap), or the Wilshire 5000 (r-e-a-l-l-y broad) and others to confirm trends. If the Dow is making new highs or new lows, a technical analyst might conclude that we are in either a bull or a bear market. Remember that the number included in the index's name usually refers to how many stocks make up the index. So, the Wilshire 5000 covers many more stocks than the S&P 500. The Dow Jones Industrial Average is comprised of only 30 industrial stocks; the Dow Jones Composite is made up of only 65 stocks. The theory is that however these indexes move is how the overall market will move.

Or not.

The so-called Dow Theory places major importance on the movement in the DJIA and the DJ Transportation Index. Believers of the Dow Theory preach that a major trend is confirmed only when both of the aforementioned indices reach a new high or low.

INVESTMENT STYLES, OBJECTIVES

GROWTH

Perhaps you have heard of "growth funds" and "value funds" before. Both invest in stock, but for different reasons. A growth fund is a mutual fund that invests in companies whose earnings are expected to grow rapidly. Trouble is, those earnings have inconveniently not actually been earned yet, so if we base a stock's price on how much it *should* or *will probably* earn over the next 5–10 years, that stock price is propped up by the shaky crutch of speculation. The company reports earnings every quarter—what if the Wall Street analysts have predicted earnings of one penny per share but the "growth company" actually reports a *loss* of one penny per share?

Usually, the stock drops faster than a big-league curve ball. Growth stocks are expensive, which means they trade at high "P/E ratios" or "high multiples." Starbucks, for example, is trading today for about 55 times earnings. Valero, a company that turns oil into gasoline, trades at just 9 times earnings.

VALUE

A "growth index" would track stocks trading at high P/E ratios. A "value index" would track stocks trading at lower P/E ratios. Simply put, value stocks trade at lower multiples than growth stocks. Why are they trading so cheap? Usually, because the company has hit a snag, or maybe it operates in an industry that is currently taking it on the chin. A value investor sees that an old established company is now trading at a very low price-to-earnings (P/E) ratio. Why? Maybe the earnings have been flat or shrinking lately. Maybe the company purchased a competitor and is having trouble integrating it. Whatever the case may be, the value investor might decide that the stock in this company is still worth more than people realize. He says its "intrinsic value" is $50 a share while the market is selling it for about $42 per share and, therefore, he loads up his shopping cart with it like my Aunt Barbara at a Big Lots back-to-school sale.

Long-established companies are the ones likely to pay dividends. And, even though a dividend *could* be cut or suspended, that doesn't happen very often. Why not? First, the headlines will make the company look really lame. Second, the board of directors—who declare dividends—are almost always huge shareholders themselves. If you owned 10 million shares of stock, would you vote to cut or suspend the dividend?

Probably not. So, since dividends usually stay the same or increase over time, when these value stocks start trading cheaper and cheaper, their dividend yields are increasing. Therefore, the exam could point out that value stocks offer higher yields. They are also, generally, not as volatile as growth stocks. See, when a stock pays regular income, that always takes some of the volatility out of holding the stock. Similarly, when you throw a dinner party, your guests might start getting volatile if it's taking too long for the main course to show up. Well, to reduce the volatility of the crowd, you can always feed them some appetizers now. That's pretty much how dividend income works. So, since growth stocks seldom pay any income, investors can get a little testy as they wait for this supposed feast that's supposed to show up any year now.

INCOME

An "income investor" is, surprisingly, an investor seeking income. Where is the best place to seek income? Debt securities. Is that the only place? No—equities also pay income, which explains why there are equity income funds. An equity income investor would purchase stocks that pay consistent or generous dividends. Most folks would just buy an "equity income fund" and let the portfolio managers decide which stocks pay the best dividends. Either way, the main objective here is the dividend income. Capital appreciation is only a secondary goal.

Income investors will also purchase preferred stock, since that dividend has to be paid before any dividends can be paid to common stock. But, generally, the phrase "income investor" describes a gentleman or lady who prefers bonds. A corporation has to pay bond interest, while a dividend can always be cut or suspended entirely. Plus, if you buy bonds issued by state governments or Uncle Sam, the chance of default is usually quite remote in the case of the states and virtually nonexistent in the case of the United States Treasury.

Just how much income an income investor will end up seeking depends on her risk tolerance, objectives, and time horizon. As we'll soon see, bonds with long maturities usually offer higher yields, but they present more risk in terms of rising interest rates. Low-rated bonds yield more than high-rated bonds, but they also subject the investor to the risk of further credit downgrades or outright default.

CAPITAL PRESERVATION

I suppose capital preservation could be the only objective of an investor, but any time he seeks capital preservation, he ends up earning some income, too. He would preserve his capital with U.S. Treasury securities, primarily. And, while he knows the principal value of the investment will be paid out at maturity, he will also earn interest on the T-bills, T-notes, and T-bonds. A U.S. Government Securities mutual fund would likely say that its objective is "**preservation of capital** and income consistent with that goal." How much income can you seek on things that are guaranteed by the U.S. Treasury? Not much—but what do you want? High yield or sleep? You can't have both.

Whether someone chooses T-bills, T-notes, T-bonds, or STRIPS has to do with time horizon and risk tolerance. If an investor is very concerned that rates will rise, stick her in T-bills and call it a day. If she wants to avoid reinvestment risk, stick her into STRIPS, which return all the interest at the very end. If she has a time horizon of 2–10 years, recommend T-notes. A longer time horizon would make T-bonds more suitable.

LIQUIDITY

If an investor plans to buy a house over the next several months or few years, keep their money out of the stock market. While you could put them into a short-term bond fund, I wouldn't recommend that, either. Why not? If rates rise, even short-term bond funds will see their NAVs drop. Put this investor, instead, into the money market. She'll earn relatively low rates of interest compared to long-term corporate and junk bonds, but that's okay. She'll also be able to cut checks against the value of her money market mutual fund investment, where the share price is magically maintained at $1.

The most *illiquid* investment would be a limited partnership (DPP). Generally, the more complex and innovative the investment, the less liquid it is. Variable life settlements, and even CMOs, do not have highly liquid markets, meaning you might not be able to sell at all, or sell at a decent price. Thinly traded securities (some municipal bonds, OTC Bulletin Board stocks) also present more liquidity risk simply because there aren't as many buyers creating demand for the securities. So, "How soon might you need to access this money?" is a real good question to ask before deciding whether to put somebody into a money market mutual fund or a long-term bond fund. Note that FINRA rules on suitability say that you can't recommend investments unless the customer has provided financial information to you, unless you're just talking about money market mutual funds.

INVESTMENT RISKS

One of the best ways to understand investment risks is to read through the first pages of several different mutual fund prospectuses. I'm looking at the prospectus for a growth fund right now, which declares that its investment goal is "growth of capital." It then says that "dividend income, if any, will be incidental to this goal." In other words, the fund invests in growth stocks but some companies that are expected to grow will also pay dividends and this fund is not too proud to cash the check. The "principal strategy" tells me that the fund focuses on companies with $5 billion or more of market value (mid- or large cap, depending on whom you talk to) and uses fundamental analysis to determine which companies show strength in terms of EPS, revenue, profit margins, etc. The next section is called "important risks," and this prospectus lists investment risks such as:

> Stock market risk, or the risk that the price of securities held by the Fund will fall due to various conditions or circumstances which may be unpredictable

The exam might refer to the above "stock market risk" as **market risk** or **systematic risk**. In any case, market/systematic risk is the risk that an investment will lose its value due to an overall market decline. As the prospectus says, the circumstances may be unpredictable. For example, no one can predict the next war or where the next tsunami or hurricane will hit, but when events like that take place, they can have a devastating effect on the overall stock market. Whether they panic because of war, weather, interest rate hikes, inflation, etc., the fact is that when sellers panic, stock prices plummet. The test might bring up the fact that market risk or "systematic risk" is measured by the beta coefficient. The "beta" shows how volatile a particular stock is compared to the S&P 500, which measures the overall market. A beta of .6 means that when the market goes up or down, this stock only moves 60% as much. A beta of 1.5 means that when the market moves, this stock jumps 1.5 times as much. So, a beta of less than 1 means the stock is less volatile than the market, while a beta of more than 1 means the stock is more volatile than the overall market. And, of course, the overall market is already plenty freaking volatile.

What can an investor do to combat market or "systematic" risk? Bet *against* the market. That's right—buy puts on NASDAQ 100 or the S&P 500. Or, use the ETFs that track those indices and sell the suckers short. Now, if the market rises, your stocks make money. And, if the market drops, your little side-bet makes money. To bet the other way, remember, is called "hedging." If you own Microsoft common stock, you can buy puts on Microsoft or sell covered calls to hedge your position. That would protect against "non-systematic risk," or the risk of one stock dropping. If you own a broad spectrum of the overall market, you can buy puts or sell calls on the S&P 500 index, or you can sell Spiders short to profit from the possible market decline in order to protect against market or systematic risk.

And you thought the Series 7 was going to be boring!

Basically, any risk that can affect the overall market can be called "systematic." So, the following risks can be safely placed in this category: interest rate risk, inflation risk, stock market risk. On the other hand, there are risks that affect a particular security as opposed to the overall market. This type of risk is called **non-systematic.** For example, buying stock in any company presents **business risk.** Business risk would be exemplified by the risk of competition or the risk that the company is getting into VHS right as DVDs are taking off. The risk of poor management (which we Krispy Kreme shareholders are still trying to recover from), of better competitors, or of products/services becoming obsolete are all part of business risk. The exam might also equate business risk with non-systematic risk, since it is company-specific.

My handy prospectus also mentions that "foreign securities carry additional risks including currency, natural event and political risk." Well said. See, the American business climate and financial markets are pretty darned dependable, especially when compared to, say, Libya. Of course, we might occasionally want to raise the bar a little bit, but you get the point. Remember that **political risk** is part of the package if you want to invest in emerging market funds. An emerging market by definition is in a country where the markets are still, you know, emerging. They're not fully developed, a little awkward, a little bit volatile, basically like teenagers—bright future, but some days you really aren't sure if they're going to make it. You could buy 1 million shares of a networking startup company headquartered in Baghdad. That would certainly be a growth opportunity where everybody's talking about "getting in on the ground floor." Trouble is, the political insurgents in Iraq may turn that ground floor into a pile of rubble, and if the rebels take over the country and nationalize all industry, those 1 million shares might not be worth the paper they're printed on. Also, since most countries use a different currency from the American dollar, **foreign exchange risk** is also part of the package. The value of the American dollar relative to foreign currencies, in other words, is a risk to international and emerging markets investors. So, even if it's a developed market, such as Japan, if you're investing internationally into Japanese stocks, the value of the yen versus the dollar presents foreign exchange or currency risk. The natural event risk is fairly self-explanatory, as it refers to the fact that a tsunami, earthquake, hurricane, etc., could have a devastating effect on a country's economy, possibly the economy of an entire area such as Europe or Southeast Asia.

Marketability or liquidity has to do with the ability to sell an investment quickly and at a fair price. Money market securities are easy to buy and sell at a fair price; municipal bonds, DPPs (limited partnerships), hedge funds, and thinly traded stocks are not. How much money could you make on your house if you had to sell it today? Might have to drop your asking price pretty severely, unless there were, like, 10 buyers pounding on your door for an opportunity to put in a bid, right? So, thinly traded securities have **liquidity risk** or **marketability risk** compared to securities with more active secondary markets.

Legislative or **regulatory risk** means that if laws change, certain companies could be greatly affected. Suddenly, Microsoft® has to give away its operating systems for free. Ouch. That would certainly impact the stock price, right? Or, what if an investor bought a bunch of dividend-paying stocks in order to reap the rewards of a Republican-inspired lower tax rate on dividends, only to see a Democrat take office and rescind the tax rate?

Hate it when that happens.

So, to review, the following risks are specific to particular securities and are, therefore, referred to as non-systematic risk: business risk, political risk, currency exchange risk, marketability or liquidity risk, and legislative/regulatory risk.

RISKS TO BONDHOLDERS

This section is a review of what I presented in the chapter Debt Securities, but I felt it would not hurt for you to see it twice. Investing in bonds is inherently less frightening than investing in stocks, as mutual fund prospectuses will list as an accepted assumption. For example, the prospectus I'm reading right now says that the growth fund might be suitable if you "can accept the risks of investing in a portfolio of common stocks." See? It's like one of Jefferson's self-evident truths—stocks are inherently more volatile than bonds. Of course, there are still many risks involved with bond investing. Since the prospectus for this "growth fund" brings up the fact that the fund also invests in fixed-income securities, naturally it has to disclose the risks that fixed-income securities present. For example:

> The value of any fixed-income security held by the Fund is likely to decline when interest rates rise

What the prospectus is talking about is called **interest rate risk**, which is the risk that rates will suddenly shoot up, sending the market price of your bond down. The longer the term on the bond, the more volatile its price. When rates go up, all bond prices fall, but the long-term bonds suffer the most. And, when rates go down, all bond prices rise, but the long-term bonds go up the most. So, a 30-year government bond has no default risk, but carries more interest rate risk than a 10-year corporate bond. As we'll mention later, "duration" is how we measure a bond's price volatility given a small change in interest rates.

Bet you can't wait. In any case, the reason we see short-term and intermediate-term bond funds is because many investors want to reduce interest rate risk. Maybe they have a shorter time horizon and will need this money in just a few years—they can't risk a huge drop in NAV due to a sudden rise in long-term interest rates. They will probably sacrifice the higher yield offered by a long-term bond fund, but they will sleep better knowing that rising rates won't be quite as devastating to short-term bonds.

The prospectus I'm looking at actually covers several of the family's funds. In the bond fund prospectus, we see that the important risks include:

> Risk that the value of the securities the Fund holds will fall as a result of changes in interest rates, an issuer's actual or perceived creditworthiness or an issuer's ability to meet its obligations

The first part of that statement is the interest rate risk we just discussed. The second part has to do with **credit/default risk**. What if S&P and Moody's decide to downgrade the bond ratings? Hate it when that happens, and so does this mutual fund. Unfortunately, neither of us has figured out how to prevent it. Notice how they separate the "perceived" from the "actual" creditworthiness—in other words, if the markets perceive the bonds as shaky, their price will plummet whether the company ever misses an interest or principal payment. And, if the issuer actually *does* discover they, like, can't pay you, that would also tend to be a problem. Of course, U.S. Treasury securities have no default risk, but some municipal securities and most corporate bonds carry default/credit risk to a certain degree.

The bond fund prospectus then writes, "**call risk**, or the risk that a bond might be called during a period of declining interest rates." Most municipal and corporate bonds are callable, meaning that when interest rates drop, the issuer will get tired of paying you the higher fixed rate they started out paying. Just like a homeowner refinancing from a 9% to a 6% mortgage, corporate and municipal bond issuers will borrow new money at the lower rate and use it to pay you off much sooner than you expected. First, your bond price stops rising in the secondary market once everyone knows the *exact* call price that will be received. Second, what do you do with the par value they give you? Reinvest it, right? And, where are interest rates now? Down—so you probably take the proceeds from a 9% bond and turn it into a 6% payment going forward. Hmm—you used to get $90 per year; now you can look forward to $60. Couldn't you protect yourself by buying non-callable bonds? Sure—and they'll offer you lower rates than callable.

Purchasing power risk has to do with inflation. If inflation erodes the value of money, an investor's return simply ain't worth what it used to be. Fixed-income investments carry purchasing power risk, which is why investors often try to beat inflation by investing in common stock. The ride might be a wild one, but the reward is that we should be able to grow faster than the rate of inflation; whereas, a fixed-income payment is, well, fixed, even when inflation rises. Note that high inflation does not *help* stocks. It's just that in a period of high inflation, stock will probably perform better than fixed-income securities. So, during an expansion, where inflation tends to rise, you're better off in equities/stock. During a period of decline/contraction, bonds are the place to be, since their price will rise as interest rates fall due to the cooling demand for money/capital.

Remember that bonds paying regular interest checks force investors to reinvest into new bonds every few months or so. What kind of rates/yields will debt securities be offering when they go to reinvest the coupon payments?

Nobody knows, which is why it's a risk. In other words, it's very annoying to take a 9% interest payment and reinvest it at 3%, but it does happen. To avoid reinvestment risk buy a debt security that gives you nothing to reinvest along the way—zero coupons, i.e. Treasury STRIPS.

Notice how bondholders can get hit comin' or goin'. If it's a corporate bond—and even some municipal securities—you could end up getting stiffed (default risk). If rates go up, the price of your bond gets knocked down (interest rate risk). If rates go down, callable bonds are called (call risk), and the party's over, plus you have to reinvest the proceeds at a lower rate than you were getting (reinvestment risk). And, even if none of the above calamities strikes, inflation could inch its way up, making those coupon payments less and less valuable (purchasing power risk).

Oh well. If you want fixed income, you take on these risks to varying degrees, depending on which bond you buy and when you buy it.

PRACTICE

1. **Which of the following would be of least interest to a technical analyst?**

   A.   advance/decline line

   B.   historical prices

   C.   daily trading volumes

   D.   P/E ratio

2. **A fundamental analyst would be concerned with all of the following except**

    A. current ratio

    B. working capital

    C. income statements

    D. open short positions

3. **XXR common stock has a dividend payout ratio of 40%, EPS of $3.00 and a P/E ratio of 12. What is the market price of XXR common stock?**

    A. $12

    B. $20

    C. $36

    D. $15

4. **RRT Corp. had Net Income of $10,000,000 last year. After the company pays $1,000,000 in preferred dividends, an owner of one of the company's 1,000,000 common shares would notice an EPS of**

    A. $10

    B. $9

    C. $3.33

    D. $5

5. **When a company issues long-term convertible debentures, all of the following are affected except**

    A. current assets

    B. accounts payable

    C. total assets

    D. working capital

6. **Where would an investor go to determine if a change in accounting methods has had a material effect on a company's reported earnings?**

    A. statement of cash flows

    B. footnotes

    C. corporate charter

    D. CNBC

7.   A company's net profit margin is

A.   higher than its gross margin

B.   always the same as its gross margin

C.   net income divided by revenues

D.   net income divided by interest expense

8.   A company's gross margin would include revenue and

A.   bond interest

B.   federal taxes

C.   cost of goods sold

D.   paid-in surplus

9.   The theoretical liquidation value of a share of common stock is known as the

A.   liquidation ratio

B.   book value

C.   par value

D.   market value

ANSWERS

1.   **D,** if it has to do with the company in any way, it's not a concern for technical analysts. They only care about stock prices and what other traders are doing: volume, advance/decline, support/resistance.

2.   **D,** the fundamental analyst doesn't care whose shorts are open. He/she cares about companies and industries—not traders.

3.   **C,** P/E just means "price to earnings." If the price is 12 times the earnings, the price of the stock must be 12 x $3, or $36.

4.   **B,** EPS is simply "earnings available to common" divided by the number of outstanding shares. After paying the preferred dividend, the pie would be worth $9,000,000 cut into 1,000,000 slices. Each slice of equity is worth $9 in earnings.

5.   **B,** if you issue securities, you sell them for cash, which affects current assets, total assets, and

working capital right there. How would that affect "accounts payable"? It wouldn't. Those are the bills the company owes their suppliers.

6. **B,** footnotes explain things that will affect how someone might read and understand the numbers presented in a quarterly or annual report.

7. **C,** like most fancy-sounding terms, net margin is simpler than it sounds. It just means, "how much are you left with on the bottom line compared to what you started with on the top line?"

8. **C,** revenue – cost of goods sold = gross "profit." Divide that by the revenue to get "gross profit margin."

9. **B,** sure hope all those assets are listed accurately on the balance sheet.

CHAPTER 13

Customers & Brokerage Procedures

OPENING ACCOUNTS

You have heard their names on TV or seen them in elaborate print advertisements in magazines: Morgan Stanley, Charles Schwab, TD Ameritrade, E-trade, Goldman Sachs, Fidelity, etc. Maybe you've seen branch offices for such firms at the mall, or on one of the floors at your office building. What is happening inside these offices? Customers are investing in the stocks, bonds, and mutual funds that we have looked at in earlier chapters. Maybe the customer was pulled in by an advertisement. Maybe she was recommended by a friend. Maybe the customer was simply buying a three-hundred-dollar pair of pumps at Nordstrom and happened to see the broker-dealer's sign on the door on her way to Starbucks. Whatever pulled her toward the front door, your job is to get her to sign up for a new account.

NEW ACCOUNT FORM

You, the registered representative, will fill out the new account form (card), often over the telephone. You should obtain the following information from the new customer:

- Full name and address
- Home and work phone numbers
- Social security or Tax ID number
- Employer, occupation, employer's address
- Net worth
- Investment objectives (speculation, growth, income, growth & income, preservation)
- Estimated annual income
- Bank/brokerage firm reference
- Whether employed by a bank or broker-dealer
- Third-party trading authorization (if any)
- Citizenship (doesn't have to be an American)
- Whether the customer is of legal age (not a minor child)

- How account was obtained (referring broker-dealer, investment adviser)
- Whether client is an officer, director, or 10% shareholder of a publicly traded company

As a registered representative for a broker-dealer, you are supervised by **principals**, people who have passed not only their Series 7 but also their Series 24, 9/10, what have you. The principal has sign-off power over all kinds of important stuff. One thing a principal must always sign off on is a new account. So, the registered representative signs the new account form, and the principal/branch manager signs it too. Believe it or not, there is no rule that says the customer has to sign it. And, of course, that statement is always true except when it isn't. What we mean is that the customer can open a **cash account** without signing the new account form, but if she's opening a **margin account** or wants to trade options, she will have to sign it. Now, even though the customer does not have to sign the new account form for a pay-as-you-go cash account, she does need to verify that the information recorded is accurate, and she must sign that acknowledgment. Remember that the firm needs to send the customer a *copy* of the new account form (new account card) within 30 days of opening the account and within 30 days of any major change in the information. Every 36 months the firm must verify the customer's information, too. Why? Making suitable recommendations to clients is your main job. If you're looking at customer information that is no longer accurate, your recommendations will most likely be unsuitable. For example, one of your customers used to trade a lot of speculative stocks because he owned a seat on the Chicago Board of Trade and had an annual income of just under $2 million. Turns out, the guy went bust last year, had his 70-foot yacht repossessed, did a short sale on a high-rise condominium, and is now living in his mommy's basement in Western Springs. So, if you're still recommending high-risk securities to this guy, you're probably making unsuitable recommendations. As we'll see in a later chapter, unsuitable recommendations frequently lead to fines and suspensions from FINRA, and customers have been known to recover the money they lost by filing an arbitration claim. So, as the NYSE has been saying for centuries, the first rule for the registered representative is to "know thy customer." Since customers' situations change frequently, you and your firm need to keep up with the changes.

The Series 7 will likely ask you some questions based on the bullet list above. For example, can the customer list only a PO Box? No, and this is tricky so pay attention. Even though your firm can send correspondence to the customer's PO Box—account statements, proxy statements, trade confirmations—your firm still needs to get a residential/street address from the customer. What if the customer refuses to provide a social security or other tax ID number? First of all, good luck getting any further cooperation from this guy, and, secondly, notify him that the IRS is going to demand that a certain percentage of any interest, dividends, or capital gains will have to be withheld by the broker-dealer—known as a **backup withholding.** Yes, if the customer sells 1,000 shares of ABC for a profit, he won't be able to pull all of it out in cash at this time; rather, a percentage will go to your friends and mine at the IRS.

Believe it or not, even in today's climate, customers can actually open **numbered accounts.** Now, this does not mean that the customer remains anonymous. Rather, it means that the customer does not want a lot of people at the firm talking about his or her financial business. So, instead of titling the account *Sandra Bullock,* the firm can assign the account a number. Ms. Bullock would need to sign a written statement acknowledging that she owns the account identified only with a number, and your firm must keep that on file. And, you would still get all the information listed in the above bullet points. It's just that Ms. Bullock can now have, say, a $10 million investment account and execute large buy and sell orders without everybody at the broker-dealer asking each other if they saw how much money "Sandra" is making on index options this week. Whether an account is identified by a name or a number, remember that account information is considered confidential. This is the customer's personal business, and you know how touchy some folks get over financial matters. So, the information you obtain on a customer can only be released with the customer's written permission, or if there is a legal requirement to turn it over—the SEC, FINRA, a divorce or probate court, or your state regulator, for example, have subpoenaed the information. But, if somebody calls up claiming to be Sandra's fiancée and just wants to know how much dividend income Sandra should expect this month, do not release any information to him.

Believe it or not, sometimes customers end up losing money by following the recommendations of their registered representatives. Sometimes, the customer assumes the rep was not at fault. Other times, this being America, the customer demands her money back. FINRA has a system in place to handle such disputes, called **arbitration.** Members of the securities industry are automatically required to use arbitration to handle disputes between firms or between registered representatives and their employing broker-dealers. But a customer only has to use arbitration if she has signed a **pre-dispute arbitration agreement.** If your firm somehow failed to get her signature on that agreement, the customer would be free to sue you and your firm in civil court, where her attorneys could keep filing appeal after appeal until you cry uncle. To avoid the lengthy and expensive process of civil court, broker-dealers use arbitration—much as Major League Baseball does. The pre-dispute clause has to make it clear that the customer generally gets only one attempt at arbitration—no appeals—and that the arbitrators do not have to explain their decisions, and that many of them come from the industry. So, if she loses, say, $100,000 following her registered representative's recommendations, the arbitrators could decide a whole range of outcomes. Maybe she gets $100,000, maybe she shares half the blame and gets $50,000. Maybe she gets nothing at all, and the arbitrators won't even explain why they decided against her. You can probably see why this arbitration thing needs to be clearly explained before the firm tries to hold the customer to the process by signing on the dotted line.

Finally, if the test asks about the customer's educational background, remember that it is not relevant. Educated people frequently do the dumbest things with their money, and high school dropouts have been known to make money in the market even as all the MBAs, CFAs, and CFPs consistently lose their shirts. So, you won't have to ask for the customer's educational level or record it on the new account form.

INSTRUCTIONS FOR SECURITIES, CASH, MAIL

Securities

When a customer buys securities, somebody has to hold them. There are three basic ways this can happen:

- Transfer and ship
- Transfer and hold in safekeeping
- Hold in street name

Maybe Grandma wants to put the cute, colorful Disney stock certificates right over the baby crib in the spare bedroom. If so, she'll request that you register the certificates in her name and ship them—**transfer and ship**. I, myself, don't want the responsibility of protecting the certificates from damage or misplacement. I mean, I could get them re-issued by the transfer agent if I lost them, but that's a pain in the neck, and there will be fees involved. So, rather than having the securities shipped, I could have the broker-dealer transfer the securities into my name and then hold them in the firm's vault (**transfer and hold**). The firm would likely charge a fee to do that. So, what I actually do is what most customers do these days—have the broker-dealer hold the securities in **street name.** The exam might say that the firm in this case is the "nominal owner" and the customer is the "beneficial owner" of the securities. However we phrase it, the fact is that most customers these days have never seen a stock or bond certificate because their broker-dealer holds them in street name (name of the firm) and may actually have them on deposit at centralized "depositories" such as the Depository Trust Company. From there, the securities are transferred through book/journal entries only, which explains why many registered representatives have also never seen a stock or bond certificate. It also explains why good record keeping is such a concern for your firm's principals, and their friendly-but-fastidious regulators known as FINRA.

Cash

Stocks have been known to pay dividends. Bonds and money-market securities pay interest to the account. So, if the securities are held in street name by the broker-dealer, the customer needs to indicate whether the firm should credit her account or send a check. Also, customers will sell securities from time to time, so the customer needs to indicate what should be done with the cash in the account. It can be "swept" into a money-market account (usually a government/Treasury money market account for ultimate safety and horrible yields). Alternatively, the cash can be sent to the customer, or it can simply be credited to her cash balance until she decides how to reinvest the proceeds into more securities.

Mail

The firm will be sending the customer monthly or (at least) quarterly **account statements** confirming the positions in the account and the value of the securities and the cash. Also, any time the customer buys or sells, a **trade confirmation** (sort of like an invoice) will be mailed to the customer's address of record. These days, statements and confirmations are often sent by email, but a customer would have to sign off on this method, which is much faster and cheaper for the firm to use. Confirmations and statements have to be sent to the customer, unless the customer has instructed the firm in writing to send them elsewhere, e.g., his financial planner/investment adviser. If a customer will be traveling, she can send a written request to the firm to hold her mail while she is away. If traveling domestically, mail can be held for 2 months; if traveling abroad, 3 months. Now, just in case you fall prey to that awful Series 7 panic mode, please note that the broker-dealer does not, like, stop by the client's house, open her mailbox and bring all her magazines, junk mail, etc., to the firm. I'm merely saying that instead of mailing out a trade confirmation, account statement, proxy statement, or annual report, the firm can hold that material as described.

TYPES OF ACCOUNTS

There are five basic types of customer accounts:

- Individual
- Joint
- Corporate
- Partnership
- Third party/fiduciary

INDIVIDUAL ACCOUNTS

If an individual opens an account, the firm will only take orders from that individual. Not his wife, or his secretary, or even his bowling buddy—only the individual. Surprisingly enough, we call these **individual accounts**. The only way you'll take buy or sell orders from somebody other than the individual is if the individual has granted 3rd-party **trading authorization** or "**power of attorney**" to someone else and you have that on file. The first account you opened for Michelle Madsen was an individual account, and you would only take orders from Michelle on that one. If she later gets remarried and wants her husband to put in trades on her behalf, you can do that, but only after she grants him trading authorization in writing.

A special type of individual account is called the **transfer on death (TOD) account.** Maybe a grandmother wants to use the account while she's alive but then transfer the assets to her grandson upon her death. If so, she opens the individual account as "TOD," and then when she meets her maker, the assets will bypass the probate court process and go directly to the named beneficiary. Notice how I didn't say that estate taxes are avoided—a TOD account makes the transfer of assets faster and simpler, but if the deceased person's estate is of a certain amount, the estate will be liable for estate taxes. Grandma in this example can also change the beneficiary whenever she feels like it. And—in case you're really nervous at the testing center—only the assets in the brokerage account transfer upon death. In other words, Grandma's house and Ferrari are not assets held by the broker-dealer. Finally remember that there might be two people involved on a TOD account, but this is not a joint account, which is explained in the paragraph immediately below this one.

JOINT ACCOUNTS

Two or more adults can open a joint account. If two (or more) individuals want to share an account, they will open it either as JTWROS or JTIC. JTWROS stands for **joint tenants with rights of survivorship**. "Rights of survivorship" means that the survivor gets the assets if the other party dies. They go straight to the surviving owner(s), bypassing probate, should the exam try to get all legalistic on you.

A **joint tenants in common** account is a little different. Here the assets are split according to the customers' instructions. Michelle Madsen, for example, and her sister Christina recently set up a joint account as "**tenants in common.**" If Christina dies, then her share of the assets goes to her estate rather than directly to Michelle, and vice versa. If Michelle gets married again, she may decide to open a JTWROS account with her husband. That way, if he turns out to be another abusive jerk who dies in a bizarre gardening accident, all the assets will pass directly to Michelle.

If it's a joint account, orders will be accepted from any party listed on the account. Mail can be sent to either party. But if you're talking about cutting a check, the check has to be made out to all names on the account. You wouldn't cut a check, for example, to Michelle Madsen and remind her to settle up with Christina next time she sees her. The check would be made out to, "Michelle Madsen and Christina Madsen, Joint Tenants in Common." The securities would be registered in more than one name, so all parties would have to sign the certificates or stock powers when transferring ownership.

Even though there are two or more customers sharing this account, remember that there is only one account number, and only one social security or tax ID number used for tax reporting.

CORPORATE ACCOUNTS

Businesses also open investment accounts. If it's a corporation, the registered rep needs to look at the **corporate resolution** to verify which parties have the authority to trade and withdraw assets from the account. Why? Well, you'd feel mighty silly if some disgruntled employee managed to open an account through you in the name of a corporation, fund it with a forged check, and then pull out, say, $300,000 before any of the authorized persons at the corporation found out what's going on. Right? So, make sure that these people are actually authorized to do business in the name of the corporation, and that the corporation actually, you know, exists. The officers of the corporation who have authority to transact business must sign a "certificate of incumbency" within 60 days, and your firm needs to keep that on file. If a corporation wants to trade on margin, you need to look at their **corporate charter** to see if that's allowed.

PARTNERSHIP ACCOUNTS

We talked about partnerships in the exciting DPP chapter. If you open an investment account for a partnership, you need to obtain information about each partner and get each partner's signature whenever a signature is required. You also need to obtain a partnership agreement, stating which partner(s) may enter orders. If the partnership wants to trade on margin, you'll need to make sure it's allowed by the partnership agreement.

THIRD PARTY/FIDUCIARY ACCOUNTS

Then there are accounts where somebody manages the assets for the benefit of somebody else. These are known as **fiduciary accounts**, which is a fancy term meaning, basically, that somebody manages the assets for the benefit of somebody else. Or, we can call them **third party accounts**, since a third party manages the assets on behalf of someone else. Generally, you'll have to verify that the fiduciary has the authority to manage the account. They will either have "full power of attorney" or "limited power of attorney." Limited power of attorney allows them to enter buy and sell orders. Full power of attorney allows them to have cash and/or securities withdrawn from the account. The fiduciary always has to act solely for the benefit of the other party. They can charge reasonable expenses to administer the account, as banks obviously didn't set up those giant trust departments purely for philanthropic purposes. And if a fiduciary does not follow **prudent investor standards** or is using the account to, say, make little loans to his various side businesses, the beneficiaries of the account have legal grounds to sue.

Trust Account

Let's start with the trust account. If you're a movie buff, perhaps you remember that Orson Welles' character in *Citizen Kane* was set up with a fat trust account early on, which largely explained why he later said, "It might be fun to own a newspaper." Of course, not all trust accounts are for budding millionaires, but I sure as heck never had one when I was growing up and didn't know anyone else who did. Later, I started attending Grateful Dead concerts during that foggy period known as "college," which is when I met hundreds of trust fund hippies selling cucumber and granola sandwiches from the back of Mommy and Daddy's spare Beemer. In any case, in a trust account, a trustee is managing the assets for the benefit of a third party. The rep needs to look at a copy of the trust agreement to make sure the trustee actually has the authority to manage the account and what limitations have been placed on the trustee's authority. For example, the grantor who funded the trust might have stipulations against options trading, or buying penny stocks. A trust account also will only be set up as a margin account if the trust agreement specifically permits such foolishness.

UGMA/UTMA Accounts

A minor child is not considered a "legal person," as you'll see when preparing for that nasty little exam that comes next: the Series 63 or Series 66. That means that a minor cannot open up an investment account, so an adult opens an account for the benefit of the child. When the child becomes an adult, the assets will be re-registered to the new adult, but until then we'll have an adult custodian manage the account. If a donor wants to donate money for the benefit of a minor, all she has to do is set the account up as either an UGMA or UTMA (depending on the state) account, which doesn't require any supporting documentation. The rep just opens it as either UGMA or UTMA, making sure there's just one adult custodian and one minor child per account. That's highly testable. If you see "Michelle and Javier Madsen as custodians for....," stop right there. You can't have two adults as custodians. And you can't have more than one minor child per account. You also can't have a corporation or a partnership acting as the custodian—only an adult human being can serve in that role. A proper title for an UTMA account would look something like this:

Michelle Madsen, Custodian F.B.O. Alicia Rodriguez under California's Uniform Transfers to Minors Act

F.B.O. means "for benefit of." If you've ever done a direct rollover from a 401(k) to another plan, the check they cut named the new custodian followed by "F.B.O." and then your name.

The gifts cannot be taken back once given, even if the child turns out to be an underachieving little brat. In other words, the gifts are all "irrevocable and indefeasible." The "indefeasible" part means you cannot treat the gift you make as a loan the child will someday pay back. It's a gift. We used the word "defeased" in the chapter Municipal Securities when the issuer was paying off a bond issue through an advance refunding. And if you remembered that before I just reminded you, I really like your chances on this exam.

These accounts cannot be opened as margin accounts and states may have lists of allowable investments for UGMA/UTMA accounts. Since Michelle's niece won't be needing the money for, say, eight years, surely she can sort of "borrow" from the account from time to time as needed, as long as she repays her, right?

Sure, as long as she doesn't get caught. Remember, these accounts receive special tax consideration, so if she's pretending the account is an UTMA account, but actually uses it to get interest-free loans, well, the IRS might start talking about tax fraud, back taxes, penalties-plus-interest, and various other phrases that no one ever wants to hear from the Internal Revenue Service. Some students get confused when asked if securities could be sold to cover an 11-year-old's attendance at a summer music camp. Of course—this account is for the benefit of the minor. Just make sure the custodian isn't enriching herself or taking back gifts. The exam may point out that it is the minor's social security number listed on the account, and that after a certain amount, the income is taxable. Use the parents' tax bracket until the kid is 14; after that, use the child's tax bracket.

For "UTMA" just remember that the "T" stands for "transfer." Under the Uniform Transfer to Minors Act, the transfer of assets can be pushed back to as late as 25 years of age. Maybe you want the kid to get his master's degree before you re-register the account in his name. Or maybe you just oppose giving 19-year-olds an account worth $1.1 million on general principles. Most states are UGMA, some are UTMA.

Finally, if the minor child dies, the assets do not pass to the custodian, the donor, or the parents. They pass to the minor's estate, should the exam be in a morbid mood the day you take it.

Guardian Account

As much as we wish it weren't so, parents do die or become incapable of raising their children. If the parents are unable to care for their children, a court will appoint an adult as guardian. You may open a guardian account, as long as the guardian provides a court appointment no more than 60 days old. If the court appointment is older than that, you'll need a new one before opening the account. A guardian (a.k.a. conservator) account is also used when an adult is declared mentally incompetent by a court of law.

Estate Account

The executor or administrator of an estate may open an investment account. If so, you'll need a copy of the will and the court appointment (letters of office). You'll also need a copy of the death certificate. The court appointment naming the executor/administrator must be no more than 60 days old. Estate accounts are, generally, only open for a few months, maybe two years. T-bills and other money market securities are the usual recommendation for such accounts. Michelle is named as executor in her grandmother's will, so when her grandmother passes away, Michelle may need to open an account in the name of the estate. The account would have its own tax ID number, just like a corporation or other legal entity, and might be registered as:

Michelle Madsen Independent Executor for the Estate of Rosalie M. Madsen

Discretionary Account

The registered rep might be appointed as a third party manager. We call these discretionary accounts because buying and selling decisions will be up to the registered representative's and the firm's discretion. That means if the registered representative wants to buy 1,000 shares of MSFT for the customer's account, he can do so without even bothering to call the customer. The customer would have to sign a trading authorization form to make the account "discretionary," and the account would be reviewed more frequently, but that's about it. From then on, the registered rep and the firm can choose any of the following three A's:

Action
Asset
Amount

That means they can choose whether to buy or sell, what to buy or sell, and how much to buy or sell without contacting the customer. Without discretionary authority a registered rep can never determine any of the three A's. Unless the account is a discretionary account, the only thing a rep can determine is the time or price at which to execute a transaction. So, if a client calls you up and says, "Buy me some computer chip manufacturers today," do you need discretionary authority before you buy 100 shares of Intel?

You bet. If you choose the asset, that constitutes discretion.

If a client calls up and says, "Pick up 1,000 shares of INTC today," do you need discretion? No, your client has chosen the asset (INTC), the action (buy), and the amount (1,000 shares). Only thing left for you to decide is the best time and price to do it, and time/price does not equal discretion.

Each discretionary order ticket would be marked "discretionary," by the way, and a particular principal would be assigned to make sure the securities purchased are appropriate and that the rep isn't churning in order to win the big trip to Hawaii. If a registered representative purchases unsuitable investments for a discretionary account, it's not just a bad idea—it's a violation of FINRA rules. Just this morning, I read that the regulators recently imposed a censure and a 6-month bar on a registered representative who misused his discretionary authority over an account. FINRA reminds firms that in a discretionary account before purchasing certain complex and/or high-risk securities, the firm may need to get the customer's written approval before entering the transaction. Investments in hedge funds, distressed debt, equity-linked notes, CMOs, and other complex products would generally require a higher suitability obligation, and the firm should probably get the customer to sign a disclosure statement that they know how crazy the investment is and are okay with it anyway.

WRAP ACCOUNT

Some customers like to pay for an investment adviser to manage the account, usually as a percentage of the assets—1% is a fairly typical advisory fee. To cover the cost of portfolio management, custody of the assets, and execution of the trades, a **wrap fee** is often charged. A wrap fee is one fee covering all of these services and is more suitable for accounts that are frequently traded. Why? If there is a built-in fee for execution of trades, that fee would be a waste of money for a customers whose account only gets traded here and there throughout the year.

DEATH OF A CUSTOMER

What should you do if one of your clients dies?

1. Cancel all open orders
2. Mark the account "deceased"
3. Freeze the account
4. Await proper legal papers

The proper legal papers authorizing you to transfer or sell securities are:

- Letters testamentary
- Inheritance tax waivers
- Certified copy of death certificate

If it's a discretionary account, the discretion is immediately revoked/terminated. If it's an UGMA account (sad, but it happens, unfortunately), the exam may expect you to know that the assets are not immediately transferred to the child's parents. Rather, they become part of the child's estate. And, if it's a transfer on death (TOD) account, you do need to verify that the owner is actually, you know, dead.

ACCOUNTS FOR INDUSTRY PERSONNEL, IMMEDIATE FAMILY

The new account card asks if the customer, spouse, or the customer's minor child work for a broker-dealer. If so, the employer will be notified in writing. If the member firm belongs to the NYSE, permission to open the account is required. For MSRB and FINRA firms, notification is required before the firm opening the account can proceed. For NYSE and MSRB firms, duplicate trade confirmations will automatically be sent to the employer, but for FINRA firms, duplicates are sent only upon request from the employer.

Just to keep things nice and simple.

ACCOUNT TRANSFERS

Clients have been known to get huffy and transfer their account to another firm. This is generally done through something called an **ACAT**, which stands for **Automated Client Account Transfer**. The ACAT provides instructions to the broker-dealer for transfer and delivery. The firm receiving the request has one business day to validate the instructions or take exception to them. The following are the reasons that the firm might "take exception" to the transfer instructions:

- Customer's signature is invalid or missing
- Account title does not match the carrying firm's account number
- Social security number does not match
- Account number is wrong

Once the account and positions have been validated, the firm has three additional business days to complete the transfer. To avoid depriving you of FINRA's snappy prose, broker-dealers also need to be aware that:

> The receiving member and the carrying member must immediately establish fail-to-receive and fail-to-deliver contracts at then-current market values upon their respective books of account against the long/short positions that have not been delivered/received and the receiving/carrying member must debit/credit the related money

```
amount. The customer's security account assets shall thereupon be
deemed transferred.
```

In English, they're saying that at this point, both sides need to establish what has not been received or delivered in terms of money and securities, based on current market prices, and at that point the account is deemed to have been transferred, even if the carrying broker-dealer has to send cash and/or securities at a later date.

SIPC

I mentioned that my broker-dealer was holding my cash and securities. What if it turned out that they were on the brink of bankruptcy and started pledging my securities and draining my cash position to keep their creditors off their backs? If the firm went belly-up, the folks who now have my cash and/or securities aren't likely to let go of them.

Luckily, my accounts are covered by SIPC. Perhaps you've seen the little "SIPC" sign in the office of a broker-dealer? It stands for the Securities Investor Protection Corporation, a non-profit, industry-funded insurance company. It provides coverage of each customer account up to a total of $500,000, of which only $250,000 may be cash. So, if the investor has securities worth $200,000 and a cash position of $300,000, SIPC will cover all the securities but only $250,000 of the cash. Remember that commodities are not considered securities and are not covered. Mutual funds are held by the transfer agent, so if your broker-dealer fails, they weren't holding your mutual fund shares, anyway.

If a broker-dealer goes belly up, a trustee is appointed and on that day we value each account and cover each separate customer up to the full amount. A separate customer means a separate account title. So Michelle Madsen's individual account is covered up to 500K. Her JTIC account with her sister Christina is covered as a "separate customer." Her IRA is treated as a "separate customer." The UGMA she manages for her niece is covered separately. The only accounts that get combined are cash and margin accounts for the same person.

One of the most important points about SIPC is that it is *not* the same thing as the FDIC. In fact, at SIPC's website (www.sipc.org) there is a link under "Who We Are" called "Why We are NOT the FDIC." I could easily picture a test question related to the fact that securities investments are not protected by FDIC. You have probably seen that warning on the first page of most mutual fund prospectuses, too. FDIC insures bank deposits. When a bank also sells securities, they have to use disclaimers such as "No bank guarantee," "not FDIC insured," or "may lose value" so that customers understand just how far they have wandered from the safety and security of a bank deposit, CD, etc., even if they are in the same building.

BROKERAGE OFFICE PROCEDURES

SERVICING CUSTOMER ACCOUNTS

Other People's Money Counts

As much as I disparage the cheesy little memory joggers that Series 7 candidates use, some of these things are great. For example, to remember the four separate departments through which a customer order passes, in order, remember that "Other-People's-Money-Counts. That should help you remember that an order passes through the:

- Order Room
- Purchasing and Sales
- Margin
- Cashiering

When you, the registered rep, finally talk your customer into buying 10,000 shares of ABC, you will present the order for execution to the **order room**. Since everything needs at least two names on this exam, we also call this the "wire room" because the order is then wired to the appropriate exchange. Once the order has been executed, the order room forwards a confirmation or "execution report" back to you and also to the next department—purchasing & sales. After the order has been executed the "P&S" department inputs the transaction to the customer's account. The "P&S" department also mails (or emails) the trade confirmation to the customer, and that trade confirmation must be delivered no later than the settlement date, which is always T + 3 except when it isn't. **Purchasing and sales** is also responsible for billing. Now, you might think that something called the **margin department** would only handle transactions in margin accounts. No, that would make way too much sense. All transactions are sent through the margin department, whether for cash or margin accounts. The margin or "credit" department calculates the amount owed by the customer and the date the money is due. This department also calculates any money due to a customer. The **cashiering department** (**cashier**) processes all securities and payments delivered to the firm. This department also issues checks to customers. When the margin department issues a request, the cashiering department also forwards certificates (stocks, bonds) to the transfer agent. Basically, the cashiering department handles all receipts and distributions of cash and securities.

Another department that the test might bring up is the **reorganization department**, sometimes referred to Wall Street hipsters as "reorg." When a merger takes place, shareholders of, say, Gillette, have to replace their shares with a certain number of shares of Procter & Gamble. The reorganization department makes this switch. It also handles bond calls and tender offers.

We wrote that the registered representative presents an order to the order/wire room. He does so by filling out and submitting an **order ticket/trade ticket**. An order ticket would contain at least the following information:

- Account number
- Registered representative number
- Buy or Sell
- If a sell: long or short
- Stock or bond symbol
- Number of shares, bonds
- Exchange where security should be executed
- Special instructions (if any)
- Whether solicited, unsolicited, or discretionary

That last bullet item is a potential powder keg. See, some unscrupulous registered representatives have been known to place customer orders that no customer ever ordered. They do this by marking the order ticket "unsolicited" and pretending that the customer actually called in the order. I guess they're hoping the customer doesn't watch his account closely, but all it takes is one customer to notice a trade he never placed and suddenly the registered rep is being disciplined for executing unauthorized transactions. It is not uncommon for such a registered representative to be barred from any further association with any FINRA firm, as he probably should be. It's the Wall Street equivalent of spending your friend's money without his permission.

If you would like to view a "real world" trade ticket, we have one at www.passthe63.com/extra.

Finally, the exam might ask a question about what information a registered representative needs to maintain. If so, tell it that a registered representative must maintain a record of each individual client's current holdings and also a cross-indexed list of securities owned across the board with the names of clients and number of shares associated with it. So, he needs a list of which securities Joe Smith owns: MSFT, IBM, and ORCL. He also needs a cross-indexed list that shows, for example, MSFT and then who owns how many shares of that stock.

Customer Mail

A brokerage firm is a busy place to work. With registered representatives taking customer orders by telephone and/or reviewing the orders placed online, what are the odds that some of these transactions will end up getting hosed? Pretty high. That's why every trade has to be confirmed with the customer.

Trade Confirmations

Now, what would this industry call a document that confirms a trade? Would you believe, a **trade confirmation**? The confirmation below is one of my actual trade confirmations, exactly as it exists in the real world, except for the parts I like totally made up.

Account #	Transaction #	Capacity	Account Executive	
26597-5	006530698	Agent	GH	

Activity	Quantity	CUSIP	Price	Principal Amt.
Bought	10,000	3890227	$25.49	254,900.00

Trade Date	Settlement Date	Interest	Commission	Net Amount
04/22/2003	04/25/2003	N/A	$10.99	254,910.99

Symbol	Trade Description
LGTO	Legato Systems, Inc.

Notice how this document confirms the trade and tells the customer everything he needs to know about the transaction: the stock, the number of shares, the price of the stock, the commission, the total price paid or received on the transaction, etc. I basically just think of it as an invoice—a bill of sale; this is what we did for you, this is what it cost you, please keep this as a record of the transaction. Trade confirmations must be delivered no later than settlement, which is the completion of the transaction (T + 3 for stock, corporate bonds, and municipal bonds). Confirmations are often delivered by email these days, a much faster and cheaper method. Also, when we said that the firm can hold customer mail, this is one of the pieces of mail that might need to be held. Customers should also save their trade confirmations, to make it easier to report capital gains and losses each year, or to straighten out a sloppy broker-dealer who suddenly claims that you don't actually own 10,000 shares of IBM anymore. Oh yeah? Well here's my confirmation of the purchase—unless you guys have confirmation of a sale, guess what—I own 10,000 shares of IBM, as my attorneys will gladly explain to you.

Execution Errors

The registered rep has to check execution reports with order tickets. If the customer wanted to buy 1,000 shares of Cisco and ended up buying 1,000 shares of Sysco, well that's not what the customer ordered and is not, therefore, the customer's trade. The firm would have to eat that one. Likewise, if the customer had entered a buy-limit @30 but the firm accidentally bought the stock for more than $30 a share, the customer would not have to accept the transaction. Or, if she had ordered 100 shares but the firm bought 10,000 shares, those extra zeroes would not be her problem. Firms have to maintain an error account to keep track of and deal with, these errors that can and do occur.

A single customer might have several different accounts at the firm. Or, maybe the firm has 10 customers named Joe Smith. Whatever the case, sometimes a security is purchased for the wrong account. If so, the registered representative needs to talk to a principal. The principal can grant permission to **"cancel and re-bill"** the transaction, which means to simply put the transaction in the proper account and keep good notes.

Reporting Errors

So, an error in the execution of the trade is one thing. On the other hand, if the registered rep merely gives the customer a mistaken report when the firm, in fact, did exactly as instructed, that's just a mistaken report. If the customer's order was filled as instructed, it's the customer's trade. Even if the firm sent a trade confirmation that was erroneous, that confirmation can be fixed and re-sent. The customer doesn't get to walk away from the trade based on some minor technicality.

Account Statements

At the least, a broker-dealer has to send account statements to their customers quarterly. It would only be that infrequently if there had been no activity in the account. Since there is usually activity in the account, most account statements are sent monthly. If any of the following had occurred in the account during the month, a monthly statement would be sent:

- Purchases or sales of securities
- Dividend and/or interest received
- Addition or withdrawal of cash or securities
- Margin interest charged to a margin account (don't worry, that chapter's next)

The account statement shows:

- All positions in the account (for example a "1,000" next to "Abbott Labs" and the symbol "ABT" to remind me just how much I have riding on that company)
- All activity since the last statement (purchases, sales, interest and dividends received, etc.)
- All credit and debit balances (don't worry, margin accounts are coming up, as promised)

Account statements have to contain a message to customers asking them to verify the statement and promptly report any discrepancy or error that they notice. This way, unauthorized transactions or plain old mistakes can be spotted and fixed sooner. As in, I don't remember talking to anyone about buying 1,000 shares of XYZ—what's going on here? And, it also ties in with SIPC protection. Remember that a customer's account is protected based on their account balance as of the day the trustee is appointed. The customer will need to show his/her account balance, and it would be a really bad time to discover a major error *after* the broker-dealer had already gone belly up. *No, but I could have sworn I owned two hundred and fifty thousand dollars worth of ORCL* isn't going to cut it. FINRA tells broker-dealers that they must:

```
advise all new customers that they may obtain information about
SIPC, including the SIPC brochure, by contacting SIPC. Such members
also must provide SIPC's Web site address and telephone number.
Members must provide this disclosure to new customers, in writing,
at the opening of an account and also must provide customers with
the same information, in writing, at least once each year.
```

Proxies

Back in olden days small shareholders weren't likely to cast votes at the annual meeting, unless they happened to live near corporate headquarters. The Securities Exchange Act of 1934 covered a whole lot of ground, and part of the ground covered had to do with public corporations/issuers letting shareholders vote by proxy. This way, I don't have to travel from Chicago to Redwood Shores, California, just to throw in my two cents about Oracle's employee stock incentive plan or Larry Ellison's desire to buy up yet another annoying rival. I can just fill out the little form I get from my broker-dealer and let them vote per my instructions. Usually these proxies go ahead and tell you how management thinks you should vote. I'm not saying they'd take me out back if I voted the wrong way. I just often figure the Board of Directors knows what they're doing and vote according to their recommendation. Of course, I can vote however I want with my insignificant number of shares. Or if I sign the proxy and fail to indicate how I want to cast my votes, then the board of directors/management of the company gets to use those votes as they see fit. If the matter is of no major importance, the broker-dealer can cast the votes on behalf of their customer, if the customer has failed to return the proxy at least 10 days prior to the annual meeting. A major issue, such as whether HP and Compaq should merge, would be a different matter. We're talking more like the decision to retain KPMG as the firm's auditor. The Act of '34 also requires public companies to report quarterly and annually. So, the broker-dealer will end up forwarding those reports as well as proxy materials to their customers, but they won't charge the customers. This stuff is all a cost that the issuer has to bear, ever since that embarrassing little fiasco known as the 1920s. Another name for a proxy is an "absentee ballot," just to make sure it also has at least two names.

Oh, and just in case you've been told that what you're learning only matters in the "test world" not the "real world," I attended the Northern Trust annual shareholders meeting in the spring of 2006. The very first item of business was that the Board of Directors planned to switch from cumulative to statutory voting. An angry shareholder stood up and tried to shame the board for taking away the power that minority shareholders have with cumulative voting. How he, himself, first got elected to a corporate board through cumulative voting, which—as the test wants you to know—provides a benefit to small/minority shareholders, who can pool all of their votes for just one candidate.

The board listened patiently to the impassioned plea of the pro–cumulative-voting shareholder, paused three seconds out of respect, and then promptly approved their plan to switch to statutory voting.

Why send in a proxy statement when you can attend such fascinating drama in person? Of course, the Northern Trust headquarters is just a 25-minute El ride for me—I'm not getting on one of those hideous four-hour West Coast flights just to cast a vote or attend the meeting for Oracle, Intuit, etc. With proxy voting, I don't have to.

Annual Reports

As we said, most broker-dealers hold customer securities in "street name," which is the name of the broker-dealer, for benefit of the customer. My stocks, for example, are registered to TD Ameritrade, FBO Robert Walker. Shareholders have to receive annual reports from the issuers whose securities they hold, and the issuing corporations will send the reports to the broker-dealer, who must be sure the customer receives them. I have a thick stack of annual reports next to my desk from issuers such as Starbucks, Oracle, and a couple of REITS. TD Ameritrade mailed me those reports, just as they mail me proxy materials, either by snail- or e-mail. Again, we mentioned that customers can request a mail hold when traveling. Such mail would include trade confirmations, account statements, proxies, and annual reports.

REG T

How long does a customer have to pay for stock?

Well, the trade settles between broker-dealers at T + 3, but the customer actually has five business days before he's required to pay for the stock. Payment is requested at T + 3; it's required at T + 5, or two business days after regular way settlement, whichever is easier for you to remember. On the third business day following the trade date, the buying broker-dealer sends the money to the selling broker-dealer regardless of what the customer does. If the customer still hasn't paid for the transaction two business days after that, the broker-dealer can either request a five day extension from their SRO, or just sell the stock that the other side has delivered to get whatever they can get for it. If they end up losing money on the deal, they'll hold the customer responsible for the loss. Either way, they'll **"freeze"** the account for 90 days, which just means the customer won't be able to pull this trick on them anytime soon. For 90 days, no purchase orders will be accepted unless the cash is already sitting in the account. And, if we're talking less than $1,000, that's chump change in this business so we don't have to freeze the account.

Also, a customer should really make payment for a security before selling it. So, if a customer buys securities and then sells them before making payment by the deadline, he can still get the money sent to him, but his account will be frozen for 90 days.

If the exam brings up the phrase **free credit balance,** remember that this is the amount of cash that belongs to the customer and can be requested at any time by the customer. When a sale of securities has settled, the proceeds are now part of the customer's "free credit balance." Broker-dealers may not delay the paying out of customers' free credit balances. Why would they want to? The unused cash in customer accounts is actually an asset of the broker-dealer, who earns interest on that cash. They might be tempted to hang onto that cash just a few days or weeks longer, but the regulators will not allow such nonsense.

DELIVERY OF SECURITIES

Customers have a longer time frame when it comes to delivering the securities they have sold through the broker-dealer. If you get a question on this, tell the exam that the customer has 10 business days from the settlement date to deliver the securities. If they fail to do so, the broker-dealer has to perform a "buy-in" of the securities, which means they have to buy the securities and deliver them to the other side. If they have to pay more than the trade was executed for, they're going to be ticked, and they can take the difference from their customer.

UNIFORM PRACTICE CODE

As boring as the nit-picky rules of baseball are, the game would descend into chaos if different teams could not agree on a common set of rules. No, you can't have 10 players this inning; no, you don't get four strikes this time. That's not uniform practice. There may be a designated hitter for one league and not the other, but after that everything is uniform, just as NYSE member firms used to do things slightly different from their NASD (now FINRA) counterparts. But, essentially, everybody was on the same page when it came to procedures involving customer confirmations, delivery of securities, endorsements/signatures, settlement dates, etc. FINRA's **Uniform Practice Code** does exactly what its name implies—it's the code that keeps the industry practices uniform among broker-dealers. So, we're not talking about conduct rules yet, where violations lead to sanctions and fines from FINRA. We're just talking about the uniform or standard way in which broker-dealers do business with each other.

SETTLEMENT

Broker-dealers place orders for their customers and then have to settle up with the other side. The Uniform Practice Code requires firms to send written confirmations to the other broker-dealer on the first business day following the trade/transaction. These dealer-to-dealer confirmations must contain an adequate description of the transaction to ensure that both sides know what each other is talking about. Sometimes there is a disagreement—the number of shares, the execution price, the existence of the trade itself—and if so, the broker-dealer receiving confirmation needs to send the other side a **DK (don't know) notice.** A DK notice means that the other broker-dealer thinks the transaction is erroneous. The firm can cancel the trade after notice to and approval from FINRA. In other words, there is a uniform way to handle trades that both sides do not recognize as legitimate.

Let's make sure you understand what we mean by "settlement/clearing" of a securities transaction. When a customer places a trade online to buy, say, 100 shares of ABC, a few seconds later the customer will see the position in his account. At this point, however, it's just data on a computer screen. Similarly, if he sells 1,000 shares of XYZ for $20,000, his computer screen will indicate that his cash balance just went up by $20,000. But, again, that is just data on a computer screen. What do I mean? I mean the transaction has not settled or cleared yet. The customer does not officially own those 100 shares of ABC until the trade has settled between the two sides. And, if the customer wants that $20,000 after selling the shares of XYZ, he'll have to wait until the transaction has cleared/settled. As you may recall, we were yakking away about "regular way" and "T + 3" way back in the Equity Securities chapter. For corporate and municipal securities regular way settlement is also T + 3. The Trade Date is the "T," so if you trade on Monday, the transaction settles on Thursday, assuming there are no holidays to mess it up. Watch out for that, by the way. If a trade occurs on, say, Friday, June 30th, the 4th of July is going to be a factor. For the exam, please remember that the 4th of July typically occurs on the fourth day of July. When Treasury securities (bills, notes, bonds, STRIPS) are traded, they settle next business day or "T + 1." That's always "regular way settlement," which means, surprisingly, that this is the regular way.

Of course, you can already see where this is headed—securities transactions always settle "regular way," except when they don't.

Cash Settlement

When you absolutely, positively must settle the trade *today*, some broker-dealers will arrange a "**cash settlement**" for you. A "cash settlement" settles "same day," meaning the day you buy it is the day that settlement occurs. Of course, you have to have the cashier's check, wire transfer, or suspicious brown bag of cash ready to go, and the seller has to have the securities available for delivery on the day of the trade. If the trade happens before 2:00 pm, it settles by 2:30 pm. If the trade happens after 2:00 pm, it settles within 30 minutes, which sounds like the same thing but really isn't.

Next Day

This one is tricky. For a next day settlement, would you believe the cash and securities have to be available by—get this—the next day?

Seller's Option

In case the exam hasn't met its quota of useless information, it may ask you about a **seller's option**. This is where the seller likes the price they can get today but—for whatever reason—won't be able to come up with the securities for a while. In this case the seller specifies the date on which they will be able to deliver the securities and may not deliver sooner than the fourth business day following the trade (I guess it would be T + 3 if it were any earlier, right?). If the seller specifies a certain date but ends up wanting to deliver the securities earlier, they have to give the buyer a one-day written notice of their intention.

Buyer's Option

The buyer could also specify the date when payment will be made for securities and accept delivery, which is pretty much the flip-flop of the seller's option.

RVP/DVP/COD

RVP stands for **Receipt Versus Payment.** Institutional investors—say a large trust or a corporation—often use this method of settlement whereby payment on the transaction is made when delivery of the securities is received and accepted. In this case, the customer has sold securities to a broker-dealer. When an institutional investor buys securities from a broker-dealer, **DVP** or **Delivery Versus Payment** is often used, meaning that payment will be made when the securities involved in the transaction are delivered and accepted. So, rather than talking about a certain number of days before settlement, RVP and DVP methods of settlement happen when the terms of this very particular settlement process are met.

GOOD DELIVERY

So, the buy side has to remit the funds to pay for the transaction. The sell side has to deliver the securities to the buy side. Remember that some customers still choose to have their securities "transferred and shipped." So when they sell stock, they have to deliver the certificates. Usually, it's the broker-dealer for the seller delivering the certificates, but, either way, if the stock or bond certificate is registered to Joe B. Kuhl, then it has to be signed exactly as: Joe B. Kuhl. Under no circumstances, can the customer sign the certificate *Joey Kuhl*, no matter how cool he may, in fact, be.

If a client forgets to endorse the certificate, should you put it back in the mail? No, just send her a **stock power** and have her sign that instead. If it's a bond, guess what you'd send her?

A bond power.

These are also known as **powers of substitution** because everything in the securities industry has to have at least three names. In any case, it's usually the power of substitution that gets signed, rather than having the customer sign the back of the stock or bond certificate. That way, if the customer messes up the signature, they haven't really destroyed anything of value. They can always try again until they get it right. The transfer agent has to accept the signature as valid, so, a **signature guarantee** is used. This is a medallion/stamp that NYSE member firms have, as well as bank officers. The stamp means that the elite holders of the sacred stamps have verified that this signature is valid.

The transfer agent would reject the following signatures:

- Signature of a minor child
- Signature of an individual now deceased
- Signature of one person in a joint account (gotta' have all signatures)

When you study for the Series 63, you'll remember that minors and dead individuals are not "legal persons," but we'll save that excitement for a later date.

When certificates come in, the back office has to be able to separate round lots (100s) from odd lots (<100). So, if the trade is for 540 shares, what we'd like to see is 5 certificates good for 100 shares each and 1 certificate for 40 shares. We could also take a certificate for 90 shares and immediately stack it with a certificate for 10 shares—that would make a round lot, right? So, if we received 5 certificates for 90 shares, 5 certificates for 10 shares, and one certificate for 40 shares, that would be good delivery, too. We'd take a 90 and a 10 and make a round lot five times; then we'd have the odd lot of 40 separated all by itself.

What about 6 certificates for 90 shares each? Six times ninety = 540, right?

Yes, but it's not good delivery. If you take a certificate for 90 shares and stack it with another one for 90 shares, you do not have a round lot. It has to be stackable into round lots without exceeding a round lot.

If we had a certificate for 200 shares and one for 300 shares, that would be fine. 200 and 300 are immediately "breakable" into round lots of 100, right?

Did we mention this stuff is crazy?

Bond certificates delivered between broker-dealers must be $1,000 or $5,000 par value. If there are coupons (bearer, principal-only) missing, that's a problem. The receiving broker-dealer would actually cop such an attitude that if the missing coupon represented $60 of interest, they would deduct $60 from the money they send to the other firm. So there. If it's a municipal bond, the legal opinion has to be attached. If there was no legal opinion obtained, the certificate needs to be stamped "ex-legal." Ex- means "without," as in "ex-dividend," which means the stock is trading without the dividend.

Delivery can be rejected by the firm representing the buyer if:

- Certificates are mutilated
- Certificates don't comply with the weird round lot thing we just looked at
- All attachments are not present (affidavit of domicile, stock power, etc.)
- Signature is invalid
- Signatures are not guaranteed
- Securities are delivered prior to the settlement date

Think back to our exciting chapter called "Equity Securities." Remember what we said on page 13, paragraph 3, line 1? No? Okay, we were talking about the whole "DERP" thing. If a stock is purchased on or after the ex-dividend date, the seller is entitled to the dividend, and if the stock is purchased before the ex-date, the buyer is entitled to the dividend. Sometimes things get screwed up. The buyer purchases the stock before the ex-date, but the seller still ends up getting the dividend. In this case, the customer's broker-dealer would send a **due bill** for the dividend to the other broker-dealer and would expect them to fork over the cash that is due. The exam might also want you to point out that when securities are sent to a broker-dealer and are not in good delivery form, the broker dealer should file a **reclamation** with the other side. As the name indicates, it's time to reclaim things here and get them right.

PRACTICE

1. **Which of the following is required on the New Account Form?**

   A. registered rep's signature

   B. customer's signature

   C. neither A nor B

   D. both A and B

2. **Which of the following would be considered the most important when opening an account?**

   A. customer is over 30 years old

   B. customer's wife works for an FINRA member firm

   C. customer prefers bonds

   D. customer is a registered Democrat

3. **Which of the following is a true statement concerning the opening of a new account?**

   A. The customer cannot be asked for bank or brokerage references.

   B. The customer cannot be asked to provide net worth and income level.

   C. The customer does not have to sign the new account form.

   D. The customer's spouse is automatically granted trading authorization.

4. **When opening a new account, if your customer wants to trade options,**

   A. he must submit to a polygraph administered by an FINRA member

   B. he must submit to a polygraph administered by a licensed law enforcement professional

   C. he must provide information to help determine suitability

   D. he may not trade options if his net worth is below $1.5 million

5. **If a customer refuses to provide a tax ID number or social security number:**

    A.   the account cannot be opened under FINRA rules

    B.   the account cannot be opened under SEC rules

    C.   backup withholding will result

    D.   she must pre-file electronically

6. **Without contacting the customer, a registered rep managing a discretionary account could purchase all of the following except:**

    A.   common stock

    B.   preferred stock

    C.   speculative options

    D.   municipal bonds where a control relationship exists

7. **Your customer tells you to buy 1,000 shares XYZ at a good price today. This order**

    A.   cannot be executed under any circumstances

    B.   cannot be executed 10 minutes before market close

    C.   is discretionary

    D.   is not discretionary

8. **Your customer has read an enticing article extolling the many advantages of investing in real estate; therefore, she calls and says, "I want you to buy as many REITs as you think I can afford right now." This is an example of**

    A.   painting the tape

    B.   frontloading

    C.   a discretionary order

    D.   a non-discretionary order

9. **When the account is non-discretionary, the registered representative may not determine**

    A.   number of shares

    B.   time

    C.   price

    D.   all of the above

10. **All of the following may open discretionary accounts except**

    A.   individuals

    B.   corporations

    C.   partnerships

    D.   fiduciaries

11. **If a corporation wishes to open a trading account as a margin account,**

    A.   this cannot occur under any circumstances

    B.   this can only occur if the NYSE and FINRA approve the arrangement

    C.   the corporate charter and bylaws must be provided

    D.   only U.S. treasury and agency securities may be purchased

12. **When you discover that one of your customers has died, you must do all of the following except**

    A.   marked the account "deceased"

    B.   freeze the account

    C.   cancel all sell stop and buy limit orders

    D.   liquidate all positions

13. **The husband of a customer calls and tells you his wife wants to sell 1,000 shares of ORCL immediately. What should you do?**

    A.   refuse the order

    B.   mark the order "unsolicited"

    C.   mark the order "joint and several"

    D.   execute the order in a timely fashion

14. **A registered rep learns that two former college roommates now sharing an investment account as joint tenants in common have each moved to opposite coasts and rarely see each other. The representative holds a conference call and discovers that JoAnne, in Philadelphia, prefers dividends while Barbara, in San Rafael, prefers interest payments. Therefore, the rep decides to start sending checks to JoAnne for the dividend income and checks to Barbara for the interest income received in the account. This is**

    A.   standard operating procedure

    B.   a violation known as "painting the tape"

    C.   improper procedure for joint accounts

    D.   perfectly acceptable as long as the agreement is duly notarized

15. **As the custodian for her nephew's account, Marilyn Mason would rather not charge a fee for her services. Rather, she would like to receive 10% of the account's appreciation each year so that she receives no benefit in poor performing years. This arrangement is**

   A.   standard operating procedure

   B.   a violation known as "painting the tape"

   C.   improper procedure for UGMA/UTMA accounts

   D.   perfectly acceptable as long as the agreement is duly notarized

16. **None of the following statements are true concerning SIPC except**

   A.   covers market risk

   B.   does not cover government securities exempt from Regulation T

   C.   covers losses in commodity futures

   D.   is an industry-funded, non-profit insurance company

ANSWERS

1.   **A,** we don't need the customer's signature on the new account form. The rep and his/her supervisor must sign the form. The exam might call the rep's boss the principal, supervisor, or branch manager, because everything needs at least three names on this test.

2.   **B,** whenever the customer or the customer's spouse works for an FINRA member firm, certain special handling of the account must be undertaken. For example, these customers are prohibited from buying new issues under FINRA Rule 2790.

3.   **C,** you definitely ask for financial information, including bank and brokerage references. The spouse does not automatically have trading authorization. If they want to set that up, they have to fill out the proper form(s).

4.   **C,** doesn't "C" just look like the right answer? Polygraphs? Those things aren't even admissible in court—can you picture registered reps administering these things and how badly the test would be abused in order to get the customer cleared for trading?

5.   **C,** no idea why someone would refuse to give you a tax number or why you'd open an account for somebody so uncooperative, but if they don't give that information, the firm will have to withhold some income every year for your friends and mine at the IRS.

6.   **D,** just another MSRB rule to memorize.

7. **D,** time/price do NOT equal discretion.

8. **C,** the rep would have to choose the Asset (which REITs) and the Amount (how many shares), so this is definitely a discretionary order. Without discretion, all the rep can choose is time of day and the price to pay.

9. **A,** without discretion, all the rep can choose is time of day and the price to pay.

10. **D,** a fiduciary is responsible for making decisions for a third party. Fiduciaries include trustees in a trust account, or a custodian for an UGMA account. These folks can't pass off their responsibility to a registered rep by granting him/her discretion. They can take advice from the rep, but they can't let the rep choose the Activity, Asset, or Amount.

11. **C,** memorize it.

12. **D,** don't liquidate positions yet. Just stop trading the account, which is called "freezing" the account. And don't start passing anything out until the appropriate legal documents have come in: death certificate, trust document, will, etc.

13. **A,** only accept this order if the husband has been granted trading authorization (power of attorney) and you have that on file.

14. **C,** all "distributions" have to be made out to all names on the account. The firm doesn't send part to one tenant and part to another. They're joint tenants—it's not your problem how they share things. Just send the proceeds to both names on the account.

15. **C,** if the custodian for the UGMA is appointed by a donor, then a reasonable fee can be charged to the account. But no way can the custodian receive gains or appreciation on the account.

16. **D,** SIPC doesn't cover commodities, because those aren't securities.

CHAPTER 14

Margin Accounts

Maybe you've purchased a house before. Chances are you didn't just buy the thing outright. If the house cost $200,000, maybe you put down $20,000 and then borrowed the rest from the mortgage lender. Why was the mortgage lender willing to spot you $180,000 on a house worth $200,000? Two reasons. One, they're going to charge you interest on that loan for many years to come. And, two, if you can't pay them back, they'll just sell the house.

When the collateral we're pledging is real estate, we can easily put down just 10%, or even less, and then borrow the rest by pledging the house to the lender. When we buy stock "on margin," we have to start out by putting down 50% of the purchase price. If you want to buy $200,000 of stock, the broker-dealer can loan you ½ of that, or $100,000, and you can put down just $100,000. Pretty neat, huh? If the stock pays dividends, you get dividends on twice as many shares. If the stock goes up 10%, you make 10% of $200,000 rather than the mere $100,000 you could have afforded in a **cash account**. Also, whatever upside this stock delivers belongs solely to you—you're just going to pay back the broker-dealer what they lent you and pay interest on the balance until it's paid off. When this stock increases, that increase is all yours.

So, broker-dealers love **margin accounts**. It opens up a whole new line of business—suddenly they're credit card companies, and they don't even have to issue the little plastic cards. Plus, credit card companies have no collateral from their customers—your VISA account is backed up solely by your tendency to repay. In a margin account, you pledge the assets you're buying on credit to the lender, the broker-dealer. If things turn south on you, they can sell the stock or bond to recover the money they lent you. So, the interest rate they charge is actually lower than what you'd pay on a credit card.

People talk about the "equity" in their houses all the time. That means that maybe they bought the house for $200,000 and borrowed $180,000 to do that. If so, their account starts out like this:

$200,000   MARKET VALUE
-$180,000   MONEY OWED

=$20,000   EQUITY

Just remember that **equity** simply equals the difference between what somebody owns (assets) and owes (liabilities). In any case, let's say that this home's value increased 15% for three years running—remember when that used to seem "normal"?. Believe it or not, when an investment of that size compounds for just three years at 15%, it is suddenly worth $304,175. To check my math, just take $200,000 times 1.15, times 1.15, times 1.15. That's the formula for "future value" that many of you will work with on your Series 66, and there's no law that says it can't show up on your Series 7, either. Anyway, part of each monthly mortgage payment knocks down the principal that was borrowed, and maybe these homeowners diligently overpaid each month by a few hundred dollars. Suddenly, the value of their asset has risen while the amount owed has dropped. Their account now looks like this, maybe:

$304,175	MARKET VALUE
-$170,000	MONEY OWED
=$134,175	EQUITY

What can these happy homeowners do with that equity? They can transfer all the high-interest credit card debt they've foolishly accumulated to a home equity loan and start funding that debt at a lower interest rate. Or, they can borrow money and put on a second-story addition. That's just what comes to mind as an example; frankly, nobody cares what they do with the money. They have some equity, let them play with it a little. You only go around once, right?

In a margin account, you aren't buying houses; you're buying stocks and bonds. What if you had bought JDSU at $250 a share on credit, and then the stock dropped to $2.50? You would have had yourself a serious collateral problem. That broker who hasn't returned a phone call in three weeks is suddenly going to be paging you, emailing you, cell-phoning you, text-messaging you, and possibly even sending out a team of Navy SEALS to locate you and get you to put some more money on the table in order to stay in this high-stakes game called margin trading.

This is, of course, where margin accounts get their bad name, but they're not all bad. I have one myself. As with a big bottle of Jack Daniels, the trick is to party responsibly. My margin account entitles me to a cash advance of exactly $6,141.53 this morning. Or, I could buy $17,206.00 worth of stock completely on *credit*. But, nobody's holding a gun to my head either, so I just keep paying 100% in my so-called "margin account." Basically, to be approved for options, you also turn your account into a margin account. Why? If you want to exercise a call, you'll need to come up with a bunch of cash in a hurry, so having the account approved for margin is real handy. Or, if you write puts, you will occasionally have to buy a bunch of stock, and margin accounts let you buy twice as much stock as you would otherwise be able to purchase. Same for the call seller who has to suddenly purchase a really expensive stock to deliver to a really happy call holder. Without trying to blow your mind completely, I will tell you that even though an options account is also approved for margin, options are not actually purchased "on margin." Rather, they are paid in full, probably because they can fluctuate 40–80% in the space of an afternoon. So, a "margin account" is simply a different type of account than a "cash account." In a **cash account**, you have to pay in full when you purchase securities, and you cannot sell short in a cash account. If your account is approved for margin trading, you can buy securities on credit and sell them short if you really like to party.

REG T

The Securities Exchange Act of 1934 gave the Federal Reserve Board the authority to regulate margin accounts. The "Fed" regulates credit, and one form of credit is the margin account, in which the broker-dealer fronts the customer half the purchase price. In the 1920s, too many customers were holding stock on margin without putting down enough money. When the prices of those stocks collapsed, they ended up owing money with nothing to show for it all. The Fed would sort of like to prevent another 1929-style market crash if at all possible. So, to purchase stock on margin, the broker-dealer follows **Regulation T (Reg T)**, which states that a listed stock can be pledged as collateral by the customer in exchange for a loan from the broker-dealer of half the market value. That sure is a long way to say that the customer has to put down half, isn't it? But Reg T really tells broker-dealers how much credit they can extend to their customers—that percentage has been 50% for quite some time. The industry sometimes refers to the amount that a customer puts down as the "Fed call." For a test question, when a customer buys $200,000 of stock, he puts down ½ or $100,000. The other ½ or $100,000 is provided by the broker-dealer, who looks forward to charging interest on that $100,000 for just as long as the customer would like to go on owing them. The amount that the customer puts down is referred to as "the margin." **Margin** simply means "percent," but sounds more sophisticated somehow.

Regulation T requires 50% of the purchase price to be deposited by the customer within two business days after the settlement date of the transaction. Any market price change between the purchase of the security and the required payment would not affect the amount of the deposit the customer has to make. If the stock purchased on margin rises from, say, $50 to $60, or drops from, say, $50 to $40, the margin call is still based on $50 per share; it's figured at the time of purchase.

RUNNING THE NUMBERS

Say a customer went long 1,000 shares @40 and made the required Reg T deposit of half or $20,000. At that point the customer's account looks like this:

LMV	-	Dr	=	Equity	Reg T Deposit
$40,000		$20,000		$20,000	$20,000

LMV stands for "long market value." It could just be referred to as "market value" or "current market value," to make sure you have three names for the same darned thing. The "Dr" stands for "debit register," which can also be called the "debit balance." This is simply the amount the customer borrowed and still owes his broker-dealer, like the mortgage balance that the homeowner still owes the lender. So, the long market value of the stock he bought is $40,000. He made the required Reg T deposit of half—20K—so the broker-dealer fronted him the other half. Do you suppose the broker-dealer wants that money back?

You bet, so it's a debit (Dr) to the client's account until he pays it off.

He "owns" an asset worth 40K and he owes 20K to the lender. That's why his equity is $20,000. Just like if you owed $80,000 on your mortgage when your house was worth $100,000—the difference of $20,000 would be your equity.

So, the investor has $20,000 of equity. What happens if the stock rises, to, say, $50 a share? The account looks like this:

$$LMV \quad - \quad Dr \quad = \quad Equity$$
$$\$50,000 \qquad \$20,000 \qquad \$30,000$$

The amount owed to the broker-dealer (Dr) didn't change. The long market value of the stock went up, increasing the equity dollar-for-dollar. Now, let's compare the equity of $30,000 to Reg T, which is 50% of the market value or "LMV." Reg T wants to see 50% equity in the account. Does this customer have at least half his "LMV" as equity? More, actually. Half of 50K is $25,000. The customer has $30,000 of equity. That's **excess equity** of $5,000. Like this:

$$LMV \quad - \quad Dr \quad = \quad Equity \quad - \quad Reg\,T \quad = \quad Excess\ Equity$$
$$\$50,000 \qquad \$20,000 \qquad \$30,000 \qquad \$25,000 \qquad \$5,000$$

You know how a lot of homeowners used to borrow more money long before they really started to pay off their mortgage? Well, in a margin account you can do the same thing. Since this customer has excess equity of $5,000, we certainly wouldn't require him to do something crazy and, like, pay back the lender. Heck no. Instead, the customer has $5,000 credited to a special little line item called "**SMA**." SMA, which stands for **Special Memorandum Account,** is just a line of credit that the customer can tap. I mean he can withdraw $5,000 of his cash, like it's in a savings account, right? Not at all. The $5,000 is just a number—as with Social Security there's actually no money there. But, if the customer wants to borrow that *amount* of money, he can. And whenever he borrows from SMA, that amount is added to the debit balance/debit register. See why customers love margin accounts, especially when the markets are moving in the proper direction? The customer can just tell the broker-dealer to cut him a check for $5,000, which will be added to his tab, like this:

$$LMV \quad - \quad Dr \quad = \quad Equity$$
$$\$50,000 \qquad \$25,000 \qquad \$25,000$$

Borrowing the cash didn't affect the long market value of the securities. We added the amount borrowed to the debit balance, which reduced equity and wiped out the SMA. SMA can be used as a cash advance that will be repaid with interest. Or, SMA can be used as an initial margin requirement for the purchase of more stock. So, instead of borrowing the cash, the customer could have used the $5,000 SMA credit to purchase $10,000 of stock. If so, the account would have looked like this:

$$LMV \qquad Dr \qquad Equity \qquad SMA$$
$$\$60,000 \qquad \$30,000 \qquad \$30,000 \qquad \$0$$

If the customer buys more stock, that definitely adds to the market value of securities held long in the account. Why did his Dr go up by $10,000? Because the $5,000 of SMA is not the customer's cash—it's just a line of credit. Funny money, no different from your line of credit on a credit card. You can use the credit, but since it isn't your money, it has to be paid back, with interest. The customer in our example used his line of credit (SMA) as his margin deposit, and the broker-dealer fronted him the other half, or $5,000, which is also added to the Dr along with the $5,000 he borrowed for the deposit from SMA. So, he borrowed $5,000 from his line of credit (SMA), plus $5,000 that the broker-dealer fronted him for the additional stock purchase. In other words, when the stock moves your way, you can end up using borrowed money in order to borrow more money. Also note that when dividends, interest, or capital gains distributions from mutual funds come into the account, that income is applied to/pays down the debit balance. Therefore, SMA is affected by such income being applied to the debit.

Reg T absolutely demands that a customer put up 50% of the long market value initially. After that, it really only sort of requests or prefers that the customer have 50% equity. What happens if the customer's equity dips below 50%?

Not much. Even though the account is called "**restricted**," there really aren't many restrictions. The customer has to put up ½ in order to buy more stock. If the customer sells stock, he can still withdraw/borrow ½ the proceeds. So the test question might show an account with less than 50% equity and ask you how much cash the customer can withdraw if he sells a certain amount of stock.

Half. The proceeds pay down the Dr; and half that amount is credited to SMA, where it can be promptly withdrawn. But, remember, no cash has been moved to SMA. Just a number. No different from a credit card issuer raising your line of credit.

Maybe we should take a look at the numbers there. The market value of the long position is $20,000, and the Dr is $13,000. That means the customer controls a $20,000 asset with not a lot of skin in the game. His equity or ownership is really only $7,000. Half of his long position would be $10,000, but his equity is below that. Therefore, we call this a "restricted account." Let's say he sells $5,000 of stock. The broker-dealer takes the $5,000 raised by selling the stock and pays down the debit by $5,000, since that debit is the money the customer owes them. So, the LMV becomes $15,000, and the Dr becomes $8,000. How much money can the customer borrow after making this sale? Half of the sale, or $2,500. And, if he did that, he'd end up with LMV of $15,000 and a Dr of $10,500. As we'll see, that's pushing it, since his equity is now just 30% of his long position. The **SROs** won't let the firm allow him to drop below 25% equity, so this guy is apparently a real party animal. Oh well. If the firm will allow him to control a position with just 30% equity, everything is just hunky dory.

Also, check this out. <u>When the market value of a securities position drops, that does not affect SMA</u>. It certainly reduces the market value of the stock and, therefore, the equity, but SMA is just a line of credit. It does not get taken away. One of the best cheesy memory joggers I've ever heard comes from an instructor who would tell his students that excess equity is the water in the tub. When the excess equity rises, it makes a ring around the tub called "SMA." When the water drains away, the SMA is still here to stay.

SMA does not go away due to a drop in market value. The customer can always use SMA as long as using it does not take him below the minimum maintenance requirement, which we're about to look at right now.

MINIMUM MAINTENANCE

Reg T tells us what to put down on an initial transaction, and any excess above Reg T gives the customer "SMA." But, SMA and excess equity are, by definition, terms used when the market is cooperating with the margin customer. What happens when the market goes the wrong way?

Suddenly, the customer's equity is deficient, and he either has to throw more cash on the fire or start liquidating securities. See, Reg T requirements apply initially and then help us figure if the customer has any SMA to play with. The customer's larger concern is the SRO 25% **minimum maintenance requirement**. The regulators say that a customer's equity can never go lower than 25% of the long market value. If it does, the customer gets a maintenance call to bring the equity up to the minimum 25%. If the customer can't deliver the cash, the firm sells/liquidates securities equal to four times the amount of the maintenance call. The following numbers should help to clarify the concept of the minimum maintenance requirement:

LMV	Dr	Equity	Minimum	Call	Liquidate
40,000	20,000	20,000	10,000	0	0

At this point, the customer has twice as much equity as the minimum (25% of long market value). If the stock goes from 40K down to 30K, we're still okay:

LMV	Dr	Equity	Min.	Call	Liquidate
30,000	20,000	10,000	7,500	0	0

But, if the long market value falls to 24K, we're in trouble:

LMV	Dr	Equity	Min.	Call	Liquidate
24,000	20,000	4,000	6,000	2,000	8,000

The SROs demand $6,000 in equity, which is ¼ of $24,000, and the customer has only $4,000. So, the customer gets a maintenance call informing him that he needs to deliver $2,000. If the customer does that, the account looks like this:

LMV	Dr	Equity	NYSE	Call	Liquidate
24,000	18,000	6,000	6,000	0	0

He paid down the debit by $2,000 and now he has $6,000 in equity, the bare minimum of 25% of market value. If he didn't have the cash, the firm would have liquidated $8,000 worth of securities. If so, the account would have looked like this:

LMV	Dr	Equity	Minimum Maintenance
$16,000	$12,000	$4,000	$4,000

Whereas, it used to look like this:
this:

LMV	Dr	Equity	Minimum Maintenance
24,000	20,000	4,000	6,000

Selling the $8,000 worth of securities reduced the LMV and the Dr by an equal amount, leaving the customer with exactly 25% equity. Remember, all we're doing here is selling $8,000 of stock and using the $8,000 to pay down the debit. By the way, since the firm might have to sell a customer's stock in a hurry, they hold the customer's securities in "street name," which we looked at in the chapter Customers & Brokers. That means the securities are registered in the name of the firm for the beneficial ownership (FBO) of the customer, who hasn't exactly paid for them yet. Also, the 25% requirement is the *minimum* maintenance. That means the broker-dealer can be only that loose about things. Many broker-dealers require a higher minimum maintenance than just 25% to protect themselves from a bunch of dead-beat speculators.

How low can a customer's long market value go before he gets a maintenance call? The test might refer to this as the **"account at maintenance."** All you do is take the Dr and divide it by .75. If you want to know why, it's because .75 is the "complement" of 25%. Either way, just take the Dr and divide it by .75. That tells you exactly how low the LMV can go before a customer has to worry about a maintenance call. So, if the account looked like this:

LMV	Dr	Equity
40,000	20,000	20,000

To find the lowest LMV or the account "at maintenance," just take the Dr of 20,000 and divide it by .75 to get $26,667. As long as the LMV doesn't dip below that amount, the customer is properly margined. We can check the numbers, too:

LMV	Dr	Equity
26,667	20,000	6,667

Isn't the equity exactly 25% of the LMV in that case?

Yes. So, the customer would still be okay. If the LMV kept falling, he'd get a maintenance call. If it hangs tough or increases, the pressure starts coming off. See how it works?

Also, please understand that there is no way that a customer can use SMA to meet a maintenance/margin call. Why not? By definition, a margin call comes in when the customer's debit balance is too high; tapping SMA adds to the very debit he's trying to pay down. Unless you're a member of the United States Congress, you should be able to see the inherent problem here.

DEPOSITING STOCK

In a margin account, the customer can deposit cash equal to the Reg T requirement ("Fed call"), or they can pledge fully paid securities. If the margin purchase is for $50,000, Reg T is 50% of that. Therefore, the customer can deposit $25,000 cash, or pledge fully paid securities with a market value of $50,000. Under Reg T, securities have a loan value of ½ (50%) of their current market value. A customer's fully-paid securities must be segregated (separated clearly) from those of the firm and other customers. Also, customers who pledge fully paid securities must be informed that these securities may be withdrawn at any time.

MARGINABLE SECURITIES, ACCOUNTS

Not everything can be purchased "on margin," but that doesn't mean it can't be purchased within a margin account. A "margin account" is really just an account that has been approved for margin. I have one, myself. Luckily, I rarely use it to borrow money, much as I usually shred all those little pretend checks my credit card companies keep sending me. No thanks. Not interested in paying interest on purchases—I'm looking to make money, thank you. Well, if I really wanted to purchase securities "on margin," these are the securities I could buy by depositing half:

- NYSE, NASDAQ, AMEX stocks
- OTC securities on the FRB's approved list

The following can be purchased inside my margin account, but I'd have to pay for them in full:

- Non-NASDAQ OTC securities
- Options
- IPOs or any new issue for 30 days
- Mutual fund shares

Watch out re: the above bullet list. If the exam question asks if options can be purchased "on margin," the answer is no. If the question asks if options can be purchased "in a margin account," the answer is yes.

I doubt the test would be this mean, but if it is, remember that those funky, long-term options called LEAPS allow me to purchase them by putting down 75%. If you get that question, please watch out for black cats, spilled salt, ladders, and cracked mirrors, as your luck has apparently just run out completely.

Also, a retirement account can not be set up as a margin account, since it would be rather crazy to let retirees lose money that quickly, losing perhaps more than they initially deposit into the account. UGMA/UTMA accounts also may not be established as margin accounts. We saw in Customers & Brokerage Procedures that for corporations and partnerships to trade on margin, the firm has to verify the documents that govern those business structures actually allow it, as the firm must do when opening a trust account. Something that has always amazed me is that a discretionary account, in which the registered rep can enter purchase and sale orders without even talking to the client first, can also be a margin account. Perhaps I'm cursed with too much empathy, but I can not imagine having to call my customer to inform him that not only have my boneheaded trades brought his account value down 60%, but if he doesn't send $50,000 in ASAP, we'll have to liquidate the rest of the positions at fire-sale prices.

EXEMPT FROM REG T

Just to keep things nice and simple, they decided to make certain securities exempt from the Reg T requirement of 50%. For government securities, the customer can put down 1–7% of the par value (depends on the broker-dealer). For municipal securities, the customer can deposit the greater of 7% of par or 15% of market value. Agency securities also have much lower requirements. So, if the test asks you who sets margin requirements for exempt securities, the example is the SRO's (**self-regulatory organizations).**

SHORT POSITIONS

Short accounts work a little different. Remember that when a customer sells short, he is selling borrowed securities in anticipation that he can buy them back to replace them at a lower price. So, if he wants to sell short $10,000 worth of securities, he has to deposit half that value, or $5,000 to meet the Reg T requirement. If he did so, his account would look like this:

Cr	$15,000
SMV	-$10,000
Equity	$5,000

The "**Cr**" stands for the "**credit**" and the "**SMV**" stands for "**short market value,**" or, perhaps, we could just call it the "market value." In any case, when the customer sells short $10,000 worth of securities, that $10,000 is credited to the customer's account. Remember, he sold some stock—somebody paid him $10,000 for that stock. That somebody doesn't know or care that the seller is "short" the stock; to the buyer of the stock the other side is simply a seller.

So, our investor gets the proceeds from the sale and also deposits 50% of that to meet the Reg T requirement, which is added to the $10,000 he took in for selling the stock for a total credit of $15,000. For the exam questions "Cr" will remain unchanged; it's the "SMV" or "short market value" that fluctuates. Think about that for a second—which numbers move in a margin account? The ones with "MV" in their name, which stands for "market value." Market value is what changes in a margin account, whether long (LMV) or short (SMV). And, equity is always a percentage of market value or "MV."

If the "SMV" goes down, as the investor hopes, he'll end up with more equity. For example, if the SMV dropped to just $5,000, the customer's equity would increase by $5,000, like this:

Cr	$15,000
SMV	-$5,000
Equity	$10,000

Remember, the credit didn't change. He started with a credit of $15,000, and that's all the credit he's going to have. It's the market value (SMV) that changed, dropping in the desired direction for our short seller.

And if the market value of the securities sold short were to increase (ouch!), his equity would shrink, like this:

Cr	$15,000
SMV	-$11,000
Equity	$4,000

How high can the SMV go before a customer gets one of those nasty maintenance calls? For short accounts, customers need 30% of their SMV as equity. If the customer's SMV is $11,000, he needs at least $3,300 in equity. You can find the highest SMV at maintenance by taking the "Cr" and dividing it by 1.3. Since the customer has a credit of $15,000, just divide that by 1.3, and you see that the highest SMV without a maintenance call would be $11,538. As long as the securities' value doesn't exceed that number, his account will remain properly margined.

COMBINED EQUITY

Keep this simple. To find combined equity just find the equity for the long positions and add it to the equity for the short positions. You can also remember that the formula for combined equity would be:

$$LMV \quad + \quad Cr \quad - \quad Dr \quad - \quad SMV$$

Which is just another way of saying, "Add the two things that go on top and subtract the two things that go on the bottom." So if a customer had an LMV of $20,000, a Cr of $20,000, a Dr of $10,000, and SMV of $10,000, his combined equity would be $20,000:

LMV	+	Cr	-	Dr	-	SMV
20,000	+	20,000	-	10,000	-	10,000

In other words, he has $10,000 equity on the long positions, and $10,000 equity on the short positions. He has to have 25% equity for the long, and 30% for the short. This customer is okay on both fronts. Each day the markets are open, the margin department that we mentioned in Customers & Brokerage Procedures recalculates requirements by **marking to the market.** If market values have gone the wrong way, the customer might receive a margin call. If market values have gone the right way, the customer might see SMA increase.

PORTFOLIO MARGINING

Recently, a program was introduced under which margin requirements are based on the net risk of the entire portfolio, rather than on the individual securities inside the portfolio. Margin requirements figured this way are usually lower that those calculated conventionally. I'm hoping that your exam will not delve too far into this; with any luck, the question would expect you to know the concept rather than running any calculations. And, as always, I can't guarantee or prove that it will.

INITIAL REQUIREMENTS

SHORT POSITIONS

For an initial transaction in a short account, the customer has to put up at least $2,000, end of story. If they sell short $3,000 worth of stock, half of that would be $1,500. Too bad, they still put up $2,000. Otherwise, it's just half of the SMV, which gets added to the proceeds of the short sale to make the Credit. You can also think of the Cr as being 150% of the SMV, or "half again" as much after the customer makes the required Reg T deposit. When the per-share stock price is low, things get a little tricky. Remember that to sell stock trading below $5 per share short, the customer must deposit $2.50 per share or 100% of the market value, whichever is higher. To sell stock trading above $5 short, the customer must deposit 30% of the market value.

LONG POSITIONS

For long positions it's a little trickier. Of course, the customer has to put down ½ the LMV for the Reg T deposit. If the securities are worth $5,000, he deposits half, or $2,500. But, if he wants to buy $3,600 worth of stock, half of that falls short of the SRO minimum $2,000 deposit. In this case, he'd put down $2,000.

And, if the total value of the securities is below $2,000, he has to put down 100% of their value. So, if he buys $1,800 worth of securities, he just pays the full $1,800.

Simple, right? So, if the first trade is worth more than $4,000, the customer puts up half. If the first trade is between $2,000 and $4,000, the customer puts up the minimum of $2,000. And, if the first trade is less than $2,000, the customer puts down 100% of the securities' value.

Might help to remember the following chart:

Initial Purchase	Customer Deposits
> $4,000	50% of purchase price
$2,000–$4,000	$2,000 SRO minimum
< $2,000	Full purchase price

OPENING A MARGIN ACCOUNT

When a customer opens a margin account, he will be asked to sign the following:

- Credit agreement
- Hypothecation agreement
- Loan consent

The **credit agreement** states the terms and conditions for the credit extended to the customer. It includes information about how interest is charged and which interest rate it will be tied to (LIBOR, broker call rate, prime rate, etc.). The **hypothecation agreement** pledges the customer's securities purchased on margin as collateral for the loan. It also allows the broker-dealer to re-hypothecate those securities as collateral for a loan at a bank to obtain-the-money they're going to front the customer. If you speak Spanish, you probably know the word "hipoteca," which would be on a sign for a business that makes loans. Hypothecate/hipoteca. As usual, Spanish is pretty close to the Latin that many English words are based on. To **hypothecate** securities means to pledge them as collateral for a loan. Finally, the **loan consent** is not something the customer has to sign, unlike the credit agreement and hypothecation agreement. But, if the customer does sign the loan consent, the broker-dealer can lend out their securities to customers who want to sell short.

DOUBLE OR NOTHING

So, are margin accounts a really good thing, or a really bad thing?

Absolutely.

Like the Jack Daniels sitting on the shelf, it all depends on who opens it. Basically, a margin account allows you to maximize your gains but also your losses. Let's look at two more scenarios to drive this point home, and then I promise to lay off the numbers for a while. Say that you purchase 1,000 shares @20 ($20,000) using just $10,000 of your own money. Put down $10,000, broker-dealer fronts you the other $10,000. You get lucky, the stock rises to $25 per share (25,000), and you sell it. After paying back the broker-dealer their $10,000, you walk away with $15,000, which is an extra $5,000. How did you do? You put down $10,000 and made a 50% profit. If you had only been able to buy the $10,000 worth, or 500 shares, you would have put down $10,000 and sold for $12,500, which is only a 25% profit.

With margin, your profit was doubled.

Then again, let's say that after putting down $10,000 for 1,000 shares of stock trading at $20, the stock took an inconvenient nosedive. Instead of going up like it's supposed to, the stock drops to $15 per share. You freak out and sell it for $15,000. You give the broker-dealer back their $10,000, and you're left with $5,000.

Wait a minute, you put down $10,000 and are now left with just $5,000? Isn't that a net loss of 50%? Sure is. And, it wouldn't have been so ugly if you had just bought $10,000 of that stock. If you had purchased 500 shares @20 with your $10,000, and then sold the 500 shares at $15 ($7,500), you would have lost $2,500, or just 25%.

So, with margin you can make twice as much but also lose twice as much. The broker-dealer makes their interest charges, either way, and they help you to buy twice as much stock as you otherwise would have. So, it's definitely a win-win situation for the broker-dealer. The customer will also come out ahead.

Unless he loses.

Because of this high-risk nature of margin account trading, broker-dealers have to provide all margin customers with a **margin risk disclosure document**, much the way that options customers have to receive the OCC disclosure document. This margin risk disclosure document must be provided when the account is opened and also provided annually to margin customers. It must disclose the inherent risks of doubling your gains *and* doubling your losses—the customer can lose more than he invests in the account. And, it must explain that the broker-dealer does not have to consult with the customer about which securities to liquidate if the equity shrinks below the minimum maintenance.

PRACTICE

1. **If the value of securities increases in a long account, all of the following are affected except**

   A. LMV

   B. equity

   C. SMA

   D. Dr

2. **If the value of securities decreases in a long account, which of the following are affected?**

   I. SMA

   II. Dr

   III. LMV

   IV. equity

   A. I, II only

   B. I, II, III, IV

   C. III, IV only

   D. IV only

3. **If a customer sells $2,000 of securities in a restricted account, all of the following are affected except**

   A. Dr

   B. SMA

   C. equity

   D. LMV

4. **If a customer uses SMA to buy stock, all of the following are affected except**

   A. LMV

   B. SMA

   C. Dr

   D. equity

5. **If a customer borrows SMA, all of the following are affected except**

    A. LMV

    B. SMA

    C. Dr

    D. equity

6. **In a new margin account, a customer buys 100 shares ABC @38 and makes the required Reg T deposit. Three months later ABC is @47. What is the equity?**

    A. $2,900

    B. $2,700

    C. $900

    D. none of the above

7. **A new margin customer purchases 200 ART @48 and meets the Fed call. Seven and one-half months later—with Reg T at 50%--ART rises to $64 per share. What is the customer's buying power?**

    A. $3,200

    B. $6,400

    C. $2,000

    D. $9,600

ANSWERS

1. **D,** the word "value" is a clue. If the "value" goes up, then the Long Market Value (LMV) is affected, right? As LMV increases, so does equity. If an increase in market value creates excess equity, then SMA is also affected. Dr is just the amount the customer owes the broker-dealer.

2. **C,** remember that SMA is the ring around the tub. Excess equity can drain away, but SMA is still here to stay. Once it's credited, it can't be taken away by a drop in the securities' value. Customer has to borrow or use it to buy more stock; otherwise, SMA is here to stay. As the securities' value decreases, so does the equity in the account.

3. **C,** obviously, when the customer sells securities, the LMV goes down, right? The proceeds pay down the debit, so Dr is affected. Since the full amount pays down the debit, equity remains the

same. LMV goes down 2K, so does the Dr, leaving equity unchanged. Half of the amount of the sale is credited to SMA, which is the amount that can be borrowed, even in a restricted account.

4. **D,** the question tells us the customer "uses" SMA, so SMA is definitely affected. It's used to buy more stock, so the LMV goes up. Is SMA free? Nope. It's added to the Dr, so the Dr is also affected. If the customer has $4,000 in SMA and uses it to buy $8,000 of stock, both the LMV and the Dr will be increased by $8,000, which is why equity is not affected.

5. **A,** borrowing SMA as a cash advance doesn't affect LMV, since we aren't buying any stock. We're just taking the cash advance. That's a line of credit to the customer and when it's used it's added to the debit register. The customer owes that money, which is why Dr is affected. If LMV stays the same and the Dr is increased, that affects the equity by lowering it, dollar-for-dollar, by the amount added to the Dr.

6. **A,** now that's a tricky question! If the customer buys $3,800 worth of stock, she'll have to put down $2,000, leaving her with a Dr of $1,800. $4700 - $1800 = $2900 equity.

7. **A,** the customer put down half initially, or $4,800, leaving a Debit balance of $4800 (it's easy when there are 200 shares—just multiply by half of them). So, when the stock is now worth $12,800, the equity is $8,000. Reg T is $6,400 (half of LMV) so the $1,600 above that is excess equity. Multiply that by two to get the buying/purchasing power.

CHAPTER 15

Rules & Regulations

There is no perfect way to organize a Series 7 textbook. Because there are rules and regulations connected to equity securities, debt securities, municipal securities, customer accounts, etc., we could have placed all the related rules and regulations only within those chapters. Or, we could have left out all mention of the rules in those chapters and placed them, instead, in this one. I have opted to do a little of both. The only downside here is that you may end up revisiting some of the rules and federal securities acts that have been mentioned earlier. I'm thinking if that's our downside, we're going to be just fine. Too many Series 7 students make the mistake of working only on options and maybe municipal securities when they could probably boost their scores even more by learning the federal securities acts and the industry rules and regulations inside out. Remember, you can learn the information in this chapter without possessing any math skills or financial background whatsoever. Anybody interested in boosting his or her score?

THE SEC

The SEC is the ultimate securities regulator. The NYSE, FINRA, MSRB, etc., all answer to the SEC, which stands for the "Securities and Exchange Commission." This is not a mere "SRO" or "national securities association" that can regulate its own members. This is an arm of the federal government. Created with the passage of the Securities Exchange Act of 1934, the SEC has five commissioners, with no more than two from a particular political party. The President of the United States gets to name the commissioners (with the "advise and consent" role played by Congress) and he gets to appoint the Chairman, which is why it's always stacked 3-to-2 in favor of the party occupying the White House.

Why does the federal government regulate the securities markets? It has to do with interstate commerce. See, when commerce takes place all within one state, that state has authority over the activity. A state highway here in Illinois is the domain of IDOT (Illinois Dept of Transportation), but there are also many interstate highways running through this state, which are the domain of the federal government's USDOT. That's because when commerce becomes "interstate commerce," the federal government steps in and lets everyone know they're in charge. In other words, if the commerce is not conducted within just one state, it's not just one state's responsibility—it's the federal government's responsibility. The federal government explains why they have the authority to regulate the securities markets in the Securities Exchange Act of 1934:

> Transactions in securities as commonly conducted upon securities exchanges and over-the-counter markets are affected with a national public interest which makes it necessary to provide for regulation and control of such transactions and of practices and matters related thereto…in order to protect interstate commerce, the national credit, the Federal taxing power, to protect and make more effective the national banking system and Federal Reserve System, and to insure the maintenance of fair and honest markets in such transactions.

A very important concept is that the federal government views the purpose and implementation of securities regulations as follows:

> Whenever pursuant to this title the Commission is engaged in rule-making and is required to consider or determine whether an action is necessary or appropriate in the public interest, the Commission shall also consider, in addition to the protection of investors, whether the action will promote efficiency, competition, and capital formation. (Securities Act of 1933, Section 2[b])

The SEC is basically an army of attorneys with the authority to crack the whip whenever somebody tries to manipulate the markets or sell securities fraudulently, or provide investment advice without getting registered, or many, many other things that threaten investors and the markets themselves. They can expel firms and agents from national securities exchanges. They can go after CEOs who provide bogus income statements in their quarterly and annual reports. When they kick somebody out of the industry or investigate a renegade company, they are engaged in civil enforcement. That means they take you to federal court and sue the heck out of you. Since they are part of the federal government, they can also refer criminal cases to the U.S. Department of Justice, which means you might be sweating it out with a roomful of FBI agents in dark suits and side arms if you aren't careful. That's why we've seen so many executives squirming in the courtroom in recent times. If you lie on your quarterly and annual reports filed with the SEC, you are committing securities fraud, which carries stiff monetary penalties and scary jail time. We're talking 20 years if the fraud is egregious enough. And, how are quarterly and annual reports circulated? By wire and by mail. This is just a suggestion, but I strongly recommend keeping "wire and mail fraud" off your U4 for as long as possible.

Let's examine the actual verbiage on the criminal penalties, which I've borrowed and abbreviated from the Securities Exchange Act of 1934, Section 32(a) –

> Any person who willfully violates any provision of this title, or any person who willfully and knowingly makes, or causes to be made, any statement in any application, report, or document required to be filed under this title, which statement was false or misleading with respect to any material fact, shall upon conviction be fined not more than $5,000,000, or imprisoned not more than 20 years, or both.

Wow.

No thanks.

FEDERAL SECURITIES ACTS

When I hear the phrase "Roarin' 20s," I immediately picture shaky film reels of flappers dancing the Charleston and people partying in speakeasies, but then it always turns ugly, with ruined men jumping out of skyscrapers when the stock market crashes in October 1929. Up to this point the stock market had pretty well ruled itself, but then the Great Crash caused people to lose faith in the whole concept of investing. Well, the federal government is definitely interested in helping to foster a strong capital market that provides much-needed cash to corporate issuers, state and local governments, not to mention the biggest issuer of all—the federal government itself. The securities/capital markets are inherently linked with the banking system, employment, tax revenues, political stability, etc. So, in 1933 the federal government decided that most securities would have to register with a new organization that would be called the **Securities and Exchange Commission**, which would make sure that investors get a lot more and a lot better information from issuers before turning over their hard-earned money for strange pieces of paper called "stocks" and "bonds."

SECURITIES ACT OF 1933

The **Securities Act of 1933** regulates the primary market. This so-called "Paper Act" is all about registering a security (the paper) with the SEC, which then gives the company the green light to sell or "issue" their paper to the public. As an investor, before you buy a brand new share of stock, you have to be provided with a prospectus that discloses everything you need to know about the company issuing the paper. That prospectus has been registered with the SEC. In it you can read about the company's history, its products and services, its chances for success, and its chances for failure. You can look at the balance sheet and the income statement. You'll still be taking a risk if you buy—because all securities carry risk—but at least you'll be able to make an informed decision because of this full and fair disclosure of material information.

If you had gotten in on that IPO for Frank & Emma's Fruit Pies (FREM), the prospectus you received would have talked about how the company was founded in 1947 by Francis R. Funkmeyer, who used his GI bill to earn a business degree from Ohio State University and started the company from the money he'd saved up working the night shift at a local tool-and-die shop. You would have read how the company was now run by third-generation owners, and how the company had bold plans to expand its reach and market share. You could have looked at the financial statements and read all the risks involved with buying stock in a company with many larger competitors who were much better financed and better known on the national stage. Product liability, union slowdowns, fuel costs, penny-pinching customers like Walmart driving down profit margins...any negative thing imaginable was detailed in the risk disclosure section. You could read about the board of directors and the three officers of the company: Jeremy, CEO, Jennifer, CFO, and Jason, COO. You'd see where they went to college, where they got their M.B.A. degrees, how much of the company's stock they own, etc.

You'd get a pretty good picture of the company before deciding if you want to buy a little slice of its profits in the form of common stock. And that's the whole purpose of the Securities Act of

1933—giving investors enough information to give them a fair shot. Sometimes we refer to the Securities Act of 1933 as the "Paper Act," because it governs how "paper" gets issued for the first time. When a corporation wants to raise cash by selling securities, they have to get a group of underwriters together and fill out a bunch of paperwork for the federal government in the form of a registration statement, or "S1." Part of this information will become the prospectus, which is the disclosure brochure that the public will be provided with. An "underwriter" is just a broker-dealer that likes to take companies public, by the way. Another name for an underwriter is "investment banker," but they don't act like a traditional bank. No deposits or checking offered here.

Here is how the Act of '33 defines the terms *issuer* and *underwriter*:

> The term "issuer" means every person who issues or proposes to issue any security

> The term "underwriter" means any person who has purchased from an issuer with a view to, or offers or sells for an issuer in connection with, the distribution of any security, or participates or has a direct or indirect participation in any such undertaking, or participates or has a participation in the direct or indirect underwriting of any such undertaking

Hmm. Thanks for clearing that up, huh?

Oh well, that's partly why I have a job. Anyway, notice how the term "issuer" includes people who have not yet issued a security. Seems goofy, but they have to write it that way so that as soon as you file your paperwork to issue a security, you have "proposed to issue a security" and are now defined as an "issuer." Therefore, you have to follow all the rules on issuers spelled out by the piece of legislation. If you weren't clearly defined as an issuer at that point, the law wouldn't be able to touch you. The law really does want to touch you at this point. As we saw earlier, as soon as you register your paper, you go into a cooling-off period, where only certain things are allowed. That's because you're an issuer now that you have proposed to issue securities. By the way, your Series 63 may ask you to define "issuer," and the definition should look exactly as we just saw.

The definition of "underwriter" is just sad. There are surely better ways to express that idea, such as:

- An "underwriter" means any person who has purchased securities from an issuer with intent to distribute the securities, working either on their own or as part of a group

Anyway, once the underwriters and the issuer file the registration papers, they go into a "cooling-off" period, which will last a minimum of 20 days. This process can drag on and on, but no matter how long it takes, the issuing corporation and its underwriters can only do certain things during this "cooling-off" period. Number one, they can't sell anything. They can't even advertise. They can announce that a sale is going to take place by publishing a tombstone ad in the financial press. A tombstone ad is just a boring rectangle with some text—looks like a tombstone. You can see them in the *Wall Street Journal* fairly often, or in most any newspaper at least once in a while. It announces that a sale will take place and informs the reader where he/she can obtain a prospectus. But it is neither an offer nor a solicitation. Remember that for the exam—if somebody reads a tombstone and calls up wanting to buy the securities, nothing has been offered for sale yet. Once the prospectus has been delivered/sent to the client, *now* an offer to sell securities has been made. And, if anybody said or did anything deceptive at this point, we could have a case of fraud on our hands, which is the single most important topic on the Series 63.

But, we'll save the excitement of the Series 63 for a later date.

The underwriters can send out a preliminary prospectus/red herring to certain clients to see if anyone wants to give an indication of interest, but those aren't sales. Just names on a list. The red herring, by the way, contains almost everything that the final prospectus will contain except for the effective date and the final offering price or "POP." The registered rep may NOT send a research report along with the red herring and may not highlight or alter it in any way.

The issuer and the underwriters hold due diligence meetings during the cooling-off period, which just means they make sure they provided the SEC and the public with accurate and full disclosure.

Nothing gets sold until the SEC "releases" the security on the release or effective date. But, even though the SEC makes issuers jump through all kinds of hoops, they don't approve or disapprove of the security. They don't guarantee accuracy or adequacy of the information provided by the issuer and its underwriters. In other words, if this whole thing goes belly up because of inaccurate disclosure, the liability still rests squarely on the shoulders of the issuers and underwriters, not on the SEC. And, there has to be a disclaimer on the prospectus that says something scary like this:

```
These securities have not been approved or disapproved by the Secu-
rities and Exchange Commission nor has the Commission passed upon
the accuracy or adequacy of this prospectus. Any representation
to the contrary is a criminal offense.
```

They're a very serious bunch this SEC. Let's hope you never find out exactly how serious yourself.

THE SECURITIES EXCHANGE ACT OF 1934

The Act of '33 is about new issues only. The **Securities Exchange Act of 1934** covers just about everything else. It is often referred to as the "People Act," which is easy to remember, because it dictates how people may act in the securities markets. Before the Act can tell the players what they can and can't do, though, it has to clearly define the players and clearly define the term "security." That's no different than how we'd have to write a set of rules for the game of basketball, right? We couldn't begin to outlaw "goal tending" unless we first clearly define terms such as goal, rim, net, backboard, shot, and who knows what else?

Here is how the Securities Exchange Act of 1934 defines such terms:

- The term "broker" means any person engaged in the business of effecting transactions in securities for the account of others.

- The term "dealer" means any person engaged in the business of buying and selling securities for such person's own account.

When you sit for the Series 63 or 66, you'll see why they very cleverly fused those two bullet points together to define the entity known as a "broker-dealer," which is, "Any person engaged in the business of effecting transactions in securities for the account of others or its own account."

Since this is, after all, the <u>Securities</u> Exchange Act of 1934, it only covers securities. That's why it has to carefully define what a security is. Basically, a security is anything that can be exchanged for value where the investor's fortunes are at risk and are bound up with other investors' fortunes in some common enterprise, where the investors will benefit solely through the efforts of others. That could clearly define common stock, where millions of investors are bound together in their investment in, say, Microsoft, and they'll all benefit solely through the efforts of others, since few investors could write a line of code to save their lives.

And, the beauty of this rather loose definition is that it could include a 10% ownership stake in a racehorse. Or a 15% stake in somebody's soybean farming operation. That way, the regulators can regulate a very broad array of investments, should investors end up getting bilked by shady operators.

This rather broad definition comes from a Supreme Court case referred to as the "**Howey Decision**," by the way. In that decision, the term "investment contract" was clarified as we just discussed, and an investment contract is specifically mentioned as one example of a "security." The definition of "security" even goes so far as to include, "anything commonly known as a security." In other words, if it looks like and walks like a security, it's a security. That means it will probably have to register, and the agents and broker-dealers who sell it will also probably have to register.

The Securities Exchange Act of 1934 has a lot to say about broker-dealers and registered reps having to register. As you might already know, "**associated person**s" such as registered reps and principals have to register with a "member firm" through a **U4** form. So the firm is the member; you, the registered rep, are an associate of the member firm.

If there were troubling bits of news on that U4, the individual trying to register with a member firm could be disqualified by statute, which, we very cleverly call a "**statutory disqualification**." Sounds impressive, but it's no more complicated than you and some friends trying to organize a summer soccer league. Who can play and who can't? Maybe any kid over 12 is too old and, therefore disqualified by the statutes/rules that your soccer club lays down. Statutorily disqualified. Maybe if any kid has had a conviction for gun possession or felony amounts of narcotics, he/she can't join the soccer club. That would be another statutory disqualification.

The Act of 1934, basically, says that if the firm trying to associate with an SRO, or the individual trying to associate with a firm, has been convicted of any felony during the past 10 years, or any misdemeanor that involves fraud, theft, embezzlement, perjury—that kind of stuff—he/they will most likely be disqualified. Also, if other regulators have slapped sanctions/penalties on the firm or individual during the past 10 years, they probably aren't going to get registered, either. That includes foreign authorities, the commodity futures regulators, and state securities regulators (called "The **Administrator**" on the Series 63/65/66 exams).

Notice how a felony is a felony. One's just as bad as another. But, the misdemeanors that could keep somebody out are spelled out like so:

- involves the purchase or sale of any security, the taking of a false oath, the making of a false report, bribery, perjury, burglary, any substantially equivalent activity however denominated by the laws of the relevant foreign government, or conspiracy to commit any such offense;

- arises out of the conduct of the business of a broker, dealer, municipal securities dealer, government securities broker, government securities dealer, investment adviser, bank, insurance company, fiduciary, transfer agent, foreign person performing a function substantially equivalent to any of the above, or entity or person required to be registered under the Commodity Exchange Act (7 U.S.C. 1 et seq.) or any substantially equivalent foreign statute or regulation;

- involves the larceny, theft, robbery, extortion, forgery, counterfeiting, fraudulent concealment, embezzlement, fraudulent conversion, or misappropriation of funds, or securities, or substantially equivalent activity however denominated by the laws of the relevant foreign government

So, if the misdemeanor involved deceit or leaving somebody feeling they'd been robbed, cheated, bilked, or otherwise mistreated in a financial sense, things aren't looking too good for this candidate. Probably going to be disqualified by statute, "statutorily disqualified."

The Act of 1934 talked about insider trading, warning investors not to pass around or use non-public information. The penalties were raised in 1988 with the so-called **"Insider Trading Act of 1988."** Because of this legislation, any person who uses inside information can be penalized under the Securities Exchange Act of 1934 up to three times the amount of the profit made or loss avoided. For "controlling persons" overseeing an inside trader, the penalty can go up to $1 million. Plus, the Justice Department might make a criminal case out of it.

How would anybody catch you? The SEC can pay bounties up to 10% of whatever they extract from the people stupid enough to both use inside information and get caught.

Many securities are exempt (excused) from having to register under the Securities Act of 1933. For example, T-bonds and bank securities don't have to register. Neither do church securities. A few Sundays ago I actually picked up an offering circular for some church bonds on a back table. The first page of the offering circular declares:

The offer and sale of these securities have not been registered with the Securities and Exchange Commission…these securities have not been approved or disapproved by the Securities and Exchange Commission or the securities authorities of any state, nor has the Securities and Exchange Commission or any state securities authority passed upon the accuracy or adequacy of this offering circular. Any representation to the contrary is a criminal offense.

So, the fixed-rate and the adjustable-rate debt securities being offered by this religious organization did not have to be registered with the SEC or state regulators. Goody for them. They are still *securities*, which means that if anyone makes any material misstatement of fact or omits to state a necessary fact in connection with the offer, sale, or purchase of these (or *any*) securities, that would be fraudulent and altogether not a good idea. For example, if this offering circular overstates the cash this religious organization has in the bank in order to falsely raise my confidence in their ability to pay me back, that would be securities fraud. This offering circular has been distributed by the U.S. mail, and whether you're wearing a tight black leather jacket or an off-white satin robe, you can be busted for mail and securities fraud.

Which is bad.

So, the exam might point out that while some securities are exempt from registration under the Securities Act of 1933, *all* securities are subject to the Securities Exchange Act of 1934's anti-fraud provisions. State law could also come down on anyone connected to the offer, sale, or purchase of any security, should that person decide to use deceptive, misleading, or fraudulent means.

The Securities Exchange Act of 1934 also gave the Federal Reserve Board the power to regulate margin. Reg T stipulates how much credit a broker-dealer can extend to a margin customer (50%); Reg U stipulates how much credit a bank can extend to a broker-dealer or public customer (140% of the customer's debit balance). Finally, proxies have to be sent to investors at the issuer's expense to enable shareholders to vote without having to attend the annual shareholder meeting in Keokuk, Iowa.

FINRA

FINRA is a self-regulatory organization organized along four major bylaws:

- rules of fair practice
- uniform practice code
- code of procedure
- code of arbitration

The rules of fair practice describe how to deal with customers without getting the regulators all bent out of shape. Commissions, markups, recommendations, advertising, sales literature, etc., are covered here. These are often referred to as "member conduct rules." The uniform practice code is the code that keeps the practice uniform. Go figure. Settlement dates, delivery of securities, the establishment of the ex-date…all that stuff is covered here. The exam might refer to the uniform practice code as "promoting cooperative effort," which it does. Just keeping the broker-dealers in Boston on the same page as the broker-dealers in Austin. As we'll see a few pages later, violations of **conduct rules** are investigated and handled under **Code of Procedure**, while disputes among members (usually concerning money) are handled under **Code of Arbitration**.

FINRA MEMBERSHIP

If your firm wants to join FINRA, they must:

- meet net capital requirements (must be solvent)
- have at least two principals to supervise the firm
- have an acceptable business plan detailing its proposed activities
- attend a pre-membership interview (sort of like Rush Week)

If your firm pledges the fraternity, they must agree to:

- abide by the rules of the "Association"
- abide by all federal and state laws
- pay dues, fees, and membership assessments

What are these fees the firm must pay?

- Basic membership fee
- Fee for each rep and principal
- Fee based on gross income of the firm
- Fee for all branch offices

MEMBERSHIP, REGISTRATION AND QUALIFICATION REQUIREMENTS

Since we had so much fun looking at actual MSRB rules in the Municipal Securities chapter, let's look at some actual FINRA rules and definitions related to registration and qualification requirements. The "Commission" is shorthand for the SEC. The "Association" is shorthand for FINRA. Notice how the "Association" frequently uses the same phrase used by the MSRB, NYSE, and CBOE: *conduct inconsistent with just and equitable principles of trade*. That means FINRA expects member firms to conduct themselves in a manner that is fair and honest. If they do something inconsistent with that, they've probably broken a rule and will probably hear from FINRA at its earliest convenience. By the way, you can look at a copy of the FINRA Manual by visiting www. FINRA.org and we highly recommend doing that.

No, seriously.

First off, firms have to register, and they also have to register their representatives and principals. When they do so, FINRA reminds them not to file misleading information. Basically, it doesn't look good when you're lying before we've even let you into the club, so, as the FINRA Manual says:

Filing of Misleading Information as to Membership or Registration

The filing with the Association of information with respect to membership or registration as a Registered Representative which is incomplete or inaccurate so as to be misleading, or which could in any way tend to mislead, or the failure to correct such filing after notice thereof, may be deemed to be conduct inconsistent with just and equitable principles of trade and when discovered may be sufficient cause for appropriate disciplinary action.

COMMENT: don't file misleading or incomplete applications, and if we're nice enough to point out your mistake, fix it.

Failure to Register Personnel

The failure of any member to register an employee, who should be so registered, as a Registered Representative may be deemed to be conduct inconsistent with just and equitable principles of trade and when discovered may be sufficient cause for appropriate disciplinary action.

COMMENT: register your representatives. That's why they're called "registered representatives." Who "should be so registered"?

FINRA lays that out, too:

Definition of Representative

Persons associated with a member, including assistant officers other than principals, who are engaged in the investment banking or securities business for the member including the functions of supervision, solicitation or conduct of business in securities or who are engaged in the training of persons associated with a member for any of these functions are designated as representatives.

There are different categories of "registered representative," too. A **General Securities Representative** has a Series 7 and can sell individual stocks, bonds, munis, options…generally just about anything. A person with a Series 6 is called a Limited Representative–Investment Company and Variable Contracts Products. This allows the individual to sell only mutual funds and variable contracts, plus something that seldom gets mentioned: a Series 6 holder can also be part of an underwriting for a closed-end fund. Just the underwriting, though, which is done through a prospectus. Once they start trading in the secondary market between investors, they're just shares of stock, and a Series 6 holder can't sell individual shares of stock. Everything they sell has to come with a prospectus.

So, if you fit the definition of "representative," you have to be registered, as FINRA indicates below:

All Representatives Must Be Registered

All persons engaged or to be engaged in the investment banking or securities business of a member who are to function as representatives shall be registered as such with FINRA in the category of registration appropriate to the function to be performed as specified in Rule 1032. Before their registration can become effective, they shall pass a Qualification Examination for Representatives appropriate to the category of registration as specified by the Board of Governors.

As you probably know, you are registered through a U4 form, which asks a bunch of personal questions about your residential history and professional background. A principal has to sign the application and certify that he/she has reviewed your information. Which is why it's not a good idea to use a fictional work history—they, like, check up on that. Lots of representatives try to conceal their criminal records by, like, forgetting to report them on the U4. When FINRA finds out, they usually bar the representative permanently from association with any member firm. If you decide to leave your firm, a **U5** must be filled out and submitted to FINRA within 30 days. You can't just transfer your registration from one firm to the next. The firm you're leaving completes a U5, and the firm that is hiring you completes a U4. If the exam uses the phrase "termination for cause," that means the registered rep gave the firm a good reason to fire him. Good reasons to fire a registered representative include:

- Violating the firm's policies
- Violating the rules of the NYSE, FINRA, SEC, or any other industry regulator
- Violating state or federal securities laws

If the registered representative is the subject of an investigation by any securities industry regulator, the firm cannot terminate the rep until the investigation is completed. Otherwise, a shady supervisor could say, "Oh, you're being investigated by the State of New York? No problem, we'll just terminate you for cause and make the whole thing go away."

Not.

Recently, FINRA changed some of the questions on and procedures for the U4. It used to be that if a customer wanted to win an arbitration claim, it was sort of understood that they needed to name the firm—not the individual representative—in the claim. This way, when the customer got paid, the registered rep didn't have to have something to report on a U4 or U5 form. The information on the U4 and U5 are available to the public through "broker check" at www.finra.org, so it can make your sales efforts really difficult if your next appointment already has her laptop out, with a PowerPoint presentation based on your recent arbitration awards to wronged customers and disciplinary proceedings for breaking the rules. Now, the firm has to add the arbitration or civil litigation (lawsuit) award to the registered representative's U4/U5 form even if he or she isn't specifically named in the arbitration award. But, FINRA did raise the threshold to $15,000 (from $10,000) for the firm to report the settlement. FINRA and the SEC are also especially concerned about "willful violations" of securities law, and the new questions under the disclosure section are specifically designed to find out about those. As you might expect, if your U4 contains information about "willful violations" of securities law—maybe executing transactions that your customers don't even know about, or misleading people about the mutual funds you sold them—it can be very tough to stay in the business. FINRA uses "statutory disqualification," which means that by statute you are—yep—disqualified.

After becoming a registered representative, you will also need to put in some time earning continuing education requirements. Let's see what FINRA has to say about that:

Continuing Education Requirements

This Rule prescribes requirements regarding the continuing education of certain registered persons subsequent to their initial qualification and registration with FINRA. The requirements shall consist of a Regulatory Element and a Firm Element as set forth below.

The Regulatory Element is described like so:

Each registered person shall complete the Regulatory Element on the occurrence of their second registration anniversary date and every three years thereafter, or as otherwise prescribed by FINRA. On each occasion, the Regulatory Element must be completed within 120 days after the person's registration anniversary date.

What if you don't complete the Regulatory Element in that time frame?

(2) Failure to Complete

Unless otherwise determined by the Association, any registered persons who have not completed the Regulatory Element within the prescribed time frames will have their registrations deemed inactive until such time as the requirements of the program have been satisfied. Any person whose registration has been deemed inactive under this Rule shall cease all activities as a registered person and is prohibited from performing any duties and functioning in any capacity requiring registration.

The Firm Element is described like this by the FINRA Manual:

(2) Standards for the Firm Element

(A) Each member must maintain a continuing and current education program for its covered registered persons to enhance their securities knowledge, skill, and professionalism. At a minimum, each member shall at least annually evaluate and prioritize its training needs and develop a written training plan.

Active Military Duty

On the Series 7 exam you will see several questions about the registration of representatives and principals of a broker-dealer. One question might ask what happens when a registered representative volunteers or is called into active military duty. If he or she is away from the firm more than two years, does the license expire? Does he have to take continuing education courses in some cave in Afghanistan? Does she lose all the commissions she could have made on her "book of business"?

Not surprisingly, FINRA and the SEC are extremely accommodating when a registered rep or principal is called away from the firm to serve Uncle Sam. Here are the basic facts:

- license is placed on "inactive status"
- continuing education requirements waived
- dues, assessments waived
- two-year expiration period does not apply—exam might refer to this as "tolling"
- can earn commissions, usually by splitting them with another rep who will service the book of business
- the "inactive" rep cannot perform any of the duties of a registered rep while on inactive status

You could see a question about a "sole proprietor" called into active military duty. If so, tell the test that the same bullet points above would apply.

Investment Banking Representative (Series 79)

A relatively new category of registered representative has been created for individuals whose activities relate only to investment banking (primary market) and not the trading of securities (secondary market). As FINRA states in their notice to members:

FINRA has developed this exam to provide a more targeted assessment of the job functions performed by the individuals that fall within the registration category. The exam will be required in lieu of the current General Securities Representative (Series 7) exam or equivalent exams by the individuals who perform the job functions described in the new registration category.

The individuals who will take this new test instead of the Series 7 are those whose activities involve:

(1) advising on or facilitating debt or equity securities offerings through a private placement or a public offering, including but not limited to origination, underwriting, marketing, structuring, syndication, and pricing of such securities and managing the allocation and stabilization activities of such offerings, or (2) advising on or facilitating mergers and acquisitions, tender offers, financial restructurings, asset sales, divestitures or other corporate reorganizations or business combination transactions, including but not limited to rendering a fairness, solvency or similar opinion.

This registration category does not apply to those who work only in public finance (municipal securities) or direct participation programs. The test contains 175 questions, and candidates have 5 hours to complete them. Are there any exam materials available for these people to, like, study? Actually, this is not a concern for FINRA, who frequently gives exams for which no study material yet exists.

Seriously.

Principals

Member firms need principals who review correspondence, approve every account, initial order tickets, handle written customer complaints, and make sure there's a procedural manual for the office to use. In other words, somebody at the firm is ultimately responsible for the business of the firm—that person is the principal.

FINRA says:

All Principals Must Be Registered

All persons engaged or to be engaged in the investment banking or securities business of a member who are to function as principals shall be registered as such with FINRA in the category of registration appropriate to the function to be performed as specified in Rule 1022. Before their registration can become effective, they shall pass a Qualification Examination for Principals appropriate to the category of registration as specified by the Board of Governors.

COMMENT: those of you who have been asked to take the Series 24—that would make you one of these principal-type-people.

Here is how FINRA defines a principal:

Definition of Principal

Persons associated with a member who are actively engaged in the management of the member's investment banking or securities business, including supervision, solicitation, conduct of business or the training of persons associated with a member for any of these functions are designated as principals.

COMMENT: that one's pretty clear as is.

Also note that, in general, each member must have at least two principals taking care of the stuff that principals are supposed to take care of:

- New accounts
- Trades (transactions)
- Advertising
- Sales literature
- Correspondence

And, making sure there is a written supervisory and procedural manual.

Research Analysts

Registration of Research Analysts

(a) All persons associated with a member who are to function as research analysts shall be registered with FINRA.

Comment: a research analyst prepares and approves the research reports put together by the firm. You know all those "strong buy" or "market outperform" ratings and the accompanying reports that tell people whether to buy or back off a particular stock? Well, those are prepared by a research analyst. To become a research analyst you generally have to get the Series 7 and then pass another license exam specifically for research analysts (Series 86 and 87). Also note that a *supervisory analyst* has to approve all research reports.

More on Registration Requirements

Many people in my classes ask, "If I stop selling for a while, can I just park my license at the firm until I'm ready to use it again?"

Here is how FINRA answers that:

No.

Actually, they go into more detail:

> A member shall not maintain a representative registration with FINRA for any person (1) who is no longer active in the member's investment banking or securities business, (2) who is no longer functioning as a representative, or (3) where the sole purpose is to avoid the examination requirement prescribed in paragraph (c).

COMMENT: if you're out for two years or more, you have to take this exam again, so (3) is saying that your firm had better not pretend you're associated just so you can skip the Series 7 requirement.

A broker-dealer also could not sponsor someone for the Series 7 exam just so the person could sit for the test. As the rules say:

> A member shall not make application for the registration of any person as representative where there is no intent to employ such person in the member's investment banking or securities business.

Many of my students remind me during the class, "But, Bob, I'm not actually going to be selling." To which FINRA says, "Close enough." An "assistant representative" will also have to get a license, because of the following:

> **All Assistant Representatives-Order Processing Must Be Registered**
>
> All persons associated with a member who are to function as Assistant Representatives--Order Processing shall be registered with the Association. Before their registrations can become effective, they shall pass a Qualification Examination for Assistant Representatives--Order Processing as specified by the Board of Governors.
>
> (b) Definition of Assistant Representative-Order Processing
>
> Persons associated with a member who accept unsolicited customer orders for submission for execution by the member are designated as Assistant Representatives-Order Processing.

Exemptions from Registration

Of course, not everybody has to register. The following have been granted exemptions from the painful process you're undergoing right now:

Persons Exempt from Registration

(a) The following persons associated with a member are not required to be registered with the Association:

(1) persons associated with a member whose functions are solely and exclusively clerical or ministerial;

(2) persons associated with a member who are not actively engaged in the investment banking or securities business;

(3) persons associated with a member whose functions are related solely and exclusively to the member's need for nominal corporate officers or for capital participation; and

(4) persons associated with a member whose functions are related solely and exclusively to:

(A) effecting transactions on the floor of a national securities exchange and who are registered as floor members with such exchange;

(B) transactions in municipal securities;

(C) transactions in commodities; or

(D) transactions in security futures, provided that any such person is registered with a registered futures association.

COMMENT: if you're just doing filing/temp work, you're not involved with underwriting or trading securities, you're just sitting on the board for a golfin' buddy, or you're a member of a futures or stock exchange filling orders for the firm, you don't have to register as a "registered representative."

Oh well. I guess we didn't find an exemption for you anywhere above, so you can keep on reading this exciting material and keep that appointment at the testing center.

Outside Business Activities

By the way, were you thinking of selling securities as sort of a "part-time job"? Maybe so, but your firm still has to know what you're up to outside the firm. As FINRA makes clear:

> No person associated with a member in any registered capacity shall be employed by, or accept compensation from, any other person as a result of any business activity, other than a passive investment, outside the scope of his relationship with his employer firm, unless he has provided prompt written notice to the member. Such notice shall be in the form required by the member.

So, whenever you have a chance to make money outside the firm, remember to notify the firm in writing. A "passive investment" is not the same thing as working, so if the question talks about a registered representative buying a limited partnership interest (DPP), remember that that's different.

Supervision

FINRA makes sure that principals are actually supervising registered representatives. The member firm has to establish and maintain written procedures to supervise the various types of business it's engaged in and has to supervise the activities of registered representatives. They must also designate a principal responsible for supervising each type of business in which the firm engages, and they must designate an "OSJ" (Office of Supervisory Jurisdiction), which is pretty much an office with, like, supervisory jurisdiction.

The firm has to perform internal inspections, and I'll just let FINRA explain this one:

> Each member shall conduct a review, at least annually, of the businesses in which it engages, which review shall be reasonably designed to assist in detecting and preventing violations of and achieving compliance with applicable securities laws and regulations, and with the Rules of this Association. Each member shall review the activities of each office, which shall include the periodic examination of customer accounts to detect and prevent irregularities or abuses and at least an annual inspection of each office of supervisory jurisdiction. Each branch office of the member shall be inspected according to a cycle which shall be set forth in the firm's written supervisory and inspection procedures.

Without getting bogged down in the amazing amount of verbiage used by FINRA, this is how they define office of supervisory jurisdiction (OSJ) and **branch office**:

> Branch office: any location identified by any means to the public or customers as a location at which the member conducts an investment banking or securities business

> OSJ: "Office of Supervisory Jurisdiction" means any office of a member at which any one or more of the following functions take place:

> (A) order execution and/or market making;

> (B) structuring of public offerings or private placements;

> (C) maintaining custody of customers' funds and/or securities;

> (D) final acceptance (approval) of new accounts on behalf of the member;

> (E) review and endorsement of customer orders

> (F) final approval of advertising or sales literature for use by persons associated with the member

(G) responsibility for supervising the activities of persons associated with the member at one or more other branch offices of the member.

Exam Confidentiality

Some individuals become upset when they discover that my practice questions can only mimic the actual exam—I didn't actually pay a fraternity brother to, like, steal an old exam for me. How serious is FINRA about protecting the surprise element in their exams? Let's see:

> FINRA considers all of its Qualification Examinations to be highly confidential. The removal from an examination center, reproduction, disclosure, receipt from or passing to any person, or use for study purposes of any portion of such Qualification Examination, whether of a present or past series, or any other use which would compromise the effectiveness of the Examinations and the use in any manner and at any time of the questions or answers to the Examinations are prohibited and are deemed to be a violation of Rule 2110.

Since that's the case, I decided to start a side business whereby I would text message my customers at the testing center for $100 per correct answer (no fee for incorrect answers). Unfortunately, FINRA says:

> An applicant cannot receive assistance while taking the examination. Each applicant shall certify to the Board that no assistance was given to or received by him during the examination.

Use of the FINRA Logo

Member firms may not use the FINRA logo in any manner; however, a firm may refer to itself as a "FINRA Member Firm" or "Member of FINRA." Also, if a firm refers to its FINRA membership on its website, it has to provide a hyperlink to FINRA's website, which is www.finra.org.

MEMBER CONDUCT RULES

Violating the member conduct rules leads to fines and sanctions that can get a firm expelled or a rep suspended or barred, for example. There are many ways to mistreat customers or try to operate outside the watchful eye of your principal and firm. I recommend *not going there* in the real world, although—really—my job is just to help you pass the test. So promise you'll at least tell the regulators what they want to hear when you sit for your exam.

Standards of Commercial Honor and Principles of Trade

A member, in the conduct of his business, shall observe high standards of commercial honor and just and equitable principles of trade.

Often other rules will state something like, "doing such and such would be considered conduct inconsistent with high standards of commercial honor and just and equitable principles of trade." For example, not paying an arbitration award would be a violation, or cheating on your Series 7 exam. So would:

Trading Ahead of Customer Limit Order

If you enjoyed those limit orders we examined in "Trading Securities," you'll recall that a customer might want to buy 1,000 shares of Oracle @$15. When the customer enters that order, maybe the firm is trading for its own account in Oracle, too. So, they have the customer order to buy 1,000 shares of Oracle @15 and when they see that the ASK is $15 and the size is (10) or 10 round lots, they go ahead and buy the stock...for their own trading account.

What about the customer who wanted to buy the stock at that price?

Screw him, the guy's a jerk, right?

Wrong. This FINRA Rule states:

> ...will require members to handle their customer limit orders with all due care so that members do not "trade ahead" of those limit orders. Thus, members that handle customer limit orders, whether received from their own customers or from another member, are prohibited from trading at prices equal or superior to that of the limit order without executing the limit order.

Then there is further clarification of that with the following:

> A member firm that accepts and holds an unexecuted limit order from its customer (whether its own customer or a customer of another member) in a NASDAQ or exchange-listed security and that continues to trade the subject security for its own account at prices that would satisfy the customer's limit order, without executing that limit order, shall be deemed to have acted in a manner inconsistent with just and equitable principles of trade.

When you're about to place some huge customer order to buy a bazillion shares of Google, you can pretty well guess that the price is about to go up. So, why not buy some Google for yourself, your firm, your wife, etc.? Because that's a violation called front-running, or taking advantage of an order you're about to place by buying some of the stock for yourself first. As FINRA states:

> **Front Running Policy**
>
> It shall be considered conduct inconsistent with just and equi-table principles of trade for a member or person associated with a member, for an account in which such member or person associated with a member has an interest, for an account with respect to which such member or person associated with a member exercises

investment discretion, or for certain customer accounts, to cause to be executed:

(a) an order to buy or sell an option or a security future when such member or person associated with a member causing such order to be executed has material, non-public market information concerning an imminent block transaction in the underlying security, or when a customer has been provided such material, non-public market information by the member or any person associated with a member; or

(b) an order to buy or sell an underlying security when such member or person associated with a member causing such order to be executed has material, non-public market information concerning an imminent block transaction in an option or a security future overlying that security, or when a customer has been provided such material, non-public market information by the member or any person associated with a member; prior to the time information concerning the block transaction has been made publicly available.

How do we know if the order is a "block transaction"? Luckily, the rule defines that as:

A transaction involving 10,000 shares or more of an underlying security, or options or security futures covering such number of shares is generally deemed to be a block transaction, although a transaction of less than 10,000 shares could be considered a block transaction in appropriate cases.

If you're a big Wall Street broker-dealer the research reports your analysts put out encouraging folks to buy or sell a particular security can have a huge impact on the price of the stock. So, if your research department is about to issue a "strong buy" recommendation and a glowing report on Google tomorrow morning, why not buy a boatload of Google shares today, and then release the report tomorrow? Won't that be fun? Your customers will want to buy the stock tomorrow at higher and higher prices and, heck, you'll be right here to sell it to them, at higher and higher prices.

As FINRA states:

Trading Ahead of Research Reports

The Board of Governors, under its statutory obligation to protect investors and enhance market quality, is issuing an interpretation to the Rules regarding a member firm's trading activities that occur in anticipation of a firm's issuance of a research report regarding a security. The Board of Governors is concerned with activities of member firms that purposefully establish or adjust the firm's inventory position in NASDAQ-listed securities, an exchange-listed security traded in the OTC market, or a derivative security based primarily on a specific NASDAQ or exchange-listed security in anticipation of the issuance of a research report in that same security. For example, a firm's research department may prepare a research report recommending the purchase of a particular NASDAQ-listed security. Prior to the publication and dissemination of the report, however, the trading department of the member firm might purposefully accumulate a position in that security to meet anticipated customer demand for that security. After the firm had established its position, the firm would issue the report, and thereafter fill customer orders from the member firm's inventory positions.

The Association believes that such activity is conduct which is inconsistent with just and equitable principles of trade, and not in the best interests of the investors. Thus, this interpretation prohibits a member from purposefully establishing, creating or changing the firm's inventory position in a NASDAQ-listed security, an exchange-listed security traded in the third market, or a derivative security related to the underlying equity security, in anticipation of the issuance of a research report regarding such security by the member firm.

See? These regulators take all the fun out of the business.

We saw that firms can't trade ahead of their customer limit orders, and it's basically the same deal with customer market orders.

Trading Ahead of Customer Market Orders

(a) A member must make every effort to execute a customer market order that it receives fully and promptly.

(b) A member that accepts and holds a market order of its own customer or a customer of another broker-dealer in a NASDAQ or exchange-listed security without immediately executing the order is prohibited from trading that security on the same side of the market for its own account, unless it immediately thereafter executes the customer market order up to the size and at the same price at which it traded for its own account or at a better price.

This next FINRA rule is shocking in its draconian reach:

Use of Manipulative, Deceptive or Other Fraudulent Devices

No member shall effect any transaction in, or induce the purchase or sale of, any security by means of any manipulative, deceptive or other fraudulent device or contrivance.

So, apparently, FINRA is in full agreement with that whole anti-fraud stuff in the Securities Exchange Act of 1934.

Communications with the Public

The first part of this rule defines "sales literature," "advertising," "correspondence," etc., but before we distinguish the various types of communications, let's understand the main points:

- A principal (compliance officer) has to approve the firm's communications and file them.
- The communications had better not be misleading in any way, shape or form.

(1) Standards Applicable to All Communications with the Public

(A) All member communications with the public shall be based on principles of fair dealing and good faith, must be fair and balanced, and must provide a sound basis for evaluating the facts in regard to any particular security or type of security, industry, or service. No member may omit any material fact or qualification if the omission, in the light of the context of the material presented, would cause the communications to be misleading.

(B) No member may make any false, exaggerated, unwarranted or misleading statement or claim in any communication with the public. No member may publish, circulate or distribute any public communication that the member knows or has reason to know contains any untrue statement of a material fact or is otherwise false or misleading.

(C) Information may be placed in a legend or footnote only in the event that such placement would not inhibit an investor's understanding of the communication.

(D) Communications with the public may not predict or project performance, imply that past performance will recur or make any exaggerated or unwarranted claim, opinion or forecast. A hypothetical illustration of mathematical principles is permitted, provided that it does not predict or project the performance of an investment or investment strategy.

(E) If any testimonial in a communication with the public concerns a technical aspect of investing, the person making the testimonial must have the knowledge and experience to form a valid opinion.

Okay. Seems fair enough—don't mislead your clients with a bunch of misleading communications. The exam may also want you to know the different types of communication. Understand that all communications have to be at least monitored by the firm, but that your correspondence with customers would only have to be monitored, while the advertising and sales literature produced at the firm would have to be approved before it went out. Either way, the communications had better not be misleading.

But, let's just let FINRA define their own terms at this point:

(a) Definitions

For purposes of this Rule and any interpretation thereof, "communications with the public" consist of:

(1) "Advertisement." Any material, other than an independently prepared reprint and institutional sales material, that is published, or used in any electronic or other public media, including any Web site, newspaper, magazine or other periodical, radio, television, telephone or tape recording, videotape display, signs or billboards, motion pictures, or telephone directories (other than routine listings).

(2) "Sales Literature." Any written or electronic communication, other than an advertisement, independently prepared reprint, institutional sales material and correspondence, that is generally distributed or made generally available to customers or the public, including circulars, research reports, market letters, performance reports or summaries, form letters, telemarketing scripts, seminar texts, reprints (that are not independently prepared reprints) or excerpts of any other advertisement, sales literature or published article, and press releases concerning a member's products or services.

(3) "Correspondence" consists of any written letter or electronic mail message distributed by a member to:

(A) one or more of its existing retail customers; and

(B) fewer than 25 prospective retail customers within any 30 calendar-day period.

(4) "Institutional Sales Material" consists of any communication that is distributed or made available only to a:

(A) governmental entity or subdivision thereof;

(B) employee benefit plan that meets the requirements of Section 403(b) or Section 457 of the Internal Revenue Code and has at least 100 participants, but does not include any participant of such a plan;

(C) qualified plan, as defined in Section 3(a)(12)(C) of the Act, that has at least 100 participants, but does not include any participant of such a plan;

(D) FINRA member or registered associated person of such a member; and

(E) person acting solely on behalf of any such institutional investor.

(5) "Public Appearance." Participation in a seminar, forum (including an interactive electronic forum), radio or television interview, or other public appearance or public speaking activity.

(6) "Independently Prepared Reprint."

(A) Any reprint or excerpt of any article issued by a publisher, provided that:

(i) the publisher is not an affiliate of the member using the reprint or any underwriter or issuer of a security mentioned in the reprint or excerpt and that the member is promoting;

(ii) neither the member using the reprint or excerpt nor any underwriter or issuer of a security mentioned in the reprint or excerpt has commissioned the reprinted or excerpted article; and

(iii) the member using the reprint or excerpt has not materially altered its contents except as necessary to make the reprint or excerpt consistent with applicable regulatory standards or to correct factual errors;

If you read all that exciting text closely, you noted that a letter or email to fewer than 25 prospects is considered "correspondence," what the test might call "group correspondence." But if the number is 25 or more, now it's "sales literature." Why would it matter? Sales literature has to be pre-approved. And, if it concerns investment companies, sales literature and advertising have to be filed with FINRA within 10 days of first use. A new firm would actually pre-file that stuff for the first year, in case the exam has absolutely lost its mind and expects everyone to be the Rain Man coming in.

(1) Date of First Use and Approval Information

The member must provide with each filing under this paragraph the actual or anticipated date of first use, the name and title of the registered principal who approved the advertisement or sales literature, and the date that the approval was given.

This is also self-explanatory:

(7) Spot-Check Procedures

In addition to the foregoing requirements, each member's written and electronic communications with the public may be subject to a spot-check procedure. Upon written request from the Department, each member must submit the material requested in a spot-check procedure within the time frame specified by the Department.

As is this:

(2) Record-keeping

(A) Members must maintain all advertisements, sales literature, and independently prepared reprints in a separate file for a period of three years from the date of last use. The file must include the name of the registered principal who approved each advertisement, item of sales literature, and independently prepared reprint and the date that approval was given.

(B) Members must maintain in a file information concerning the source of any statistical table, chart, graph or other illustration used by the member in communications with the public.

Market letters usually discuss recent economic developments as they relate to the stock or bond markets and maybe—just maybe—encourage the recipients to contact the firm for some help. FINRA decided recently that calling a **market letter** "sales literature" automatically might have slowed down the flow of valuable information to investors, since sales literature requires pre-approval. Therefore, market letters can be treated as "correspondence" instead, as long as they conform to the definition of correspondence. That means that if the market letter goes to existing retail customers or to fewer than 25 retail prospects, it qualifies as "correspondence," not subject to pre-approval by a principal.

A recent change says that firms who are intermediaries in selling investment company products (e.g., mutual funds, annuities) do not have to approve or file sales material that was already filed by someone else, usually the distributor of the fund. The intermediary selling the products could not alter the material significantly; otherwise, they would have changed it enough to require re-approval and re-filing, which is what they're trying to avoid in the first place.

We've seen that corporate stock, corporate bonds and municipal bonds settle "T + 3," and that the broker-dealer has to deliver a trade confirmation by settlement, or what the passage below calls "completion of each transaction." Here it is in the original legalese:

Confirmations

A member at or before the completion of each transaction with a customer shall give or send to such customer written notification disclosing (a) whether such member is acting as a broker for such customer, as a dealer for his own account, as a broker for some other person, or as a broker for both such customer and some other person; and (b) in any case in which such member is acting as a broker for such customer or for both such customer and some other person, either the name of the person from whom the security was purchased or to whom it was sold for such customer and the date and time when such transaction took place or the fact that such information will be furnished upon the request of such customer, and the source and amount of any commission or other remuneration received or to be received by such member in connection with the transaction.

This next one doesn't seem to require much explanation, so let's enjoy it in its original state:

Disclosure of Control Relationship with Issuer

A member controlled by, controlling, or under common control with, the issuer of any security, shall, before entering into any contract with or for a customer for the purchase or sale of such security, disclose to such customer the existence of such control, and if such disclosure is not made in writing, it shall be supplemented by the giving or sending of written disclosure at or before the completion of the transaction.

My online broker holds my securities in "street name," which means in the name of their clearing company. I am the beneficial owner. Therefore, when the companies whose stock I own send out proxy materials and annual reports, my broker has to forward them to me, as we see below:

Forwarding of Proxy and Other Materials

(a) A member has an inherent duty to forward promptly certain information regarding a security to the beneficial owner (or the beneficial owner's designated investment adviser) if the member carries the account in which the security is held for the beneficial owner and the security is registered in a name other than the name of the beneficial owner.

This next rule seems to make perfect sense to me—if the member firm is holding my cash and securities, maybe I'd like to see how their financial condition is looking.

Disclosure of Financial Condition to Customers

(a) A member shall make available to inspection by any bona fide regular customer, upon request, the information relative to such member's financial condition as disclosed in its most recent balance sheet prepared either in accordance with such member's usual practice or as required by any state or federal securities laws, or any rule or regulation thereunder.

(b) As used in paragraph (a) of this Rule, the term "customer" means any person who, in the regular course of such member's business, has cash or securities in the possession of such member.

There is a big difference between an unsolicited order and an investment that your client makes based on one of your recommendations. If you're recommending an investment, you have to make sure that the investment is suitable for the client, based on her time horizon, investment objectives, risk tolerance, etc. This next rule is perfectly clear as is:

Recommendations to Customers (Suitability)

(a) In recommending to a customer the purchase, sale or exchange of any security, a member shall have reasonable grounds for believing that the recommendation is suitable for such customer upon the basis of the facts, if any, disclosed by such customer as to his other security holdings and as to his financial situation and needs.

(b) Prior to the execution of a transaction recommended to a non-institutional customer, other than transactions with customers where investments are limited to money market mutual funds, a member shall make reasonable efforts to obtain information concerning:

(1) the customer's financial status;

(2) the customer's tax status;

(3) the customer's investment objectives; and

(4) such other information used or considered to be reasonable by such member or registered representative in making recommendations to the customer.

Notice a few things above. First, you base your recommendations on "the facts, if any, disclosed by such customer." That means if your client discloses assets of $300,000, then that is the number you're working with, even if everyone at the corner tavern swears she's worth five million easy. Also note that they used the words "non-institutional customer," which would be an individual, not a bank, trust department, mutual fund, insurance company, etc. These are the folks who need your recommendations, and FINRA needs you to know why you're recommending this particular investment to this particular client. Notice also that if the "investments are limited to money market mutual funds," you don't really need the customer's financial picture. The money market funds will just be a safe holding place to generate whatever short-term interest rates happen to be at the time until the investor decides what to do with her cash.

FINRA is, again, very clear in the rule below:

Fair Dealing with Customers

(a)(1) Implicit in all member and registered representative relationships with customers and others is the fundamental responsibility for fair dealing. Sales efforts must therefore be undertaken only on a basis that can be judged as being within the ethical standards of the Association's Rules, with particular emphasis on the requirement to deal fairly with the public.

(2) This does not mean that legitimate sales efforts in the securities business are to be discouraged by requirements which do not take into account the variety of circumstances which can enter into the member-customer relationship. It does mean, however, that sales efforts must be judged on the basis of whether they can be reasonably said to represent fair treatment for the persons to whom the sales efforts are directed, rather than on the argument that they result in profits to customers.

The part I underlined often shocks some of my students—hey, they say, as long as the guy makes money, why not? Well, FINRA takes the radical view that your sales efforts be judged on whether they represent fair treatment to your customers, so we'll work with that notion, shall we?

FINRA really gets hot with this next series of examples of how you can end up being unfair to your customer and, therefore, without a license.

(1) Recommending Speculative Low-Priced Securities

Recommending speculative low-priced securities to customers without knowledge of or attempt to obtain information concerning the customers' other securities holdings, their financial situation and other necessary data.

The principle here is that this practice, by its very nature, involves a high probability that the recommendation will not be suitable for at least some of the persons solicited. This has particular application to high pressure telephone sales campaigns.

(2) Excessive Trading Activity

Excessive activity in a customer's account, often referred to as "churning" or "overtrading." There are no specific standards to measure excessiveness of activity in customer accounts because this must be related to the objectives and financial situation of the customer involved.

(3) Trading in Mutual Fund Shares

Trading in mutual fund shares, particularly on a short-term basis. It is clear that normally these securities are not proper trading vehicles and such activity on its face may raise the question of Rule violation.

(4) Fraudulent Activity

(A) Numerous instances of fraudulent conduct have been acted upon by the Association and have resulted in penalties against members. Among some of these activities are:

(i) Fictitious Accounts

Establishment of fictitious accounts in order to execute transactions which otherwise would be prohibited, such as the purchase of hot issues, or to disguise transactions which are against firm policy.

(ii) Discretionary Accounts

Transactions in discretionary accounts in excess of or without actual authority from customers.

(iii) Unauthorized Transactions

Causing the execution of transactions which are unauthorized by customers or the sending of confirmations in order to cause customers to accept transactions not actually agreed upon.

(iv) Misuse of Customers' Funds or Securities

Unauthorized use or borrowing of customers' funds or securities.

(B) In addition, other fraudulent activities, such as forgery, non-disclosure or misstatement of material facts, manipulations and various deceptions, have been found in violation of Association Rules. These same activities are also subject to the civil and criminal laws and sanctions of federal and state governments.

(5) Recommending Purchases Beyond Customer Capability

Recommending the purchase of securities or the continuing purchase of securities in amounts which are inconsistent with the reasonable expectation that the customer has the financial ability to meet such a commitment.

Recent Concerns

FINRA puts out notices to their member firms to remind them of their responsibilities, update them on rule changes, etc. One of the more recent topics concerning suitability has to do with the tricky situation of a firm hiring an established registered representative who brings with him a book of business in which the customers own mutual funds and/or annuities that the new firm can't service. See, as another rule points out, distributors have to have a written sales agreement with any broker-dealer who wants to sell, and get paid on, their mutual funds and/or annuities. So, what should the firm and their newly hired registered rep do? They should probably just liquidate all the investments and put the clients into mutual funds/annuities that the firm and the rep can service and get paid on, right?

Not right. No way can the firm and the rep even *consider* the fact that they can receive "trail commissions" on the new funds/annuities they want to sell when making such a recommendation that a customer sell/liquidate his current holdings. Don't even factor that into your suitability determination. However, the fact that the rep and the firm can offer *service* on the new investments, and not the existing holdings, can be one—among many—suitability factors considered. So, if the new funds/annuities meet all the suitability requirements, then the rep and the firm can factor their ability to offer <u>service</u> on the new investments into their suitability determination. But, if they talk the client into liquidating a perfectly good annuity and incurring a stiff surrender charge just so the rep and the firm can get paid…nothing good can come of that. The firm and the rep would both probably pay five times more in disciplinary fines than they could possibly make on the annuity switch, not to mention the whole, you know, ethical thing.

Another *really* big concern the regulators have concerning suitability has to do with selling to senior citizen investors. Not to lump "senior citizens" into one big, neat category, but FINRA is reminding anyone who'll listen that senior citizens often have big needs for liquidity and cannot afford big investment losses, period. They should not be hustled into deferred annuities (variable or indexed) with long surrender periods and steep surrender charges, since their liquidity needs are so high. And, they had better understand that the "subaccounts" are tied to the stock and bond markets which have been very dangerous and scary places from time to time. Some firms and agents are so aggressive that they'll talk senior citizens into taking home equity loans or second mortgages to free up some money for high-risk, speculative investments. Or, they'll talk seniors into making big withdrawals from their IRAs in order to roll the dice maybe on oil & gas drilling partnerships, or complex derivatives no one understands.

Don't go there, FINRA is saying, especially if you might get caught.

FINRA is also concerned about "variable life settlements," which are usually pitched to senior citizens. With home values and investment accounts depressed, many senior citizens are tempted to sell their variable life insurance policy to an intermediary to get their hands on a big chunk of cash-money right now. FINRA reminds people that if the broker-dealer wants to get into this line of business, they must file a material change in business operations notice to FINRA. And, in case there is any doubt, a transaction involving *variable* life insurance is a securities transaction that requires proper licensing of individuals and registration of the securities. Firms who want to get into the variable life settlement line need to keep suitability in mind and be sure to fully inform customers that selling a variable life policy can trigger tax consequences, decreased access to insurance coverage, ineligibility for Medicaid, and the release of their private medical information. Also, there are transaction costs involved that the parties might not fully understand—FINRA wants firms and their registered representatives to be upfront and clear about such costs.

After purchasing variable life policies, the intermediary then sells the investment product to investors, and FINRA is concerned that retail investors will be attracted to the higher yields offered without understanding that the investment is almost completely illiquid—meaning, it can't be sold to anyone else. So, what if you want your money after holding the investment, say, seven years?

Too bad. You're waiting for the insured to die. The sooner he or she does so, the higher your yield. I kid you not. Although I doubt this topic will play a big role on your Series 7 exam, it does happen to be interesting in a ghoulish sort of way, so let's dig just a little deeper. FINRA notifies members firms:

> Also, the yield on a related product may be adversely affected by the parties structuring the related product—by an inexpert or incomplete actuarial analysis or an incomplete assessment of the medical conditions of any insured(s) covered by any policy in which an investor has an interest, or by a failure to follow applicable law regarding life settlements that may result in legal challenges at the time a death benefit is payable. External developments, such as advances in medical research and treatment regarding certain diseases, also may reduce the yield of related products.

Basically, FINRA is saying in their lawyerly manner that the yield an investor receives on a "life settlement" is related to how long it takes the insured to die. That's what they mean by "advances in medical research and treatment," which could be really good for the insured but would, by definition, reduce the yield to the investor, who has to keep waiting and waiting for the macabre security to mature. Also, even if the insured conveniently dies quickly, the investor may not be able to collect due to legal challenges based on faulty structuring of the product.

I am not making this up. However, we have already devoted too much time to this topic, so let's keep moving.

Remember that even though an "institutional investor" such as a pension fund or mutual fund is almost by definition sophisticated, FINRA reminds firms and their agents that they still have suitability requirements when servicing their institutional clients. If the products they're pitching are so new and so inherently complex that even the institutional buyers don't or couldn't reasonably understand the risks, then the firm and the agent have a responsibility to explain it in detail. And, if the buyer—institutional or not—still doesn't seem to understand the risks, don't sell it to him. CMOs and other mortgage derivatives are too complex for even the big Wall Street firms to understand, as we found out back in 2008. Many readers now work at firms who were rescued by bigger players with stronger balance sheets in one of the most bizarre shake-ups ever on "the Street." So, don't tell FINRA that institutional investors are by definition, you know, smart.

Believe it or not, the regulators feel that broker-dealers should get their customers the best possible price when they buy and when they sell. As FINRA explains:

Best Execution and Interpositioning

(a) In any transaction for or with a customer, a member and persons associated with a member shall use reasonable diligence to ascertain the best inter-dealer market for the subject security and buy or sell in such market so that the resultant price to the customer is as favorable as possible under prevailing market conditions. Among the factors that will be considered in determining whether a member has used "reasonable diligence" are:

(1) The character of the market for the security, e.g., price,

volatility, relative liquidity, and pressure on available communications;

(2) the size and type of transaction;

(3) the number of primary markets checked;

(4) location and accessibility to the customer's broker/dealer of primary markets and quotations sources.

This is why a very likely Series 7 question would have you answer that a customer order to buy should be filled at the lowest ask/offer price possible and a customer order to sell should be filled at the highest bid price possible at the time.

The violation called "**interpositioning**" has to do with unnecessarily inserting yourself into a transaction. As FINRA explains:

> (b) In any transaction for or with a customer, no member or person associated with a member shall interject a third party between the member and the best available market except in cases where the member can demonstrate that to his knowledge at the time of the transaction the total cost or proceeds of the transaction, as confirmed to the member acting for or with the customer, was better than the prevailing inter-dealer market for the security. A member's obligations to his customer are generally not fulfilled when he channels transactions through another broker/dealer or some person in a similar position, unless he can show that by so doing he reduced the costs of the transactions to the customer.

The member firm needs to be careful what they do with the securities they're holding for their customers:

Customers' Securities or Funds

c) Authorization to Lend

No member shall lend, either to himself or to others, securities carried for the account of any customer, which are eligible to be pledged or loaned unless such member shall first have obtained from the customer a written authorization permitting the lending of securities thus carried by such member.

Remember how short sellers borrow securities? That's partly what the above is talking about—get the loan consent form signed before you go loaning your customers' securities, okay?

The firm needs to keep their assets separate from the assets that clearly belong to the customer, as we see in the next item:

d) Segregation and Identification of Securities

No member shall hold securities carried for the account of any customer which have been fully paid for or which are excess margin securities unless such securities are segregated and identified by a method which clearly indicates the interest of such customer in those securities.

In case the exam wants to play really rough concerning the segregation of customer securities, let's throw the following clarification into the mix:

FINRA rules require members to segregate and identify by customers both fully paid and "excess margin" securities. With regard to a customer's account which contains only stocks, it is general practice for firms to segregate that portion of the stocks having a market value in excess of 140% of the debit balance therein.

So, if the "Dr" or "debit register" in a margin account is $5,000, 140% of that would be $7,000, and anything above that would be considered "excess margin" securities. How you could be allowed to sell securities without first knowing that, I have no idea, but thank God the testing committee is here to threaten you with a question even that trivial.

As you already know, you and your firm do not guarantee customers against losses, nor could you afford to.

(e) Prohibition Against Guarantees

No member or person associated with a member shall guarantee a customer against loss in connection with any securities transaction or in any securities account of such customer.

Can you share or "go halvsies" with your clients? Let's see what FINRA thinks about "sharing" with customers:

(f) Sharing in Accounts; Extent Permissible

(1)(A) Except as provided in paragraph (f)(2) no member or person associated with a member shall share directly or indirectly in the profits or losses in any account of a customer carried by the member or any other member; provided, however, that a member or person associated with a member may share in the profits or losses in such an account if (i) such person associated with a member obtains prior written authorization from the member employing the associated person; (ii) such member or person associated with a member obtains prior written authorization from the customer; and (iii) such member or person associated with a member shares in the profits or losses in any account of such customer only in direct

proportion to the financial contributions made to such account by
either the member or person associated with a member.

And then, just to keep things nice and simple, FINRA says, "Well, that whole proportionate sharing thing doesn't *always* apply," as we see right after the above otherwise clear passage:

(B) Exempt from the direct proportionate share limitation of paragraph (f)(1)(A)(iii) are accounts of the immediate family of such
member or person associated with a member. For purposes of this
Rule, the term "immediate family" shall include parents, mother-
in-law or father-in-law, husband or wife, children or any relative
to whose support the member or person associated with a member
otherwise contributes directly or indirectly.

Remember that the most important thing for a registered rep to do if he wants to "share in the profits and losses of the account" is to check his firm's compliance manual and get the firm's written permission. Some firms are more permissive than others on this issue, but the bottom line is to let the compliance department of your firm make this determination, as opposed to just going ahead and opening a joint bank account with a customer or passing envelopes of cash under the table at the corner bar.

FINRA rules require broker-dealer member firms to send account statements to clients no less frequently than every quarter. However, it is almost always going to be at least once per month, because if there has been any "account activity," the statement has to go out monthly. As we see from their definition of "account activity," it's pretty tough to imagine an account without any of that over the period of one month:

(c) Definitions

For purposes of this Rule, the following terms will have the stated
meanings:

(1) "account activity" includes, but is not limited to, purchases,
sales, interest credits or debits, charges or credits, dividend
payments, transfer activity, securities receipts or deliveries,
and/or journal entries relating to securities or funds in the
possession or control of the member.

Even if you're not trading every month, chances are you receive an interest payment or dividend. If you're in a margin account, there will be interest debited to your account, so account statements will always be sent monthly except when they're sent quarterly. What, exactly, is an "account statement"? FINRA defines it as:

[an account statement is a document]. . . containing a description
of any securities positions, money balances, or account activity
to each customer whose account had a security position, money

balance, or account activity during the period since the last such statement was sent to the customer.

As we know, margin trading is just a little high-risk, so lots of disclosure is, naturally, required:

Margin Disclosure Statement

(a) No member shall open a margin account, as specified in Regulation T of the Board of Governors of the Federal Reserve System, for or on behalf of a non-institutional customer, unless, prior to or at the time of opening the account, the member has furnished to the customer, individually, in writing or electronically, and in a separate document, the margin disclosure statement specified in this paragraph (a). In addition, any member that permits non-institutional customers either to open accounts on-line or to engage in transactions in securities on-line must post such margin disclosure statement on the member's Web site in a clear and conspicuous manner.

Some broker-dealers now operate in the same physical space used by banks, which is pretty shocking, if you think about it. Kind of like going to the local pharmacy and finding an opium den operating just behind the cold and flu remedies. I mean, sure, it all fits under the heading of "drugs," I guess, but one type is tightly regulated while the other form is just, you know, *partying*. Anyway, bank deposits are guaranteed by the FDIC. Banks are very safe, which is why we have phrases such as, "it's money in the bank," or, "you can bank on it." Stocks and bonds are associated with the word "broker," and that is probably not just a coincidence. In any case, FINRA is just a little nervous about bank customers not understanding that they have wandered far from the umbilical safety of FDIC-insured deposits when they visit the friendly broker-dealer up on the 11th floor:

(c) Standards for Member Conduct

No member shall conduct broker/dealer services on the premises of a financial institution where retail deposits are taken unless the member complies initially and continuously with the following requirements:

(1) Setting

Wherever practical, the member's broker/dealer services shall be conducted in a physical location distinct from the area in which the financial institution's retail deposits are taken. In all situations, members shall identify the member's broker/dealer services in a manner that is clearly distinguished from the financial institution's retail deposit-taking activities. The member's name shall be clearly displayed in the area in which the member conducts its broker/dealer services.

(2) Networking and Brokerage Affiliate Agreements

Networking and brokerage affiliate arrangements between a member and a financial institution must be governed by a written agreement that sets forth the responsibilities of the parties and the compensation arrangements. The member must ensure that the agreement stipulates that supervisory personnel of the member and representatives of the Securities and Exchange Commission and the Association will be permitted access to the financial institution's premises where the member conducts broker/dealer services in order to inspect the books and records and other relevant information maintained by the member with respect to its broker/dealer services.

(3) Customer Disclosure and Written Acknowledgment

At or prior to the time that a customer account is opened by a member on the premises of a financial institution where retail deposits are taken, the member shall:

(A) disclose, orally and in writing, that the securities products purchased or sold in a transaction with the member:

(i) are not insured by the Federal Deposit Insurance Corporation ("FDIC");

(ii) are not deposits or other obligations of the financial institution and are not guaranteed by the financial institution; and

(iii) are subject to investment risks, including possible loss of the principal invested; and

(B) make reasonable efforts to obtain from each customer during the account opening process a written acknowledgment of receipt of the disclosures required by paragraph (c)(3)(A).

(4) Communications with the Public

(A) All member confirmations and account statements must indicate clearly that the broker/dealer services are provided by the member.

(B) Advertisements and sales literature that announce the location of a financial institution where broker/dealer services are provided by the member or that are distributed by the member on the premises of a financial institution must disclose that securities products: are not insured by the FDIC; are not deposits or other obligations of the financial institution and are not guaranteed by the financial institution; and are subject to investment risks, including possible loss of the principal invested. The shorter, logo format described in paragraph (c)(4)(C) may be used to provide these disclosures.

(C) The following shorter, logo format disclosures may be used by members in advertisements and sales literature, including material published, or designed for use, in radio or television broadcasts, Automated Teller Machine ("ATM") screens, billboards, signs, posters, and brochures, to comply with the requirements of paragraph (c)(4)(B), provided that such disclosures are displayed in a conspicuous manner:

--Not FDIC Insured

--No Bank Guarantee

--May Lose Value

The Series 7 will likely ask a few questions about borrowing from or lending to customers. Those words make the regulators a little nervous—I mean, how, exactly, does that registered representative define "borrowing" from a customer? Is this like an actual loan from a bank that happens to be his customer? Or, is this like a little old lady who seldom monitors her account and, therefore, probably won't even notice that the $50,000 was missing for a few weeks? We're talking, of course, about:

Borrowing From or Lending to Customers

(a) No person associated with a member in any registered capacity may borrow money from or lend money to any customer of such person unless: (1) the member has written procedures allowing the borrowing and lending of money between such registered persons and customers of the member; and (2) the lending or borrowing arrangement meets one of the following conditions: (A) the customer is a member of such person's immediate family; (B) the customer is a financial institution regularly engaged in the business of providing credit, financing, or loans, or other entity or person that regularly arranges or extends credit in the ordinary course of business; (C) the customer and the registered person are both registered persons of the same member firm; (D) the lending arrangement is based on a personal relationship with the customer, such that the loan would not have been solicited, offered, or given had the customer and the associated person not maintained a relationship outside of the broker/customer relationship; or (E) the lending arrangement is based on a business relationship outside of the broker-customer relationship.

How do they define "immediate family" here? Quite broadly, actually:

(c) The term immediate family shall include parents, grandparents, mother-in-law or father-in-law, husband or wife, brother or sister, brother-in-law or sister-in-law, son-in-law or daughter-in-law, children, grandchildren, cousin, aunt or uncle, or niece or nephew, and shall also include any other person whom the registered person supports, directly or indirectly, to a material extent.

As with sharing, the most important thing is to get your firm's permission before borrowing or lending with *any* customer. A registered representative who borrows money "under the table" from a customer will usually end up getting suspended by FINRA.

Being a member of FINRA is a big deal. Such a big deal that if somebody is *not* a member, your firm had better not extend any of the membership privileges to this mere civilian, as we see in the following FINRA rule:

Dealing with Non-Members

(a) No member shall deal with any non-member broker or dealer except at the same prices, for the same commissions or fees, and on the same terms and conditions as are by such member accorded to the general public.

So, if you let me buy a mutual fund below the NAV, I would be forever grateful, but FINRA would be forever on your ass.

We already mentioned that registered reps can receive **continuing commissions** in some cases. Let's see how FINRA explains this rather good piece of news:

Continuing Commissions Policy

The Board of Governors has held that the payment of continuing commissions in connection with the sale of securities is not improper so long as the person receiving the commissions remains a registered representative of a member of the Association.

However, payment of compensation to registered representatives after they cease to be employed by a member of the Association — or payment to their widows or other beneficiaries — will not be deemed in violation of Association Rules, provided bona fide contracts call for such payment.

Also, a dealer-member may enter into a bona fide contract with another dealer-member to take over and service his accounts and, after he ceases to be a member, to pay to him or to his widow or other beneficiary continuing commissions generated on such accounts.

An arrangement for the payment of continuing commissions shall not under any circumstances be deemed to permit the solicitation of new business or the opening of new accounts by persons who are not registered. Any arrangement for payment of continuing commissions must, of course, conform with any applicable laws or regulations.

Keep the charges reasonable between you and your customers, and keep the charges fair *among* your customers, as we see here:

Charges for Services Performed

Charges, if any, for services performed, including miscellaneous services such as collection of moneys due for principal, dividends, or interest; exchange or transfer of securities; appraisals, safe-keeping or custody of securities, and other services, shall be reasonable and not unfairly discriminatory between customers.

Member broker-dealer firms have to give customers fair and reasonable prices when taking the other side of the transaction, and we looked at the 5% markup policy, with all the relevant factors, in the fascinating chapter on Trading Securities.

Another rule covers discretionary accounts, which we covered when we were talking about—go figure—discretionary accounts. Just means that the firm needs to have the discretionary authorization in writing before executing the first transaction. The transactions need to be suitable and if, God forbid, you and your firm start executing excessive transactions just to enrich yourselves... well, you'd never do a thing like that or be dumb enough to get caught, right?

And, again, time/price are not a big deal. So, if I ask you to "buy 1,000 shares of a software company," that's a discretionary order. If I tell you to "buy 1,000 shares of Oracle today," that requires no special authorization. It's a "market not held" order, as we mentioned, where you or the floor broker down on the NYSE floor can wait until the time and the price are right before executing the transaction.

Rules on analyst reports attempt to clean up the abuses of the go-go '90s, where firms would issue "strong buy" reports on a particular stock, not because it was a good investment for their retail customers, but because the "strong buy" recommendation would help prop up the stock price long enough to let some big-shot CEO exercise his stock options for a nice $10 million profit. Then, since that guy is pleased as punch, perhaps he'll use the firm's investment banking department for his next merger or additional offering of stock. See? The CEO guy is rich and happy, the firm is rich and happy, and the retail investors...well, as PT Barnum said, there's one born every minute.

From now on, investment banking can have no say over the compensation of a research analyst, who had better NOT be promoting a company's stock just to help land investment banking business or to pay some company back after using the firm's investment bank. We'll actually see the same rule under NYSE rules, so let's save the excitement for a few pages in order to keep this page-turner humming along.

Speaking of the go-go '90s, as it turns out, there were two basic types of IPOs: the ones where people made millions of dollars in an afternoon as easily as shooting fish in a barrel, and those that the public actually got to buy. So, since the big players in the industry decided to pass out hot

IPOs to their agents, their agents' wives, husbands, mothers-in-law, etc., FINRA has had to crack the whip. Reminds me of high school, when the whole school would lose weight room privileges because two or three chuckleheads thought it would be a good idea to set off an M-80 directly under the supine bench press apparatus. In any case, there is almost no way for you or your immediate family to buy an IPO now, as we see from the rule below:

Restrictions on the Purchase and Sale of Initial Equity Public Offerings

(a) General Prohibitions

(1) A member or a person associated with a member may not sell, or cause to be sold, a new issue to any account in which a restricted person has a beneficial interest, except as otherwise permitted herein.

(2) A member or a person associated with a member may not purchase a new issue in any account in which such member or person associated with a member has a beneficial interest, except as otherwise permitted herein.

b) Preconditions for Sale

Before selling a new issue to any account, a member must in good faith have obtained within the twelve months prior to such sale, a representation from:

(1) Beneficial Owners

the account holder(s), or a person authorized to represent the beneficial owners of the account, that the account is eligible to purchase new issues in compliance with this rule;

Who are these "restricted persons," you might ask?

10) "Restricted person" means:

(A) Members or other broker/dealers

(B) Broker/Dealer Personnel

(i) Any officer, director, general partner, associated person, or employee of a member or any other broker/dealer (other than a limited business broker/dealer);

(ii) Any agent of a member or any other broker/dealer (other than a limited business broker/dealer) that is engaged in the investment banking or securities business; or

(iii) An immediate family member of a person specified in subparagraph

(B)(i) or (ii) if the person specified in subparagraph (B)(i) or (ii):

a. materially supports, or receives material support from, the immediate family member;

b. is employed by or associated with the member, or an affiliate of the member, selling the new issue to the immediate family member; or

c. has an ability to control the allocation of the new issue.

(C) Finders and Fiduciaries

(D) Portfolio Managers

(i) Any person who has authority to buy or sell securities for a bank, savings and loan institution, insurance company, investment company, investment advisor, or collective investment account.

(ii) An immediate family member of a person specified in subparagraph (D)(i) that materially supports, or receives material support from, such person.

(E) Persons Owning a Broker/Dealer

(vi) An immediate family member of a person specified in subparagraphs (E)(i)-(v) unless the person owning the broker/dealer:

a. does not materially support, or receive material support from, the immediate family member;

b. is not an owner of the member, or an affiliate of the member, selling the new issue to the immediate family member; and

c. has no ability to control the allocation of the new issue.

And, just how does *this* rule define "immediate family"? Also very broadly:

"Immediate family member" means a person's parents, mother-in-law or father-in-law, spouse, brother or sister, brother-in-law or sister-in-law, son-in-law or daughter-in-law, and children, and any other individual to whom the person provides material support.

"Material support" means directly or indirectly providing more than 25% of a person's income in the prior calendar year. Members of the immediate family living in the same household are deemed to be providing each other with material support.

FINRA RULE. VARIABLE CONTRACTS.

This rule tells member firms that when they accept payment from a customer for a variable contract, the price at which the money is invested is the price next computed when the payment is accepted by the insurance company. Just an obvious restatement of the "forward pricing" concept you already know for mutual funds, which are the same thing as variable annuities minus the tax-deferral and death benefit. The member firm has to transmit the application and payment promptly to the insurance company. No member who is a principal underwriter may sell variable contracts through another broker/dealer unless the broker-dealer is a member, and there is a sales agreement in effect between the parties. The agreement must also provide that the sales commission be returned to the insurance company if the purchaser terminates the contract within seven business days. Sorry, that rule doesn't favor you very much, but it is what it is. Also, member firms can only sell variable annuities if the annuity/insurance company promptly pays out when clients surrender their contracts.

Associated persons (you) may not accept compensation from anyone other than the member firm. The only exception here is if there is an arrangement between you and the other party that your member firm agrees to, and your firm deals with a bunch of other requirements. Associated persons (you) may not accept securities from somebody else in exchange for selling variable contracts. The only non-cash compensation that can be offered or accepted would be:

- gifts that do not exceed an annual amount per person fixed periodically by the Association and are not preconditioned on achievement of a sales target. The gift limit is still $100, by the way.
- an occasional meal, a ticket to a sporting event or the theater, or comparable entertainment which is neither so frequent nor so extensive as to raise any question of propriety and is not preconditioned on achievement of a sales target.
- payment or reimbursement by offerors in connection with meetings held by an offeror or by a member for the purpose of training or education of associated persons of a member.

For that last bullet, remember that the associated person (you) would have to get your firm's permission to attend and that your attendance and reimbursement of expenses cannot be preconditioned on your meeting a sales target. Only you—not your guest—can have your expenses reimbursed, which is a rule just begging to be bent like a freakin' pretzel but let's keep moving. The location of the meeting has to be appropriate, too, meaning if the offeror's office is in Minneapolis, it looks real suspicious when the meeting is held in Montego Bay, mon. And—as always—the record keeping requirements are tougher than we'd like. As the rule states, your:

```
member firm shall maintain records of all compensation received by
the member or its associated persons from offerors. The records
shall include the names of the offerors, the names of the asso-
ciated persons, the amount of cash, the nature and, if known, the
value of non-cash compensation received.
```

Your firm can give you non-cash compensation for selling variable contracts, but they can't compensate you more for selling one variable contract than for another. This rule states that the non-cash compensation arrangement requires that the credit received for each variable contract security is equally weighted.

FINRA RULE. INVESTMENT COMPANY SECURITIES

Mutual funds and variable annuities are both investment companies covered under the Investment Company Act of 1940. Since they are so similar, it's not surprising that this FINRA rule on investment company securities is very similar to the one we just looked at on variable contracts. Like the previous rule, this one tells member firms who act as underwriters/distributors of investment companies that they need to have a written sales agreement between themselves and other dealers. If the other dealer is not an FINRA member, they would have to pay the full public offering price, which would make it real tough for them to make a profit. As before, member firms need to transmit payment from customers to the mutual fund companies promptly.

Excessive Charges

This rule also tells member firms not to offer or sell shares of investment companies if the sales charges are excessive. What makes the sales charges excessive? Well, you already know that 8.5% of the public offering price is the maximum sales charge. Also note that if the fund does not offer breakpoints and rights of accumulation that satisfy FINRA, the fund cannot charge 8.5%. As you already know, it would be a violation to describe a mutual fund as being "no load" or as having "no sales charge" if the investment company has a front-end (A shares) or deferred (B shares) sales charge, or whose 12b-1 fees exceed .25 of 1%.

Withhold Orders

Although I would have thought this truth were self-evident, this FINRA rule states that, "No member shall withhold placing customers' orders for any investment company security so as to profit himself as a result of such withholding." Another part of this rule says that member firms can only purchase investment company shares either for their own account or to fill existing customer orders—they can't just pick up a batch of shares and then see if anybody wants them, in other words.

Anti-Reciprocal Rule

This next thing seems highly testable to me. Broker-dealers cannot decide to sell particular investment company shares based on how much trading business the investment company does or would consider doing through the firm. The old "pay to play" method is a big no-no, in other words. Be very broad in your understanding of this rule—if it looks at all as if a member firm is tying the promotion of particular funds to the amount of trading commissions they receive when the fund places trades through them, it's not passing the smell test. This would also apply to a member firm offering to compensate their branch managers and reps more for selling the shares of those investment companies who execute transactions through the firm, generating fat commissions.

So, I just told you that a broker-dealer (member firm) cannot sell mutual fund shares if the mutual fund trades through the broker-dealer, generating commissions for the member firm, right?

No. What I'm saying is that the firm can't tie the promotion/sale of the mutual fund to the level of trading the fund does or intends to do through the firm. Similarly, firms definitely compensate their branch managers and representatives for selling mutual fund shares; they simply can't compensate them more for selling the shares of the funds willing to "pay to play."

Interestingly, as I look at FINRA's website this morning, I see that the regulators just fined a firm over $12 million for placing mutual funds on a "preferred list" in exchange for those funds doing lots of lucrative trading business through the firm. The news release calls it a "shelf space program," which is a great name for it. See, in the supermarket, all the products you see are there because the company paid a fee for "shelf space." Well, that's okay for cookies and crackers, but not for mutual funds.

This all boils down to the fact that a broker-dealer should recommend a mutual fund because it's the best investment for a particular client, not because the broker-dealer will make money from the mutual fund when it executes its trades through the firm.

If a transaction involves the purchase of shares of an investment company that imposes a deferred sales charge when the investor redeems the shares some day, the written confirmation must also include the following legend: "On selling your shares, you may pay a sales charge. For the charge and other fees, see the prospectus." The legend must appear on the front of a confirmation and in, at least, 8-point type.

I am not making that up. 8-point type. What's more, I understand that the members of the rowdy 9-point-font faction of the rules committee had to be forcibly restrained several times before finally bowing to the demands of their relentless, 8-point-font-favoring colleagues.

Finally, everything I told you about the FINRA rule concerning receipt of payment from other sources, including non-cash compensation, holds true here, too. So, assuming you haven't fallen asleep or died of boredom yet, you might want to do a quick review of that section.

FINRA takes the radical view that firms must supervise their principals and their representatives. If they don't supervise them, FINRA will kick out the whole bunch. In fact, it's somewhat amusing to me (as one not subject to any FINRA action of any type) to see that when a firm gets busted for breaking a rule, they also get busted for not having better written procedures and/or processes that could have prevented the nonsense that happened from happening. It's like a little bonus violation that punishes the crazy reps who were pushing high-risk securities on senior citizens and the principals in charge who should have been smart enough to prevent that crap from happening. As this rule states:

b) Written Procedures

(1) Each member shall establish, maintain, and enforce written procedures to supervise the types of business in which it engages and to supervise the activities of registered representatives, registered principals, and other associated persons that are reasonably designed to achieve compliance with applicable securities laws and regulations, and with the applicable Rules of FINRA.

The very next item below that informs firms that if FINRA notifies you that because certain of your reps come from **"disciplined firms,"** your firm must now tape-record every word that passes between them and your customers. Sounds like a pain in the neck for the firm, don't it? They'd not only have to tape-record all conversations and keep them on file the usual three years, but also file regular reports with FINRA to assure them that while these two reps did have a brief career with Soprano and Aprile Securities, they're actually keeping the churning in check quite nicely at this point and have only used threats of violence twice in the immediately preceding fiscal quarter.

In other words, if you have a bunch of disciplinary problems in your past, it's time to find a new career.

MARKET MANIPULATION

As we've seen, the federal government is very interested in maintaining a fair and efficient capital market. If a few cheaters are allowed to manipulate the markets for their own advantage, the entire financial system suffers. Therefore, the exam might bring up terms such as **painting the tape,** a technique whereby individuals acting together repeatedly sell a security to one another without actually changing ownership of the securities. This is intended to give an impression of increased trading volume that can drive up the market price of their holdings. Other forms of **market manipulation** include **capping** and **pegging.** Capping is the illegal technique of trying to keep a stock price from rising above the "cap," while pegging involves trying to move a stock up to a particular price. A shady call option writer, for example, might want to help ensure that the calls expire by artificially conspiring to keep the price of the underlying stock from rising (capping).

MONEY LAUNDERING

Money laundering is the process of turning illegal profits into what appears to be legitimate, "clean" money. For example, Tony Soprano routinely pays money launderers to take the money he makes through his various illegal rackets and turn them into what appear to be legitimate funds. If he and Silvio take in, say, $1 million cash money back in the office of the Ba-Da-Bing, the IRS would get sort of suspicious if they tried to report that as income from the bar. I mean, you can only turn in so many phony receipts from liquor distributors to make that income pass the smell test. So, criminals with far more creative financial minds than anyone you're likely to meet this week, use elaborate schemes to take that "dirty" money and make it "clean." The exam may bring up the three distinct phases of money laundering:

- Placement
- Layering
- Integration

Placement is the first stage in the cycle in which illegally generated funds are placed into the financial system or are smuggled out of the country. The goals of the money launderer are to remove the cash from where it was acquired in order to avoid detection from the authorities, and to then transform it into other assets, e.g., travelers' checks, money orders, etc. **Layering** is the first attempt at disguising the source of the ownership of the funds by creating complex layers of transactions. The purpose of layering is to disassociate the dirty money from the source of the crime through a complicated web of financial transactions. Typically, layers are created by moving money in and out of offshore bank accounts of shell companies, through electronic funds' transfers (EFT). Because there are over 500,000 wire transfers circling the globe every day, most of which is legitimate, there isn't enough information disclosed on any single wire transfer to know how clean or dirty the money is. This provides an excellent way for money launderers to move their dirty money. Other forms used by launderers are complex dealings with stock, commodity and futures brokers. Given the sheer volume of daily transactions, and the high degree of anonymity available, the chances of transactions being traced is insignificant. In other words, broker-dealers are great places to launder money, which is why broker-dealers need to help the federal government clamp down on terrorists and other criminals trying to layer dirty money through a flurry of trading activity. **Integration** is the final stage in the process. In this stage the money is integrated into the legitimate financial system. Integration of the now-clean money into the economy is accomplished by making it appear to have been legally earned. By this stage, it is very difficult to distinguish "clean" financial assets from "dirty."

Okay, so the federal government sort of insists that broker-dealers do not open up accounts for Osama Bin Laden or anyone who funnels money to the wacky multimillionaire cave dweller. FINRA lays out the rules for preventing money laundering:

Anti-Money Laundering Compliance Program

On or before April 24, 2002, each member shall develop and implement a written anti-money laundering program reasonably designed to achieve and monitor the member's compliance with the requirements of the Bank Secrecy Act (31 U.S.C. 5311, et seq.), and the implementing regulations promulgated thereunder by the Department of the Treasury. Each member's anti-money laundering program must be approved, in writing, by a member of senior management.

The Bank Secrecy Act (BSA) authorizes the U.S. Treasury Department to require financial institutions such as banks and broker-dealers to maintain records of personal financial transactions that "have a high degree of usefulness in criminal, tax and regulatory investigations and proceedings." It also authorizes the Treasury Department to require any financial institution to report any "suspicious transaction relevant to a possible violation of law or regulation." These reports, called "Suspicious Activity Reports," are filed with the Treasury Department's Financial Crimes Enforcement Network ("**FinCEN**").

This is done secretly (thus the law's middle name), without the consent or knowledge of bank customers, any time a financial institution determines that a transaction is suspicious. The reports are made available electronically to every U.S. Attorney's Office and to 59 law enforcement agencies, including the FBI, Secret Service, and Customs Service.

Recently, the U.S. Treasury Department used the Bank Secrecy Act (BSA) to require that for transmittals of funds of $3,000 or more, broker-dealers are required to obtain and keep certain specified information concerning the parties sending and receiving those funds. In addition, broker-dealers must include this information on the actual transmittal order. Also, any cash transactions over $10,000 require the same type of uptight record keeping. For these, broker-dealers must file a **Currency Transaction Report (CTR)** with FinCEN.

Why? Because terrorist and other criminal organizations fund their operations through money laundering. Since broker-dealers are financial institutions, they're lumped in with banks and required to do all kinds of record keeping to help the government prevent these operations.

With the passage of the "USA Patriot Act" broker-dealers and other financial institutions have to help the government monitor suspicious activity that could be tied to money laundering. Broker-dealers now have to report any transaction that involves at least $5,000 if the broker-dealer knows, suspects, or has reason to suspect that it doesn't pass the smell test. FINRA spells out four specific characteristics that would make a broker-dealer file a **suspicious activity report (SAR)**. An SAR would be filed if the transaction falls within one of four classes:

- the transaction involves funds derived from illegal activity or is intended or conducted to hide or disguise funds or assets derived from illegal activity;
- the transaction is designed to evade the requirements of the Bank Secrecy Act
- the transaction appears to serve no business or apparent lawful purpose or is not the sort of transaction in which the particular customer would be expected to engage and for which the broker/dealer knows of no reasonable explanation after examining the available facts; or
- the transaction involves the use of the broker/dealer to facilitate criminal activity

Broker-dealers now have to have a "**customer identification program**" whereby they require more information to open an account. They now have to get the customer's date of birth. If the customer is not a U.S. citizen, the firm will need:

- taxpayer ID number
- passport number and country of issuance
- alien ID card
- other government-issued photo ID card

Even the U.S. citizen may need to show a photo ID, just as you do when you go take your Series 7 exam.

Finally, the federal government now maintains an **Office of Foreign Asset Control (OFAC)** designed to protect against the threat of terrorism. This office maintains a list of individuals and organizations viewed as a threat to the U.S. Broker-dealers, and other financial institutions now need to make sure they aren't setting up accounts for these folks, or—if they are—they need to block/freeze the assets.

REGULATION S-P

Sharing customer information with law enforcement officials is one thing. Providing it to tele-marketers and identity thieves is quite another. To fight identity theft and to protect customers from having too much of their information shared with people they've never met, the SEC enacted Regulation S-P to put into place a requirement from the Gramm-Leach-Bliley Act. Basically, "a financial institution must provide its customers with a notice of its privacy policies and practices, and must not disclose nonpublic personal information about a consumer to nonaffiliated third parties unless the institution provides certain information to the consumer and the consumer has not elected to opt out of the disclosure." A "**consumer**" is basically a prospect, someone interested in establishing some type of account. A "**customer**" is someone who has now opened a financial relationship with the firm. Broker-dealers now have to deliver initial and annual notices to customers about their privacy policies and practices, and about the opportunity and methods to opt out of their institution's sharing of their nonpublic personal information with nonaffiliated third parties. The initial notice must be provided no later than when the firm establishes a customer relationship with the individual. Broker-dealers and financial advisers also need to have written supervisory procedures dealing with the disposal of consumer credit report information. Since firms typically look at a consumer's credit history before opening accounts—especially margin accounts—selling annuities, or providing financial planning services, the firms need to safely dispose of the information rather than just setting it all in a big box out back.

FINRA RULE, FIDELITY BONDS

This next rule is self-explanatory, which is good, because if you think *you're* getting bored reading this crap, imagine having to write it:

Fidelity Bonds

(a) Coverage Required

Each member required to join the Securities Investor Protection Corporation who has employees and who is not a member in good standing of the American Stock Exchange, Inc.; the Boston Stock Exchange; the Midwest Stock Exchange, Inc.; the New York Stock Exchange, Inc.; the Pacific Stock Exchange, Inc.; the Philadelphia Stock Exchange, Inc.; or the Chicago Board Options Exchange shall:

(1) Maintain a blanket fidelity bond, in a form substantially similar to the standard form of Brokers Blanket Bond promulgated by the Surety Association of America, covering officers and employees which provides against loss and has agreements covering at least the following:

(A) Fidelity

(B) On Premises

(C) In Transit

(D) Misplacement

(E) Forgery and Alteration (including check forgery)

(F) Securities Loss (including securities forgery)

(G) Fraudulent Trading

FINRA RULE, OUTSIDE BUSINESS ACTIVITIES OF AN ASSOCIATED PERSON

Many students seem shocked when I tell them that they'll need to notify their employing broker-dealer before doing any type of work outside the firm. As this rule stipulates:

No person associated with a member in any registered capacity shall be employed by, or accept compensation from, any other person as a result of any business activity, other than a passive investment, outside the scope of his relationship with his employer firm, unless

he has provided prompt written notice to the member. Such notice
shall be in the form required by the member.

FINRA RULE. PRIVATE SECURITIES TRANSACTIONS OF AN ASSOCIATED PERSON

Some people who attend my live classes seem to imagine that they'll be maintaining their independence and autonomy even after associating with a member firm. They can't believe they'd have to tell the firm about the landscaping business they're planning to open with their brother-in-law Joey next spring. They're appalled that, say, Ameritrade would have the audacity to inform their employer that they just opened an investment account at their firm. They also don't see why they can't join up with a member firm but continue to offer whatever type of investment opportunity comes up to their clients.

Well, FINRA wants all activities of a registered representative to be monitored, so if the registered representative is sitting in his office offering investors a chance to invest in his sister's new diner down the street without telling his firm, there is no way the firm could monitor his wacky sales activities. That could even be the answer to a Series 7 question that asks why **selling away** is a violation—because it gives your principal/firm no opportunity to supervise your activities. It also gives them no opportunity to say, "Are you out of your f*#*#in' mind, you little piece of #*#*?" before calmly explaining the spirit and applicability of FINRA rules to your renegade little attitude. So, a registered representative cannot be offering securities to investors that his firm knows absolutely nothing about. As this rule makes clear:

> No person associated with a member shall participate in any manner in a private securities transaction except in accordance with the requirements of this Rule.
>
> (b) Written Notice
>
> Prior to participating in any private securities transaction, an associated person shall provide written notice to the member with which he is associated describing in detail the proposed transaction and the person's proposed role therein and stating whether he has received or may receive selling compensation in connection with the transaction.

Once you've provided written notice to your employer they can either approve or disapprove of your little plan. If they approve your activities the transaction must be recorded on the books and records of the member and the member has to supervise the rep's participation in the transaction as if the transaction were executed on behalf of the member. In other words, your boss is going to be enjoying free meals at your sister's diner for perpetuity, on the odd chance that he'll let you offer shares in the company at all. What if the firm says they disapprove of your activity?

Don't do it. And if you do, don't get caught. Otherwise, we'll see you up on the FINRA website with words like "selling away," "suspension," and "conduct inconsistent with just and equitable principles of trade."

FINRA RULE. TRANSACTIONS FOR OR BY ASSOCIATED PERSONS

On the new account form, we ask if the customer is associated with a member firm. If your broker-dealer knows that the customer is associated with a member firm, or if an associate of a member firm has discretion over the account, your firm must:

- notify the employer member in writing, prior to the execution of a transaction for such account, of the executing member's intention to open or maintain such an account;
- upon written request by the employer member, transmit duplicate copies of confirmations, statements, or other information with respect to such account; and
- notify the person associated with the employer member of the executing member's intention to provide the notice and information required

You will soon be an associate of a member firm, so when you want to open an investment account with another firm, first of all, what the heck are you thinking? Do you understand *nothing* about office politics? Secondly, this FINRA rule states:

> A person associated with a member, prior to opening an account or placing an initial order for the purchase or sale of securities with another member, shall notify both the employer member and the executing member, in writing, of his or her association with the other member; provided, however, that if the account was established prior to the association of the person with the employer member, the associated person shall notify both members in writing promptly after becoming so associated.

As in baseball, disputes in the sport known as investing are settled in arbitration. In other words, member firms can't sue each other in civil court if an underwriting turns sour and one member of the syndicate is convinced they are owed an additional $1 million from another member, who acted as syndicate manager in the IPO. That sort of dispute must be submitted to arbitration. That means you get one shot, no appeals. As we saw earlier, firms get their customers to sign pre-dispute arbitration agreements, but they have to be very upfront about what the heck that means in the document they're getting the customer to sign. The rule stipulates that the warning has to look like this:

> This agreement contains a pre-dispute arbitration clause. By signing an arbitration agreement the parties agree as follows:
>
> (A) All parties to this agreement are giving up the right to sue each other in court, including the right to a trial by jury, except as provided by the rules of the arbitration forum in which a claim is filed.
>
> (B) Arbitration awards are generally final and binding; a party's

ability to have a court reverse or modify an arbitration award is
very limited.

(C) The ability of the parties to obtain documents, witness statements and other discovery is generally more limited in arbitration
than in court proceedings.

(D) The arbitrators do not have to explain the reason(s) for their
award.

(E) The panel of arbitrators will typically include a minority of
arbitrators who were or are affiliated with the securities industry.

(F) The rules of some arbitration forums may impose time limits
for bringing a claim in arbitration. In some cases, a claim that
is ineligible for arbitration may be brought in court.

(G) The rules of the arbitration forum in which the claim is
filed, and any amendments thereto, shall be incorporated into this
agreement.

Only by getting the customer to sign this agreement would your firm know that when somebody loses a bunch of money selling stock short or trading like a fiend, that somebody will not be able to drag them through civil court, with appeal after appeal. Arbitration is faster and cheaper for all involved.

FINRA rules make sure that your firm provides you, the registered rep, with the same written disclosure that you are bound by FINRA Arbitration whenever you are asked to sign a U4 or U5 form.

EXAGGERATING YOUR EXPERTISE

It's already, of course, a violation of FINRA rules to offer/sell securities by using manipulative/deceptive methods. But, specifically, FINRA and the state regulators are concerned about registered representatives giving themselves titles that make them sound like experts, when, in fact, maybe they're not at all. For example, FINRA warns firms that agents have been known to pay a marketing company to write a book on some financial topic and put the agent's name and bio on it, as if he wrote the thing. Kind of misleading, wouldn't you say? Or, maybe a marketing company could produce something that looks like an important financial magazine with a worldwide distribution with articles apparently written by or about *you* all over the place. Kind of misleading, too, right? And, what with the World Wide Web and all, some reps will put out webcasts that sound like radio interviews when, in fact, somebody they're paying is just feeding them questions like an infomercial. I mean, it's an excellent marketing strategy, no doubt about that. It's just, you know, misleading as far as the regulators are concerned.

So is giving yourself a credential that you sort of made up or sort of purchased from a marketing company selling certificates with credentials on them. Check your firm's compliance department before getting all creative with your marketing, especially when marketing to senior citizen investors. Putting the word "senior" into a credential you plan to use is a very dangerous thing. I'm not saying it's always bad; just saying be careful. I am saying that if you send out a form letter telling people you are "specially licensed to provide investment advice to senior citizens," you will probably be receiving a letter by registered mail from FINRA and/or your state securities regulator very soon.

CODE OF PROCEDURE

So, FINRA has member conduct rules that you really, really do not want to break, especially if you end up getting caught. FINRA investigates violations of the conduct rules through **Code of Procedure**, which spells "COP." Just like on the street, if somebody breaks the rules, you can call a COP. When we mentioned words such as "suspend, expel, bar, and censure," those are all part of this Code of Procedure. Maybe a staff member of FINRA found out some rather disturbing information during a recent routine examination of a firm, or maybe one of your customers got ticked about losing 90% this year and then found out you were breaking rules along the way. Either way, you'll be notified and asked to respond to the charges in writing. All requests for information must be met within 25 days, so start writing. Remember that you have to cooperate with the investigation, producing documents or testimony as required. And if it's decided that you broke a rule, you could be censured, fined, suspended, expelled, or barred.

Which is bad.

You would get to appeal, assuming you can afford the legal fees. The appeals first go to the National Adjudicatory Council (NAC), then to the SEC, and even into the federal courts.

But it would be easier if you didn't get in trouble in the first place.

What is the maximum fine FINRA can impose? Trick question—for a major violation, they've never actually set a cap. If it's a "minor rule violation," there is a maximum fine (which changes from time to time, approx. $5,000), but no maximum will ever be set for the big violations. You would receive an offer from FINRA to use what they call "summary complaint procedure," and if you want to avoid a hearing as much as they apparently do, you need to accept it within 10 business days. Minor rule violations typically involve the failure to pay fees or file reports in a timely fashion. If you reject their offer to play nice, there will be a hearing, where any of these penalties can be assessed:

- Censure
- Fine (any amount)
- Suspension (up to 1 year) from the member firm or all member firms
- Expelled (up to 10 years, for firms only)
- Barred (game over, history, toast)

I doubt the test would mess with you on this point, but although "acceptance, waiver, and consent" is often used for minor rule violations (MRVs), it is also used for larger fines when the respondent does not want a hearing.

Now, if you like to see how this test world stuff works in the real world, simply go to www. FINRA.org and look for links to "regulation" or "disciplinary actions" and see the amazing audacity of registered representatives who run afoul of the SRO rules and regulations. You can probably find real world examples of most of the violations we just examined in just a few minutes.

CODE OF ARBITRATION

When broker-dealers are arguing over money, they have to take it to "arbitration." Under the **Code of Arbitration** members of FINRA must resolve money disputes with an arbitrator or arbitration panel, which cuts to the chase and makes their decision quickly. There are no appeals to arbitration. If they say your firm owes the other side one million dollars, your firm will have to open their checkbook and cut a check for one million dollars. End of story. A customer is free to sue a firm or registered rep in civil court unless the customer signs the arbitration agreement. Once that's signed, the customer is also bound by the Code of Arbitration, which means they can't sue you in civil court. Which is why most firms get their customers to sign arbitration agreements when the new account is opened. Civil court is too costly and time-consuming. Arbitration can be very painful, but at least it's quick. Like a root canal. Or being crushed by a 10-ton truck.

If the arbitration claim is for $100,000 or less, Simplified Industry Arbitration is used. Here there is just one "chair-qualified" arbitrator and no hearing. The claims are submitted in writing, and the arbitrator reaches a decision.

Larger amounts of money are handled by three or five arbitrators, some from the industry and some from outside the industry. Evidence and testimony is examined and the arbitration panel makes a final determination. Maybe they say the lead underwriter owes your firm $1 million. Maybe they say they owe you nothing. All decisions are final and binding in arbitration, unlike civil court where the appeal process can go on and on. So, if the arbitration panel says you owe somebody $50,000, you have to, like, pay them. Failure to comply with the arbitration decision could lead to a suspension, and now you're really not having a good day.

The bylaw doesn't specifically mention the word "money." The precise wording looks like this:

```
any dispute, claim, or controversy arising out of or in connection
with the business of any member of the Association, or arising
out of the employment or termination of employment of associated
person(s) with any member
```

So, money is the first "dispute, claim or controversy" that pops into my mind. Because, if it isn't money *per se*, there's still probably a 99% chance that the dispute led to somebody losing money or not making what they expected to. Anyway, the exam is likely to refer to it in the dry language "dispute, claim or controversy," while I prefer to call it what it usually is: money.

A recent rule change says that, while arbitrators generally don't have to explain their decision, FINRA now requires arbitrators to explain their decision if both parties make a joint request. The parties to the arbitration are required to submit any joint request for an explained decision at least 20 days before the first scheduled hearing date. The chairperson of the arbitration panel writes the explained decision and receives an additional honorarium of $400 for doing so. And if you get *that* test question, I'm afraid your time on this planet is just about up, my friend.

As we mentioned, if a registered representative violates sales practice rules, and a customer makes an arbitration claim after losing money, the firm has to report it on the registered (or formerly registered) representative's U4/U5 forms. If the amount of the award is $15,000 or more, the public will be able to find out about it, even if the plaintiff (customer) names the firm and not the registered rep specifically. Of course, if you treat your customers fairly, chances are, no one will ever even think about taking you to arbitration. Unless...the markets tank and they lose a bunch of money.

MORE FEDERAL SECURITIES ACTS

Now let's look at some other pieces of federal legislation that are within the scope of the Series 7.

TRUST INDENTURE ACT OF 1939

To protect bondholders, Congress passed the Trust Indenture Act of 1939. If a corporation wants to sell $5,000,000 or more worth of bonds that mature outside of a year, they have to do it under a contract or indenture with a trustee, who will enforce the terms of the indenture to the benefit of the bondholders. In other words, if the issuer stiffs the bondholders, the trustee can get a bankruptcy court to sell off the assets of the company so that bondholders can recover some of their hard-earned money. Sometimes corporations secure the bonds with specific assets like airplanes, securities, or real estate. If so, they pledge title of the assets to the trustee, who just might end up selling them off if the issuer gets behind on its interest payments. So just remember that an indenture is a contract with a trustee, who looks out for the bondholders.

THE INVESTMENT COMPANY ACT OF 1940

The Investment Company Act of 1940 classified investment companies as face amount certificate companies, UITs, or management companies. Remember that the "management companies" are the open- and closed-end funds. This is the act that sets rules for registration and operation of mutual funds, separate accounts, etc. It also gives the SEC the authority to continuously revise rules and write new ones to stay on top of an ever-changing marketplace. For example, the SEC can and has written a rule telling a tax-exempt bond fund that under normal circumstances 80% of its assets are actually, you know, tax-exempt. Or, in order to protect investors perhaps a mutual fund's board of directors has to be a majority, or even 75% "non-interested." This is the Act that gives the SEC the authority to regulate the mutual fund industry, or at least go back and forth like an old married couple with the industry's powerful lobbying group called the "Investment Company Institute."

INVESTMENT ADVISERS ACT OF 1940

If you want to give people your expert advice on their specific investment situation and charge a fee, you have to register under the Investment Advisers Act of 1940. Only registered advisers can charge "wrap fees," too, because those fees contain a component for advice. Investment advisers are the individuals/companies managing mutual funds and separate accounts, as well as managing money for other customers. With your Series 7 you will be paid a commission when executing customer buy and sell orders. If you worked for the investment advisory unit of your firm, you would be paid as a percentage of the assets your client has under the firm's management. In fact, many readers will take the Series 66 after the Series 7 because they will be serving accounts that pay commissions for trading securities as well as accounts that pay a percentage of assets. Charging a percentage of assets is part of the investment advisory business, and most states require that you have the 65/66 (same license) in order to get paid that way. Since you would be representing an investment adviser, you would be considered an "investment adviser representative."

Some people like to compensate you and your firm for a percentage of assets as opposed to paying commissions every time they buy and sell. See, when you convince me to buy a really hot stock, you get a commission when I do. What if the stock tanks after that? Sucks to be me, but you can now call me up and convince me to sell that dog, and if I do, you get the same commission all over again. Plus, now that I'm sitting on some cash, why not take another one of your hot stock tips so that you can make another commission off me? In other words, no matter how my investments work out, you get a commission when I buy and a commission when I sell. Is it good for me to buy and sell frequently? Probably not—but how else can you get paid as my agent?

You can't, unless your firm is charging a percentage of assets and you have the Series 65/66 license for "IARs." Now, I'll just let one of your portfolio managers run my portfolio and pay you guys maybe 1% of whatever the assets are worth. Each quarter you would deduct .25% of my account value as a "management fee," and it will be like having my own little private mutual fund. No sales charges or other operating expenses—I just pay my fees to your firm based on the value of the assets you're managing for me. If you do a good job and my account grows, your 1% annual fee gets bigger, too. And, when your stock and bond picks stink, your 1% will be a smaller and smaller number. I'm thinking that might get your attention, so maybe I prefer paying a percentage of assets rather than getting charged every time I buy and sell a security.

So, which billing method should a financial services firm use? Whichever one makes the most sense for the client. If the regulators feel that your firm is sticking people into a fee- or percentage-based billing structure just because it puts more money in the firm's pocket, they will take swift and harsh action. Your firm has to explain the difference to clients and steer them toward the method that would be most economical for them. See, if someone only trades a few times a year, their commissions might represent significantly less than 1% or whatever the management fee is. Then again, someone who trades more frequently or someone who needs a lot more advice/supervision, might be better off paying 1%–2% of assets.

The reason many readers are getting both their Series 7 and Series 65/66 is so that they can serve the client whether she chooses to pay commissions per transaction or just pay a percentage of assets for portfolio management and related services.

INSIDER TRADING & SECURITIES FRAUD ENFORCEMENT ACT OF 1988 (ITSFEA)

Although the Act of 1934 talked about insider trading, apparently it didn't quite get the message across. So in 1988 Congress passed the **Insider Trading & Securities Fraud Enforcement Act** of 1988 and raised the penalties for insider trading, making it a criminal offense with stiff civil penalties as well. If your brother-in-law happens to be the Chief Financial Officer of a public company and over a few too many martinis lets it slip that his company is going to miss earnings estimates badly this quarter, just pretend like you didn't hear it. Tell your principal and no one else. If you start passing out that information, or if you—God forbid—buy a bunch of puts on the stock, you could go to federal prison. More likely, the SEC would just sue the heck out of you in federal court and try to extract a civil penalty of three times the amount of the profit made or loss avoided.

How would they ever catch me, though?

Interestingly enough, those words have been carved into many federal prison cell walls since they passed the Insider Trading and Securities Fraud Enforcement Act of 1988. As we mentioned earlier, the SEC offers bounties of up to 10% of the amount they get out of the inside traders. Any material information the public doesn't have, that's inside information. Don't pass it around, don't use it. People who violate the act can be held liable to what they call "contemporaneous traders." That means that if you're dumping your shares based on an inside tip, and that hurts me, we might need to have a little talk with our attorneys.

The investment banking arm of a broker-dealer has access to all kinds of material non-public information. To prevent that sensitive information from flowing to other areas of the firm, the broker-dealer is required to create a **Chinese Wall** around departments that obtain such information. No, they don't build an actual wall. They just try to prevent the investment bankers working on a merger from revealing some good trading tips to the registered representatives working the telephones.

REG FD

Issuers of common stock routinely speak to broker-dealer analysts through conference calls and webcasts. In order to level the playing field between analysts and public investors, **Reg FD** requires that any material nonpublic information disclosed to analysts or other investors must be made public. If the disclosure was intentional, the information must be simultaneously disclosed to the public. If unintentional, the public disclosure must be made within 24 hours. One method of meeting this public disclosure requirement is to file a Form 8-K with the SEC.

TELEPHONE CONSUMER PROTECTION ACT

The Telephone Consumer Protection Act of 1991 is not specific to the securities business. This act sets rules on cold calling. When calling a prospect, you must identify yourself and the firm you represent. If the prospect rejects your offer and asks to be taken off your call list (put on the "don't-call" list), your firm may not contact this individual again. You may only call prospects Monday through Friday between 8 am and 9 pm in the prospect's time zone (unless they've indicated in writing that it's okay to call them at other times, though I don't know why you'd make a sales call outside that time frame). All faxes must contain contact information of the firm sending them so that prospects can call up and ask to be put on the don't-call list if they want. And, the caller must identify who she is, who she works for, and the fact that she is trying to interest the person in securities investments. Non-profits are exempt from these restrictions, as is legitimate debt collection. So if VISA™ calls you about your $20,000 credit card balance, you will not be able to say, "I'm not interested. Please put me on your don't-call list."

Well, I guess you can *say* it. It just won't help you very much.

SARBANES-OXLEY ACT, 2002

After several accounting scandals at public companies, Sarbanes-Oxley was introduced in order to clean up the reporting of bogus financial statements that defraud public investors. Because of this federal legislation, the officers and directors of public companies have to attest to the accuracy of financial reports with their signatures. Which means if the 10-K, for example, contains a bogus earnings statement or leaves out important risks, the board members and the officers could be civilly liable (sued) or criminally liable (screwed). Sarbanes-Oxley also requires broker-dealers to clean up abuses in the form of dishonest and conflicted "research" from their analysts, who used to frequently issue glowing reports on a company's stock as a favor to that company, who would then use the firm for investment banking, which happened to be the department who set the compensation and bonuses for the research analysts. No longer can investment banking have any control over the research analysts, and no longer can research analysts use their "research" as a favor to be granted to the CEO of some public company.

Yes, the regulators often take all the fun out of the business by insisting that firms do business, you know, honestly.

PRACTICE

1. **Which of the following securities would have to be registered with the SEC prior to an initial public offering?**

    A.   ADRs

    B.   XXR Corporation's preferred stock

    C.   XXR Corporation's common stock

    D.   all of the above

2. **Which of the following securities would have to be registered with the SEC prior to an initial public offering?**

    A.   church bonds

    B.   T-notes

    C.   Chicago 7% General Obligation bond

    D.   none of the above

3. **The Securities Act of 1934 addressed all the following except**

    A.   fraudulent offers, sales of securities

    B.   registration of broker-dealers

    C.   registration of agents

    D.   registration of new issues

4. **Which of the following parties have capital at risk in a transaction?**

   A. principal

   B. dealer

   C. market maker

   D. all of the above

5. **Which of the following parties have capital at risk in a transaction?**

   A. agent

   B. underwriter

   C. registered representative

   D. broker

6. **FINRA**

   A. is an SRO

   B. is a DEA

   C. was created by a merger of NYSE regulators and NASD

   D. all of the above

7. **The SEC is**

   A. an SRO

   B. a government body

   C. the Securities Ethical Committee for FINRA

   D. none of the above

8. **The sponsor of a mutual fund is trying to increase sales. She visits 50 broker-dealers and offers to award $400 to the registered representative who sells the most shares of the fund. This is**

   A. a great way to increase sales

   B. permissible so long as prior notice is filed with FINRA

   C. permissible so long as prior notice is filed with the SEC

   D. not acceptable

9. **FINRA's Conduct Rules prohibit which of the following?**

   A.   choosing the price paid for a security after a non-discretionary customer has named the action, asset, and amount of shares

   B.   splitting commissions with other registered representatives

   C.   choosing the security to be bought/sold in the absence of discretionary authority

   D.   all of the above

10. **FINRA's Conduct Rules prohibit which of the following?**

   A.   borrowing money from a bank customer

   B.   borrowing money from an S&L customer

   C.   making projections for mutual fund performance

   D.   all of the above

11. **All of the following securities would need to be registered with the Securities and Exchange Commission except a**

   A.   T-bond

   B.   mutual fund

   C.   closed-end share during the offering period

   D.   variable annuity

ANSWERS

1.   **D,** all securities have to be registered with the SEC, except for all the securities that don't have to be registered with the SEC. The ones that don't have to register are "excused" or "exempt" from the pain-in-the-neck process of registration. The excused securities are: Treasuries, Munis, Banks, Charitables, Small Business Investment Companies (VC firms), and short-term promissory notes.

   Since we don't see any of that in this question, nobody has an excuse; everybody registers.

2.   **D,** all securities have to be registered with the SEC, except for all the securities that don't. The ones that don't have to register are "excused" or "exempt" from the pain-in-the-neck process of registration. The excused securities are: Treasuries, Munis, Banks, Charitables, Small Business Investment Companies (VC firms), and short-term promissory notes.

3.   **D,** registration of securities was covered by the Securities Act of 1933, which is the only thing that

Act covers. The Act of 1934 has a much broader scope: anti-fraud regulations, registrations of firms and associates, margin, yada, yada.

4. **D,** in the sense of "money at risk," these are basically synonymous terms.

    Note that agent/representative/broker do NOT have money at risk.

5. **B,** only the underwriter has money at risk here. The other three terms are synonymous, and these individuals (like yourself) do not have $ at risk. Only your jobs.

6. **D,** a gift of a question--always accept the few gifts the test is giving away for free.

7. **B,** it oversees the SROs, but the SEC is a government body. The President appoints the chairman.

8. **D,** maximum gift to a person in the business is $100.

9. **C,** choosing time/price does not involve discretion. Discretion involves choosing the security, the number of shares, and whether to buy or sell. You can split commissions with registered agents at your firm or a firm under common control.

10. **C,** no projections for mutual funds. Usually, the agent can't borrow from a client—unless the client is a lending institution or an immediate family member. Even there, inform the firm and/or consult their written policy on borrowing/lending activities with customers.

11. **A,** Treasuries are exempt from the Act of 1933.

Dealing with Test Questions

There is no substitute for knowing the material. Unfortunately, that will only take you so far on the Series 7. In order to pass your exam, you need to sharpen your test-taking skills as much as possible. See, the test is very tricky. It likes to lead you down a false path and then ditch you, just to see if you can get yourself out of the forest. Many test-takers panic when they encounter unexpected forks in the trail, or unforeseen obstacles in their path. That's why we've provided this section on test-taking strategies. The following strategies will provide a sort of compass that can help guide you through all the nasty twists and turns you'll encounter on your exam.

LESSON ONE: WEED OUT THE UNNECESSARY INFORMATION.

The exam loves to give test-takers more information than they need to answer a question. If a test-taker needs three numbers, the exam will be sure to provide more like five or six.

Like this:

> On August 12 August Augustus bought an XYZ Aug 50 put @ 3 when XYZ Corporation's common stock was trading at $52. On August 15, when the underlying stock is trading at $45, August buys the stock on the open market and exercises his Aug 50 put. What is August's gain or loss on the Aug 50 put that he purchased on August 12?
>
> A. $300 gain
> B. $300 loss
> C. $200 gain
> D. none of the above

Do you really need all that information given in the question? Of course not. That's why they gave it to you. So let's get rid of what we don't need. First of all, you could remove the word "August" and all the abbreviations thereof from the question.

So now it looks like this:

> An investor bought a 50 put @ 3 when XYZ Corporation's common stock was trading at $52. When the underlying stock is trading at $45, the investor buys the stock on the open market and exercises his put. What is the investor's gain or loss?

Much easier to read now, right?

But there are still more weeds to pull. Do you need to know what XYZ Corporation's common stock was trading at when the investor bought the put?

Nope.

So now we're down to this:

An investor bought a 50 put @ 3. When the underlying stock is trading at $45, the investor buys the stock on the open market and exercises his put. What is the investor's gain or loss?

That's all the information we need to answer what used to look like a hard question. By weeding out the inessential noise from the essential information, we just reduced a 64–word question down to a 36–word question, a reduction of 44%.

So, are you ready to attack the question now that we've got the upper hand?

Good. Break out Mr. T-chart and let's knock this thing out. The investor bought the put for 3. That's money-out, so let's place $3 in the money-out column. He buys the stock at the market price of $45, so let's place $45 in the money-out column as well. He exercises his put, which gives him the right to sell the stock at the strike price of $50. So, let's place $50 in the money-in column. Then total it up. $48 went out, and $50 came in. Sounds like a gain of $200, doesn't it? So, the answer is C.

LESSON TWO: BEWARE OF TRAP DOORS.

Sometimes the exam can get downright nasty. You will encounter questions that intentionally mislead you. In fact, that's one of the main techniques used to test Series 7 candidates. The idea is to see if candidates can hang onto what they've learned, in spite of various tricks and traps that might spring up along the way. Sort of an intellectual obstacle course, if you will.

So, all we need to do is get in shape. Let's start with this one:

XYZ Corporation issued 1,000,000 shares of non-cumulative 6% preferred stock in June of 1997. Two years ago preferred stockholders received $2 in annual dividends. Last year XYZ's board of directors declared no dividends. This year, the board has declared the full 6% dividend. How much does the company have to pay in dividends on the 1,000,000 shares of preferred stock before dividends can be paid to common shareholders?

A. $6

B. $16

C. $20

D. $26, plus interest and back taxes

Careful! The question is misleading you. They've presented a scenario where dividends have been missed in the past. Well, holders of cumulative preferred stock would have to receive missed dividends plus current dividends before anybody else received a dime. But this question is talking about NON-cumulative preferred stock, which is why the correct answer is A, $6. Non-cumulative preferred stockholders either receive the stated 6%, or they don't. This year they do. The two previous years, they didn't. See how the whole question turned on the prefix "non?"

Careful. The Series 7 can get really tricky if you let it. By the way, why did the question give you the information that the stock was issued in June of 1997? Only one reason—to distract you. So, you had to apply Lesson One and Lesson Two to handle this one.

LESSON THREE: TURN ROMAN NUMERALS INTO AN ADVANTAGE.

Roman numeral questions intimidate some test takers, but they're really the easiest type to answer. If you can use the process of elimination effectively, you'll end up with an edge over these seemingly tough questions.

The following are considered to have an equity position in a corporation.

I.   common stockholders

II.   preferred stockholders

III. convertible bondholders

IV. mortgage bondholders

A.   I and II

B.   I, II and III

C.   II and III

D.   I, II, III and IV

The question asks for "equity positions," right? Equity equals "ownership."

Bondholders aren't owners, they're creditors. So all you need to do is read the word "bondholders," and eliminate any choice that contains III or IV. That gets rid of choices B, C, and D in one fell swoop.

With those choices gone, you're left with only:

A.   I and II

Why? Because every other choice contained choice III.

See how quickly you can annihilate the Roman Numeral questions? Find something you know is false and eliminate all choices that contain that one. Like this:

Which of the following are true concerning bonds that are both callable and convertible?

I.   If called, the owners have the option of retaining the bonds and will continue to receive interest.

II.   After the date it is called, interest will cease.

III. Upon conversion, there will be dilution.

IV. The coupon rate would be less than the rate for a nonconvertible bond.

A.   I and III

B.   I, III and IV

C.   II, III and IV

D.   II and IV

When you read, "If called, the owners have the option of retaining the bonds and will continue to receive interest," a red flag should go up. You know that when a corporation calls a bond, that's it. Turn in your bonds, everybody, take the premium above par, and that's that. So choice I is completely false. Knowing that, we can eliminate any choice that contains Roman Numeral I.

So, now we're down to just:

C. II, III and IV

D. II and IV

At this point, we just went from a 25% chance to a 50% chance, doubling our odds of success very quickly. So now what's different about choices C and D?

Right, both contain II and IV, so all we have to do is read choice III, which says, "Upon conversion, there will be dilution."

That's true of convertible bonds, right? If bondholders convert to common stock, there will be more shares of common stock. The corporation's earnings/profits don't change, but there are more shares to cut the earnings pie into. That's dilution. That's why III is in and choice C is correct.

Although I prefer the "negative approach," whereby I find something that's false and eliminate any answer choice that contains that one, you can also use the "positive approach." Here, you find something you're pretty sure is true and eliminate anything that does not contain that one.

Let's look at the same question from this angle:

Which of the following are true concerning bonds that are both callable and convertible?

I. If called, the owners have the option of retaining the bonds and will continue to receive interest.

II. After the date it is called, interest will cease.

III. Upon conversion, there will be dilution.

IV. The coupon rate would be less than the rate for a nonconvertible bond.

A. I and III

B. I, III and IV

C. II, III and IV

D. II and IV

Which one of the four Roman Numeral choices looks like it's true? Choices III and IV are kind of tough, right? What about choice II? You're pretty sure that once the bond is called, interest payments cease, right?

Okay, so if the answer choice does not contain a II, let's eliminate it.

Choice A is gone. Choice B is gone.

And now we're right where we were before, trying to decide if choice III is correct. Why choice III? Because, once we eliminate A and B, our final answer will contain II and IV. Does it also contain a III?

If you know that converting a bond into shares of stock will increase the number of slices the earnings pie must be cut into, you know the answer does contain a III, which is why the answer is, again, C.

See how easy that is? Just do it step-by-step. If you aren't sure about the choices, find one you are sure about and use it to eliminate other choices.

LESSON FOUR: TRY READING THE LAST SENTENCE FIRST.

Long test questions are not always harder than short test questions. Usually, a long question is designed to confuse test-takers. Reading from left to right, we take in all the irrelevant information provided in the question only to discover that the last sentence is leading us in a completely different direction. So, we get frustrated and have to read the whole paragraph over, conscious that the clock is still ticking.

Try reading the last sentence first, since that's usually where the question is located. For example:

In early October, an active options investor named Shirley went long 10 XXR Oct 60 calls @ 4.75 when the underlying stock was trading @61. After little movement in the stock's market price, Shirley continues to hold the calls, which she eventually expects to exercise close to expiration. How many shares of stock would change hands if Shirley exercised her calls?

See how the question appears to be about gains/losses but actually ends up asking about something else? All the question wants you to know is that 100 shares are covered in each equity option contract. So, if 10 options are exercised, we're talking about 1,000 shares changing hands. If we had read the last sentence first, we would have seen that right off and not been distracted by all the irrelevant verbiage in the first two sentences.

Another technique is to read the choices before you even look at the question. The four choices usually tell you what the question is about, whether it's about numbers, definitions, rules and regulations, taxes, etc. If you have a sense of where the question is going before you read it, you'll probably go in with a major advantage.

LESSON FIVE: DON'T MAKE THE QUESTION HARDER THAN IT IS.

Many of the exam questions are very difficult. Some are moderately challenging. Some are downright easy. Like a skilled big-league pitcher, the Series 7 throws a devastating mix of fast balls, curve balls, and changeups. Just when you get used to doing tricky questions on rules and regulations, the exam will throw an easy question on variable annuities. Swing too fast, and you'll strike out every time. So, if you encounter an easy question, don't assume you need to turn it into a hard question.

For example, you could see something like:

A standardized equity options contract covers 100 shares of the underlying instrument. If Carol Calloway holds 10 QRS Nov 50 puts, how many options does she own?

A. 100
B. 1,000
C. 10
D. 10,000

Maybe you caught the trap right away, but many test-takers would use the information provided in the first sentence and read it into the second sentence, which is a trap. If you do that, you end up thinking about how many *shares* of stock are covered in Carol Calloway's 10 QRS puts. Her 10 contracts cover 1,000 shares, but the question asks how many options does she own?

Ten.

The correct answer is C, 10. See? It's an easy question. It's just being asked in a tricky way.

Practice Exam

250 questions

NOTE: before embarking on this 250-question practice exam, please know the following:

- Most of the following questions are addressed in the text of this book, but some will force you to use educated guessing, just as you will have to do on the actual Series 7 exam
- The following questions are not lifted from the actual Series 7 test bank. If anyone tells you that they have "actual Series 7 questions," they are lying. FINRA would sue anyone who somehow obtained actual questions from the test bank
- While the following 250 questions are helpful, they are not intended to provide all the practice questions needed to prepare for the exam. For more practice questions see www.passthe7.com and/or www.solomonexamprep.com.

1. FINRA defines a form letter as a communication sent to 25 or more prospects in a 30-day period. All of the following statements concerning form letters are true except

    A. they are considered sales literature
    B. prior principal approval is required
    C. they are subject to filing requirements
    D. they are considered advertising

2. The principal in a member firm's Office of Supervisory Jurisdiction (OSJ) has all of the following responsibilities except

    A. must ensure that all rules in the firm's policy and procedure manual are followed by all employees
    B. must write all advertising and sales material
    C. must review and approve new accounts
    D. all of the choices listed

3. Which of the following is/are defined as "advertising" by FINRA?
    I.   video kiosks
    II. telephone directory listings
    III. cold calling scripts
    IV. computer slide shows

    A. I only
    B. II only
    C. I, II only
    D. I, II, III, IV

4. The investment adviser for a mutual fund is compensated based on which of the following?

    A. profits of the fund
    B. net assets of the fund
    C. number of shares of the fund sold to investors
    D. all of the choices listed

5. **Under FINRA's Code of Procedure, violations of member conduct rules are handled and sanctions may be applied if deemed appropriate. Which of the following represents the least severe of the sanctions?**

   A. lethal injection

   B. censure

   C. bar

   D. expulsion

6. **All of the following are self-regulatory organizations except**

   A. SEC

   B. FINRA

   C. MSRB

   D. CBOE

7. **If material information is intentionally misstated in a prospectus, which of the following may be held liable to investors?**

   A. officers of the issuer

   B. attorneys connected with the offering

   C. anyone who signed the registration statement

   D. all of the choices listed

8. **If a member firm presents a report concerning the performance of past recommendations, which of the following must be contained in the report?**

   A. statement as to general market conditions

   B. similar recommendations over the past year

   C. whether the firm participated in an underwriting of any of the securities

   D. all of the choices listed

9. **Which of the following may contain performance figures?**

   A. tombstone

   B. generic advertising

   C. advertising prospectus

   D. all of the choices listed

10. **Concerning a registered representative's discussions with a customer about equity options, which of the following represents an accurate statement?**

    A. The OCC disclosure document must be received by the customer before such discussions may begin.

    B. In every discussion about the benefits of trading options, a statement must also be made about the corresponding risks.

    C. Writing covered calls is considered sufficiently conservative to waive delivery of the OCC disclosure document.

    D. all of the choices listed

11. **Under ERISA, at what age must an employee be allowed to participate in a qualified plan?**

    A. 18

    B. 21

    C. 25

    D. 19

12. **All of the following retirement plans involve immediate vesting except**

    A. SEP-IRA

    B. SIMPLE IRA

    C. 401(k)

    D. Traditional IRA

13. **An investor who seeks to maintain minimum market risk and capital preservation would most likely invest in**

    A. general obligation bonds rated AA or higher

    B. revenue bonds rated AA or lower

    C. money market mutual funds

    D. 10-year high-grade corporate bonds

14. **All of the following tax-deferred savings plans provide for tax-free withdrawals except**

    A. Roth IRA

    B. SEP-IRA

    C. Education Savings Account (Coverdell)

    D. 529

15. **An investor is 53 years old. If she withdraws money from her non-qualified variable annuity in order to take care of a family emergency, she will**

    A. pay capital gains taxes

    B. pay ordinary income taxes

    C. pay penalties and ordinary income taxes on the amount withdrawn representing her growth/earnings

    D. pay a 25% early withdrawal penalty

16. **Which of the following could reduce the amount that an individual may contribute to a Traditional IRA?**

    A. Roth IRA contributions made for the year

    B. high income level

    C. participation in an employer-sponsored plan

    D. all of the choices listed

17. **Mutual funds attempt to achieve many different types of objectives. Some seek capital appreciation/growth, others seek income, and some seek a combination of both, not to mention international, emerging market, option income, and many other funds that have absolutely nothing to do with the rest of this question. If an investor has long-term growth as an objective and is also concerned about taxes and expense ratios, which of the following types of mutual funds would you MOST likely recommend?**

    A. small cap growth fund with a high portfolio turnover rate

    B. high-income bond fund

    C. international growth fund with high portfolio turnover rate

    D. small cap no-load growth fund with a low turnover rate and low management fees

18. **Which of the of the following represent(s) breakpoint selling, a violation of FINRA member conduct rules?**

    A. encouraging an investor to split an investment into several installments without a letter of intent in force

    B. encouraging an investor to invest in three growth and income funds issued by three fund families

    C. remaining mum when the investor suggests that she invest an amount that is $10 from the next breakpoint

    D. all of the choices listed

19. **Carol recently completed a graduate degree in comparative literature. Even worse, she has $20,000 in outstanding student loan debt. If Carol asks for your investment recommendation, you should**

    A. recommend high-income corporate bonds and BB-rated municipal securities

    B. insist that she invest in growth stocks only

    C. recommend that she invest in money market mutual funds and pay down the student loan as soon as reasonably possible

    D. advise her to sell Treasury notes short

20. **Which of the following properly lists investments from the most liquid to the least liquid?**

    A. stocks and bonds, money market funds, annuities, CMOs

    B. real estate, stocks and bonds, money market funds, annuities, CMOs

    C. money market funds, stocks and bonds, mutual funds, annuities, real estate

    D. annuities, mutual funds, money market funds

21. **A registered representative must maintain which of the following?**

    A. a record of each individual client's current holdings

    B. a cross-indexed list of each client's holdings, listed by securities owned

    C. neither choice listed

    D. both choices listed

22. **Which of the following represent(s) violations?**

    A. a broker-dealer gives a gift valued at $95 to an agent of another member firm

    B. a broker-dealer opens an account for a customer identified only by a number, with a letter from the customer attesting to ownership

    C. an agent of a member firm takes a part-time job paying less than $5,000 without informing his supervisor

    D. all of the choices listed

23. **What is required to open a guardian account?**

    A. declaration papers

    B. affidavit of domicile

    C. stock power

    D. trust document

24. **If a trustee enters orders for the owners of the account, the account is a(an)**

    A. custodial account

    B. fiduciary account

    C. trading account

    D. proxy account

25. **All of the following are true of an account that grants the registered representative the authority to purchase and sell securities without first consulting the client except**

    A. it is called a discretionary account

    B. the account is reviewed more frequently

    C. the client is bound by the transactions made by the representative

    D. discretion survives the death of the client and the representative

26. **In the event that the beneficial owner of an UGMA account dies, what happens to the assets in the account?**

    A. they revert to the parents

    B. they revert to the custodian

    C. they become the property of the minor's estate

    D. they are deposited in the account of a sibling or parent

27. **For a new investor which of the following choices are available for holding securities purchased in the account?**

    A. transfer and ship

    B. hold in street name

    C. transfer and hold for safekeeping

    D. all of the choices listed

28. **If a registered representative has limited power of attorney over a customer's account, the account is**

    A. frozen

    B. discretionary

    C. custodial

    D. restricted

29. Which of the following represents a false statement concerning UGMA accounts?

A. The nominal owner of the account is the custodian.

B. Withdrawals are tax-free when used for the beneficiary.

C. The minor's social security number is required.

D. The beneficial owner of the account is the minor.

30. If a registered representative reports to her customer that 100 shares of XYZ were just bought @22.15 for the customer's account, when, in fact, the trade was executed at 22.55, as indicated on the trade confirmation, which of the following is true?

A. The firm must make up the $40 difference.

B. The registered rep must forego the first $40 in commissions from the transaction.

C. The trade is executed at $22.55.

D. The customer has no obligation to pay the higher price.

31. All of the following statements accurately describe a securities exchange except

A. Only listed securities trade on a securities exchange.

B. Securities prices are set by negotiation between interested parties.

C. Issuers may be de-listed if they fail to file their 10-K with the SEC.

D. The highest bid and lowest asked prices prevail.

32. In order to receive a dividend distribution for a mutual fund, the investor must purchase shares

A. on or after the Ex-Date

B. on or after the Record Date

C. on or before the Record Date

D. by the Payable Date

33. Which of the following funds is most susceptible to interest rate risk?

A. short-term municipal bond fund

B. intermediate term corporate bond fund

C. long-term government bond fund

D. small cap fund

34. **Which of the following statements is/are true concerning a mutual fund investor's decision to receive dividend and capital gains distributions rather than reinvesting into more shares?**

I.   proportional ownership of the portfolio will increase

II.   tax liability will increase

III. proportional ownership of the portfolio will decrease

A.   I, III only

B.   II only

C.   I, II, III

D.   III only

35. **Which of the following SEC rules covers the sale of restricted securities by the CEO of a public corporation?**

A.   145

B.   144

C.   G-13

D.   13-d

36. **An investor has been using dollar cost averaging to purchase shares of a balanced fund the past three years. If the NAV has been consistently dropping, she would notice that:**

A.   her deposits are purchasing fewer shares as NAV drops

B.   her deposits are purchasing more shares as NAV drops

C.   her strategy is locking in a minimum level of profitability

D.   her strategy is more tax-efficient

37. **Reading the prospectus for a growth fund, you notice that the portfolio turnover ratio is 50%. You would conclude that**

A.   total holdings are replaced every two years

B.   total holdings are replaced every year

C.   ½ of the stocks in the portfolio increased over the year

D.   50% of the board of directors is independent/non-interested

38. XYZ Growth & Income fund has a NAV of $10.00 and a POP of $10.50. The sales charge equals:

A. 5%

B. 4.8%

C. 4.0%

D. 3.5%

39. Which of the following constitute(s) an offer to sell securities?

A. tombstone ad

B. prospectus

C. both choices given

D. neither choice given

40. As a representative of XYZ Broker-Dealer, you would like to help a client purchase 1,000 shares of ARQ, which is going public next week. Your head trader calls the syndicate manager to inquire if your firm can get an allocation of 1,000 shares. If so, your firm will be paid:

A. selling concession

B. total spread

C. manager's fee

D. a markup

41. Which of the following information is not found in a prospectus for an IPO?

A. effective date

B. intended use of the proceeds raised by the offering

C. names of all syndicate members

D. likely price range for secondary market trading after the offering period

42. If the SEC would like more clarification of key points in an issuer's registration statement, the Commission would most likely

A. issue a letter of deficiency

B. issue a cease & desist order

C. issue an injunction

D. contact the lead underwriter

43. **Which of the following can be determined solely from the balance sheet?**

    A.   working capital

    B.   net profit margin

    C.   earnings per share

    D.   all of the choices listed

44. **If a corporation's assets have remained unchanged while shareholders' equity has dropped, what must have happened?**

    A.   total liabilities decreased

    B.   total liabilities increased

    C.   the company has changed auditors

    D.   stock has been repurchased for the treasury

45. **All of the following represent "defensive" stocks except stocks in companies that produce/sell:**

    A.   milk

    B.   energy

    C.   automobiles

    D.   snack chips

46. **How is Gross Domestic Product (GDP) best defined?**

    A.   net interest expense divided by revenues

    B.   net new claims for unemployment divided by CPI

    C.   overall health of a nation's economy

    D.   a nation's aggregate indebtedness

47. **All of the following are established by the Federal Reserve Board except**

    A.   discount rate

    B.   monetary policy

    C.   government spending

    D.   margin requirements

48. **What is the theoretical liquidating value of a share of common stock?**

    A.   par value

    B.   book value

    C.   fair market value

    D.   notional value

49. The market prices for which of the following would probably fall the fastest during an inflationary period?

    A.   T-bills

    B.   T-bonds

    C.   7-year debentures

    D.   T-notes

50. Which two of the following does "beta" measure?

    I.   volatility

    II.   risk

    III. reward

    IV. yield spreads

    A.   I, II

    B.   I, III

    C.   II, III

    D.   II, IV

51. If you notice a consistent increase in the CPI, you would associate this with all of the following, generally, except

    A.   rising consumer prices

    B.   rising bond yields

    C.   rising bond prices

    D.   rising interest rates

52. Which of the following is generally negative/bearish for the stock market?

    A.   rising interest rates

    B.   increased government spending

    C.   loose money supply

    D.   falling inventories

53. All of the following would be considered negative indicators except

    A.   falling S&P 500

    B.   falling claims for unemployment

    C.   rising inventories

    D.   high consumer debt

54. Checking a financial periodical, you note that a large number of odd lot purchases are reported. You would take this as an indication of

A.   a market top

B.   a market bottom

C.   a market on close

D.   consolidation

55. If a technical analyst notices that a stock has declined sharply the past quarter and has a high short interest, he would consider this

A.   insignificant

B.   bearish

C.   bullish

D.   Keynesian

56. An investor who wants to grant her registered representative the authority to place trades on her behalf without first discussing suitability would

A.   be required to open a margin account

B.   be required to present a letter of authorization from an attorney

C.   be required to sign a power of attorney granting the representative discretionary authority

D.   not be allowed to trade options in the account

57. A limited partner has invested $100,000, which represents a 10% interest in the partnership. If the partnership secures a $300,000 non-recourse loan, the maximum loss that the investor may realize is

A. $300,000

B. $100,000

C. $30,000

D. $130,000

58. Which of the following characteristics of limited partnership investments is generally considered the most advantageous?

A.   immediate diversification of holdings

B.   guaranteed rate of return

C.   flow through of income and expenses

D.   professional management

59. **The Bond Buyer publishes the "placement" or "acceptance ratio," which is found by**

    A. dividing the dollar amount of general obligation bonds purchased on the secondary market by the dollar amount of revenue bonds sold

    B. dividing the dollar value of new issues sold by the dollar value of new issues offered the previous week

    C. dividing the dollar amount of revenue bonds purchased on the secondary market by the dollar amount of general obligation bonds sold

    D. dividing the visible supply by the number of new bonds absorbed on the primary market the previous week

60. **A limited liability company (LLC) is taxed differently than a corporation and must, therefore, avoid or "fail" at least two corporate characteristics. Which TWO of the following are most likely to be avoided by the LLC?**

    I. freely transferable interests
    II. limited liability
    III. centralized management
    IV. continuity of life

    A. I, III
    B. I, IV
    C. II, III
    D. II, IV

61. **A direct participation program's offering circular states that a reversionary working interest is in place. This means that**

    A. the limited partners absorb all of the expenses and the general partner does not receive payments until the LPs have recovered their costs

    B. the general partner has an overriding royalty interest

    C. the limited partners will maintain management responsibilities

    D. the limited partners will provide some labor to the operation

62. **An investor purchases $20,000 in a new margin account and makes the required Reg T deposit. Three weeks later, the account is charged $100 in interest and receives $150 in dividends. The debit balance for this account is now:**

    A. $12,500
    B. $19,900
    C. $9,500
    D. $9,950

63. In a direct participation program, all of the following may be depreciated except

    A.   buildings

    B.   computers

    C.   raw land

    D.   assembly line equipment

64. If the XYZ Corporation makes a new offering of securities not registered with the Securities and Exchange Commission to accredited investors, this type of offering is called a

    A.   private placement

    B.   144 offering

    C.   registered secondary offering

    D.   unregistered secondary offering

65. When helping to determine suitability for a DPP investment, which TWO of the following characteristics would you consider least significant?

    I.   tax advantages of the investment

    II.   liquidity

    III.   safety

    IV.   profitability

    A.   I, IV

    B.   II, III

    C.   I, III

    D.   II, IV

66. If your real estate limited partnership takes out a recourse loan, as a limited partner

    I.   you can be held liable for a portion of it

    II.   you cannot be held liable for any portion of it

    III.   this can increase your cost basis

    IV.   this cannot increase your cost basis

    A.   I, III

    B.   I, IV

    C.   II, III

    D.   II, IV

67. An investor seeking tax advantages inquires about investing in a limited partnership interest in a wildcatting/oil exploration program. You would inform him that the tax advantages will be generated primarily through

   A.   tax credits

   B.   intangible drilling costs

   C.   cost of management

   D.   depreciation

68. To open an investment account on behalf of a corporation, which of the following documents must the account executive obtain?

   A.   corporate resolution

   B.   corporate charter

   C.   corporate bylaws

   D.   all of the choices listed

69. Which of the following required documents for a margin account must be signed by the customer in order to grant the member firm the power to pledge securities as collateral?

   A.   corporate resolution

   B.   corporate charter

   C.   hypothecation agreement

   D.   loan consent

70. The Visible Supply published in the Bond Buyer

   A.   is required by the SEC under the Securities Act of 1933

   B.   indicates the dollar value of new issues to be offered over the next 30 days

   C.   lists the total dollar amount of revenue bonds sold the previous 30 days

   D.   indicates the acceptance/placement of new issues over the previous week

71. Pursuant to a declared dividend, all of the following orders would be reduced except

   A.   open buy limit

   B.   open sell stop

   C.   order marked DNR

   D.   order marked GTC

72. If a market maker is unable to resolve a trade issue with another market maker, the situation must be reported to NASDAQ Market Operations within

    A.   5 minutes

    B.   15 minutes

    C.   30 minutes

    D.   1 hour

73. Your customer has placed an order to sell 100 XYZ at 85 stop limit 82 GTC. After the close of trading, XYZ announces disappointing earnings, and the stock opens at 72 the next morning. What is true of your customer's order?

    A.   it was canceled when it did not execute the day before

    B.   it has been triggered and is currently a limit order

    C.   it has been elected and filled

    D.   it has been canceled, since the market price opened below the stop price

74. How often must customer GTC orders be reconfirmed?

    A.   daily

    B.   quarterly

    C.   semi-annually

    D.   annually

75. If you open a joint account (tenants in common) for three investors, financial information should be obtained on

    A.   the investor granted trading authorization by the other two owners

    B.   at least two of the three investors

    C.   the investor owning the largest percentage of the assets in the account

    D.   all three investors

76. An investor purchases 100 shares of GRZ @35 on January 1st. If she sells them for $36.15 in March, her profit, excluding commissions will be:

    A. $15

    B. $115

    C. $230

    D. $.15

77. **A customer asks you to explain what the following display on the NYSE tape means:**

ABC 50.50.2s55

You would tell the customer that

A. you actually used to know this for your Series 7

B. 5,050 shares were traded at $25.50 per share

C. 100 shares of ABC traded at $50.50, followed by another 200 shares at $50.55

D. don't pick this answer unless you want to get the question wrong

78. **An open sell order entered below the current market price of a stock is a:**

A. market not held order

B. GTC order

C. stop order

D. limit order

79. **Which of the following information is provided in the Pink Sheets?**

A. prices for all new municipal bonds coming to market over the next 30 days

B. bid and asked quotes for stocks, and the dealers making a market in the stocks

C. prices for all revenue bonds

D. prices for corporate stock trading on the AMEX

80. **What is true about an NYSE specialist "stopping stock"?**

A. specialist guarantees a price on a specific number of shares

B. the broker may continue to seek a better price on the trading floor

C. stock may be "stopped" for customers of NYSE member firms

D. all of the choices listed

81. **A "market on close" order (MOC) is**

A. executed at the closing price for the day

B. executed as close to the closing price for the day, if not the closing price

C. cancelled if trading in the stock is halted

D. all of the choices listed

82. **A market participant is considered bearish if he:**

    A. purchases put options
    B. establishes short stock positions
    C. establishes a credit call spread
    D. all of the choices listed

83. **A market maker for a NASDAQ stock is compensated with**

    A. the spread
    B. commissions
    C. fees
    D. commissions plus fees

84. **Which of the following may a specialist do?**

    A. accept a not held order
    B. allow the spread to become excessive in light of the stock's volume
    C. trade for their own account between the bid and ask
    D. refuse to purchase securities for their own account in the absence of public buy orders

85. **FINRA has the authority to take which of the following actions against a registered representative or principal who violates the member conduct rules?**

    A. indictment in those cases where the violation was criminal in nature
    B. imprisonment in those cases where the sum of money involved represents a felony in the state of occurrence
    C. permanent bar from associating with any member firm in any capacity
    D. none of the choices listed

86. **If a customer fails to pay for a transaction within Reg T time limits, what is the FIRST action the member firm must take?**

    A. liquidate the security
    B. close the account
    C. freeze the account
    D. file a report with the SEC

87. When does a "cash transaction" settle?

A. no later than 12:30 PM Eastern Time for trades executed before noon, and in 30 minutes for trades executed after noon.

B. no later than 2:30 PM Eastern Time for trades executed before 2 PM Eastern Time, and in 30 minutes for trades executed after 2:00 PM Eastern Time

C. T + 3

D. T + 5

88. List the following dates from first to last for a dividend paid on XYZ common stock:

I. record date

II. payable date

III. ex-date

IV. declaration date

A. I, II, III, IV

B. IV, III, I, II

C. II, I, III, IV

D. I, IV, II, III

89. If a customer cannot pay for a transaction in time

A. the member firm may request an extension after the fifth business day following the trade

B. the member firm may request an extension in writing to their Self-Regulatory Organization before the fifth business date following the trade

C. the customer must pledge tangible assets equal to the trade

D. the customer must transfer title of real property at 1.5 times assessed value to secure any deficit in the trading account

90. The Federal Reserve Board Regulation T, under the Securities Exchange Act of 1934, stipulates that an investor must pay for a stock transaction

A. T + 1

B. T + 3

C. T + 5

D. T + 2

91. Which TWO of the following may guarantee a signature?

    I.   bank officer

    II.   principal of a member firm

    III. transfer agent

    IV. spouse of the customer

    A.   I, III

    B.   I, II

    C.   II, III

    D.   II, IV

92. A customer fails to pay for a stock purchase and the member firm liquidates the account. Five weeks later, the customer wants to purchase stock. What must happen first?

    A.   customer must deposit the full purchase price before the trade is executed

    B.   customer must open a new account

    C.   FRB must send an authorizing amendment for the account

    D.   customer must submit fingerprints to the SEC

93. Which of the following are true statements concerning customer trade confirmations?

    A.   no charge may be added for odd lot purchases/sales

    B.   the confirmation must be delivered next business day

    C.   the confirmation must contain the registered rep's AE number

    D.   settlement date, but not trade date, must be disclosed

94. Trade confirmations are sent by which of the following departments?

    A.   cashiering

    B.   order

    C.   P&S

    D.   margin

95. The reorganization department of a firm would handle all of the following except

    A.   bond calls

    B.   tender offers

    C.   arbitrage

    D.   preferred stock redemption

96. A member firm may charge for which of the following?

    A.   lack of trading activity in the account

    B.   collection of dividends

    C.   safekeeping of securities

    D.   all of the choices listed

97. Account statements must be sent at least monthly for all of the following reasons except

    A.   penny stocks are held in the account

    B.   trading activity has occurred

    C.   no trading activity has occurred in a cash account

    D.   long positions are held on margin

98. A customer purchases 1,000 XYZ two days before the ex-date. If the seller delivers after the record date, all of the following will occur except

    A.   the selling member will receive the dividend

    B.   the buying member will send a due bill

    C.   the buyer will be owed the dividend

    D.   the seller may keep the dividend

99. A broker-dealer receives delivery of securities and may use all of the following to reject delivery EXCEPT

    A.   signature on stock certificate not guaranteed

    B.   certificate is not legible

    C.   bearer bond is missing coupons

    D.   customer has determined that the investment is unsuitable

100. While in the past many investors retained possession of their stock certificates, typically most investors choose to have their broker-dealer hold securities in "street name." All of the following statements concerning this practice are true except

    A.   the corporation will send proxies to the broker-dealer

    B.   the broker-dealer will forward proxy materials to the customer

    C.   the issuing corporation will not reimburse the broker-dealer for forwarding proxies

    D.   if the investor attends the annual meeting to cast a vote, the proxies are voided

101. Which of the following broker-dealer personnel must register?

    A.   clerk who inputs new account information into the firm's computer

    B.   webmaster posting information on market conditions to the firm's public website

    C.   sales assistant who accepts fewer than 3 customer orders per month

    D.   public relations assistant

102. Melissa is the principal of XYZ Broker-Dealers. When Melissa hires a new registered representative, she must

    I.   attest to the employee's character

    II.   sign the U4 prior to submission

    III. confirm the rep's employment for the past 3 years

    IV. administer a polygraph in the presence of an FBI agent

    A.   I, IV only

    B.   I, II only

    C.   III only

    D.   I, II, III only

103. If a customer cannot deposit the Reg T requirement by the fifth business day following the trade, all of the following may occur except

    A.   a "DK" may be sent to the contra party

    B.   margin call for less than $1,000 may be waived

    C.   broker-dealer may apply for an extension

    D.   forced liquidation of the position

104. All of the following information must be included on an order ticket EXCEPT

    A.   registered representative's number

    B.   commission

    C.   customer's name

    D.   account number

105. A customer retains stock certificates for XYZ in her safe deposit box at the local bank. If the customer places an order for your firm to sell the stock, the certificates must be delivered

    A.   immediately

    B.   by settlement

    C.   within 15 days of settlement

    D.   directly to the buyer of the stock

106. **When must the official statement be delivered to a purchaser of a municipal bond primary offering?**

   A. before accepting payment

   B. at or before confirmation

   C. T + 3

   D. prior to submitting an order

107. **In a municipal securities offering, the issuer prepares an official statement, which discloses all of the following EXCEPT:**

   A. purpose of the issue

   B. feasibility statement

   C. sources of collateral, if any

   D. name of the managing/lead underwriter

108. **According to MSRB General Rule #15 (G-15), when a member firm executes an order for a customer, all of the following information must be contained on the trade confirmation except:**

   A. CUSIP #

   B. capacity the firm acted in

   C. extended principal

   D. legal opinion

109. **Appleton has a statutory debt limit of $100,000,000. Currently, there is $85,000,000 of debt outstanding. Therefore, if a convention center is to be built with the proceeds of a revenue bond, which of the following is a true statement?**

   A. only $15 million of the bonds may be issued

   B. the full amount of new bonds may be issued

   C. the issue must first be approved by voters

   D. all of the choices listed

110. **An investor owning a CMO should know that:**

   A. as interest rates rise, mortgage repayments will slow, causing him to receive his principal more slowly than anticipated

   B. as interest rates fall, prepayment risk rises

   C. what he owns is referred to as a "tranche"

   D. all of the choices listed

111. Your client bought 10M of New York 8% F & A bonds on Monday Nov 3rd at 104. She will pay a total, excluding commissions, of:

  A. $10,400

  B. $1,400

  C. 10,611.11

  D. 10,606.67

112. Upon request, an MSRB member firm must provide to a customer

  A. current list of the firm's 401(k) holdings

  B. all trading records

  C. MSRB Rule Book

  D. commission runs

113. In the vernacular of municipal securities trading, a "round lot" is

  A. $100,000 par value

  B. $10,000 par value

  C. $5,000 par value

  D. $50,000 par value

114. When the member of a municipal bond underwriting syndicate fills an order for a client, the firm will receive

  A. manager's fee

  B. total spread

  C. total takedown

  D. selling concession

115. How far is a MSFT Jan 90 call in-the-money with MSFT trading at $85?

  A. $5

  B. $90

  C. $87.50

  D. $0

116. **An investor is long an IBM Mar 90 call @3. With IBM @94.75, the investor closes the option for its intrinsic value. He has a**

    A.   loss of $175

    B.   gain of $175

    C.   loss of $300

    D.   gain of $475

117. **One of your firm's customers has been depositing $8,000 cash every Thursday into his account. Therefore, your firm would**

    A.   notify CBOE by close of business

    B.   file a Currency Transaction Report (CTR)

    C.   notify the Federal Bureau of Investigation (FBI)

    D.   file a Suspicious Activity Report (SAR)

118. **An IBM Mar 75 put @3 has how much time value with IBM @74?**

    A. $1

    B. $3

    C. $2

    D. $0

119. **An investor writes an XYZ Mar 75 put @4. With XYZ @74, he closes the contract for its intrinsic value. He has a**

    A.   gain of $400

    B.   gain of $100

    C.   loss of $400

    D.   gain of $300

120. **When a broker-dealer underwrites securities for a client, the broker-dealer is responsible for which of the following?**

    A.   advising the issuing corporation on how best to use the proceeds of the offering

    B.   filing the registration statement with federal and/or state securities regulators

    C.   making a market for the security in the secondary market

    D.   advising the issuing corporation on the type of security to be offered

121. Your customer owns 100 shares of MSFT. To generate income, he should

    A. buy a call

    B. buy a put

    C. sell a call

    D. sell a put

122. Long 100 shares XYZ @40. Short XYZ Oct 50 call @2.25.
What is the maximum loss in this position?

    A. unlimited

    B. 12.25 per share

    C. 10.00 per share

    D. 37.75 per share

123. One of your investors has both long and short stock positions in her margin account. Today, if the value of the long positions increases by $4,000 and the value of her short positions increases by $2,000, the combined equity will

    A. increase by $6,000

    B. increase by $2,000

    C. decrease by $2,000

    D. decrease by $6,000

124. Short IBM Mar 90 call
Long IBM Mar 100 call
The investor will profit if the difference in premiums

    A. narrows

    B. expires

    C. elongates

    D. widens

125. Which type of option can be exercised only at expiration?

    A. call

    B. put

    C. American

    D. European

126. **Which of the following is most suitable for a young investor starting an IRA with a deposit of $4,000?**

    A. penny stocks

    B. growth stocks

    C. government bonds

    D. money market securities

127. **An investor writing an ABC Apr 45 put @ 2.50 will break even if ABC common stock trades at**

    A. parity

    B. $47.50

    C. $45.00

    D. $42.50

128. **A large loan is made with the interest rate expressed as "One point above LIBOR." LIBOR stands for**

    A. London Interbank Offered Rate

    B. Locked In Before Redemption

    C. Leveraged-Incentive Basic Outstanding Rate

    D. Last In Before Ordered Reclamation

129. **Which of the following is true concerning a Letter of Intent?**

    A. the letter covers a period of 13 months

    B. it is a binding agreement between the investor and the mutual fund

    C. if backdated 90 days, the agreement would cover 16 months

    D. accumulation counts toward the amount stated in the LOI

130. **When a limited partnership is liquidated, which of the following parties is last to receive distributions?**

    A. general creditors

    B. secured creditors

    C. limited partners

    D. general partners

131. Limited partners are allowed to do all of the following except

A. sue the general partner for negligence

B. vote to remove the general partner

C. make loans to the partnership

D. sell partnership assets to pay creditors

132. An investor sells 500 shares of XYZ at a loss on March 1. On March 25 he would be able to establish which of the following positions without causing a "wash sale"?

A. long 5 XYZ May calls

B. long 10 XYZ debentures convertible @20

C. long 100 shares XYZ preferred convertible at $20

D. none of the choices listed

133. An investor purchases a T-bond Mar 110 call at 1.24. The investor's breakeven point is:

A. 108.16

B. 118.84

C. 111.24

D. 1.24

134. When opening a new account for a customer planning to trade options, the following steps would occur in which order?

I. obtain essential information on customer's finances, investment goals, experience, etc.

II. ROP approves the account

III. obtain signed options agreement from customer

IV. first trade

A. I, II, III, IV

B. I, III, IV, II

C. I, II, IV, III

D. III, II, I, IV

135. An investor has shorted XYZ @70 and notices that the stock is currently trading at $50. Which of the following would you recommend to help the customer protect his paper profit?

    I.   enter a sell-stop @45

    II. enter a buy-stop @51

    III. buy XYZ Oct 55 calls

    IV. sell XYZ Oct 45 puts

    A. I

    B. III

    C. II, III

    D. I, II, III, IV

136. Which of the following statements is true concerning the purchase of a Treasury note?

    A. the investor retains capital risk

    B. the investor retains credit risk

    C. the investor retains purchasing power risk

    D. the investor retains no risk

137. There are many ways to measure an investor's return. Some factor in volatility, others factor in risk. The so-called "real rate of return" is the rate:

    A. of inflation

    B. earned that exceeds the rate of inflation

    C. charged on debit balances within margin accounts

    D. that the prime rate exceeds the broker-call loan rate

138. A Treasury bond trading at 102.20 has a nominal yield of 8%. Therefore, the current yield is

    A. 9%

    B. 10%

    C. 7.82%

    D. 7.79%

139. Which of the following best defines Gross Domestic Product (GDP)?

    A. real interest rate divided by inflation

    B. output of goods produced domestically

    C. CPI times an interest rate multiplier

    D. output of goods and services produced domestically

140. An investor has an account with an investment advisory that charges one fee covering execution of transactions, management fees, and other services. What is true of this account?

    A. it is unlawful

    B. it is considered unethical

    C. it is referred to as a wrap account

    D. all of the choices listed

141. Which of the following statements concerning REITs is/are true?

    I.   may trade on the first or second market

    II. are exempt under the Securities Act of 1933

    III. may not be held within a 401(k) or Keogh plan

    IV. may pass through income but not losses to investors

    A. I, II

    B. III

    C. II, III

    D. I, IV

142. A customer calls this afternoon stating that she recently noted the beta on one of her current holdings is .5. How would you explain this to the customer?

    A. beta is of no significance

    B. this represents a high beta stock and is not appropriate for most investors

    C. this stock will typically underperform a bull market and outperform a bear market

    D. beta and alpha are synonymous

143. Horatio Hackelmeyer is a customer of Arashay Investments, a broker-dealer properly registered in the state of Vermont, where Horatio resides. Horatio then moves to Oregon to start a winery. If Arashay is registered solely in Vermont, what is true of this situation?

    A. Horatio may continue to be a customer of the firm.

    B. The firm may service the account as long as an officer or director resides in the state of Oregon.

    C. The firm may service the account as long as Horatio maintains a PO box in Vermont.

    D. Arashay will not be able to maintain the account for Horatio.

144. **One of your margin customers has an account with $20,000 long market value, a debit of $16,000, and an SMA of $2,000. What is true of this situation?**

   I.   The account is at maintenance.

   II. The customer may apply the SMA to the debit balance.

   III. The customer may bring the account back to maintenance with a cash deposit of $1,000.

   A. I

   B. II, III

   C. III

   D. I, II, III

145. **The volatility of a stock compared to the overall market is known as its**

   A. alpha

   B. beta

   C. standard deviation

   D. Sharpe ratio

146. **Your customer needs to know the purchase price, excluding commissions, on a T-bond 98 call with a premium of 1.24. You would inform him that the premium is**

   A. $124 per contract

   B. $1,240 per contract

   C. $1,750 per contract

   D. $1,000 per contract

147. **One of the investors on your new book of business is holding shares of stock that have appreciated nicely over the past several years. The investor is considering ways to deal with what he anticipates may be a tough financial quarter at the company in whose stock he is invested. Which of the following strategies would be least appropriate in helping the investor deal with a possible temporary drop in market value?**

   A. write covered calls against the stock

   B. enter a sell-stop order

   C. buy puts on the stock

   D. sell straddles

148. One of your customers calls this morning, wondering if she's too late to make her annual IRA contribution. An investor should know that an IRA contribution for Tax Year 2011 may be made

    A.   no later than Dec 31, 2011

    B.   no later than April 15, 2011

    C.   no later than April 15, 2012

    D.   no later than April 1, 2012

149. All of the following are NRSROs (Nationally Recognized Statistical Ratings Organizations) that assign credit ratings to debt securities except

    A.   Fitch

    B.   S&P

    C.   Moody's

    D.   MBIA

150. Which of the following will provide the largest amount of deductions for an oil and gas drilling program during the first year?

    A.   depletion

    B.   depreciation

    C.   intangible drilling costs

    D.   appreciation

151. Which of the following statements concerning exercise limits for listed equity options is/are true?

    A.   the limits are applied to all of a customer's accounts, even if held at different brokerages

    B.   the limits cover the maximum number of contracts that may be exercised over a 5-business-day period

    C.   long puts and short calls on the same underlying stock are counted on the "same side of the market," as are long calls and short puts

    D.   all of the choices listed

152. Which of the following statements is/are true concerning callable debentures?

    I.   they are typically called during a period of falling yields

    II.   they are typically called during a period of rising bond prices

    III. bonds subject to a partial or "sinking fund" call feature are called at random

    IV. if a bond is called, investors owning the bond less than three years may retain the bonds and receive accrued interest for two years

    A.   II only

    B.   IV only

    C.   I, II, III only

    D.   I, II, III, IV

153. All of the following are true concerning index options tracking an index such as the S&P 500 or Dow Jones Industrial Average except

    A.   expirations are monthly

    B.   upon exercise, the holder may receive shares in the underlying index

    C.   when exercised, intrinsic value is relative to the closing value of the index for that trading day

    D.   exercise involves receiving cash from the writer of the contract

154. Jill, a registered representative with an FINRA member firm, appears before the Hearing Panel, which decides on a fine of $10,000 and a 90-day suspension. Jill may appeal this decision to:

    A.   no one

    B.   SEC

    C.   NAC

    D.   NYSE

155. Which of the following are associated with a deflationary period?

    A.   rising unemployment

    B.   falling interest rates

    C.   decreasing GDP

    D.   all of the choices listed

156. An underwriting firm participating in a municipal securities offering has sold their allotment of bonds. The syndicate letter states that the additional takedown is 1/4 point, and the concession 1/2 point. Together, this amount is known as the

A. spread

B. total spread

C. total takedown

D. notice of sale

157. An investor in a margin account purchases 100 XYZ @80 and writes
1 XYZ Nov 85 call @2.
Therefore, the customer must deposit:

A. $8,200

B. $4,200

C. $3,800

D. $4,000

158. Mia, Marta, and Maria share a joint account registered as Tenants in Common. Marta has passed away; therefore, which of the following correctly explains the handling of this account?

A. the account will become Joint Tenants with Rights of Survivorship

B. Mia and Maria will each receive 50% of Marta's ownership

C. the Estate of Marta will typically become the third owner of the account

D. all of the choices listed

159. Which of the following orders will accept a partial execution?

A. AON

B. IOC

C. FOK

D. NH

160. Which of the following, according to MSRB rules, must be approved by a principal before being sent to a customer?

A. official statement

B. preliminary official statement

C. research report

D. firm's offering list

161. A customer sells stock currently held in a safe deposit box. If the customer fails to deliver the certificates on time, SEC rules mandate that her broker-dealer must:

A. freeze the account

B. report the action to the state securities regulator

C. buy in the securities within 10 days following the trade date

D. buy in the securities within 10 days following settlement

162. A municipal securities dealer purchased a block of 5% municipal bonds at a 5.00 basis. Which of the following represent reoffering prices/yields most likely to be deemed reasonable?

I. 3.00 basis

II. 4.70 basis

III. 106

IV. 101

A. I, III

B. I, IV

C. II, III

D. II, IV

163. The official statement for an Ohio Sports Authority revenue bond states that debt service will be paid after operating and maintenance expenses. This represents a

A. non-forfeiture clause

B. net revenue pledge

C. gross revenue pledge

D. prior lien bond

164. A customer at your firm would have to present a letter stating that he or she is not a "restricted person" before buying a new issue of which of the following securities?

A. participating preferred shares

B. common stock

C. subordinated debentures

D. all of the choices listed

165. The amount that an issuer will pay above par to retire bonds prior to maturity is known as a(n)

 A. call premium

 B. put premium

 C. arbitrage settlement

 D. adjustment allowance

166. A member firm holds 1,000 shares AXQ, which it purchased at $30.
If the firm sells the stock to the customer, the amount (and fairness) of the markup will be based on the

 A. highest bid displayed on NASDAQ system

 B. lowest offer displayed on NASDAQ system

 C. $30 purchase price

 D. dealer's best judgment of fairness

167. When diversifying a portfolio of bonds, which of the following is not a concern?

 A. price

 B. quality

 C. maturity

 D. geographic location of the issuers

168. A customer's margin account has a long market value of $40,000 and a debit balance of $12,000. FRB initial margin requirement is 50%. What is the purchasing power in the account?

 A. $13,000

 B. $16,000

 C. $36,000

 D. 0

169. JoAnne Robinson originally invested $52,000 in the XYZ Conservative Income fund, in order to reach the first breakpoint. Over the past several years, JoAnne has reinvested dividend distributions of $3,000 and capital gains distributions of $1,500. If JoAnne sells all of her fund shares this year, her cost basis should be reported as

 A. $52,000

 B. $53,500

 C. $55,000

 D. $56,500

170. **For a non-discretionary customer of a member firm, the account executive may decide:**

    A. the security purchased or sold

    B. the time to enter the order

    C. whether to purchase or sell

    D. the number of shares to be purchased if the customer specifies the security

171. **If a registered representative has not completed the regulatory element training within 120 days of his registration anniversary, which of the following will be the result?**

    A. The broker-dealer will be suspended.

    B. The rep will be sanctioned and fined.

    C. The rep will be placed in inactive status.

    D. The rep has 60 days to complete the requirement.

172. **An investor who buys put options will lose most or all of his investment if, at expiration:**

    I. the strike price is equal to the market price of the underlying security

    II. the strike price is significantly lower than the market price of the underlying security

    III. the strike price is significantly higher than the market price of the underlying security

    A. I

    B. II

    C. I, II

    D. III

173. **A bond investor could hedge against interest rate risk by purchasing:**

    I. interest-rate option calls

    II. interest-rate option puts

    III. yield-based option calls

    IV. yield-based option puts

    A. I, III

    B. I, IV

    C. II, III

    D. II, IV

174. If ABC splits their common stock 2:1, which of the following will also be adjusted?

    A. warrants

    B. calls

    C. par value of the common stock

    D. all of the choices listed

175. A customer enters an order that is good for one week. If the order is not executed, who is responsible for canceling the order at the end of the week?

    A. the specialist

    B. the customer

    C. the exchange where the security trades

    D. the brokerage firm that entered the order

176. A tombstone ad states that Iowa Gas & Electric is issuing $50 million of 5% first mortgage bonds at par. The bonds are secured by

    A. the full faith and credit of the State of Iowa

    B. the full faith and credit of Iowa Gas & Electric

    C. a lien on property owned by Iowa Gas & Electric

    D. a lien on property owned by the State of Iowa

177. For purposes of position limits which of the following are considered to be on the "same side of the market"?

    I.   long calls

    II.   long puts

    III. short calls

    IV. short puts

    A. I, III

    B. I, IV

    C. II, IV

    D. III, IV

178. Which of the following orders may an account executive accept from a non-discretionary retail customer?

A. buy 1,000 shares of a manufacturer today

B. buy shares of three technology stocks today

C. buy 1,000 shares of GE today

D. buy as much IBM as I can realistically afford

179. Which of the following actions on the part of the FRB/FOMC would be associated with "loose" or "easy money"?

A. lowering the discount rate

B. buying Treasuries from primary dealers

C. relaxing the reserve requirement

D. all of the choices listed

180. Which of the following actions on the part of the FRB/FOMC would be associated with "tight money"?

A. lowering the discount rate

B. buying Treasuries from primary dealers

C. relaxing the reserve requirement

D. selling Treasuries to primary dealers

181. You are discussing ABC common stock with one of the retail clients on your book of business. As the account executive, which of the following statements would be permissible?

A. The company's financials are so solid that this is really a can't-miss opportunity.

B. Our chief equities analyst has assured me that ABC will appreciate no less than 10% this year.

C. Our chief equities analyst just issued a report estimating 20% revenue and earnings growth over the next five years; therefore, I think ABC represents a good investment opportunity for your account.

D. If ABC doesn't advance at least 3 points this year, my principal has promised to refund your money.

182. A trader who writes a JJJ Jun 45 call @3.50, if assigned, would report proceeds for purposes of tax reporting of

A. $45

B. $48.50

C. the price paid for the security delivered to the buyer upon exercise

D. $41.50

183. A pension fund would trade securities directly with a mutual fund on which of the following markets?

  A. exchange

  B. OTC

  C. fourth

  D. any of the choices listed

184. The City of Central Falls, North Dakota, issued revenue bonds this year to finance the construction of a new sewer system. If revenues fall short of debt service requirements, a provision is in place to seek emergency funding from the state legislature. This describes which of the following?

  A. general obligation bond

  B. double obligation bond

  C. moral obligation bond

  D. double barreled bond

185. When an NYSE specialist informs a floor broker that she has been "stopped at 32 and a half," this means that

  A. the floor broker may not purchase shares for less than $32.50

  B. the floor broker must purchase at least 10 round lots for $32.50

  C. the floor broker is guaranteed the price of $32.50 and may seek a better price from the crowd

  D. the specialist is engaging in insider trading

186. Which of the following has the responsibility for stating whether a municipality has the legal authority to issue bonds?

  A. SEC

  B. FINRA

  C. MSRB

  D. bond counsel

187. During a busy trading day a customer of your firm places a market order to sell 1,000 XYZ. When the transaction is executed, the customer is told via telephone that the shares were sold at $37.50. Unfortunately, this price was erroneous due to a clerical error. The 1,000 shares of XYZ common were, in fact, sold at only $36. Therefore,

  A. the firm must make up the difference to the customer

  B. the customer will receive only $36 per share

  C. the transaction will automatically be rescinded

  D. the customer may accept or reject this transaction

188. How many shares of underlying stock are represented by the following?
25 TOY Mar 35 puts @2.50

A. 3500

B. 100

C. 2500

D. 250,000

189. When comparing AAA-rated debt securities to BBB-rated, which of the following are true?

I.   AAA-rated securities carry a higher market price

II. BBB-rated securities carry a higher market price

III. AAA-rated securities are higher yielding

IV. BBB-rated securities are higher yielding

A. I, III

B. I, IV

C. II, III

D. II, IV

190. Settlement occurs when the purchaser is recognized as the owner of the security. Which of the following represent(s) true statement(s) concerning settlement dates?

A. Treasury notes and bonds settle regular way T + 3

B. index options settle regular way T + 2

C. options purchases and sales settle regular way T + 1

D. all of the choices listed

191. A member firm receives confirmation of a trade that does not appear on its records. The firm should

A. send a DK to the contra broker-dealer

B. ignore the erroneous confirmation

C. send a DK to the SEC

D. send a DK to FINRA

192. Which of the following factor into the premium of a listed option?

A. volatility of the underlying instrument

B. time to expiration of the contract

C. value of the underlying instrument relative to the strike price of the option

D. all of the choices listed

193. **If an options holder chooses to exercise the contract, which of the following best describes the process?**

    A. broker-dealer for the options holder submits an exercise notice to the OCC, who assigns the contract to a member firm on a random basis

    B. broker-dealer for the options holder submits an exercise notice to the OCC, who assigns the contract to a member firm on a LIFO basis

    C. broker-dealer for the options holder assigns the contract to any investor at the firm who has written that series of option

    D. broker-dealer for the options holder sends an assignment notice to the SEC

194. **Which of the following represent a violation of MSRB rules?**

    A. a registered rep contacts a municipal bond mutual fund and offers to promote the fund to his book of business if the mutual fund will direct more trades for execution with the registered rep's firm

    B. a municipal securities dealer's trade confirmation indicates that the firm acted in a principal capacity on a transaction with a retail investor

    C. a municipal securities dealer allows an apprentice to execute transactions for an institutional client

    D. all of the choices listed violate MSRB rules

195. **Underwriting securities, an activity engaged in by a broker-dealer's investment banking department, may be performed on several different bases with various issuers. Which of the following represent types of underwriting commitments rather than some nonsense we're trying to trick you with?**

    I. standby

    II. firm commitment

    III. best efforts

    IV. all or none

    A. I, II

    B. III

    C. II, III, IV

    D. I, II, III, IV

196. Securities of which of the following issuers would back a Collateralized Mortgage Obligation (CMO)?

A. GNMA

B. FNMA

C. FHLMC

D. all of the choices listed

197. Which of the following are typically associated with "growth stocks"?

I. high dividend payouts

II. low dividend payouts

III. high P/E ratios

IV. low P/E ratios

A. I, III

B. II, III

C. I, IV

D. II, IV

198. When an issuer effects a forward stock split, which of the following is/are decreased?

I. number of outstanding shares

II. price per share

III. par value

IV. conversion prices on convertible bonds/preferred stock

A. I, II, III, IV

B. II, III, IV

C. III

D. IV

199. Which of the following typically is issued with the longest time before expiration?

A. ordinary calls

B. ordinary puts

C. LEAPS

D. warrants

200. When determining suitability of a DPP investment, you and your client should first consider

    A. MACRS

    B. economic viability

    C. tax advantages

    D. liquidity

201. If a registered representative leaves the firm, all of the following are true except

    A. customer accounts transfer to the employing member firm

    B. new account forms do not need to be completed for the agent's customer accounts

    C. customer account records will be amended to reflect that a new registered representative has been named account executive

    D. the firm completes a U5

202. One of your clients is a partnership with three partners. If one of the partners dies, what should you, the registered representative do?

    A. freeze the assets of the account

    B. liquidate all open positions

    C. allow the account to continue trading

    D. transfer to the assets to separate accounts established by the remaining partners

203. Where would you look to read the additional bonds covenant for a revenue bond?

    A. legal opinion

    B. official statement

    C. bond indenture

    D. syndicate agreement

204. Which of the following represents an inaccurate statement concerning penalties and Individual Retirement Accounts?

    A. premature withdrawals are subject to a 10% penalty tax on the amount withdrawn

    B. excess contributions are subject to a 6% penalty on the excess plus any earnings associated with it

    C. an investor who fails to withdraw sufficient funds by April 1 following the year he/she turns 70½ is subject to a 50% penalty

    D. the owner of a Roth IRA would be penalized for any withdrawals from the account during the first five years.

205. Which two of the following are TRUE when opening new customer accounts?

I. On the new account form a P.O. Box may be listed as the customer's address.

II. A street address must be shown on the new account form.

III. Customer correspondence may be sent to a P.O. Box.

IV. Customer correspondence may not be sent to a P.O. Box.

A. I and III

B. I and IV

C. II and IV

D. II and III

206. All of the following affect the marketability of a block of municipal bonds except

A. credit rating

B. maturity

C. dated date

D. yield to maturity

207. A T-bond call option is quoted at 2-24. The premium is, therefore:

A. $224

B. $2,240

C. $2,750

D. $20,750

208. Which of the following securities makes interest payments to the investor?

A. commercial paper

B. banker's acceptance

C. Treasury note

D. Treasury bill

209. All of the following represent negotiable securities except

A. municipal General Obligation bonds

B. jumbo CDs

C. commercial paper

D. EE Savings Bonds

210. **When opening an account, all of the following account types would require supplemental documentation except:**

    A. guardian

    B. trust

    C. Uniform Gifts to Minors

    D. estate account

211. **If an account executive opens an account for the client of an investment adviser, all of the following are required except:**

    A. written authorization from the client

    B. a listing of all the investment adviser's clients

    C. the client's name

    D. the client's social security number

212. **Which of the following would normally represent taxable income?**

    A. interest earned on school bonds issued within the investor's state of residence

    B. unrealized capital appreciation on stock held more than one calendar year

    C. tips earned waiting tables

    D. annual contributions to a SEP or SIMPLE IRA

213. **Dale has written call options on XYZ common stock. All of the following could cover this position except**

    A. escrow receipt for the stock

    B. bond convertible into a like number of shares

    C. shares equal to the contract size

    D. short position in the stock

214. **All of the following municipal bonds are trading at a 5.00 basis. Which one is most susceptible to call risk?**

    A. 5% nominal, 10-year maturity

    B. 6% nominal, 10-year maturity

    C. 6% nominal, 15-year maturity

    D. 5% nominal, 5-year maturity

215. **This morning you receive a telephone call from a Mr. Joe Elroy, informing you that Joe's mother, Barbara, one of your customers, has died. Joe has been named independent executor of the estate and would like you to re-title the account "The Estate of Barbara M. Elroy." Which of the following should you do as account executive?**

    A. refuse to change the account title

    B. change the account title immediately

    C. request a copy of the death certificate and letters of office from Joe and only then transfer assets into the estate account

    D. insist that Joe put the request in writing and then re-title the account

216. **When a limited partnership is liquidated, limited partners would typically receive distributions before**

    A. secured creditors

    B. general creditors

    C. general partner

    D. all of the choices listed

217. **If the annual dividend paid drops by 2% and the market price of the stock drops 4%, what happens to the stock's dividend yield?**

    A. it widens

    B. it narrows

    C. it increases

    D. it decreases

218. **What are the effects of a reverse stock split?**

    A. more shares outstanding

    B. fewer shares outstanding

    C. lower EPS

    D. fully diluted EPS

219. **An M & S Municipal Bond trades Thursday, July 20th. For how many days of accrued interest will the buyer pay the seller?**

    A. zero

    B. 160

    C. 145

    D. 144

220. When a municipal dealer sells municipal bonds to a customer from the dealer's inventory, it must

   A.   comply with the 5% markup policy

   B.   consider the total dollar amount of the transaction when determining the markup

   C.   attach the legal opinion to the customer's trade confirmation

   D.   disclose the amount of the commission on the customer's trade confirmation

221. The portfolio manager for the XYZ Technology Fund should hedge market risk by:

   A.   buying broad-based index calls

   B.   selling broad-based index puts

   C.   buying narrow-based index puts

   D.   buying broad-based index puts

222. Which of the following securities is the most sensitive to interest rate changes?

   A.   common stock

   B.   warrants

   C.   debentures

   D.   convertible debentures

223. Your investor is most concerned with income. You would recommend any of the following except:

   A.   adjustment bonds

   B.   money market funds

   C.   GNMAs

   D.   T-bonds

224. The General Partner bears the non-deductible costs for an oil-drilling program, while the Limited Partners bear the IDCs. This sharing arrangement is known as:

   A.   abusive

   B.   inconsequential

   C.   functional allocation

   D.   reversionary assignment

225. **How long must a customer hold shares of a primary offering before pledging them as collateral?**

    A. 1 year

    B. 30 days

    C. 25 days

    D. 90 days

226. **Under ERISA, at what age must an employee be allowed to participate in a qualified plan?**

    A. 18

    B. 21

    C. 25

    D. 19

227. **When is the last day to purchase shares of a mutual fund and still receive the upcoming dividend?**

    A. declaration date

    B. ex-date

    C. record date

    D. payable date

228. **The initial margin requirement for T-bonds is set by**

    A. Reg T

    B. FRB

    C. SROs

    D. all of the choices listed

229. **Mrs. Smith purchased 1,000 shares RRR @50 and simultaneously wrote 10 RRR May 55 calls @2. Therefore her breakeven is**

    A. $50

    B. $52

    C. $57

    D. $48

230. If a corporation enters bankruptcy protection and must be liquidated, which of the following creditors would have the highest priority?

    A.   debenture holders

    B.   secured bond holders

    C.   preferred stockholders

    D.   common stockholders

231. If an options investor chooses to establish a short position, she will enter

    A.   an opening purchase

    B.   a closing sale

    C.   a closing purchase

    D.   an opening sale

232. Which of the following are subject to FINRA's 5% markup rule?

    A.   limited partnerships

    B.   variable annuities

    C.   mutual funds

    D.   stock trading on the OTC BB

233. How far is a MSFT Jan 85 call in-the-money with MSFT trading at $90?

    A. $5

    B. $90

    C. $87.50

    D. $0

234. An investor is long an IBM Mar 90 put @3. With IBM @94.75, she closes the option for its intrinsic value. She has a

    A.   loss of $300

    B.   gain of $300

    C.   gain of $175

    D.   loss of $175

235. An investor is short an IBM Mar 90 call @3. With the underlying security trading @92, she closes the contract for its intrinsic value. She has a

    A.   loss of $100

    B.   gain of $100

    C.   loss of $9,000

    D.   gain of $9,000

236. An IBM Mar 75 put @3 has how much intrinsic value with IBM @74?

    A. $2

    B. $1

    C. $0

    D. $3

237. An investor purchases an XYZ Mar 75 put @4. With XYZ @74, he closes the contract for its intrinsic value. He has a

    A.   gain of $100

    B.   loss of $300

    C.   loss of $400

    D.   gain of $300

238. Your customer is long 100 shares of MSFT. For best protection, what should he do?

    A.   buy a call

    B.   sell a call

    C.   sell a put

    D.   buy a put

239. Your customer sold 100 shares of MSFT short. To generate income, he should

    A.   buy a call

    B.   buy a put

    C.   sell a call

    D.   sell a put

240. **Long 100 shares XYZ @40. Short XYZ Oct 50 call @2.25. What is the breakeven on this position?**

    A. $47.25

    B. $37.75

    C. $2.25

    D. unlimited

241. **Long IBM Mar 90 call. Short IBM Mar 100 call. The investor will profit if the difference in premiums**

    A. narrows

    B. expires

    C. elongates

    D. widens

242. **The longer the investor's time horizon, the greater the danger of**

    A. investment loss

    B. interest rate risk

    C. loss of purchasing power

    D. volatility

243. **Sue Smarmek owns 100 shares ARZ @50. If ARZ undergoes a 3:2 split, Sue will be:**

    A. up 30%

    B. up 32%

    C. long 150 ARZ @$33.33

    D. long 300 shares @$50

244. **Which of the following securities represent equity in a company?**

    I. non-cumulative preferred stock

    II. common stock

    III. convertible debentures

    IV. convertible preferred stock

    A. II, III

    B. I, II, III

    C. I, II, IV

    D. I, II, III, IV

245. The record date is Tuesday, August 7th. Therefore, the ex-date is

    A. Monday, August 6th

    B. Friday, August 10th

    C. Friday, August 3rd

    D. next business day

246. The right of common stockholders to claim company assets in a bankruptcy proceeding is known as:

    A. residual right

    B. creditorial right

    C. bottom line right

    D. demand payment right

247. Which of the following investors is most likely to have voting rights?

    A. debenture holder

    B. convertible debenture holder

    C. secured bond holder

    D. common stock holder

248. Which of the following is a true statement concerning Eurodollar bonds?

    A. They are registered with the Securities and Exchange Commission.

    B. They are zero coupon issues only.

    C. Payment is made in a currency other than the U.S. dollar.

    D. They are issued outside of the United States.

249. A quarter percent is equivalent to how many basis points?

    A. 25

    B. 250

    C. .25

    D. 2.5

250. To whom must a customer direct a request for a copy of the MSRB rulebook?

    A. SEC

    B. MSRB

    C. broker-dealer

    D. FINRA

Practice Exam Answers

1. **ANSWER:** D

   WHY: anything that is sent to a targeted/controlled audience is sales literature. Advertising is material that is available to a general audience—billboard, TV, radio, etc.

2. **ANSWER:** B

   WHY: the principal approves things; he or she doesn't have to be the one doing the writing. Why use highly paid principals to do the writing when there are plenty of hungry, underemployed English majors out there?

3. **ANSWER:** A

   WHY: cold calling scripts and computer slide shows represent sales literature, where the audience is more targeted/controlled/known. Anyone could stumble across your touch-screen kiosk on IRA rollovers at the mall, but only the audience you invited to the seminar would see your computer slide show. A "listing" in a telephone directory would not be sales literature or advertising, but a display advertisement would, of course, be considered advertising. As always, read the questions very carefully.

4. **ANSWER:** B

   WHY: the management fee is a percentage of the net assets of the fund. 25 to 50 basis points is a typical management fee for equity mutual funds.

5. **ANSWER:** B

   WHY: a censure is a reprimand that people can see at www.FINRA.org , but it's not as bad as having to take a time-out for a little while (suspend), or forever (bar).

6. **ANSWER:** A

   WHY: the SEC is a government body. The other organizations self-regulate, so they went ahead and named themselves "self-regulatory organizations."

7. **ANSWER:** D

    WHY: the Securities Act of 1933 leaves the ringleaders of the fraud civilly liable to the investors that were duped by their shenanigans.

8. **ANSWER:** D

    WHY: sounds reasonable, right? Can't let the firm pick out one or two great picks, while they conveniently exclude the losers. And, if they have an underwriting relationship with any of the companies they're recommending, we should know that, in case they're just cheerleading as a payback for much appreciated underwriting business.

9. **ANSWER:** C

    WHY: and if they ask you which federal act allowed advertising prospectuses to contain performance figures, tell it NSMIA.

10. **ANSWER:** B

    WHY: after the registered representative discusses suitability issues concerning options, he or she sends out the OCC disclosure document. Covered call writing is not risk-free; remember that the stock owned can drop to zero. The premium collected would only partially offset that loss.

11. **ANSWER:** B

    WHY: that's according to ERISA, by the way under the section on "eligibility."

12. **ANSWER:** C

    WHY: in the 401(K) it usually takes a few years to become fully vested, at which point you're entitled to 100% of your employer's contributions. For the others, the contributions belong immediately to the employee for the SEP/SIMPLE, and to the individual in the Traditional IRA.

13. **ANSWER:** C

    WHY: if the guy is a total wimp and can't stand to watch his investment go down for a while, put him in-the-money market so you can both get some sleep at night. Money market shares are priced at $1, period.

14. **ANSWER:** B

    WHY: for the SEP, contributions go in pre-tax and come out fully taxable.

15. **ANSWER:** C

    WHY: what is a "family emergency," by the way? If they let annuitants take money out for "family emergencies," would that include you daughter's dire need for a $700 prom dress?

16. **ANSWER:** A

WHY: if you were going too fast, you might have been tricked by this one. The other choices only affect how much can be deducted from the contribution, but anyone with earned income can contribute to their Traditional IRA.

17. **ANSWER:** D

WHY: a low turnover ratio means that the fund doesn't spend so much money trading securities and probably doesn't have to pay the investment adviser quite as much, lowering the fees that otherwise reduce an investor's returns. They don't generate as much in capital gains, lowering the investor's tax liability. No-load also means the 12b-1 fee cannot exceed 25 basis points.

18. **ANSWER:** D

WHY: is the rep helping the customer achieve a lower sales charge or not? If not, it's breakpoint selling, a major no-no at FINRA.

19. **ANSWER:** C

WHY: the test assumes that people will pay down their debts before risking money on stocks and bonds. Earn some interest in-the-money market, pay off the student loans, and then we'll think about investing in growth stocks, corporate bonds, etc.

20. **ANSWER:** C

WHY: if you put money market first in terms of liquidity, you're done with this question.

21. **ANSWER:** D

WHY: some things simply are what they are. This one is what it is.

22. **ANSWER:** C

WHY: you can't work outside your firm without notifying your supervisor. The firm does not have to approve it, but they can deny it—in case the question goes in that direction.

23. **ANSWER:** A

WHY: yet another factoid to memorize.

24. **ANSWER:** B

WHY: "fiduciary" just means that someone is acting on behalf of someone else and for that someone else's best interests. If you take the 65/66, you'll see the word "fiduciary" all over the place and I know you can't wait for that.

25. **ANSWER:** D

    WHY: it's reviewed to make sure the transactions are suitable and that no churning is going on. The exam might try to trick you into saying all transactions have to be approved in advance by a principal—no. Also, when the client dies, the firm and the rep need to stop trading, period, and definitely are not entering several quick discretionary trades just to churn out some commissions while no one's really watching.

26. **ANSWER:** C

    WHY: something to memorize. The assets would become part of the estate rather than passing directly to the parents.

27. **ANSWER:** D

    WHY: the exam may still talk about "transfer and ship" even though most investors have never seen a stock or bond certificate in their lives. Letting the custodial broker-dealer hold your securities in street name (their name, for your benefit) is very common. Also remember that mutual fund shares are typically not held by either the customer or the broker-dealer. Rather, they are held by the transfer agent for the fund.

28. **ANSWER:** B

    WHY: you may have noticed how many ways there are to say the same thing in this industry. Power of attorney/discretion/trading authorization…they all basically mean the same thing— someone has granted the authority to make investment decisions to someone else.

29. **ANSWER:** B

    WHY: the income generated from an UGMA account might be taxed favorably, but withdrawals could represent capital gains, which would be taxable to the account.

30. **ANSWER:** C

    WHY: a mistaken report is still the customer's trade. If you'd bought the wrong stock, that's different. But you're not lying about anything. You filled the order at a particular price. You got it wrong on the phone—the confirmation has it right.

31. **ANSWER:** B

    WHY: the "second" or "OTC" market is associated with "negotiated market." Exchanges (first market) are considered "auction markets," where the highest bid and lowest ask prices would represent the best market for a security. If an issuer listed on an exchange does not remain current with its financial reports, the exchange begins to hassle them—the stock symbol changes and sometimes the company ends up getting kicked off the exchange.

32. **ANSWER:** C

WHY: mutual fund shares don't trade between investors, and they usually aren't being held in people's safe deposit boxes somewhere. So there's none of that T + 3 thing going on, and, there-fore, the DERP you learned for stocks trading on exchanges doesn't apply. For a mutual fund, you settle same-day, so just buy it on or before the deadline—the record date—and you'll get your dividend.

33. **ANSWER:** C

WHY: good chance the exam will want you to know that long-term debt securities carry more interest rate risk than intermediate- or short-term. And, credit quality is not a concern, which is why we made you choose a U.S. Government bond as being the riskiest in terms of "rates up-price down." You're welcome.

34. **ANSWER:** D

WHY: it makes no difference what you do with your dividends and capital gains from a mutual fund—either way, they will be taxed. A related question would point out that, since you are taxed, you add the reinvestment to your cost basis so that you don't get taxed on it later when you sell for a capital gain.

35. **ANSWER:** B

WHY: the big guys use Form 144 to report their sales to the SEC. That way, if they keep dumping one million shares the day before a bad earnings announcement, it saves the SEC enforcers lots of time and effort when enforcing insider trading rules.

36. **ANSWER:** B

WHY: if you put a fixed dollar amount in every month, your fixed dollar amount will buy more shares when the price is down and fewer when the price is up. This is why the average cost works out so well—most of the shares are purchased at low prices and only a few are purchased at high prices.

37. **ANSWER:** A

WHY: a 100% turnover ratio means the portfolio gets "turned over" every year. In other words, the account balance also represents the dollar amount of trading that has taken place over the year. 50% means it takes two years, since only half the account balance is traded in a year. 200% would mean it gets turned over twice a year. I've read many disciplinary orders against agents who not only engaged in unauthorized transactions but were churning their customers' accounts without their knowledge with turnover rates as high as 13 times! Imagine if you discovered that your mother's $10,000 brokerage account had seen trading activity representing $130,000, all without her knowledge.

38. **ANSWER:** B

WHY: the difference is the sales charge. How much of the customer's check (POP) is the sales charge? 50 cents or 4.8%. The exam can refer to the POP as the "gross amount invested" also.

39. **ANSWER:** B

WHY: a tombstone is just an announcement that a certain issuer is offering a certain number of shares to the public. There is a disclaimer on the tombstone that this announcement is not to be construed as an offer to sell—all offers are made by the prospectus only. A prospectus IS an offer. If I call you up and request a prospectus based on the tombstone ad, this is so far an unsolicited order. But, once you send me the prospectus, you have OFFERED me the security. This is a Series 63 concept, too.

40. **ANSWER:** A

WHY: assume that a broker-dealer who can help the syndicate sell securities will make the selling concession.

41. **ANSWER:** D

WHY: no one can predict where the stock will trade among investors after the offer period. The intended use of the proceeds is very important—if a company tells investors the money is being used to buy equipment, but the money actually gets handed out to the top sales reps or the board members, the regulators will come down hard.

42. **ANSWER:** A

WHY: and, of course, the exam could say it the other way around: "deficiency letter." Please try to be flexible in that regard—many terms will be similar to what you're comfortable with, but you'll have to adjust to the language used on the actual exam.

43. **ANSWER:** A

WHY: working capital is "current assets – current liabilities," which is why the exam would probably rather say "current liabilities subtracted from current assets," since the exam likes to play rough. The other items are from the income statement. A quick visit to a financial website would allow you to view a company's balance sheet and income statement.

44. **ANSWER:** B

WHY: if you know that the formula is Assets – Liabilities = Shareholder Equity (net worth), you have to assume that liabilities increased. If assets didn't move, the only way for the other side of the equation to go down is for liabilities to go up.

45. **ANSWER:** C

WHY: the stuff people buy for a few bucks every day without thinking about it—that stuff is sold by companies whose stocks are "defensive," meaning that even in a recession people turn on the heat, buy milk and snack chips, etc. But an automobile can usually go another year or two given an ample supply of duct tape.

46. **ANSWER:** C

WHY: another way to define Gross Domestic Product would be to refer to the value of all goods and services produced and consumed over a financial quarter. GDP is generally considered to be the best measurement of current economic health. About 2/3 of its value comes from consumer spending, by the way.

47. **ANSWER:** C

WHY: the President and Congress decide how the U.S. Government spends money. The "Fed" is appointed by the government and is given amazing autonomy. It does not, however, get to decide tax and spend policies—only elected officials get to do that.

48. **ANSWER:** B

WHY: the book value represents the hard, tangible value that a share of stock represents. As a worst-case scenario, if the company went bankrupt, they could liquidate tangible assets like land and equipment to pay off the bondholders and preferred stockholders, and then this amount of cash would go to each share of common stock. Though, of course, you wouldn't actually buy a share of common stock if you thought the company was going bankrupt, but, as the question said, this is a theoretical or hypothetical value.

49. **ANSWER:** B

WHY: yet again, you're being asked to remember that long-term bonds carry more interest rate risk, but notice how we can ask it with many different spins and angles. This time we only said "inflationary" just in case you forgot how that related to interest rates.

50. **ANSWER:** A

WHY: beta measures how much a share of stock or a portfolio moves up or down compared to the movement of the overall market. It measures volatility, which is considered to be the same thing as "risk" by investment professionals.

51. **ANSWER:** C

WHY: rising CPI (inflation) leads to higher interest rates. Rates up—price down. Yields and rates are the same thing.

52. **ANSWER:** A

WHY: rising interest rates crush the market price of existing bonds, and they don't do much good for stock prices either. Rising rates mean that the cost of expanding or starting a business is going up. Also, consumers aren't as likely to be walking around with fat stacks of "cash out" money from refinancing their overpriced, speculative home purchases. Remember, all we really need is for consumers to be able to BUY stuff. If rates are low, buying stuff gets easier. If rates are high, buying stuff gets tougher.

53. **ANSWER:** B

WHY: read carefully on this exam. Low unemployment is the same thing as high employment, which is a good thing. If people are working, they're making money and probably buying stuff. That's a healthy economy, especially if interest rates are nice and low.

54. **ANSWER:** A

WHY: I guess you have to show some faith in the odd lot theory to get this one right. Oh well. Do you know any non-professional investors who like to get into a hot stock after it's already made its big advance?

55. **ANSWER:** C

WHY: sounds backwards, but if a lot of people will have to buy the stock back to replace the shares they sold short, that buying pressure could push the stock price up.

56. **ANSWER:** C

WHY: discretionary authorization could be referred to as "power of attorney," but that doesn't mean it comes from an attorney. A discretionary account could be approved for options trading, although I would sure hate to be the registered rep who has to make the phone call after losing $30,000 writing calls and puts without, you know, even talking to the customer first.

57. **ANSWER:** B

WHY: always look for the set-up. The numbers in this question were trying to pull you in—yeah, just take 10% of $300,000, ignore the word "non-recourse" and get the question wrong.

58. **ANSWER:** C

WHY: there is no reason to assume that investing in an exploratory oil drilling program makes the investor "immediately diversified." Immediately sleepless, sure, but not immediately diversified. There is no guaranteed rate of return on any security, really, so you have to eliminate at least two choices in this question.

59. **ANSWER:** B

WHY: underwriters reading the Bond Buyer want to know how well new issues were "absorbed" or "placed" the previous week on the primary market. This metric is called the "placement ratio" or the "acceptance ratio."

60. **ANSWER:** B

WHY: you probably didn't choose "limited liability," which would be really tough to avoid in a "limited liability company."

61. **ANSWER:** A

WHY: remember that limited partners are investors only—they have no work or management responsibilities. It's a passive investment.

62. **ANSWER:** D

WHY: all that happened here is that the customer had an extra $50 come in, which we applied to the debit balance of 10K.

63. **ANSWER:** C

WHY: raw land ought to be appreciating—not depreciating—right? But an old apartment building isn't as desirable as a brand new one, and old equipment loses value, too.

64. **ANSWER:** A

WHY: Rule 144 is how the shares might be sold later on the secondary market, but this offering is a private placement. There is a holding period, and there cannot be a general solicitation of investors who have no relationship with the broker-dealers in the syndicate. It's a private offering of securities. Remember that the word "secondary" means that someone other than the issuer receives the proceeds, like the former CEO or a board member, for example.

65. **ANSWER:** B

WHY: this is just a way of saying that DPPs aren't liquid and usually aren't all that safe. If you need liquidity and safety, you should be in-the-money market, which is on the opposite side of the spectrum in these regards.

66. **ANSWER:** A

WHY: that's what "recourse" means—the creditors have recourse to take a percentage of the debt from your own personal bank account.

67. **ANSWER:** B

WHY: an IDC is something we pay and are left with nothing tangible to show for it. Paying for the geological survey and the labor = intangible drilling costs (IDCs). The tangible stuff, such as the oilrig, would be called a "capitalized cost." If the exam asks you which sharing arrangement allocates the IDCs to the LPs and the capitalized costs to the GP, tell it "functional allocation."

68. **ANSWER:** D

WHY: "account executive," by the way, is another name for you, the registered representative, a.k.a. agent.

69. **ANSWER:** C

WHY: if you speak Spanish, you might have noticed how close "hypothecation" is to hipotecas, which are loans. You pledge your stock as collateral to secure the margin loan—you hypothecate your securities, in other words.

70. **ANSWER:** B

WHY: municipal securities are exempt from the Securities Act of 1933, so eliminate that choice. Choice "D" describes the placement ratio, so eliminate that one, too. The "visible supply" looks forward, showing the volume of bonds to be offered over the next 30 days. An underwriter would want to know how many other bonds are going to be competing for investors' dollars as they take an issue to the primary market.

71. **ANSWER:** C

WHY: "DNR" stands for "Do Not Reduce," as in—do not reduce the order price for a cash dividend .

72. **ANSWER:** C

WHY: I would be surprised if the exam got that nasty and expected you to memorize something like that. But, I wouldn't be totally shocked, which is why I threw it in.

73. **ANSWER:** B

WHY: this is exactly why some traders make their stop orders stop LIMIT orders. If the stock opens way down one day, they don't want it sold at a low price. This order hasn't been filled yet and can't be until we can find a buyer (bid price) willing to pay at least $82. And, the order doesn't get canceled just because the stock opens lower.

74. **ANSWER:** C

WHY: twice a year. And, if the exam wants the months, tell it April and October.

75. **ANSWER:** D

WHY: always obtain financial information on your investors, period. No reason to assume that just one investor can place trades. Percentage of ownership will be indicated by the account owners in the joint account agreement.

76. **ANSWER:** B

WHY: $1.15 per share times 100 shares = $115 gain.

77. **ANSWER:** C

WHY: review the section in Trading Securities on reading the consolidated tape, as you will likely get up to two questions on this topic.

78. **ANSWER:** C

WHY: a sell stop or stop loss order is placed below the current market value.

79. **ANSWER:** B

WHY: the Pink Sheets are OTC (over-the-counter) stocks that do not meet the requirements for NASDAQ. The exam might refer to Pink Sheet and "Bulletin Board" stocks as "Non-NASDAQ OTC securities."

80. **ANSWER:** D

WHY: the question is simply designed to teach you about "stopping stock." It doesn't mean that trading has stopped—just that the specialist is freezing a price for somebody as a courtesy.

81. **ANSWER:** A

WHY: another point to memorize. MOC orders must be placed at least 20 minutes prior to the closing time of the market or exchange.

82. **ANSWER:** D

WHY: a "credit call spread" could be read as "selling calls," which, like buying puts and shorting stock, is a bearish sentiment/position.

83. **ANSWER:** A

WHY: the spread is the difference between the price that the market maker pays for a stock and sells the stock for. If he's willing to pay $10 and sell that sock for $10.25, the 25 cents per share is the spread, or his compensation for "making a market."

84. **ANSWER:** C

WHY: the bid and ask prices are the highest buy-limit and lowest sell-limit orders on the specialist's book. He can trade in between those two prices.

85. **ANSWER:** C

WHY: read the disciplinary actions at www.finra.org, where they provide monthly and quarterly wrap-ups. You'll see many instances of permanent bars being issued against somebody. Unauthorized trades, forging client signatures, misappropriating client funds or securities…these violations often lead to a permanent bar against the individual. FINRA has no authority to pursue criminal cases.

86. **ANSWER:** A

WHY: they would sell or "liquidate" the security, since they have to pay for it in order to settle the transaction with the other broker-dealer whose customer sold the security. The account would not need to be liquidated, although a "freeze" would be placed on the account. When an account is "frozen," the customer has to have the cash in the account before placing any purchase orders for the next 90 days.

87. **ANSWER:** B

WHY: chances are, you would only have to know that cash transactions settle on the day of the trade. But, it would be fun to correctly answer even a question this specific.

88. **ANSWER:** B

WHY: DERP is the order in which the dates go chronologically.

89. **ANSWER:** B

WHY: they need to request the extension before the 5-day deadline, just like in college you had to request an extension before the due date for the assignment.

90. **ANSWER:** C

WHY: the broker-dealers have to settle regular way at T + 3, but the customer has two more business days to pay, if the firm feels like being that nice. Does the customer pay "T + 5," within one calendar week, or two business days after regular way settlement? Yes. Basically, those are three ways of saying the same thing.

91. **ANSWER:** B

WHY: that's who can guarantee a signature. If I'm the executor of an estate, I have to get a signature guarantee to get the securities re-titled in the name of the estate. I can go to my broker-dealer or my bank for this special stamp called a "signature guarantee."

92. **ANSWER:** A

WHY: the broker-dealer is freezing the customer's credit temporarily when the account is "frozen." The account can still be traded, and cash can be withdrawn. If a dividend or interest payment is received, he can have that cash immediately. He just can't buy any stock for a while without having the cash in the account.

93. **ANSWER:** C

WHY: "AE" stands for "account executive," which is another name for a registered representative in charge of a customer's account. Another good test question is, "when must the confirmation be delivered?" Answer: no later than settlement.

94. **ANSWER:** C

WHY: "P & S" stands for "purchasing and sales."

95. **ANSWER:** C

WHY: the point is not to get you to remember the thing about "arbitrage" but to help you remember the other three things, which are handled by this department.

96. **ANSWER:** D

WHY: one thing they can't charge for—forwarding proxy materials on behalf of the issuer. The issuer pays that cost under the Act of 1934.

97. **ANSWER:** C

WHY: if no trading or other account activity has taken place, the account statement is sent at least quarterly for a cash account. For a margin account monthly statements are required in order to reflect the interest being charged on the debit balance.

98. **ANSWER:** D

WHY: the buyer is entitled to the dividend if he bought the stock before the ex-date. Mistakes like this happen all the time; part of FINRA's role is to provide procedures under the Uniform Practice Code to help firms work it out.

99. **ANSWER:** D

WHY: buyers of stock do not get to change their minds and return the merchandise if it doesn't quite fit or clashes with other items in the portfolio.

100. **ANSWER:** C

WHY: under the Act of '34, issuers have to pay the cost of forwarding/soliciting proxies to the shareholders.

101. **ANSWER:** C

WHY: it's the people who are dealing directly with customers who need to be registered. If they're taking orders, we definitely need them to be licensed. In fact, for some of you, this is why you're taking the test. The sales rep you work for is actually better at golf, while you're better at doing actual work. Which is why he's willing to split everything with you 80/20 right down the middle just as soon as you get your license.

102. **ANSWER:** B

WHY: I think you can safely rule out any answer choice with the word "polygraph" in it. Residential history is disclosed for 5 years and employment history for the past 10 years on the U4. Since people have been known to make up jobs and stretch the dates, these things need to be verified. And, of course, if a new hire is caught lying to the firm on her U4, she's done.

103. **ANSWER:** A

WHY: a "DK" (don't know) is used when a firm does not recognize a trade that another firm thinks was executed with them. In this case a "DK" would be a big, fat lie.

104. **ANSWER:** B

WHY: let's get the order filled before we worry about the sales rep's commission.

105. **ANSWER:** B

WHY: deliver the certificates by settlement. Another name for settlement is "clearing" of the trade.

106. **ANSWER:** B

WHY: the answer is the same if the question asks when a final prospectus must be delivered to the purchaser of a primary offering—no later than the due date for settlement or clearance of the transaction, the exam might say.

107. **ANSWER:** D

WHY: the official statement gives the financial picture for the issue of bonds and/or the issuer of the bonds in general. The lead underwriter is irrelevant to whether the bonds are on solid ground or not.

108. **ANSWER:** D

WHY: good one to memorize—and no reason you can't read all the G (General) rules yourself at www.msrb.org. Investors don't really care about the legal opinion—that is something obtained by the issuer and of interest only to the syndicate members.

109. **ANSWER:** B

WHY: revenue bonds are self-supporting, meaning they're backed by the revenues generated by the project that the bonds built. So, they have nothing to do with a debt limit, which is solely for GOs.

110. **ANSWER:** D

WHY: memorize it and know that rising rates lead to what could be called "extension risk." Meaning, the time it takes to get all of your principal will be extended. If rates go down, you'll get your principal sooner, but then you'll have to reinvest it at lower rates (prepayment risk).

111. **ANSWER:** C

WHY: choice "B" is eliminated, since the "10M" means 10 bonds. Step 1 is to find the settlement date—Thursday, November 6th. Now, go back to "A" or August and count 30 days for August, 30 days for September, 30 days for October, plus 5 days for November. The seller owned the bonds through the fifth day of November, right up until ownership transferred on the sixth day of November. The buyer gets the next interest check, but the seller's portion of that check has to be paid upfront. If the coupon rate is $80 per year, divide that by 360 days to get a daily rate of 22.2 cents. The buyer has to pay 22.2 cents times 95 days. That's $21.11 per bond, plus $1,040, as indicated by the quote "104," times 10 bonds.

112. **ANSWER:** C

WHY: the firm would send the MSRB rulebook upon request.

113. **ANSWER:** A

WHY: $100,000 par value is a round lot. A question could refer to this as a "block" of bonds.

114. **ANSWER:** C

WHY: only the managing underwriter gets the manager's fee, and only that firm could earn the total spread—since everyone else has to cough up the manager's fee to that firm. The selling concession goes to any firm who makes a sale, and since this firm is credited with a sale to their customer, they keep the concession as well as the additional takedown that is earned whenever one of their bonds is sold by any firm. The concession and the additional takedown = the "total takedown." And that is a lot to know for just one or two Series 7 questions.

115. **ANSWER:** D

WHY: that is how one writes a trick question. If we write "how FAR is the option in-the-money," you naturally assume it is, in fact, in-the-money. But, in fact, these options are way OUT of the money. Do you want the right to buy at 90 when the thing is only worth 85? Read carefully, and don't trust the set-up to the question.

116. **ANSWER:** B

WHY: you can easily double-check your answer to a question such as this. Just find the buyer's breakeven point. If the stock moved more than that, he makes the difference. The BE was $93. If the stock goes to $94.75, he keeps the $175 difference.

117. **ANSWER:** D

WHY: a Currency Transaction Report (FinCen 104) would be filed for deposits of cash > $10,000. This regular cash deposit could be suspicious, so your firm should fill out an SAR (suspicious activity report).

118. **ANSWER:** C

   WHY: the intrinsic value is the amount the option is in-the-money. If the stock is trading at $74, the right to sell it at $75 is worth that $1 difference. The other $2 in the premium must be time value.

119. **ANSWER:** D

   WHY: a basic T-chart question. Put the "short/write/sell" in the credit column. So, $4 comes in. Then, the trader pays the $1 intrinsic value to close the contract, and keeps the $3 per share difference, or $300 total.

120. **ANSWER:** D

   WHY: the issuing corporation knows what to do with the money they raise, but they may need advice from the underwriter on which type of securities to issue—common stock, convertible preferred stock, bonds-with-warrants-attached, etc. The underwriters may or may not make a market in the stock once it starts trading among investors. Even though the underwriters will probably help fill out the registration statement—maybe even do it for the client—it is the issuing corporation's responsibility to file the registration statement.

121. **ANSWER:** C

   WHY: do these hedging suitability questions step by step. Step 1 is to figure out the risk on the stock position—that it could go DOWN. So, the two options have to be bearish, pointing down. To hedge, you identify what can hurt you and bet some money on that outcome, too. So, you sell a call or buy a put in this case, the two bearish options. Sell a call for income; buy a put for protection.

   To generate income, you SELL an option.

122. **ANSWER:** D

   WHY: don't assume the stock will be sold. If the stock drops, all the covered call writer got was the premium to offset the almost total loss on the stock.

123. **ANSWER:** B

   WHY: remember that you want the value of a short position to drop. It's nice that the long position advanced $4,000, but that was reduced by the $2,000 advance in the short position's value.

124. **ANSWER:** A

   WHY: which option is worth more? The right to buy stock at…$90. If she sold that one, she has a credit spread.

   Credit spreads are profitable if the spread narrows.

125. **ANSWER:** D

WHY: associate the "E" in "European" with the "E" in "Expiration." Associate the "A" in "American" with the "A" in "any time." In case you didn't already have enough associations to keep track of.

126. **ANSWER:** B

WHY: a young investor isn't going to tap the money in her IRA until at least age 59½ and doesn't have to start until 70½. So, go for long-term growth on a question like this.

127. **ANSWER:** D

WHY: "breakeven" is neither good nor bad. A seller would rather not go anywhere NEAR the breakeven, because he starts out winning. Well, he won $2.50 a share here and will be back to where he started if the stock falls below the strike price by that much. The buyer of the put, who started out the loser, would now be up to his breakeven point.

And neither one is buying drinks tonight, because neither one has made money yet.

128. **ANSWER:** A

WHY: there's really no limit to the amount of details this exam feels entitled to throw at you. Maybe LIBOR will pop up, maybe not. Sure would be nice to have an idea what it stands for.

129. **ANSWER:** A

WHY: every other statement has got it wrong. An LOI is non-binding. The fund just holds the extra shares purchased as a result of the reduced sales charge in "escrow." If the customer doesn't pay up, those shares are gone, and the customer gets exactly as many shares as her investment entitled her to. If you backdate the later (max of 90 days), you only get 13 months from that date. LOIs are based on new dollars, too, not on accumulation. Rights of accumulation, remember, has nothing to do with an LOI.

130. **ANSWER:** D

WHY: the GP has all the responsibility and liability—he can't compete, commingle, or borrow from the partnership. And when the thing goes belly up, he's last in line. Of course, the bankers are first in line, especially the ones with collateral securing the loan.

131. **ANSWER:** D

WHY: a management decision such as selling assets has to be made by the GP. The LPs are just passive investors.

132. **ANSWER:** D

WHY: all of these positions could immediately result in the investor buying 500 shares of XYZ in a hurry, right? That's what they mean by "substantially identical."

133. ANSWER: C

WHY: the price of T-bonds needs to move by 1.24. Each contract covers $100,000 par value, so if the price goes up by 1.24, that represents what the buyer pays/seller receives.

134. ANSWER: C

WHY: as soon as the ROP approves the account, the first trade can occur. But if the firm doesn't get the signed options agreement within 15 business days, no new positions may be established, only closing transactions.

135. ANSWER: C

WHY: if someone has already shorted stock, don't tell the exam he needs to sell some stock again. Eliminate sell orders, and there's no reason to purchase puts, which give him the "right to sell."

136. ANSWER: C

WHY: you will get your interest and principal, but it's a fixed-income security. Therefore, you have no protection from inflation or rising interest rates, which usually go hand-in-hand.

137. ANSWER: B

WHY: the word "real" means "inflation-adjusted." Your investment needs to return more than the rate of inflation. Otherwise, you're falling behind.

138. ANSWER: D

WHY: take the $80 of annual income and divide that by the price of the bond. "102.20" is $1,020 plus 20/32nds or $1,026.25. $80 divided by $1,026.25 = 7.79%. If you chose 9% or 10%, you weren't using your understanding of the bond see-saw.

Price up—yield has to be down.

139. ANSWER: D

WHY: just a common definition of GDP.

140. ANSWER: C

WHY: the account "wraps" everything together.

141. ANSWER: D

WHY: the exam is likely to make sure you know that REITs don't pass through losses/provide tax shelter. That's what real estate limited partnerships (DPPs) do.

142. **ANSWER:** C

WHY: a beta of 1 would mean the stock is exactly as volatile as the overall market, no more no less. If the beta is less than 1, the stock goes up less than the overall market, but also falls less than the overall market.

143. **ANSWER:** D

WHY: if the firm wants to deal with individual customers in other states, they'll have to get registered in those states. Also a Series 63 question.

144. **ANSWER:** C

WHY: as in many households, the debt is too high. You don't always have to wait for the market to raise the value of your asset—you can also build equity by paying down the debt. So, to get the equity up to $5,000, the customer would pay down the Debit Balance by $1,000.

145. **ANSWER:** B

WHY: that's the definition of beta, which measures market risk or "volatility."

146. **ANSWER:** C

WHY: the "1" means $1,000. Each 32nd is worth $31.25.

147. **ANSWER:** D

WHY: one of the worst things you could do to your long stock position is write either a straddle or a put. If you do that, what happens if your stock goes to zero? You have to buy the worthless stock again for the strike price.

148. **ANSWER:** C

WHY: IRA contributions have to be made by April 15th of the following year (or the deadline for filing taxes).

149. **ANSWER:** D

WHY: MBIA insures issues of municipal securities against default risk.

In the real world, you'll sometimes see the word "pure" attached to, say, an AA rating. That means, the issue is AA all by itself, rather than bolstered by the insurance backing against default. See? There's just no end to the fascinating details you get to learn for your Series 7.

150. **ANSWER:** C

WHY: just something else for you to memorize. IDCs represent items such as the geological survey and the labor. The equipment will be depreciated gradually; it's the intangible costs that will represent the biggest deductions early on.

151. **ANSWER:** D

> **WHY:** position limits cover the number of contracts that can be held on the bull or bear side, and they also cover the number of contracts that can be exercised in a 5-day period.

152. **ANSWER:** C

> **WHY:** if a bond is called, the investor does not have the option of holding it—the money is going to be paid out in exchange for the bond, period. Remember that falling yields and rising bond prices are the same darned thing, so the answer had to include both of those choices.

153. **ANSWER:** B

> **WHY:** index options are always settled in cash—the writer does not hold the properly weighted shares of 30 or 500 companies in his pocket. Also, no one exercises in the morning, since the value of the option is based on where the index closes—and the DOW can easily fluctuate 200 points or more in one trading day.

154. **ANSWER:** C

> **WHY:** the first appeal is to the NAC, and it needs to be filed within 25 days. This is Code of Procedure. Remember that under Code of Arbitration there are no appeals.

155. **ANSWER:** D

> **WHY:** the economy is being deflated, just like a tire with a leak. Nothing good is happening… unless you're a bondholder who owns a bunch of non-callable bonds. Rates down/price up.

156. **ANSWER:** C

> **WHY:** something to memorize—the members of the syndicate can make the "total takedown" when a sale is credited to them. The "total takedown" is the additional takedown plus the concession.

157. **ANSWER:** C

> **WHY:** the call premiums collected reduce the amount of cash that needs to be deposited. It would have been $4,000 without the $200 coming in. Careful here—if the question had asked what the Reg T requirement is, the answer would have been $4,000. The amount of CASH to deposit is $3,800.

158. **ANSWER:** C

> **WHY:** in a TIC account (tenants in common), the assets go to that party's estate, not to the other account owners. The account agreement also spells out the percentages owned by each account owner.

159. **ANSWER:** B

WHY: IOC stands for "Immediate Or Cancel." Maybe the customer wants 10,000 shares @50. If only 4,000 shares can be bought at the limit price, then that number of shares is purchased and the rest of the order is canceled.

160. **ANSWER:** C

WHY: official statements are prepared by the issuer. A list of offerings is not narrative that can easily be misinterpreted. The principal approves correspondence, sales literature, and advertising because people could misconstrue those messages.

161. **ANSWER:** D

WHY: usually an exam question would focus on making sure you understand what a buy-in is as opposed to the precise number of days within which something has to happen. But, actually, exam questions can go either way, so be prepared.

162. **ANSWER:** D

WHY: the yield should be just a bit lower than the 5.00%. Otherwise, the price is being unfairly jacked up. The price should not be $60 above the dealer's purchase price. Basically, we're just presenting the bond's market value in terms of its yield, and also its price. A price of "106" is way above par. And, to push a yield from 5% to 3% is just another way of saying that they're jacking up the price on the unsuspecting client.

163. **ANSWER:** B

WHY: "net" means that something else gets subtracted first. If that seems strange, take a look at a recent paycheck stub. See all those subtractions before your "net income"?

164. **ANSWER:** B

WHY: this rule prevents people in the securities industry from buying initial public offerings. It only applies to offerings of common stock.

165. **ANSWER:** A

WHY: if a bond is callable at 104, that extra $40 above par is the call premium. Not to be confused with the premium you pay to buy a call option, which is also a "call premium."

166. **ANSWER:** B

WHY: the inside market is the highest bid and lowest offer among all market makers quoting a particular stock. If the firm is selling, it has to be in line with the lowest offer…within about 5%, according to the FINRA markup guideline.

167. **ANSWER:** A

WHY: you wouldn't get diversification by buying a few bonds at 102 and a few at 98. Yield is what you're trying to diversify…price doesn't really mean anything unless we know the coupon rate and, therefore, the yield.

168. **ANSWER:** B

WHY: Reg T is used as a measuring stick to see if there is excess equity. The equity is 28K and Reg T (50%) is 20. So, there is $8,000 SMA and $16,000 buying power.

169. **ANSWER:** D

WHY: cost basis is the money you've already paid taxes on. JoAnne paid taxes on the reinvested dividends and cap gains distributions, so they are added to her cost basis.

170. **ANSWER:** B

WHY: time and price don't really trouble the regulators. It's the 3 A's that represent a major decision: asset, activity (action), amount.

171. **ANSWER:** C

WHY: don't blow off the Regulatory Element, in other words.

172. **ANSWER:** C

WHY: easy to misread this one. If the STRIKE PRICE is significantly lower than the market price, the put expires. If you read that as saying "MARKET price is significantly lower," you fell for the trap. Try not to do that. Read skeptically, carefully.

173. **ANSWER:** C

WHY: Step one, interest rate risk is "rates up/price down." To hedge, I bet that way. Rates up/yields up (buy a call on the yield). Rates up/price down (buy a put on the price).

174. **ANSWER:** D

WHY: everything tied to the company's stock price has to be adjusted. Otherwise, the company could really stick it to somebody. They find out that the guy who mouthed off at the annual shareholder meeting is holding a bunch of convertible bonds, convertible at $50. So, when the stock hits $50, they do a 10:1 stock split, and suddenly the stock is trading at $5. No way. They can do the 10:1 split, but they have to lower the conversion price on the bonds proportionally.

175. **ANSWER:** D

WHY: the exam might point out that the specialist won't accept "good for a week" orders. If a broker-dealer wants to deal with that order, they will have to cancel the order if it's not executed.

176. **ANSWER:** C

WHY: we just put the word "Iowa" in there to see if you'd assume it's backed by the state of Iowa. No, a utility is a company in the private sector, even if they use the name of the state in their own corporate name. Remember that a "mortgage bond" is secured by a lien on the property, just like a homeowner's mortgage is.

177. **ANSWER:** B

WHY: you just need to find a pair that are both bullish or both bearish. We could have paired up long calls–short puts or long puts–short calls.

178. **ANSWER:** C

WHY: time and price don't make regulators nervous. Discretionary authorization is required when the rep and the firm are left to decide the asset, action, or amount.

179. **ANSWER:** D

WHY: loose money stimulates a sputtering economy. Tight money slows down an over-expanding economy before it over-inflates and explodes in chaos.

180. **ANSWER:** D

WHY: Tight money slows down an over-expanding economy before it over-inflates and explodes in chaos. Monetarists raise short-term interest rates to fight inflation and lower them to stimulate a sluggish economy. Selling Treasuries will pull money out of the money supply, raising interest rates, and tapping the brakes on the economy.

181. **ANSWER:** C

WHY: registered representatives can't use language such as "can't miss," because it implies a sense of surety that can't exist. Any stock can go to zero, and any corporate bond can default. Period.

182. **ANSWER:** B

WHY: the writer of the call takes in the strike price of the call when he sells, and he also keeps the premium. So, that's his total proceeds. His cost basis is the market price for the stock he has to buy and deliver to the buyer of the call.

183. **ANSWER:** C

WHY: direct institutional trading takes place electronically on the so-called "fourth market." INSTINET is a good example. These are often referred to as "ECNs" for "electronic communications network."

184. **ANSWER:** C

WHY: there are plans for seeking emergency funding from the state legislature in a "moral obligation bond." Sure makes me sleep better knowing my investment is backed up by the morals of my state politicians.

185. **ANSWER:** C

WHY: the price is "stopped," but trading in the stock continues. The specialist sometimes "stops stock" for a public customer order as a courtesy to a commission house broker, which means he gives them a price that's good temporarily, while the broker is free to seek a better price from the floor traders in the crowd.

186. **ANSWER:** D

WHY: bond counsel, as in "counselor at law."

187. **ANSWER:** B

WHY: seems like a pretty common testable point—an error in reporting is different from an error in execution. If the customer puts in a market order, she pays or receives the best available price, period. We can fix the report either before we send the confirmation, or we can fix the confirmation. But the firm executed the transaction as instructed.

188. **ANSWER:** C

WHY: there are 100 shares per contract, so just add two zeroes to the number of contracts—25, in this case.

189. **ANSWER:** B

WHY: people pay more for AAA-rated debt because it's safer and more reliable. People pay less for low-rated debt because it's unsafe and unreliable. Price and yield are inverse, so high-rated debt is low-yielding and vice versa for low-rated debt (low price/high yield).

190. **ANSWER:** C

WHY: Treasuries traded on the secondary market settle T + 1. Options also settle T + 1.

191. **ANSWER:** A

WHY: believe it or not "DK" stands for "don't know." The broker-dealer does not recognize a trade that another broker-dealer thinks was actually executed between the two firms.

192. **ANSWER:** D

WHY: an option is worth more as the stock trades closer and closer to the strike price. It's worth more if the underlying stock is volatile, meaning likely to jump around in somebody's favor. And the more time that is left on the contract, the more valuable it is. The premium basically reflects a buyer's chance of winning.

193. **ANSWER:** A

WHY: the OCC assigns the notice to any firm with a customer who wrote the series. They do so at random. The broker-dealer who gets the notice from the OCC would assign the contract to anyone at the firm who wrote that particular series at random, according to FIFO, or any other fair method.

194. **ANSWER:** A

WHY: the only violation here would be the one in which somebody promises to promote mutual fund shares in exchange for trading business from the fund's investment adviser, who, of course, has to trade somewhere, right? Trade confirmations must indicate whether the firm acted as principal or agent for the customer, and municipal bonds are often "principaled" with both retail and institutional investors. An apprentice can do transactions with institutional investors, not retail or "public" investors. You can read the "G/general" rules at www.msrb.org.

195. **ANSWER:** D

WHY: all four are types of underwriting. Mini-max could also have been an answer choice.

196. **ANSWER:** D

WHY: CMOs typically hold mortgage-backed securities and then create some mind-blowing investment products few people understand. They call it a "tranche," and then they start selling you PACs, TACs, Z-tranches and a bunch of other stuff we hope doesn't show up much on the exam.

197. **ANSWER:** B

WHY: you pay a lot for growth, and the gratification—if any—is seriously delayed. I'm still waiting for Howard Schultz to pay me my first dividend on SBUX, and if he could do something about the low share price—maybe give it a couple shots of espresso—that would also be great.

198. **ANSWER:** B

WHY: the number of shares increases after a forward stock split. A "forward split" means the first number in the ratio is bigger…5:4, 2:1, etc. So, we take the earnings pie and cut it into more slices. Only way that can happen is to make the size of the slices smaller. It's the difference between sharing a medium pizza among 5 people and 10 people. With 10 people, I hope no one's real hungry, right?

So, the price of the stock goes down, bringing down everything else attached to it: par value, conversion terms, calls, puts, warrants, etc.

199. **ANSWER:** D

WHY: a warrant is good for 5–10 years, typically. Some are perpetual. Longer even.

200. **ANSWER:** B

WHY: even though the client will be salivating over tax advantages in the real world, tell the exam that economic benefits are first and foremost on everyone's mind.

201. **ANSWER:** A

WHY: the member firm has to fill out a U5. With any luck, the registered rep is simply getting out of the business or getting a better job; if he's being fired after signing customer signatures to important documents or entering unauthorized trades, that will have to be indicated on the U5. The accounts belong to the firm—a new "account executive" will simply be assigned to the former rep's accounts.

202. **ANSWER:** A

WHY: death of a partner terminates a partnership agreement, which has to be re-written and signed by the remaining partners.

203. **ANSWER:** C

WHY: think of a bond indenture as a contract where the issuer states everything they'll do for the investor to make sure the interest and principal get paid.

204. **ANSWER:** D

WHY: the tax deferral is nice, but you have to play by all the little rules of the IRA. If you put in too much, you pay 6%. If you take it out too soon, you pay 10%. If you take it out too late you pay 50%. The Roth IRA allows the owner to remove up to the amount he's contributed (his cost basis) without penalty, though why the regulators would want to advertise that, I've no idea.

205. **ANSWER:** D

WHY: we need a physical address somewhere for this customer, even if the mail is then sent to a P.O. Box.

206. **ANSWER:** C

WHY: the dated date has to do with accrued interest, which is never really of importance when deciding to buy a bond. Whatever you pay up front you get back with the first interest payment.

207. **ANSWER:** C

WHY: the "1" or the "2" for a premium on a T-bond option would equal $1,000 or $2,000. Each

32nd is worth $31.25. So, the premium costs $2,000 plus $750. Also, note that 24/32nds is the same as 3/4ths of $1,000.

208. **ANSWER:** C

WHY: money market securities are simply issued at a discount and pay out the higher par value upon maturity. Commercial paper is no different from my asking you to give me $97,000 today, and I'll give you $100,000 in 3 months.

209. **ANSWER:** D

WHY: the word "negotiable" means that the investment can be traded on a secondary market. You don't trade you bank CDs, your checking account, you savings account, or your savings bonds. They aren't negotiable. In fact, your checks announce that they are not negotiable—take a look.

210. **ANSWER:** C

WHY: UGMA/UTMA accounts are a snap to set up. If you have the child's social security number, you're halfway there. The other accounts would require documentation, such as a trust agreement, a death certificate, letters of office (court appointment), etc.

211. **ANSWER:** B

WHY: the broker-dealer would only need information on the client for whom the adviser is opening an account.

212. **ANSWER:** C

WHY: tips and wages are ordinary income. The other stuff would either be tax-free or tax-deductible.

213. **ANSWER:** D

WHY: when Dale writes the calls, he can only cover himself by having the stock or having the ability to get it at a set price. Selling calls and shorting stock are really the same thing—you're betting against the stock.

214. **ANSWER:** C

WHY: yet another way to factor in the bond see-saw concept. Bonds trading at a premium are likely to be called, so if the bonds are trading at a 5.00 basis, the bonds with HIGHER coupon rates/ nominal yields are trading at a premium. Now you're down to the two bonds with 6% coupon rates. Which mortgage would you want to refinance first, the one that sticks you with payments for 15 years, or the one that sticks you with payments for 10 years? You'd get rid of the 15-year mortgage first, which is why that debt is the most likely to be "called."

215. **ANSWER:** C

   WHY: to open an estate account, you have to see proof that Barbara has died (death certificate) and court papers showing that Joe is the executor. These court papers can be referred to as "letters of office" or a "court appointment." A copy of the will might also be requested.

216. **ANSWER:** C

   WHY: the creditors get paid first, then the limited partners. The GPs are last in line.

217. **ANSWER:** C

   WHY: if you don't like abstract math, start with $1 over $10, which is 10%. What would happen if you reduced the $1 by 2% and the stock price by 4%. You'd have 98 cents divided by $9.60. That would be a 10.2% yield, which is higher than where you started? How did you come up with $1 over $10? Creative problem-solving.

218. **ANSWER:** B

   WHY: a forward split creates more shares, and a reverse split reduces the number of shares. Neither one dilutes anybody's equity—we're just slicing the same earnings pie into more or fewer slices. Everybody ends up owning the same amount of pie.

219. **ANSWER:** D

   WHY: the trade settles T + 3, which would be on Tuesday, July 25th. So, there are 24 days for July (don't include the settlement date, since on that day the buyer is the rightful owner). M & S stands for March and September. 30 days for March, 30 for April, 30 for May, and 30 for June. That's 120 days plus 24 days = 144 days. And you thought the Series 7 was going to be boring.

220. **ANSWER:** B

   WHY: the 5% mark-up policy does not apply to municipal bonds. A commission is not charged when the firm acts as a dealer by selling from inventory. The total dollar amount of the transaction must be considered, as well as the services offered by the firm, the liquidity for the security, etc.

221. **ANSWER:** C

   WHY: a technology fund is focused on one narrow section of the stock market. So a narrow-based index is what we need.

222. **ANSWER:** C

   WHY: convertible debentures get part of their value based on the movement of the common stock. A debenture that doesn't convert is simply tied to interest-rate movements.

223. **ANSWER:** A

WHY: another name for the adjustment bond is the "income bond," which is evil, since it sounds like an "income investor" should purchase one of those "income bonds." No, these bonds only pay income if the issuer can afford to. Typically, these are companies coming out of bankruptcy, struggling to get back on their feet. Their creditors are willing to be patient to allow that to happen.

224. **ANSWER:** C

WHY: they are allocating the costs according to function. Some costs function as expenses, others are depreciated slowly over time.

225. **ANSWER:** B

WHY: as with mutual funds, IPO shares need to be held fully paid for 30 days before being pledged as collateral in a margin account.

226. **ANSWER:** B

WHY: just a fact to memorize. Also memorize "1 year of full-time service," which only requires 1,000 hours of work. So, if the employee has put in 1,000 hours over the first year and is at least 21, she is eligible to participate in the qualified plan.

227. **ANSWER:** C

WHY: purchases of mutual fund shares settle same-day. To get any dividend, the buyer simply needs to settle no later than the record date.

228. **ANSWER:** C

WHY: exempt securities such as Treasuries and municipal bonds aren't covered by Reg T, so the SRO (FINRA) would set the requirement.

229. **ANSWER:** D

WHY: if she paid $50 for the stock and received $2 for writing calls against it, she would still be even if the stock dropped to $48. After that, she could lose everything down to zero, which is why her maximum loss would be $48 per share. The strike price of the covered call only comes into play if you're asked for her maximum gain.

230. **ANSWER:** B

WHY: secured creditors have assets pledged to secure the loan. Just like a mortgage lender doing a foreclosure, secured creditors recoup at least some of their money. Unsecured lenders, like credit card companies, often get nothing when the borrower defaults. Common stock is, of course, the most junior security issued by the corporation, with preferred above common stock but below all the bond holders (creditors).

231. ANSWER: D

WHY: "short" and "opening sale" mean the same thing. Whether shorting stock or options, the investor starts out by selling and would close by buying the position back.

232. ANSWER: D

WHY: the 5% markup is for over-the-counter stocks trading among investors. Anything sold to an investor with a prospectus would be exempt from this rule, since those transactions are taking place on the primary market, between the issuer and the investor. The markup rule is for trades among investors, effected through broker-dealers, or for trades between investors and the broker-dealers, who can add a "markup" when acting in a principal (dealer) capacity. Knowing how all this stuff works (primary, secondary, markup, commission, principal, agent, etc.) is extremely important on the Series 7.

233. ANSWER: A

WHY: this question might look similar to an earlier one, but now the option is in-the-money. The right to buy a $90 stock for $85 is a good thing—in-the-money by $5.

234. ANSWER: A

WHY: the put would expire worthless at any price of $90 or higher.

235. ANSWER: B

WHY: sold the option for $300; buys it back for $200. $200 is what the 90 call would be worth with the stock at $92, right?

236. ANSWER: B

WHY: the stock can be sold for $1 more than it's worth."

237. ANSWER: B

WHY: he paid $400 for the put, but it's only worth $100 if the stock drops only to $74. Pay $400; receive $100; lose $300.

238. ANSWER: D

WHY: if you're holding stock, your risk is that it could drop and force you to sell at a horrible price. So, buy a put and lock in a sale price. That's protection.

239. ANSWER: D

WHY: short sellers can buy a call for protection or sell a put for income and limited protection.

240. **ANSWER:** B

WHY: the breakeven is never "unlimited." Only a max gain or max loss could be unlimited. If you pay $40 and take in $2.25 per share, you'll be even at $37.75. That number, by the way, is also the maximum loss on this position.

241. **ANSWER:** D

WHY: step one—which option is worth more? The right to buy @90. If he BOUGHT that more expensive option, he starts with a debit. Debit = widen, exercise.

242. **ANSWER:** C

WHY: the longer the investor's time horizon, the better he can withstand investment loss or volatility. Interest rate risk is greatest on long-term bonds, but that doesn't really address the question. Inflation or loss of purchasing power is a serious risk, since even a "mild" inflation rate of 2 or 3% per year becomes devastating over 20 or 30 years.

243. **ANSWER:** C

WHY: for a forward split, just look for more shares at a lower price. And make sure it still represents the same total value.

244. **ANSWER:** C

WHY: equity = stock. Bonds are never considered to represent equity in the corporation.

245. **ANSWER:** C

WHY: the ex-date would be two business days before the Record Date.

246. **ANSWER:** A

WHY: they have the right to claim all the residuals. Unfortunately, there is generally nothing left after the creditors have been satisfied to varying degrees.

247. **ANSWER:** D

WHY: for the exam, assume that common stock is voting stock. Preferred stock has a higher claim on dividends but generally has no voting rights attached.

248. **ANSWER:** D

WHY: if the question is talking about a "Eurobond," those pay interest in foreign currencies. But, "Eurodollar bonds" pay interest and principal in U.S. dollars. They are issued outside the U.S. and not subject to SEC registration.

249. **ANSWER:** A

   WHY: 25 basis points is .25%. 50 basis points is .50%. 100 basis points is 1%.

250. **ANSWER:** C

   WHY: broker-dealers have to provide the MSRB rulebook upon request.

Glossary

1035 contract exchange: a tax-free exchange of one annuity contract for another, one life insurance policy for another, or one life insurance policy for an annuity. The contracts do not have to be issued by the same company.

1099-DIV: a tax form sent to investors showing dividends and capital gains distributions from a mutual fund for the tax year.

12b-1 fee: annual fee deducted quarterly from a mutual fund's assets to cover distribution costs, e.g., selling, mailing, printing, advertising. An operating expense, unlike the sales charge that is deducted from the investor's check.

200-day moving average: average closing price over the previous 200 days for a stock or an index.

401(k) plan: qualified defined contribution plan offering employer-matched contributions.

403(b): qualified plan for tax-exempt, non-profit organizations.

529 Plans: education savings plans offering tax-deferred growth and tax-free distributions at the federal level for qualified educational expenses. Pre-paid tuition plans allow clients to purchase a certain number of tuition credits at today's prices to be used at a school within a particular state. 529 Savings Plans allow clients to contribute up to the current gift tax exclusion without paying gift taxes. Earnings grow tax-deferred and may be used for qualified education expenses (more than just tuition) later without federal taxation. States can tax the plans—so know the customer's situation!

72(t): a neat trick under IRS tax code allowing people to take money from retirement plans including annuities without paying penalties, even through they aren't 59½ yet.

75-5-10 rule: diversification formula for a fund advertising itself as "diversified." 75% of the portfolio must have no more than 5% of assets invested in any one security, and no more than 10% of a company's outstanding shares may be owned.

A

A-Shares: mutual fund shares sold with a front-end sales load/charge. Lower annual expenses than B- and C-shares.

Account at maintenance: the point at which a customer's equity in a margin account is just high enough to avoid a margin call.

Account Executive (AE): another name for a registered representative or agent.

Account Statement: document sent to a broker-dealer customer showing the recent value of all cash and securities, plus all recent activity in an investment account.

Accounts Payable: what the company owes its vendors, a current liability.

Accounts Receivable: what customers owe a corporation, a current asset.

Accredited Investors: large institutional investors, and individuals meeting certain income or net worth requirements allowing them to participate in, for example, a private placement under Reg D of the Securities Act of 1933, or hedge funds.

Accretion: increasing the cost basis of a discount bond for tax purposes

Accrued Interest: the interest that the buyer of a debt security owes the seller. Bond interest is payable only twice a year, and the buyer will receive the next full interest payment. Therefore, the buyer owes the seller for every day of interest since the last payment up to the day before the transaction settles.

Accrued Taxes: taxes that are owed by a corporation, a current liability.

Accrued Wages: wages that are owed by a corporation, a current liability.

Accumulation Stage/Period: the period during which contributions are made to an annuity, during which the investor holds "accumulation units."

Accumulation Units: what the purchaser of an annuity buys during the pay-in or accumulation phase, an accounting measure representing a proportional share of the separate account during the accumulation/deposit stage.

Ad Valorem: property tax. Literally "as to value."

Additional Takedown: the piece of the spread that goes to the various members of the syndicate when the bonds they've been allotted are sold.

Adjustable Rate Preferred Stock: preferred stock whose dividend is tied to another rate, often the rate paid on T-bills.

Adjusted Gross Income (AGI): earned income plus passive income, portfolio income, and capital gains. The amount upon which we pay income tax.

Adjustment Bond: another name for an "income bond," on which the issuer may skip interest payments without going into default.

Administrator: (1) the securities regulator of a particular state; (2) a person or entity authorized by the courts to liquidate an estate.

ADR/ADS: American Depository Receipt/Share. A foreign stock on a domestic market. Toyota and Nokia are two examples of foreign companies whose ADRs trade on American stock markets denominated in dollars. Carry all the risks of owning stocks, plus "currency exchange risk."

Advance/Decline Line: the number of stocks whose market prices increased versus the number of stocks whose market prices decreased during a trading session.

Advance Refunding/Pre-refunding: issuing new bonds and depositing part of the proceeds in escrow ahead of the first legal call date on the existing bond issue.

Advertising: communications by a member firm directed at a general, uncontrolled audience, e.g., billboard, radio/TV/newspaper ads, website.

Affiliated Person: anyone in a position to influence decisions at a public corporation, including board members (directors), officers (CEO, CFO), and large shareholders (Warren Buffett at Coca-Cola or Wells Fargo).

Affiliated Investor: a person who is an officer or director of the issuer, or a 10%+ owner of its common stock.

Agency Issue (Agency Bond): a debt security issued by an agency authorized by the federal government but not directly backed by the federal government.

Agency Transaction: a securities transaction in which the broker-dealer acts as an agent for the buyer or seller, completing the transaction between the customer and another party.

Agent: an individual representing a broker-dealer or issuer in effecting/completing transactions in securities for compensation. What you will be after passing your exams and obtaining your securities license.

Agreement Among Underwriters: a document used by an underwriting syndicate bringing an issue of securities to the primary market. This document sets forth the terms under which each member of the syndicate will participate and details the duties and responsibilities of the syndicate manager.

AIR: Assumed Interest Rate. Determined by an actuary, representing his best estimate of the monthly annualized rate of return from the separate account. Used to determine value of annuity units for annuities and death benefit for variable life contracts.

All or None: a type of underwriting in which the syndicate will cancel the offering if a sufficient dollar amount is not raised as opposed to being responsible for the unsold shares (as in a "firm commitment"). Also a type of order on the secondary market in which the investor wants the order to be canceled if the broker can not acquire the full number of shares on one attempt.

American Stock Exchange (AMEX): a private, not-for-profit corporation that handles roughly 20% of all securities trades in the U.S. One of the big secondary markets, along with NYSE, and the various NASDAQ markets.

American Style: an option that can be exercised at any time up to expiration.

Amortize: reducing the cost basis on an intangible item, i.e. a bond premium.

AMT (Alternative Minimum Tax): tax computation that adds certain "tax preference items" back into adjusted gross income. Some municipal bond interest is treated as a "tax preference item" that can raise the investor's tax liability through the AMT.

Annual Compliance Review: a broker-dealer's annual compliance meeting that is mandatory for principals and registered representatives.

Annual Report: a formal statement issued by a corporation to the SEC and shareholders discussing the company's results of operations, challenges/risks facing the company, any lawsuits against the company, etc. Required by the Securities Exchange Act of 1934.

Annuitant: the person who receives an annuity contract's distribution.

Annuitize: the process of changing the annuity contract from the "pay-in" or accumulation phase to the "pay-out" or distribution phase. Defined benefit pension plans, such as the ones that have done so much good for GM and Ford, generally offer their pensioners either a lump sum payment or the chance to annuitize. Hint to all pensioners—take the LUMP SUM!

Annuity: a contract between an individual and an insurance company that generally guarantees income for the rest of the individual's life in return for a lump-sum or periodic payment to the insurance company.

Annuity Units: what the annuitant holds during the pay-out phase. Value tied to AIR.

Anticipation Notes: short-term debt obligations of a municipality typically held primarily by tax-exempt money market mutual funds.

Appreciation: the increase in an asset's value that is not subject to tax until realized.

Arbitrage: a word that has no business being mentioned on the Series 7. Arbitrage involves taking advantage of the disparity of two things. If you think GE will buy a small company, you can make a bet that GE will temporarily drop and the small company's stock will skyrocket. Then, when you make your fantastic and fortuitous gain, you can explain to the SEC how you happened to make that bet.

Arbitration: settling a dispute without going to an actual court of law.

Arbitration Award: the decision rendered through FINRA Arbitration.

Ask, Asked: the higher price in a quote representing what the customer would have to pay/what the dealer is asking the customer to pay. Customers buy at the ASK because dealers sell to customers at the ASK price. Ask/asked is also called "offer/offered."

Assessed Value: the value of property used to calculate property tax. For example, a home with a market value of $300,000 might have an assessed value of $150,000 against which the rate of tax is applied.

Assets: something that a corporation or individual owns, e.g., cash, investments, accounts receivable, inventory, etc.

Asset Allocation: maintaining a percentage mix of equity, debt, and money market investments, based either on the investor's age (strategic) or market expectations (tactical).

Associated Person: a registered representative or principal of a FINRA member firm.

Assumed Interest Rate: see AIR.

Auction Market: the NYSE, for example, where buyers and sellers simultaneously enter competitive prices. Sometimes called a "double auction" market because buying and selling occur at the same time.

Auction Rate Securities: debt securities with a variable rate of interest or preferred stock with a variable dividend rate that is re-set at regular auctions.

Authorized Stock: number of shares a company is allowed to issue by its corporate charter. Can be changed by a majority vote of the outstanding shares.

Automated Client Account Transfer (ACAT): a system that provides instructions among broker-dealers for transfer and delivery of customer assets.

Automatic Reinvestment: a feature offered by mutual funds allowing investors to automatically reinvest dividend and capital gains distributions into more shares of the fund, without paying a sales charge.

Average Cost Basis: a method of figuring cost basis on securities for purposes of reporting capital gains and/or losses. The investor averages the cost for all purchases made in the stock, as opposed to identifying particular shares to the IRS when selling.

B

B-Shares: mutual fund shares charging a load only when the investor redeems/sells the shares. Associated with "contingent deferred sales charges." B-shares have higher operating expenses than A-shares by way of a higher 12b-1 fee. Although the back-end load or "contingent deferred sales charges" decline over time, the higher 12b-1 fee usually makes B-shares appropriate only for investors who lack the ability to reach the first or second breakpoint offered on A-shares.

Backdating: pre-dating a letter of intent (LOI) for a mutual fund in order to include a prior purchase in the total amount stated in the letter of intent. LOIs may be backdated up to 90 calendar days.

Backing Away: a violation in which a market maker fails to honor a published firm quote to buy or sell a security at a stated price.

Back-end Load: a commission/sales fee charged when mutual fund or variable contracts are redeemed. The back-end load declines gradually, as described in the prospectus. Associated with "B-shares" and, occasionally "C-shares."

Backup Withholding: a required withholding from an investment account that results when the customer refuses/fails to provide a tax identification number.

Balanced Fund: a fund that maintains a mix of stocks and bonds at all times. Asset allocation funds are a type of balanced fund (or so darned close that they should be).

Balance Sheet: a financial statement of a corporation or individual showing financial condition (assets vs. liabilities) at a particular moment in time.

Balance Sheet Equation: Assets – Liabilities = Shareholders' Equity, or Assets = Liabilities + Shareholders' Equity.

Banker's Acceptance (BA): money-market security that facilitates importing/exporting. Issued at a discount from face-value. A secured loan.

Bank Qualified Municipal Bond: municipal bonds that allow banks to deduct 80% of the interest costs incurred to buy them.

Bar: the most severe sanction that FINRA can impose on an individual, effectively ending his/her career

Basis Points: a way of measuring bond yields or other percentages in the financial industry. Each basis point is 1% of 1%. Example: 2% = .0200 = 200 basis points. 20 basis points = .2% or 2/10ths of 1%.

Basis Quote: the price at which a debt security can be bought or sold, based on the yield. A bond purchased at a "5.50 basis" is trading at a price that makes the yield 5.5%.

Bearish, Bear: an investor who takes a position based on the belief that the market or a particular security will fall. Short sellers and buyers of puts are "bearish." They profit when stocks go down. Seriously.

Bear Market: a market for stock or bonds in which prices are falling and/or expected to fall.

Bear Spread: a call or put spread in which the investor benefits if the underlying instrument's value drops. For example, an investor who buys the ABC Aug 50 call and sells the ABC Aug 45 call establishes a bear spread. The spread would also happen to be a "credit spread" in this case.

Bearer Bond: an unregistered bond that pays principal to the bearer at maturity. Bonds have not been issued in this way for over two decades, but they still exist on the secondary market.

Beneficiary: the one who benefits. An insurance policy pays a benefit to the named beneficiary. IRAs and other retirement plans, including annuities, allow the owner to name a beneficiary who will receive the account value when the owner dies. A 529 plan names a beneficiary, who will use the money for educational expenses someday.

Best Efforts: a type of underwriting leaving the syndicate at no risk for unsold shares, and allowing them to keep the proceeds on the shares that were sold/subscribed to. Underwriters act as "agents," not principals, in a best efforts underwriting.

Beta: a way of measuring the volatility of a security or portfolio compared to the volatility of the overall market. A beta of more than 1 is associated with an investment or portfolio that is more volatile than the overall market. A beta of less than 1 is associated with an investment or portfolio that is less volatile than the overall market.

Beta Coefficient: another way of referring to "beta."

Bid: what a dealer is willing to pay to a customer who wants to sell. Customers sell at the bid, buy at the ask.

Bid Form: document used by the syndicate to submit a competitive bid to the issuer.

Blend Fund: a fund that can't decide if it wants to be a growth fund or a value fund.

Blind Pool Offering: a direct participation program in which the sponsor does not identify the assets of the partnership.

Blue Chip: stock in a well-established company with proven ability to pay dividends in good economic times and bad. Lower risk/reward ratio than other common stock.

Blue Sky: state securities law, tested on the Series 63 exam

Board of Directors: the group elected by shareholders to run a mutual fund or a public company and establish corporate management policies.

Bond: a debt security issued by a corporation or governmental entity that promises to repay principal and pay interest either regularly or at maturity.

Bond Anticipation Note (BAN): a short-term municipal debt security backed by the proceeds of an upcoming bond issue. Often found in tax-exempt money market funds.

Bond Buyer: daily publication covering the municipal securities industry.

Bond Counsel: tax law firm that guides a municipal issuer through the legal process of issuing bonds.

Bond Fund: a mutual fund with an objective of providing income while minimizing capital risk through a portfolio of—get this—bonds.

Bond Point: 1% of a bond's par value. 1 bond point = $10.

Bond Rating: an evaluation of a bond issue's chance of default published by companies such as Moody's, S&P, and Fitch.

Bond Resolution: a document that legally authorizes the process of issuing municipal bonds for a specific purpose.

Bond Swap or Tax Swap: taking a loss on a bond and replacing it with a substantially different bond to avoid tax problems.

Bonus Annuities: annuities with special riders/features attached.

Book Entry: a security maintained as a computer record rather than a physical certificate. All U.S. Treasuries and many mutual funds are issued in this manner.

Branch Office: any location identified by any means to the public or customers as a location at which the member conducts an investment banking or securities business. The small Charles Schwab or E-Trade office at the nearby mall or office complex is a "branch office."

Breakeven: the price at which the underlying security is above or below the strike price of the option by the amount of the premium paid or received. For example, an ABC Aug 50 call @2 has a "breakeven" of $52 for both the buyer and the seller.

Breakpoint: a discounted sales charge or "volume discount" on mutual fund purchases offered on A-shares at various levels of investment.

Breakpoint Selling: preventing an investor from achieving a breakpoint. A violation.

Broad-based Index: an index such as the S&P 500 or the Value Line Composite Index that represents companies from many industries.

Broker: an individual or firm that charges a commission to execute securities buy and sell orders submitted by another individual or firm.

Broker's Broker: a firm that holds no inventory and executes securities transactions exclusively with other broker-dealers and not with public investors.

Broker-Dealer: a person or firm in the business of completing transactions in securities for the accounts of others (broker) or its own account (dealer).

Broker Call Loan Rate: interest rate that broker-dealers pay when borrowing on behalf of margin customers.

Bullish, Bull: an investor who takes a position based on the belief that the market or a particular security will rise. Buyers of stock and call options are bullish.

Bull Market: a market for stocks or bonds in which prices are rising and/or expected to rise.

Bull Spread: a call or put spread in which the investor will benefit if the underlying instrument rises in value. If the investor is "long the lower strike price," he has established a "bull spread." For example, if he buys the ABC Aug 50 call and sells the ABC Aug 55 call, he establishes a "bull spread." The spread would also happen to be a "debit spread" in this case.

Bulletin Board: OTC stocks too volatile and low-priced for NASDAQ.

Business Cycle: a progression of expansions, peaks, contractions, troughs, and recoveries for the overall (macro) economy.

Business Risk: the (non-systematic) risk that the company whose stock or bond you own will not be successful as a business. Competition, poor management, obsolete products/services are all examples of business risk.

Buy Limit: an order to buy a security at a price below the current market price, executable at a specified price or lower/better.

Buy Stop: an order to buy a security at a price above the current market price triggered only if the market price hits or passes through the stop price.

C

C-Shares: often called "level load" because of the high 12b-1 fee. Usually involve no front-end load, sometimes have a contingent deferred sales charge for 1 or 1.5 years. Appropriate for shorter-term investing only.

Call (n.): a contract that gives the holder the right to buy something at a stated exercise price.

Call (v.): to buy.

Call Premium: the price paid and received on a call option. Or, the amount above the par value paid by the issuer to call/retire a bond.

Call Protection: the period during which a security may not be called or bought by the issuer, usually lasting five years or more.

Call Provision: agreement between the issuer and the bondholders or preferred stockholders that gives the issuer the ability to repurchase the bonds or preferred stock on a specified date or dates before maturity.

Call Risk: the risk that a callable bond or preferred stock will be forcibly called when interest rates fall.

Call Spread: buying and selling a call on the same underlying instrument where the strike price, the expiration, or both are different.

Callable: a security that may be purchased/called by the issuer as of a certain date, e.g., callable preferred, callable bonds. Generally pays a higher rate of return than non-callable securities, as it gives the issuer flexibility in financing.

Capital: a fancy word for "money." When a corporation raises cash by offering stocks/bonds to investors on the primary market, we dignify the cash by calling it "capital."

Capital Appreciation: the rise in an asset's market price. The objective of a "growth stock investor."

Capital Gain: the amount by which the proceeds on the sale of a stock or bond exceed your cost basis. If you sell a stock for $22 and have a cost basis of $10, the capital gain or profit is $12.

Capital Gains Distribution: distribution from fund to investor based on net capital gains realized by the fund portfolio. Holding period determined by the fund and assumed to be long-term.

Capital Loss: loss incurred when selling an asset for less than the purchase price. Capital losses offset an investor's capital gains and can offset ordinary income to a certain amount.

Capital Structure: the make-up of a corporation's financing through equity (stock) and debt (bonds) securities.

Capped Index Options: options that are automatically exercised when the underlying instrument moves by a certain amount known as the "cap interval."

Capping: a form of market manipulation. A violation.

Cash Account: an investment account in which the investor must pay for all purchases no later than 2 business days following regular way settlement. Not a margin account.

Cash Dividend: money paid to shareholders from a corporation's current earnings or accumulated profits.

Cash Equivalent: a security that can readily be converted to cash, e.g., T-bills, CDs, and money market funds.

Cash Flow: net income plus depreciation/amortization.

Cash Settlement: same-day settlement of a trade requiring prior broker-dealer approval. Not the "regular way" of doing things.

Cash Value: the value of an insurance policy that may be "tapped" by the policyholder through a loan or a surrender.

Catastrophe Call: a provision in a municipal bond issue providing for an automatic call of the bonds due to a disaster, e.g., hurricane, flood, etc.

CEO: chief executive officer. Individual ultimately responsible for a corporation's results.

Certificate of Limited Partnership: a document filed by the general partner of a direct participation program with a state disclosing who the partnership is and what it does.

CFO: chief financial officer. Individual in charge of a corporation's financial activities.

Check-writing Privileges: a privilege offered by mutual funds, especially money market funds, by which investors can automatically redeem shares by writing checks.

Chinese Wall: the separation that is supposed to exist between the investment banking department and the traders and registered representatives in order to prevent insider trading violations.

Churning: excessive trading in terms of frequency and size of transactions designed to generate commissions without regard for the customer.

Clearing Rate: the interest rate established by auction in connection with auction rate securities.

CLN: construction loan note, a type of municipal note backed by the proceeds from a construction loan for a new building project.

Closed-end Fund: an investment company that offers a fixed number of shares that are not redeemable. Shares are traded on the secondary market at a price that could be higher or lower than NAV (or even the same as NAV).

CMO: Collateralized Mortgage Obligation: A complicated debt security that few people actually understand. Based on a pool of mortgages or a pool of mortgage-backed securities. Pays interest monthly but returns principal to one tranche at a time.

Code of Arbitration: FINRA method of resolving disputes (usually money) in the securities business. All decisions are final and binding on all parties.

Code of Procedure: FINRA system for enforcing member conduct rules.

Collateral Trust Certificate: a bond secured by a pledge of securities as collateral.

Collection Ratio: the amount of taxes collected by a municipality divided by the amount of taxes assessed.

Combination: a multiple options position that is neither a straddle nor a spread. For example, if an investor buys an ABC Aug 45 call and sells an ABC Aug 50 put, he has established a combination.

Combination Privilege: allows investors to combine purchases of many funds within the mutual fund family to reach a breakpoint/reduced sales charge.

Combined Offering: an offering of securities in which both the issuer and other large shareholders will be selling to the public.

Commercial Paper: a short-term unsecured loan to a corporation. Issued at a discount from the face value. See "money market securities."

Commissions: a service charge an agent earns for arranging a security purchase or sale.

Commission House Broker: a broker who works for a particular member of the exchange filling orders for the firm and receiving a commission per-order.

Common Stock: the most "junior security," because it ranks last in line at liquidation. An equity or ownership position that usually allows the owner to vote on major corporate issues such as stock splits, mergers, acquisitions, authorizing more shares, etc.

Competitive Floor Traders: members of the NYSE who buy and sell exchange-listed securities for their own account.

Competitive, Sealed Bids: process used for most general obligation bonds in which the underwriting business is awarded to the syndicate who turns in the lowest cost of borrowing to the issuer.

Compliance Department: the principals and supervisors of a broker-dealer responsible for making sure the firm adheres to SEC, exchange, and SRO rules.

Concession: the amount that the seller of a new issue of municipal bonds receives, whether a syndicate member of a selling group member.

Conduct Rules: an SRO's rules for member conduct that, if violated, may lead to sanctions and fines.

Conduit Theory (Tax Treatment): a favorable tax treatment achieved if a company (REIT, mutual fund) distributes 90%+ of net income to the shareholders.

Confirmation: document stating the trade date, settlement date, and money due/owed for a securities purchase or sale. Delivered on or before the settlement date.

Consolidation: a stock trading in a narrow price range.

Consolidated+ Quotation Services (CQS): system used for trading in the third market.

Consumer: for purposes of Regulation S-P, a consumer is someone considering a financial relationship with a firm.

Consumer Price Index (CPI): a measure of inflation/deflation for basic consumer goods and services. A rising CPI represents the greatest risk to most fixed-income investors.

Constant Dollar Plan: a defensive investment strategy in which an investor tries to maintain a constant dollar amount in the account, meaning that securities are sold if the account value rises and purchased if it goes down.

Constructive Receipt: the date that the IRS considers an investor to have put his grubby little hands on a dividend, interest payment, retirement plan distribution, etc. For example, IRA funds are not taxable until "constructive receipt," which usually starts somewhere between age 59½ and 70½.

Contingent Deferred Sales Charge: associated with B-shares, the sales charge is deducted from the investor's check when she redeems/sells her shares. The charge is deferred until she sells and is contingent upon when she sells—the sales charges decline over time, eventually disappearing after 7 years, at which point the B-shares become A-shares in order to keep everything nice and simple.

Continuing Commissions: the practice of paying retired registered representatives and principals commissions on business written while still employed with the firm, e.g., 12b-1 fees on mutual funds and annuities.

Contraction: phase of the business cycle associated with general economic decline, recession or depression.

Contribution: the money you put into a retirement plan subject to the limits imposed by the plan.

Conversion/Exchange Privilege: a feature offered by many mutual funds whereby the investor may sell shares of one fund in the family and use the proceeds to buy another fund in the family at the NAV (avoiding the sales load). All gains/losses are recognized on the date of sale/conversion for tax purposes.

Conversion Ratio: the number of shares of common stock that the holder of a convertible bond or preferred stock would receive upon conversion. A bond "convertible at $50" has a conversion ratio of 20 (20 shares of stock per $1,000 par value).

Convertible: a preferred stock or corporate bond allowing the investor to use the par value to "buy" shares of the company's common stock at a set price.

Cooling-off Period: a minimum 20-day period that starts after the registration statement is filed with the SEC. No sales or advertising allowed during this period, which lasts until the effective or release date.

Corporation: the most common form of business organization, in which the business's total value is divided among shares of stock, each representing an ownership interest or share of profits.

Correspondence: under FINRA rules = a letter/fax/email to existing clients, or a letter, fax, or email sent to fewer than 25 prospects in a 30-day period.

Cost Basis: the amount that has gone into an investment and has been taxed already. For stock, includes the price paid plus commissions. For a variable annuity, equals the after-tax contributions into the account. Investors pay tax only on amounts above their cost basis, and only when they sell or take "constructive receipt."

Coterminous: municipal issuers who overlap, e.g., a village and a school district.

Coupon Rate: a.k.a. "nominal yield." The interest rate stated on a bond representing the percentage of the par value received by the investor each year. For example, a bond with a 5% "coupon rate" or "nominal yield" pays $50 per bond to the holder per year. Period.

Covered Call: a position in which an investor generates premium income by selling the right to buy stock the investor already owns, and at a set price.

CPI: Consumer Price Index, a measure of inflation/deflation for basic consumer goods and services. A rising CPI represents the greatest risk to most fixed-income investors.

Credit Agreement: document that must be signed by a margin customer in which all finance charges are explained in connection to the margin account.

Credit Risk: a.k.a. "default" or "financial" risk. The risk that the issuer's credit rating will be downgraded, or that the issuer will default on a debt security.

Credit Spread: selling a more valuable call/put and simultaneously buying a less valuable call/put on the same underlying instrument. For example, an investor who sells an ABC Aug 50 put for $400 and buys an ABC Aug 45 put for $100 establishes a "credit put spread" for a net credit of $300.

Crossover Point: the point at which a limited partnership has exhausted the tax shelter and is now beginning to show a profit.

Cum Rights: term used when a stock trades with rights, meaning that buyers of the stock will receive rights to subscribe to the upcoming additional offer of stock.

Cumulative Preferred Stock: preferred stock where missed dividends go into arrears and must be paid before the issuer may pay dividends to other preferred stock and/or common stock.

Cumulative Voting: method of voting whereby the shareholder may take the total votes and split them up any way he chooses. Said to benefit minority over majority shareholders. Total votes are found by multiplying the number of shares owned by the number of seats up for election to the Board of Directors.

Currency Exchange Risk: the risk that the value of the U.S. dollar versus another currency will have a negative impact on businesses and investors.

Currency Transaction Report (CTR): a reported submitted to the US Treasury by a broker-dealer when a customer deposits more than $10,000 cash.

Current Liability: a debt to be paid by a corporation in the short-term, usually one year or sooner.

Current Ratio: a short-term measure of a corporation's liquidity found by dividing current assets by current liabilities; the higher the number, the more liquid the corporation.

Current Yield: annual interest divided by market price of the bond. For example, an 8% bond purchased at $800 has a CY of 10%. $80/$800 = 10%.

CUSIP number: an identification number/code for a security.

Custodial Account: an investment account in which a custodian enters trades on behalf of the beneficial owner, who is usually a minor child.

Custodian: maintains custody of a mutual fund's securities and cash. Performs payable/receivable functions for portfolio purchases and sales. In an UGMA, the custodian is the adult named on the account who is responsible for the investment decisions and tax reporting.

Customer: a person who opens an investment account with a broker-dealer.

Cyclical Industry: a term of fundamental analysis for an industry that is sensitive to the business cycle. Includes: steel, automobiles, mining and construction equipment.

D

Dated Date: the date on which interest begins to accrue on a new issue of municipal bonds.

Dealer: a person who buys or sells securities for his/its own account, taking the other side of the trade. A dealer buys securities from and sells securities directly to a customer, while a broker merely arranges a trade between a customer and another party.

Death Benefit: the amount payable to the beneficiary of a life insurance (or annuity) contract, minus any outstanding loans and/or unpaid premiums.

Debenture: an unsecured corporate bond backed by the issuer's ability (or inability) to pay. No collateral.

Debit Spread: buying a more expensive call/put and selling a less expensive call/put on the same underlying instrument. If an investor pays $500 to buy an XYZ Jan 50 call and receives $200 for selling an XYZ Jan 55 call, he has established the debit call spread at a net debit of $300.

Debt Limit: a self-imposed restriction on the total amount of general obligation debt that an issuer may have outstanding at any one time.

Debt Per Capita: a measure that shows a bond analyst how much general obligation debt is outstanding divided by the number of residents of the municipality.

Debt Security: a security representing a loan from an investor to an issuer. Offers a particular interest rate in return for the loan, not an ownership position.

Debt Service: the schedule for repayment of interest and principal on a debt security.

Debt Statement: a statement in which a municipal issuer lists all of its outstanding debts.

Declaration Date: the date the Board declares a dividend.

Default: when the issuer of the bond stiffs you.

Default Risk: the risk that the issuer of the bond will stiff you. Measured by S&P and Moody's (AAA, Aaa and on down the scale).

Defensive Industry: a company that can perform well even during rough economic times. For example, food and basic clothing represent two products purchased through both good and bad economic times; therefore, stocks of food and basic clothing companies would be "defensive" investments.

Deferred Annuity: an annuity that delays payments of income, installments, or a lump sum until the investor elects to receive it. Usually subject to surrender charges during the deferral period.

Deferred Compensation Plan: a non-qualified business plan that defers some of the employee's compensation until retirement.

Deficiency Letter: SEC notification of additions or corrections that an issuer must make to a registration statement before the offering can be cleared for distribution.

Defined Benefit Plan: a qualified corporate pension plan that, literally, defines the benefit payable to the retiree.

Defined Contribution Plan: a qualified corporate plan that defines the contribution made on behalf of the employee, e.g., profit sharing, 401(k).

Deflation: a general drop in the level of prices across the economy, usually connected to an economic slump.

Delivery: the change in ownership of a security that takes place when the transaction settles. The seller delivers the securities purchased to the buyer.

Department of Enforcement: FINRA enforcers of the member conduct rules, a group you never want to hear from, especially by certified mail.

Depression: six quarters (18 months) or longer of economic decline.

Designated Examining Authority: another name for an SRO or Self-Regulatory Organization, e.g., CBOE or FINRA.

Developmental Program: an oil or gas drilling program in an area in which reserves are known to exist.

Dilution: a reduction in the earnings per share of common stock, often due to convertible bonds or preferred stock being converted to common stock.

Direct Debt: the general obligation debt of a municipal issuer for which it is solely responsible.

Direct Participation Program (DPP): an investment in a limited partnership or similar pass-through entity in which the investor receives a share of income and expenses.

Discount: the difference between the (lower) market price for a bond and the par value.

Discount Bond: any bond traded below the par value, e.g., @97.

Discount Rate: interest rate charged by the 12 Federal Reserve Banks to member banks who borrow from the FRB.

Discretion: authority given to someone other than the account owner to make trading decisions for the account.

Disintermediation: a situation in which money is being withdrawn from banks and savings & loans by depositors in order to reinvest the funds into higher yielding money market instruments (Treasury bills, certificates of deposit, money market funds). Disintermediation would occur when interest rates at savings banks are lower than money market instruments. The cause could be that the FRB is pursuing a "tight money policy," which is causing a rise in interest rates, creating a demand for the higher yielding money market securities.

Distribution: the money you take out of a retirement plan.

Distribution Expenses: the cost of distributing/marketing a mutual fund, including selling, printing prospectuses and sales literature, advertising, and mailing prospectuses to new/ potential clients. Covered by sales charges/12b-1fees.

Distribution (annuity) Stage: the period during which an individual receives payments from an annuity.

Distributor: a FINRA member firm that bears distribution costs of a fund, profiting from the sales charges paid by the investors; a.k.a. "sponsor," "underwriter," "wholesaler."

Diversification: purchasing securities from many different issuers, or industries, or geographic regions, to reduce "nonsystematic risk."

Diversified Mutual Fund: complies with an SEC rule so that no more than 5% of assets are invested in a particular stock or bond and so that the fund does not own more than 10% of any issuer's outstanding stock. Often called the "75-5-10 rule," where the 75 means that only 75% of the assets have to be diversified this way just to keep things nice and simple.

Dividend: money paid from profits to holders of common and preferred stock whenever the Board of Directors is feeling especially generous.

Dividend Payout Ratio: the amount of dividends paid divided by the earnings per share. Stocks with high dividend payout ratios are typically found in "equity income" funds.

Dividend Yield: annual dividends divided by market price of the stock. Equivalent to current yield for a debt security.

Dividend/Income Distributions: distributions from a fund to the investors made from net investment income. Typically, may be reinvested at the NAV to avoid sales charge.

DK notice: a notice sent to the other broker-dealer when a firm does not recognize a transaction.

Dollar Cost Averaging: investing fixed dollar amounts regularly, regardless of share price. Usually results in a lower average cost compared to average of share prices, as investors' dollars buy majority of shares at lower prices.

Donor: a person who makes a gift of money or securities to another.

Do Not Reduce (DNR): a buy-limit or sell-stop order that will not be reduced for the payment of a cash dividend.

Double Barreled: a municipal bond backed by both the issuer's full faith and credit and revenues.

Dow Jones Industrial Average (DJIA): an index comprised of 30 large companies.

Dual-Purpose Fund: a closed-end fund with two classes of stock: income shares and capital shares. The income shares receive dividends and interest, while the capital shares receive capital gains distributions.

Due Bill: document sent by a broker-dealer when a dividend payment was sent to the wrong party and belongs to the broker-dealer's customer

Due Diligence: meeting between issuer and underwriters with the purpose of verifying information contained in a registration statement/prospectus

DVP: a form of settlement in which payment will be made when the securities involved in the transaction are delivered and accepted.

E

Earned Income: income derived from active participation in a business, including wages, salary, tips, commissions, and bonuses. Alimony received is also considered earned income. Earned income can be used toward an IRA contribution.

Earnings per Share (EPS): the amount of earnings or "net income" available for each share of common stock. A major driver of the stock's price on the secondary market.

Eastern/undivided Account: a syndicate account in which participants are responsible for a percentage of all bonds, even if they sell their allotment.

Education IRA: another name for the Coverdell Education Savings Account in which after-tax contributions may be made to pay qualified education expenses for the beneficiary.

Effective Date: date established by SEC as to when the underwriters may sell new securities to investors; a.k.a. "release date."

Electronic Communications Networks (ECNs): electronic trading platforms that allow institutional investors to buy and sell securities directly.

Eligibility: a section of ERISA that outlines who is/is not eligible to participate in a qualified plan. Those 21 years old who have worked "full time" for one year (1,000 hours or more) are eligible to participate in the plan.

Emerging Market: the financial markets of a developing country. Generally, a small market with a short operating history, not as efficient or stable as developed markets. For example, Brazil, China, India.

Equipment Leasing Program: a direct participation program that leases computers, mining equipment, etc.

Equipment Trust Certificate: a corporate bond secured by a pledge of equipment, e.g., airplanes, railroad cars.

Equity: ownership, e.g., common and preferred stock in a public company.

Equity Funds: mutual funds that primarily invest in equity securities.

Equity Income Fund: a mutual fund that purchases common stocks whose issuers pay consistent and, perhaps, increasing dividends. The fund has less volatility than an equity fund with "growth" as an objective.

Equity Options: standardized options giving the holder the right to buy or sell the underlying stock at a set price (strike/exercise price).

Equity-indexed Annuity: an insurance product offering a minimum guaranteed rate and the opportunity to participate in some of the gains of a particular index, usually the S&P 500.

ERISA: the Employee Retirement Income Security Act of 1974 that governs the operation of most corporate pension and benefit plans.

Escrowed to Maturity: a municipal bond issue in which the issuer has deposited funds sufficient to retire the bonds on the original maturity date.

Estate: a legal entity/person that represents all assets held by a deceased person before he died.

Estate Tax: an annoying tax on estates over a certain amount, often called the "death tax" by those who don't like it.

ETF: or "Exchange-Traded Fund," a fund that trades on an exchange, typically an index fund tracking the S&P 500, the Dow Jones Industrial Average, etc. Unlike an open-end index fund, the ETF allows investors to sell short, trade throughout the day, and even purchase shares on margin.

European Style: an option that may be exercised at expiration only.

Excess Equity: the amount of equity above the Reg T requirement in a margin account.

Exchanges: any electronic or physical marketplace where investors can buy and sell securities. For example, NASDAQ, NYSE, AMEX.

Exchange-listed Security: a security that has met listing requirements to trade on a particular exchange such as NYSE, AMEX, or NASDAQ.

Exclusion Ratio: method of determining which part of an annuity payment is taxable, and which part represents the tax-free return of the annuitant's after-tax cost basis.

Ex-Date: two days before the Record Date for corporate stock. The date upon which the buyer is not entitled to the upcoming dividend. Note that for mutual funds, this date is established by the board of directors, usually the day after the Record Date.

Exempt Security: a security not required to be registered under the Securities Act of 1933. Still subject to anti-fraud rules; not subject to registration requirements, e.g., municipal bonds and bank stock.

Exempt Transaction: a transactional exemption from registration requirements based on the manner in which the security is offered and sold, e.g., private placements under Reg D.

Exercised: on option that the buyer has used to purchase or sell securities at the strike price.

Existing Properties: a direct participation program that purchases operating real estate.

Expansion: phase of the business cycle associated with increased activity.

Expense Ratio: a fund's expenses divided by/compared to average net assets. Represents operating efficiency of a mutual fund, where the lower the number the more efficient the fund.

Exploratory Programs: a direct participation program that drills for oil or natural gas.

Ex-rights: the term used when a stock begins to trade without rights attached.

Extension Risk: the risk that interest rates will rise, and the holder of a CMO or mortgage-backed security will have to wait longer than expected to receive principal.

F

Face-Amount Certificate: a debt security bought in a lump-sum or through installments that promises to pay out the stated face amount, which is higher than the investor's purchase price.

Face-Amount Certificate Company: one of the three types of investment company under the Investment Company Act of 1940. Issues face-amount certificates. Not a UIT of "management company."

Fair and Orderly Market: what the specialist at the NYSE is charged with maintaining.

FDIC (Federal Deposit Insurance Corporation): federal government agency that provides deposit insurance for member banks and prevents bank and "thrift" failures. Bank deposits are currently insured up to $250,000, a number that could have changed by the time you read this definition. A trip to your local bank will give you the updated number.

Feasibility Study: a study put together by a consulting firm analyzing the economic merits of a facility to be financed by revenue bonds.

Federal Covered: a security or an investment adviser whose registration is handled exclusively by the federal government (SEC)

Federal Farm Credit System: organization of privately owned banks providing credit to farmers and mortgages on farm property.

Federal Open Market Committee (FOMC): council of Federal Reserve officials that sets monetary policy based on economic data. The money supply is tightened to fight inflation, loosened to provide stimulus to a faltering economy.

Federal Reserve Board: a seven-member board directing the operations of the Federal Reserve System.

Federal Reserve System: the central bank system of the United States, with a primary responsibility to manage the flow of money and credit in this country.

Fed Funds Rate: interest rate charged on bank-to-bank loans. Subject to daily fluctuation.

FHLMC: a.k.a. "Freddie Mac." Like big sister Fannie Mae, a quasi-agency, public company that purchases mortgages from lenders and sells mortgage-backed securities to investors. Stock is listed on NYSE.

Fiduciary: someone responsible for the financial affairs of someone else, e.g., custodian, trustee, or registered rep in a discretionary account.

FIFO: first-in-first-out. An accounting method for valuing a company's inventory or for determining the capital gain/loss for an investor. Using FIFO, an investor indicates that, for example, the 100 shares of ABC that were sold at $55 are the first 100 shares that he purchased.

Filing Date: the date that an issuer files a registration statement with the SEC for a new issue of securities.

Fill or Kill (FOK): a specialized order to buy or sell securities at a set price that will be canceled if all the securities are not available at once at the specified price.

Final Prospectus: document delivered with final confirmation of a new issue of securities detailing the price, delivery date, and underwriting spread.

Financial Risk: another name for "credit risk," or the risk that the issuer of a bond could default.

FinCEN: U.S. Treasury's "Financial Crimes Enforcement Network." Suspicious Activity Reports must be provided to FinCEN if a broker-dealer notices activity in accounts that appears suspicious or possibly related to fraud or money laundering activities.

FINRA (Financial Industry Regulatory Authority): the SRO formed when the NASD and the NYSE regulators merged.

Firm Commitment: an underwriting in which the underwriters agree to purchase all securities from an issuer, even the ones they failed to sell to investors. Involves acting in a "principal" capacity, unlike in "best efforts," "all or none," and "mini-max" offerings.

Firm Quote: a quote by a dealer representing a price at which the dealer is prepared to trade.

First-In-First-Out (FIFO): an accounting method used to value a company's inventory or to determine capital gains/losses on an investor's securities transactions.

First Market: another name for the exchange market, where the NYSE is the model.

Fiscal Policy: Congress and President. Tax and Spend.

Fixed Annuity: an insurance product (not a security) in which the annuitant receives fixed dollar payments, usually for the rest of his or her life.

Fixed Assets: long-term assets that generate revenue but are not intended to be sold. For example, a printing press.

Flexible Premium: a premium that is flexible. Characteristic of "universal" insurance. Allows the policyholder to adjust the premiums and death benefit according to changing needs.

Flow of Funds: a statement for a revenue bond issue showing the priority of payments to be made with revenue generated from the facility.

FNMA: a.k.a. "Fannie Mae." Like little brother Freddie Mac, Fannie buys mortgages from lenders and sells mortgage-backed securities to investors. A quasi-agency, a public company listed for trading on the NYSE.

FOMC: the Federal Reserve Board's Federal Open Market Committee. Sets short-term interest rates by setting discount rate, reserve requirement and buying/selling T-bills to/from primary dealers.

Foreign Currency Options: standardized options in which the underlying instrument is a foreign currency, e.g., the Yen, the Euro, etc.

Foreign Exchange Risk: the risk to an American ADR holder that the American dollar will strengthen versus the currency used by the foreign corporation. For example, an American holding the Toyota ADR is at risk that the US dollar will strengthen versus the Yen.

Forward Pricing: the method of valuing mutual fund shares, whereby a purchase or redemption order is executed at the next calculated price. Mutual fund shares are bought and sold at the next computed price, not yesterday's stale prices.

Fourth Market, INSTINET: an ECN (electronic communications network) used by institutional investors, bypassing the services of a traditional broker. Institutional = INSTINET.

Fractional Share: a portion of a whole share of stock. Mutual fund shares typically are issued as whole and fractional shares, e.g., 101.45 shares.

Fraud: using deceit to wrongfully take money/property from someone under false pretenses.

Free Credit Balance: the cash in a customer account that can be withdrawn.

Free-Look: period during which a contract or policyholder may cancel and receive all sales charges paid. Not a popular phrase among seasoned insurance and annuity salespersons.

Free-riding & Withholding: a violation in which underwriters fail to distribute all shares allocated in an offering of a "hot issue."

Front-end Load: a mutual fund commission or sales fee charged when shares are purchased (A-shares). The amount of the load is added to the NAV to determine the public offering price (POP).

Frozen Account: an account in which purchase orders will be accepted only if the cash is in the account due to the customer's failure to comply with Reg T.

Funding: an ERISA guideline that stipulates, among other things, that retirement plan assets must be segregated from other corporate assets.

Fungible: interchangeable, e.g., $20 bills or shares of stock, where one is just as good as another.

Full Faith and Credit: a phrase used to denote that there are no specific assets backing a bond issue, only the issuer's ability to repay the loan.

Fully Registered Bonds: bonds whose principal and interest payments are tracked/registered for purposes of taxation. A physical certificate with the owner's name, and interest payable automatically by the paying agent (no coupons).

Funded Debt: another term for corporate bonds backed by a sinking fund as opposed to collateral.

G

GAN – grant anticipation note: short-term debt obligation of a municipal issuer backed by funds to be received in a grant, usually from the federal government.

GDP: Gross Domestic Product, the sum total of all goods and services being produced by the economy. A positive GDP number is evidence of economic expansion.

General Account: where an insurance company invests net premiums in order to fund guaranteed, fixed payouts.

General Obligation Bond: a municipal bond that is backed by the issuer's full faith and credit or full taxing authority.

General Partner: the manager of a DPP with unlimited liability and a fiduciary obligation to the limited partners.

General Securities Representative: an agent who passed the Series 7 and may sell virtually any security, unlike a Series 6 holder, who sells mutual funds and variable contracts only.

Generic Advertising: communications with the public that promote securities as investments but not particular securities.

Gift Tax: a tax paid when a gift exceeds the current exclusion limit.

Global Fund: a mutual fund investing in companies located and doing business all across the globe, including the U.S.

GNMA: a.k.a. "Ginnie Mae," nickname for Government National Mortgage Association. A government agency (not a public company) that buys insured mortgages from lenders, selling pass-through certificates to investors. Monthly payments to investors pay interest and also pass through principal from a pool of mortgages. Recall that bonds pay interest and return principal only at maturity, while "pass-throughs" pass through principal monthly.

Good Faith Deposit: the deposit required by a municipal issuer for all syndicates submitting bids for an issue of bonds. Typically 1-2% of par value.

Green Shoe Clause: an agreement allowing the underwriters to sell additional shares if demand is high for an offering of securities.

Gross Margin: gross profit divided *into* revenue. For example, a company with $100 million in revenue and cost-of-goods-sold of $70 million has a gross margin of 30%.

Gross Profit: a company's revenues minus their "cost of goods sold." For example, a company with $100 million in revenue and cost-of-goods-sold of $70 million has a gross profit of $70 million.

Gross Revenue Pledge: less common method used by revenue bond issuers in which debt service is paid even before operations & maintenance.

Growth: investment objective that seeks "capital appreciation." Achieved through common stock, primarily.

Growth Funds: mutual funds investing in stocks expected to grow faster than the overall market and trading at high price-to-earnings multiples.

Growth & Income: a fund that purchases stocks for growth potential and also for dividend income. Less volatile than pure growth funds due to the income that calms investors down when the ride becomes turbulent.

Guaranteed Bond: bond that is issued with a promise by a party other than the issuer to maintain payments of interest and principal if the issuer cannot.

Guardian: a fiduciary who manages the financial affairs of a minor or a person declared mentally incompetent by a court of law.

H

Head and Shoulders: a chart pattern used by technical analysts to determine that a bull or bear trend is about to reverse.

Hedge: to bet the other way. If you own stock, you can hedge by purchasing puts, which profit when the stock goes down.

Hedge Fund: a private investment partnership open to accredited investors only. Illiquid investments that generally must be held one or two years before selling. Typically charge a management fee plus the first 20% of capital gains in most cases.

High-Yield: an investment whose income stream is very high relative to its low market price. A high-yield bond is either issued by a shaky company or municipal government forced to offer high nominal yields, or it begins to trade at lower and lower prices on the secondary market as the credit quality or perceived credit strength of the issuer deteriorates.

Holding Company: a company organized to invest in other corporations, e.g., Berkshire-Hathaway, which holds large stakes in other companies such as Coca-Cola, See's Candy, Dairy Queen, and Wells Fargo.

Holding Period: the period during which a security was held for purposes of determining whether a capital gain or loss is long- or short-term.

Howey Decision: a U.S. Supreme Court decision that defined an "investment contract" as "an investment of money in a common enterprise where the investor will profit solely through the efforts of others."

HR-10: a reference to a Keogh plan.

Hypothecate: to pledge securities purchased in a margin account as collateral to secure the loan.

Hypothecation Agreement: document that gives a broker-dealer the legal authority to pledge a margin customer's securities as collateral to secure the margin loan.

I

IDR: "Industrial Development Revenue Bond," a revenue bond that builds a facility that the issuing municipality then leases to a corporation. The lease payments from the corporation back the interest and principal payments on the bonds.

Immediate Annuity: an insurance contract purchased with a single premium that starts to pay the annuitant immediately. Purchased by individuals who are afraid of outliving their retirement savings.

Immediate or Cancel Order: an order to buy or sell securities in which the customer will accept any part of the order that becomes available at a certain price, with the remainder of shares to be canceled.

Income: investment objective that seeks current income, found by investing in fixed-income securities, e.g., bonds, money market, preferred stock. An equity income fund buys stocks that pay dividends; less volatile than a growth & income fund or a pure growth fund.

Income Bond: a bond that will pay interest only if the issuer earns sufficient income and the board of directors declares the payment. AKA "adjustment bond."

Income Programs: a direct participation program that invests in existing producing oil and/or natural gas wells.

Income Statement: a financial statement showing a corporation's results of operations over the quarter or year. Shows revenue, all expenses/costs, and the profit or loss the company showed over the period. Found in the annual shareholder report among other places.

Indenture: a contract that spells out the responsibilities and rights of an issuer in connection with a bond issue.

Index: a theoretical grouping of stocks, bonds, etc., that aids analysts who want to track something. The Consumer Price Index is a theoretical grouping or "basket" of things that consumers buy, used to track inflation. The Dow Jones Industrial Average is a theoretical grouping of 30 large-company stocks that analysts use to track the stock market. The S&P 500 index tracks the stock of 500 large companies and represents the overall stock market for many calculations, including beta.

Index Option: a call or put option based on the value of a particular index, e.g., the Dow Jones Industrial Average or the S&P 500.

Indication of Interest: an investor's expression of interest in purchasing a new issue of securities after reading the preliminary prospectus; not a commitment to buy.

Individual Retirement Account (IRA): also called an "individual retirement arrangement" to make sure it has at least two names. A tax-deferred account that generally allows any individual with earned income to contribute 100% of earned income up to the current maximum contribution allowed on a pre-tax basis that reduces the current tax liability and allows investment returns to compound.

Inflation: rising prices, as measured by the Consumer Price Index (CPI). Major risk to fixed-income investors (loss of purchasing power).

Inflation Risk: also called "constant dollar risk" or "purchasing power risk," it is the risk that inflation will erode the value of a fixed-income stream from a bond or preferred stock.

Initial Public Offering (IPO): a corporation's first sale of stock to public investors. By definition, a primary market transaction in which the issuer receives the proceeds.

Inside Information: material information about a corporation that has not yet been released to the public and would likely affect the price of the corporation's stock and/or bonds. Inside information may not be "disseminated" or acted upon.

Insider: for purpose of insider trading rules, an "insider" is anyone who has or has access to material non-public information. Officers (CEO ,CFO), members of the board of directors, and investors owning > 10% of the company's outstanding shares are assumed to possess and have access to inside information. As fiduciaries to the shareholders, insiders may not use inside information to their benefit.

Insider Trading and Securities Fraud Enforcement Act (ITSFEA) of 1988: an Act of Congress that addresses insider trading and lists the penalties for violations of the Act. Insider traders may be penalized up to three times the amount of their profit or their loss avoided by using inside information.

Insurance: protection against loss of income due to death, disability, long-term care needs, etc.

Insurance Covenant: promise by a revenue bond issuer to keep the facility properly insured.

Institutional Investor: not an individual. An institution is, for example, a pension fund, insurance company, or mutual fund. The large institutions are "accredited investors" who get to do things that retail (individual) investors often do not get to do.

Integration: the final stage in the money laundering process.

Interdealer: among dealers. The "interdealer market" is the highest bid and lowest asked price for a security among all dealers/market makers.

Interest Rate Options: options based on the price or yield of US Treasury securities.

Interest Rates: the cost of a commodity called money. In order to borrow money, borrowers pay a rate called an interest rate on top of the principal they will return at the end of the term. A one-year loan of $1,000 at 5% interest would have the borrower pay $50 on top of the $1,000 that will be returned at the end of the year.

Interest Rate Risk: the risk that interest rates will rise, pushing the market value of a fixed-income security down. Long-term bonds most susceptible.

Interpositioning: unnecessarily inserting another party between the broker-dealer and the customer. A violation.

Internal Revenue Code (IRC): tax laws for the U.S. that define, for example, maximum IRA contributions, or the "conduit tax theory" that mutual funds use when distributing 90% of net income to shareholders, etc.

Internal Revenue Service (IRS): an agency for the federal government that no one seems to like very much. Responsible for collecting federal taxes for the U.S. Treasury and for administering tax rules and regulations.

International Fund: a mutual fund investing in companies established outside the U.S.

Interstate Offering: an offering of securities in several states, requiring registration with the SEC.

In-the-money: a call option allowing an investor to buy the underlying stock for less than it's worth or a put option allowing an investor to sell the underlying stock for more than it's worth. For example, if ABC trades @50, both the ABC Oct 45 calls and the ABC Oct 55 puts are "in-the-money."

Intrastate Offering: an offering of securities completed in the issuer's home state with investors who reside in that state, and, therefore, eligible for the Rule 147 Exemption to registration with the SEC. Intrastate offerings generally register with the state Administrator.

Intrinsic Value: the amount by which an option is in-the-money. For example, if ABC trades @50, an ABC Oct 45 call has $5 of intrinsic value, regardless of what the premium might be.

Inventory: finished goods that have not yet been sold by a corporation. A current asset that is included in the current ratio but excluded in the quick ratio.

Inverse Relationship: when one goes up, the other goes down, and vice versa. Interest Rates and Yields are inversely related to Bond Prices. Your rate of speed is inversely related to your travel time to and from the office.

Investment Adviser: a business or professional that is compensated for advising others as to the value of or advisability of investing in securities. The entity that manages mutual funds/separate accounts for an asset-based fee. Financial planners are also advisers.

Investment Banker: see "underwriter." A firm that raises capital for issuers on the primary market.

Investment Banking: the business of helping companies with mergers and acquisitions, performing IPOs and additional offerings. In other words, investment bankers raise capital for issuers not by loaning money (like a traditional bank) but by finding investors willing to contribute to the cause.

Investment Company: a company engaged in the business of pooling investors' money and trading in securities on their behalf. Examples include unit investment trusts (UITs), face-amount certificate companies, and management companies.

Investment Company Act of 1940: classified Investment Companies and set rules for registration and operation.

Investment Grade: a bond rated at least BBB by S&P or Baa by Moody's. The bond does not have severe default risk, so it is said to be appropriate for investors, as opposed to the speculators who buy non-investment grade bonds.

Investment Objective: any goal that an investor has including current income, capital appreciation (growth), capital preservation (safety), or speculation

Investment Style: an approach to investing, such as active, passive, or buy-and-hold.

IRA: Individual Retirement Account. A retirement account/arrangement for any individual with earned income. The Traditional IRA offers pre-tax contributions while the Roth IRA is funded with after-tax contributions.

Issued Shares: the number of shares that have been issued by a corporation.

Issued Stock: the shares that have been issued to investors by the corporation at this time. Often a lower number than the number of shares authorized.

Issuer: any individual or entity who issues or proposes to issue any security. For example, the issuer of Google common stock is Google.

Issuing Securities: raising capital by offering securities to investors on the primary market.

J

Joint Account: investment account owned by more than one individual. Account owners sign a joint account agreement that stipulates which % of the assets is owned by each individual. Joint accounts are either "tenants in common" or "tenants with rights of survivorship."

Joint With Last Survivor: a settlement/payout option on an annuity that requires the insurance company to make payments to the annuitants as long as they are alive.

JTIC (Joint Tenants In Common): account where the assets of the deceased party pass to the deceased's estate, not the other account owner(s)

JTWROS (Joint Tenants With Rights Of Survivorship): account where the assets of the deceased party pass to the other account owner(s).

Junk Bond: a bond backed by a shaky issuer. It was either issued by an entity with shaky credit, or is now trading at a frightfully low price on the secondary market because the issuer's credit has suddenly or recently been downgraded. Since the price is low, given the low quality of the debt, the yield is high. High-yield and junk are synonymous.

K

Keogh: qualified retirement plan available to sole proprietorships.

K-1: a tax form required of people who own direct participation interests (limited partnership, S-corp).

Keynesian Economics: economic school of thought that advocates government intervention through fiscal policy as a way to stimulate demand for goods and services.

L

Layering: the phase of money laundering in which the first attempt at disguising the source of the ownership of the funds is made by creating complex layers of transactions.

Large Cap: a stock where the total value of the outstanding shares is large, generally greater than $10 billion. For example, GE, MSFT, IBM.

Last-In-First-Out (LIFO): an accounting method used for random withdrawals from an annuity. The IRS assumes that all withdrawals represent part of the taxable "excess over cost basis" first.

LEAPS: long-term standardized options.

Legal Opinion: the opinion of the bond counsel attesting to the municipality's legal authority to issue the bonds as well as the tax status of the bonds.

Legislative Risk: the risk to an investor that laws will change and have a negative impact on an investment. For example, if municipal bonds lose their tax-exempt interest, their value would plummet.

Letter of Intent: LOI, a feature of many mutual funds whereby an investor may submit a letter or form expressing the intent to invest enough money over 13 months to achieve a breakpoint.

Level Load: an ongoing asset-based sales charge (12b-1 fee) associated with mutual fund C-shares. Appropriate for short-term investments only.

Leverage: using borrowed money to increase returns. Debt securities and margin accounts are associated with "leverage."

Liabilities: what an individual or corporation owes, e.g., credit card debt, bonds, mortgage balance, accounts payable.

Life Only/Life Annuity: a payout option whereby the insurance/annuity company promises to make payments only for the rest of the annuitant's life.

Life With Joint and Last Survivor: a payout option whereby the insurance/annuity company promises to make payments to the annuitant for the rest of his life, then to the survivor for the rest of her life.

Life With Period Certain: a payout option whereby the insurance/annuity company promises to make payments to the annuitant for the rest of his life or a certain period of time, whichever is greater.

Life With Unit Refund: a payout option whereby the insurance/annuity company promises to make at least a certain number of payments to the annuitant or beneficiary.

Limited Liability: an investor's ability to limit losses to no more than the amount invested. Holders of common stock and limited partnership interests enjoy "limited liability," which means they can only lose 100% of what they invest.

Limit Orders: orders to buy or sell a security at a specified price or better.

Limited Partner: a person who owns a limited partnership interest. Has no managerial responsibility and is shielded from debts of—and lawsuits against—the partnership.

Limited Partnership: a form of business ownership in which income and expenses flow through directly to the partners rather than to a separate business entity.

Limited Representative: what one would be after passing the Series 6 and getting registered to represent one's broker-dealer. You will be a "general securities representative" once you pass the Series 7 exam.

Limited Tax Bonds: general obligation bonds backed by a tax whose rate may not be increased above a certain limit.

Limited Trading Authorization: an authorization for someone other than the account owner to enter purchase and sale orders but make no withdrawals of cash or securities.

Liquidation Priority: the priority of claims on a bankrupt entity's assets that places creditors (bondholders) ahead of stockholders and preferred stockholders ahead of common stockholders.

Liquidity: ability to quickly convert an investment to cash and get a fair price. A home is not a liquid investment—100 shares of GE are extremely liquid. Mutual funds are very liquid, since the issuer has to pay the NAV promptly. The most liquid investment imaginable is the money market mutual fund—just write checks and the fund redeems enough shares to cover it.

Liquidity Risk: the risk of being unable to sell a security quickly for a fair price. AKA "marketability risk."

Loan Consent: a document that when signed gives the broker-dealer the permission to lend a customer's securities to short sellers.

Long: to buy or own.

Long Straddle: a position created by purchasing a call and a put with the same strike price in order to bet on the volatility of the underlying instrument.

Long-Term Gain: a profit realized when selling stock held for at least 12 months plus 1 day. Subject to lower capital gains tax rates than short-term gains.

Long-Term Liability: a debt to be repaid in the long-run, i.e. the principal value of an outstanding bond issue.

Long-Term Loss: a loss realized when selling stock held for at least 12 months plus 1 day. Used to offset long-term capital gains.

Long-Term Options (LEAPS): standardized options contracts with expiration terms of several years, unlike ordinary options, which expire in nine months or sooner.

Lump Sum Payment: a settlement/payout option for annuities or insurance where the annuitant or beneficiary receives a lump sum payment. Go figure.

M

Maintenance Covenant: a promise of a revenue bond issuer to keep the facility properly maintained.

Maloney Act: An amendment to the Securities Exchange Act of 1934 creating the NASD as the self-regulatory organization (SRO) for the over-the-counter (OTC) market.

Management Company: one of the three types of Investment Companies, including both open-end and closed-end funds.

Management Fee: the % of assets charged to a mutual fund portfolio to cover the cost of portfolio management.

Manager's Fee: typically the smallest piece of the spread, paid to the managing underwriter for every share sold by the syndicate.

Margin: amount of equity contributed by a customer as a percentage of the current market value of the securities held in a margin account.

Marginal Tax Rate: the tax rate applied to the next dollar of income earned.

Markdown: the difference between the highest bid price for a security and the price that a particular dealer pays an investor for her security.

Market Letter: a publication of a broker-dealer sent to clients or the public and discussing investing, financial markets, economic conditions, etc. Can be considered correspondence if sent to a limited number of clients; otherwise, considered sales literature and subject to pre-approval.

Market Maker: a dealer in the OTC market maintaining an inventory of a particular security and a firm Bid and Ask price good for a minimum of 100 shares. Acts as a "principal" on transactions, buying and selling for its/their own account.

Market Manipulation: the illegal process of using deception to move securities prices in favor of the conspirators. Includes terms such as "painting the tape" or "pegging."

Market Order: an order to buy or sell a security at the best available market price.

Market Risk: also called "systematic risk," the risk inherent to the entire market rather than a specific security. The risk that the stock market may suffer violent upheavals due to unpredictable events including natural disaster, war, disease, famine, credit crises, etc. Market risk can be reduced by hedging with options or ETFs.

Marketability: a.k.a. liquidity; the ease or difficulty an investor has when trying to sell a security for cash without losing his shirt. Thinly traded securities have poor marketability.

Marketability Risk: the risk of being unable to sell a security quickly for a fair price. AKA "liquidity risk."

Marking to the Market: process of calculating margin requirements based on the most current market values for the securities in a margin account.

Markup: the difference between the lowest ask/offer price for a security and the price that a particular dealer charges.

Material Information: any fact that could reasonably affect an investor's decision to buy, sell, or hold a security. For example, profits and losses at the company, product liability lawsuits, the loss of key clients, etc.

Maturity Date: the date that a bond pays out the principal, and interest payments cease. Also called "redemption."

Member Firm: a broker-dealer and/or underwriting firm that belongs to FINRA or other securities association (MSRB, CBOE).

Millage Rate: the property tax rate used to calculate a property owner's tax bill.

Mini-Max: a type of best efforts underwriting where the syndicate must sell a minimum amount and may sell up to a higher, maximum amount.

Minimum Death Benefit: the minimum death benefit payable to the insured, regardless of how lousy the separate account returns are in a variable policy.

Minimum Maintenance Requirement: the minimum amount of equity that a margin customer must maintain on either a short or a long position.

Monetary Policy: what the FRB implements through the discount rate, reserve requirement, and FOMC open market operations. Monetary policy tightens or loosens credit in order to affect short-term interest rates and, therefore, the economy.

Money Laundering: the process of turning profits from illegal enterprises into seemingly legitimate assets.

Money Market: the short-term (1 year or less) debt security market. Examples include commercial paper, banker's acceptance, T-bills.

Money Market Mutual Fund: a highly liquid holding place for cash. Sometimes called "stable value" funds, as the share price is generally maintained at $1. The mutual funds invest in—surprisingly—money market securities.

Money Purchase: a retirement plan in which the employer must contribute a set percentage of the employee's salary, regardless of profitability.

Moody's Investors Service: one of the top three credit rating agencies for corporate and municipal bonds as well as stocks.

Moral Obligation Bond: type of revenue bond with a provision to seek emergency funding from the state legislature should the issuer run into financial problems.

Mortality Guarantee: a promise from an insurance company to pay out no matter how soon the insured dies, or to pay an annuitant no matter how long he lives.

Mortgage Bond: a corporate bond secured by a pledge of real estate as collateral.

Municipal Bond: a bond issued by a state, county, city, school district, etc., in order to build roads, schools, hospitals, etc., or simply to keep the government running long enough to hold another election.

Municipal Bond Fund: a mutual fund that invests in municipal bonds with an objective to maximize federally tax-exempt income.

Municipal Note: a short-term obligation of a city, state, school district, etc., backed by the anticipation of funds from revenues, taxes, or upcoming bond issues, e.g., TAN, RAN, BAN.

MSRB (Municipal Securities Rulemaking Board): the self-regulatory organization overseeing municipal securities dealers.

Mutual Fund: an investment company offering equity stakes in a portfolio that is usually managed actively and that always charges management fees and other expenses.

N

Narrow-based Index: an index focusing on a particular industry or geographic region, i.e. a transportation index.

NASD (National Association of Securities Dealers): former name of the SRO empowered with the passage of the Maloney Act of 1938. Regulates its own members and enforces SEC rules and regulations. Now called FINRA after a merger with the regulators from the NYSE.

NASDAQ: National Association of Securities Dealers Automated Quotation system. The main component of the OTC market. Stocks that meet certain criteria are quoted throughout the day on NASDAQ, e.g., MSFT, ORCL, and INTC.

National Adjudicatory Council: NAC, the first level of appeal for a party sanctioned by the DOE under FINRA's Code of Procedure.

NAV: the net asset value of a mutual fund share. Assets – Liabilities/Outstanding Shares.

Negotiable: the characteristic of a security that allows an investor to sell or transfer ownership to another party. For example, savings bonds are not negotiable, while Treasury Bills are negotiable (able to be traded).

Negotiated Market: another name for the "second" or "over-the-counter" market.

Negotiated Underwriting: a municipal bond—usually a revenue bond—underwritten without a competitive, sealed bid.

Net Income: the "bottom line" of a corporation's income statement. Revenue minus all expenses. Also known as a "profit" or a "loss," depending on whether it's a positive or negative number.

Net Interest Cost: a measure of a municipal issuer's total cost of borrowing money by issuing bonds.

Net Investment Income: the source of an investment company's dividend distributions to shareholders. It is calculated by taking the fund's dividends and interest collected on portfolio securities, minus the operating expenses. Funds using the "conduit tax theory" distribute at least 90% of net investment income to avoid paying taxes on the amount distributed to shareholders.

Net Overall Debt: a municipal issuer's direct debt plus their overlapping debt.

Net Revenue Pledge: the more common method used by the issuer of a revenue bond in which operations & maintenance are covered before debt service.

Net Worth: the difference between assets and liabilities. For example, the difference between the market value of a home and the mortgage balance still owed would represent the total net worth for many Americans. Other components would be checking, savings, and retirement accounts minus credit card debt. Add the pluses, subtract the minuses, and you have the individual's financial net worth.

New Account Form: the form that must be filled out for each new account opened with a broker-dealer. The form specifies, at a minimum, the name of the account owner, trading authorization, method of payment, and the type of investment securities that are appropriate for this particular account.

New Construction: a type of DPP in which the partnership builds and then sells housing units.

New Issue Market: the primary market, where securities are issued to investors with the proceeds going to the issuer of the securities. Initial public offerings (IPOs), for example, take place on the "new issue market."

NHA – New Housing Authority (bonds): revenue bonds issued by a municipal government but ultimately backed by the United States Government, who guarantees rental payments for the residents of the housing project.

NYSE: New York Stock Exchange, an auction market where buyers and sellers shout out competitive bid and asked/offered prices throughout the day.

No-load Fund: a mutual fund sold without a sales charge, but one which may charge an ongoing 12b-1fee or "asset-based sales charge" up to .25% of net assets.

Nominal Yield: the interest rate paid by a bond or preferred stock. The investor receives this % of the par value each year, regardless of what the bond or preferred stock is trading for on the secondary market.

Non-accredited Investor: an investor who does not meet various SEC net worth and/or income requirements. For a Reg D private placement, accredited investors may participate, but only a limited number of non-accredited investors may purchase the issue.

Non-cumulative Preferred Stock: a type of preferred stock that does not have to pay missed dividends (dividends in arrears).

Non-discrimination Covenant: a promise by a municipal revenue bond issuer that all users of a facility must pay to use it, including VIPs of the municipality.

Non-diversified Fund: a fund that doesn't care to meet the 75-5-10 rule, preferring to concentrate more heavily in certain issues.

Non-equity Options: standardized options based on things other than equity securities, e.g., indexes or foreign currency options.

Non-NASDAQ OTC Securities: over-the-counter securities that do not meet the requirements of NASDAQ. For example, Pink Sheet securities.

Non-systematic Risk: the risk of holding any one particular stock or bond. Diversification spreads this risk among different issuers and different industries in order to minimize the impact of a bankruptcy or unexpected collapse of any one issuer.

Not Held (order): AKA "market not held." A market order in which the customer allows the broker-dealer to enter the trade when they feel the price is right, as opposed to a market order, which is filled as soon as possible.

Note: a short-term debt security.

Nolo Contendere: a phrase you hope you've never uttered in open court when it comes time to complete the U4. Curious? Look it up under item 14 on Form U4. Latin for "no contest," which means, "Yeah, I done it—now what?"

Numbered Account: an account identified with a number rather than a name. Allowed if the owner files a statement with the broker-dealer attesting to ownership.

O

Odd Lot: an order for fewer than 100 shares of common stock or 5 bonds.

Offer: another name for "ask," or the price an investor must pay if he wants to buy a security from a dealer/market maker.

Offer of Settlement: a respondent's offer to the disciplinary committee of FINRA to settle his or her recent rule violations.

Officers: high-level executives at a public corporation, e.g., the Chief Executive Officer (CEO), Chief Financial Officer (CFO), and the Chief Operating Officer (COO).

Official Notice of Sale: advertisement in the Bond Buyer in which a municipal issuer hopes to attract potential underwriters.

Official Statement: the document that discloses detailed information about a municipal bond issuer's financial condition.

OID: original issue discount. A bond purchased for less than the par value on the primary market, i.e. a zero coupon bond.

Omitting Prospectus: an advertisement for a mutual fund that typically shows performance figures without providing (omitting) the full disclosure contained in the prospectus. Therefore, it must present caveats and encourage readers to read the prospectus and consider all the risks before investing in the fund.

Open-End Fund: an investment company that sells an unlimited number of shares to an unlimited number of investors on a continuous basis. Shares are redeemed by the company rather than traded among investors.

Operating Expenses: expenses that a mutual fund deducts from the assets of the fund, including board of director salaries, custodial and transfer agent services, management fees, 12b-1 fees, etc.

Option: a derivative giving the holder the right to buy or sell something for a stated price up to expiration of the contract. Puts and calls.

Order Room: AKA "wire room." The department of a broker-dealer that places trades.

Order Ticket/trade ticket: a ticket filled out by a registered representative when placing an order to buy or sell securities.

Ordinary Income Rate: tax rate paid on earned income and some forms of investment income, i.e. corporate or Treasury bond interest.

OTC/Over-the-Counter: called a "negotiated market." Securities traded among dealers rather than on exchanges. Includes NASDAQ and also Bulletin Board and Pink Sheet stocks, plus government, corporate, and municipal bonds.

Outstanding Shares: the number of shares a corporation has outstanding. Found by taking Issued shares minus Treasury stock.

Overlapping Debt: the debt that a municipal issuer is responsible for along with a coterminous issuer.

P

PACs – planned amortization class. A type of CMO (collateralized mortgage obligation) that provides more protection against extension risk vs. a TAC.

Paid-In Surplus: the amount above the par value that investors paid when purchasing the company's initial public offering. For example, if the stock has a par value of $1 and was sold to investors at a public offering price of $5, the paid-in surplus is $4 per share.

Painting the Tape: a form of market manipulation in which bogus trades are reported in order to affect the market price of a security. A violation.

Par, Principal: the face amount of a bond payable at maturity. Also, the face amount of a preferred stock. Preferred = $100, Bond = $1,000.

Partial Surrender: life insurance policyholder cashes in part of the cash value. Excess over premiums is taxable.

Participating Preferred Stock: preferred stock whose dividend is often raised above the stated rate.

Participation: provision of ERISA requiring that all employees in a qualified retirement plan be covered within a reasonable length of time after being hired.

Partnership Agreement: the agreement between the LPs and the GP for a direct participation program.

Pass-Through Certificate: a mortgage-backed security (usually GNMA) that takes a pool of mortgages and passes through interest and principal monthly to an investor.

Passive Income: as opposed to "earned income," the income derived from rental properties, limited partnerships, or other enterprises in which the individual is not actively involved.

Payable (or Payment) Date: the date that the dividend check is paid to investors.

Payroll Deduction: non-qualified retirement plan offered by some businesses.

Peak: the phase of the business cycle between expansion (good times) and contraction (bad times).

Pegging: a form of market manipulation. A violation.

Penny Stock Cold Calling Rules: rules to protect consumers receiving telemarketing pitches to buy risky stocks trading below $5 a share. Rules require special disclosure and investor signatures when selling penny stocks.

Pension Plan: a contract between an individual and an employer that provides for the distribution of benefits at retirement.

Performance Figures: total return for a mutual fund over 1, 5, and 10 years, and/or "life of fund." Only past performance may be indicated, and there must be a caveat that past performance does not guarantee future results.

Periodic-Payment Deferred Annuity: method of purchasing an annuity whereby the contract holder makes periodic payments into the contract. The pay-out phase must be deferred for all periodic payment plans.

Permanent Insurance: life insurance other then "term."

PHA – Public Housing Authority (bonds): another name for NHA/New Housing Authority municipal revenue bonds.

Pink Sheets: a virtually unregulated part of the OTC market where thinly traded, volatile stocks change hands.

Placement: the first stage in the cycle of money laundering in which illegally generated funds are placed into the financial system or are smuggled out of the country.

Placement Ratio: a statistic published in the Bond Buyer showing the dollar amount of municipal securities sold on the primary market out of the dollar amount offered the previous week. AKA the "acceptance ratio."

Political Risk: the risk that a country's government will radically change policies or that the political climate will become hostile or counterproductive to business and financial markets.

POP: public offering price. For an IPO, this includes the spread to the underwriters. For a mutual fund, this includes any sales loads that go to the underwriter/distributor.

Portfolio: a batch of stocks, bonds, money market securities, or any combination thereof that an investor owns.

Position Limit: maximum number of options contracts that a trader can have on the same side of the market (bull/bear) and/or may exercise over a five day period.

Power of Substitution: a document that when signed by the security owner authorizes transfer of the certificate to another party.

Pre-dispute Arbitration Agreement: an agreement signed by the customer of a broker-dealer in which the customer agrees to use arbitration rather than civil court to settle disputes.

Pre-emptive Right: the right of common stockholders to maintain their proportional ownership if the company offers more shares of stock.

Preferred Stock: a fixed-income equity security whose stated dividends must be paid before common stock can receive any dividend payment. Also gets preference ahead of common stock in a liquidation (but behind all bonds and general creditors).

Preliminary Official Statement: the official statement for a municipal bond issue subject to further additions and changes.

Preliminary Prospectus: a prospectus that lacks the POP and the effective date; a.k.a. "red herring." Used to solicit indications of interest.

Premium Bond: a bond purchased for more than the par value, usually due to a drop in interest rates.

Prepayment Risk: the risk that the mortgages underlying a mortgage-backed security/pass-through will be paid off sooner than expected due to a drop in interest rates. Investors reinvest the principal at a lower rate going forward.

Preservation of Capital: an investment objective that places the emphasis on making sure the principal is not lost. Also called "safety."

Price-based Options: standardized interest rate options based on the price of various US Treasury securities.

P/E or Price-to-Earnings Ratio: the market price of a stock compared to the earnings per share. Stocks trading at high P/E ratios are "growth stocks," while those trading at low P/E ratios are "value stocks."

Primary Market: where securities are issued to raise capital for the issuer.

Primary Offering: offering of securities in which the proceeds go to the issuer.

Prime Rate: interest rate charged to corporations with high credit ratings for unsecured loans.

Principal-Protected Fund: a mutual fund for people who want their principal protected. Involves holding the investment for several years, at which point the fund guarantees that the value of the investment will be equal to at least what the investor put in.

Private Placement: an exempt transaction under Reg D (Rule 506) of the Securities Act of 1933, allowing issuers to sell securities without registration to accredited investors, who agree to hold them for a required period that is subject to change by the SEC before selling them through Rule 144.

Private Securities Transaction: offering an investment opportunity not sponsored by the firm. Requires permission from the firm and any disclosure demanded; otherwise, a violation called "selling away."

Proceeds Transaction: using the proceeds from a sale of securities to buy other securities on the same day.

Profit Sharing: a defined contribution plan whereby the company shares any profits with employees in the form of contributions to a retirement account.

Progressive Tax: a tax that increases as a percentage as the thing being taxed increases, including gift, estate, and income taxes. Not a flat tax.

Prospectus: a disclosure document that details a company's plans, history, officers, and risks of investment. It's the red herring plus the POP and the effective date.

Protective Covenants: promises from the issuer of a revenue bond to the bondholders designed to protect the bondholders against default.

Proxy: a form granting the power to vote according to a shareholder's instructions when the shareholder will not attend the meeting.

Prudent Investor Standards: guidance provided to fiduciaries investing on behalf of a third party, i.e. trustees or custodians of UTMA accounts.

PSA Model: a method of estimating the speed of prepayments on a CMO investment.

Public Appearance: addressing an audience on topics related to securities. Before speaking at a local Chamber of Commerce function, for example, registered representatives need prior principal approval.

Public Offering: the sale of an issue of common stock, either an IPO or an additional offer of shares.

Public Offering Price (POP): the price an investor pays for a mutual fund or an initial public offering. For a mutual fund = NAV + the sales charge.

Purchasing Power Risk: also called "constant dollar" or "inflation" risk, the risk that a fixed payment will not be sufficient to keep up with rising inflation (as measured through the CPI).

Put (n.): a contract giving the owner the right to sell something at a stated exercise price.

Put (v.): to sell.

Put Spread: the act of buying and selling puts on the same underlying instrument where the two options are different in terms of strike price, expiration, or both.

Q

Qualified Dividend: a dividend that qualifies for a lower tax rate vs. ordinary income.

Qualified Institutional Buyers: investors meeting certain SEC criteria allowing them to participate in certain investment opportunities not open to the general public.

Qualified Plan: a retirement plan that qualifies for deductible contributions on behalf of employers and/or employees and covered by ERISA. For example, 401(k), defined benefit, Keogh. Must meet IRS approval, unlike more informal "non-qualified plans."

Qualified Opinion: opinion by the bond counsel for a municipal issuer in which some doubt or reservations are expressed.

Quick Ratio: a more stringent measure of liquidity than the current ratio. Inventory is excluded from current assets before comparing to the company's current liabilities.

Quote, Quotation: a price that a dealer is willing to pay or accept for a security. A two-sided quote has both a bid and an asked/offer price.

R

Random Withdrawals: a settlement option in an annuity whereby the investor takes the value of the subaccounts in two or more withdrawals, rather than one lump sum.

Rate Covenant: a promise that the issuer of a revenue bond will raise rates if necessary to cover the debt service.

Rating Service: e.g., S&P and Moody's; a company that assigns credit ratings to corporate and municipal bonds.

Raw Land: unimproved real estate providing no cash flow and no depreciation. A speculative investment in land.

Reclamation: document sent by a broker-dealer when delivery of securities is apparently in error.

REIT (Real Estate Investment Trust): a corporation or trust that uses the pooled capital of investors to invest in ownership of either income property or mortgage loans. 90% of net income is paid out to shareholders.

Realized Gain: the amount of the "profit" an investor earns when selling a security.

Recession: two quarters (6 months) or more of economic decline. Associated with rising unemployment, falling interest rates, and falling gross domestic product.

Record Date: the date determined by the Board of Directors upon which the investor must be the holder "of record" in order to receive the upcoming dividend. Settlement of a trade must occur by the record date for the buyer to receive the dividend.

Recourse Note: an obligation of a limited partnership for which a limited partner is responsible personally.

Red Herring: a.k.a. "preliminary prospectus." Contains essentially the same information that the final prospectus will contain, minus the POP and effective date.

Redeemable Security: a security that may be redeemed or presented to the issuer for payment, i.e. open-end (but not closed-end) funds.

Redemption: for mutual funds, redemption involves the sale of mutual fund shares back to the fund at the NAV (less any redemption fees, back-end loads). For bonds, the date that principal is returned to the investor, along with the final interest payment.

Redemption Fee: a charge to a mutual fund investor who sells her shares back to the fund much sooner than the fund would prefer.

Refunding: replacing an outstanding bond issue by issuing new bonds at a lower interest rate. Also known as "calling" a bond issue.

Reg A: a laid-back and predictable form of island music. Also, an exempt transaction under the Securities Act of 1933 for small offerings of securities ($5 million issued in a 12-month period).

Reg D: an exempt transaction under the Securities Act of 1933 for private placements.

Reg FD: legislation requiring that any material non-public information disclosed by a public corporation to analysts or other investors must be made public.

Reg T: established by the FRB as the amount of credit a broker-dealer may extend to a customer pledging a security as collateral for a margin loan. In a margin account, customers must put down ½ of the security's value, or at least $2,000.

Reg U: established by the FRB as the amount of credit a bank may extend to a broker-dealer or public customer pledging a security as collateral.

Registered as to Principal Only: a bond with only the principal registered. Interest coupons must be presented for payment.

Registered Representative: an associated person of an investment banker or broker-dealer who effects transactions in securities for compensation.

Registered Secondary: an offering of securities by persons other than the issuer. For example, the former CEO of a corporation may offer a large block of restricted (unregistered) stock to the public through a broker-dealer.

Registrar: audits the transfer agent to make sure the number of authorized shares is never exceeded.

Registration Statement: the legal document disclosing material information concerning an offering of a security and its issuer. Submitted to SEC under Securities Act of 1933.

Regressive Tax: any flat tax, i.e. sales or gasoline taxes.

Regular Way Settlement: T + 3, trade date plus three business days. T + 1 for Treasury securities.

Regulated Investment Company: an investment company using the conduit tax theory by distributing 90% or more of net investment income to shareholders.

Reinstatement Privilege: a feature of some mutual funds allowing investors to make withdrawals and then reinstate the money without paying another sales charge.

Reinvestment Risk: the risk that a fixed-income investor will not be able to reinvest interest payments or the par value at attractive interest rates. Happens when rates are falling.

Regressive Tax: a flat tax, e.g., gasoline, sales, excise taxes.

Release Date: date established by the SEC as to when the underwriters may sell new securities to the buyers; a.k.a. "effective date."

Repurchase Agreement: an agreement in which one party sells something to the other and agrees to repurchase it for a higher price over the short-term.

Required Minimum Distribution (RMD): the required minimum distribution that must be taken from a retirement plan to avoid IRS penalties. Usually April 1st of the year following the individual's 70½th birthday.

Reserve Requirement: amount of money a bank must lock up in reserve, established by the FRB.

Residual Claim: the right of common stockholders to claim assets after the claims of all creditors and preferred stockholders have been satisfied.

Restricted Person: a person who is ineligible to purchase an equity IPO, including members of the brokerage industry and their immediate family members.

Restricted Stock: stock whose transfer is subject to restrictions, i.e. a holding period. Stock purchased in private placements is an example of restricted stock.

Revenue: the proceeds a company receives when selling products and services.

Revenue Anticipation Note (RAN): a short-term debt obligation of a municipal issuer backed by upcoming revenues.

Revenue Bond: a municipal bond whose interest and principal payments are backed by the revenues generated from the project being built by the proceeds of the bonds. Toll roads, for example, are usually built with revenue bonds backed by the tolls collected.

Reverse Repurchase Agreements: an agreement between two parties to buy and sell securities for a set price.

Rights: short-term equity securities that allow the holder to buy new shares below the current market price.

Rights Offering: additional offer of stock accompanied by the opportunity for each shareholder to maintain his/her proportionate ownership in the company.

Rights of Accumulation: feature of many mutual funds whereby a rise in account value is counted the same as new money for purposes of achieving a breakpoint.

Riskless Principal Transaction: transaction in which a broker-dealer chooses to act as a principal when they could have acted as an agent for the customer.

Rollover: moving retirement funds from a 401(k) to an IRA, or from one IRA to another. In a "60-day rollover," the check is cut to the individual, who must then send a check to the new custodian within 60 days to avoid early distribution penalties.

Roth IRA: individual retirement account funded with non-deductible (after-tax) contributions.

All distributions are tax-free provided the individual is 59½ and has had the account at least five years.

Round Lot: the usual or normal unit of trading. 100 shares for common stock.

RTRS: a trade reporting system used for transactions in municipal securities on the secondary market.

Rule (and Form) 144: regulates the sale of "control stock" by requiring board members, officers, and large shareholders to report sales of their corporation's stock and to adhere to volume limits. The form is filed as often as quarterly and no later than concurrently with the sale.

Rule 144a: rule that allows restricted securities to be re-sold to institutional investors including banks, insurance companies, broker-dealers, investment advisers, pension plans, and investment companies without violating holding period requirements.

Rule 145: rule that requires corporations in a proposed merger/acquisition to solicit the vote of the shareholders of both the purchasing and the acquired corporation.

Rule 147: exemption under the Securities Act of 1933 for intra-state offerings of securities.

RVP: receipt versus payment, a method of settlement whereby payment on the transaction is made when delivery of the securities is received and accepted.

S

Safety: an investment objective that seeks to avoid loss of principal first and foremost. Bank CDs, Treasury securities, and fixed annuities are generally suitable.

Sales Charge, Sales Load: a deduction from an investor's check that goes to the distributors/sellers of the fund. Deducted from investor's check, either when she buys (A-shares) or sells (B-shares).

Sales Literature: communications of a member broker-dealer delivered to a targeted, controlled audience, e.g., brochures, research reports, cold calling scripts.

Savings Bond: a U.S. Government debt security that is not "negotiable," meaning it can't be traded or pledged as collateral for a loan. Includes EE and HH series bonds.

Scheduled Premium: life insurance with established, scheduled premium payments, e.g., whole life, variable life. As opposed to "universal" insurance, which is "flexible premium."

Secondary Offering/Distribution: a distribution of securities owned by major stockholders—not the issuer of the securities.

Secondary Market: where investors trade securities among themselves and proceeds do not go to the issuer.

Sector Fund: a.k.a. "specialized." A fund that concentrates heavily in a particular industry or geographic area, e.g., "The Japan Fund," or the "Technology Fund." Higher risk/reward than funds invested in many industries.

Secured Bond: a corporate bond secured by collateral, e.g., mortgage bond, collateral trust certificate, equipment trust certificate.

Securities Act of 1933: a.k.a. "Paper Act," regulates the new-issue or primary market, requiring non-exempt issuers to register securities and provide full disclosure.

Securities and Exchange Commission: SEC, empowered by passage of Securities Exchange Act of 1934. A government body, the ultimate securities regulator.

Securities Exchange Act of 1934: prevents fraud in the securities markets. No person and no person exempt from anti-fraud regulations. Created/empowered the SEC. Requires broker-dealers, exchanges and securities associations to register with SEC. Requires public companies to report quarterly and annually to SEC.

Security: an investment of money subject to fluctuation in value and negotiable/marketable to other investors. Other than an insurance policy or fixed annuity, a security is any piece of securitized "paper" that can be traded for value.

Self-Regulatory Organization: SRO, e.g., FINRA. An organization given the power to regulate its members. Not government bodies like the SEC, which oversees the SROs.

Sell Limit: on order to sell placed above the current market price that may be executed only if the bid price rises to the limit price or higher.

Sell Stop: an order to sell placed below the current market price, activated only if the market price hits or passes below the stop price.

Selling Away: a violation that occurs when a registered representative offers investment opportunities not sponsored by the firm.

Selling Concession: typically, the largest piece of the underwriting spread going to the firm credited with making the sale.

Selling Dividends: a violation where an investor is deceived into thinking that she needs to purchase a stock in order to receive an upcoming dividend.

Selling, General, and Administrative: general operating expenses listed on the company's income statement.

Selling Group: certain broker-dealers with an agreement to act as selling agents for the syndicate (underwriters) with no capital at risk.

Semi-Annual: twice per year, or "at the half year," literally. Note that "bi-annually" means "every two years." Bond interest is paid semi-annually. Mutual funds report to their shareholders semi-annually and annually. Nothing happens "bi-annually" as a general rule of thumb.

Senior Security: a security that grants the holder a higher claim on the issuer's assets in the event of a liquidation/bankruptcy.

Separate Account: an account maintained by an insurance/annuity company that is separate from the company's general account. Used to invest clients' money for variable annuities and variable insurance contracts. Registered as an investment company under Investment Company Act of 1940.

SEP-IRA: pre-tax retirement plan available to small businesses. Favors high-income employees (compared to SIMPLE). Only employ-er contributes.

Series EE Bond: a nonmarketable, interest-bearing U.S. Government savings bond issued at a discount from the par value. Interest is exempt from state and local taxation.

Series HH Bond: a nonmarketable, interest-bearing U.S. Government savings bond issued at par and purchased only by trading in Series EE bonds at maturity. Interest is exempt from state and local taxation.

Series I Bond: a savings bond issued by the U.S. Treasury that protects investors from inflation or purchasing power risk.

Settlement: final completion of a securities transaction wherein payment has been made by the buyer and delivery has been made by the seller.

Settlement Options: payout options on annuities and life insurance including life-only, life with period certain, and joint and last survivorship.

Share Identification: a method of calculating capital gains and losses by which the investor identifies which shares were sold, as opposed to using FIFO or average cost.

Shelf Registration: registering securities that will be sold gradually on the primary market.

Short Interest Theory: theory that a high level of short sales is a bullish indicator, as it creates potential buying pressure on a particular security.

Short Sale: method of attempting to profit from a security whose price is expected to fall. Trader borrows certificates through a broker-dealer and sells them, with the obligation to replace them at a later date, hopefully at a lower price. Bearish position.

Short-Term Capital Gain: a profit realized on a security held for 12 months or less.

Short-Term Capital Loss: a loss realized on a security held for 12 months or less, deductible against Short-Term Capital Gains.

Signature Guarantee: an official stamp/medallion that officers of a bank affix to a stock power to attest to its validity.

SIMPLE IRA: a retirement plan for businesses with no more than 100 employees that have no other retirement plan in place. Pre-tax contributions, fully taxable distributions. Both employer and employees may contribute.

Simple Trust: a trust that accumulates income and distributes it to the beneficiaries annually.

Simplified Arbitration: a method of resolving disputes involving a small amount of money (currently $25,000).

Single-Payment Deferred Annuity: annuity purchased with a single payment wherein the individual defers the payout or "annuity" phase of the contract.

Single-Payment Immediate Annuity: annuity purchased with a single payment wherein the individual goes immediately into the payout or "annuity" phase of the contract.

Sinking Fund: an account established by an issuing corporation or municipality to provide funds required to redeem a bond issue.

SIPC: Securities Investor Protection Corporation, a non-profit, non-government, industry-funded insurance corporation protecting investors against broker-dealer failure.

SLGS: special securities created by the US Treasury to help municipalities do an advance refunding and comply with IRS rules and restrictions on such transactions.

Small Cap: a stock where the total value of all outstanding shares is considered "small," typically between $50 million and $2 billion.

Solvency: the ability of a corporation or municipality to meet its obligations as they come due.

Special Assessment Bonds: revenue bonds backed by an assessment on only those properties benefiting from the project.

Special Memorandum Account (SMA): a line of credit in a margin account.

Special Tax: a tax on gasoline, hotel and motel, liquor, tobacco, etc.

Special Tax Bond: a revenue bond backed by taxes on gasoline, hotel and motel, liquor, tobacco, etc.

Specialist: NYSE member that maintains a fair and orderly market in a particular exchange-listed security.

Specialized Fund: another name for a sector fund, e.g., "Telecommunications Fund," or "Financial Services Fund" focusing on a particular industry sector.

Specified Program: a direct participation program in which the assets of the partnership are identified.

Sponsor: the party who puts together a direct participation program.

Spousal Account: an IRA established for a non-working spouse.

Spread: generally, the difference between a dealer's purchase price and selling price, both for new offerings (underwriting spread) and secondary market quotes. For underwritings the spread is the difference between the proceeds to the issuer and the POP.

Spread Load: sales charges for a mutual fund contractual plan that permits a maximum charge of 20% in any one year and 9% over the life of the plan.

Stabilizing/Stabilization: the surprising practice by which an underwriting syndicate bids up the price of an IPO whose price is dropping in the secondary market.

Standby Underwriting: a commitment by an underwriter to purchase any shares that are not subscribed to in a rights offering.

Statute of Limitations: a time limit that, once reached, prevents criminal or civil action from being filed.

Statutory Disqualification: prohibiting a person from associating with an SRO due to disciplinary or criminal actions within the past 10 years, or due to filing a false or misleading application or report with a regulator.

Statutory Voting: method of voting whereby the shareholder may cast no more than the number of shares owned per candidate/item.

Stock: an ownership or equity position in a public company whose value is tied to the company's profits (if any) and dividend payouts (if any)

Stock Dividend: payment of a dividend in the form of more shares of stock; not a taxable event.

Stock Power: document used to transfer ownership of a stock.

Stock Split: a change in the number of outstanding shares designed to change the price-per-share; not a taxable event.

Stop Loss: another name for a sell-stop order. So named because an investor's losses are stopped once the stock trades at a certain price or lower.

Stop Order: an order that is activated only if the market price hits or passes through the stop price. Does not name a price for execution.

Stop-limit Order: a stop order that once triggered must be filled at an exact price (or better).

Stopping Stock: a courtesy in which the specialist will guarantee a price for execution and allow the participant to seek a better price.

Straddle: buying a call and a put on the same underlying instrument with the same strike price and expiration…or selling a call and a put on the same underlying instrument with the same strike price and expiration. For example, an investor who buys an ABC Aug 50 call and buys an ABC Aug 50 put is establishing a "long straddle."

Straight Life Annuity: a settlement option in which the annuity company pays the annuitant only as long as he or she is alive. Also called "straight life" or "life only."

Straight Preferred: a preferred stock whose missed dividends do not go into arrears, a.k.a. "non-cumulative preferred."

Street Name: in the name of the broker-dealer holding securities on behalf of customers.

Strike Price or Exercise Price: the price at which a call or put option allows the holder to buy or sell the underlying security.

STRIPS: Separate Trading of Registered Interest and Principal of Securities. A zero coupon bond issued by the U.S. Treasury in which all interest income is received at maturity in the form of a higher (accreted) principal value. Avoids "reinvestment risk."

Subaccount: investment options available within the separate account for variable contract holders. Basically, these are mutual funds that grow tax-deferred.

Subchapter M: section of the Internal Revenue Code providing the "conduit tax treatment" used by REITs and mutual funds distributing 90% or more of net income to shareholders. A mutual fund using this method is technically a Regulated Investment Company under IRC Subchapter M.

Subject Quotes: quotes in which the dealer/market maker is sharing information and not yet ready to trade at those prices.

Subordinated Debenture: corporate bond with a claim that is subordinated or "junior" to a debenture and/or general creditor.

Subscription Price: the price that all buyers of a new issue will pay to buy the security being offered on the primary market.

Suitability: a determination by a registered representative that a security matches a customer's stated objectives and financial situation.

Supervision: a system implemented by a broker-dealer to ensure that its employees and associated persons comply with federal and state securities law, and the rules and regulations of the SEC, exchanges, and SROs.

Surrender: to cash out an annuity or life insurance policy for its surrender value.

Syndicate: a group of underwriters bringing a new issue to the primary market.

Syndicate Letter: another name for the agreement among underwriters. The document detailing the terms of operation for an underwriting syndicate.

Systematic Risk: another name for "market risk," or the risk that an investment's value could plummet due to an overall market panic or collapse. Other "systematic risks" include inflation, interest rate, and natural event risk.

T

T + 3: regular way settlement, trade date plus three business days.

TACs – targeted amortization class: a type of CMO (collateralized mortgage obligation) that leaves the investor with greater extension risk as compared to a PAC (planned amortization class).

Tax and Revenue Anticipation Note (TRAN): a short-term debt obligation of a municipal issuer backed by future tax and revenue receipts.

Tax Anticipation Note (TAN): a short-term debt obligation of a municipal issuer backed by future tax receipts.

Tax Credit: an amount that can be subtracted from the amount of taxes owed.

Tax-Deferred: an account where all earnings remain untaxed until "constructive receipt."

Tax-Equivalent Yield: the rate of return that a taxable bond must offer to equal the tax-exempt yield on a municipal bond. To calculate, take the municipal yield and divide that by (100% – investor's tax bracket).

Tax-Exempt Bonds: municipal bonds whose interest is not subject to taxation by the federal government.

Tax Preference Item: certain items that must be added back to an investor's income for purposes of AMT, including interest on certain municipal bonds.

Tax-Sheltered Annuity (TSA): an annuity funded with pre-tax (tax-deductible) contributions. Available to employees of non-profit organizations such as schools, hospitals, and church organizations.

T-bills: direct obligation of U.S. Government. Sold at discount, mature at face amount. Maximum maturity is 1 year.

T-bonds: direct obligation of U.S. Government. Pay semi-annual interest. Quoted as % of par value plus 32nds. 10–30-year maturities.

T-notes: direct obligation of U.S. Government. Pay semi-annual interest. Quoted as % of par value plus 32nds. 2–10-year maturities.

Technical Analysts: stock traders who rely on market data to spot buying and selling opportunities.

Telemarketing: to market by telephone. Assuming you can get past the caller ID.

Telephone Consumer Protection Act of 1991: federal legislation restricting the activities of telemarketers, who generally may only call prospects between 8 am and 9 pm in the prospect's time zone and must maintain a do-not-call list, also checking the national registry.

Tenants in Common: see Joint Tenants in Common, a joint account wherein the interest of the deceased owner reverts to his/her estate.

Tender Offer: an offer by the issuer of securities to repurchase the securities if the investors care to "tender" their securities for payment.

Term Life Insurance: form of temporary insurance that builds no cash value and must be renewed at a higher premium at the end of the term. Renting rather than buying insurance.

Third Market: exchange-listed stock traded OTC primarily by institutional investors.

Third-Party Account: account managed on behalf of a third party, e.g., trust or UGMA.

Time Value: the value of an option above its intrinsic value. For example, if XYZ trades @50, an XYZ Oct 50 call @1 has no intrinsic value but has $1 of time value.

Timing Risk: the risk of purchasing an investment at a peak price not likely to be sustained or seen again. Timing risk can be reduced through dollar cost averaging, rather than investing in a stock with one purchase.

Tippee: the guy who listened to the insider information.

Tipper: the guy who told him.

Tombstone: an advertisement allowed during the cooling-off period to announce an offer of securities, listing the issuer, the type of security, the underwriters, and directions for obtaining a prospectus.

Total Return: measuring growth in share price plus dividend and capital gains distributions.

Total Takedown: the additional takedown plus the concession.

Trade Confirmation: a document containing details of a securities transaction, e.g., price of the security, commissions, stock symbol, number of shares, registered rep code, trade date and settlement date, etc.

Trade Date: the date that a trade is executed.

Trade Reporting and Compliance Engine (TRACE): system used to report corporate bond transactions in the secondary market.

Trading Authorization: a form granting another individual the authority to trade on behalf of the account owner. Either "limited" (buy/sell orders only) or "full" (buy/sell orders plus requests for checks/securities) authorization may be granted. Sometimes referred to as "power of attorney."

Traditional IRA: individual retirement account funded typically with tax-deductible contributions.

Tranche: a class of CMO. Principal is returned to one tranche at a time in a CMO.

Transfer Agent: issues and redeems certificates. Handles name changes, validates mutilated certificates. Distributes dividends, gains, and shareholder reports to mutual fund investors.

Transfer and Hold in Safekeeping: a buy order for securities in which securities are bought and transferred to the customer's name, but held by the broker-dealer.

Transfer and Ship: a buy order for securities in which securities are purchased and transferred to the customer's name, with the certificates sent to the customer.

Transfer on Death (TOD): individual account with a named beneficiary—assets transferred directly to the named beneficiary upon death of the account holder.

Treasury Bill: see T-bill.

Treasury Bond: see T-bond.

Treasury Note: see T-note.

Treasury Receipts: zero coupon bonds created by broker-dealers backed by Treasury securities held in escrow. Not a direct obligation of U.S. Government.

Treasury Securities: securities guaranteed by U.S. Treasury, including T-bills, T-notes, T-bonds, and STRIPS.

Treasury Stock: shares that have been issued and repurchased by the corporation. Has nothing to do with the U.S. Treasury.

True Interest Cost: a measure of a municipal issuer's total cost of borrowing money by issuing bonds. Unlike net interest cost, true interest cost factors in the time value of money.

Trough: phase of the business cycle representing the "bottoming out" of a contraction, just before the next expansion/recovery.

Trustee: a person legally appointed to act on a beneficiary's behalf.

Trust Indenture: a written agreement between an issuer and creditors wherein the terms of a debt security issue are set forth, e.g., interest rate, means of payment, maturity date, name of the trustee, etc.

Trust Indenture Act of 1939: corporate bond issues in excess of $5 million with maturities greater than 1 year must be issued with an indenture.

TSA: Tax-Sheltered Annuity. A retirement vehicle for 403(b) and 501c3 organizations.

Two-dollar Broker: an independent broker on the floor of the NYSE.

U

UGMA: Uniform Gifts to Minors Act. An account set up for the benefit of a minor, managed by a custodian.

UIT: Unit Investment Trust. A type of investment company where investments are selected, not traded/managed. No management fee is charged. Shares are redeemable.

Underwriter: see "investment banker." An underwriter or "investment banker" is a broker-dealer that distributes shares on the primary market.

Underwriting Spread: the profit to the syndicate. The difference between the proceeds to the issuer and the POP.

Unearned Income: income derived from investments and other sources not related to employment, e.g., savings account interest, dividends from stock, capital gains, and rental income.

Unfunded Pension Liabilities: obligations to retiring municipal workers that outweigh the funds set aside to actually pay them.

Uniform Practice Code: how FINRA promotes "cooperative effort," standardizing settlement dates, ex-dates, accrued interest calculations, etc.

Uniform Securities Act: a model act that state securities laws are based on. Designed to prevent fraud and maintain faith in capital markets through registration of securities, agents, broker-dealers, and investment advisers. Main purpose is to provide necessary protection to investors.

Unit of Beneficial Interest: what an investor in a Unit Investment Trust (UIT) owns.

Universal Life Insurance: a form of permanent insurance that offers flexibility in death benefit and both the amount of, and method of paying, premiums.

Unqualified opinion: an opinion issued by the bond counsel expressing no doubts and requiring no qualifiers.

Unrealized Gain: the increase in the value of a security that has not yet been sold. Unrealized gains are not taxable.

Unsecured Bond: a debenture, or bond issued without specific collateral.

User Fee: AKA "user charge," a source of revenue used to retire a revenue bond, e.g., park entrance fees, tolls, skybox rentals, etc.

UTMA: just like UGMA, only the kid has to wait as late as 25 years of age to have the assets re-registered solely in his/her name. The "T" stands for "transfer."

V

Value: as in "value investing" or a "value fund," the practice of purchasing stock in companies whose share price is currently depressed. The value investor feels that the stock is trading below its "estimated intrinsic value" and, therefore, sees an opportunity to buy a good company for less than it's really worth. Like a "fixer-upper" house in need of a little "TLC." With a few quick improvements, this property is going to be worth a lot more than people realize.

Value Funds: mutual funds investing in stocks currently out of favor with investors.

Variable Annuity: an annuity whose payment varies. Investments allocated to separate account as instructed by annuitant. Similar to investing in mutual funds, except that annuities offer tax deferral. No taxation until excess over cost basis is withdrawn.

Variable Insurance: insurance whose death benefit and cash values fluctuate with the investment performance of the separate account.

Variable Life Insurance: form of insurance where death benefit and cash value fluctuate according to fluctuations of the separate account.

Variable Universal Life Insurance: flexible-premium insurance with cash value and death benefit tied to the performance of the separate account.

Vesting: a schedule for determining at what point the employer's contributions become the property of the employee.

Viatical Settlement: a.k.a. "life settlement," the sale and purchase of a life insurance policy wherein the investor buys the death benefit at a discount and profits as soon as the insured dies.

Visible Supply: total par value of municipal bonds to be issued over the next 30 days, published in the Bond Buyer.

Volatility: the up and down movements of an investment that make investors dizzy and occasionally nauseated.

Volume: total number of shares traded over a given period (daily, weekly, etc.)

Voluntary Accumulation Plan: a mutual fund account into which the investor commits to depositing amounts of money on a regular basis.

Voter Approval: the process of approving the issuance of a general obligation bond by referendum.

VRDO – variable rate demand obligation: a debt security whose interest rate is regularly re-set and which can be "put" or sold back to the issuer or a designated third party for the par value plus accrued interest.

W

Warrants: long-term equity securities giving the owner the right to purchase stock at a set price. Often attached as a "sweetener" that makes the other security more attractive.

Wash Sale: selling a security at a loss but then messing up by repurchasing it within 30 days and, therefore, not being able to use it to offset capital gains for that year.

Western/divided account: a syndicate account in which each participant is responsible for their share of the bonds only.

When-issued confirmations: confirmations of a purchase on the primary market delivered before the bonds have been issued.

Whole Life Insurance: form of permanent insurance with a guaranteed death benefit and minimum guaranteed cash value.

Withdrawal Plan: a feature of most mutual funds that allows investors to liquidate their accounts over a fixed time period, or using a fixed-share or fixed-dollar amount.

Working Capital: difference between a company's current assets and current liabilities measuring short-term liquidity.

Wrap Account: an account in which the customer pays one fee to cover the costs of investment advisory services, execution of transactions, etc.

Wrap Fee: the fee charged in a wrap account, believe it or not.

Y

Yield: the income a security produces to the holder just for holding it.

Yield-based Options: standardized options based on the yield of various US Treasury securities.

Yield to Call: the yield received on a bond if held to the date it is called.

Yield to Maturity: calculation of all interest payments plus/minus gain/loss on a bond if held to maturity.

Z

Zero Coupon Bond: a bond sold at a deep discount to its gradually increasing par value.

Z-Tranche: the last tranche to receive principal in a CMO.

Index

T

V

Value 568
Variable Annuities 198, 211-216, 219, 224-
    226, 229, 230, 255, 268, 287, 290,
    292, 424, 438, 532, 568
  Regulations 227
  Tax Treatment of 287
Variable Annuity Contract
  Features of the 215
Variable Life Insurance 222, 225, 569
  Advantages of 226
  Regulations 227
Variable Rate Demand Obligation 74
Variable Universal Life Insurance 225, 569
Variable vs. Whole Life Insurance 224
Vesting 207, 437, 569
Viatical Settlement 569
VLI 225. *See also* Variable Life Insurance
Volatility 43, 67, 138, 139, 142, 143, 183-
    185, 273, 317, 321, 397, 445, 463,
    465, 475, 494, 506, 526, 537, 569
Voluntary Accumulation Plan 569
Voting Rights 217
VUL 225, 226. *See also* Variable Universal
    Life Insurance

W

Warrants 18, 19, 25, 46, 261, 269, 300,
    308, 472, 477, 482, 503, 512, 513,
    569
Wash Sales 197, 285, 462, 569
  Taxation of 285
Whole Life Insurance 223, 224, 569
Wire Room 337
Withdrawal Plans 197, 219, 569
  Systematic 197
Withhold Orders 408
Working Capital 311
Wrap Account 334
Wrap Fee 334

Y

Yield 22, 23, 30-35, 39-41, 97, 105, 162,
    163, 179, 184, 300, 301, 509, 533,
    535, 542, 552, 565, 570
Yield Curves 40, 300

Yield Spread 41
Yield to Maturity 31, 32, 39, 570
YTC 32, 33, 106
YTM 31-35, 40, 97, 106

Z

Zero Coupon Bond 53, 66, 93, 94, 281,
    564, 567, 570
Z-tranche 59